History of Plains, Georgia

History Book Committee
Left to Right: Steve Short, Milton Raven, Willie Raven, Annette Wise, President Jimmy Carter, Jimmy Bagwell, Jack Cox, Dan Ariail, Earline Cox, Allene Haugabook, C. G. Haugabook, Jr. Not Present: Fred Boyles, Mary Minion, and Amy Wise. Photo credit: Lonnie Wise

Compiled by
Plains Historical Preservation Trust, Inc.

The Cover

The cover picture was painted by Donna Wills Mosteller and is a limited edition print. Donna Mosteller especially likes to paint old town scenes, churches, homes and farm scenes. She is in her twenty-eighth year of teaching public school art and currently teaches in the Lee County School System, where she was named 2002 Teacher of the Year for Twin Oaks Elementary School. She holds a Bachelor of Fine Arts degree from Valdosta State College and a Masters degree in Art Education from the University of Georgia. Her husband, Martin, teaches fifth grade at Twin Oaks Elementary School and their daughter, Margo, is a student at Mercer University.

Plains Historical Preservation Trust © 2003
All rights reserved

Library of Congress Catalog Card Number
2003113073

ISBN 1-883793-62-9

Additional copies of
History of Plains, Georgia
may be ordered from:
Plains Historical Preservation Trust
P. O. Box 17
Plains, Georgia 31780

ⅅℍⅅ

Wolfe Publishing
P. O. Box 8036
Fernandina Beach, FL 32035

Dedication

This book is gratefully dedicated to all the contributors who used this avenue to express their love and interest in their families and in the history of Plains, Georgia.

Plains
Historical Preservation Trust

"The objective and purpose of the organization is to own, lease, operate, renovate, use, and/or maintain real and personal property of historic significance in and about the City of Plains, Georgia, and to cooperate with other persons, firms, corporations, and government agencies to that end."

Board of Directors 2002
Front Row: Ruby Watson, P. J. Wise, Martha Harris, Frank Williams, Eunice Griggs, Allene Haugabook. Back Row: Annette Wise, President Jimmy Carter, Rosalynn Carter, Mary Evelyn Moncus, Gwen Wise, Jan Williams, Jo Medlock, Bob Moss, Lonnie Wise, Dan Ariail. Not Present: Mary Minion, Millard Simmons and Jimmy Bagwell. Photo credit: Annette Wise

History of The Trust

Plains is a small community with a rich history. Years before the first white settlers established homes here, Indians made this fertile land with its many creeks and streams their home. Even today reminders of the past can be found on farmland as fragments of flint and arrowheads appear after the deep plowing of farm tractors or a washing rain uncovers a treasure from the past.

Our community is indebted to Milton Leander Hudson who donated the land for the town of Plains and the train depot. The train ensured prosperous times for merchants and landowners of this agricultural community for many years. As our community changed, the depot sat silently, a reminder of the past. It was an important part of our heritage, but an exciting event was in store, as it became the backstage for an event which no one expected. As those famous words rang throughout the nation, "My name is Jimmy Carter and I am running for President of the United States of America," the depot and Plains were thrown into an unexpected arena of world publicity.

Thousands of people poured into the town of Plains in hopes of a glimpse of Jimmy Carter and a chance to learn more about him. The depot was the perfect place to greet the news media and visitors as they streamed into town. Many changes had occurred in our community, but nothing could compare to Jimmy Carter's presidential announcement.

Some of the residents of Plains began to look at the community and decided that the presidential announcement would only be the beginning of many changes that would occur in the future. After much discussion and planning, the decision was made to form the Plains Historical Preservation Trust. The mission of the Trust would be to own, lease, operate, preserve, renovate, use and/or maintain real and personal property of historic significance in and about the City of Plains, Georgia, and to cooperate with other persons, firms, corporations, and government agencies to the same end.

Plains Historical Preservation Trust was officially incorporated by Ben W. Fortson, Jr., Secretary of State of Georgia, on October 11, 1977. Through the years, the Trust has worked diligently to secure land and buildings of historic significance in cooperation with the City of Plains and the National Park Service. Presidents of the Trust include: Buford Reese, P.J. Wise, Maxine Reese, Steve Smith, Ellen Harris, and Annette Wise.

The Trust believes the history of our community is significant due to our heritage and ancestors. Our history is also unique since the 39th President and First Lady of the United States of America were born, raised, and continue to live here. Members of the Trust have dedicated many hours researching and conducting oral histories for this book. We are very appreciative of Mrs. Beth Walters, who wrote the first History of Plains in 1985 and gave us permission to use her research. This book has indeed been an effort of love and commitment as we share our pride for our hometown with you.

Annette Wise
President, PHPT
1999-2003

Contents

Foreword

The writing and publishing of this book has truly been a community project, and its success has been another demonstration of the ability of Plains citizens to work together harmoniously to achieve a worthwhile goal.

Our town is special in many ways. We have never lost our vitality and eagerness to improve; our population has enjoyed a slow but steady growth during the last century; we've always enjoyed harmony among our citizens; and the basic character and appearance of the town has been cherished and maintained by many citizens who represent five or more generations that have lived here.

We've been intensely reminded of these facts as we compiled the history of our families and friends and reexamined what has happened here since the railroad first generated the marriage of three rural communities into the one that this book will describe.

This has been a time of reassessment of our citizens' personal roles as we deliberately resurrected joyful and painful memories, and often learned for the first time about similar feelings among our friends and neighbors. Only a few of us knew anything about the earliest days of Plains, and there is little doubt that in the learning we have come to appreciate its special values.

As far as Rosalynn and I are concerned, there has always been a special attraction here that brought us back home from the United States Navy, the Governor's Mansion, and the White House. News reporters have asked us often to explain what the magnet has been, and we've had trouble devising answers that others could understand. In the preparation of this history, the reasons have become clearer than ever to us. The closeness of our families, friends, and land has always been apparent, but there is more than that. There is something especially attractive about Plains, and particularly the good relationship among our people and the harmonious melding of modern progress and preservation of the best aspects of the past. These are just a few reasons why we have always considered this to be a personal refuge, in which we have found fellowship, pleasure, inspiration – and also challenge and adventure!

We realize also, of course, that Plains is one of the most famous small towns in the world, and that many people will be interested in visiting with us and in reading this book about our families and the political and social events that have shaped our history.

I wrote a poem about our town a decade ago, and the last few lines summarize my feelings:

"Together, we have learned we must depend
On one another. Though the town is small,
We cherish it as haven, home and friend.
And won't let strife or mischance bring to all
Our dreams – our modest, tempered dreams – an end."

Jimmy Carter

Acknowledgements

Book Committee

Co-Chairpersons: Dr. Dan Ariail and Dr. Jimmy Bagwell
Coordinator: Annette Wise
Copy Editor: Steve Short
Formating Editor: C. G. Haugabook, Jr.
Committee Members:
Fred Boyles
President Jimmy Carter
Jack and Earline Cox
Allene Haugabook
Mary Minion
Milton and Willie Raven
Amy Wise

Sources for Pictures

The Jimmy Carter Presidential Library
The Georgia Department of Archives and History
Jimmy Carter National Historic Site
Alan Anderson
Lawrence Smith
and
Friends of Plains

Section I: History

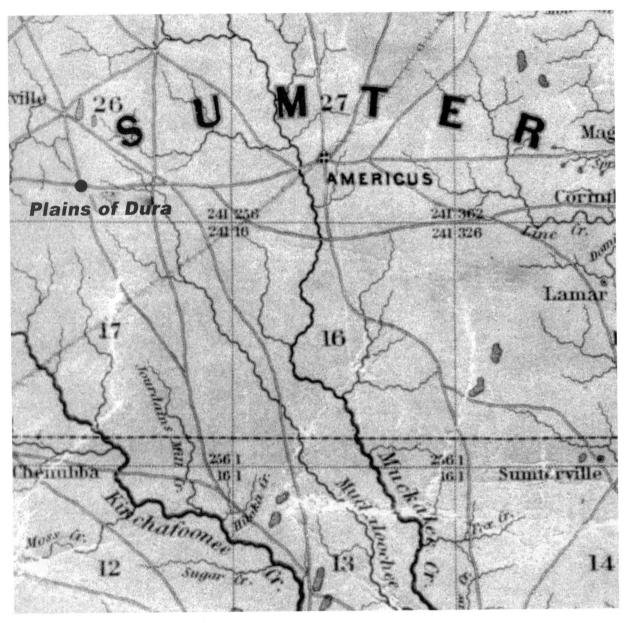

1847 Bonner Map of Georgia showing Plains of Dura
Photo credit: Georgia Department of Archives and History

Chapter 1: Early Beginnings

Submitted by Jack F. Cox

The area had been in the possession of the Indians before the advent of the White settlement. This area was occupied by the Creek Nation, where the center of government was located at Coweta, 60 miles northwest of Plains near present day Columbus. The Creeks, a civilized group of people, were highly opposed to surrendering any of their communal held lands to white encroachments. Indeed, in 1823 the Creek Council prescribed death for any members giving up land without Council approval.

At the Treaty of Indian Springs in 1825, Chief William McIntosh, a mixed blood chief of the Lower Creeks, signed the treaty giving land for white settlement. As a result, he was killed by the Upper Creeks.

As a result of their treaty, under the terms of the treaty of Washington in 1826, the Creeks ceded their lands in exchange for lands in the Indian Territory. The Lower Creeks migrated to these lands soon thereafter and in 1828 six whites and a free black couple crossed the Flint River to settle in what later became Sumter County.

This new territory, which included the lands between the Flint and Chattahoochee rivers, was divided into the counties of Muscogee, Troup, Coweta, Lee, and Carroll. To dispose of this vast tract of land an Act was passed by the Georgia Legislature on June 9, 1825, which gave the following requirements for persons to be eligible for a draw in the Lottery to dispose of the land:

(1) White males above 18, who had been residents of the state for 3 years

(2) Revolutionary soldiers, widows of Revolutionary soldiers, orphans, and others who had not drawn land in previous lotteries

(3) Men who had been wounded and disabled in the late wars with Great Britain or the Indians, shall be entitled to one additional draw.

Thus the stage was set for the influx of settlers who would populate this area. Additional counties were created from these original five and Sumter County was created in December 1831.

The land lottery draws were for land lots consisting of 202½ acres and the fortunate drawer could either move to their new land or sell the lots. Many of these winners sold their lots, so the people who drew the lots where Plains was later located did not come here to settle but sold their lots to people who would later populate the county.

Sumter County was given formal status in December 1831 and Americus, the county seat, was founded in 1832. The first mention of the Plains of Dura was in the recorder of the United States Postal Service where there is a record of a post office at Plains of Dura in 1839. Names of the postmasters and dates of service will be found in later chapters.

In these early years the post office was kept in the home or on the property of the postmaster so there is no absolute record of where the Plains of Dura was physically located. Early maps in the 1840s show a Plains of Dura and there is mention of the town in the 1850s in the Sumter Republican, the earliest newspaper of which we have records.

The name "Plains of Dura" was a Biblical reference, taken from Daniel 3:1- the plain where Nebuchadnezzar II set up his golden idol that the Israelites Meshach, Shadrach, and Abednego refused to worship and were cast into a burning furnace from which they emerged above and unhurt as a sign of God's favor.

Several small settlements were in the area and when the railroad came, their settlements lost significance as the town on the railroad became the most important place.

Mossy Dell School
Photo credit: Lottie Wise Tanner

Southeast of Plains on what is now Salters Mill Road was the Providence community. A church was there and nearby was Davison Mills. Mossy Dell School educated the children of the area until it was incorporated into Plains school in 1920. The only remnant of the settlement left is the Providence cemetery located near Pessell Creek. In their cemetery are the graves of John W. Caldwell, his wife, sister-in-law and three of his children. In one of the most sickening crimes ever committed in Sumter County, Caldwell slew all the above. The lonely graves bear mute witness to a man's passion.

Another community of note in the area was Magnolia, or Mineral Springs, located on Magnolia Springs Road northwest of Plains. A thriving community in the 1850s, Magnolia Springs had a very reputable school, the Magnolia Male and Female Institutes, which was run by Mr. and Mrs. J.E. Rylander and advertised: "The mineral virtues of our spring are no longer questionable; many invalids in the last two summers having realized its power to heal." Their

advertisement appeared in the November 21, 1855, edition of the Sumter Republican.

In an 1854 announcement the trustees were: Judge James Glass, Dr. Wm. J. Reese, J.H. Black, G.H. Harper, and George Torbit, and some students were Mary Pickett, Sallie Black, Sarrie Glass, Sophia A. Clark, Pollie Russell, Emma Glass, Eudora A. Russell, Sallie Pickett, Martha J. Pierce, and Amanda A. Wooten.

In addition to the thriving school, there was also the Methodist Church and a very popular Masonic organization, Mineral Springs Lodge #230, which was chartered in 1858. The names of its members will be found in another section of this history.

The Springs was a popular gathering place for area residents for well over a century and the swimming pool was remembered as having ice-cold water even in the hottest days of summer.

Of this settlement the only remains are the overgrown Methodist cemetery and the no longer in use swimming pool. All the surrounding buildings have been victims of time.

Historical landmark on Bond's Trail
Photo credit: Lawrence Smith

Bottsford, located southwest of Plains on Highway 45, was a thriving village as early as the 1850s. As early an 1850 a Masonic lodge, Furlow Lodge #124, was established with Littlebury L. Causey a worshipful Master, John B. Thomas as Senior Warden, Carey Thomas Cox as Junior Warden, John R. Evans as Treasurer and John Mathis Cox as secretary. Twenty-eight charter members were farmers and planters in the vicinity. Rural Hill Methodist provided the spiritual guidance and the burial ground for their earliest settlers.

In the late 1860s a migration of Lutherans from South Carolina began to trickle into the Bottsford area. In "A History of the Lutheran Church in South Carolina" is the comment: "One congregation (of Lutherans) in Edgefield County, St. Mark's, was so depleted by removals to Georgia that the emigrants felt it only proper to carry the congregational name with them. They organized St. Mark's, Plains, Georgia in 1870."

The description of the actual organization of St. Mark's appears in the Old Record Book, pages 1 and 2: "The members of the Evangelical Lutheran Church who had recently moved to this portion of the state from South Carolina, being desirous of adhering to the church of the Reformation solicited the services of Rev. John P. Margart of Eufaula, Alabama, who responded favorably to our call and preached his first sermon in the Methodist Episcopal Church at Bottsford on the third Sunday in March, 1870, the Methodists having kindly offered the use of their church until we could build one of our own. We organized ourselves on the first Sunday in May, 1870 under the title and designation of St. Mark's Evangelical Lutheran Church

and appointed John McNeary, L.C. McNeary, David Wise, and Joel Wise to serve as elders during the succeeding years."

Thus did the Jennings, Wise, Addy, and other leading families of Plains come to Sumter County and, later, to Plains.

There was probably a settlement of some sort where Lebanon Cemetery is now located. The Lebanon Baptist Church, forerunner of Plains Baptist, was located here in the 1850s and there was usually a settlement around a church.

On the Jack Slappey Road, just off Highway 45, was the Universalist Church and cemetery. Known as "Devil's Half Acre," it probably had a settlement around it. Rev. George Harper, whose descendants still live in Plains, was an early Universalist minister.

These early communities faded when the railroad came and Plains became the town.

St. Mark's Lutheran at Bottsford
Photo credit: C. G. Haugabook, Jr.

Fleeta Wise Smith age 20, grandmother of Horace Seymour Jr., and the students she was teaching in 1897 in front of school at Magnolia Springs. Photo credit: Horace Seymour, Jr.

Chapter 2: 1886–1929

Submitted by Steve Short

The arrival of the railroad in rural areas of Georgia and the South after the Civil War and into the 1880s provided a means of not only survival, but prosperity.[1] Plains owes its existence to the railroad and Milton Leander Hudson (1853-1912), the man who served as the town's first railroad agent. M.L. Hudson donated land for the town itself and the depot that followed.

Milton Leander Hudson
Photo credit:Hudson family album

When the depot was constructed in 1888 in the center of town, Plains began to grow. Residential neighborhoods developed to the north and south of the railroad tracks. The construction of the tracks running east and west in the sparsely-settled region led to the founding of a significant small town.[2] The depot, like in other Georgia towns, influenced the growth and development of the new town that had combined the communities of Plains of Dura, Magnolia Springs and Lebanon.[3]

A 36-foot-by-70-foot rectangular wood frame building with an asphalt shingled, front gable roof, the 1888 Plains depot typified the roots of small towns.[4] The railroad and depot provided a frame of development and encouraged the growth of businesses, schools, churches and homes in the vicinity.[5]

The railroad's arrival also encouraged the cultivation of cash crops. Railroads provided area farmers with a way to transport their crops to distant markets, thus increasing sales.[6] Small-scale landowners in the Plains area responded by increasing the size of their farms and cash crops. The railroad and the financial power of Plains merchants created a place where merchants led political and community affairs.[7] Among the most influential residents in the area in the mid-1880s were the Coxes, Davenports, Hudsons, Simpsons and Wises.

The establishment of the railroad, however, didn't go without blemish. Originally the Americus-Preston-Lumpkin (A.P.L.) Railroad, the name was changed to the Savannah-Americus-Montgomery (S.A.M.) Railway on December 26, 1888. In 1895, it became the property of the Georgia and Alabama Railway. By 1902, it was acquired by the Seaboard Air Line Railway through stock ownership.[8]

Despite its rocky beginnings, overall the railroad provided a location for the development of a central core of stores, businesses and other establishments to support the agricultural community.[9] Town leaders had agreed to move to the present location because the railroad promised economic growth.[10]

S.A.M. train
Photo credit: Ann Jennings Singer

Incorporation and Laws

Though it existed in its present location for a few years, the town of Plains was not incorporated until 1896. The first charter was dated December 17, 1896.[11] Town leaders officially shortened the town's biblical name to Plains.[12] The first election was held in January 1897. A mayor and four councilmen were chosen. Dr. B.T. Wise was elected mayor, and R.S. Oliver, W.L. Thomas, E. Timmerman, Sr., and L.D. Wise were elected councilmen.[13]

Immediately, the settlement established social and legal parameters to spur development.[14] Dozens of laws for residents to abide by were incorporated that year. Residents had to have resided in the town for 60 days to be eligible to vote. It was the duty of the marshal "to execute all processes directed to him and all orders of the Mayor or Mayor and Councilmen or Police Court. He shall patrol the town and see that the peace and good order thereof are preserved."

Among the ordinances adopted were the following:

• A license fee of $2.50 per quarter or $5 per year were required for livery and sale stables. A $5 per year fee for "each animal or vehicle for hire for transportation in the town" also was required.

• "Any transient photographer who shall open an office or gallery within the corporate limits of this city" was required to pay the clerk, on application, $2.

Other ordinances called for civic duties to be carried out. One read "The Marshal, at the beginning of each year, shall make out a list of persons between the ages of sixteen and 50 years, residing in the city, liable to work the streets ... Any person subject to street duty could relieve himself of the same by paying to the Marshal, when called on, such a street tax as the Board shall annually fix."

Among the more "colorful" ordinances:

• Concerning exhibitions and shows, another decree stated "No person, or persons, shall within the limits of the town of Plains, act, represent, perform, or exhibit wire works, or rope dancing, or other exercise thereon, beating or playing on musical instruments, have concerts of vocal or instrumental music, fire works, theatrical exhibitions, exhibition of wild beasts, sleight of hand, or other kind of amusement, show or whatever, without first paying the Marshal a sum of not less than one, nor more than twenty-five dollars, at the option of the Mayor, for each day's performance, exhibition, or continuance of such show or amusements; provided that nothing in this ordinance shall relate to schools or colleges, or any associated corps for amusement, resident in the city."

• Another ordinance indicated "hides shall not be cured inside the city limits, where the same may be offensive to any person."

• Vagrants were to be kept off the streets. All residents were forbidden from throwing heavy materials from windows that in any manner would "endanger or annoy any person."

• Punishment was warned for any person who provoked another to fight. No person could "vend any spirituous or fermented liquors in the town of Plains; or anything that will intoxicate."

• It was unlawful for any person or persons "to use sling shots, flips, or bow and arrows within the corporate limits."

• No person, merely for sport, and when there was no intention to become a passenger, was allowed to jump on the cars of any train in motion.

• Inside the city limits, no person was allowed to fight "except in self defense."

Character played an important role in the new town. Sec. 92 of the ordinances referred to Houses of Ill Fame and read, "No person shall keep in said town, any house of ill fame. No person shall permit any house under his control to be inhabited by disorderly persons of an immoral character."

Crowd control and orderliness were of key importance in 1897. Any person or persons who engaged "in playing ball, or throwing and catching balls on any public streets without the consent of the Mayor, shall, upon conviction, be fined."

Sec. 108 of the adopted ordinances stated "No person or persons shall be permitted to obstruct the sidewalks of this city by standing in crowds on the same, to the inconvenience and annoyance of the public." No locomotives or cars could "obstruct the streets of the city by standing across the same for a longer time than ten minutes."

Businesses also had rules to follow. Sec. 114 stated all businesses were "required to close their doors at 12 o'clock each night." Every person "found on the streets after that time shall be required to give satisfactory cause for being out."

The form of judgments against defenders included paying a fine. In default of such payment, the offender could be imprisoned in the calaboose or a work-gang.[15]

As prudish as some of these ordinances seem today, they kept Plains an orderly town. And families continued to move in and build homes. Some of the families who moved to the community around the turn of the century or shortly thereafter were the Clarks, Wellonses, Spanns, Andrewses, Howells and Carters.

Early Homes and Residents

After M.L. Hudson built the first house in present-day Plains in 1884, a succession of others followed.[16] Two of the dominant builders were R.S.

M. L. Hudson House
First house built in Plains. Photo credit: Lawrence Smith

Oliver and A.C. Wellons, both of whom had dwellings built for themselves and their children. Notable homes in Plains through its first 40 years were occupied by Dr. Frank Cato, Alex Chappell, Jim Chappell, W.H. Crawford, Ross Dean, Armstid Dodson, George Hiller, Joe Hiller, James Ira Howell, George Jennings, Leonard Jennings, M.M. Jennings, Sr., C.C. Lunsford, J.A. McDonald, George W. Montgomery, Ernest Spann, Will Thomas, Alvin Timmerman, Edwin Timmerman, Frank Timmerman, Jesse Timmerman, Seaborn J. Walters, Aletus Wellons, Broadus Wellons, Ernest Wellons, Dr. B.T. Wise, David Wise, Luther David Wise, Phillip Joseph Wise, and Samuel Wise.

By 1900, Plains had grown to a population of 345. The 1900 U.S. Census, enumerated by William S. Moore between June 1 and June 7, 1900, showed the population of "Plains Village" nearly evenly split between white and black residents.[17] In 1900, Plains was billed as "a busy little town with fine schools and churches."[18]

Buildings and Businesses

Although the business section of Plains began in 1885 with three small wooden buildings on the south side of the railroad tracks, Plains as it looks today traces its roots to the first brick building built in 1896. The first three wooden buildings, according to old records, were built by R.E. Webb, Jesse Clark and Capt. B.R. Mayes,[19] the maternal great-grandfather of Betty Jennings Carter. These buildings and two more wooden buildings that served as a cafe, barbershop, post office, general store and filling station anchored what was to become Main Street and be completed after 1910.

Town of Plains in early 1900s

The first substantial building in town went up in 1896 and was built by R.S. Oliver. It was known as the Oliver-French-Shields Co. general store. It is the second brick building on the west end of the contiguous Main Street structures. Mr. French left the firm in 1902 and started a business with Lunsford & Timmerman. John McDonald joined Oliver and the store became the Oliver-McDonald Co. and was used as a furniture store.[20] About 1929, Ross Dean operated a funeral home in the building. The building became part of the Plains Mercantile Co. about 1934. In 1971, the building and the one

beside it became Hugh Carter's Antiques.[21] In 2002, the building reopened as the Plains Inn and Antiques Mall.

In 1901, the Plains Bank building was completed and began business. One source says it was the second bank in town, the first being organized by the Timmerman family in a building on the east side of Bond Street at an earlier date. R.S. Oliver was the first president of Plains Bank. B.T. Wise was the bank's vice president and C.C. Lunsford the cashier. After a period of prosperity, the bank hit hard times and closed in January 1919. In the 1920s, the post office moved into the structure. In 1928, it was purchased as an addition to Plains Mercantile Co. Later the offices of the Carter Worm Farm,[22] it reopened in May 2002 as the Old Bank Café.

About 1902, three more brick buildings were added to the growing town. R.H. Forrester operated a general store in the building on the far east end of Main Street. After a succession of owners, Earl Carter, the father of President Carter, purchased the store in 1919 and operated it as a grocery for several years.[23] He sold the business to Plains Cotton Warehouse. For years it was used as storage. In more recent years, it was known as the Peanut Patch.

In 1902, Edwin Timmerman, Everett Lunsford, and John E. French built what was known as the "General Store," the fifth contiguous building from the west end of Main Street. Alton Carter bought this store in 1909 and renamed it Plains Mercantile Co. Hewlette Carlton purchased the building in 1934 and in 1939, H.B. Moman bought the store and called it the M&M Cash Store. In later years, it was known as Turner's Hardware, owned by Ernest and June Turner.[24] Today it is the Plains Trading Post.

Also in 1902, the Oliver-McDonald Co. built the third brick building from the west end of Main Street that later became Walters' Grocery. The original business sold farm equipment and supplies and general merchandise. C.L. Walters, Jr. became owner in 1949.[25] Today, the building is home to Windham Castings, run by Debbie Young.

About 1907, an addition on the west side of the Oliver-McDonald building was added as Plains continued to grow.[26] This building later was part of Hugh Carter's Antiques and reopened in 2002 as part of the Plains Inn and Antiques Mall.

In 1912, Ross Dean Funeral Home opened in the site of the second building on the east end of Main Street. The building later was used as a cotton and peanut warehouse. It became known more recently as the Peanut Museum.[27] The last of the Main Street structures was built in 1916. This building, third and fourth establishments from the east end, was known originally as Wise Sanitarium No. 1, or the A.C. Wellons Building. Intended as a hotel, it housed both retail on the first floor and the Wise Sanitarium on the second floor. The Wise brothers used this building until moving to the new hospital in 1920. Earl Carter rented the building in 1934 and began his peanut warehouse business here. He purchased the east portion of the building (now known as Plain Peanuts and run by Bobby Salter) in 1943. This building housed President Carter's senatorial and gubernatorial campaigns.[28]

Religion and Churches

By the time most of the Main Street buildings were completed, Plains had grown into a thriving agricultural community. Residents took pride in strong Christian heritage and conservative social and political beliefs.[29] In no town was the influence of church more widespread than in Plains.

A new Baptist church was constructed in 1906, followed by a Lutheran church in 1907 and a Methodist church in 1910. Plains' leading residents held memberships in each of the churches. No one denomination held superiority over the others, though membership in the Baptist church usually exceeded those of the other congregations.

The present Plains Baptist Church was erected on the north side of town at a cost of $6,000. The church traces its history to a building built in 1849 at a cost of $300 near the center of what is Lebanon Cemetery. In 1870, a second church was built at a cost of $2,200. In 1889, the church building was moved to Plains on the south side of town below the railroad tracks.[30] This building and lot were sold in 1906 when the new church was built.[31] Rev. A.C. Wellons, a contractor and former pastor of the church in the 1890s, constructed the building, which often is recognized as the most impressive structure in town.

W.W. Arnold served as first pastor in the new building, through 1908. The name of the church was changed from Lebanon Baptist Church to Plains Baptist Church in 1909 with 158 members on roll.[32] It was inside this building that Jimmy Carter was ordained as a deacon and taught Sunday school before his presidency.[33]

In 1907, the year after Plains Baptist was built, St. Andrew's Evangelical Lutheran Church was officially established under Rev. Charles A. Phillips. This building was built across the street from Plains Baptist. On June 20, 1907, a program was held for the laying of the cornerstone. The cornerstone is made of white marble.[34] Fourteen antique Gothic stained glass windows imported from Germany are dedicated to some original member.[35] The church is built of handmade blocks.

St. Andrew's traces its beginnings to 1870 when a Lutheran church was started at St. Mark's in Bottsford, a few miles south of Plains. In 1885, a congregation of Lutherans was organized in Plains after the railroad opened. On August 27, 1905, in a congregational meeting, a vote was taken to build a church in Plains, and it was carried by a large majority. Rev. Phillips served both parishes in Plains and Bottsford until 1918. In 1966, St. Mark's of Bottsford voted to unite with the congregation of St. Andrew's of Plains.[36]

The third significant church building erected after the turn of the century was Plains United Methodist Church, built in 1910. The Methodist church in Plains traces its beginnings to 1888, when the congregation moved to the new settlement on property given by M.L. Hudson, and changed its name to Plains.[37] Originally, the church was known as the Tabernacle and sat on land near the home of George and Louise Whitten north of town.[38]

The building in 1910 replaced a frame church first used in Plains. E.R. Stewart served as Sunday school superintendent for 50 years, and was succeeded by C.L. Walters, Jr. The old building was bought by R.S. Oliver and rebuilt into a dwelling house. The first wedding in the new structure, in 1911, united Ophie Markette and George Stafford Addy.[39] Thirty-five years later, former President Carter and first lady Rosalynn Smith Carter were married here.

As late as 1910, when this church was built, the majority of Georgia's population continued to work in agriculture. The post-Civil War plantation system remained the basis for the state's economy. Unlike today, the bulk of Georgia's population remained in the central and southwest counties. Tenancy and the automobile provided farm owners with more freedom and access to towns like Plains where they opened general stores, cotton gins and other small businesses.[40]

Schools and Education

As farm owners became more involved in town activities, they increased participation in local affairs through politics, church and education. Increased movement to small towns in the early 20th century fueled what many historians called the Progressive Movement in the South. This movement created a concern for education and related social reforms.[41] In education, Plains exceeded the norm for a small town.

Miss Julia Coleman (far left) and group of children in front of old Plains School. Photo credit: Hudson family album

Before 1886, a four-room school at Magnolia Springs was the dominant educational institution in western Sumter County. In 1887, Plains residents decided a new school was necessary. Capt.

G.M. Patterson and Mrs. W.L. Thomas were instrumental in carrying out the plans.

In 1891, a public subscription for funds to build a new building was begun. A Board of Education was named to guide the policies. Members of the board were R.B. Evans, E. Timmerman, M.L. Hudson, J.W. Oliver, C.C. Jernigan and W.L. Thomas.

Plains residents contributed $1,800 toward the enterprise and a two-story wooden building with four rooms on the lower floor was constructed. A professor Jarrell took the reins as first superintendent. The Masonic Lodge paid part of the expenses for the building and, in turn, was allowed to use the upper floor for a lodge room. [42]

At about this time, Planters Academy, three miles south of town, consolidated with the new organization. Around the turn of the century, the county took over and began supporting the school by taxation.[43] Some of the earliest families to graduate from the Plains School included the Fletchers, Murrays and Clarks.

In 1919, Mossy Dell, a school seven miles south of Plains, decided to "cast its lot" with the Plains School, thus consolidating the western part of Sumter County under one solid school. In 1920, a bond issue for $50,000 was approved for building a new high school, as Plains took a step as a leader in public education during that time.[44] Between 1900 and 1920, Southern states increased funding for public education by nearly 300 percent, in addition to adopting compulsory education laws.[45]

In 1921, the Classic Revival-style Plains High School building in a symetrically-arranged H plan measuring 208 feet by 132 feet was opened.[46] The concrete keystone over the front door is inscribed with "1921." This building provided the beginning of educational enhancement for the town and surrounding area.

Construction of the school allowed for the sale of the old wooden building. Bishop William D. Johnson and the A.M.E. Church purchased the old

building for $500.[47] Johnson moved the building to the Archery community and it became the Johnson Home Industrial College, a school for black students under the direction of Johnson.[48] The school had begun in 1912 and offered male and female students primary, high school, collegiate and vocational classes.[49] Some of the families who attended were the Kleckleys, Lasters, Johnsons, Ravens, Schleys and Wakefields. The school bell from the old building was loaded on a wagon and also hauled to Archery to be used by the black students.[50]

The opening in town of the new brick building marked a milestone for Plains. The class of 1922 was the first to graduate from the new building. The principal was Thomas Morgan. This class was the first one to use the school for graduating due to a fire which occurred in the old building before completion in January 1922 (or soon after that). The graduation was in the auditorium.[51]

The room teacher was Miss Lucy Kate Clark (1896-1957), a graduate of Bessie Tift College and the daughter of John Bartow Clark and Mary Spann Clark. Lucy Kate Clark, like all five of her siblings, graduated from Plains High School, and unusual for their time, earned college degrees. Three of the Clark sisters – Amise, Berta Will and Lucy Kate – all taught in Plains, and are believed to be the only three sisters in the town's history to have done so. A fourth sister – Mary – taught in Richland before marrying and moving to Florida.[52]

Other teachers played important and historic roles in the

Marguerite "Tot" Hudson, teacher

Plains School. Miss Tot Hudson, a daughter of M.L. Hudson, taught three generations of Plains schoolchildren. However, no two teachers had a bigger impact than Miss Julia L. Coleman and Young Thompson Sheffield. Julia Coleman (1889-1973) began teaching in 1908 at Friendship. A graduate also of Tift College, she had come to Plains as a small child, the daughter of a Baptist minister father and schoolteacher mother. In 1912, she returned to Plains to teach English. She spent the rest of her career, except for one year, in Plains before retiring in 1958.[53]

Y.T. Sheffield (1904-1967) came to Plains as assistant principal in 1928. He worked with Julia Coleman in the capacities of superintendent and principal until 1949, when she stepped down to teach English only. Plains High School prospered under Y.T. Sheffield's hand as teacher and coach for nearly 38 years.[54]

"Mr. Y.T.," as he was known, was basketball and baseball coach during most of his tenure in Plains and coached several title-winning teams. According to his obituary, his squads played a record 2,082 regular season games. He had attended

Top Row: Coach Y.T. Sheffield, Richard Salter, Raymond Gaines, Durelle Anderson, Everett Chambliss, B.T. Wishard, Herbert Howell, Joe Moore. Middle Row: Millard Simmons, Rembert Forrest, Harold Taylor, Ross Oliver, Richard Smith, Joe Hendrix, Billy Parker. Bottom Row: Lavon Turner, Fred Foster, Joe Smith, Donald McDonald, Unknown. Photo credit: Millard Simmons

Mercer University in Macon and graduated from Carson-Newman College in Jefferson City, Tenn. At Mercer, he was a teammate of Wally Butts, the legendary football coach at the University of Georgia.

Y.T. Sheffield was a charter member and first president of the Plains Lions Club. The beloved teacher and coach also was a Sunday school superintendent and deacon at Plains Baptist Church. It was because of the leadership of both him and "Miss Julia" that Plains High School prospered in its 1921 building for decades to come.

Health Care and Healers

In addition to education, another Progressive era reform in the South extended into the field of health care.[55] As good as educational advancements were in Plains, perhaps no attainment matched the progression of a town as small as Plains in the early 1900s as did health care. It was welcome relief, because both poor and well-to-do alike had suffered tragedies.

By the turn of the century, for example, town founder M.L. Hudson had lost his wife and four children to untimely deaths. One of his daughters died at age 3 in 1884 when she fell into a pot of lye soap. A son died at age 5 months in 1897; a second son died at age 7 in 1898. A third son, Stewart Hudson, died at age 20 in January 1900, only 11 days into the new year, in a freak horse accident in his parents' yard. Yet sickness killed far more residents than did accidents during this time.

A lack of services – including garbage disposal, water quality control and sewerage conditions – combined with hot Georgia climate and poor medical care had led to a plethora of diseases. Tuberculosis, diptheria, yellow fever, malaria, smallpox, typhoid, hookworm and pellagra were common.[56]

The first hospital in Plains in 1912,[57] which occupied the present-day Plains Pharmacy building, dealt with these maladies and more. Before

this time, Dr. Burr Thomas Wise, and before him, Dr. James F. Cato and Dr. T.W. Stewart, served the area.[58]

Dr. Burr T. Wise, who owned the first car in town,[59] died in 1910 at age 51. After his death, his oldest son, Dr. Burr Thaddeus Wise, resumed his father's business.[60] This move marked the beginning of a period in which Plains boasted a leading hospital under the Wise brothers that was called "the Mayo Clinic of the South."[61]

Dr. Burr T. Wise and his wife, Laura Rachel Addy Wise (1864-1943), were the parents of three sons – Dr. Thad Wise (1882-1956), Dr. Sam Wise (1884-1943) and Dr. Bowman Wise (1888-1951) – all of whom graduated from Tulane Medical College in New Orleans. Dr. Thad returned to Plains in 1908; Dr. Sam returned in 1911, and Dr. Bowman in 1914. They set up the small hospital in 1912 to accommodate up to 15 patients. They later moved to a location where they could care for 20 patients.[62] In 1917, the hospital was moved to the rooms above the present-day Plains Trading Post and its adjoining building. The original rooms were used to house boarding nurses.[63] An accredited training school for nurses operated in Plains from 1917 to 1934.[64] Among those who trained as nurses were Lottie Thomas Meadows, Jewel Sears, Gussie Abrams, Betty Pennington, Ethel Vaughn,

Nurses in training at Wise Sanitarium
Photo credit: C.A. Stead, Jacksonville, FL.

Grace McConnell, Bonnie Dominick, Effie McArthur, and Lillian Gordy, the mother of the future president.[65]

In 1921, the same year the new high school opened, the 60-bed Wise Sanitarium, run by the three brothers, opened its doors. The one-story hospital had an X-ray and radium department and included a building annex for black patients. This hospital was one of the first less than 100-bed hospitals to be accredited by the American College of Surgeons and the American Medical and Hospital Association.[66] In the late 1920s, the Wise Sanitarium served as the S.A.M. hospital. Following a train wreck in Savannah, 10 to 15 patients were brought in for treatment and all eventually returned home.[67]

The Wise brothers occupied Wise Sanitarium until the building was damaged by fire in January 1936, at which time patients were moved to the hospital in Americus. A new wing was added to the hospital to accommodate the overflow of patients from Plains.

Wise Clinic in Americus. Photo credit: Georgia Department of Archives and History

In 1936, the brothers moved their offices to the Wise Clinic Building in Americus and established a diagnostic clinic there. Dr. Thad and Dr. Sam moved to Americus to live, but Dr. Bowman continued to live in Plains until his death in 1951.[68]

Because of their skill and expertise, Plains was known throughout the Southeast for its medical care. Dr. Thad, a pioneer in surgery, completed an outstanding surgical career; Dr. Sam assisted him in surgery and did general practice in what today would be labeled internal medicine; and Dr. Bowman specialized in obstetrics and anesthesiology.[69]

Dr. Thad Wise inspired confidence, many said, by his "thoroughness, interest and sincerity." He was a strong believer in that any information he obtained belonged to his patient and should be given to the patient even when the prognosis was hopeless if the patient wished to know his condition. Dr. Thad used his wisdom and insight into human beings for the good of mankind. As an old black man once said, it has been written, "He is a good man, a real doctor, and he don't have to reckon. He knows."[70]

Other than the Wises, another doctor who made an impact on Plains in the early 20th century was Dr. J. Colquitt Logan (1880-1965). Dr. Logan, for whom the present-day downtown park through which the railroad track runs is named, graduated from the Atlanta College of Medicine and Surgeons (Emory University College of Medicine) in 1910. He began practice in the Plains area with his father, Dr. A.J. Logan, who lived five miles north of town on Highway 45. In 1913, he moved into the Logan Clinic building on the east side of the intersection of Bond and Main streets. He later did post-graduate work in Atlanta and New York.[71]

Dr. Logan was the first doctor to treat and cure a Rocky Mountain spotted fever patient. A medical book was written about the feat that involved patient Malcolm Hogg. Dr. Logan received the General Practitioners Award of the Year from the state of Georgia.

Dr. Logan, a Methodist church member, later served as mayor of Plains for 14 years.[72] He died in 1965 after more than 50 years of service.[73]

With the arrival of Dr. Logan in 1913 and the three Wise brothers came a new pharmacy in Plains, which complemented the medical care. Plains Pharmacy, which today has been run by the same family for 85 years, opened in either 1913 or 1914 and occupied the entire ground floor of the building at Hudson and Main streets. It was owned by M.M. Jennings, Sr.[74] An earlier pharmacy was begun in the 1890s under the direction of Alex Chappell.[75]

In 1917, Dr. J.H. Monts and L.E. Godwin, Sr. purchased an interest in the business and it was operated as a partnership. Three pharmacists were employed full-time. After the partners opened the Clinic Drugstore in Americus in 1928, the partnership eventually dissolved. In its heyday, the drugstore was the center of community life. A Victrola provided music and a soda fountain offered refreshments. An old-fashioned ceiling fan provided setting and cooling on hot days.[76] The store also sold paint, seeds, automobile tires, and gas and oil.[77] What prescriptions could not do for the body, atmosphere did for the soul.

Growth Amid Hardships

After its incorporation in 1896, Plains prospered through its schools, churches, transportation and medical care, but not without difficulty.[78] At one time, four day and two night trains served the town.[79] The railroad went bankrupt, but bounced back.

In 1902, when only 8 percent of U.S. homes had a telephone and a three-minute call from Denver to New York City cost $11, permission was given to Southern Bell Telegraph Co. to erect poles and conductors in Plains with free use for police and fire alarms.[80]

In 1904, a summer drought devastated crops.[81] In 1905, a smallpox epidemic hit Plains. It was noted in council minutes that all houses infected with the disease had to be quarantined for 18 days.[82] Again, Plains bounced back. By 1906, the town boasted "a tannery, shoe factory, a bank, a telegraph service, a school, a post office and several stores."[83]

By 1907, a City Water Works was established and that same year, a 25-year franchise was given to the Plains Telephone Co.

In 1912, the Hercules Light Co. of Chattanooga built an electrical plant.[84] By January 5, 1914, there was a mention of two banks in town.[85] In 1919, Plains installed a light system that was run by a diesel-driven generator, replacing the kerosene lamps in homes and the gas lights on the streets. A celebration was held the night the lights were turned on. Mr. Snow Bowers came to manage the new system. His job included reading the meters and making out monthly bills.[86]

Also in 1919, on the west corner of Logan Park, a 50,000-gallon water tank was erected by Scholfield Iron Works of Macon. It replaced a small well with a tank on the north side of the A.C. Murray House on South Bond Street. The first city well pump had been located between the Baptist pastorium and the home of Mrs. Alice Green and had been dug in 1906.[87]

Individual Successes

Business prospered in the early decades for many individuals. Luther James Cranford began his cotton gin operation in the 1910s on the west side of South Hudson Street. His gin covered an acre and was surrounded by a high fence. Cranford had been a teacher and farmer before coming to Plains from Marion County.[88]

George W. Montgomery owned and operated Planters Warehouse in the 1910s in a brick building on South Bond Street.[89] He also served as mayor. Brothers Broadus and Ernest Wellons ran the first barbershop in town on the northern end of South Bond Street in the 1910s.[90] Dr. Seymour Evans, a half-brother of veterinarian Jack Slappey, was the town's first dentist.[91]

The Murray family owned and operated the telephone company in Plains from the early 1900s

Plains Telephone Exchange

to about 1940. During these years, service was provided by a magneto manual switchboard, as were all exchanges of this era. Norman Murray helped his father operate and maintain the exchange.[92]

Elsewhere in the early 1900s, Plains Cotton Warehouse was started under the name of Timmerman and Wise. The partners in this firm were Luther D. Wise and E. Timmerman. Frank F. Timmerman also worked in the business, handling fertilizer, seed, cotton and bricks. Beginning in 1926, the firm was known as Timmerman and Williams. In later years, O.A. Williams, Sr. operated Plains Cotton Warehouse as the sole owner.[93] It is still owned by the Williams family today.

Plains Mercantile Co. was bought and established in 1909 by Alton Carter, uncle of President Carter.[94] Ross Dean's funeral home, which opened in 1912, and other businesses thrived.[95]

For years, Plains was home to a two-story hotel. Built in the 1910s, it was run by Ernest and Rosa Dean. An Aiken family ran the hotel next, followed by the Walter Kennedy family. Later, Flora Markette Kendrick (1873-1950) was hotel

Chautauqua Group in Plains. Plains Hotel, left corner. Photo from Walters family

manager. Boarders, renters, transients, salesmen and actors enjoyed the friendliness and good food at the hotel.[96] The building later was home to the Hewitt family. It was dismantled in 1952 and replaced by a filling station that in the 1970s was run by Billy Carter.[97]

Farming Came First

Despite the success of diverse businesses, farming remained first and foremost the dominant Plains commodity. Agriculture dominated the livelihoods. Even professional people maintained farming operations in addition to their respective careers.[98]

By 1910, Sumter County ranked second in the state in the number of acres of cotton planted and bales produced.[99] One of the first attempts to diversify the agricultural economy of Plains and the area occurred when a northern farmer planted an experimental peanut crop on a Sumter County farm in 1910-11. A Plains cotton merchant purchased the hand-picked peanuts for seed, making the crop readily available to local farmers. By 1916, candy manufacturers regularly purchased peanuts from Plains. The first peanut mill in Georgia opened in nearby Randolph County in 1916.[100] Cotton gins processed peanuts for peanut oil using the same method employed for cottonseed.

Over the years, farmers benefitted from having the railroad in town. By 1919, Plains was described as an agricultural settlement boasting a shipment of 76 boxcars of hogs and cattle. That number was the largest amount shipped from any point of local production in the United States at the time.[101]

The Roaring '20s

With the boom in agricultural production came an influx of new residents to the town. In 1920, Plains' population was recorded at 611 residents, 173 black and 438 white.[102] Though many families had moved to the area several years earlier, including the Carters in 1904,[103] the decade around 1920 brought several families from North Georgia, including the Turners and Kennedys. Others who picked Plains were the Hobgoods, Smiths, Fosters and Medlocks. To some, Plains had become a "boom" town.[104] It was a major trade center for both its residents and area farm families. On Saturdays, its streets were lively and filled with shoppers.[105]

A gasoline station was operated at the time on East Church Street by Charlie C. Lunsford.[106] In the 1920s, garages were run by Edgar Smith and Mark Chambliss, and Bernard and Robert Ratliff.[107] In the late 1920s, Earl Carter even operated a dry cleaning business on Main Street.[108]

By this time, many of Plains' black residents also enjoyed a taste of prosperity.

The black college at Archery thrived during the 1920s. For younger black students, a school had been built in July 1915 on the outside corner of Lebanon Baptist Church in Plains, called the Plains Institutional School. Rosa Lee Pullum was the first known principal of this school, and Mrs. Lenny Rogers was the teacher in the two-room building. In 1922, the school was rebuilt to accommodate more students and was named Rosenwald Elementary School.[109]

As in most U.S. towns during this period, black residents and white residents remained segregated.[110] The white residents of Plains typically dominated Plains' successful ventures. Though Jim Crow laws of the 1890s firmly entrenched segregation and discrimination until the 1960s civil rights movement,[111] some black residents still experienced financial good fortune. Well into the 20th century, black businesses found their ambitions served by a cluster of four small segregated stores just south of the intersection of Main and South Hudson streets.[112]

Joe Kater ran the first barbershop for black people in the early 1900s. At the turn of the century, merchants such as Peter Floyd and Oscar Thommie, Sr. operated businesses in the section a block south of the depot.

According to local legend, Mr. Floyd was the first black man to build his own home in Plains. Joe Kater hired out as a skilled carpenter in addition to operating his barbershop. Tom King owned and operated a cotton gin. Putt Tondee ran a shoe shop. Alex Tatum also operated a barbershop.

Thad Chappell owned a snack shop.[113] In the 1920s, General Myers and John Graham had a thriving mercantile business at the south side of the pharmacy building. They are remembered as having high reputations.[114]

In addition to businesses, Plains' black residents also enjoyed three congregations at which to worship. St. John A.M.E. Church, which was organized in the late 1800s;[115] Lebanon Baptist Church, which broke away from the white division of the church in the 1870s;[116] and the House of God, which started in Plains in 1916,[117] all offered blacks a place of worship by the 1920s.

Recreation and Good Times

As important as church, business and school were to both black and white families at the time, all found ways to recreate. From the simple acts of flying kites, climbing trees and swimming that children enjoyed[118] to the hunting, fishing and poker games undertaken by adults,[119] Plains and the surrounding area was a vibrant place.

By the 1920s, Magnolia Springs, northwest of Plains, had become a very popular "resort" escape enjoyed by white residents. The icy cold water of the springs and the fellowship of other visitors lured people there for decades. Magnolia Springs featured cottages, a pavilion, a dance floor and a swimming pool. Many visitors went early enough to cook breakfast at the springs.[120]

For other residents, a skating rink on South Bond Street that was run by Gurley Davis, a railroad agent, offered another means of enjoyment. It drew soldiers during World War I from Souther Field in Americus. In the late 1920s, brothers J.F. Plexico and Perry Plexico operated a mini-golf course in the Grove downtown.[121] Tennis courts complemented the means of having fun. Years later, a bowling alley run by Oliver Spann provided more recreation.[122]

Jim and Leila Mae Wishard Forrest. Jim is in World War I uniform. Photo from James Forrest

During the '20s, Plains' medical community was known for its revelry. Sumter County's social life reportedly included excessive drinking during this time, some older residents recall. Parties were a highlight of weekend activity for many in Plains.[123]

However, for whites and blacks alike, the 1920s boomed only for a time. The impact of an agricultural depression was felt in the early '20s, years before the rest of the country and 1929.[124] The post-World War I depression of 1921 was felt,[125] though not as severely as World War II decades later. Fewer Plains men served in World War I. Among those who did were Drs. Sam and Bowman Wise, who were in the U.S. Army.[126] Earl Carter also served from 1917-18, returning to Plains after the war.[127]

Depression Years

The 1929 Depression hit Plains the hardest. Southerners, who experienced a significant rise in income because of increased industrialization and strong agricultural prices after 1910, mainly because of the effects of World War I, felt the impact of agricultural depression by the early 1920s.[128] The boll weevil devastated many farms. When the Great Depression hit in 1929, the town of Plains lost much of its prosperity. Plains assumed the role of a quiet Southern community.[129]

From 1929-32, per capita income in the South fell 44 percent.[130] Though Plains, like other Georgia towns, was hurting by the time 1930 rolled around, its people carried on with a steel resolve. In the 1930s, Ernest Spann built and operated Spann's Service Station at Hudson and Church streets.[131] In 1937, Jennings Service Station opened in a wooden building at the end of Main Street.[132] Overall, however, business was slowing with the agricultural difficulties. Because of two traits – desire and determination, through a strong religious faith and educational system under fearless leaders – Plains persevered.

By 1929, the town had lost its first settler and postmaster, first mayor, and first physician. Yet the

Murray Smith holding L. E. "Boze" Godwin. Old hotel in background. Mill Jennings' first service station to right. Photo credit: L. E. "Pete" Godwin, Jr.

strength of its leaders helped sustain a modicum of success.

Church was important. People were still close to the land, and agriculture remained important. Education remained important to everyone in the community.

And as 1930 rolled in, the man who would grow up to be president was about to enter first grade.

Endnotes

[1] United States Department of the Interior/National Park Service, National Register of Historic Places, Registration Form, Prepared by Jill K. Hanson, (Atlanta, Georgia: Southeast Support Office, Atlanta Federal Center,1924 Building,100 Alabama St. S.W., Atlanta, GA 30303, May 1998), p.7

[2] United States Department of the Interior/National Park Service, National Register of Historic Places, Inventory-Nomination Form, Pepared by Andrea Niles,(Atlanta, Georgia: Georgia Department of Natural Resources, 270 Washington Street, S.W., Atlanta, Georgia 30334, April 23, 1984.), p.8

[3] Hanson. p.15

[4] Hanson, p.2

[5] Hanson, p.15

[6] Hanson, p.7

[7] Hanson, p.7

[8] Carter, Ruth, *A History of the Railroad in Plains, Georgia*, (Copyright by Ruth Carter, July 26, 1986)

[9] Hanson, p.28

[10] Hanson, p.16

[11] Walters, Beth, *The History of Plains*, 1885-1985 (Americus,Georgia: Gammage Print Shop, 1985), p.2

[12] Hanson, p.15

[13] Walters, p.2

[14] United States Department of the Interior, *Special History Study*, written by William Patrick O'Brien,(Jimmy Carter National Historic Site and Preservation District, National Park Service, November 1991), p.22

[15] *Act of Incorporation and Ordinances of the Town of Plains, Georgia*, 1897, (Americus, Georgia. Herald Job Department. March 1, 1897), pp.4-30

[16] Walters, p. 127

[17] Anderson, Alan, Interviewed by Steve Short, June 6, 2002

[18] Klenbort, Marcia and Daniel –Text, Smith, Jack, Drawings and Map of Plains, Klenbort, Photos, *The Road to Plains: A Guide to Plains and Nearby Places of Interest in Southwest Georgia*, (Atlanta, Georgia: Avery Press, P.O. Box 7396. 1977), p.5

[19] Walters, p.2

[20] O'Brien, p.77

[21] Gibson, Dot Rees, *Plains, Georgia. Carter Country, U.S.A*, Book 4 of the Historic Classics Series,(Waycross,Georgia:Dot Gibson Publications, 1977), p.5

[22] O'Brien, p.78-79

[23] O'Brien, p.80

[24] O'Brien, p.81

[25] Walters, pp.55,57

[26] Gibson, p.5

[27] Gibson, p.6

[28] O'Brien, p.90-91

[29] Hanson, p.16

[30] _____, *History of Plains*, (Americus,Georgia:Gammage Print Shop, Published under auspices of Lebanon Baptist Church, Plains Baptist Church, Plains United Methodist

Church, St. Andrew's Evangelical Lutheran Church, St. John A.M.E. Church, The House of God, October 1976),10

[31] Cox, Jack F., *History of Sumter County, Georgia,* (Roswell,Georgia:Wolfe Publishing, In association with the Sumter Historic Preservation Society, 1983), p.67

[32] O'Brien, p.83

[33] Cox, p.68

[34] Cox, p.76

[35] Ariail, Dan, *A Self-Guided Tour of Plains, Georgia,* Published by Plains Historical Preservation Trust, P.O. Box 17, Plains, Georgia 31780, No. 3

[36] Cox, pgs.175-78

[37] Cox, p.68

[38] _____, History of Plains, p.12

[39] Cox, p.69

[40] Hanson, p.10

[41] Hanson, p.10

[42] Cox, p.28

[43] Cox, p.28

[44] Cox, p. 28

[45] Hanson, p.11

[46] Hanson, p.2

[47] Walters, p.95

[48] _____, *The Johnson Home Industrial College History* ,(unpublished paper in possession of Milton Raven)

[49] Wise, Amy, *Colored Schools of Plains,Georgia,* (Unpublished paper, July, 2002).

[50] Cox, p. 28

[51] Walters, p.94

[52] Bagwell, Mary Carol, Interviewed by Steve Short, June 2002.

[53] Walters, p.93

[54] Cox, p.29

[55] Hanson, p.11

[56] Hanson, p.11

[57] Gibson, p.11

[58] Walters, p.97

[59] Walters, p.2

[60] _____, *History of Plains,* p.45

[61] Gibson, p.11

[62] Gibson, pgs.10-11

[63] _____, *History of Plains,* p. 45

[64] Cox, p.26

[65] Walters, p. 101

[66] _____, *History of Plains,* p.43

[67] Walters, p.101

[68] _____, *History of Plains,* p.43

[69] Cox, p.26

[70] _____, *History of Plains,* p.44

[71] Walters, p.99

[72] Cox, p.27

[73] Cox, p. 27

[74] _____, *History of Plains,* p.37

[75] Walters, p.46

[76] Walters, p.47

[77] _____, History of Plains, p.37

[78] O'Brien, p.22

[79] Carter, Ruth, p.2

[80] O'Brien, p.22

[81] Cox, p.69

[82] Bagwell, Dr. James E., *Of Time and Mayors: A Sketched History of Plains Mayors and the World Beyond,* Professor of History, Georgia Southwestern State University, Mayor 1984-1985, City Council 1978 to present, p.1

[83] O'Brien, p.22

[84] O'Brien, p.22

[85] Walters, p.5

[86] Walters, p.5

[87] Walters, p.5

[88] Walters, p.37

[89] Walters, p.41

[90] Walters, p.31

[91] Walters, p.46

[92] _____, *History of Plains,* p.33

[93] _____, *History of Plains,* p.37

[94] _____, *History of Plains,* p.39

[95] Walters, p.52

[96] Walters, p.69

[97] Walters, p.69

[98] O'Brien, p. 98

[99] Walters, p.7

[100] O'Brien, p.23

[101] Cox, p.25

[102] Anderson, (Interview)

[103] Carter, Jimmy, *An Hour Before Daylight.*(New York,NY.: Simon & Schuster. Rockefeller Center, 1230 Avenue of the Americas,2001) p.135

[104] O'Brien, p.27

[105] Haugabook, Allene, *Remembering Plains in the 1930s,1940s, 1950s and a Little Beyond,*(Americus,Georgia: Copyright 1996), p.17

[106] Walters, p. 49

[107] Walters, p.54

[108] Walters, p.49

[109] Wise, p.1

[110] O'Brien, p.24

[111] Hanson, p. 17

[112] O'Brien, p.24

[113] O'Brien, p.43

[114] Walters, p.57

[115] _____, *History of Plains,* p.18

[116] _____, *History of Plains,* p.8

[117] _____, *History of Plains*, p.20

[118] Carter, Jimmy, p.93-94

[119] Morris, Kenneth E., *Jimmy Carter, American Moralist*, (Athens, Georgia: The University of Georgia Press,1996), p.30

[120] _____, *History of Plains*, p.58

[121] Walters, p.78

[122] Spann, Oliver, Interviewed by Steve Short, March 2002.

[123] Morris, pgs.42-44

[124] Hanson, p.12

[125] O'Brien, p.27

[126] _____, *History of Plains* ,(1976), p.43

[127] Morris, p.26

[128] Hanson, p.7

[129] _____, *History of Plains*, p.6

[130] Hanson, p.12

[131] Spann, Oliver, Interviewed by Steve Short, 2002.

[132] Walters, p.50

Chapter 3: 1930–1974

Submitted by Allene Timmerman Haugabook

Beginnings in the 1930s

By the time the '30s arrived, Plains was a very well established town. The stores were all built as well as many of the homes, which were very attractive and substantial, showing that the citizens took great pride in the town they had established.

Just before the decade of the '30s, the stock market crashed which ushered in what has become known as "The Great Depression." Great it was, as it affected not only the people of Plains, but also those of the entire nation. The people who grew up during the depression have a different way of thinking and living than those of any other era. Many people lost everything they had. Banks failed; businesses closed; some families lost not only their jobs, but their homes and farms. Many people committed suicide, unable to face the stigma of owing money they could never repay. Those growing up during this time were taught many hard lessons that have stayed with them for life. Lessons learned were to do on very little or simply to do without. Nothing was thrown away. However, even though times were hard, very hard, the people of Plains were a very close-knit group. The business area of the town had been finished and one of the businesses was the bank. It was housed in the only one-story brick building on Main Street. The bank "broke," in 1926, causing hardships carrying over into the 1930s. Many of the houses went unpainted, no new houses were built, and things were pretty much at a standstill.

Health Care

Wise Sanitarium, the only hospital in southwest Georgia during the '20s and early '30s, caught fire in the kitchen area and partially burned in 1935. From this time on it was no longer used as a hospital. It had served the people of this area since it was built in 1921. Before that time a hospital had

East side of Wise Sanitarium 1924
Photo credit: Georgia Department of Archives and History

been located in the upstairs of one of the downtown buildings. What a loss, not only to Plains, but the entire area. Dr. Burr Thomas Wise had become a prominent doctor in Plains, and was the first mayor of the town. His three sons, Thad, Sam and Bowman, settled in Plains and built the hospital. When it burned in 1935, Dr. Thad and Dr. Sam established their medical practice in Americus. However, Dr. Bowman stayed on until his death. He and his wife, Mozelle, and their daughter, Marguerite, lived in the first house built in Plains. It is the first on the right as you come into Plains from Americus, and was built by M.L. Hudson, one of the founding fathers of Plains.

The Wise Sanitarium building was used as apartments for a number of families after it partially burned. Then, in 1956 the building was bought by a Dr. Barber, repaired and reopened as Plains Convalescent Home with a fifty-patient capacity. In 1957, it was sold to Plains Convalescent Home, Inc. with S.H. Greenwald as administrator until his retirement in 1958. His partner, Linton Earl Godwin, Jr., became the administrator, assisted by his wife, Dorothy Oliphant Godwin, as Director of Nursing. It was remodeled in 1960 and in 1978 an entire new wing was added, making it a facility for housing one hundred patients.

In 1958 Plains Citizens bought shares and built a small brick clinic building on West Main Street, just east of the Post Office. The first doctor to serve in the clinic was Dr. Carl Sills. He practiced in Plains until 1962, at which time he moved to Cuthbert, Ga., to practice medicine there. In 1979 an addition was made to the building. At the time of the writing of this book, another addition has been made to the building and the people of the Plains area are well served by the staff of this clinic.

Churches

By the time of the '30s the three churches for white people had already been built, this taking place not long after the turn of the century. These churches were St. Andrew's Lutheran, Plains Baptist and Plains Methodist. However, the churches originally had only a sanctuary but didn't have Sunday school annexes. Plains Baptist began to build its Sunday school annex in 1924. It was still unfinished when the depression years descended upon the nation and town. In 1936, fire damaged part of the Sunday school annex. The front part of the second story and the basement went unfinished until just after World War II when times got better and more financial stability was realized.

The Methodist church was fortunate in that Mrs. Mamie McDonald Bradley, only daughter of J.A. McDonald, one of the prominent early founders of the town, gave money for building the Methodist Sunday school annex in 1937. "Miss" Mamie was a widow and had no children. She was the only person the writer of this portion of the history ever knew who made a trip to Europe during those times. She also owned a Cadillac car, which she kept hidden away in the garage behind her house. Children of the neighborhood took delight in going to the door of the garage and peeping in at "Miss" Mamie's Cadillac. It was the only one we knew about. She never drove it. It just sat there, later being bought by George Cannon of Americus.

The Lutheran church didn't have an annex in those years. The little white wooden building just behind the church was a part of the old Plains High School that was moved to Archery. This small building was used as a music building after the brick school building was built in 1921. Mrs. Frank (Ida Lee) Timmerman taught piano in that building during the '20s. The Lutheran church added a social hall in 1952. The wooden building is now used as a pastor's study.

The three churches for whites were not what we referred to as "full-time" churches. The Lutheran Church and Plains Baptist Church had services on first and third Sundays, while Plains Methodist, which was on a charge, had services on second and fourth Sundays. Citizens of the town were very diligent in attending the church of their own denomination when services were being held. However, on the Sundays that services were held in the other denominations, many people visited the churches of which they were not a member. Plains Baptist Church shared its minister with Preston Baptist until becoming "full-time" under the ministry of Rev. Tommie Jones on October 1, 1954.

The Methodist church continued as a circuit for several more years, becoming a full-time charge in 1978, when Rylander, the last of the churches on the circuit joined its membership with the Plains church.

Infrastructure

The streets of Plains during this time were dirt, with ditches on each side of the streets. These ditches were used by the children to build "frog houses" and to play in after rains. Until 1938-39, the only paved road into Plains was Highway 280 going to Americus. It was at this time that a new road was cut to Preston and was paved. Prior to this time the road went by Lebanon Cemetery, the home of J.A. Bacon, the Carter home, the home of the Watson family, Archery and on over into Webster County joining the road already there just about where the Herlovitch family home was located. During the year of 1938 and '39 a highway crew moved families into Plains in order to work on the "new road," as it was called for many years. This was an exciting time at the school, as many of the grades had new pupils, something that didn't ordinarily take place. Then in 1956 the streets of Plains were paved, also. This was quite a "step forward." Dr. J.C. Logan was mayor at that time.

Plains did not have electricity provided by Georgia Power until sometime in the 1940s. However, the town was fortunate in having electricity before the advent of Georgia Power Co. There was a power plant located in the area of what is now Windham Castings. This plant, according to the history written by Beth Walters, was built in 1919. Many citizens called this "the putt-putt plant" as it made a putt-putt noise when running. The writer remembers her mother telling that when the town first received electricity from this plant, how exciting it was to have lights burning all over the house. The brightness was astounding.

Plains had telephone service for many years, being served by "on the wall" phones with a telephone operator, known as "Central," taking calls and connecting citizens to the person to whom they wished to speak. How exciting, when in 1940, Mr. Thad Jones opened Citizens Telephone Co. and dial phones became available. Now, rather than having a telephone number consisting of two numbers, residents had three numbers. Children took great delight in calling each other. They didn't have much to say, other than "What are you doing?" The answer was obvious. They were enjoying each other's company by way of the new phenomenon in town. What great fun!

Household trash was picked up from the street in an ox-drawn cart, driven by Chick Tyson. If there was a regular schedule or a fee charged I have no record of it.

Most houses at the beginning of this era did not have electric refrigerators. Some had iceboxes and were dependent on blocks of ice being delivered to their homes by way of an ice truck. Hence, families were dependent of blocks of ice being delivered to their homes by way of an ice truck.

Children delighted in following the truck down the street, scraping up the ice chips and eating them. This was, perhaps, one way of keeping cool on a hot day.

The Post Office

In the early 1930s, the Plains Post Office was housed in one of the small wooden buildings at the west end of the street of stores. Sometime in either the late '30s or early '40s the post office was relocated to the building that was formally the Plains Bank. For sure it was in the bank building during World War II, as the children would leave school on occasion and go to the post office in order to purchase war stamps to build toward a war bond. At other times, the students purchased their war stamps on the stage of the auditorium. This was their small way of helping the "war effort." Mail came in on the train twice a day. There was a mail wagon, a flatbed affair with a long tongue, which was pulled over to the depot and mailbags put on it in order to be pulled back to the post office building and put into individual boxes. These boxes did not have a key, but had a particular combination in order to be opened. The newspaper, "The Americus Times-Recorder," was also delivered to the post office and put in boxes in the afternoon. Sometimes the paper only arrived after the post office was closed, at which time the papers were left on a table in the main part of the post office where subscribers could leaf through and find the paper with their name on it.

Post Office in early 1930s. S.H. Timmerman in mail cart. Photo credit: Bettie T. Lorentzson

The Plains Post Office moved into a new building in 1964. This was the first time Plains had a post office built especially for the purpose of receiving and delivering mail. The building is lo-cated on West Main Street. Robert McGarrah was Postmaster at this time and Mrs. Allie M. Smith, mother of first lady Rosalynn Carter, was clerk. Others who helped there were Betty Moss and Irma Wise. Plains had the distinction of being the first new building on which the zip code was posted. Dedication was held August 23, 1964, with addresses being given by Rep. E.L. (Tic) Forrester and Glenn L. Krause, a postal service officer. Rep. Forrester presented the flag, which was raised by Boy Scout Troop 25. Some members of this troop were Murray Walters, Mill Simmons (son of Millard Simmons, a later postmaster), Wayne Murray, Jeff and Steve Smith (twins), Jack Carter (son of President and Mrs. Jimmy Carter), John Williams, Millard English and the leader, Rev. Charles Culbreth, pastor of Plains United Methodist Church.

After the old bank building was vacated and the post office relocated to the new building the old bank building became the office for The Carter Worm Farm, owned and operated by Ruth and Hugh Carter. The Carters shipped so many worms from the post office in Plains that the classification of the post office was raised from C to B.

Public Transportation

The train that came through the town, bringing mail, passengers, and freight was called "The Butt Head." It came through going east at approximately 12:00 noon, and came again going west around 3:00 in the afternoon. The sound of the train whistle was a very familiar one to all the Plains citizens. Prior to the '30s, according to citizens living then, there had been more passenger trains passing through. Mr. Alton Carter reported in a taped talk at St. Mark's Lutheran Church in 1977 that at one time there had been three passenger trains going east and three going west.

During the '40s and '50s citizens were provided public transportation by the Atlantic Trailways Bus system. The bus station was located in what is now City Hall and was operated by the Booker family, along with the service station there.

Another means of traveling back and forth to Americus was on the Shirt Factory bus operated by Margaret Harris. This enabled the people in Plains who worked at the Manhattan Shirt Factory to ride to and from work there, as well as for other people who worked in Americus, and day students going to Georgia Southwestern College. The Shirt Factory was opened in the late '30s and provided work for many people in the area. After Miss Harris' marriage to Foster Cooper, her sister, Carolyn Harris, drove the bus.

Schools

Plains High School was the focal point of the town and surrounding community. Though it has always been known as Plains High School, it had an elementary school, too. There were only eleven grades until 1952, at which time the twelfth grade was added. Two county schools fed into Plains School when the students of Concord and Thompson joined with the Plains students for their four high school years. Concord School was about six miles north of Plains and Thompson School was located about six miles south of Plains.

Perhaps the students and even the citizens of the area didn't realize what a treasure we had in the leaders of our school. Miss Julia Coleman had been a teacher, principal and superintendent for years. However, in 1927 Mr. Y.T. Sheffield, a young man from Pinehurst, Georgia, joined the faculty. He became a permanent fixture in our community until his death in 1967. He taught subjects related to mathematics, but one of his main duties was to coach basketball, both the girls' and boys' teams. The mascot for the teams was the buffalo. The reason for the name was because our town was Plains and the buffalo roamed the plains of the West. This seemed a fitting name for the mascot. At this time, basketball was an important

activity in small towns. Schools in these small towns were classified as "C" schools.

Each Tuesday and Friday nights ballgames were held in the towns. Nearly the entire population came out to cheer their home team. Mr. Sheffield led many of his teams to victory, not only

The second gym at Plains High School built in 1949. Photo credit: Michael Mallard

in the 3rd District West, but also to some wins in the state playoffs. Mr. Sheffield was so loved and respected in the town that in the early '30s a basketball court, called "The Shell," was built. When completed, it became known as Sheffield Stadium. What a sad day for our community when, in 1940, the stadium burned to the ground. Our school was without a place to play basketball until a new gymnasium was built in 1949. This was built right behind the present school building. By the time the school building was restored, the 1949 stadium was in a bad state of repair, and since it was not there during the '30s and '40s, the years that are depicted at the school, it was torn down.

Many programs were held at the school at night. This also brought in the whole community. Graduation night was a *big* event. Girls were dressed in their long white dresses and carried large bouquets of red roses grown in the flower gardens of local people. For this grand occasion, the boys wore white pants and dark dress coats. On Sunday morning, prior to Monday night's graduation exercises, the baccalaureate service was held in the school auditorium. The churches of the community called off their morning worship service in order to attend this event. The school was segregated until 1970 at which time the school became integrated, and students of both the white and black communities could attend school together.

During the '30s and '40s many of the teachers at Plains School were young ladies just finishing their college education. Since Plains was declared a Model School of Georgia in 1937, young teachers were anxious to teach here. At this time, many of the teachers boarded with families out in town. Some were from Americus, but even being that close by, they still boarded in Plains. Teachers did not own their own cars and, hence, could not commute to teach here. This enabled them to be an integral part of the community. It was always exciting to learn at the beginning of the school year who the new teachers would be. Some married Plains men and became permanent citizens of the town.

A very interesting thing that brought the citizens closer together was Friendship Garden at Plains High School. Miss Julia was instrumental in getting different citizens to donate plants, which were then planted at the school in honor or in memory of citizens. One part of the garden was "Baby Row." Upon the birth of a new citizen of the town, an Arbor Vita (meaning tree of life) was planted in his or her honor. This was before the days of integration of the races, so the plants were only in honor of the white babies born here. The planting of the shrubs was another element that brought families of the community in close contact with each other.

In 1941, Plains High School became one of the first schools in the area to have a lunchroom. Prior to this time the students who rode the bus to school

brought their lunches. Students who lived in town could walk home to eat what was at that time called "dinner." The schedule of the day allowed a one-hour period for the dinner break.

The Parent Teacher Association was quite active in these years. Parents, as well as grandparents and friends, were encouraged to attend the meetings and stand up for some particular student who had invited them to attend.

In 1954 the United States Supreme Court decreed that no longer could the people of this country have separate schools for the black and white

Friends in Friendship Garden
Clockwise from top: Allene Timmerman, Joyce Dozier, Billie Morgan, Ruth Carter, Carolyn Harris, Betty Cranford. Photo credit: Allene T. Haugabook

citizens. The schools had been called "separate but equal." Separate they were, but equal they were not. This was to have far-reaching impact on the country and certainly upon the people of Plains and Sumter County. Total integration began in 1970. For several years before this, there had been freedom of choice for those of the black race to choose to go to a school that had previously been for whites only. Plains High School was totally integrated in 1970. The school closed in 1979, at which time the high school students went to Americus and the elementary grades were housed on the south side of Plains at what had previously been the school for black children. The name of this school became Westside Elementary, built in the late 1950s.

In the 1930s and 1940s, Plains High School had a canning plant located behind the building. Here citizens of the town came to can the many vegetables grown on their farms or in the home garden which many of the people had in their own back yards. Also, in these back yards, chickens, cows, and sometimes pigs were raised. The owners of the cows would milk them and sell the milk to other citizens of the town. The milk was not required by law or health standards to be pasteurized at that time. Usually, the chickens were killed, cleaned and eaten in the homes. The eggs provided a bit of income for the families. The grocery stores downtown would buy eggs from local people and sell them to other local people.

The Stores

What a delight when in the late 1940s Plains got a freezer locker. This business was located on the site of the present police station. This was something quite new and unique. The freezer locker was owned and operated by Roy Brannen and Millard Simmons. Here, people could take the meat from cows or hogs that were raised on their farms and killed for eating. Before the advent of the freezing plant, hogs had to be killed in the dead of winter and cured. Now, meat could be taken to town and frozen. This was certainly a modern convenience for the people of Plains.

One might say that Plains was a self-contained little village at that time. Nearly all of our needs could be provided for right here. There were always several grocery stores. These stores would deliver groceries to your door, free of charge. We always had a drug store, Plains Pharmacy. Through the years the Godwin family provided for our needs in the field of medicine. First there was Dr. L.E.

Godwin, Sr., followed by his son, L.E. Godwin, Jr., called "Pete," and then L.E. Godwin, III, called "Boze." Pete and Boze have both served as mayors of the town.

Plains circa 1950s
Photo credit: Georgia Department Archives and History

Service stations were located in three places in the town. Ernest Spann's station was located in the building that now houses City Hall. In the rear of the building, Mr. Spann's son, Oliver, had a bowling alley for a short time in the 1930s. This station was later operated by the Julian Booker family.

Sinclair Service Station
Photo credit: Bettie T. Lorentzson

Another station was located on the corner of Bond's Trail and Highway 280. This building faced Bond's Trail, now called Bond Street. The station was operated by S.H. Timmerman and later by Bobby Timmerman, Ernest Fussell and also, George A. Harper for a short time.

Mill Jennings had a station located where Citizens Bank is today. He later relocated to Highway 280. After Mill's death this station was bought by Billy Carter and became world famous when Billy's brother, Jimmy, became President of the United States.

Barbershops were run by Broadus Wellons, William Spires and Loren Blanton.

Plains citizens could count on Ross Dean to attend to their needs upon the event of a death in a family. His undertaking business was located in the last brick store building to the west of the downtown area. In this building was an elevator used in the funeral business. It still remains in the building, which at the time of this writing is part of The Plains Inn and Antiques Mall. Mr. Dean trained many young men in Plains in the embalming and mortuary business. Some were J.C. Webb, II, James Cranford, and James Wise. Mr. Dean and his wife, Carrie, had no children, but Mr. Dean was always an encourager to the young people of Plains. He died in 1941 and the funeral business was in Plains no more.

The drugstore building was, for many years, a two-story building. On the top floor Ann Gay operated a beauty parlor. Ann came here in the summer of 1939. She also became a permanent citizen when she married Clarence Dodson in 1945. She opened her shop and had a contest for people to help her name it. Mrs. Alice Timmerman won a free permanent for naming it "Ann's Beauty Parlor." The beauty shop was in the southeast corner of the upstairs and in the front part of the upstairs, Dr. Bowman Wise had his medical practice. Another doctor in town, Dr. J.C. Logan, had his medical practice in a building on Bond's Trail, now called Bond Street.

In the 1940s, Mr. H.B. Moman established a dry goods business downtown. There, on the east side of the store, groceries could be bought, while on the west side, needs in the area of cloth and patterns could be provided. Mr. and Mrs. Moman built a brick house on Highway 280 in Plains. This was, perhaps, the first house built in town after the onset of The Great Depression.

A few doors down from M&M Cash Store, as the Moman store was called, was Plains Mercantile, run by Alton Carter. Again, groceries could be bought here. Also, cloth for making dresses was available, while upstairs ready-made clothes could be bought. Mrs. Floyd Burnette, better known as "Miss" Mary Lou, waited on customers in this area and could even decorate hats to the taste of those buying them. Groceries being ordered from Plains Mercantile were delivered to the homes by means of a horse and dray driven by Booker Schley.

Another grocery store was Oliver's, run by "Miss" Katie Oliver, daughter-in-law of R.S. Oliver, one of the founding fathers of Plains. She sold this store to C.L. Walters, Jr. in the late 1940s. During the time of its being Oliver's and Walters', clerks stood behind the counter and waited on customers as the customer read out the list of items needed. If you were not inclined to go to town, all that was needed was to call and order. Pretty soon these items would be delivered to your door. Stores stayed open from about sunup until sundown. However, on Saturdays sundown passed while the streets were still full of customers. The stores remained open until about midnight. This was the time when rural people could come to town, make purchases and visit with friends they did not often see.

There was a store on South Hudson Street just south of the drugstore run by John Graham, a very responsible black man. He sold nice material for making dresses and I can remember going there with my mother from time to time to buy cloth.

Also, at this time, there was a shoe shop operated by Hugh "Bud" Walters. It was located just west of the drugstore.

In these days cotton was king, which necessitated several cotton warehouses in Plains. One was

Timmerman and Williams operated by Frank Timmerman and Oscar Williams. In 1939 the Williams family became the sole owners of this business after the death of Frank Timmerman.

Billy and Sybil Carter at Carter's Warehouse in the 1970s. Photo credit: Georgia Department Archives and History

Another cotton warehouse was operated by George Montgomery and one by Earl Carter. Upon Mr. Carter's death, his son, Jimmy, returned to Plains and operated this warehouse. During Jimmy's years in Washington, the warehouse was operated by his brother Billy.

Bales of cotton often lined the streets of Plains, providing much entertainment for the children as they played on top of the bales, jumping from one bale to another. The cotton bales above had been ginned by L.J. Cranford and when stored in the Timmerman and Williams Warehouse overflowed into the street.

In most towns during the '30s and '40s, a livery stable was almost a necessity. This was an establishment dealing in the sale of mules and horses. Since mules were a vital part of farming before the advent of tractors, this was a needed trade. The stable in Plains was located on Bonds Trail just

Oscar Williams and bales of cotton on Bond's Trail in Plains. Photo credit: Larry Williams

Stable operated by John Woodruff
Photo credit: Georgia Department of Archives and History

beyond Timmerman/Williams Warehouse. The proprietor of this stable was a Mr. John Woodruff.

Also, dealing in the trade of mules was Alton Carter. About once a year a number of families moved into Plains, setting up tents in what was known as "The Grove," now Maxine Reese Park, living there for at least a month. These peole were mule traders and dealt with Mr.Carter. Local people called them "gypsies," as they traveled from place to place. The name of many of the families was Sherlock.

Very few needs of families in Plains could not be met in the little village.

World War II

On December 7, 1941, something happened that alarmed the entire world. The Japanese made an attack on Pearl Harbor, causing the United States to declare war. World War II impacted our town and nation as nothing before or since has done. Many of its young men and a few young women were enlisted in the armed services. Food, gas and clothes were rationed. People joined together in helping in every way possible to help the "war effort." Victory gardens were planted to help with providing food. Children went about their neighborhoods collecting scrap iron. Gas was very

scarce and people were unable to do much traveling. All were happy to join in to help in any way they could to make this war a short war. Even with all their efforts, the war lasted nearly four years.

After the war, servicemen and women began coming home, establishing homes of their own and starting businesses. The future began to look brighter for all.

Clubs

The Plains Lions Club was organized in 1946. One of their great accomplishments was the building of a swimming pool for the citizens to enjoy. Prior to this time, swimming was done at Magnolia Springs, a pool about three miles northwest of

Magnolia Springs picnic
Photo credit: Georgia Department of Archives and History

World War II Soldiers: Charles Hall, Albert Williams, and L.B. Johnson. Photo credit: Allene T. Haugabook

Plains. Water for this pool came from an artesian well and was icy cold. At Magnolia Springs picnics were held, as well as the Junior/Senior prom for the students of Plains High School. Many happy times were enjoyed there, but having a pool in Plains was a great convenience. Women of the town took turns keeping the pool open for Plains citizens to go swimming. These were the days of segregation and this pool was for white children only, though this was not a stated law. In those days, it was just an accepted fact.

Plains had many other clubs. During the '30s and '40s there was a Literary Club, a Rook Club, a Sewing Circle, and in the early 1930s the Stitch and Chat Club was organized, and is still in existence at the writing of this history in 2002.

The Experiment Station

In 1951, 456 acres of land just east of Plains were purchased from the family of Dr. Bowman Wise, on which the Southwest Georgia Branch Experiment Station was to be built. The reason for choosing Plains was because of Sumter County's intense interest in experimental work and also because the soil on the farm was typical of the soil all over Southwest Georgia. In the beginning, N.D. McRainey was superintendent with Howard Dupree as foreman. These two men, along with a few helpers, began tests on vegetables, grains and other crops grown in the area, primarily peanuts, cotton and corn. Mr. McRainey was followed by Robert B. (Bob) Moss, Sr., who served as superintendent from 1962-1992. Upon Mr. Moss' retirement, Stan Jones became the third superintendent, serving in that capacity from 1992 until the present. The McRainey family moved away from Plains, but the Moss family has remained in Plains, being very helpful citizens in many areas. Stan Jones is a Plains native, having grown up in the 17th District just south of Plains. He is the son of Jack and Lorraine Stanford Jones.

Community Award

In 1956 Plains was named first-place winner in the "Better Hometown Contest," sponsored by the Georgia Power Co., competing with cities and towns throughout the state. Plains entered four areas and won first place in two of them and second place in the other two. The four areas were beautification, education and religion, youth work and municipal development. Chairpersons of these four areas were: Mrs. J.C. Logan, Rev. I.L. Bishop, Jimmy Carter and Mayor J.C. Logan. More than 100 people were present for the awarding of $1,000 in prize monies and four beautiful plaques to chairmen of particular divisions of the contest. J.W. Sewell was president of the Plains Lions Club, sponsor of the overall project.

A Governor Elected

Things went along in Plains at a slow pace in the late 1940s and early 1950s. However, in 1953 former citizens of Plains returned to make their home here, which forever changed the complexion of the community. Jimmy and Rosalynn Carter decided to come home to the place of their birth to become residents again. Jimmy first became a member of the Sumter County School Board. Then in 1962, he made the decision to run for state senator. This was quite a story in itself. He first lost the election from our district. However, it was revealed that many wrongdoings had taken place in Georgetown and Quitman County with dead people being registered and voting. Upon a recount of the votes it was determined that Jimmy Carter was the winner and he went on to serve four years in the Georgia State Senate. In 1966, more excitement was in store for Plains. Jimmy Carter decided to run for governor of Georgia. This was an exciting time, but to the dismay of many, he lost to Lester Maddox.

When the time came for another state election, Carter decided to run again. The year was 1970.

This time he was successful in his bid for office. He was elected governor of Georgia and was inaugurated in 1971, serving until 1975. This was a very meaningful time for the citizens of Plains, and a sign was put up over downtown stores in his hometown declaring that this was the home of Jimmy Carter, Governor of Georgia.

The Peanut Special
Sara and Edwin Timmerman and children, Frank and Miriam. Allene and C. G. Haugabook, Jr. and daughters, Beth and Amy. Photo credit: Allene T. Haugabook

home in the White House. Many citizens boarded the train dubbed "The Peanut Special" and headed for Washington, D.C., to see their native son inaugurated as the 39th President of the United States.

Governor Jimmy Carter 1970-1974
Picture given to Mrs. Ida Lee Timmerman

This event was great, but had much less impact on the town and state as when Carter announced that he would run for the office of President of the United States. The total complexion of the town changed as tourists began coming to town to see the small village that hoped to produce a president. Some thought this entirely impossible, but they were proved wrong, for in November 1976, Jimmy Carter and his wife were destined to make their

Top picture: Sign when Carter was Governor. Photo credit: Georgia Department of Archives and History. Bottom picture: Sign when Carter was running for President.

At the time of the writing of this article the sign reads, "Plains, Georgia, Home of Jimmy Carter 39th President of the United States." However, the sign has read "Home of Jimmy Carter, Our Governor," "Home of Jimmy Carter, Our Next President," followed by "Home of Jimmy Carter, Our President."

Many changes took place from the dark days of depression and World War II. The 1950s and '60s saw improvements in the town. Some new houses were built, but the population remained relatively the same. Little did the citizens realize what lay ahead, as thousands of visitors began pouring into the town of Plains that had been referred to as a "sleepy little village."

Chapter 4: 1975–1981

Submitted by Jimmy Bagwell

As the 1970s dawned, Plains lay unchanged from the previous decades. "In summer, the sun was white with glare and fiery hot. There was absolutely nothing to do – one may as well go down to the edge of town and listen to the road gang sing."[1] Magnolias and oaks mingled with pine trees, gnats, pecans, peanuts, and cotton. Life was unhurried, peaceful – a place where time stood still. The townspeople liked this, not given to the hurley-burley of city life. Existence centered on home, school and church. This style was a part of them, bone and marrow.

It was a wonderful world where past and present inextricably intertwined. Miss Julia and Mr. Sheffield had just died, one could still remember Mr. Moman's hardware store and the C. L. Walters' grocery store on Main Street still stayed open on Saturday nights until 11:00, and if Christmas, later. People came to buy groceries on Saturday and stayed late socializing. Many a fight broke out with the help of Jim Beam and "cuttings" were a regular occurrence. On one occasion when the new Methodist preacher hit town, the good pastor, Rev. Charles Culbreth, still wet behind the ears from seminary, went into the store one night to get a quart of milk. The store was jammed and two incidences occurred simultaneously: the lights went out for a moment, and one could hear Mr. C. L. shout, "Keep your hands in your pockets." When light returned, a fight broke out; two women were swinging "co-cola" crates. Mr. C. L. broke it up, but the poor pastor, who was caught in the middle of the fracas, lost his milk and made a quick retreat home. The rest of us lay low.

Then, this place of calm demeanor was jolted. The town was stood on its head, topsy-turvy. But, it was a pleasant shock, indeed, a titillatingly exciting shock, for one of its natives, Jimmy Carter, had received the Democratic Party's nomination for President of the United States. The year was 1976. The town began to take on a singular demeanor, a collective voice that said, "What if he wins?" No one is supposed to know a president. And, what shall we call him? "Jimmy, as always" was the answer.

Jimmy had begun running two years before when he left the governor's office. He was virtually an unknown when he announced his candidacy. A news commentator remarked, "Jimmy Carter, a nobody from the South is running for President of the United States."[2] Most people underestimated Jimmy; his campaign manager was Hamilton Jordan from Albany, Georgia. This young man did a superb job masterminding the run for the presidency.

In understanding Jimmy's winning the presidency, his past is very important. His roots run deep into the red earth of Sumter County, a fact he has always appreciated. He was born on October 1, 1924, in Plains at the Wise Sanitarium, the first president to be born in a hospital. The Carter family lived on a farm in nearby Archery, the small community slightly west of Plains. As a child, Jimmy was free to play with black children, although he attended segregated school and church. He helped work in the fields and at the age of five began selling boiled peanuts on the streets of Plains.

Jimmy's father, James Earl Carter, Sr., was a farmer, peanut broker, local public official, and conservative Democrat. Earl and his wife, Lillian Gordy Carter, did not see eye to eye on racial matters. Many times he left the house when she had black guests. He served in the Georgia Legislature and on the Sumter County Board of Education. He died of cancer at the age of 59. It was this event that

Dot and L.E. "Pete" Godwin, Jr., members of the Peanut Brigade. Photo credit: Pete Godwin

forced Jimmy to resign his commission in the Navy and return home to Plains.

Jimmy married Rosalynn Smith of Plains on July 7, 1946. She and Jimmy became partners for life, doing almost everything together. They had three sons, Jack, Chip, and Jeff. They had one daughter, Amy. Rosalynn proved to be a most gracious and effective First Lady.

Jimmy Carter's first brush with politics came in 1963, when he was elected to the Georgia Senate. He was very successful in this position as he was back home as a peanut and cotton warehouseman. He ran for governor in 1966, and was defeated by Lester Maddox. In 1970, however, he again ran and won the governorship. In this top state job, he directed himself toward administrative governmental reorganization.

It was after the Democratic Convention of 1972 that he began to think seriously about running for president. One of his thoughts was: "I am a farmer, that lives in the Deep South, and no Southerner has been elected President in more than one hundred years."[3] In politics, timing is everything and Jimmy Carter picked the right time to seek the

country's highest office. The country, coming off of the Watergate years, was ready for a change and he was poised to take advantage of the situation. He shocked observers with early victories in the Iowa caucuses and the New Hampshire primary. One at a time he knocked out the other contenders in the areas of their strength. He stopped former Gov. George Wallace of Alabama in Florida, Rep. Morris Udall of Arizona in Wisconsin, and Sen. Henry Jackson of Washington in Pennsylvania. Gov. Jerry Brown of California upset Carter in the Maryland and California primaries, but by then it was too late to stop Jimmy and his faithful followers. Carter had the Peanut Brigade behind him. This was a group of Georgians that had campaigned for him since his initial decision to run for president.

As Democrats gathered in New York in July 1976, Carter had more than the 1,054 delegates that

Plains Depot Presidential Campaign Headquarters Photo credit: Georgia Department of Archives and History

Jimmy Carter speaks at Presidential Campaign Headquarters in Plains, November 1976. Photo credit: Georgia Department of Acrchives and History

were needed to win. He was nominated on the first ballot with 2,238½ votes to 329½ for Udall, 300½ for Brown, and the rest were scattered about. Sen. Walter Mondale of Minnesota was nominated for vice president. The symbol of Carter as a candidate of unity was reinforced for television viewers with the spectacle of George Wallace, and Coretta Scott King and other prominent blacks joining Carter on the victory platform. In his acceptance speech, he continued to stress unifying themes: it was time to honor and strengthen families, neighbors, diverse cultures, and customs. Jimmy Carter was elected President of the United States on November 2, 1976. He heard the good news of victory while he was in Atlanta. He then left to come back to Plains in the early morning hours. His faithful supporters welcomed Carter back home. His vote total was 40,825,039 (50%) to 39,147,770 (48%). The electoral vote for Carter was 297 and 240 for Gerald Ford. Jimmy won the electoral votes of the District of Columbia and the following states: Alabama, Arkansas, Delaware, Florida, Georgia, Hawaii, Kentucky, Louisiana, Maryland, Massachusetts, Minnesota, Mississippi, Missouri, New York, North

Carolina, Tennessee, Texas, West Virginia, and Wisconsin. Carter's ability to win votes was evident, especially in the South. He was particularly popular with blacks, who gave him 90 percent of their votes.

Jimmy Carter in his Inaugural Address, on January 20, 1977, stated: "You have given me a great responsibility – to stay close to you, to be worthy of you, and to exemplify what you are. Let us create together a new national spirit of unity and trust. Your strength can compensate for my weakness, and your wisdom can help to minimize my mistakes."[4] Jimmy's election had a phenomenal effect on Plains. The campaign had been exceptionally wonderful and electrifying.

Maxine Reese ran the Georgia campaign from the now famous depot in Plains. She was a human dynamo with a lot of political savvy. She had connections all over the world, setting up conferences for Jimmy, Rosalynn, Billy and Miss Lillian. She talked to the European, Asian and African press. Congressmen called en masse from all over the United States. Maxine talked with them relating Jimmy's ideas, policies, and agenda. She took to this like a "duck on a junebug" – a regular

Lillian Carter, Maxine Reese, family and friends celebrate Jimmy's victory. Photo credit: Georgia Department of Archives and History

Theodore Roosevelt and Louis XIV, with a touch of Machiavelli. She was truly a legend in her own time. Jimmy, indeed, owed her much.

In addition to her thoroughness and determination to get Jimmy elected president, she could be quite humorous. She once told this author that whenever she fried a chicken, she fried two – the first, for her to eat while she fried the second one. Another time, she asked, "Why do people come up and say, Maxine you are so fat. Well, I know I'm fat, but they seem to think I don't know it. Also, people never seem to walk up to thin people and tell them, they are so thin." Moreover, it is remem-

Ann Dodson, Plains Garden Club. Chairman of the White House Decorating Committee

bered when a stray dog took up at the depot campaign headquarters. Many workers there suggested various names for the cur. Maxine proclaimed the perfect name, "Jimmy Who." So the dog became the now famous "J-Who," who lies buried across from the depot under a granite slab, which bears his name.

Continuing with the election's effect on Plains, there were the crowds – how they descended upon the little hamlet. They came by the hundreds and thousands each day, with car and pedestrian congestion being the order of the day. Sen. Herman Talmadge got caught up in the hurly burly while visiting and quipped, " I never thought I'd get into a traffic jam in Plains."

Then, there was the time when a group of ladies from the Plains Garden Club went to Washington to decorate the White House. Mrs. Ann Dodson was chair of the committee. "Miss Ann," as Plainsites fondly called her, came to Plains in the early 1940s from Flowery Branch, Georgia. She opened up a beauty parlor downtown on the second floor over the drugstore. She was a fixture in Plains.

In January 1977, the ladies trooped to Washington to use their decorating expertise. They went into every room of the White House decorating it exquisitely. Rosalynn Carter later wrote," The freshest, most beautiful flowers I have ever seen came from Plains to the White House the afternoon that Jimmy was sworn in as President, January 20, 1977."[5]

The only negative aspect, perhaps, of all of this notoriety for Plains was the effect it had on the local businesses. Nice, long-standing stores like the hardware store, the Mercantile, and Walters Grocery changed for the worse. Their owners succumbed to the "trinket fever" of the moment. Local purchasers could not get to the stores as before, for hundreds and thousands of tourists flooded the business section, taking all the parking places. Fresh vegetables, meats, hammers, saws, flour, dry goods, etc. disappeared and in their places came cheap trinkets, capitalizing on the recent election and the Carter phenomenon. The locals disliked them; the tourists loved them. Two convenience stores appeared away from the main business area that supplied a few of the needful items that had been lost. They were *Maxine's* and *The Peanut Gallery.* At least, now, residents didn't have to go to Americus or Preston for a loaf of bread. But, caught up in it all, none really seemed to mind. It was all part of this great new wonderful whirlwind that had gripped Plains so completely. Moreover, the "Smiling Peanut" was not a trinket; it was

The Smiling Peanut
Used at Carter rally in Evansville, Indiana, later given to Plains. Photo credit: Annette Wise

stationary. The locals and tourists alike loved it. It has been repaired twice and still stands proudly in front of Davis E-Z Shop (formerly Maxine's). It is a 13½-foot, 250-pound statue of a peanut, with Carter teeth – smiling.

Perhaps the most trying time during this period was the split in the Plains Baptist Church. As Jimmy became more and more famous in the latter days of the campaign and when he beat Gerald Ford for the presidency, tremendous pressures manifested themselves upon the congregation, which were used to worshipping God in its own unassuming ways. But, the crowds came en masse to the church – some came more for notoriety than for worship. To attend church with a president, especially a new one, was quite thrilling. Visitors stood in the pews to take pictures; some, for a souvenir, tore out front pages of the hymnals that had Plains Baptist Church printed on them; they crowded in the back and huddled around the walls of the church. Moreover, when the church was filled to overflowing, a bigger crowd hovered outside to catch a glimpse and a snapshot of the president and his family as they emerged at the end of the service. True worship under these circumstances was hard to come by and seemed elusive, especially to the faithful members who had worshipped there all their lives. Added to all these pressures and distractions internal differences of opinion concerning congregational policy began to arise in the church. Pursuant to this, approximately 35 members decided to leave the congregation and build another church down the road on North Bonds Trail. President and Mrs. Carter chose to go with this new congregation, which evolved into the present day Maranatha Baptist Church. Perhaps the split was a blessing in disguise, for now Plains has two flourishing churches out of one, both doing God's will. The Lord works for good in wonderful and mysterious ways for those who love Him and meet in His name.

When Jimmy and Rosalynn went to Washington, Plainsites were "pleased as punch." They were very proud of them and the thought of the inaugural parade moving down Pennsylvania Avenue conjures up the mental picture of the "special pair" superbly dressed, Jimmy in topcoat and Rosalynn in an absolutely stunning, exquisite aqua coat with black accessories. Plains was proud of its native son and so was the world. Much was expected from this new president from the Deep South.

The aftermath was good for Plains; the crowds dwindled to a comfortable number that the citizens could handle. Plains people could afford to be friendly and display that hospitality for which Southerners are so well known. The presidential years passed with triumphs and tragedies. The high point was the Middle-East peace accord signed at Camp David by Menachem Begin and Anwar Sadat of Israel and Egypt, respectively. Another plus was Jimmy's "human rights policy" that was spread around the world. But, in this vale of tears, nothing is perfect, not even the administration of a well-meaning president.

Tragedies and defeats came as surely as the triumphs. A fanatical Shiite holy man, who became dictator of the country and the state church, toppled America's good friend, Reza Shah, ruler of Iran. Thus, a theocracy was formed that boded ill for Iran, the United States and the world. Pursuant to this, the dastardly act occurred of taking American hostages by order of the Ayatollah Khomeini. Months passed and an American nation nervously waited, hoping for a breakthrough of miracle proportions. President Carter negotiated the release of the hostages during his last three days as president. Khomeini released them five minutes after Carter's term expired.

After returning from the White House, Jimmy has continued to do his good works, and has won acclaim as the most effective former president in the history of this country. No other president has contributed so much after leaving the presidency.

History will place accolades on Jimmy for this, and Plains continues to be "pleased as punch."

Endnotes

[1] Carson McCullers, *The Ballard of the Sad Café and Other Stories* (Boston: Houghton Mifflin Company, 1951), 3,4.
[2] Jenny McCorkle, *Jimmy Carter and the 1976 Presidential Election* (unpublished manuscript December 1, 2000), 1. In private collection of James E. Bagwell, Plains, Georgia.
[3] Jimmy Carter, *Why Not the Best* (Nashville, TN: Broadman Press, 1975), 138.
[4] William A. Degregorio, *The Complete Book of U. S. Presidents* (New York: Brigade Books, Inc., 1984), 624.
[5] *Flowers from Plains to the White House* (Privately published pamphlet, 1977) n.a., 2.

One of four arrangements in the ground floor corridor of the White House. Arranged by Mrs. Sam (Ann) Singer

Chapter 5: 1981–2002

Submitted by Jimmy Carter

President And First Lady Return Home

On January 21, 1981, Plains entered a new era. The town's famous son and daughter came back home – from the White House. Although the weather was cold and raining, the community was warm with excitement and friendship. Maxine Reese called the event "the world's largest covered-dish dinner." Thousands of people jammed Main Street, and

![President Jimmy Carter and Rosalynn Carter accompanied by White House Appointments Secretary, Phil Wise.]

President Jimmy Carter and Rosalynn Carter accompanied by White House Appointments Secretary, Phil Wise. Photo credit: Jimmy Carter Library

broke into cheers when Jimmy and Rosalynn Carter arrived. The electrifying news had already swept the nation: the hostages had been released after being held for 444 days in Iran! When the man stood before us with his family, we realized that he had been president only a few hours earlier, and he stated in a choked voice how much he appreciated the support of his neighbors, and then announced that he would rest for a few hours and then leave for

Wiesbaden, Germany, so he could personally greet the released hostages. After that day of mixed excitement and happiness was over, our town settled into a much quieter existence, eager in many ways to revert back to the life we knew before being in the world's spotlight.

Carter greets released hostages.
Photo credit: Jimmy Carter Library

World Leaders Visit Plains

Later that year, world leaders continued to visit our community, each time welcomed by public and private receptions, a flock of news reporters, and major speeches of international importance. In August, Egypt's President and Mrs. Anwar Sadat came to visit us, followed just a month later by Israel's Prime Minister Menachem Begin. Another visitor was Japanese Prime Minister Fukuda, followed later by presidents of Paraguay, Dominican Republic, and other countries.

Carter Administration Reunion

The first major reunion of the Jimmy Carter presidential administration was held in Plains in September 1981. Vice President Walter Mondale, Press Secretary Jody Powell, and other key players in White House affairs reminisced about the four years they shared in Washington.

Lillian Carter Laid To Rest

In October 1983, Rev. Fred Collins gave a brief eulogy at the funeral of Mrs. Earl Carter, known throughout the world as "Miss Lillian." He said, "Although she was a friend of the rich and powerful, she retained a love of all humanity. Besides being a great mother and matriarch of a large family, this was the sum total of her life: caring for other people. This woman was full of good works." Lillian Gordy (1898-1983) moved from Richland to Plains to enter nursing training at Wise Sanitarium, and married Earl Carter in 1923. She was the mother of Jimmy, Gloria, Ruth, and Billy Carter.

Plains High School Will Be Renovated

Citizens of Plains began almost immediately to prepare for a future that would not only bind us together and preserve our history, but also make our town more interesting to visitors. P.J. Wise, Maxine Reese, and John Pope were our leaders, and a dynamic group began to seek support in the U.S. Congress for a partnership – between our town and the U.S. Park Service. Our goal was to renovate Plains High School, which many of us had attended during its years of service. Now vacant and partially dilapidated, the cost of repair was approximately $5,000,000. The new law provided that 40% of the cost would have to be provided from local sources, and in 1990 the community went to work. We raised money with cake sales, square dances, music concerts, contributions from alumni and others, and inmates from the local corrections centers joined local citizens in doing much of the

P.J. Wise, Fred Boyles, Maxine Reese and John Pope, instrumental in historic preservation in Plains. Photo credit: Mary Wise

work. We even sold small packages of dirt from Jimmy Carter's front yard, and portions of boards from the schoolhouse signed by the former president. Generous manufacturers donated many of the necessary supplies and equipment. The project was to be completed in October 1996 and the beautiful old building will contain a visitor's center, offices for the Park Service, an auditorium for movies and public events, and a museum that presented three eras in the life of the former first family. Soon thereafter, in April 1997, PHS would become the Official State School of Georgia.

We Celebrate Our Centennial

In May 1985, Plains celebrated its centennial. It would be the first of our town's annual celebrations, either on the same date in late spring or later, as a peanut festival in September, during harvest season. Each year our community hosted thousands of visitors, with dances, display booths, softball games, road races, auctions, and entertainment. Most people would agree that the centennial concert by Willie Nelson on the school's baseball field was the all-time highlight. He contributed all the proceeds from the event to our town for its future development. Our celebration was widely publicized, including coverage by Walter Cronkite and Larry King.

Centennial parade on Main Street in Plains
Photo credit: Allene Haugabook

1953 home of Jimmy and Rosalynn Carter
Photo credit: Annette Wise

Railroad Depot Given To Plains

The first building in Plains and the headquarters for the Jimmy Carter presidential campaign was the railroad depot in the center of town. In July 1986, Seaboard Air Line Railroad and CSX contributed the building and surrounding property to the Park Service to be preserved as a historic site. Because of an original reversionary clause in the original deed, this actually means that heirs of M.L. Hudson Estate still own an interest, and it will take a number of years before clear title can be transferred. (Title cleared in 2002)

Carters' Apartment 9A Dedicated

In January 1987, Unit 9A in the Plains Public Housing Project was dedicated as part of the U.S. Park Service. This is where Jimmy, Rosalynn, Jack, Chip, and Jeffrey lived when they returned to Plains from the U.S. Navy in October 1953. The apartment is now used by the Plains Historical Preservation Trust, and is commemorated by a chained area, plaques, and photographs for visitors to peruse.

A Visit From Tibet's Dalai Lama

In September 1987, Tibet's Dalai Lama visited Plains. He is one of many dignitaries to be our guests, along with presidents and prime ministers of nations in Africa, Asia, and Latin America, movie actors, journalists, presidential candidates, and other well-known people. We always extend to them a warm welcome and make them feel at home, because they do not cause a furor among citizens who have become accustomed to visitors who are famous.

Plains To Be A National Historic Site

With strong support, congressional legislation was passed and signed into law in December 1987 to designate Plains as the Jimmy Carter National Historic Site. The official designation within the town would include the schoolhouse, railroad depot, the former president's ranch-style home, and the façade of the old Wise Sanitarium, where Jimmy became the first future president to be born in a hospital. The historic area would also include enough acreage in the Archery community to encompass the boyhood home, barn, blacksmith shop, and other buildings. It is expected that the National Park Service will have overall supervision of the 650-acre designated site. Most of the property, including the former president's current home, will be donated to the U.S. government.

Simmons Retires, White Will Serve

After thirty years with the U.S. Postal Service, Millard Simmons retired as postmaster in May 1990. He had served in that capacity since December 1979, after having begun as a rural mail carrier twenty years earlier.

Clarence Johnson of Cuthbert acted as postmaster for approximately three months, after which a postal clerk, Polly White, received the permanent appointment. Simmons said he plans to "wear out a lot of fishing rods."

Plains Products, Inc. Opens

In May 1991, Allen Mountjoy, manager, was joined by Mayor Boze Godwin and Sumter County Chief Administrative Officer Barbara McCarty in a ceremony to announce the opening of a new business in Plains. Former President Jimmy Carter and his wife Rosalynn made brief remarks and clipped the ribbon to open the plant, which will manufacture furnishings to be used in the manufacture of mobile homes. The new plant is expected to employ between fifty and a hundred workers.

Superintendent Robert Moss Retires

Southwest Georgia Experiment Station superintendent Robert Moss retired after thirty years of service with the University of Georgia Department of Agriculture. He had replaced N.D. McRainey as superintendent upon his retirement in 1963. The people of Plains were delighted to learn that Superintendent Moss will continue to make his permanent residence in our community.

Jacksons Get New Home

Following several weeks of hard work by volunteers, a new home was completed for Curtis and Martha Jackson late at night on Christmas Eve. This was one of the many homes being built in Sumter County under auspices of Habitat for Humanity. The old home, next door on the same lot, was bought by Curtis for $100 in the early 1960s and moved to the site. It will be destroyed when the Jackson's furniture is transferred to the new home. Jackson said, "This is a wonderful Christmas gift for me and Martha, and we thank all the people who made it possible."

Bobby Salter Opens Plain Peanuts

Bobby Salter is the owner of the town's newest business, Plain Peanuts, which officially opened the first Saturday in April 1992. Special comments were made during the dedication program by P.J. Wise, president of Plains Historical Preservation Trust, Sumter County Commission representative George Ellis, Fred Boyles, and former President Jimmy Carter. A.B. Jackson represented the Plains City Council. Located in the old Carter's Warehouse office on Main Street, the store will offer Plains souvenirs and a wide variety of delicious peanut products, including five flavors of peanut brittle.

Jimmy Carter speaks at the opening of Plain Peanuts in 1992. Photo credit: Bobby Salter

Fire Guts Plains Store

In May 1992, a fire almost totally destroyed Simply Southern Antiques Shop, owned by Frances Irlbeck, and threatened to destroy the entire Main Street. Sheriff Randy Howard announced that, in his opinion, it was a case of arson, and the fire apparently started at the rear of the store. At the same time, two windows had been broken down the street at the Plains Post Office. The sheriff gave full credit to the Plains Fire Department, which responded promptly to the conflagration, discovered by a night watchman at about 3:30 a.m.

Our Citizens In A Movie!

Some of our local residents became movie actors in 1993, when Hallmark came to town and filmed "To Dance With the White Dog," starring Jessica Tandy and Hume Cronyn, partially on the streets of Plains. It was exciting to watch the process of making a high-quality movie, and even more so when all of us viewed the film to see our neighbors or ourselves on the screen.

Our Worst Flood In History

Our community suffered its worst flood in history in July 1994, when a tropical hurricane lingered over this part of Georgia and poured 21 inches of rain on us in one day. Thirty-one people were drowned in floodwaters from broken dams and the Flint River's spilling over its banks, fifteen of them in Sumter County. More than two dozen homes in Plains were flooded, and the downpour damaged many other buildings. As part of a disaster area, we received funds to put new roofs on all the downtown buildings, and to repair and paint the awning over our sidewalk.

Park Service Acquires Carter Home

The National Park Service announced the acquisition of the boyhood home of Jimmy Carter. The U.S. Congress had authorized this purchase in 1987, to commemorate the history of the community where the 39th president was born and spent his early life.

Plains Receives Award

The National Park Service and its Foundation announced in April 1996 that the Jimmy Carter National Historic Site, Plains Historical Preservation Trust, and the City of Plains received one of their most prestigious awards. The citation recognizes the outstanding partnership contributions of private and public entities in advancing the mission of the National Park Service. The essence of the accomplishment has been the close cooperation among the three honorees in achieving common goals in the Plains community.

Olympic Torch In Plains

One of the most memorable sporting events came to our town – or at least passed through Plains – in July 1996, when we were chosen to be on the Olympic torch route from Athens, Greece, to Atlanta, Georgia. On the stage, Stan McWhorter of Leesburg passed the torch to Ethel Marshall of Plains, who carried it on westward toward Preston.

Annette Wise Appointed State Teacher

The Jimmy Carter National Historic Site Education Program began in August 1996 with Annette Wise being appointed as the official State Teacher. The education program is a partnership between the Georgia Department of Education, Sumter County Schools, and the National Park Service. Student classes will visit the renovated Plains High School, and will enjoy the unique experience of learning how their parents and

Annette Wise working with students
Photo credit: Keith Wishum

grandparents learned in classrooms of the 1930s. They will also have an opportunity to visit other historic places in the Plains community. Mrs. Wise described the opportunity as "Exciting! It will be a thrill to teach students in this setting." She has twenty years experience as a teacher, and holds a master's degree in early childhood education.

Amy Carter Wed

One of the highlights of Plains social life was the wedding of Amy Lynn Carter to James Wentzel in September 1996. The entire bridal party spent several days at the Pond House, where they enjoyed music, dancing, horseshoes, badminton, fishing, and boating. The bridesmaids and groomsmen also decorated the outdoor wedding site, baked the wedding cake, and made other preparations for the ceremony. A private group of about 150 attended the wedding, after which the bride and groom spent their honeymoon night in the bridal suite at the Windsor Hotel.

PHS Dedicated

The Plains High School building was officially dedicated in October 1996, with one of the largest ceremonies our community has ever seen. Following a $5 million renovation project, hundreds of school alumni, friends, contributors, and dignitaries assembled to share the history of the building and to learn about its future as a welcome center, museum, and place for community meetings.

Arafat Makes A Late Visit

In March 1997, the third major player in the Middle East came for a visit, after an interesting trip to our town that caused him to arrive almost two hours late. In a large airplane furnished by the government of Saudi Arabia to bring the Palestinian leader down from New York, the pilot first circled

Plains High School dedicated
Photo credit: Keith Wishum

over Atlanta. When Yasir Arafat looked down on our capital city's skyscrapers, he told the pilot that it didn't look like the town that President Carter had described to him as his hometown, but they finally landed at one of its large airports. It was only after they obtained directions to Souther Field in Americus that the plane took off again and brought the entourage to the correct destination. The Palestinian leader was welcomed by Mayor Boze Godwin and other dignitaries, and expressed his commitment to peace between his own people and the Israelis.

Plains Depot A Campaign Museum

In September, the Carter Campaign Museum opened in the depot, which was headquarters for the nationwide presidential campaign. For two years, the Carter Political Items Collectors worked with the U.S. Park Service to prepare a presentation of this era in the life of Plains. In addition to representatives of these two organizations, Jimmy and Rosalynn Carter and Maxine Reese reminisced about interesting and humorous events of the campaign, when hundreds of news reporters and thousands of visitors filled our town.

Photographs Tell Our Town's History

In September 1997, photographs of all the mayors of Plains were unveiled in the City Hall.

Peanuts, And A Great Play!

The same week, many visitors joined our home folks as we attended the first of a series of annual Peanut Festivals, which continued the previous springtime celebrations and inaugurated remarkable performances of "If These Sidewalks Could Talk." This is an original play each year, written by Kim Fuller with music and lyrics composed by Dr. Dan Ariail. We look forward each year to a delightful evening of songs, jokes, and anecdotes dramatized by dozens of our own citizens.

"If These Sidewalks Could Talk"
Group of cast members. Back row: Eola Mae Jennings, Josh Speir, Virginia Williams. Front row: Evelyn English, Allene Haugabook as Miss Julia, Carrie Wise and Joni Stelly Westberry

Experts Plan Our Future

A team of experts came from the University of Georgia to Plains in 1998 to examine our community, talk to dozens of our interested neighbors, and record their compliments, criticisms, and suggestions. In July, at a public meeting, we received their well-considered advice on ways that our town could be beautified and increase tourism, employment, governance, and relations with the surrounding rural areas, always with great care not to change the basic character or appearance of where we live.

An Old-New Coca-Cola Sign

A month later, the Coca-Cola company refurbished its huge sign on the east side of South Bond Street, which had first been painted in 1927.

New Recreation Center Opens

A new recreation center was dedicated in September on the western side of Plains, following a community-wide effort to raise money and provide workers. A complete plan has been followed, primarily with the involvement of the children who will be enjoying the facility. The installations included a swimming pool, bathhouse, playground, and a basketball court. The next project will be completion of a community building for a Boys and Girls Club and classes and other activities for adults.

Jimmy Carter working on Plains Boys and Girls Club. Photo credit: Allene Haugabook

Bishop William Johnson Honored

Our most famous (and wealthy?) citizen six or seven decades ago was Bishop William Decker Johnson, who actually lived in nearby Archery. He was justifiably famous as a churchman, educator, world traveler, and publisher who never forgot his roots in our community. After a year of raising funds and making careful plans led by Johnny Raven and Eugene Edge, a historical roadside marker was dedicated in Archery in February 1999, extolling Bishop Johnson's virtues and describing his achievements. A highlight of the ceremony was a letter read from Bishop

Johnson's 94-year-old daughter, Fannie Johnson Hill, with speeches by Rep. Jimmy Skipper, Simeon Wakefield, Rev. Walter Washington, and Milton Raven, Sr. At the bottom of this bronzed litany is a simple statement that the 39th President of the United States also lived in Archery.

Committee members at unveiling of the Archery marker honoring Bishop William Johnson. Photo credit: Allene Haugabook

Plains Becomes A Better Hometown

After applying for designation as a Georgia Better Hometown in 1997 and 1998, Plains achieved this coveted honor from the Georgia Department of Community Affairs on the third try, in 1999. Working on the successful application were City Clerk Penny Smith, Chrissy Marlowe, Department of Community Affairs, and Bill Russell, University of Georgia Business Outreach Services. This prized designation is awarded only when a community has demonstrated proven cooperation and civic spirit. Affiliated legally with the City of Plains, a group of citizens comprise the Better Hometown Committee, which will attempt to carry out some of the recommendations of the team from the University of Georgia and from our own citizens. Major projects will include completion of the comprehensive recreation center for our children, a new restaurant, increased employment opportunities, and the preservation and beautification of the downtown area.

Boys and Girls Center Opened

Working closely with Habitat for Humanity and volunteers from our own community, we completed and designated a beautiful building that will house the final stages of a difficult and exciting project. We first built a swimming pool and bath house, and later a multi-goal basketball court, playground, and now a complete building complex. A Boys and Girls program will be conducted in the new center, along with instructional programs for adults who learn to read, operate computers, speak a second language, or complete a high school education.

Mom's Kitchen Opens

The next major project was to provide a permanent and high quality restaurant in Plains. Our Better Hometown Committee bought an old building, renovated it, and sold it to Maggie Crimes and her family. For eighteen years, they have operated a popular restaurant in nearby Preston, and our community was delighted when they opened Mom's Kitchen in our town in June 2000.

Better Hometown Committee at ribbon cutting opening of Mom's Kitchen. Photo credit: Allene Haugabook

Boyhood Home Dedicated

Following a seven-year effort, the U.S. Park Service was proud to dedicate the Boyhood Home of

Jimmy Carter in November 2000. A crowd of several thousand people assembled to examine the farm site and to hear addresses by Secretary of Agriculture Dan Glickman, Congressman Ralph Regular (R-Ohio), and the former president. The property was first acquired in 1994, carefully assessed by skilled archaeologists, and restored to its 1937 condition. Combined with the museum presentations in the depot and schoolhouse, this will give visitors a unique understanding of rural life during the Great Depression days.

Maxine Reese Honored

In March, the people of Plains gathered at our city park to dedicate the lovely site to Maxine Reese. She has been the key driving force in our community, always willing to do most of the work in challenging projects, but equally able to induce others to perform duties. An attractive path will surround a commemorative marker, so that a maximum number of visitors and local citizens will always be reminded of how much we all appreciate

Maxine Reese
Photo credit: Mary Wise

her wonderful leadership and dedication. The honoree said, "I never dreamed of anything like this. It's really unreal to believe that these people that you love and have worked with so long would do something like this for you." Tragically, Maxine Reese died two months later.

Windham Castings Officially Opens

A large crowd attended the official opening of Debbie Young's Windham Castings Company in October 2000. Realizing that we needed more job opportunities in our town, our Better Hometown group acquired the buildings formerly housing the cotton gin, storage warehouses, and commercial peanut shelling

plant of Carter's Warehouse, and they were offered to Debbie Young as a new home for Windham Castings. We were delighted when she decided to acquire the buildings, renovate them, and begin producing some of our nation's finest patio furniture. Subsequently, Debbie has received a series of honors as one of Georgia's most successful entrepreneurs.

Excursion Train On The Way

The Georgia General Assembly authorized $7 million in February 2001 to acquire and refurbish the old CSX railroad track, part of which will permit an excursion train to begin operation between Cordele and Jimmy Carter's boyhood home west of Plains. Heavily damaged during the 1994 flood, the tracks have permitted trains to travel at only ten miles per hour, but planned repairs will increase the speed limit to thirty-five miles per hour. Stops are contemplated at Veterans' State Park, the telephone museum in Leslie, Habitat for Humanity's Global Village in Americus, downtown Plains, and the boyhood home. Unloading platforms and other facilities will have to be prepared by the affected communities before the passenger coaches and dining cars can begin regular runs in late summer of 2002. State Sen. George Hooks said, "This will be a major economic development and tourism boost for our entire area."

Excursion train
Photo credit: Annette Wise

Miss Julia Coleman Honored

Perhaps the most beloved person who lived in our community was Miss Julia Coleman, the dedicated superintendent of Plains High School who inspired us and helped to shape many of our lives. In March 2001 we were thrilled when Miss Julia was inducted into the Hall of Fame for Women of Achievement in Georgia at Wesleyan College in Macon.

Miss Julia's nephew, David Crenshaw, and wife Marialice at induction ceremony honoring Julia L. Coleman. Photo credit: Allene Haugabook

PHS Commemorated

A historical marker was erected and dedicated in April 2001, near the entrance to Plains High School. This bronze plaque informs visitors that they are approaching the official Georgia State School, and provides some historical information about the site. Annette Wise, Allene Haugabook, Eunice Griggs, Virginia Williams, Ruby Watson, and Fred Boyles comprised the committee responsible for this achievement.

Habitat's 100,001st!

Habitat for Humanity has been a major force in our community, providing decent houses for poor families in need. It was completely appropriate that the 100,001st Habitat house was built here in September 2001, by our own volunteers. Most of the funds were contributed by Maranatha Baptist Church, and other congregations joined in the effort.

First African-American School Remembered

Dignitaries assembled near Lebanon Baptist Church on a cold and windy day in February 2002 to dedicate a historical marker on the site of the First Formal School for African-American children in Plains.

Declaration Of Independence In PHS

Plains received a special honor in April 2002, when one of the original copies of the Declaration of Independence was displayed in Plains High School. Film producer Norman Lear purchased this copy at auction for $8 million, and decided that it should be made available for viewers at the presidential libraries of Ronald Reagan, George Bush, Jimmy Carter, and Gerald Ford. Mr. Lear made a special exception by sending the extraordinary document to our community. A steady stream of adults and students not only viewed the national treasure, but had an opportunity to enjoy additional displays of memorabilia relating to the days of the Revolutionary War.

A New Antique Mall And Historic Inn

The Plains Historic Inn and Antiques Mall were dedicated in May 2002. Gov. Roy Barnes was the keynote speaker, and a crowd of other dignitaries and guests attended. Special recognition went to a group of prison inmates who have done much of the carpentry and masonry work. After the ceremony, the future excursion train made several runs to the Jimmy Carter Boyhood Farm – a precursor to trips that will be a regular attraction later in the summer.

The renovation of downtown Plains was one of the most ambitious projects of the Plains Better Hometown committee. After the former Plains Mercantile

Gov. Roy Barnes and Jimmy Carter cutting ribbon at opening of Plains Historic Inn. Photo credit: Annette Wise

Co. property was purchased from the heirs of Hugh Carter last November, the two main buildings were completely restored and transformed into a street-level antique mall with 25 booths and an upstairs inn. Each of the seven hotel suites is beautifully furnished and decorated to commemorate a different decade, from the 1920s to 1980s. The eighth apartment is a common room available for the enjoyment of all guests, which opens onto a balcony over the sidewalk.

Two old warehouses have become a community center that will be used for antique auctions, performances, dances, family reunions, and com-

munity meetings. The garden clubs of Plains have landscaped a lovely stamped concrete courtyard between the center and the mall. Also included in the project was the old Plains Bank, completed in 1901. The building was later the town's post office and then Hugh Carter's worm farm office. The new facility was dedicated in July as the Old Bank Café, with a patio on the south end equipped with beautiful furniture from Windham Castings.

Nobel Peace Prize

October 11, 2002, Acceptance Statement from President Carter in Plains for Nobel Peace Prize:

"I am deeply grateful for this honor. I want to thank the Nobel Committee and the many people at The Carter Center who have worked side by side with me and my wife, Rosalynn, to promote peace, health, and human rights."

"People everywhere share the same dream of a caring international community that prevents war and oppression. During the past two decades, as Rosalynn and I traveled around the world for the work of our Center, my concept of human rights has grown to include not only the right to live in peace, but also to adequate health care, shelter, food, and to economic opportunity."

"I hope this award reflects a universal acceptance and even embrace of this broad-based concept of human rights."

"This honor serves as an inspiration not only to us, but also to suffering people around the world, and I accept it on their behalf."

Plains Depot Exhibit

On October 11, 2002, the M.L. Hudson exhibit was unveiled at Plains Depot. The small parcel of land on which the Depot sits was formerly received by the National Park Service at a marker dedication ceremony. Several members of the

Hudson family attended the ceremony for the unveiling of an exhibit which tells the story of the Hudson family. The street in front of the depot was renamed M.L. Hudson Street in memory of this dedicated citizen who donated land for the town of Plains in the 1800s and assisted in the planning and development of the town.

Jimmy and Rosalynn Carter in Plains after giving Nobel acceptance speech. Photo credit: Lawrence Smith

Descendants of M.L. Hudson with Carters at unveiling of M.L. Hudson Exhibit at the Plains Depot. Photo credit: Lawrence Smith

Chapter 6: Chronology

Submitted by Alan Anderson and Rebecca Wise

	1820s	Chief Philema, or Fillimmee, ruled over three Creek towns on Muckalee and Philema Creeks in south central Sumter County.
February	1825	Treaty of Indian Springs opened land between Flint and Chattahoochee Rivers for settlement.
December 26,	1831	Sumter County created, named for Thomas Sumter, the "Fighting Gamecock" of South Carolina, last surviving Revolutionary War general.
September 4,	1839	Plains of Dura post office is established with David W. Robinet appointed as Postmaster.
November	1842	Pleasant Plain Baptist Church newly constituted.
November	1843	Bottsford Baptist Church admitted to Bethel Association.
March	1845	Americus Methodist Circuit: Americus, Rocky Mount, Shiloh, Salem, Bethesda, Bethel, Andrew Chapel, Concord, Danville and Tabernacle.
September	1846	Methodist Church Tabernacle and Camp Ground located on 5 acres (south side Young's Mill Rd. between Ga. 45 and Magnolia Springs Rd.), Charles J. Malone, Joseph Wood, Humphrey Drury, John W. Tommey, David Laseter, James Glass and George W. Varner, trustees.
December	1848	Lebanon Baptist Church constituted by presbyters Francis F. Seig and John U. Fletcher at the Plains of Dura, Rev. Jesse Stallings, pastor, with sanctuary built in 1849 for $300.
February	1855	John Coker donated 2 acres to New Hope Universalist Church trustees Micajah B. Pickett and George R. Harper, "except the graveyard" (Lot 79, 26th Dist.).
January	1861	Henry Davenport, Jr., of Plains of Dura, and Timothy M. Furlow and Willis A. Hawkins, of Americus, Sumter's delegates to the Secession Convention in Milledgeville, voted for severing Georgia's union with the United States of America.
February	1864	James H. Raven sold one and a half acres in Bottsford for Rural Hill Methodist Church, Henry Lassiter, James Lassiter, James H. Raven, Matthew E. Rylander, Jackson Laney, trustees.
April	1864	Bethlehem Baptist Church established in 17th District, west side of Thomas Mill Rd. at Pessell Creek, one of the county's oldest black churches.
November	1866	Lebanon Baptist Church granted letter of dismission from Bethel Association.

May	1870	St. Mark's Lutheran Church organized in Bottsford, with sanctuary built 1872, Rev. J.P. Margart, pastor (Lot 10, 17th Dist.), merged with St. Andrew's of Plains in 1966.
December	1870	Lebanon Baptist Church dedicated its new sanctuary, Rev. James H. Cawood, pastor (moved to south side of railroad in 1889).
February	1871	Sumter County School Board organized, William A. Wilson, D.G. Patterson, William T. Toole, Timothy M. Furlow, David Bagley, George W. Huckabay, Samuel T. Feagin, William M. Threlkeld, John F. Bolton, Henry Davenport, members.
May	1871	"Lebanon Colored Baptist Church" organized in Plains of Dura.
November	1871	Mrs. Cassandra Pickett Windsor Durham, of Plains of Dura, Reformed Medical College, of Macon, graduate, became Georgia's first woman licensed as a doctor.
December	1871	Sumter County Board of Commissioners of Roads and Revenues created, now the county commission, James H. Black, Samuel Heys, James W. Furlow, Amos K. Schumpert and Seth K. Taylor.
May	1876	Providence Post Office established at W.H. Davison's, south of Plains of Dura, in the 17th District.
June	1884	Samuel Hugh Hawkins, Esq., established Georgia's only privately financed railroad, the Americus, Preston, and Lumpkin (name changed to better known Savannah, Americus, and Montgomery, or SAM, in Dec. 1888); John Pullum sold one acre (Lot 117, 17th District) to St. John's A.M.E. Church, James Pullum, Lewis King and G.W. Crawford, trustees.
July	1884	Milton L. Hudson sold the right of way to the A.P. & L. Railroad that became the town of Plains.
September	1886	Earthquake in Sumter County.
October	1890	Ed Timmerman sold St. Paul's A.M.E. Church its land (northeast corner Della Glass Rd. and Logan Store Rd.), Charles E. Little, Prince Sanders, Edmond Little, Godfrey Kleckley, Henry Evans, John King and Jackson Hicks, trustees.
November	1890	Sumter County 15th most populous, with 21,948 residents.
April	1891	Competing "Times" and "Recorder" consolidated into "Times-Recorder," Bascom Myrick, publisher.
June	1892	Grand opening of Windsor Hotel (originally named Alhambra); electric street cars resumed operation until August; Sumter County jail completed, between and behind courthouse and City Hall, another G.L. Norrman creation.
September	1896	Legislative bill introduced to incorporate Plains.
December	1896	Plains adopted its first charter.

January	1897	Plains' first city council: Dr. Burr Thomas Wise, Mayor, Rodolphus S. Oliver, William L. Thomas, Edwin Timmerman, Sr., and Luther D. Wise, councilmen.
January	1902	Bank of Plains incorporated: R.S. Oliver, president, W.L. Thomas, cashier, and directors R.S. Oliver, T.M. Merritt, W.L. Thomas, J.E. French, B.T. Wise, and Frank Sheffield.
August	1902	Oliver-French Co. Building completed and J.E. French & Co. Building started, both in Plains 1906. Cotton crop of T.L. McLendon averaged 55 bales to 60 acres; Lebanon Baptist Church relocated to its present sanctuary.
November	1906	Announcement of Sumter's selection as site of Third District Agricultural & Mechanical College, to be built in Americus (now Georgia Southwestern University).
June	1907	Cornerstone ceremony for St. Andrew's Evangelical Lutheran Church in Plains, Rev. Charles A. Phillips, pastor.
January	1908	Formal opening of Third District Agricultural and Mechanical School.
May	1908	Booker T. Washington spoke at Americus Institute.
June	1909	Lebanon Baptist Church changed its name to Plains Baptist Church.
July	1910	Cornerstone ceremony for Plains Methodist Church, J.P. Dickerson, pastor.
March	1912	Four new homes near completion in Plains for Mr. W.L. Thomas, Mr. Tom Lawson, Mr. Edmund Oliver, and Mr. Ernest Wellons.
April	1912	Presidential candidate Woodrow Wilson made a whistle stop speech at Central Depot, Cotton Avenue and McGarrah Street in Americus.
August	1912	Drs. Burr Thaddeus and Samual Paul Wise, brothers, opened Plains' first hospital, T.O. Lawson, contractor.
	1912	Rodolphus Silas Oliver and John Archibald McDonald were listed in the prestigious book of *Men of Mark,* Vol. VI.
August	1913	Edwin Timmerman, Sr. and L.D. Wise, who have for eighteen years been identified with the cotton trade in Plains, will soon open a new brick warehouse, housed with a concrete floor and equipped with water connection and chemical fire apparatus, thus insuring protection against possible fire.
March	1917	U.S. Vice President Thomas Riley Marshall gave a speech from the balcony at the Windsor Hotel for Woodmen of the World Convention.
May	1918	Maj. Carlyle Wash, in machine #1778, flew first plane at Souther Field.
July	1918	Formal opening of Souther Field, U.S. Army installation, northeast of Americus (also served as training camp, then German P.O.W. camp, in World War II).
June	1919	William Jennings Bryan, three-time Democratic presidential nominee, visits Sumter County for a speech supporting the League of Nations and the anti-saloon league, at First Baptist Church of Americus.

December	1919	Drs. Wise announce a decision to stay in Plains and construct a new $75,000 structure which will be located between the Lutheran church and the Plains-Americus Highway and in plain view from the S.A.L. Railroad.
September	1920	Miss Ruth Clark became the first woman to register to vote in the county's history.
May	1921	Opening of Wise Sanitarium in Plains, Drs. B.T. and S.P. Wise (destroyed by fire Jan. 23, 1936).
May	1923	John Alden Wyche, owner of S & W Airplane Co., sold Charles A. Lindbergh the "Lone Eagle," his first plane, a World War I surplus "Jenny," for $500, at Souther Field, where he made his first solo flight.
February	1928	Franklin D. Roosevelt, Governor of New York, spoke to Chamber of Commerce dinner at Windsor Hotel in Americus and spent the night, returning to Warm Springs the next day.
March	1929	Plains stuck by tornado from southwest to northeast, missing high school and Wise Sanitarium by 300 yards; one killed.
December	1931	Sumter County celebrated its centennial with parades and programs attended by thousands.
April	1933	Americus Normal College (now Georgia Southwestern University).
January	1935	Miss Julia Coleman, Plains High School principal, invited by First Lady Eleanor Roosevelt to luncheon at White House.
June	1936	Death of Plains resident Rev. William Decker Johnson, A.M.E. Bishop of South Carolina, with burial at Archery community, Webster County.
October	1936	A.S. Staley High School, for blacks, opened on site of Americus Institute (east side N. Lee between Patterson and Primitive Streets).
June	1937	Plains High School designated "model school" by State Board of Education.
January	1939	Miss Thaisa Gardner, of DeSoto, returned from Hollywood after playing a munchkin in "The Wizard of Oz."
June	1939	First REA power line, 6 miles between Thomas' Store and Tom Finch's farm on Americus-Dawson Road.
November	1942	Clarence Jordan and Martin England founded Koinonia Farms, in the 17th District, as a non-profit, religious corporation that was fully integrated racially.
November	1944	German P.O.W. camp established at Souther Field, the prisoners working on local area farms (closure and repatriation in December 1945).
February	1946	Plains Lions Club chartered, Young T. Sheffield, president, Drue P. Murray, Jr., first vice president, O. Albert Williams, second vice president, L.L. Spence, secretary-treasurer.
October	1947	First-in-the-nation FmHA loan to Robert A. Hale, Sumter County farmer.

December	1947	Plains' first black Boy Scout Troop organized, Rev. C.M. Huff, scoutmaster.
May	1948	Formal opening of South Georgia Trade and Vocational School (now South Georgia Technical College).
March	1950	Grand opening of Sunset Drive-In Theater (south side US 280 west of U.S. 19).
September	1951	Dedication ceremony for site of new Southwest Georgia Experiment Station, Duncan McRainey, supervisor (south side Ga. 27, just east of Plains).
July	1954	Ed Jones, son of Plains Mayor Peter B. Jones, was program assistant for Edward R. Murrow's "See It Now" CBS television series.
January	1955	Mrs. Annie Mae McNeill, Mrs. Earl Carter, Mrs. John F. Williams, Mrs. Jewell D. Wallis, and Mrs. Buena Vista Malloy were the first women to ever serve on a Federal Court jury in Americus.
September	1955	Plains gets paved streets.
February	1956	Plains awarded first place in 1955 Better Home Towns competition sponsored by Georgia Power Co.
July	1957	Plains Convalescent Home formally dedicated by Gov. Marvin Griffin.
March	1958	Miss Julia Coleman retired after fifty years at Plains High School.
December	1963	West Central Georgia Area Planning and Development Commission (now Middle Flint) formally organized, Jimmy Carter, chairman.
June	1966	State Sen. Jimmy Carter announced for Democratic gubernatorial nomination after abandoning congressional race.
January	1971	Jimmy Carter sworn in as Georgia's 76th governor; Gov. Jimmy Carter formally dedicated Lt. Col. T.C. Tillman, Jr. National Guard Armory (northwest corner Adderton and Armory) in Americus.
March	1971	First-ever local telecast on cable TV channel; Gov. Jimmy Carter formally dedicated new auditorium for Southwest Georgia Experiment Station near Plains.
May	1971	Americus' last scheduled passenger train, the "City of Miami," pulled out, ending an era begun in 1854; half of Sumter County's students boycotted attendance protesting private school advocates on school board; Calvary Baptist Church of Leslie formally constituted.
April	1972	Gov. Jimmy Carter joined 40 Sumter County litigants in federal court to recall school board members.
May	1972	Groundbreaking ceremony for Africana Village subdivision in Plains.
December	1972	Henry Jackson became first black ever elected to Plains City Council in its 86-year history.
August	1974	Windsor Hotel closed after 82 years of operation.
December	1974	Gov. Jimmy Carter formally entered presidential race.
March	1975	Johnny Cash and wife, June Carter, visited Plains.

March		1976	Dedication ceremony for Lake Blackshear Regional Library, Gov. Jimmy Carter, keynote speaker (south side Lamar between Hinkle and Oliver Streets in Americus).
November		1976	Television personalities Mike Douglas and Barbara Walters interviewed Jimmy Carter in Plains.
November		1976	Jimmy Carter elected president of United States.
December		1976	Americus native Griffin Boyette Bell appointed U.S. Attorney-General.
January		1977	James Earl "Jimmy" Carter, Jr., of Plains, became President of the United States, the first native Georgian so honored.
July		1977	Maranatha Baptist Church constituted at Plains after racial integration split at Plains Baptist, Rev. Fred Collins, pastor.
November		1977	Actor Victor French, of television's "Carter Country," visited Plains.
January	1,	1981	The Carters return to Plains.
August		1981	Anwar Sadat, President of Egypt, visited former President Jimmy Carter at his Plains home, just two months before Sadat's assassination.
September		1981	Menachem Begin, Prime Minister of Israel, visited at former President Jimmy Carter's Plains home.
		1985	Plains Country Days began.
May	17,	1985	Plains Centennial Celebration (Willie Nelson performs).
May	19,	1990	Plains High School Sheffield-Coleman Reunion of 1923-1967 classes.
September		1991	Grand reopening of the Windsor Hotel after $5 million dollar restoration.
October		1992	Formal dedication of Lindbergh Statue, at Souther Field.
November		1992	Mrs. Irene King Edge and Mrs. Carolyn Whitehead became first black women elected to political office in Sumter county, both on the county school board.
August		1993	Hume Cronyn, Jessica Tandy, and Esther Rolle filmed Hallmark Hall of Fame movie, "To Dance With the White Dog."
July		1994	The 500-year flood, Georgia's worst-ever natural disaster, killed 15 in Americus and Sumter County, half the state's total death toll, after 21 inches of rain fell in 24 hours.
December		1994	Americus City School System ceased to exist as its charter lapsed, becoming one with the Sumter County School System.
		1995	Big effort to raise money for restoration of Plains High School.
March		1995	Painting of stores in downtown Plains by volunteers
June		1995	Jimmy Carter National Historic Site film made for auditorium at Plains High School with local citizens interviewed.
1996 to present			International Friendship Exchange between Sumter County Schools and Konu, Japan. Annual visits take place at P.H.S. in August.

April		1996	Jimmy Carter National Historic Site, Plains Historical Preservation Trust and the City of Plains shared National Park Partnership Leadership Award from National Park Foundation and National Park Service, for preservation of Plains High School.
July	12,	1996	Olympic Torch comes through Plains.
October	1,	1996	State Superintendent of Education Linda Schrenko visits Plains High School for grand opening of its visitor center.
December	22,	1996	First community sing at Plains High School inviting all churches in Plains.
		1997	Country Days changed to Peanut Festival.
April		1997	Gov. Zell Miller signed into law Plains High School's designation as Official State School of Georgia.
May	6,	1997	Palestinian Authority President Yasser Arafat visited former President Jimmy Carter at home in Plains
September	8,	1997	Unveiling of pictures of Mayors of Plains at City Hall.
September	25,	1997	First "If These Sidewalks Could Talk" folk play, written by Kim Fuller, performed at PHS.
June		1998	Archaeological dig at Boyhood Farm.
July	12,	1998	Design Team for UGA studied town and made recommendations for growth.
August	8,	1998	First Plains Peanut Pageant.
September	28,	1998	Education Program at PHS selected as a Georgia Partnership for Excellence in Education.
February	27,	1999	Archery Historical roadside marker dedicated.
August		1999	Jimmy Carter awarded Presidential Medal of Freedom by President Bill Clinton at White House ceremony.
September		1999	Boys and Girls Club opens.
October	1,	1999	Rylander Theater gala organized by Plains citizens for Jimmy Carter's 75th birthday.
March	18,	2000	Maxine Newberry Reese Park in Plains dedicated, Boze Godwin, mayor.
May	25,	2000	Maxine Reese died.
June		2000	Mom's Kitchen opens; Jimmy Carter awarded Eisenhower Medallion by People to People International, founded by President Dwight D. Eisenhower.
September		2000	Jimmy and Rosalynn Carter and Millard and Linda Fuller completed Sumter County Initiative's elimination of all substandard housing with construction of "Victory House" for Vera Thomas family.
November	17,	2000	U.S. Secretary of Agriculture Dan Glickman spoke at dedication of the Jimmy Carter Boyhood Home in Archery as a National Historic Site.
February		2001	PHS historical marker dedication for PHS being State School of Georgia.

March		2001	Gov. Roy Barnes presents Rebecca Wise with first-place trophy for state-wide Georgia History Day Essay Contest.
May	29,	2001	Julia Coleman inducted into Hall of Fame for Women of Achievement in Georgia.
June		2001	Statewide conference on Prevention of Targeted School Violence held at PHS. Conference presenter included U.S. Department of Education and Secret Service's National Threat Assessment Center.
January		2002	Jimmy Carter officiated at groundbreaking ceremony for Habitat for Humanity International's Global Village project on Church Street in Americus.
February	23,	2002	Historic marker placed at First Formal School for African-American children in Plains.
April		2002	Declaration of Independence Road Show at Plains High School, a Dunlap broadside dated 1776.
May	11,	2002	Grand opening of Plains Historic Inn and Antiques Mall.
July	21,	2002	Groundbreaking ceremony for new site of St. John's A.M.E. Church, Walter Washington, pastor.
October	11,	2002	Jimmy Carter awarded the Nobel Peace Prize.
October	11,	2002	M.L. Hudson Street and exhibit unveiled at Depot with members of the Hudson family attending.

Section II: Community

Chapter 7: Churches

Greater Cedar Springs Baptist Church

Cedar Springs was organized the year of 1908. It was a brush arbor. Rev. A.L. Mansfield was the founder of Cedar Springs. The church was down a dirt road near a creek with some cedar trees near where the church was at that time and after a few years the name Cedar Springs was given. The deacons at that time were Tom Patterson and Abe Hill. After years passed there was a number of members who worked every way they could to have a house to go to praise God in.

Greater Cedar Springs Missionary Baptist Church. Photo credit: Annette Wise

There have been 18 pastors for this church. Under the leadership of Rev. G.W. Nealy in 1968 the construction of a building began in May for our church. By the first Sunday in October we were in our new church house. At this time the word Greater was added. Our name to this day still remains

Greater Cedar Springs Baptist Church. We thank God for all the blessings and all the people in the community for their help.

These have served as pastors of our church: A.L. Mansfield, C.S. Reed, B.J. Jorden, E.J. Thomas, W.M. Starkes, E.S. Manns, R.C. Camble, W.H. Harvey, G.A. Moore, W.M. Thomas, S.A. Fullwood, S.M. Massey, J.L. Leanier, Ulysee Broeldn, G.W. Nealy, B.L. Roberson, Christer O. Brayent, and our present pastor is Rev. R.L. Duncan.

There have been 18 deacons. The older deacons were: Anderson Battle, Jackson Majors, Major Evans, Roy Jackson, Essie Lewis, Ander Butts, Elbert Germany, R.D. Laster, Mose White, James Simpson, Earnest Hicks, Robert Laster, Perry Burton, Clyde Angry, Frankie Laster, Dean Hicks, and Johnnie Laster.

Under the leadership of Rev. B.L. Robinson we enlarged our annex and added a pastor's study. We have also added heat and air conditioning, put carpet on the floor and added a porch.

—Submitted by Greater Cedar Springs Church

Greater New Lebanon Missionary Baptist Church

New Lebanon Baptist Church was founded in 1902 under the leadership of the late Rev. Baldwin Schley with the land being donated by the late J. W. "Captain" Murray, grandfather of former first lady Rosalynn Smith Carter. We pause to salute the pioneers of this great effort who, without a doubt, put God in front and were able to push forward.

The first deacons were Tom Williams and Mose White. The first members were the Smith family: Jane Smith, Minnie Smith, Robert Smith, Lewis Smith, and Mary Jane Smith. We salute those pioneers who have been called from labor to reward.

Before this present church was built, Sister Rachel Clark was united to this board of Christian workers. We bow our heads in thanksgiving to God for this faithful servant who, despite trials and tribulations, stayed on board this old ship and landed safely at the port in 1986.

New Lebanon Church was located at Bottsford. The congregation moved to what is now Greater New Lebanon Missionary Baptist Church on Highway 308 South. Photo credit: Mary Minion

There were several ministers who served as pastor. Rev. Baldwin Schley was the first pastor. He organized and built the first church. We thank God for this wonderful leader who left footprints on the sand of time. The next pastors were Rev. Wiley Jenning, Rev. N.C. Murray, Rev. Freeman, Rev. Cegues, Rev. Allen Daniels, Rev. Eli Brown, Rev. Aarron Callaway, Rev. Holloway, Rev. Jack Jackson, Rev. E.T. Thomas, and Rev. W.H. Stokes, who led this flock for only a short while. Rev. A.J. Major was shepherd of this flock for 13 years.

Under his leadership, the present church was built and painted. After finishing his work here, he was called from labor to reward. Then came Rev. J.L. Wilson, who stood as a great wall of strength and a friend to mankind. He was shepherd of this flock for 17 years. Under his leadership, the vestibule was added, the church was painted, lights were installed, the front awning put on, and cement steps, new floors and rugs were added. The next pastors were Rev. C.T. Anderson, Rev. C.G. Green, Rev. H.C. McGray and Rev. H.E. Ross, who all served for a short while.

In 1965, we set sail under the leadership of the late Rev. E.B. Clark. Under his administration, the floors were carpeted, a piano was installed, the church was painted, an annex was added, a new well was installed, bathrooms were installed, new pews were purchased for the church, a pastor's study was built and carpeted and an air conditioning unit was installed. New Lebanon has licensed one minister and ordained one.

December 17, 1982, the Lord saw fit to call Rev. E.B. Clark home. In August 1983, the Lord sent us Rev. W.B. Washington. Under his leadership, we purchased a new vacuum cleaner, new directional signs to the church, a refrigerator, and a tithes box; a new top was put on the church, the outside was painted, and a water cooler was installed. In March 1986, we lost the mother of our church, Sister Rachel Clark. Our present mother of the church is Sister Alma Solomon.

In February 1987, the Lord blessed us with our present pastor, Rev. James Milledge. Under his leadership, the church has been painted on the inside. But most important of all, he has drawn sheep to the fold with his loving and open arms of teaching the word of the Lord. We salute you, Rev. Milledge, for your endurance to lead this flock of sheep. May the Lord bless you and keep you.

In October 1989, the New Lebanon Church family began to look at our future and decided that it was time to begin to relocate our church. Due to the deterioration and upkeep of the road, we began to look for a new location. The deacon board set sail to look for such a place for a new church site.

In 1990, New Lebanon had a lot of ups and downs, but the Lord brought us through the storm. The Lord blessed us with a new member to our deacon board. Calvin Mansfield was ordained in December 1990. Our present deacon board members consist of Sam Dodson, Chairman Walter Jackson, James Wright, Robert Mansfield, Calvin Mansfield, Clyde Jackson, Edward Hicks, and Walter Jackson.

In 1991, after tears, hard struggles, and prayers, the Lord heard and answered our cry. The deacon board found a spot of land that the church could purchase. In March of 1991, New Lebanon members were blessed to be able to purchase land on Highway 308, outside Plains, for a new church site. In July 1991, we began to clear the land and in September 1991, we began construction on our new church.

Greater New Lebanon Missionary Baptist Church.
Photo credit: Annette Wise

This journey has not been easy, but the Lord has truly blessed our church. New Lebanon has a new outlook on the future - one that we will work hard to pass on to the younger generation. We take this time to salute our pilgrims and our present leader and most of all God for this wonderful blessing in preparation to seek His kingdom.

The year 1994 we were blessed with seven new members and the reorganization of the youth department. In July 1994, the community had the opportunity to experience something that most of us, in our lifetime, have never experienced and that was the Great Flood of 1994. Since that day, we were unable to go back to our old ground for worship, but the Lord blessed us with a temporary home. The Cedar Springs Baptist Church opened its doors to us for worship. We are blessed to have friends like this. It is an old saying, "God always has a ram in the bush." We are thankful for the members' hospitality giving us a place to worship as we prepared a new home for our church.

In 1995, under the leadership of Rev. Milledge, we moved into our new church in August. The road has not been easy, there have been many setbacks, but we have put our trust in the Lord, and He has not brought us this far to leave us now.

—Submitted by Mary Minion

Lebanon Baptist Church

On the site of today's Lebanon Cemetery once stood the original Lebanon Baptist Church, which served both the white and black congregation of the community. It had been the tradition of the congregations to worship at separate times and on different Sundays of the month.

This all changed on October 24, 1871, when a letter of dismissal was sent by the white division to the colored members. This was received with rejoicing and praise for the black people could worship the Lord in their own way and in their own place.

An advisory committee of the black congregation was drawn up for the purpose of meeting with the white deacons to get advice on the scripture and to resolve logistical problems. From this group evolved the first deacons of Lebanon Baptist Church. These were be-

These were believed to have been deacons: Alex Lowery, Hanson Schley, Washington Kennedy and Daniel Tatum.

Lebanon Baptist Church before it was rebuilt. Photo credit: Mary Minion

The black congregation retained the name Lebanon Baptist Church and eventually erected the first sanctuary on today's site. Other members coming from the white division of the church were as follows: Elias Davenport, Alex Lowery, Harvey Fuller, Macklin Biggins, Prince Clark, Janey Champion, Green Prince, Sady Pickett, Ann Stallings, Beatrice Rylander, Henrietta Picket, Frances Cato, James Chappell, Caroline Clark, Mary Hawkins, Elias Rylander, Mary Minyard, Zenith McIntyre, Ella Minyard, Isabelle Harper, Miller Berry, Eliza Tatum, Lorinda Mumble, Leott Clark, Luke Smith, Joseph McGrady, Charles Jenkins, James Prince, William Parker, Warrock Jones, Eliza Jones, Cahterine Jenkins, Willie Black, Viola Griffin, Jane Chappell, Rudie Marshall, Fannie Chapel, Flora West, Dicy Rylander, Susan Prince, Vina Bozeman, Rachel Napien, Nancy Jones, Rebecca Boler, Louise McIntyre, Clorapale Mayes, Albert Clark, John Cutts, Jack Forth, Benly Bryant, Hanson Schley, Aaron Wright, King Tatum, Hanson Davenport, Mart Evans, Mary Biggins, Mary Pickett, Rudy Marshall, Mira Boler, Ann White, Cassis Moran, Janey Jackson, Katie Monroe and Mary Jane Schley.

The church has had 29 pastors during its 130 years. Rev. Macklin Biggins was a member and the first pastor of Lebanon Baptist Church. Other pastors of Lebanon Baptist Church were: Reverends Richard Pittman, Eli Smith, N.A. Jones, Jimmie Jones, E.L. Thomas, C.S. Johnson, C.S. Cartwright, Shivers, A.S. Bostie, C.H. Young, W.T. Hillsman, N.B. Wright, J.B. Boyd, J.W. Lowe, B.J. Owens, O.C. Green, W.B. Mathis, S.M. Mosley, J.E. Brown, C. Waters, E.D. Hill, J.N. Williams, and Hosie Waters. The church has had two assistant pastors: Reverends S.M. Warren and Jack McGrady.

The church has licensed and ordained the following seven ministers: Reverends Hansel Schley, W.J. Jennings, P.H. Tondee, Anderson Ross, S.M. Warren, George Edge and James C. Iverson. The church has licensed the following two ministers: Reverend Jack McGrady and Marzell Jackson. We have had 47 deacons: Alex Lowery, Daniel Tatum, Clark Biggins, Daniel Stallings, Jim Williams, Moses Maye, Henry Statham, Walter Harvey, Sampson Johnson, Hanson Schley, Joe Glad, Gus Combs, West Minyard, Peter Floyd, George White, Joe Jones, Clark Biggins, Jr., J.G. Myers, Washington Kennedy, George Kitchens, Adam Prince, Alex Harvey, Galor Johnson, J.H. Giles, Phil Mugerson, Alex Tatum, Amos Brown, Isaac Prince, Burlont Bryant, Sr., James Schley, Leonard Wright, Sr., B.B. Schley, Lenward Jackson, Leo McGrady, Arzell Jackson, Claude Edge, Sr., Judson Edge, Sr., and R.B. Bridges. Our present deacons are: Bowman Colwell, Chairman, Timothy Jackson, Joe H. Franklin, Sr., Charlie Hollis, Robert L. Tyson, Eugene Edge, Sr., Joe H. Franklin, Jr., Michael Edge, and Aaron Baker. One deceased board member: C.M. Maye. Our present board members are: Alphonson Baker, Wilbur Bryant, Richard Franklin, Alvin Jackson, Mack A. Polk, and James Reliford. The following members have served as clerks: Daniel Stallings, Peter Floyd, J.G. Myers, J.H.

Jiles, Lilla B. Johnson, Essie Mae Ross, Ella Ross, and presently Eloise Jackson. Assistant clerks: Burlont Bryant, Clotee Wardell, Ella Ross, Joe Franklin, Sr., Eloise Jackson, and presently Susie Henderson. One financial clerk, Frances Reliford.

Lebanon Baptist Church
Photo credit: Eloise M. Jackson

In 1976, the church continued to move forward under the leadership of Rev. Champ Waters. A new church was built on the present site. A building committee consisting of deacons Bowman Colwell, Leonard Wright, Charlie Hollis, and Judson Edge were appointed to oversee the construction. The master carpenter during the construction was Brother Joe H. Davis and the master bricklayer was Brother Clayton Floyd. The master concrete finisher was deacon Bowman Colwell. Each one of these brothers worked faithfully at a reduced rate so we could have a nice place to worship. Several members devoted their time during the weeks and on Saturdays to help build the church. The Young Men Christian Club helped with putting the top on the bulding and installation of the ceiling. Deacon Joe Franklin trimmed and painted the interior and exterior of the church. The pastor and officers worked hard for four years. The church was completed in 1976 and dedicated on April 10, 1979.

Rev. Waters was called home in 1977 but left his vision to live on. A steeple was donated by a company in Michigan in honor of President Jimmy Carter. After the completion of the church and death of Rev. Waters we have had several pastors and the work continued under each administration.

On February 20, 1983, Maranatha Baptist Church extended an invitation to our congregation to worship with them. Our pastor, Rev. J.N. Williams, delivered the message and the choir sang and a wonderful fellowship was established. These meeting continued for several years.

In March 1984 we called our present pastor, Rev. Hosie Waters of Montezuma, GA. to be our shephard. The church has continued to flourish under his leadership. Rev. Waters is an asset to us and the entire community. He served as Georgia History Day speaker and Black History speaker at Georgia Southwestern State University. He delivered the invocation at the Mondale presidential campaign in 1984. He also delivered the Plains Bicentennial sermon in 1985. He participated on the Habitat for Humanity Walk from Americus to Kansas City led by former President Carter. He has served as chaplain of the Superior and State courts and presently serves as superintendent of the Macon County school system. We are continuing to grow in membership under Rev. Waters' leadership. We presently have a membership of 400.

We will continue to reach up and outward for things that are before us.

—*Submitted by Eloise M. Jackson*

Maranatha Baptist Church

Early History

Although the media interpreted the division of the Maranatha congregation from Plains Baptist Church as stemming primarily from the issue of race, the issue was more complex than that. Several thousand visitors were arriving in Plains each day; the traffic alone nearly paralyzed this village of 700 people. Over one hundred reporters were assigned to Plains, each having to come up with enough material to justify their being here. The glare of publicity made normal life, and particularly normal church life, nearly impossible.

The group that departed from the home church held its first service on May 22, 1977, at the St. Mark's Lutheran Church building, six miles toward Dawson on Georgia Highway 45. The congregation took the temporary name of Bottsford Baptist Mission. Sunday school classes were begun on May 29, some classes meeting in cars or vans.

On June 7, 1977, Rev. Dr. Fred Collins was called as the first pastor. On July 3 the group took the name "Maranatha Baptist Church of Plains." On July 10 the congregation was constituted as a church with 29 charter members. A constitution and set of bylaws were adopted on November 2.

Maranatha Baptist Church
Photo credit: Annette Wise

On December 28 a building committee was elected. It was determined that work on the new building would be done by Northway Contractors, Inc., of Taylors, South Carolina. Groundbreaking ceremonies took place on July 4, 1978. Construction was begun on July 26. The cost of the building was $195,025 and the congregation borrowed $159,500 to equal the difference above what had been given at that point.

The building was completed in December with the first service being held on December 13. The building was formally dedicated in a service on January 14, 1979.

On July 11, 1982, Dr. Collins resigned to establish Fred Collins Revival Ministries, Inc. Rev. Jesse Bell of Preston, Georgia, was chosen to be the interim pastor. On October 3, 1982, Rev. Dr. Daniel G. Ariail began as the church's second pastor.

The first deacons of Maranatha were elected on December 5, 1982. The list included Henry Barfield, Hugh Carter, Jimmy Carter, L. E. Godwin, Jr., L. E. Godwin III, and Ralph Speegle.

The church's Woman's Missionary Union group was organized on October 12, 1983.

The final payment on the church's mortgage was made on December 4, 1991. The deed was recorded and satisfied on December 13. The formal service for burning the note in indebtedness was held on January 26, 1992, with Dr. Kirby Godsey, president of Mercer University, as speaker.

Worldwide Outreach

Maranatha is unique in that two members were once president and first lady of the United States. When President and Mrs. Jimmy Carter returned to Plains in 1981 at the end of his term of office, they united with Maranatha and became active members. He was elected a deacon and continues to teach a regular Sunday school class for Adults. They both share with other church members the task of cleaning and maintaining the building and grounds, including mowing grass and cleaning floors and restrooms. The Carters practice Christian hospitality as they remain at the front of the church following each morning worship hour to allow visitors to have their photographs taken with them.

Consequently, the church has a ministry that touches visiting persons representing many nations of the world. Since the Carters are active and visible members, Maranatha has for several years averaged about or over 10,000 visitors per year. On April 21, 1996, twenty-eight foreign countries were represented among the guests. These included persons from the Philippines, Vietnam, mainland China, Taiwan, Pakistan, Greece, Japan, Armenia, Poland, Lebanon, Puerto Rico, Turkey, Indonesia, and Canada. Rarely does a Sunday fail to bring visitors from many states.

The visitors include persons from various religious backgrounds including Mormons, Jews, Catholics, Protestants of every stripe, atheists, agnostics, Buddhists, Muslims, and others. The church is thus a true mission station but is distinctive in that persons who need to be reached are coming to the mission rather than the reverse.

The congregation has always been open to persons of all races, actively encouraging their participation and membership. The congregation has included an interracial couple and persons born in Afghanistan, India, Korea, Mexico, Taiwan, Vietnam, and Zimbabwe.

Maranatha has met a need in the Plains-Americus community largely neglected by other churches. A couple who had adopted a Korean daughter found themselves less than cordially welcomed at nearby churches but found a home here. A young Muslim husband and father born in Afghanistan came, accepted Christ and was baptized. A family from Zimbabwe who were converted to Christianity by Southern Baptist missionaries could fit in only here, and a family from India had the same experience.

Tourists, including many foreign nationals, comprise the large majority of visitors, but other groups also come. International students from nearby Georgia Southwestern State University often visit. One Japanese student wrote to the pastor that her positive experience at Maranatha had caused her seriously to consider accepting Christ. After returning home, she wrote in December, 1991, saying: "I became a Christian in May at First Baptist Church at Valdosta in Georgia. It was the greatest experience for me since I came to the United States." Usually, however, pastor and people never know what impact they have had on visitors.

At times business persons or diplomats have reason to be in the area and attend, such as philanthropist Dominique de Menil and Absalom Vusi Mamba, Ambassador of Swaziland, in 1989. Actors Bettye Ackerman and Gary Merrill have attended as has Mrs. Fred Astaire. Singers Amy Grant, Michael W. Smith, and soprano Medea Ruhadze-Namoradze of the Tbilisi State Opera of the Republic of Georgia have sung at morning worship services.

Local Involvement

Maranatha has for many years been a strong supporter of Habitat for Humanity, which was founded in Americus, Georgia, and which has since become a global organization seeking better housing for the poor. Millard and Linda Fuller, Habitat's founders, are members of the church.

While Koinonia Partners is close by, there has been little relationship between them and Maranatha except for occasional visits by residents or visitors. Only two persons who were partners have united with this church.

The church has had periodic contact with the Baptist Student Union of Georgia Southwestern State University in Americus. Maranatha ladies have provided meals at times for WATCH (Women Accepting the Challenge of Housing), a female branch of Habitat for Humanity. The church also takes part in Sumter County Initiative, another local housing improvement organization.

Maranatha has long had a strong relationship with Lebanon Baptist Church, a local black congregation which dates back to before the founding of

Plains. Several times the two churches have met together.

Maranatha also has a good relationship with Plains Baptist, Plains United Methodist, and St. Andrews Lutheran churches. These four congregations have joint worship services at Thanksgiving, Easter, and every fifth-Sunday evening when they combine for a time of musical worship. All four participate in St. Andrews' candlelight Christmas service each year.

Carter Participation

President and Mrs. Carter came home from Washington at the end of his term and united with Maranatha on January 25, 1981. He began teaching his present Sunday school class in September of that year and was elected one of the first deacons in 1982. He has served as deacon, as chairman of the Finance Committee, as a trustee, and on the Constitution and By-laws Committee.

Mrs. Carter taught the Youth Sunday school class for several years. She takes her turn several times a year providing flowers for the sanctuary. She also helps with refreshments at showers for brides and new babies.

Both are active in maintaining the building and grounds. They have duty every second month helping with housekeeping of the building and keeping the grounds tidy. They attend weddings and funerals, make visits when fellow members are hospitalized, and visit those who have lost loved ones to death. They regularly visit those who are new to Plains and may be prospects for Maranatha. They often take flowers to the sick and food to the bereaved.

President Carter has long had a hobby of working in wood. He made the church's four offering plates, turning the walnut wood in his lathe. He also made a table in the nursery, several shelves in classrooms, and two large free-standing bookcases

in the pastor's study. He often repairs sticking doors and other items around the church.

The Carters do not have a special status within the congregation that elevates them above other members. This is their home and their home church. They are accepted and treated as such by others in the congregation. They take their turn at whatever comes. But they are much loved and respected.

—Submitted by Dan Ariail

Plains Baptist Church

Lebanon Baptist Church, known today as Plains Baptist Church, was constituted on December 1, 1848, with twenty members entering into the Church Covenant and subscribing to the Articles of Faith. The following day, Rev. Jesse Stallings was called to be the first pastor. He graciously accepted and continued as pastor for eight years. The first house of worship was built in 1849 and was located one and 1½ miles west of Plains, near the center of the present day Lebanon Cemetery. Services were held monthly.

Lebanon Baptist Church held a firm belief in missions and had a "Mission Committee" as early as 1850. A Sabbath Day (Sunday school) was established in 1860. The church discussed the effects of the Civil War and on April 18, 1863, a decision was made to take a collection for army colportage (Bible distribution) for J.H. Campbell, associational missionary to Confederate soldiers.

Our "colored brethren and sisters" requested letter of dismissal, which was granted on March 19, 1870. They formed their own church and named it The New Lebanon Baptist Church.

On December 7, 1870, a dedication service was held for our second house of worship. It was erected at the same site as the first house of worship. A buggy costing $75.00 was purchased for our pastor, Rev. John H. Cawood of Preston , who served as pastor for twenty years. He was an effective preacher who was missionary minded and well informed.

Plains Baptist Church
Photo credit: Lawrence Smith

A collection was taken for Indian missions and a contribution made to the Georgia Baptist Orphans' Home in 1872. The church decided to hold weekly prayer meetings. In 1876 we purchased Sunday school literature. One hundred thirty-two members had been received by 1886. The church's first organ was purchased in 1887.

In 1889, the place of worship was moved into the town of Plains to a location south of the railroad tracks on South Bond Street. A dedication service for the new building was held in June 1890. That year, we took a special collection for the suffering in India. A Woman's Missionary Society was organized in 1892, dedicated to mission work throughout the world.

Dr. W.W. Arnold of Richland was pastor from 1895-1908. He was a stepson of William R. Calloway of the famous Calloway preachers. During his pastorate, we began holding services twice a month.

In March 1902, it was announced that the Stewart lot on North Bond Street was for sale for $500 (this is the site of the present church building.) A committee had purchased the lot by April and paid for it by September. It was discussed whether to move the old church to the lot. A decision was finally made to build a new church building which was erected in 1906 by Rev. A.C. Wellons, a local contractor and former pastor. In 1909, a committee planned for the church to be dedicated to God and that a short history of the church be given at that time. The historical sketch read by Chairman Dr. J.F. Cato stated in part, "The question of missions was always one of prime importance. For years we assisted in the support of a missionary to the Creek Indians, Reverend H.J. Buckner. Missions has ever been the motto of the church."

After years of discussion, the name of the church was changed from Lebanon Baptist Church to Plains Baptist Church on June 29, 1909. Rev. P.C. Barkley of Alabama was pastor at this time, serving from 1908-1914. There were 158 members on roll at that time. Rules were again reinforced as to dancing, card playing and other worldly amusements. Also, in 1909, A Baptist Young People Union was organized.

The Plains branch of the American Red Cross was organized at Plains Baptist Church on August 4, 1917.

Around 1924, construction began on the church annex. The annex included the basement, which was used for many years with only a dirt floor. Rev.

J.E. Hall was pastor at this time and served a total of fourteen years.

In 1926, the Women's Missionary Society (WMS) began filling jars with fruit and vegetables for the Baptist Children's Home. On January 10, 1927, the WMS agreed to organize Royal Ambassadors (missions group for boys) and Girls Auxiliary (missions group for girls.)

In 1929 we began giving to the Cooperative Program, which supports foreign, home and state missions. Also in 1929, a motion was carried to sponsor an infants nursery.

Rev. Royal Calloway was our pastor from 1932-1944. He was born into a family of 31 pastors. His brother Merril was a Baptist missionary in the Near East.

The earliest record of Vacation Bible School was in 1942. Each summer, the youth in our community attend VBS, where they learn about the Bible and God's plan of salvation.

We were delighted when construction of our two-story Sunday school annex was completed in 1944.

The Brotherhood was organized in February 1948. One of its many exceptional contributions took place in the fall of 1948 when members loaded the first freight car with produce to go to the Georgia Baptist Children's Home. This yearly activity continued for over two decades.

In 1951, Rev. Tommie Jones, who had been the camp director of Camp Pinnacle in Clayton, Ga., accepted the call as pastor. On July 18, 1954, the church voted to begin full-time services, which would start in October of that same year. Rev. Jones served from 1951-1955.

In 1952, we were at the forefront in beginning Friendship Camp. We continue to support the many activities of the camp. Work also began on a church office and library.

A visitation program was presented by Rev. J. Robert Harris and approved in October 1956 and is continued today. Brother "Bob" served as pastor for 12 years. There were 261 additions to the church, including 142 baptisms. Improvements were made in the music department, to the air conditioning and electrical system and preschool furniture was built.

Rev. John Simmons served as pastor for five years, later becoming a missionary in the state of New York under the Home Mission Board.

In December 1963 and again in 1977 representatives from our church appeared before the Sumter County Board of Commissioners to express strong opposition to the granting of a liquor license in the Plains area.

Jimmy Carter was baptized into the fellowship of this church and later ordained a deacon and was a Sunday school teacher for many years. Letters were granted for Gov. and Mrs. Carter to Northside Drive Baptist Church in Atlanta in January 1971. Four years later, they returned to Plains Baptist, but, when Jimmy became our 39th President, they moved their church membership to First Baptist Church, Washington, D.C.

Plains quickly filled with visitors during the presidential election period. Many visited our church, but we were unable to accommodate the volume of visitors and meet the needs of various media groups. After a continuous disagreement about the future direction of the church, there was a split in the church membership and about thirty members requested and were granted letters to Maranatha Baptist Church.

Rev. Donald Wilson became pastor in 1977. In 1978, the deacons started a visitation program with each deacon being responsible for visiting eleven families. A preschool building was completed in 1981 after a year of construction. A special offering was taken in February 1982 to help build the new Friendship Association Center in Americus. The Children's Church, Outreach Committee, and Hospitality Committee all began in 1996.

Our church's sesquicentennial celebration began on December 7, 1997, with a special Sunday morning worship service. The yearlong celebration ended on December 6, 1998, with a Sunday morning service of worship, praise, thanksgiving and pageantry. An abbreviated history was compiled and distributed.

Plains Baptist Church has flourished for 154 years and currently has an enrollment of 272 members. Our growth in membership and continuous mission work is attributed to the dedication and hard work of our pastors, deacons, Women's Missionary Union, the Brotherhood, directors, teachers, committees, librarians, and music directors.

The 25th anniversary of Brother Don Wilson's pastorate was celebrated in December 2002. He and his wife Linda were honored for their many years of dedication to our church.

We are grateful for our rich heritage and for our forefathers' unswerving dedication to the biblical principles on which our church was founded.

Members Ordained

Jesse Stallings, J.F. Eden, G.T. Jennings, Auston Turner, Lamar Clements, Jimmy Hayes and David McLemore

Pastors Who Have Served Plains Baptist Church

Jesse Stallings	1848	1856
George F. Cooper	1857	1858
B.L. Binnion	1858	1961
Wash Tharp	1862	1864
S.B. McJenkin	1864	1866
John H. Cawood	1867	1887
J.L. Underwood	1887	1890
B.W. Davis	1890	1891
J.W. Beck	1891	1892
A.C. Wellons	1892	1895
W.W. Arnold	1895	1908
P.C. Barkley	1908	1914
C.S. Durden	1914	1918
L.B. Johnson	1919	1921
J.C. O'Quinn	1922	1923
J.E. Hall	1923	1927
Jesse F. Ray	1928	1931
Royal Calloway	1932	1941
J.E. Hall	1941	1951
Tommie Jones	1951	1955
J. Robert Harris	1955	1967
John Simmons	1967	1972
Fred Collins	1972	1974
Bruce Edwards	1975	1976
Donald Wilson	1977	

—*Submitted by Mrs. Marian Harris and Amy Wise*

Plains United Methodist Church

Beginnings 1848 to 1899

The Plains Methodist Church (added United to the name in 1968) originated from the Tabernacle Church. The earliest record of this church, as taken from the church record book recorded by Dr. A.J. Logan, is dated March 18, 1848. It was on the Americus Circuit, which was composed of 10 churches with Rev. Daniel Fresley as pastor and Rev. Jessie Boring as presiding elder. It was a wooden frame building located about 3 miles north of the present town of Plains.

In 1865 the Tabernacle Church members bought a three-room frame school house near Magnolia Springs. The Tabenacle Church building was given to the black Methodists. The large room of the newly acquired schoolhouse was used for Sunday school, which met each Sunday. Preaching services

The Pearl Walters' history speaks of a frame church at Magnolia Springs, which was torn down when the Methoidst congregation moved to Plains. Photo credit: C. G. Haugabook, Jr.

were held the second Sunday and preceding Saturday of each month. Later the two small rooms were torn down, the large room remodeled and a small belfry added. Samuel Glass was Sunday school superintendent at this time and Rev. Samuel Anthony was pastor. The parsonage was a frame building that stood nearby and was still being used in 1951 as the home of a black man named John Burke, who repaired clocks. The church congregation moved to the Magnolia Springs area because of a large number of families living there. They included the Alec Chappell family, Arline family, Mrs. Camilla Wise and daughter, Fleeta Wise, Ralph Wise family, Phil and Loy Wise family, William and Emma Dean Wise family, Tyre Wise family, Fred Robins, Walton Walters and a Spann family.

The Beth Walters' chapter of the official church history says, "On September 18, 1888, property deeds were given by Mr. M.L. Hudson to the local Methodist Church and the Tabernacle congregation moved into the Plains settlement." There is a deed and a copy of the deed in a safety deposit box at the Plains branch of Citizens Bank of Americus that gives January 1, 1888 as the date of the gift. At this time the name of the church became Plains

Methodist Church and was the first church in Plains. The new church building was a wooden frame structure with a porch across the front supported by columns with a steeple from which the bell was rung every Sunday for Sunday school attendance. Church services were still held only on each second Sunday and the preceding Saturday. Kerosene lamps were used for lighting purposes. E.R. Stewart was the Sunday school superintendent, an office he held for 50 years. The stewards were: Zimri Markett, W.L. Thomas, W.S. Moore, T.G. Walters and E.R. Stewart. Near the church, a five-room frame parsonage with hall and two porches was built. About 20 years later, two more rooms were added. Installed were electric lights, a new stove, refrigerator and hot water heater. In 1950, butane gas was installed, having eight heaters, at a cost of $350.00.

Plains United Methodist Church
Photo credit: Lawrence Smith

Construction Projects

In 1910, the frame church building at Plains was torn down and the present beautiful brick edifice was erected. The cornerstone reads J.A. McDonald chrm., R.S. Oliver, R.M. Andrews, W.S. Moore, E.R. Stewart with Rev. J.M. Rustin as pastor. In 1912 the church was dedicated with Bishop Warren Chandler presiding. At this time, Plains began having church services twice a month, the second and fourth Sunday mornings and nights. In 1919 electricity came to Plains by a city-owned plant. At this time the church lighting was changed from gas to electricity.

In 1937 Mrs. Mamie McDonald Bradley gave a two story-brick educational building in memory of her parents, Mr. and Mrs. J.A. McDonald. The building joins the sanctuary with a front inside walkway and has an assembly room, six class-rooms, two rest rooms, and three office rooms. The building committee included Dr. J.C. Logan, chrm., R.M. Andrews, E.R. Stewart and Rev. H.S. Brooks. Rev. O.B. Chester presided at the dedication. Board of Stewards were Dr. J.C. Logan, R.M. Andrews, C.L. Walters, Sr., Charles Smith, H.B. Moman, Oliver Spann, Robert McGarrah, Thad M. Jones, C.L. Walters, Jr., L.L. Spence, and R.D. Brannen. Church trustees were J.C. Logan, R.M. Andrews, C.L. Walters, Sr., Ed Jackson and John Mask.

The need for a Fellowship Hall was realized in 1954, so during the pastorate of Rev. I.L. Bishop, a Lord's Acre project was instituted, realizing $1,060.00. The blueprint was drawn up in 1955, ground broken in March 1956 and the brick build-ing at the south side of the sanctuary was completed in 1957, valued at $15,000 and all debts paid. With the Rev. W.E. McCord as pastor, on the second Sunday in April 1957, the building was dedicated to the Lord's work at the homecoming service. District Superintendent Rev. E.J. Garbutt presided. The cornerstone shows: Pastors I.L. Bishop, W.E. McCord, Building Committee Dr. J.C. Logan chrm., Ralph Wiggins, J.W. Sewell, Charles W. Smith, H.W. Smith, treas., Leroy Young, Charlie Vaughn, and R.M. Andrews.

In July 1980, the Young family gave and built, with other members helping, a block utility house in the back yard of the parsonage.

From Circuit to Station Church

Beginning on the Americus Circuit as one of 10 churches, the Tabernacle (Plains) Church pro-gressed over the years to a station church. In 1891, Plains was on the Smithville Circuit with six churches: Benevolence, Bottsford, Concord, New Point, Pine Grove (Rylander), and Plains still known as Tabernacle. Evidently, New Point was removed, for in 1896 the history indicates that there were only four churches on the circuit, namely, Plains, Concord, Rylander, and Benevolence. In 1887, New Point was again on the circuit. The circuit was called the Plains Circuit, indicating that the Taber-nacle Church had become the Plains church. In 1899 there were five churches – Plains, Concord, Rylander, Benevolence, and New Point. Around 1952, the New Point Church was dissolved. In 1975, the Concord church left the charge and began fulltime service. Three years later, in 1978, Be-nevolence joined with Morningside of Americus to form a new charge. This left the Plains Charge with two churches, Plains and Rylander. The year 1983 was an emotional one for the Rylander church. The members faced the sad task of voting to end ser-vices. The board of the church bit the bullet and made the decision to merge with Plains effective January 1, 1984. At that date Plains became a station appointment.

Organizations

Women. In 1889 a Woman's Missionary Soci-ety was organized with seven members: Mrs. Mollie Howell, president, Mrs. Anna Markett, vice presi-dent, Mrs. Aughtry Oliver, corresponding secre-tary, Mrs. Sallie Stewart, treasurer, Mrs. Ola Evans, agent for Missionary Voice (later became World Outlook), Mrs. Rylander, honorary member, Miss Pearl Walters, secretary. Meetings were held once a month. The Jewel Gardner circle was organized in 1928 honoring the wife of Rev. T. C. Gardner. It met at night and was the first one in the South Georgia Conference to meet in the evening. The name of the Woman's Missionary Society (WMS) was changed in 1941 to Woman's Society of Chris-tian Service (WSCS), having 22 members. The

Jewel Gardner night circle name was changed to Wesleyan Service Guild with 12 members. A second name change occurred in 1968 when the WSCS became United Methodist Women (UMW).

Youth. An Epworth League was organized in the Plains church in 1897. It was disbanded in 1898. By 1928 the League had been reorganized along with a Senior League. A Juvenile Missionary Society was organized in 1901. The last recorded meeting of the JMS was June 1907.

Ministry and Recognitions

Under the guidance of Pastor Charles Culbreth, Jr. in 1960, Plains was named Rural Church of the Year on the Americus District.

An honor was given to the church in 1979 and 1980 when Plains received the World Parish Citation under the direction of Pastor Charles Houston. The honor was bestowed at the South Georgia Conference Meeting in Tifton.

In 1979 Plains was recognized as the Circuit of the Year at the South Georgia Annual Conference for its accomplishments in 1978.

In July 1981, a team of 12 went on a mission trip to Haiti. Heading the group was Rev. and Mrs. Mira Barrett with Mr. and Mrs. Doug Unger, Mr. and Mrs. Henry Coleman, Carol Walters, Deanne Young, Mary Ann Medlock, Pam Medlock, Jeff Moss and James Jackson. Church members all worked together to raise the $7,000 for the trip expense. Much inspiration was gained by carrying some help to this poverty stricken area through the strength of the Lord.

Memorable Events

Electricity came to Plains in 1919 and church lighting was changed from gas to electricity. In 1940, the church pump organ was converted to an electrical one by Rev. C.L. Glenn. In 1939, the Sunday school superintendent, E.R. Stewart, passed away, having served in this capacity for 50 years.

The enrollment at this time was 140 with average attendance of 80. Church membership was 200 with 130 active members. On the afternoon of July 7, 1946, Rev. C.M. Infinger, pastor, performed a wedding ceremony in the church sanctuary for a young couple who made national history on January 20, 1977. The groom, James Earl Carter, Jr., became the 39th president of the United States and the bride, Rosalynn Smith Carter, became first lady.

The Church Today

The average attendance at the morning worship service is 84, Sunday school 60. There are 210 persons on the roll. The annual budget is $72,343. The United Methodist Men have 12 persons on roll; the United Methodist Women 18. There is a very active United Methodist Youth Fellowship. A total of 1,160 persons have been members of the church since its inception.

—*Submitted by C. G. Haugabook, Jr.*

Endnote

Source "The Official History of the Plains United Methodist Church" as compiled by Mrs. C. L. Walters, Jr. and Rev. C. G. Haugabook, Jr.

St. Andrew's Lutheran Church

Lutherans from the Dutch Forks area of South Carolina migrated to this area during and after the Civil War. These Lutherans established St. Mark's, Bottsford in 1870. Families were named Wise, Jennings, Addy, Derrick, Dominick and Hiller.

St. Mark's first pastor was John Phillips Margart. There were small congregations in Bronwood, Magnolia Springs, and St. Paul's in Americus. St. Andrew's was built in Plains in 1907. In 1966, St. Mark's and St. Andrew's merged into one congregation. Thereafter an annual homecoming service has been held at St. Mark's,

St. Andrews Lutheran Church
Photo credit: Lawrence Smith

Bottsford. This traditionally is held on the fourth Sunday in July.

The Lutheran parish has had many honorable, hard-working members in its history. Probably some of the most famous and influential to the history of Plains were the Wise doctors. Dr. Burr Thomas Wise (the first mayor) came to Plains where he had an extensive practice until his death in 1910. His three sons, Burr Thaddeus, Samuel Paul and Bowman, all graduated from Tulane and set up medical practice in Plains. In 1912, a hospital for about 15 patients was established over the drugstore. In 1912, the Wise Sanitarium was established. It could accommodate about 60 patients. The Wise Sanitarium was known as the "Mayo Clinic of the South". Many nurses, including Lillian Carter, received training there.

St. Andrews' congregation presently has about 50 members being led by Dr. Charles Thompson of Albany.

—Submitted by Brenda Jennings

St. John A.M.E. Church

St. John A.M.E. Church was organized in the late 1800s about 3½ miles south of Plains on Bond's Trail Road at a place called Jennings Crossroads. In June 1884, the trustees purchased land from Mr. McDonald for the purpose of building a church. The land was purchased for the price of $25. The note was paid in full by November 1884. The trustees were John Pullman, Lewis King, James Pullman, and G.W. Crawford.

St. John A.M.E. Church
Photo credit: Annette Wise

The first pastor was Rev. Upshaw and the first presiding elder was F.L. Flemmings. Several ministers have served as pastor of St. John. They are the Reverends Foley, J.H. Fluellen, Henderson, W.M. Ellis, W.T. Hicks, C.W. Crawford, E.G. Harris, N.W. White, E.O. Benefield, J.W. Means, B.W. Motely, Smith and Matthews.

Over the years, our church has been under the leadership of a number of presiding elders. Some of the elders who have served on this district are Dr. Driggers, Dr. Winfield, J.E. Brown, F.M. Johnson, A.A. Duncan, James Debro, G.B. Hannah, J.E. Jackson, and C.E. Shepherd. We are happy to have Rev. J.L. Raven as our elder at this time.

On October 28, 1957, Rev. W.B. Brown was sent as our leader. Under Rev. Brown's leadership, many projects were undertaken.

A day care center organized by Mrs. Nozie B. Jackson and Mrs. Della Franklin started and was sponsored by St. John A.M.E. Church.

In 1960, a committee met and decided to build a new church. The building committee consisted of Rev. W.B. Brown, James Ross, Frank James, William Angry, Bobby Merritt, Oscar C. Tommie, Calvin Hall, S.H. Hicks, Velma Raven, Nozie Jackson, and Eva Kitchen. The first rally money raised was $1,500.

In 1963, we moved into the new church. New pews, pulpit furniture, and gas heaters were purchased. Later, a water cooler was purchased for the church. A few years later, brick veneer was added and the church was valued at $30,000. Rev. Brown served as pastor for 32 years. He was called from labor to reward in 1989.

Rev. E.X. King was sent and served for seven years. Under Rev. King's leadership, a new water cooler was installed, two heating and cooling units were added, and a keyboard and speakers were purchased. The choir was able to purchase new robes, also.

Rev. Roy Brown and Rev. Campbell served for a short time after Rev. King.

We have been blessed to have a number of faithful stewards, trustees, and stewardesses. Some of those stewards were O.C. Tommie, G.W. Hightower, John Monts Sr., George Addie, Rufus James, Calvin Hall, and Abe Hicks. Trustees were Carl Hicks, Frank James, George Hightower, G.A. Monts, D. Addie, R.E. Neeley, Oscar Tommie, Jr., George James, Calvin White and Clifford White.

Under Rev. Washington's administration, tremendous emphasis has been placed on training in the order or worship, officers' training, training of our youth and involvement in the total church on all levels. Our membership has continued to grow through converts and accessions. A youth choir has been organized and is very active.

Rev. Washington has led the church in purchasing two lots south of the church site and one lot on the north side of the church site. We are currently in the second phase of planning for the renovation and building a new church. This is a dream come true. It is our hope we will celebrate our next anniversary in our new state-of-the art building.

The current officers are: Jacqueline Slappey, church secretary; Katie Jackson, assistant secretary; and Lawrence Britt, treasurer.

Stewards are: S.H. Hicks (Pro-tem), Eugene Hollis, William Perry, Dudley Gary, Jackie Franklin, Joe Britt, Lawrence Britt, Larry Shepherd and Robert White. Shawn Gary serves as a junior steward.

Trustees are: William Perry (Pro-tem), S.H. Hicks, Dudley Gary, Eugene Hollis, Jacqueline Slappey, Joe Britt, Katie Jackson, and Commie Wright.

St. John is blessed to have prayerful warriors (pillars of the church) still on the battlefield. To name a few: Sisters Agnes Hollis, Della Franklin, Lillie Burns, Lula Britt, Velma Raven, and Agnew Angry.

We pray that the Lord will continue to bless us as we strive to work out our soul salvation.

—Submitted by Jacqueline Slappey and Mattie Washington

St. Mark A.M.E. Church

The Saint Mark African Methodist Episcopal Church was organized August 18, 1870, on the Section Place in the Archery community. Deeds were made to the trustees and the many trustees that would follow. Trustees at that time were: Brothers Alfred Rylander, James Rylander, James Pullman, Riley Harris and Jack Neal.

The church operated there for 20 years and in 1890 was sold to the railroad company and was deeded this present site by Mr. W.P. Lane. St. Mark was known as the "Mother" church of St. John, St. Paul, and St. Luke of the Bottsford community.

Some of the pastors who served in the 19th century were: the Reverends Sammie Milton, Holmes, Batey, Reynolds, Camel, J.W. Mitchel,

Davis, R.H. Tommie, Sanford, Upson, T.H. Malton, Malery and Whitaker. From 1899-1900, Rev. H. Johnson; 1901-1903, Rev. F.L.Fleming; 1904, Rev. N.W. Willams; 1905-1908, Rev. E.C. Foley; the church was rebuilt; 1901-1912, Rev. F.M. Johnson: 1913-1914, Rev. W.R. Brown; 1915, Rev. A. Bell; 1916-1919, Rev. S. Fields; the first cornerstone was laid; Rev. W.D. Johnson was made a bishop.

St. Mark A.M.E. Church
Photo credit: Old church, Milton Raven; new church, Lawrence Smith

The year 1920, Rev. J.H. Henderson, the circuit was divided. St Mark and St. Luke were left together. In 1921, Rev. Bryant; 1922-23, Rev. A.C. Kleckley,Sr.; St. Mark was made a station. 1924-26, Rev. Thomas Jefferson; 1927, Rev. L.A. Mason. He built the church that was blown down in 1952 and laid a cornerstone. Trustees serving at that time were Bishop W.D. Johnson,Sr., Brothers George Simpson,Sr., R.V. Wakefield, Johnnie Raven,Sr. and C.G. Simpson. In 1928, L. Harder; 1929, Rev. S.S. Mauldier; 1930, Rev. K.W. Shivers; 1931, Rev. Sheffield; 1932-1933, Rev. F.M. Walder; 1934, Rev. R. Battie; 1935, Rev. K.D. Shivers, again; 1936-1937, Rev. C.H. Matherson; and 1938, Rev. Henderson; he repaired the church; 1939 and 1940, Rev. J.W. McKnight; 1941, Rev. J.S. McKeller; 1942,

Rev. L.B. Harris; he died here; 1943 and 1944, Rev. S. Shack; the church was painted. In 1945, Rev. A.E. English; 1946 and 1947, Rev. K.W. Smallwood; 1948, Rev. C.H. Thompson; 1949, Rev. E.L. Wynn; 1950, Rev. E. Muckle; the church was made a circuit again; 1951 and 1952, Rev. A.W. Kemp; 1953 and 1954, Rev. H.M. Moore; he built the church after it was blown down, painted inside and out and laid a cornerstone. Trustees serving at that time were Brothers C.G. Simpson, Johnnie Raven,Sr., George Simpson,Sr., and Ulysees Hill; 1955, Rev. C. Crouch; 1956 and 1957, Rev. H.H. Braswell, he reorganized our homecoming; 1958 and 1959, Rev. E. Young; 1959-1960, Rev. E.C. Hudson. From July 1960 until May 4, 1989, Rev. W.B. Brown. He served faithfully until his death and led many souls to Christ. He was a good leader and worker who loved his church and its members. He was truly a God sent man, who tried to always do something to improve our church. Under his leadership, we made numerous improvements. A fellowship meeting was organized, and it was a successful one. During those 29 years, we put heaters, sheetrock, new floors, painted inside and outside, sealed the outside rooms, put in pews and pulpit furniture, put carpet on the floor, built an annex, put in a well, put in bathrooms and changed the front entrance. In 1988, we enlarged our sanctuary, by moving the choir stand back to where the annex was and moving the pulpit back to where the choir stand was. We built another kitchen and fellowship hall with a sliding door; a pastor's study, steward and stewardess rooms, and two more bathrooms. We also purchased chairs for the Fellowship Hall and some kitchen equipment. From June 1989 until May 1997, Rev. E.X. King. Under Rev. King's leadership, we put siding on the church, hung chandeliers, installed stained glass windows, and laid a cornerstone.

From June 1997-July 1997, Rev. J.R. Campbell; August 1997 - October 1997, Rev. Leroy Brown. From November 1997 until now, Rev. Walter L.

Washington. Under Rev. Washington's leadership, we have installed a telephone, purchased an organ, tables, and chairs. A computer was donated to the church. In December 1998, we hosted the Albany-Valdosta District Conference, with our own, Elder J.L. Raven, Jr. as presiding elder. Former President Jimmy Carter was one of the main speakers. During this time, a headstone was placed on Bishop and Mrs. W.D. Johnson's graves at the St. Mark A.M.E. Church Cemetery. In 1999, we were instrumental in renaming a portion of the Old Plains Road to Bishop Johnson Circle. In February 1999, a marker was placed at the intersection of Bishop Johnson Circle and Old Plains Road in memory of the Archery community and Bishop Johnson. The Plains Historical Preservation Trust helped us to accomplish this goal.

Our church has sent out a number of ministers. They are the Reverends Lee Raven, Abron Hill, T.R. Wakefield, Sr., Rogers Williams, Simmeon Johnson, Randolph Tommie, A.C. Kleckley, Ben Hill, W.D. Johnson, Jr. who became a presiding elder, Johnnie Raven, Jr., T.R. Wakefield, Jr. and A.L. Raven, Sr. The Reverends Johnnie Raven, Jr. and T.R. Wakefield, Jr. have become presiding elders and are now serving. Four started after they moved away. They are the Reverends Alvin Johnson, Franklin Wakefield, Harry Holley, and Christina Holley.

Trustees now serving are Brothers Milton Raven, Sr., James Merritt, Thomas Wakefield, Sr., Simeon Wakefield, Norris Holley, and Chairman-Protem Wade Wilson, Sisters Hannah Kleckley, Willie Bell Raven, Mae Frances Merritt, Thelma Holley, Addie Wright, Joesphine Thomas, and Georgia Lee King. Sisters Sallie Hill, Ola B. Wilson, Vera Gardner, Brothers Currie Dunning, Floyd Raven, Francis Raven, Jr., and James Gardner served until their death.

Our church is 131 years old. *We are pressing on the upward way*, asking for your prayers that we may continue on for the Lord. Our motto, "Keep A Going."

—*Submitted by St. Mark A.M.E. Church*

Chapter 8: Schools

Colored Schools of Plains, Georgia

Prior to 1897, the colored high school students living in the Plains area attended schools in Macon, Cordele or Columbus. In 1897, the Americus Institute, a Baptist supported boarding school, was built to accommodate the local colored students. Due to financial troubles, the school closed in 1932. Students once again went out of town to attend high school.

In July 1915, a school for black students was built next door to the New Lebanon Baptist Church in Plains. The school was given the name Plains Institutional School. The first known principal was Mrs. Rosa Lee Pullman. Mrs. Lenny Rogers was the teacher and Mrs. Lilla Johnson was the assistant teacher.

Later, after the departure of Mrs. Rogers, Will Reid took over the position of lead teacher. Mrs. Mattie Mae Mitchner followed Mr. Reid as the teacher of this institution for the black children of Plains.

In 1922, the school was rebuilt to accommodate more students. It was given the name Rosenwald Elementary School. In 1941, the school was changed from an elementary school to a junior high school. The principal at this time was G.O. Jenkins of Eatonton. Following Mr. Jenkins was Mrs. Dregger. Later Mrs. Mattie Troutman took over this position. The last principal of this school was the late Mrs. Annie B. Floyd. She earned her master's degree from Columbia University in 1955. At the time of her death, Mrs. Floyd was working toward her doctorate degree at Atlanta University.

Mrs. Floyd was admired as an exceptional educator, community leader and church leader.

In the middle of 1957, the school was rebuilt and relocated near the Lebanon Church where the Rosenwald Elementary School previously existed. It was given the name Westside Elementary School. Claude Frazier was the principal. In September, 1957, Sumter High School, a county school, opened its doors to both city and county students. James Bozeman was the first and only principal of Sumter High School.

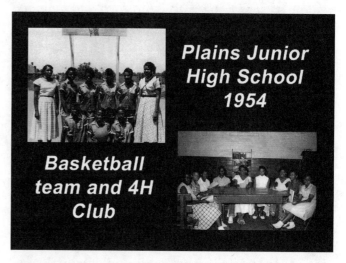

Basketball coaches Thomas and Walker. Annette Schley is fourth person from left in basketball photo. Photo credit: Robert Schley

In September 1971, the schools in Plains were consolidated. Grades one through six attended Westside Elementary School. The junior high school students grades seven and eight attended Central Junior High School, formerly Sumter High School. Plains High School then housed black and white students in grades nine through 12 until 1979 when the Sumter County schools were consolidated.[1]

—*Submitted by Amy Wise*

Endnotes

[1] History of Plains, October 1976, 1st Edition, printed by Gammage Print Shop of Americus, pages 47-48.

⌘

Will the School Instill Wisdom or Character?

1952 Commencement Address
Plains Junior High School
by Principal Annie B. Floyd

The school is not so much a place to instill wisdom as it is a place to build men and women. The boy may fail in one or many studies. Do not discourage him; if he comes out with the character of a man he has won. The girl may not lead her class, but if she comes out pure and true for life that is success.

Moral qualities live longer than intellectual ones because they have more power over the heart of the individual.

Parents, teachers, and friends, are you trying to improve upon your children and the youth of today that good manners will get one further in the world than money? Yes, money will purchase goods, but good manners will win friends and good will.

Seemingly, today's youth feel that to have good manners is old fashioned. "Thank You," "Please," "Pardon me," "Good Morning," Goodbye," etc. are words that have been taken from the language of too many homes in this fast moving age.

Children must be taught how to behave in church, at school, on the street, at the theatre, on train, trolley or bus and in all public places.

Our boys and girls are building the houses in which they are going to live and if they are not carefully guided in the selection of material their buildings will not withstand the tides of a changing world.

Education consists in action, conduct, self-control, self-culture and all that tends to discipline a man and fit him for the proper performance of duties and business of life.

To ascertain the true nature of a person, observe his deportment in public; most people contrive to conduct themselves agreeable toward the small group of acquaintance comprising their social circle. Such efforts cannot be wholly unselfish for they win them the approbation and companionship without which no human being lives happily. But how do they behave towards persons they encounter only in passing and from whom they expect no favors? Do they always think in terms of self-satisfaction or of the satisfaction of others as well?

Annie B. Floyd. Photo credit: "The Plains Site," Commencement 1952

The church must assist the home and school in character building. It is the duty of adult leaders to teach the child what is right. Give him the desire to do right and then provide ample opportunity to practice the desired act.

A friendly smile, a quiet voice and good honest eyes open many doors and hearts.

—Article taken from *The Plains Site*, a publication of the school. This was from Commencement 1952.

The Johnson Home Industrial College

The Johnson Home Industrial College was the product of the brain of William D. Johnson, D.D. Backed up by the loyal members of the Sublime Order of Archery, he was successful in building a college, and therefore opened its doors for the reception of worthy students, October 2, 1912.

Domitory for Johnson Home Industrial College which was located at Archery. Photo credit: Milton Raven

Three large buildings were erected, and much credit is and should be given to the thrift and energy put forth by Rev. F. M. Johnson, who at the time was the treasurer of the society, and by his wise counsel, and guidance of the affairs, he greatly facilitated the work of erecting the college.

The Board of Trustees elected Prof. A. J. Johnson, A.M., A.B., as its first president, and under his leadership the school prospered, both numerically and morally.

The names of the persons appearing in the charter rendered all the assistance that could be rendered, a part of whom worked with all their might for the welfare of the school.

Charter

A special term of Webster County Superior Court is hereby convened for the purpose of granting charter. This January 6, 1913.

Z.A. LITTLEJOHN, J.S.C., S.W.C.

Georgia, Webster County:

In the Superior Court of said county at special term, this 6th day of January, 1913, William D. Johnson of Muscogee County, Francis M. Johnson and J.C. Myers of Sumter County, George W. Barnes, Louis S. Raven and Andrew Johnson of Webster County and all residents of the State of Georgia, having filed in the office of the clerk of the Superior Court of said County, their petition seeking the formation of a corporation to be known as "The Johnson Home Industrial College." For the purpose of promoting the cause of education, and having complied with all the requirements of the law for such cases made and provided, and the court being satisfied that said application is legitimately within the purview and intention of the Code, the same is hereby granted, and the above named persons, their associates and successors are hereby incorporated under the said name and style of "The Johnson Home Industrial College" for and during the period of twenty years, with the privilege of renewal at the expiration of that time. That they have the right and authority to teach Normal, Industrial and Collegiate courses, to grant diplomas and confer degrees to such persons as may complete any or all of the courses prescribed by the faculty and board of trustees of said college. To own, purchase or sell real estate or personal property, to operate such mills, factories and farms as may be necessary in teaching the courses prescribed in said college and to receive gifts or endowments from the support of same, to elect a board of trustees, to make such rules and regulations, employ such teachers as may deem necessary to properly conduct said college, to charge such tuition fees as they may deem necessary to those entering; said college, to sue and to be sued, to plead and be impleaded. And said corporation is hereby clothed with all the rights, privileges and immunities, and made subject to all the restrictions and liabilities fixed by law.

This 6th day of January, 1913 Z.A. Littlejohn Judge Superior Court. Webster Co., Georgia

Situation and Means of Access

Johnson Home Industrial College is situated in the southwestern part of the State of Georgia, in the county of Webster, on the main line of the Seaboard Air Line Railway, between Americus and Richland, Georgia. The railroad company stops its trains at this place regularly. You may purchase a ticket for Archery, Georgia, and you will get off the train, and be upon a campus of over two hundred acres.

The climate is temperate throughout the year; the air is pure and unaffected with the many disease germs found in most of the large cities. The water is pure and sparkling, cool and very agreeable—pure artesian. The school is located in one of the most healthy localities within this great state.

Grounds and Buildings

The college property embraces two hundred acres of fertile land, a great part of which is well cultivated.

The buildings are of excellent architectural beauty, and contain all the modern improvements, which are necessary for the comfort and health of the students who are entrusted to the care of the authorities.

Situated as they are, upon a lofty hill overlooking the surrounding country, they command the admiration of all who may chance to see them.

Written by W.D. Johnson, Jr. (son of Bishop Johnson)

Some Graduates

The Johnson Home Industrial College was established in 1912 and began classes in 1913. The trustees were Bishop W.D. Johnson, Rev. Levi Raven, Francis Johnson, J.C. Myers, and George W. Barnes. The school was established to provide educational training for negroes. The following are names of some who attended the college:

1. Beatrice Denson
2. James Dunning, Sr.
3. Alvan Johnson
4. Semion Johnson
5. Winfred Johnson
6. Rosa Kitchen
7. Amos Kleckley
8. Hannah Smith Kleckley
9. Mary Laster
10. Ruby Laster
11. Willie Laster
12. Pauline Peterson
13. Arena Raven
14. Carrie Raven
15. Clifford Raven
16. Clinton Raven
17. Booker Schley
18. Minnie Schley
19. T.R. Wakefield, Sr.
20. Ulyses Wakefield
21. Rosa Williams

A.J. Johnson, president
Hattie Simmons, teacher
Annie Simmons, teacher
W.D. Johnson, Jr., professor
—Submitted by Milton Raven

The Site of the First Formal School for African-American Children In Plains, Georgia

Inscription on Historical Marker

On this site, black children received their education in a two-room school purchased in 1915 for $500.00 from the white community. It was named Plains Institutional School. In 1922, through the generosity of Julius Rosenwald, the school was renovated and renamed Rosenwald Elementary. The eighth and ninth grades were added in 1941 and the school was renamed Rosenwald Jr. High School. Serving as principals were Rosa Lee Pullman, Will Reid, Mattie Mae Mitchner, and Annie B. Floyd. In 1958, the wooden structure was replaced by Westside Elementary.

Some Graduates from Plains Institutional School

1932-1933
Ceola Mackey
Lura Mackey
Grace Murry
Nanie B. Tatum
Jeanett Tatum
Bernice Wright
Ozie B. Snelling
Fannie Monts
Rethemus Howard
James McGrady
Otis McGrady
L.C. McGrady
Ruby Mathis
—*Submitted by Mary Minion*

Historical marker site of first formal school for African-Americans. State Labor Commissioner Michael Thurmond, President Jimmy Carter, Annette Wise, Rev. Walter Washington and Milton Raven. Photo credit: Annette Wise

Graham School of Plains Early 1920s

Some students who attended:
Antonia Kitchens
Annie R. Kitchens
Emma Kitchens
—*Submitted by Mary Minion*

Staley High School

Once black students completed the eighth grade in Plains, to further their education they would transfer to Staley High School in Americus. The following information identifies some of the Plains students who enrolled at Staley. The school in Plains for black students was recorded in the Staley school records as Plains Rosenwald School, Plains Institute, Plains Colored School or Plains Schools.

Student	Entered	Graduated
Registering Parent/occupation		
J.C. Henderson	09-12-38 (?)	05-29-38 (?)
Curry Henderson/not listed		

Student Parent/occupation	Entered	Graduated	Student Parent/occupation	Entered	Graduated
Henry Mathis Henry Mathis/janitor	not listed	not listed	Earnestine Mathis Lillie Mathis/housewife	9-4-45	5-30-47
Jennie Mae Hicks Jennie Tatum/domestic	9-18-39	not listed	Mildred Jones Nancy Jones/housewife	9-13-43	5-30-47
Archery Whittaker Laura Henderson/cook	9-12-38	withdrew '39	Erma Hall Bertha Hall/housework	9-13-43	5-30-47
James Wright Mahaley Wright/carpenter	9-11-39	withdrew	Ned Brown Fannie Brown/housewife	9-13-43	5-30-47
Irene Perry Georgie Wilkerson/domestic	9-11-39	attended 1yr.	Ida Bell Angrish Addie Angrish/housework	11-43	withdrawn
Onnie McGarrah Relliford/laborer	9-11-39	withdrew	Clara Schley Minie Mae Schley/housework	9-9-47	5-31-48
David Harvey Ruth Harvey/domestic	9-18-39	did not return	Milton Raven Lillie Raven/farmer	9-9-46	5-31-48
William Bishop Alex Bishop/laborer	9-11-39	dropped	Jessie Hughes Carrilee Harvey/farming	9-16-46	5-31-48
Bessie Bryant Burland Bryant/farmer	9-11-40	not listed	Ruby Hicks Mozella Hicks/housework	9-17-44	5-31-48
Lucile Hicks Mazelia Hicks/laundress	9-11-40	6-2-44	Maxine Hicks Mozella Hicks/housework	9-17-44	5-31-48
Juanita Hicks Emma Lee Hicks/farmer	9-11-40	6-2-44	Almira Grimes Bertha Grimes/farmer	9-4-45	5-31-48
Mary Floyd King Leroy Miles/carpenter	9-8-41 (?)	9-8-41 (?)	William Berry Emory Berry/masonry	9-11-44	5-3-48
Irene Stevens Vernia Stephens/farmer	8-11-44	6-4-46	Elizabeth Wilson Freddie Mae Jackson/housework	9-10-45	6-3-49
Ruby Soloman Carrie Solomon/houseworker	9-20-42	6-4-46	Oscar Thomie Lillie Thomie/farming	9-10-45	not listed
James Reliford Comer Reliford/farmer	9-11-44	6-4-46	Joshua Morgan Ruth Morgan/farming	9-5-45	6-3-49
Frankie May Hawkins Ollis Hawkins/farmer	9-11-44	6-4-46	Miriam Hicks Mozelia Hicks/laundress	9-5-45	6-3-49
Lumie Mae Foster Eli Foster/farmer	10-11-43	6-4-46	Effie Schley Seagram Schley/ —	9-5-46	5-26-50
Bertel Mae Foster Eli Foster/farmer	10-11-43	not listed	Bettie L. Mathis Ed Mathis/janitor	9-5-46	5-26-50
Velma Angry Elizabeth Angry/farmer	9-14-42	6-4-46	Thelma Mae Hollis Tom Hollis/—	1948	5-26-50

—Submitted by Annette Wise

Historical Marker at Archery

Johnson Home Industrial School
Archery, Georgia

The rural community of Archery, established in the 1800s, consisted of a train stop, houses of railroad employees, the St. Mark African Methodist Episcopal (A.M.E.) Church, a school for black youth, and a store. The community was named for Sublime Order of Archery, a relief organization of the A.M.E. Church which assisted the southern black families. Two permanent white families, the Watsons and the Carters, lived here. Edward Herman Watson was the Seaboard Railroad section foreman and James Earl Carter, Sr., was the father of Jimmy Carter, 39th president of the United States who spent his youth here. The other 25 families were African-American.

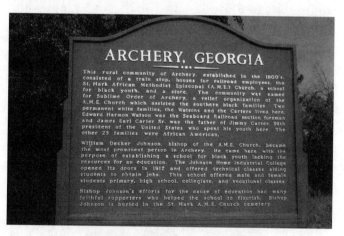

Archery Historical Marker
Photo credit: Annette Wise

William Decker Johnson, bishop of the A.M.E. Church, became the most prominent person in Archery. He came here with the purpose of establishing a school for black youth who lacked the resources for an education. The Johnson Home Industrial College opened its doors in 1912 and offered technical classes aiding students to obtain jobs. This school offered male and female students primary, high school, collegiate, and vocational classes.

Bishop Johnson's efforts for the cause of education had many faithful supporters who helped the school to flourish. Bishop Johnson is buried in the St. Mark A.M.E. Church cemetery that is located near the original site of the school three miles southwest on Old Plains Highway. Bishop Johnson lived from 1869-1936.

—*Submitted by (no name given)*

Magnolia Male and Female Institutes

Mineral Spring, Sumter County, Ga.

Board of Instructors:

J.E. Rylander, A.B., Principal of Male Dep'nt.
Wm. C. Dodd, A.B., Principal Female do.
Mrs. J.E. Rylander, Principal Primary do.
J.E. Schmidt, Principal Music do.

Rates of Tuition Per Annum:

Primary Class	$16
Third Class	$27
Second Class	$32
First Class	$40
Music on Piano or Guitar	$50
Use of Instruments	$5

The entire Female school required to take lessons in vocal music, unless objected to by the parents or guardian, for which a charge of $2.00 per annum will be made, tuition payable at the end of the Fall and Spring term. No deduction of absence except in case of protracted sickness. These schools are situated in the country, 12 miles west of Americus, in the midst of good society and in a neighborhood, proverbial for its health, morality, and religion.

The mineral virtues of our spring are no longer questionable; many invalids in the last two summers, having realized its power to heal.

Our course of instruction is thorough and practical, and embraces the branches usually taught in college.

If an extensive and thorough course of instruction, competent instructions, freedom from temptation, to vice and immorality, and healthfulness of location not surpassed, if equaled in South Western Georgia, combined with the advantages of a Mineral Spring of well known medicinal properties do not entitle us to a liberal share of patronage, we cannot offer to the public any higher inducements.

The two schools occupy houses about a quarter of a mile apart, within a few hundred yards of the spring.

Board may be had in good families; at from $7 to $10 per month.

Our next term opens on the first Monday in January, 1856. Post Office, Plains of Dura, Sumter County, Georgia.

Trustees:

M.E. Rylander

Robert Russell

Moses Pullin

H. Whitehurst

T.J. Shinholster

—Article taken from *Weekly Sumter Republican*, November 21, 1855.

⌘

Plains High School Alma Mater

O'er the plains so gently rolling,
Reared against the sky.
Proudly stands our alma mater,
As the years go by.
Forward ever – be our watchword,
Conquer and prevail.
Here's to thee, our Alma Mater,
Plains High School All Hail!

⌘

A Brief History of Plains High School

"The educational experience which shaped my life was here in the building behind us." [1] Those words were spoken by the 39th president of the United States, James Earl (Jimmy) Carter, Jr. at the reopening of Plains High School by the National Park Service and the city of Plains on October 1, 1996. The words give some indication of the significance that a small rural school played in the community of Plains, in the life of a president, and, consequently, in the shaping of world events. Few, if any, other schools may boast such a rich heritage as Plains High School.

Plains High School began as Plains School in 1890 when funds were collected for a new school for the community of Plains. Citizens contributed $1,800 and the Masonic Lodge assisted with the cost for a two-story wood frame structure that was

Student body assembled on porch of old Plains School circa 1900. Photo credit: Allene T. Haugabook

erected on the campus where the current facility stands. The new school opened in 1900 with a Professor Jarrell serving as the first superintendent.[2]

Building for today and tomorrow. Top: Jimmy Carter, Ann Montgomery. Bottom: Billy Oliver, Roy Pantall, Ross Oliver, Durell Anderson and Hortense Jennings. Photo credit: Allene Haugabook

In 1921, at a cost of $50,000, the current building was constructed. The former frame structure was sold to the all-black Johnson Home Industrial College, dismantled, and moved to nearby Archery. The new facility housed both elementary and high school through grade 11, that being the highest level required by the state of Georgia at the time. At that time, the school's two most renowned leaders were already in place. Julia Coleman served as principal from 1912 to 1927, and as superintendent from 1927 to 1949. Y.T. Sheffield, who would later serve as superintendent, was also teaching at the school when the new building was constructed.[3]

Plains school with its 10 classrooms was never a large school. In 1937, enrollment stood at 259 with 13 teachers on staff.[4] One former student recalls the excitement of events that brought new students. When road construction brought workers to Plains for a year in 1938, enrollment temporarily swelled with two new students added to fourth grade. In addition, eighth grade was an exciting milestone as two new students from Thompson school joined the existing 16 pupils in the class.[5]

While the school was small, its impact has been very large. For those who attended Plains High School, there seems to be no doubt about the reason for the school's success. Julia Lewis Coleman is constantly credited for shaping the school, its students, and to a large degree the community as well. Miss Julia, as her students called her, holds the distinction of being the only teacher ever quoted in a presidential inauguration speech.[6]

Miss Julia, daughter of a Baptist minister and a schoolteacher, moved to Plains as a small child and attended school there herself. She later graduated from Bessie Tift College in Forsyth before beginning her teaching career in 1908 at Friendship School in Sumter County. In 1912, she returned to Plains to teach English and remained at the Plains school, except for one year in LaGrange, until her retirement in 1958.[7]

Miss Julia and a student talk with Mr. Sheffield. Photo credit: Michael Mallard

Also held up as a model educator was Y.T. Sheffield. Mr. Sheffield was a graduate of Carson-Newman College in Tennessee and obtained a master's degree from Mercer University in Macon.

He arrived at Plains High in 1927 to serve as principal and coach, and in the latter capacity was noted for taking several basketball teams to championships. In addition to those duties, he is remem-

Boys involved in one of many learning activities. Back: Harold Taylor, Charles Medlock, B.T. Wishard, Rembert Forrest, Billy Oliver, Lavon Turner and Leonard Evans. Front: Henry Ratliff, Carlton Wise, A.H. "Junior" Crozier, Joe Moore and Halley Smith. Photo credit: Charles Medlock

bered for his dedication to keeping the school's coal furnace stoked so that the building would be warm for students in the wintertime.[8]

There were, of course, many other teachers who served Plains High School over the years.[9] These two, however, were the leaders of the school and set the curriculum that so significantly impacted their students. Their roles complemented each other as "Miss Julia" represented the cultural side of education, while Mr. Sheffield marshaled the mathematics and physical education courses.[10]

A typical day at Plains High School always began with all grades assembling in the auditorium for chapel. Elementary students were chosen for the honor of holding the door for others to enter as Miss Julia played the piano. High school boys and girls sat in separate rows in the center, with elementary students seated on the sides. A selection was read from the Bible and prayer was led. Many mornings included programs presented by various grades. After about 30 minutes, students were dismissed to their classes with a short recess in the mornings and an hour break for lunch.[11]

The school curriculum was broad and included, at Miss Julia's insistence, a variety of cultural subjects. Literature, composition, art, drama, and music, which included obligatory instrumental performance, were all part of Miss Julia's attempt to broaden students' horizons. In addition, math, science, shop and sports were required.[12]

The studies at Plains High were not confined to traditional classroom approaches. Former President Carter recalls that competitive exercises were an important part of motivating students to venture beyond their textbooks. He describes competing in debate, music appreciation, drama, spelling bees, and a writing contest called Ready Writing. In addition, students were required to memorize and recite long poems and chapters from the Bible.[13]

Miss Julia was also known for adapting curriculum to meet individual needs. When a student wanted to study journalism, Miss Julia took him to Athens to gather information on how to proceed and she helped him start a student newspaper. (He later became a successful journalist.) Another student (who later became a physician) wished to practice medicine, so Miss Julia taught Latin to his senior class.[14] President Carter credits Miss Julia with taking a personal interest in every student and finding some area in which that student could excel. In his own case, he recalls her encouraging him to read great books, assigning Tolstoy's *War and Peace* to him when he was 12.[15]

Not only did her students praise her innovations in later years, but Miss Julia was also recognized for her work during her tenure at PHS. In 1937, the school was designated by the Georgia Board of Education as a model school to serve as an example for other schools.[16] It was one of only four schools in the state honored in this way,[17] and Miss

1945 graduates of Plains High School dressed for baccalaureate service. Back: Harold Sproull, Joyce Dozier, Ann Wise and Billy Hogg. Front: Rev. J.A. Sanders (Lutheran pastor and teacher), Ernest Chappell, Jr., Carolyn Harris, Betty Cranford, Mattie Beth Anderson, Gloria Alston, Billie Morgan and Julian Smith. Photo credit: Billie Morgan Hart

Julia was further honored by an invitation from the Roosevelt administration to visit the White House.[18] The particular reasons for the honors are unclear, but it may be assumed that the wide variety of experiences offered to students was part of the reason for the honor. It may also be that the tremendous community involvement in the school attracted attention.

Plains High School was intricately connected to the community. "What went on in the building behind me," Carter said at the school's reopening, "was inseparable from what went on on Main Street and in the home."[19] That connection was accomplished in part by a constant parade of school programs to which parents and relatives were invited. Miss Julia brought production companies and Chautauqua programs from New York.[20] Even the Boston Celtics played an exhibition game at PHS in 1935.[21]

Miss Julia also connected the community to the school through her award-winning garden projects. Each time a former student married and

had a child, a bush or shrub was planted on "baby row" by the family.[22]

Of course, the school's connection to the community also meant that the school reflected the changes and tensions of the community. In the 1950s and 60s, segregation became a source on contention in the community. When Jimmy Carter, serving on the Sumter County Board of Education in his first elected office, proposed consolidation of white schools in 1961, he met with hostile opposition led in part by his former principal Y.T. Sheffield, a proponent of segregation, apparently believed consolidation to be a move toward integration.[23]

Similar tensions erupted in the classroom in 1963 when it was announced that President John F. Kennedy had been shot. When a teacher said, "Good," the class cheered prompting Chip Carter to throw a chair at the teacher, an incident for which he spent several days in the principal's office.[24]

With the coming of integration in the 1970s, Sumter County experienced an exodus of white students to private schools. A lack of support by wealthy white landowners led to decreased school funding and older buildings like Plains High School suffered from neglect. As schools were consolidated, it was deemed necessary to close PHS.

Plains High had played too important a role in history to be forgotten, however, and the Jimmy Carter National Historic Site and Preservation District was established by Congress in 1987 with plans to restore the school and use it for a visitor center complete with an educational program for visiting students.[25] The community spirit of Plains came alive again as the city rallied to raise funds necessary to restore the building, and the school reopened in 1996.

Under the direction of instructional specialist Annette Wise, in cooperation with the National Park Service, the educational program at PHS has the halls alive with the sounds of children once again. More than 4,000 children participated in the program in just two years as visiting fourth, fifth eighth, and 11th grade classes come to spend the day learning the history of Plains, Plains High School, and the Carters.

As new students come to Plains High School, it is hoped that new dreams are born from the old building and its story. As Governor Zell Miller said at the grand opening ceremonies, "Plains High School will show how one person can change the world."[26] As each student visits it is hoped that he will realize that he is that one person.

—Submitted by Keith Wishum

Endnotes

[1] This quotation is from personal notes taken by this writer at the reopening ceremony.

[2] Beth M. Walters, *History of Plains, Georgia, 1885-1985* (By the Author, 1985), p. 93.

[3] William Patrick O'Brien, *Special History Study* (National Park Service, 1991), p. 94-95.

[4] Ibid., p. 95.

[5] Allen T. Haugabook, *Remembering Plains in the 1930's, 1940's, 1950's and a Little Beyond* (By the Author, 1996), p. 36.

[6] National Park Service, *General Management Plan/ Development Concept Plan* (National Park Service, 1993), p. 62.

[7] Walters, p. 93

[8] Ibid., p. 95

[9] For a partial list, see Haugabook, p. 31.

[10] O'Brien, p. 40.

[11] Haugabook, p. 34-35.

[12] O'Brien, p. 40.

[13] Jimmy Carter, *Why Not the Best?* (Nashville: Broadman Press, 1975), p. 35.

[14] Haugabook, p. 37.

[15] National Park Service, p. 36.

[16] O'Brien, p. 41.

[17] National Park Service, p. 19.

[18] O'Brien, p. 41.

[19] Keith Wishum, "Plains High Reopens to Students" *SCS School Notes* (October 1996), p. 2.

[20] Walters, p. 94.

[21] Haugabook, p. 35.

[22] O'Brien, p. 95.

[23] Ibid., p. 49.

[24] Ibid., p. 40.

[25] National Park Service, p. iii.

[26] Wishum, p. 2.

BY THE GOVERNOR OF THE STATE OF GEORGIA

A PROCLAMATION
PLAINS HIGH SCHOOL

JIMMY CARTER NATIONAL HISTORIC SITE

WHEREAS: Plains High School, constructed in 1921 and integrated in 1966, maintained its commitment to the early development and educational well-being of children through the last graduating class in 1979; and

WHEREAS: Plains High School has faced many challenges through the years and inspired its students, including former President Jimmy Carter and former First Lady Rosalynn Carter, both of whom attended grammar and high school in this building, to achieve their personal best; and

WHEREAS: Plains High School's programs were cited as models for other Georgia schools and commended by various Washington, D.C. officials; and

WHEREAS: Plains High School has served as the centerpiece of the community where students enjoyed many amenities: a garden on the west lawn in which a shrub was planted each time a former student married and had children (known as "baby row"): a large library: performing arts on tour: and a marker in dedication to Miss Coleman, a teacher who taught fifty years and instilled the sense of community and duty in her students; and

WHEREAS: Plains High School represents the themes of Education, Technology, Social and Humanitarian Movements and American Ways of Life: and

WHEREAS: On October 1, 1996. Plains High School will celebrate the reopening of the school as a National Park Service Visitor Center with exhibits highlighting the life and career of former President Jimmy Carter; now

THEREFORE: I, Zell Miller, Governor of the State of Georgia, do hereby honor the **"PLAINS HIGH SCHOOL JIMMY CARTER NATIONAL HISTORIC SITE"** and extend best wishes on this grand and historic occasion.

IN WITNESS WHEREOF, I have hereunto set my hand and caused the Seal of the Executive Department to be affixed. This 1st day of October 1996.

Governor Zell Miller signs bill making Plains High School the State School of Georgia 1997. Photo credit: Annette Wise

RESOLUTION

State of Georgia
State Board of Education

WHEREAS, it is anticipated that legislation will be introduced during the 1997 Session of the Georgia General Assembly seeking an amendment to Title 20 of the Georgia Code and naming Plains High School located in Plains, Sumter County, Georgia, as the official school of Georgia, and

WHEREAS, Plains High School was erected in 1921 and served as a model school for 58 years, and

WHEREAS, the importance of Plains High School cannot be overestimated in the story of Plains and former President Jimmy Carter and Rosalynn, and

WHEREAS, the building is representative of the themes of Education, Technology, Social and Humanitarian Movements and American Ways of Life, and

WHEREAS, the proposal for education programs at Plains High School would meet the following objectives:

• Students who attend the Plains High School program will learn about the events surrounding the life of Jimmy and Rosalynn Carter, emphasizing their formative years, education and spiritual life;

• Teachers will be able to choose among several different activities so that the day is full of programs that are relevant to materials being covered by the class;

• Teachers will have available and be encouraged to use pre-visit and post-visit activities that will prepare students for their visit and ensure that topics are reinforced after the visit;

• Whenever practical, students will be exposed to critical thinking skills so that they can be stimulated and challenged to examine the events and issues associated with the Jimmy Carter National Historic Site;

• The curriculum will be a program where the students will be challenged in the same setting that challenged a president of the United States;

WHEREAS, the hallmarks of Plains High School have been unquestioned integrity and honor and unyielding commitment to all children, and

WHEREAS, Plains High School has now been renovated through the joint efforts of the National Park Service and the citizens of Plains, and

WHEREAS, such uniqueness authorizes and justifies the designation of Plains High School as the Official School of Georgia by the Georgia General Assembly.

THEREFORE BE IT RESOLVED that the members of the Board of Education of the State of Georgia, duly assembled, and it is hereby resolved by authority of the same, that this Resolution supporting an amendment to Title 20 of the Georgia Code naming Plains High School as the Official State School of Georgia be adopted and that the members of the General Assembly be notified, where appropriate, of the adoption of this Resolution by this body and of the body's support of such proposed legislation.

SO RESOLVED, this 15th day of January, 1997.

Historical Marker for Plains High School

The State School of Georgia

This school opened in 1921, racially integrated in 1966 and served students from Plains, Georgia until 1979. The school's rich history of distinguished educators and progressive curriculum earned recognition at state and national levels. Graduates from this school have made tremendous contributions to Georgia, as well as the world. Notable graduates include President Jimmy Carter and his wife, Rosalynn Smith Carter.

Historical marker for Plains High School. Lawrence Smith, Jimmy Carter, Annette Wise and Rosalynn Carter. Photo credit: Annette Wise

As a result of the consolidation of county schools, Plains High School closed in 1979. Through a partnership between the community of Plains and the National Park Service, the school was restored and reopened in 1996 as the main Visitors Center for the Jimmy Carter National Historic Site. In 1996 the Georgia Department of Education, Sumter County Schools, and the National Park Service initiated an educational program for students visiting the site. The Georgia State Board of Education approved a resolution on January 15, 1997, which noted the importance of this educational facility from 1921-1979 and recognized the significant impact of the collaborative educational venture.

The 1997 Georgia General Assembly passed a bill, which named Plains High School the State School of Georgia. The legislation recognized educators Miss Julia Coleman and Mr. Y.T. Sheffield for their outstanding leadership at the school. It also noted that President Carter and First Lady Rosalynn Smith Carter were graduates of Plains High School and that President Carter served on the Sumter County School Board as his first political office.

Governor Zell Miller signed the bill into law on April 22, 1997. At this time, Plains High School was officially designated the State School of Georgia.

A Tribute to Miss Julia and Mr. Sheffield

Backward, turn backward, oh time in your flight,
Help me recall again, just for tonight
Voices long silenced — faces long gone,
The Plains of my childhood — the place I called home.

Now in recollection I see quite a few
Who influenced us greatly — I'm thinking of two.
Mr. Sheffield, we called him, or Mr. Y.T.
Or, if out of earshot, "Teaser" 'twould be.

And another, Miss Julia— that's all! That was it!
Could you call her Miss Coleman? It just didn't fit!
Her quiet demeanor, His genial way
Have influenced our pathways for day upon day.

I can see the bright twinkle that came in his eye
Making soft, gentle wrinkles — It's those now I spy.
Her soft-spoken voice could oft become stern
Should one of her students fail his lesson to learn.

I see smiles on their faces, soft chuckles I hear,
And when life brought sadness, I've seen there a tear.
The rod of correction he used, if he must,
She chose to use words-straight forward and just.

Both modes of correction seemed to have their effect,
For you came away chastened, they gained your respect.
How often we'd listen, his footfall to hear,
They'd give to us warning — "Mr. Sheffield is near!"

At chapel each morning we'd sing as he led,
She would play the piano, then announcements were made.
Strong words from the Bible must be memorized,
"Their message," they said,"Would strengthen our lives."

They set the example for lives they would mold,
And we've looked back in awe now that we've become old.
And raised a brief prayer of thanks, as we knelt,
For the lives of those two whose influence we felt.

I've stood on the bank of a calm placid lake,
Dropped in a pebble, and watched the waves break.
I've observed, from the impact of one tiny rock,
The farthermost shore feel a brief little shock.

So it's been with the lives of those wonderful two,
Their impact's been felt in all that we do,
And the widening ring from their rippling waves
Will be felt in the future, for days upon days.

For the paths of us all have been changed very much
And destinies altered, of those whom they touched.
And our children's children, not yet to us known,
Will feel the influence of those long since gone.

And the world will be better in some minute way
Because our paths crossed here in Plains one brief day.

— by Edwin Timmerman

Plains High School Graduates

Graduating Class 1922

(June 2)

Principal: Mr. Thomas
1. Laura Caughman
2. Cecil Dodson
3. Bertha Dominick
4. Walter Kennedy
5. Irene Murray
6. Daisy Stephens
7. Rosa Stephens
8. Lillian Thomas
9. Eva Wiggins

Graduating Class 1923

1. Nelle Arnold
2. Nora Gaston
3. Paul Gaston
4. Harold Kendrick
5. Frances Lowery
6. Annola Murray
7. Norman Murray
8. C. L. Walters, Jr.
9. Mary Wise

Graduating Class 1924

1. Ed Lynn Bridges
2. Susie Mae Davis
3. James H. Dodson
4. Charlie Dozier
5. Robert Dozier
6. Mary Harris
7. John Emmette Howell
8. Bertha Jones
9. Olive King
10. Gladys Logan
11. Mildred Mackey
12. Allie Murray
13. Mary Murray
14. Ruby O'Quinn
15. R. E. Shirley
16. Martha Taylor
17. Mary Helen Thomas
18. Gladys Wiggins

Graduating Class 1925

1. Joseph Cranford
2. Elizabeth Dodson
3. Otis L. Gaston
4. Hugh Gibson
5. Felton Harris
6. James Harvey
7. Lynette Jennings
8. Nannae King
9. Carolyn Knowlton
10. Lieutishia Logan
11. Linnie Logan
12. Robert McGarrah
13. Nettie Mae McLendon
14. Bertha Alice McMath
15. Chloe Medlock
16. Ruth Medlock
17. Robert Allen Mills
18. Gladys Murray
19. Ellen Smith
20. Hazel Timmerman
21. Elizabeth Wise
22. Lake Wise

Graduating Class 1926

1. Magella Bagwell
2. Karl Campbell
3. Martha Jackson
4. Betty Jennings
5. Ethel Jennings
6. Blake Johnson
7. Lura Kennedy
8. Mildred King
9. Lillian Knowlton
10. Kathryn Logan
11. Sue McMath
12. Christine Mims
13. Aughtry Oliver
14. J. F. Plexico
15. Eva Webb
16. Josephine Wells

Graduating Class 1927

1. Reese M. Andrews
2. Bertha Mae Bridges
3. John Rufus Cook
4. Bob Dodson
5. Esther Hart
6. Hugh Jennings
7. Herschel Logan
8. Howard Logan
9. Grace McGill
10. Drue Murray
11. Perry Plexico
12. George Shirley
13. Joe Williams
14. Calvin Wise
15. J. C. Wise Jr.

Graduating Class 1928

1. Harold Andrews
2. Virgie Coggins
3. Joel Dodson

4. Guy Dominick
5. Edith Gibson
6. Paul Large
7. John Logan
8. Charles McLendon
9. Eugene Steed
10. J.W. Steed
11. Ellis Taylor
12. Pauline Taylor
13. Louise White
14. Clark Wise
15. Loris Wise
16. Louise Wise
17. L. W. Wishard

Graduating Class 1929

1. Mack Adrams
2. Marjorie Andrews
3. Stewart Campbell
4. Emmett Cook
5. Frances Israel
6. Sara Jackson
7. Marjorie Jennings
8. Mill Jennings
9. Paul Jennings
10. Elizabeth McGarrah
11. Louise Mitchell
12. Mary Lou Williams
13. Margaret Wise

Graduating Class 1930

1. Sarah Dodson
2. Stanford Hogg
3. Lynn Hogg
4. Ruth Howell
5. Ella Jean Jones
6. Lilloise Lunsford

7. Colquitt McLendon
8. Beth Murray
9. Mae Belle Salter
10. James Webb
11. Louise Webb
12. John White
13. Harriett Williams

Graduating Class 1931

1. Dorothy Andrews
2. Alice Beamon
3. Coleman Cook
4. Vera Dominick
5. Charles Fite
6. Maxine Kearse
7. Colbert McLeondon
8. George Murray
9. Etta Bell Phillips
10. Lorise Phillips
11. Sara Salter
12. Kathryn Sproull
13. Lillian Stephenson
14. Woodrow Thomas
15. James Timmerman
16. Helen Walters
17. Leo Wiggins
18. Agnes Williams
19. Mary Williams
20. James Wise
21. Ruth Wise

Graduating Class 1932

1. Clarence Dodson
2. Evelyn Jennings
3. Lillian Jennings
4. Theron McLendon
5. Nellie Phillips

6. Thomas Ragan
7. Rebecca Senn
8. Sara Smith
9. Anna Turner
10. Austin Turner
11. Nadine Wiggins
12. Allie Mae Wise
13. David Wise

Graduating Class 1933

1. Myrtle Lee Allen
2. Virginia Andrews
3. James Cranford
4. Minnie Merritt Dodson
5. Ellen Ruth Dozier
6. Frances Edwards
7. Bertha Gattis
8. Frances Howell
9. Thomas Jennings
10. Margaret Johnson
11. James Kennedy
12. Owen Markette
13. Ann McGarrah
14. Sara Eva Murray
15. Louise Price
16. Maxine Ragan
17. Alice Ratliff
18. Jerome Thaxton
19. Watson Turner
20. Emma Nell Welch
21. Dorothy Wise

Graduating Class 1934

1. Donnel Carter
2. James Crawford
3. Louise Fite
4. Lillian Harrold

5. Ruby Nell Mims
6. Ethel Mitchell
7. Albert Ratliff
8. Lucille Snider
9. Ruth Snipes
10. Oliver Spann
11. Tom Stephens
12. Joel Thomas
13. Annie Mae Watson
14. J. C. Webb
15. Virginia Wellons
16. George Wiggins
17. Eli Wilcox
18. Rachael Williams
19. Doris Wise
20. Hilda Wise

Graduating Class 1935

1. Bernice Bass
2. Chappell Dodson
3. Emily Dodson
4. Abbie Dominick
5. Henry Foster
6. Emmett Gattis
7. Lynton (Pete) Godwin Jr.
8. Cordelia Passmore
9. Raymond Phillips
10. Willard Slappey
11. Charles Smith
12. Charles Sproull
13. Henry Williams
14. Kathryn Wise
15. Thomas Wise

Graduating Class 1936

1. Karl Beamon
2. Marjorie Beamon

3. Edna Claire Blackshear
4. Kate Hogan
5. Martha Jennings
6. L. B. Johnson
7. Helen Jones
8. Carl Mask
9. Deannie Frances Mims
10. Bill Mitchell
11. William Revell
12. Kenneth Short
13. Miriam Timmerman
14. Laura Webb
15. Armstid Williams
16. Frank Williams
17. Mildred Wise
18. P. J. Wise

Graduating Class 1937

1. Bonnie Bacon
2. Hugh Carter
3. Anita Evans
4. James Forrest
5. George Harper
6. Jack Jennings
7. Laverne Price
8. Jack Smith
9. Cliff Snider
10. Gladwyn Sproull
11. Ernest Turner
12. Helen Webb
13. Sara Wise

Graduating Class 1938

1. Elliott Anderson
2. Christine Bledsoe
3. Lucille Bryant
4. Mary Foster

5. Ruth Godwin
6. Claude Harvey
7. Theron Hobgood
8. Phillip Jennings
9. Pauline Lewis
10. Sara Helen Mims
11. A. Dwight Mitchell
12. Estelle Mitchell
13. George Montgomery
14. Catherine Moore
15. Sara Ratliff
16. Annie Laurie Revell
17. Mildred Taylor
18. Edith Thomas
19. Ruth Toms
20. Eugene Wall
21. Bernice Watson
22. Clayton Watson
23. Doris Webb
24. Grady Wellons
25. Jacquelyn Wellons
26. Franklin Wiggins
27. Marvin Wiggins
28. Albert Williams
29. Alma Wise

Graduating Class 1939

1. Eola Mae Anderson
2. Earlene Bryan
3. Wynelle Bryan
4. Roy Brinkley
5. Valerie Chambliss
6. Jewell Davis
7. George Dodson
8. Margaret Harris
9. Maggie Hogan
10. Alva Israel

11. Madge Lewis
12. Marie Phillips
13. Lorraine Ratliff
14. Martha Ratliff
15. Cody Timmerman
16. Walton Wiggins
17. Carolyn Wise
18. Crawford Wise

Graduating Class 1940

1. Adrian Bacon
2. Lucille Crook
3. David Croxton
4. Eula Ann Glenn
5. Virginia Godwin
6. Frances Harper
7. Ernest Harris
8. Howard Harris
9. John Harris
10. Lorene Hendricks
11. Nelle Johnson
12. Edith Jones
13. Bobby Montgomery
14. Frank Salter
15. Earl Smith
16. Kennedy Sproull
17. Ellen Thomas
18. Joel Turner
19. Ruby Watson
20. Carolyn Webb
21. Miriam Wise
22. Morgan Wise
23. Mary Yancey

Graduating Class 1941

1. Kathryn Bacon
2. Jimmy Carter

3. Doris Cosby
4. Myrtle Crook
5. June Davis
6. Raymond Gaines
7. Kathleen Greene
8. Virginia Harris
9. L. C. Hobgood, Jr.
10. Herbert Howell, Jr.
11. Richard Johnson
12. Thaddeous Jones
13. Evelyn Lewis
14. Thomas Lowery, Jr.
15. Louise McClung
16. Eloise Ratliff
17. Richard Salter
18. Wilburn Smith
19. Lonnie Taylor, Jr.
20. Hazel Thomas
21. Doris Wiggins
22. Annie Grace Wiggins
23. Rebecca Williams
24. Billy Wise
25. Lottie Wise
26. Eugene Yarbrough

Graduating Class 1942

1. Durelle Anderson
2. Florine Anderson
3. Anne Bagwell
4. A. H. Crozier, Jr.
5. Lenora Dozier
6. Leonard N. Evans, Jr.
7. Rembert Forrest
8. Joe Hendricks
9. Grace Hewitt
10. Ollie Belle Hobgood
11. Inez Hogg

12. Harold Israel
13. Hortense Jennings
14. Frances Law
15. Grace McClung
16. Donald McDonald
17. Charles Medlock
18. Ann Montgomery
19. Joe Moore
20. Billy Oliver
21. Roy (Bubba) Pantall
22. Henry Ratliff
23. Millard Simmons
24. Halley Smith
25. Joe Smith
26. Harold Taylor
27. Annie Maude Thomas
28. Margaret Timmerman
29. Louise Toms
30. Carlton Wise
31. Edna Mae Wise
32. B. T. Wishard

Graduating Class 1943

1. Gloria Carter
2. Everett Chambliss
3. Julian Cosby
4. Mary Ann Cranford
5. Alice Hale
6. Gene Hall
7. Sara Hughes
8. Marion Mitchell
9. Ross Oliver
10. LaVilla Paradise
11. Billy Parker
12. Josephine Salter
13. Emily Smith
14. Richard Smith

15. Winifred Smith
16. Bettie Timmerman
17. Margurite Wise
18. Jack Yoder

Graduating Class 1944

1. Eunice Anderson
2. Loren Blanton
3. J.D. Clements
4. Sara Duvall
5. C.F. (Judge) Hogsed, Jr.
6. Mae Holston
7. Rae Holston
8. Doris Ivey
9. Betty Jane Jennings
10. Howard Jones
11. Robert Allen Mills
12. Grace Passmore
13. Betty Parker
14. Rosalynn Smith
15. James Wiggins

Graduating Class 1945

1. Gloria Alston
2. Mattie Beth Anderson
3. Betty Cranford
4. Ernest Chappell
5. Joyce Dozier
6. Carolyn Harris
7. Billy Hogg
8. Billie Morgan
9. Julian Smith
10. Harold Sproull
11. Ann Wise

Graduating Class 1946

1. Joe Bacon

2. Ruth Booker
3. Ruth Carter
4. Carl Chappell
5. Charlotte Forrest
6. Hazel Hobgood
7. Allman Hogsed
8. Jack Jones
9. Henry Kirkland
10. Norman Kirkland
11. Helen Lairscey
12. George Mims
13. Curtis Padgett
14. Jack Short
15. Jerry Smith
16. Allene Timmerman
17. Betty Wise
18. Harold Wise

Graduating Class 1947

1. Sara Bacon
2. Julian Booker
3. Bobby Chappell
4. Cornelia Chappell
5. Rose Gard
6. Mary Ethel Hale
7. Ruth Hand
8. Barbara Hogg
9. Charles Knight
10. Bill Medlock
11. Marilynn Mitchell
12. Mary Helen Paul
13. Paul Toms
14. Herschel Wiggins
15. Billy Wise

Graduating Class 1948

1. Betty Cosby

2. Betty Crawford
3. Thomas Hewitt
4. Elvin Matthews
5. Lamar Padgett
6. Zelma Salter
7. Peggy Short
8. Bobby Smith
9. Bobby Timmerman
10. Alice Ruth Turner
11. Dora Williams

Graduating Class 1949

1. Nell Bacon
2. Faye Beck
3. Patsy Cosby
4. Ann Dozier
5. Thelma Fox
6. Elizabeth Mask
7. Erle Mills
8. Murray Smith
9. Nancy Smith
10. Wynelle Story
11. Edwin Timmerman

Graduating Class 1950

1. Billy Bagwell
2. Barbara Dominick
3. Barbara Dowdy
4. Jimmy Foster
5. Bobby Hale
6. Bobby Hay
7. Donald Hollister
8. Billy Howard
9. Gene Jennings
10. Betty Jo Jones
11. Betty Kirkland
12. Mary Dell Kirkland

13. Dorothy Knight
14. Ted Middleton
15. Joyce Oliver
16. Earl Parker
17. Maurice Parker
18. Vivian Pugh
19. Billie Salter
20. Reese Smith
21. Sylvia Smith
22. Melba Spann
23. Covin Wiggins
24. Geraldine Wiggins
25. Luther Wise
26. Tallulah Wise

No Graduating Class 1951

12th grade added in 1952

Graduating Class 1952

1. Jane Chappell
2. Frances Cosby
3. Betty Dodson
4. Frank Hewitt
5. Burr Wise Jennings
6. Jack Jones
7. Archie Jordan
8. Jimmy Martin
9. Carol Mims
10. Ferrell Paul
11. Jean Smith
12. Lila Ruth Spires
13. Malcolm Wishard

Graduating Class 1953

1. Gene Bacon
2. Wayne Carden

3. Faye Chambliss
4. Thomas Holloway
5. Braxton Mallard
6. Carolyn Mask
7. Carolyn Mitchell
8. Bobby Moore
9. Jack Pugh
10. Mary Louise Register
11. Houston Stephenson
12. Grady Story
13. J. M. Wise
14. Leroy Young Jr.

Graduating Class 1954

1. Jacob Carlton
2. Roy Colston
3. David Crouse
4. Charlotte Davis
5. Ernest Fussell
6. Alfred Holloway
7. Betty Knight
8. Walter Matthews
9. Pat Medlock
10. Betty Middleton
11. Thelma Doris Parker
12. Lamar Paul
13. Martha Player
14. Richard Player
15. Charlene Sheffield
16. Allethea Smith
17. Shirley Smith
18. Peggy Watson

Graduating Class 1955

1. Clayton Beamon
2. Earlene Buchanan
3. Linda Buchanan

4. Billy Carter
5. Bud Duvall
6. Freda Fox
7. Gloria Ann Harrod
8. Heyward Hobgood
9. Clinton Holloway
10. Millie Jennings
11. Rene Jones
12. Nancy Kite
13. Gay McRainey
14. James Mallard
15. Mary Carol Powell
16. Barbara Sewell
17. Patsy Short
18. James Tidd
19. Barbara Ann Turner
20. Bill Young

Graduating Class 1956

1. Marie Bacon
2. Betty Blue Bagwell
3. Cecil Beamon
4. Billy Bowen
5. Thomas Carden
6. Jack Chappell
7. Sandra Chappell
8. Gwendolyn Cheek
9. Junior Davis
10. Bernice DeVane
11. Bobby Dodson
12. Bill Forrest
13. Frank Freeman
14. Roy Haynes
15. Billy Hendrick
16. Peggy Jo Jones
17. John Ed Mask
18. George Mathews

19. Wade Medlock
20. Donald Player
21. Robert Smith
22. Merry Tietjen
23. Martha Kate Toms
24. Calvin Williams
25. Mack Williams

Graduating Class 1957

1. Brooks Buchanan
2. Bobby Cooper
3. Herschel Goodin
4. Thomas Greene
5. Howard Harbuck
6. Joyce Harrod
7. Janice Hunt
8. Jimmy Jones
9. Martha Jones
10. Gerald Jordan
11. Jerry Large
12. Bobby McClung
13. Robert Mallard
14. Jimmy Melvin
15. Joyce Moore
16. Hazel Pugh
17. Carolyn Smith
18. Midred Smith
19. Coy Turner
20. C.L. Walters III
21. Oliver Wilson

Graduating Class 1958

1. Johnny Alford
2. Claude Baldwin, Jr.
3. Betty Brown
4. Ann Buchanan
5. Homer Chambliss

6. Joyce Cheek
7. Herman Davis
8. Charles Easom
9. John Forrest
10. Gloria Ann Howard
11. James Knight
12. Melanie Nicholas
13. Helen Player
14. Lee Sewell
15. Tommy Sheffield
16. Gordan Siverson
17. Tommy Surles III
18. Edgar Lee Tidd
19. Teddy Turner
20. Roy Varnum
21. Wayne Watson
22. George Whitten

Graduating Class 1959

1. Bobby Bacon
2. E.P. Bagwell
3. Jimmy Bagwell
4. J.M. Buchanan
5. John Buchanan
6. Carolyn Carden
7. Pat Cordell
8. Hardie Jo Cornwell
9. John Davis
10. George Dominick
11. Walter Dozier
12. Lynn Dupree
13. Dorothy Gaston
14. Louise Goodin
15. Carolyn Hearon
16. Johnny Hendrick
17. Ann Hogg
18. Elizabeth Jones

19. Linda Knight
20. W.C. Lamb, Jr.
21. Johnny Logan
22. Tommy Morris
23. Liza Murray
24. Barbara O'Neal
25. Bob Pilcher
26. Evie Pilcher
27. Edgar Player
28. Jerry Roberts
29. Janelle Sewell
30. Eddie Smith
31. Leroy Story
32. Madge Surles
33. W.L. (Sunny) Tietjen
34. Melanie Turner
35. John Tyler
36. John Wise Walker
37. Jane Young

Graduationg Class 1960

1. Pat Buchanan
2. Jency Carlton
3. Hugh (Sonny) Carter, Jr.
4. Margaret Colston
5. James Dozier
6. Chris English
7. Nathan Goodin
8. Jacquelyn Jennings
9. Martha Jordan
10. Frances McLendon
11. Douglas Middleton
12. Bonnie Morris
13. Clyde Murray, Jr.
14. Sherrill Murray
15. Homer Roach, Jr.
16. John Smith

17. Joyce Smith
18. Dorothy Story
19. Claudette Walters
20. Warner Webb
21. Beverly Wise

Graduating Class 1961

1. Donnie Berry
2. J.C. Buchanan
3. Anne Cordell
4. Eva Kate Davis
5. Gloria English
6. Amelia Glenn
7. Lynton (Boze) Godwin, III
8. Howard (Bud) Harrod
9. Jimmy Hogg
10. Bob Howard
11. Freddie Hurst
12. Jane Jones
13. Barbara Knight
14. Robert Logan
15. Eugene McLemore
16. James McLemore
17. Evanne Murray
18. Billy Ratliff
19. Henrietta Rigsby
20. Dock Rigsby
21. Ruth Sewell
22. Bonnie Sue Shutters
23. Mary Ann Story
24. Buddy Strickland
25. Mike Surles
26. William Earl Tidd
27. Gerald Turner
28. Donnie Tyler
29. Ronnie Tyler
30. Mattie Ward

31. Norine Wiggins
32. George Williams
33. Mary Alice Wilson

Graduating Class 1962

1. Bobby Buchanan
2. Logan Buchanan
3. Frank Bush
4. Elaine Creck
5. Barbara Lee Cromer
6. Chappell Dodson, Jr.
7. Lanny English
8. Shirley Goodin
9. Donald Holloway
10. David Jennings
11. Gail Jennings
12. Tommy Jennings, Jr.
13. Sara Johnson
14. Joe Logan
15. Nancy Jo Medlock
16. Sammy Pilcher
17. Peggy Rogers
18. C.W. (Bobo) Short
19. Donna Tanner
20. Margie Ward
21. Sandra Watson
22. Larry Wiggins
23. Roy Wise

Graduating Class 1963

1. Bobby Berry
2. Diane Chavers
3. Sarah Davenport
4. James Gaston
5. James Goodin
6. Sarah Goodin
7. Junay Harbuck

8. Ishmael Morris
9. Linda Morris
10. Richard Oats
11. Laine Pilcher
12. Ollie Player
13. Sue Redmond
14. Rebecca Ray
15. James Ryan
16. Sandra Rooks
17. Hazel Shutters
18. Rhoda Walters
19. Marion Wiggins
20. John Wilson

Graduating Class 1964

1. Maxine Berry
2. Edna Buchanan
3. Laurie Carter
4. Polly Dominick
5. Tommy Dominick
6. Ronnie Dupree
7. Corrie Gaston
8. Gene Goodin
9. Kerman Goodin
10. Tommy Hogg
11. Kaye Harper
12. Ruth Jennings
13. Lucinda Kilburn
14. Pauline Larkin
15. Frances (Cricket) Masters
16. Drue Murray
17. Griff Murray
18. Bill Revell Jr.
19. Henry Roach
20. Josaline Story
21. J.P. (Buzzy) Tanner
22. Anna Bell Thompson

23. Robert Thompson
24. Myrtice Tidd
25. Jimmy Tinker
26. Julia Ann Toms
27. Donnie Turner
28. Lonnie Tyler
29. Joy Ward
30. Thomas Ward
31. Linda Faye Williams
32. Marilyn Wise

Graduating Class 1965

1. Newt Buchanan
2. Jackie Carter
3. Jeff Cavender
4. Kathryn Davenport
5. George Easom
6. Millard English
7. Kathy Godwin
8. Shelia Greene
9. Carey Harbuck
10. Martha Laing
11. Lamar Montgomery
12. Linda Pilcher
13. Billy Rigsby
14. Jeff Smith
15. Steve Smith
16. Carol Speegle
17. David Walker
18. Janice Wiggins
19. Rocky Wiggins
20. John Williams
21. David Wise, Jr.
22. Frank Wise
23. Jerry Wise

Graduating Class 1966

1. Susie Berry
2. Ed Brown
3. Bonnie Buchanan
4. Steve Buchanan
5. Sue Dickerson
6. Barbara Goodin
7. Dave Heath
8. James Howard
9. Linda Howard
10. Martha Johnson
11. Wayne Murray
12. Patsy Parker
13. Terry Ratliff
14. Mary Jean Rogers
15. Neal Rooks
16. Martha Ann Sewell
17. Mill Simmons
18. Judy Speegle
19. Billy Stubbs
20. Cathy Toms
21. Tommy Tyler
22. Gerald Varnum
23. Murray Walters
24. Maria Weldon
25. Peggy Williams

Graduating Class 1967

1. Beth Bridges
2. Gloria Crozier
3. Walter Davenport
4. Frances Davis
5. Brenda English
6. Carol Everett
7. Clarice Greene
8. Thomas Jackson
9. Randy Johnson

10. Charles Jordan
11. Sara Logan
12. Vertis Marchant
13. Phillip Moore
14. Jackie Norman
15. Vi Pilcher
16. Carolyn Reagan
17. Janice Revell
18. Gladys Shutters
19. Linda Stokes
20. Betty Jane Storey
21. Linda Toms
22. Judy Watson
23. Brenda Wise
24. Sally Wishard
25. Nancy Woods

Graduating Class 1968

1. Benita Arthur
2. Carol Brown
3. Lou Brown
4. J.E. (Chip) Carter III
5. Susan Chappell
6. Gloria Chavers
7. Brenda Colston
8. Judy Crawley
9. Glenda Dominick
10. Joe Gerbert
11. Val Gerbert
12. Karen Hobgood
13. Lynda Hobgood
14. Danny Hollon
15. Charlie Lloyd
16. Bobby Mathis
17. Ronnie Mills
18. Brenda Oats
19. David Ratliff

20. Ann Raybon
21. Kenny Sawyer
22. Charles Smith, Jr.
23. Billy Weldon
24. DeVane (Doc) Wiggins
25. O.A. (Al) Williams, III
26. Lonnie Wise

Graduating Class 1969

1. Joe Averett
2. Jean Brown
3. Bonnie Chitwood
4. Donna Clements
5. Elizabeth Cook
6. Julian Cosby, Jr.
7. Joe Goodin
8. Dianne Hallman
9. Thomas Harris
10. Jean Buchanan Howell
11. Braunda Jarrell
12. Ronnie Jordan
13. Susan Kilburn
14. Donnie Lamb
15. Ruth Larkin
16. Tarron Layfield
17. Yvonne Marchant
18. Peggy Masters
19. Bobby McCrary
20. Angela McDonald
21. Marvelynn Murray
22. Ronnie Owen
23. Sharon Parnell
24. Janet Ratliff
25. Sherry Reese
26. Jean Rigsby
27. Hope Rogers
28. Lloyd Shaddix

29. Herbert Smith
30. Dan Smith
31. Sammy Smith
32. Pat Turner
33. June Weldon
34. Sherry Wiggins
35. Ginny Williams
36. Cheryle Wise
37. Phil Wise
38. Bill Wisham
39. Bonnie Wishard
40. Jerome Wynn
41. Mary Jo Young

Graduating Class 1970

1. Mittie Arthur
2. Roy Aycock
3. Eugene Barton
4. Shirley Wise Blanton
5. Connie Carter
6. JoAnn Coleman
7. Gail Davenport
8. Ricky English
9. Steve English
10. Elaine Everett
11. Robert Flowers
12. Maxine Griggs
13. Billy Harper
14. James Harper
15. Bob Harris
16. Alice Hatcher
17. Marlene Hobgood
18. Brenda Hollon
19. Johnny Hollon
20. Linda Hollon
21. Beverly Israel
22. H.A. (Al) Johnson, Jr.

23. Mary Jane Maloney
24. Edna Mathis
25. James Morgan
26. Glenda Ondracek
27. Linda Phillips
28. Danny Pilcher
29. Patsy Ratliff
30. Charla Smith
31. Jody Smith
32. Peggy Buchanan Smith
33. Susanne Stokes
34. Burton Thomas
35. Janice Thomas
36. Jimmy Williams

Graduating Class 1971

1. Russell Allmon
2. Cherrie Averett
3. Carolyn Brown
4. Linda Brown
5. Mary Burns
6. Chris Coleman
7. Paula Cowart
8. Carolyn Dodson
9. Beck Duncan
10. Ruedene Edmonds
11. Henry (Hank) Flowers
12. Delilah Fry
13. Louis Gardner
14. Ernest Gibson
15. Martha Ann Hollis
16. Steve Hollis
17. Jean Holton
18. Bernice Hurley
19. Bobby Jones
20. Sandra Jones
21. Carol Jordon

22. Raymond Lamb
23. David Laster
24. Rene Lockette
25. Freddy Lee Mann
26. Robert Mansfield, Jr.
27. Tommy Masters
28. Larry Middleton
29. Glenn Moore
30. Milton Tony Morgan
31. Sam Pete Muff, Jr.
32. Steve Owen
33. Tressie Pernell
34. Calvin Pope
35. Homer Reagan, Jr.
36. Eddie Rooks, Jr.
37. Larry Sheppard
38. Etheline Sims
39. Betty Speegle
40. Larry Stubbs
41. Roy Stuckey
42. Willie Bell Walton
43. Joan Waters
44. Leo Wiggens
45. Bobbie Jean Wiley
46. Fredia Williams

Graduating Class 1972

1. John Arthur, III
2. Peggy Banks
3. Yvonne Blanton
4. Raymond Bridges
5. Annie Britt
6. Mary Bryant
7. Sue Chavers
8. Brenda Chitwood
9. Eddie Davis
10. Patricia Duncan

11. Diana Edge
12. Margaret Edge
13. Yvonne Edwards
14. Donna Evans
15. Marvin Griggs, Jr.
16. Ethel Hollis
17. Margie Holton
18. Tony Jackson
19. Carolyn Jafolis
20. Brenda Jones
21. Clara Kitchens
22. James Laster
23. Annie Lockett
24. Cleveland Mann
25. Elizabeth May
26. John McCord
27. Gwen McElroy
28. Hiram Morgan
29. Elaine Morris
30. Ferrell Owen
31. Sheryl Owen
32. Ruth Ratliff
33. Eddie Revell
34. Donna Rooks
35. Shirley Sheppard
36. Annie Sims
37. Mary Sims
38. Stella Sims
39. Jeanette Slappey
40. Harvey Slocumb
41. Jerry Stokes, Jr.
42. Donna Thompson
43. Arthur Wakefield
44. Sheila Warren
45. Florine White
46. Larry Williams
47. Robby Williams

48. Thomas Williams
49. Debra Wise
50. Gwen Wise
51. Danny Wittkamper
52. Thomas Wood
53. Juillette Wright
54. Virginia Wright
55. Abbie Young

Graduating Class 1973

1. Ruthie Adams
2. Wayne Adams
3. Martha Ann Allison
4. Joe Britt
5. Debbie Chavers
6. Michael Coley
7. Ina Countryman
8. Carey Cox
9. Elaine Davis
10. Mary Jo Dodson
11. Eleanor Edge
12. Herschel Edwards
13. Marvin Floyd
14. Jacquelin Gilford
15. Clarence Harvey
16. Mike Harvin
17. Earnest Hicks
18. Clarence Hunt
19. Marilyn Jafolis
20. Chester Jordan
21. Oscar Laster
22. Mike Law
23. Elaine Little
24. William Mann
25. Diane Mayes
26. Drew Murphy
27. Lynn Peek

28. Debby Phillips
29. Margaret Pope
30. Arlene Reagan
31. Martin Rooks
32. Blanche Sheffield
33. Pete Sims
34. Grier Smith
35. Donna Everett Smith
36. Ritchie Smith
37. Wesley Smith
38. Charlene Tatum
39. Billy Volley
40. Willie Ware
41. Willie Wear
42. Mike Weldon
43. Bertha White
44. Gail Whitt
45. Marvin Wiggins
46. Alberta Williams
47. Brenda Wilson
48. George Woods
49. Jeanette Young

Graduating Class 1974

1. Pearlman Barner
2. Lee Bostwick
3. Gwen Brown
4. Gwendolyn Bryant
5. Mary Christmas
6. Arnold Cowan
7. Butch Cullison
8. Blanche Harvey
9. John Holley
10. Ellen Holton
11. Margie Jackson
12. Martha Johnson
13. Diane Larson

14. Allison Laster
15. Charlie Laster
16. John Little
17. Debra McCrary
18. Dale McDonald
19. Gail McDonald
20. Kathy Mathis
21. Lenwood May
22. Vivian Mills
23. Sandra Mitchell
24. Alphonson Moore
25. William Morgan
26. Allen Partridge
27. Allen Ratliff
28. Jessie Sims
29. Margaret Sims
30. Elaine Smith
31. Samuel Smith
32. Ricky Speegle
33. Dorothy Styles
34. Rhonda Thompson
35. Simeon Wakefield
36. Cindy Wiggins
37. Annie Williams
38. David Williams
39. Vicki Williams
40. Willie Williams
41. Bernstine Wright

Graduating Class 1975

1. Wanda Aycock
2. Richard Bradley
3. Bobby Bridges
4. Evelyn Bridges
5. Lawrence Britt
6. Shirley Byant
7. Henry Burns

8. Russell Coleman
9. Gary Cullison
10. Patricia Davis
11. Virgiria Davis
12. Bonnie Sue Dodson
13. Judson Edge Jr.
14. Leslie Franklin
15. Clifford Gardner
16. Paula Gilbert
17. Teresa Grinolds
18. Lois Hamilton
19. Harold Hargrove
20. Brian Harris
21. Maxine Hicks
22. Sherline Hicks
23. Bobbie Jean Hollis
24. Lois Hollis
25. Mescal Hunt
26. Nathelma Jackson
27. Joseph Johnson, Jr.
28. Sally Johnson
29. Rosetta Jones
30. Shirley Larson
31. Charles McElroy
32. Ellen Medlock
33. Jimmy Merritt
34. Josephine Merritt
35. Candice Miller
36. Neil Moore
37. Nadine Pope
38. MacLeon Riggins
39. Kandice Rutherford
40. Willie Sheppard
41. Gerald Smith
42. Erma Ruth Tatum
43. Howard Terri
44. Jerry Timmerman

45. Jane Turner
46. Erma Walton
47. Eunice Wilbanks
48. Ralph Wilkerson
49. Durante Williams
50. Anthony Williams
51. Vangie Williams
52. Willie Williams
53. James Wilson
54. Amy Wise
55. Walter Wooden
56. Irene Woods

Graduating Class 1976

1. Susan Anderson
2. Asa Branch
3. Irene Bridges
4. Judy Brown
5. Vera Bryant
6. Jessie Christmas
7. Mary Sue Cochran
8. Beth Dodson
9. Bobby Ann Dodson
10. Therease Edge
11. Wesley Eugene Ford
12. Bobbie Gardner
13. Marie Greene
14. Gail Griggs
15. Edward Hicks
16. Al Hurley
17. Marvin Hurley
18. Kieth Johnson
19. Elizabeth Kitchens
20. Kathleen Hale Lee
21. Johnny Little
22. Eddie May
23. Johnny Mims

24. Earnestine Monts
25. David Phillips
26. Betty Ross
27. Bryan Rooks
28. Charles Wayne Ross
29. Cynthia Schley
30. Manda Schley
31. Imogene Sims
32. Marshall Smith
33. Susie Lee Smith
34. Katherine Stanfield
35. Calvin Lamar Tatum
36. Louise Tullis
37. Cynthia Ware
38. Danny Wilbanks
39. Doc Williams
40. Pam Williams
41. Sandra Louise Wilson
42. Leonard Wright, Jr.
43. George Young
44. Katherine Young

Graduating Class 1977

1. Rose Allison
2. Selinda Battle
3. Emory Bridges
4. Diannie Bridges
5. Rose Bridges
6. Willie Brown
7. Johnny Burns
8. Thurston Clary
9. James Dodson
10. John Dodson
11. Jeff Fox
12. Brian Franklin
13. Ray Hatcher
14. Clinton Jackson

15. Doris Jackson
16. Dannie Mae Kitchens
17. Kathleen Lee
18. Laverne Little
19. Melba Little
20. Annie Ruth Martin
21. Willie Lee Merritt
22. Mary Ann Moore
23. Mary Lynn Moore
24. Renea Morgan
25. Brenda Polk
26. Harold Pope
27. Kathy Richardson
28. Mike Rushing
29. Ervin Sims
30. Deborah Slappey
31. Elaine Slappey
32. Jessie Smith
33. Teresa Stewart
34. Tammy Taylor
35. Robert Terry
36. Maxine Volley
37. Eunice Walton
38. Lee Marvin Walton
39. Ella Mae Wilkerson
40. Jan Williams
41. Sherry Wise
42. Alvin Young

Graduating Class 1978

1. Gloria Andrews
2. Ann Aycock
3. Gloria Battle
4. Marjorie Brown
5. Elizabeth Bryant
6. Andrew Clinkscale
7. Nita Coker

8. Sam Dodson, Jr.
9. Douglas Edge
10. Michael Flowers
11. Alvin Floyd
12. Joe Franklin
13. Sherrie Glover
14. Denise Harvey
15. David Hawkins
16. Soliden Hayes
17. Blake Hollis
18. Susie Jackson
19. Cindy Jennings
20. Linda Kitchens
21. Carolyn Laster
22. Dale Law
23. Donnie Lewis
24. Robert Lewis
25. Melvin Little
26. Sherry Middlebrook
27. Shelia Perry
28. Debbie Richardson
29. Jimmie Roberts
30. Natacha Searcy
31. Wendell Stanfield
32. Cassandra Tullis

33. Willie Tullis
34. Larry Tyson
35. Christine Williams

Graduating Class 1979

1. Gloria Burns
2. Eskie Christmas
3. Annie Ruth Edwards
4. Mary Elliott
5. Willie Gardener
6. Angela Green
7. Pat Hale
8. Marie Hale
9. Ronnie Harvey
10. Glenda Hawkins
11. Gloria Hurley
12. Betty Jean Jackson
13. Patricia Jackson
14. Ronnie Jenkins
15. Sonya Jenkins
16. Vickie Jones
17. Annie Lora Kitchens
18. Emory Mack
19. Charles Mathis
20. Ilean May

21. Hilda McElroy
22. Henry McGarrah
23. Debra Miller
24. Mary Oates
25. Wilma Pickett
26. Darlene Rushing
27. Mary Lene Sims
28. Nancy Sims
29. Shirley Solomon
30. Vernice Tommie
31. Calvin Ernest Tullis
32. Glenda Tullis
33. Vera Tullis
34. Mary Jean Wakefield
35. John B. Wallace
36. Brett Watson
37. Tammy Wiggins
38. Jackie Wilbanks
39. Drunell Williams
40. Mary Williams
41. Roy Williams
42. Betty Jo Wise
43. Ernestine Wright
44. Nathanie Young
—*Submitted by Eunice Griggs*

Chapter 9: Clubs

Furlow Masonic Lodge #124

Bottsford, Ga.

The following is a list of members of this lodge in the 1800s. Dates indicate the first record of membership.

ADAMS, A. H. 1868
ADAMS, A. J. 1874
ADAMS, W.D.E. 1867
ALLEN, Moses 1867
AVENT, William 1857
BARFIELD, Samuel W. 1850
BATEMAN, William F. 1850
BATTLE, Henry L. 1850
BATTLE, John R. 1850
BATTLE, Wiliam R. 1850
BEVERLY, J. J. 1867
BIGHAM, John V. 1850
BINION, Napoleon B 1852
BLACK, Jas. H. 1853
BUSH, John P. 1852
BUSH, Wm. P. 1855
CARR, D. W. 1860
CARROL, Patrick............................... 1859
CATO, J. F. 1852
CATO, J. G. F. 1856
CATO, J. G. F. 1857
CATO, J. W. 1852
CATO, James F. 1853
CATO, Jno. W. 1853
CATO, T, A, ... 1867
CAUSEY, John 1861

CAUSEY, L. B. Jr. 1868
CAUSEY, Littleberry L. 1850
CAUSEY, S. B. 1859
CAUSEY, SR., L. B. 1876
CAUSEY, T. B. 1862
CHAPPEL, J. T. 1856
CHAPPELL, J. J. 1851
CHAPPELL, James J. 1859
CHAPPELL, Jas. T. 1853
CHAPPELL, Jos. J. 1853
CHEEVER, F. H. 1856
CLAY, J. B. 1852
CLAY, John W. 1855
COCHRAN, G. A. 1867
COCHRAN, G. W. 1874
COCHRAN, Geo. A. 1868
COKER, Wm. 1852
COLEMAN, Robert W. 1853
COX, C. 1852
COX, Cary Thomas 1850
COX, Chappell 1850
COX, John M. 1850
COXE, C. 1861
CRITTENDON, Jas. 1853
CULPEPPER, Gardner 1850
DAVIS, Joseph T. 1855
DAVISON, J. C. 1852
DILLARD, George W. 1867
DOBSON, J. W. 1860
DOBSON, James 1855
DOBSON, James W. 1862
DOBSON, Jas. 1853

DURHAM, J. P.	1860	JENNINGS, Lott	1874
ELAM, A. G.	1851	JENNINGS, Phil	1874
ELAM, Augustus G.	1850	JENNINGS, Phillip	1868
ELAM, G. G.	1856	JONES, William P.	1850
ELLINGTON, W. F.	1853	JOWERS, Darling	1850
EVANS, J. R.	1858	KENDRICK, B. J.	1857
EVANS, John R.	1850	KENDRICK, Burwel J.	1855
FORD, William S.	1850	KENDRICK, I.W.	1867
FORD, Wm. L.	1853	KENDRICK, J. C.	1874
FULLER, John B.	1857	KENDRICK, J. W.	1868
GILES, E. W.	1855	KENDRICK, James C.	1857
GREEN, A. B.	1857	KENDRICK, R. J.	1856
GREEN, J.	1852	KENDRICK, Rev. J. C.	1858
GREEN, Jno.	1853	KENDRICK, W. C.	1868
GREEN, Jos. D.	1853	KERSE, J. A.	1856
GRUBBS, Wm.	1858	KINDRICK, B. J.	1859
HARDNETT, W. H.	1857	KINDRICK, Rev. J. C.	1859
HARPER, G. R., Rev.	1856	LAMAR, J. T.	1874
HARPER, George	1855	LAMAR, John T.	1867
HATFIELD, Jas.	1868	LANE, G. W.	1858
HATFIELD, Joseph	1867	LANEY, G. W.	1852
HATTOX, B. O.	1853	LANEY, George W.	1853
HAY, G. M.	1852	LANEY, Jackson	1867
HAY, George M.	1850	LANGFORD, Jno. T.	1853
HERNER, John	1876	LANSFORD, J. L.	1860
HILLER, G. E.	1874	LANSFORD, Joseph L.	1859
HILLER, J. I.	1874	LANY, G. W.	1860
HODNETT, Wm. H.	1855	LASITER, James	1858
HOLMAN, W. R.	1874	LASSETER, A.	1876
HOLMES, W. R.	1861	LASSETER, Abisha	1874
HOLMES, William R.	1867	LASSETER, Jacob	1867
HORNE, John	1874	LASSETER, James	1852
JACKSON, James J.	1850	LASSETER, Jas.	1861
JENNINGS, B. T.	1874	LASSITER, James	1853
JENNINGS, G. W.	1876	LEE, J. E.	1858
JENNINGS, George	1868	LEE, Jas. E.	1855
JENNINGS, George W.	1874	LINGO, Tallifaro	1852

LINGO, Teliaferro	1850	RANCH, S. N.	1876
LONGFORD, John	1852	RANCH, S. Sr.	1874
MARKET, B. F.	1874	RANSOM, W. A.	1856
MARKET, I. E.	1862	RANSOME, U. A.	1857
MARKET, J. E.	1861	RANSOME, Uria G.	1855
MARKET, Joseph E.	1859	RAPE, J. A.	1861
MARKET, Z. F.	1874	RAVEN, W. S.	1860
MARKETT, B. F.	1876	REESE, J. A.	1860
MARKETT, J. E.	1860	REESE, Jno. A.	1853
McGRADY, Isaac V.	1850	REESE, L. A.	1862
McGRADY, William B.	1850	RHODES, E. J.	1874
McMATH, William H.	1850	ROBERSON, Wm. M.	1868
MILLER, R. T,.	1856	ROBERTSON, W. M.	1857
MILLER, Reuben T.	1853	ROBERTSON, Wm. M.	1855
MOORE, William S.	1874	ROBINSON, William M.	1867
MURRAY, D.	1856	ROSS, E. H.	1861
MURRAY, Drury	1853	RYLANDER, Matthew E.	1855
MURRAY, J. W. F.	1856	SANDERS, F. C.	1852
MURRAY, John W.F.	1867	SAUNDERS, Ferdinand C.	1853
PARKER, E. D.	1867	SKELTON, William	1850
PARKER, W. H.	1867	SMITH, J. N.	1852
PARKER, W. J.	1852	SMITH, Joseph N.	1853
PARKER, William J.	1850	SMITH, T. C.	1862
PARKER, Wm. H.	1868	SMITH, T. E.	1858
PARKER, Wm. J.	1851	SMITH, Thomas E.	1857
PERKINS, Henry E.	1855	STALLINGS, J. S., Rev.	1852
PICKET, J. B.	1874	STALLINGS, Rev. Jesse	1853
PICKET, M. B.	1857	STALLINGS, W. B.	1852
PICKET, Micajah	1850	STALLINGS, Wm. B.	1853
PICKETT, J. B.	1857	SUMMERS, A. H.	1868
PICKETT, J. H.	1852	TANEY, G. W.	1862
PICKETT, Jeptha	1850	THOMAS, J.	1860
PICKETT, Jesse H.	1853	THOMAS, J. S.	1852
PICKETT, Rev. M.B.	1858	THOMAS, Jesse J.	1856
PRICE, L. I.	1862	THOMAS, Jesse S_	1853
PURSLEY, A.	1876	THOMAS, John B.	1850
PURSLEY, A. J.	1868	THOMAS, Joseph	1862

THOMAS, Joseph E. 1861
THOMAS. Joseph 1867
TILAY, J. W. 1858
TORBERT, J. B. 1874
TORBERT, J. M. 1860
TORBERT, James M. 1859
TORBERT, James W. 1867
TORBERT, John B. 1867
TORBET, J. M. 1862
TRACEY, C. C. 1874
WADE, W. H. 1861
WADKINS, B. E. 1861
WADKINS, R. E. 1862
WADKINS, B. E. 1867
WESSON, P. V. 1860
WEST, J. H. 1867
WHITTEN, A. 1867
WHITTEN, A. J. 1868
WILLIAMS, T. J. 1858
WILLIAMS, Thomas J. 1853
WILSON, Jas. H. 1853
WISE, Joel 1874
ZORN, H. 1852
ZORNE, H. A. 1856
ZORNE, Henry A. 1850

—*Submitted by Jack Cox*

Mineral Springs Masonic Lodge #230

Chartered 1858 thru 1878. Not all years on record

Mineral Springs is the same as Magnolia Springs. The following is a list of members of this lodge in the 1800s. Dates indicate the first record of membership.

ABRAMS, Nathaniel G. 1865
ALLEN, Thomas M. 1859
BARNS, William 1871

BLACK, James H. 1858
BLACK, James R. 1863
BLACK, T. J. 1869
BLACK, Z. J. 1869
CAPPS, John A. 1859
CHAPPELL, Alexander 1863
CHAPPELL, H. 1871
CHEEK, B. 1865
CHEEK, E. H. 1863
CHEEK, Henry A. 1859
CLARK, John 1863
COHEN, M. 1858
COKER, F. M. 1871
COKER, John 1865
COKER, P. H. 1871
COKER, Wm. 1859
COOPER, Wm. L. 1865
COOPER, W. Z. 1866
CRITENDEN, James 1859
DAVENPORT, H. T. 1865
DAVENPORT, S. 1865
DODD, Wm. C. 1859
DODSON, R. A. 1871
DREW, J. J. 1874
DUPREE, H. H. 1868
DUPREE, H. H. 1872
DUPREE, H. T. 1863
DUPREE, Hilliard J. 1859
FIELDS, W. N. 1872
FORRESTER, Redman V. 1859
GLASS, Rev. James 1859
GODWIN, R. S. 1865
GRUBBS, Wm. 1859
GUFFORD, J. P. 1871
HARPER, G. A. 1869
HARPER, G. H. 1863
HARPER, George R. 1858

HARPER, J. M. 1869
HARVEY, A. 1866
HAWKINS, S. B. 1865
HEAD, Bedford J. 1858
HELMS, J. H. 1865
HENDRICK, Rev. T. C. 1863
HILL, Wm. H. 1865
HILLIARD, M. 1863
HILLIARD, Wyatt 1874
HOBBS, J. 1874
HOBES, Jesse 1872
HYDE, Boyd 1866
HYDE, I. B. 1866
HYDE, J. 1863
HYDE, James 1865
HYDE, James B. 1863
HYDE, Thomas V. 1863
JEFFERSON, Wm. 1859
JOHNSON, Richard E. 1868
JONES, M. P. 1863
KENDRICK, Rev. J. C. 1859
LOGAN, M. G. 1872
LOGAN, Wm. H. 1859
MADDOX, T. H. 1865
McBAIN, N. 1858
McLENDON, S. D. 1866
McKENDREE, S. O. 1863
McLENDER, Simeon D. 1865
McLENDON, S. D. 1863
MOORE, N. B. 1858
NELMS, J. N. 1869
PATTERSON, G. M. 1866
PATTON, L. 1874
PICKETT, J. B. 1858
PICKETT, J. H. 1866
PICKETT, Jeptha B. 1859
PICKETT, M. B. 1859

PICKETT, N. B. 1866
PICKETT, Rev. M. B. 1863
PICKETT, T. B. 1863
PICKETT, Thomas H. 1863
PORTER, J. B. 1863
PORTER, Joseph G. 1859
PORTER, T. G. 1863
POWELL, John E. 1872
PRICE, C. 1865
PULLEN, J. H. 1865
RAFFIN, James 1859
RAINS, C. B. 1863
RANSOM, W.A. 1859
ROOK, Daniel 1872
RYLANDER, M. E. 1863
RYLANDER, M. P. 1859
SMITH, J. N. 1865
STANFIELD, P. R. 1858
TURNER, Wm. W. 1859
WALTERS, S. W. 1874
WHITEHURST, H. L. 1859
WILDER, J. A. J. 1871
WILLINGHAM, E. G. 1865
WILLINGHAM, W. 1866
WRIGHT, A. H. 1859

—*Submitted by Jack Cox*

St. Bartholomew Masonic Lodge #177 (PHA)

Free and Accepted Masons

In the year 1908 the Most Woshipful Prince Hall Grand Lodge Jurisdiction of Georgia granted a Charter to St. Bartholomew Lodge #117 F&AM in Plains. Under this charter St. Bartholomew Lodge #177 began its work as a Masonic Lodge for black Masons in Plains.

During that time in history lodges kept records in their lodge but there is no record of the first worshipful master and the lodge officers. The lodge purchased a spot of land on the north side of Lebanon Baptist Church from the Wise family in 1904 for $5.00. This was before the lodge received a chapter from the Grand Lodge.

In October 1955 the lodge sold its land to the Board of Education of Sumter County, Georgia. In Deed Book No. 47, pages 578-579, the board purchased the land for the purpose of constructing a wide, safe and adequate driveway for the new elementary school for blacks in Plains.

In November 1955, St. Bartholomew Lodge #177 purchased a tract of land on the corner of Moon Street and Bottsford Road from Ed Mathis to build a new lodge hall. The worshipful master was Ed Hicks. and William Angry, secretary. The lodge was built in 1955 but not completed until 1961 under the leadership of Ulysses Hill as worshipful master. Money was borrowed to finish the building.

Brother Hill was worshipful for 28 years until 1983. The next woshipful was Timothy Jackson, who served from 1984-1989. He was followed by Joseph Jones, 1990, Alvin Jackson, 1991, Simeon Wakefield, 1992-1994, Jeremiah Thomas, 1995, Willie J. Young, 1996, Simeon Wakefield, 1997-1998, Joseph Jones, 1999-2000, Larry Jackson, 2001-2002.

The officers for 2002 are Larry Jackson, worshipful master; Joe N. Jones, senior warden; Bobby L. Mathis, junior warden; Joseph Jones, Jr., secretary, and Alvin Jackson, treasurer.
—*Submitted by St. Bartholomew Masonic Lodge*

Plains Branch of Red Cross

Plains Branch of the Americus and Sumter County Chapter of the Red Cross was formally organized last night at a mass meeting at Plains Baptist Church. Rev. C.S. Durden acted as temporary chairman. The committee who organized the chapter includes: Charles Lunsford, Mrs. M.M. Jennings, T.M. Lowery, Mrs. L.D. Wise, Walton D. Walters, Mrs. J.R. Logan, Mrs. H.R. McGee, Dr. B.T. Wise, Mrs. R.L. Jennings, Mrs. W.L. Thomas. The permanent chairman is Rev. C.C. Phillips; vice chairman, Mrs. W.L. Thomas; secretary, Mrs. O.A. Williams; treasurer, Charles Lunsford.

Forty members were enrolled for the branch organization. Classes will be organized within a few days for preparations of surgical supplies and material for use in the military service of the United States.
—*News article from "Daily Times-Recorder," August 15, 1917*

Plains Evangelistic Club and Methodist Missionary Society

One of the most delightful social functions of the past week was on Monday evening when the Plains Evangelistic Club entertained the faculty and senior class of Plains High School. Prior to the regular outlined program for the evening, the club, composed of a large membership, with their guests, consisting of seven teachers and sixteen graduates, were ushered into the dining room of the auditorium where a delicious two course dinner was served by the ladies of the Methodist Missionary Society. Covers were laid for 55. A color scheme of the pastel shades was carried out in the profusion of lovely flowers used in the dining room.

In the center of the beautifully appointed table were silver and cut glass baskets filled with roses, sweet peas, and lilies of the valley. Arranged at intervals on the tables were silver compotes filled with mints and trays of delicious cakes.

A list of teachers present was as follows: Professor E.L. Bridges, Misses Julia Coleman, Florine Danielly, Elinor Chambliss, Pearl Langford, Marguerite Hudson, Mary Davis, and Mrs. Frank Timmerman. While the list of sweet girl graduates, daintily attired in filmy summer frocks, were Misses

Catherine Logan, Aughtry Oliver, Ethel Jennings, Elizabeth Jennings, Mag Ella Bagwell, Lura Kennedy, Lillian Knowlton, Sue McMath, Eva Webb, Christine Mims and Josephine Wells with Messrs. Karl Campbell, Blake Johnson, and J.F. Plexico completing the graduating list of 1926. Mr. and Mrs. Heyward Bridges of Harrisonburg, Virginia, were also honored guests.

—*Submitted by Carolyn H. Durham, excerpt from a newspaper article listing the 1926 graduates*

Plains Literary Club

The Plains Literary Club met with Mrs. Nina Carter on Monday afternoon. Plans for securing a lot and the building of a club house at an early date were discussed with much interest and enthusuiasm. Jno. B. Clark came before the club with a proposition concerning a lot owned by him, which the club with other offers, will take under consideration. The following program was given: Cuba and Puerto Rico. Mrs. H.R. McGee, Puerto Rico; Mrs. M.M. Jennings, Cuba; Mrs. McGill,Cuba. The next club meeting will be held with Mrs. Everett Spann on the 3rd Monday afternoon in October at 3:30.

—News article from *The Americus Times-Recorder* circa 1935.

The Stitch-n-Chat Club

May 1934 to the present

On the first Wednesday in May 1934, Ruby Calloway, recent bride of Rev. Royal Calloway, pastor of Plains Baptist Church, invited a few young ladies to afternoon tea at 3 A.M. in the pastorium.

During the afternoon, Mrs. Calloway mentioned she had not known of any social or civic organized clubs in Plains. Having lived in a large city that had many such clubs she missed them very much. She then asked the ladies if they would like

to organize a sewing club, to which they unanimously agreed. Thus began the organizing. Since most ladies like to sew and all ladies like to chat therefore, the perfect name, The Stitch-n-Chat Club was selected.

Stitch and Chat members September 11, 1996. Front: Ruby Watson, Virginia Williams, Jo Medlock, Caroline Webb and Allie Smith. Middle: Betty Moss, Allene Haugabook, Eunice Griggs and Annie Mae Vaughn. Top: Joyce Timmerman, Wynelle Chambliss, Sara Helen Bozeman, Emily Alford and Maxine Reese. Absent Ruth Carter. Photo credit: Lawrence Smith

The officers were President, Vice-Presidents, Secretary, Treasurer, Parliamentarian, and Project Chairman.

The following rules were suggested and adopted:

1. The club would meet every other Wednesday of the month at 3 P.M. the year around.
2. The dues were 25 cents at each meeting. Should any member not sew she would pay 5 cents penalty plus the dues.
3. Should a member not be able to attend the meeting she should call the hostess the day before, if not a 10 cents fine.
4. The number of members was limited to 15.

5. Should a member resign, move away or die, a regular member could suggest someone to take her place. In the beginning, voting was done by secret ballot and should there be a "no," someone else was suggested. However, a few years later the members voted openly and they were accepted.

6. Also, in the beginning, should a member miss 3 consecutive meetings without an excuse, she was dropped. This, too, had to be amended.

7. Hostesses were assigned in alphabetical order.

Among the civic duties they performed as the years passed were:

1. The purchase of uniforms for the boys and girls basketball teams and the boys baseball team.

2. Bought the time clock for the gymnasium.

3. Planted shrubbery around the school building.

4. Conducted "book fairs" for the school library.

The ladies held "clean up" days twice a year for the downtown area and the then-Ross Dean Park area (now Maxine Reese Park). Also, many baskets of food and clothing were given, at Thanksgiving and Christmas, to needy families in the community. When help was needed anywhere the Stitch-n-Chatters were there. Should someone in the community lose a home by a fire, financial support was given.

Those attending the organizing meeting were: Laura Caughman Carlton, Grace Montgomery Young, Lillian Gordy Carter, Allie Murray Smith, Irene Murray Jones, Floy Howell Bagwell, Bessie Wellons Crozier, Eva Webb, Polly Walters Nix, Caroline Channell, and Ruby Calloway. These were also the charter members.

The present members, as of February 11, 2002, are: Carol Mims Anderson, Sara Helen Mims Bozeman, Wynelle Hinson Chambliss, Allene Timmerman Haugabook, Josephine (Jo) Dupree Medlock, Betty Horne Moss, Joyce Fuller Timmerman, Annie Mae Watson Vaughn, Ruby Watson, Caroline Channell Webb and Virginia Harris Williams.

The Stitch-n-Chat Club is the only organized club to continue meeting regularly since its organization in 1934. Caroline Channell Webb is the only living original member. The members still stitch a little and chat a lot after 69 years.

—*Submitted by Caroline Channell Webb*

Plains Lions Club

A desire to improve and further develop the Plains community by a group of citizens living in the area was the motivating force that led to the chartering of the Plains Lions Club. This desire for achievement by community people working together has produced significant results during the past 50-plus years. The group was encouraged to organize as a Lions Club and become an active club by members of the Americus Lions Club. Consequently, the Americus Lions Club sponsored the Plains Lions Club to become chartered on Monday night, February 4, 1946. The dues were $3 per month. The charter members are to be commended for their vision and effort. Presently there are six of the 29 charter members still living and five of these still live in the Plains community.

The club became very active immediately by supporting the local school board and Plains school staff with various projects and working closely with the Parent-Teachers Association. Assistance was give to Future Homemakers of America, Future Farmers of America and various sports activities by providing funds, volunteer labor, materials and other ways to enhance these programs. Support was also given at this early time after being chartered to projects for helping people with sight impediments and medical research related to eye and sight problems through the State and National Lions organizations. Glasses were purchased for local people as requested and approval for the need of financial assistance was verified. The biggest project undertaken in the early 1950s was cooperating with city, county and state governments to build a gymnasium adjacent to the Plains High School to replace the one that had burned in the 1940s. The cost was over $20,000 and the club was responsible for 90 percent of this amount. The project was completed and used for many functions in addition to sports until the school was closed. It was demolished in the early 1990s to allow for restoration of the Plains school by the Plains Historical Preservation Trust and the National Park Service. The club acquired approximately five acres of land in the 1950s also to develop a swimming pool and some tennis courts. This was a very popular project at the time. Parents volunteered to assist in operating the pool and concession stand. The pool is still in use and now operates under a lease to the Rabbit Branch Recreation Association. Many young people in the area learned to swim as a result of this project.

Club members decided in 1966 it was time to start thinking about constructing a building on the property owned by the club to be used for fundraising activities, regular meetings and other community uses. Through fund-raising activities, donations, volunteer labor and borrowing $8,000 this $20,000 building was put in use in the fall of 1970. The 25th anniversary celebration was held January 25, 1971. The loan note was paid off a few years later. Recognition must also be given to the Garden Clubs, the Stitch-in-Chat Club, and the Junior Woman's Club for their assistance with this project. The Junior Woman's Club purchased the chairs, paved the parking area and offered other financial support. The Garden Clubs and Stitch-n-Chat Club assisted with landscaping and financial support. The building continues to serve a community need and is used by the Lions Club and Junior Woman's Club. A big project in the 1970s was hosting the World Tennis Tournament. Five-thousand dollars from the profit of this event was sent to Georgia Lions Lighthouse Foundation. In addition to the

previously emphasized projects, many other projects just as important have been sponsored by the club during the past 50 years. Selling brooms and mops made by blind people is still a special project. The club has always been actively involved in securing industry and supporting local health services.

The number of active members today is about one-third of the charter membership. However, the desire is still there to carry out the Lions Club Motto "We Serve." It is a goal of the club to reactivate former members living in the area and recruit new members so the rewards can continue to be significant during the years ahead. The busy world today with "50 years of change" certainly makes club reviving and growth a necessary challenge for existence and accomplishments in the future.

Plains Lions Club Presidents

1945-46	Y.T. Shefield
1946-47	Y.T. Shefield
1947-48	L.L. Spence
1948-49	Hardy Cornwell-G.F. Williams
1949-50	R.L. Montgomery
1950-51	Mark A. Chambliss
1951-52	O.A. Williams, Jr.
1952-53	C.L. Walters, Jr.
1953-54	J. Guy Dominick
1954-55	Hugh A. Carter
1955-56	J.W. Sewell
1956-57	J. Howard Dupree
1957-58	Jimmy Carter
1958-59	Clarence Dodson
1959-60	William A. Spires
1960-61	P.J. Wise
1961-62	J.D. Clements, Jr.
1962-63	Y.T. Shefield
1963-64	Elliot Anderson
1964-65	G.F. Williams

1965-66 .... Ralph W. McDonald
1966-67 .... Robert B. Moss
1967-68 .... O.A. Williams
1968-69 ..... J.W. Sewell-Clinton Holloway
1969-70 .... Clinton Holloway
1970-71 .... Theron Hobgood
1971-72 .... George Harper
1972-73 ...........................L.E. Godwin, Jr.
1973-74 .... Ted Brown
1974-75 ...........................L.E. Godwin, III
1975-76 .... C.L. Walters, III
1976-77 .... J. Marvin Griggs, Jr.
1977-78 ....Claude Frazier
1978-79 .... Mill Simmons
1979-80 ....George Williams
1980-81 .... Henry Coleman
1981-82 .... John (Buzzy) Tanner
1982-83 .... John Williams
1983-84 .... Robert B. Moss
1984-85 .... Theron Hobgood
1985-86 .... Ralph W. McDonald
1986-87 ... Joseph Respess-David Jennings
1987-88 .... David Jennings
1988-89 .... Ronny Chapman
1989-90 .... Millard Simmons
1990-91 .... Clinton Holloway
1991-92 .... Henry Coleman
1992-93 .... Bob Howard
1993-94 .... Frank Bivins
1994-95 .... Bob Howard
1995-96 .... Robert B. Moss
1996-97 .... Ethel Coleman
1997-98 .... Dr. Clinton Holloway
1998-99 .... Everette Chambliss
1999-00 .... Henry Coleman
2000-01 .... Jeff Campbell
2001-02 .... Robert B. Moss

2002-03 .... Patricia Conger

Plains Lions Club Committees

July 1995-1996

Membership, Attendance & Greeters
Bob Howard (Chair), C.L. Walters, Dewey Paradise, Pat Bivins

Sight Conservation & Health Services
Ethel Coleman (Chair), Boze Godwin

Building & Grounds
George Harper (Chair), Bob Moss, Frank Bivins, Henry Coleman, and Bob Howard

Projects & Activities
Clinton Holloway (Chair), Bubba Chambliss, Dewey Paradise, Boze Godwin, Bob Moss, and Frank Bivins

Finance, Publicity, Correspondence & Records
Henry Coleman & C.L. Walters (Co-Chairs), Ethel Coleman, and Boze Godwin

Programs and Regular Meeting Agenda
Bob Moss and all members
—*Submitted by Robert B. Moss*

Plains Supper Club

Out of the notion that Plains area citizens who did not live in town needed a means to socialize more often in the early 1950s grew the Plains Supper Club, a social club that began with six prominent couples.

The idea for the club was initiated by Ruth S. Godwin, whose husband was the town pharmacist. She saw a need to share pleasantries with her neighbors, the Duprees, and other like-minded friends who owned land in the community.

Though the club originated with 12 members, it eventually expanded to 16 members.

The original members were J.D. Clements, Sr. (1903-1990) and Ruth Moore Clements (1905-1986); J. Mallie Dupree (1879-1967) and Mary Givan Dupree (1894-1995); Dr. Lynton E. Godwin (1892-1954) and Ruth Sanborn Godwin (1897-1995); Claude Harvey (1882-1956) and Ada Patton Harvey (1881-1967); Olgia V. Hogsed (1885-1971) and Lula Looper Hogsed (1889-1973); and Frank Spann (1902-1992) and Ada Brooks Spann (1904-1987).

Later, two other couples were invited and joined the club – Ernest W. Harris (1898-1980) and Ouida Murphy Harris (1900-1969); and Rowe Bowers (1899-1969) and Evelyn Wright Bowers (1902-1983).

Club members playfully but proudly called themselves the "Country Crackers" and met once a month at each other's homes. Delicious Southern meals were their specialty. Friendship was their norm.

The Birthday and Anniversary book, published by A.D. Steinbach & Sons, Inc. of New Haven, Conn., and copyrighted in 1945, attests to the fellowship club members enjoyed. The book, now in possession of the family of Frank and Ada Spann, contains 22 basic rules of etiquette, table blessings for special occasions and gift suggestions for special occasions.

On the inside cover of the book is a quotation from Emerson: "The only way to have a fried is to be one." In the handwriting of Ada Spann are the birth dates and addresses of all club members.

The back cover of the book includes the prayer of St. Francis of Assisi, which perhaps speaks best for the Christian interests the members shared. It reads:

"Lord, make me an instrument of your peace; where there is hatred, let me sow love; where there is injury, pardon; where there is doubt, faith; where there is despair, hope; where there is darkness, light; and where there is sadness, joy.

O Divine Master, grant that I may not so much seek to be consoled as to console; to be understood as to understand; to be loved as to love; for it is in giving that we receive; it is in pardoning that we are pardoned, and it is in dying that we are born to eternal life. Amen."

Interestingly, longevity was a trademark of Plains Supper Club members. Ten of the original 12 members lived beyond age 80, as did 12 of the entire 16-member group. The last two surviving members both died in 1995.

Mary Dupree died on October 13, 1995 at age 101. Ruth Godwin, who long after the club disbanded still maintained contact with the families of her friends, died December 2, 1995. She was 98.

The following are poems written by her about the original members more than 50 years ago. Today they are treasured keepsakes in possession of the Spann family.

"Six Country Boys"

There are six country boys whose names I know
Listen carefully and I'll tell you so –
When you are lonely and nothing to do
You may recall all this as I tell it to you.
First comes "My Doc" who oft' look a fright
But look you "Crackers" he's handsome tonight!
Now Claude – He's so full of fun and dry wit
He makes us laugh 'til our sides nearly split.
Mr. Ozzie-now let me see –
He would make a good preacher, don't you agree?
Next there's Mallie – everyone's friend
And I'll tell you folk he's loyal to the end!
When we think of Frank Spann we see peanut rows

That man is a worker wherever he goes.
Last is J.D. a swing in his swagger
But listen friends – I haven't seen him stagger!

"Big Sisters Six"

The Country Crackers – Big Sisters Six
Are a bouqet of flowers – skillfully mixed.
The "Two Adas" are lilies so fair,
Smiling faces and white, shining hair.
"Our Mary" is like a Wild Rose
Shedding her radiance wherever she goes!
Then there is Lulu – A Blue Bonnet – say –
Helping and cheering those coming her way.
Last the "Two Ruths" petunias suit best –
Friendly, happy and loving the rest!
—*Submitted by Steve Short*

Plains Garden Club

"A thing of beauty is a joy forever." –John Keats

On May 8, 1957, Mrs. Clarence (Ann) Dodson invited a group of ladies to her home for the purpose of organizing a garden club, as there was not one in Plains. Those present were: Mrs. Bertha Helms, Mrs. Bertha Chappell, Mrs. Sara Chambliss, Mrs. Leila Baldwin, Mrs. Agnes McRainey, Mrs. T.J. Reid, Mrs. J.C. Wise, Sr. Mrs. Hilda Williams, Mrs. Beth Walters, Mrs. Alton Carter, Mrs. J.C. Webb II, and Mrs. Ann Dodson. All these thought this to be a great idea.

On that date, Ann Dodson organized the first garden club. Officers elected were president, 1st and 2nd vice presidents, secretary and treasurer. The name became The Plains Garden Club; club flower, the iris; colors, white and green, and the motto, "The nicest thing on earth to do is to plant a garden and share it, too."

To be recognized as a State Garden Club, a club must be recognized as a member of State Federation of Garden Clubs. The Plains Garden Club became a federation member in 1958.

Interest grew so rapidly, homes were not able to accommodate the members and a second club was formed. Members drew numbers to decide who would leave. Those drawing a 1 remained with the Plains Garden Club, and those drawing a 2 joined the new club. On June 2, 1959, Ann Dodson organized the new club with the name, Iris Garden Club.

Members of the Plains Garden Club visit Callaway Gardens, Pine Mountain, Ga., circa 1960. Front: Mrs. Walter Guy Spann, Mrs. J.C. Logan, Mrs. C.L. Walters, Jr., Mrs. W.A. Carter, Mrs. Arch Helms, Mrs. W.A. Spires and Mrs. Rufus Chappell. Back: Miss Annie Mae Brannen, Mrs.. Thad M. Jones, Miss Norma Perry, Mrs. Clarence Dodson, Mrs. Camp Perry, Mrs. Leroy Young, Mrs. Frank Campbell, Jr. and Mrs. Virgil Chambliss. Photo credit: Martha Harris

Plains Garden Club members continued to achieve much recognition both on state and national levels. They won blue ribbons, tri-color ribbons, and best of show awards in flower shows both locally and in other communities. The club had pictures of arrangements featured in the State Garden Calendar, won a state award for best poem of the year, had articles published in monthly issues of Garden Gateways, and sponsored classes on flower arranging. Ann Dodson's "country gardens" and Caroline Webb's "herb garden" were included in the state publication of Outstanding Gardens of Georgia.

Club members sold bedding plants to finance many of their projects. They bought 2,000 dogwoods, flowering cherry, and crape myrtle trees that were given to churches, schools, hospitals and all homes, on request. The club decorated Main Street and public buildings with pansies in barrels, made stockings for Central State Hospital in Milledgeville, and gave contributions to Garden Therapy, Headquarters House, and Georgia Botanical Gardens.

President and Mrs. Carter asked Ann Dodson to be chairman of a committee of Garden Club members to decorate the White House for his inauguration in 1977. All flower and greenery used in decorating came from Georgia.

Plains Garden Club is a member of the National Council of State Garden Clubs, Inc., Garden Clubs of Georgia, Inc., and Magnolias District.

A Collect written by Caroline Webb was chosen to be the official collect of Plains Garden Club, Iris Garden Club and the Magnolia District Garden Club of Georgia.

—*Submitted by Caroline Channell Webb*

Iris Garden Club

The first Garden Club was organized in Athens, Georgia in 1891 with 12 members. The first Gateway publication was in 1932: in 1934 the Brown Thrasher bird was adopted as the State Bird.

The Plains Garden Club, which was started in 1957, had so many members that they decided to split and form two clubs.

The manner in which they divided the Plains Garden Club was that everyone agreed that they would number off and the odd numbers would be one and the even numbers would be the other.

The Iris Garden Club became the new club with Ruth Carter as the first president. The first executive committee met May 18, 1959, in the home of Mrs. Clarence Dodson.

The first regular meeting was June 2, 1959, at the home of Ruth Carter. The name of the club, the flower, etc. were voted on at this meeting.

Rosalynn Carter invited Hazel Hagerson Smith and Betty Lou Hagerson to join; the club members voted them in November 1, 1960.

Mrs. Clarence Dodson was a member of our club. She also served at the district, state and national level. She contributed much to the club with her expertise in flowers – growing, arranging and in other ways.

The Iris Garden Club chose the following:

Club flower — iris

Club motto — "He who planteth a garden planteth happiness."

Club tree — dogwood

Membership to 20 persons.

Meeting Date: 1st Tuesday at 9:30 A.M. each month.

We have a long list of women who have served our club very effectively, many of whom are still active: Mrs. Ruth Carter, Mrs. Joel Thomas, Mrs. Jimmy Jones, Mr. L.C. Hobgood, Mrs. Roy Young, Mrs. Bobby Dodson, Mrs. Easter Smith, Mrs. Theron Hobgood, Mrs. Charles Medlock, Mrs. Bubba Chambliss, Mrs. Milton Hagerson, Allie Mae Cornwell, Barbara Dodson, Evelyn English, Brenda Taylor, Mary Lou Smith, Virginia Wise, Audrey Jennings, Martha Sewell Wise, Susan Elrod, Dot Godwin, Edna Heron, Christine Buchanan, Rosalynn Carter, Lorraine Jones, Jane Short, Peggy Israel, Anna Marie Nichols, Rachel Hunter and Terri Jones.

Our club has helped with several community projects through the years, including the Logan Garden, the flower bed at Plains High School, and others. We also have good programs either prepared by the members or invited guests. The Iris

Garden Club welcomes any who would like to join with us.

—*Submitted by Betty Lou Hagerson. From Mrs. Clarence Dodson & Mrs. Easter Smith*

Plains Junior Woman's Club

The Plains Junior Woman's Club, one of the most civic-minded in the town's history, was founded in 1972. Organizers were Betty Godwin, Elaine Murray, Sandra Walters, Pharis Walton and Vonnie Young.

The club serves the Plains community through projects beneficial to the betterment of the town. The group conducts a fall festival each year in October, and organizes the downtown Christmas lighting during the holiday season. Each spring in April, the club hosts the "Young at Heart" picnic for senior citizens. The club also assists with the Plains Peanut Festival each September. Also in the fall, the club joins the Sumter County Retirement Village in sponsoring a Senior Citizens Fall Dance. For the past 14 years, the Plains Junior Woman's Club has produced and sold the Plains Community Calendar that highlights the birth dates and anniversary dates of area residents. In the past 30 years, it also has provided four cookbooks for sale. A fifth cookbook currently is in the works. The club has participated in the Adopt-A-Road program, an initiative to reduce the amount of trash and signage strewn alongside Georgia highways. A philanthropic group, the organization sends scholarship money each year for two Plains area residents to attend the college of their choice.

The group is open to women 18 years old and older. Though membership fluctuates, the club boasted one of its larger memberships in October 1976 before the election that sent Jimmy Carter to the White House. A list of members then included: Mrs. Henry Barfield, Mrs. Billy Carter, Mrs. Homer Chambliss, Mrs. Harold Chavers, Mrs. Randy Coleman, Mrs. Julian Cosby, Jr., Mrs. L.E. Godwin III, Mrs. Charles Houston, Mrs. Dennis Irlbeck, Mrs. Ed Mays, Mrs. Ishmael Morris, Mrs. David Reeves, Mrs. Mill Simmons, Mrs. Charles W. Smith, Jr., Mrs. Ritchie Smith, Mrs. John Phillip Tanner, Mrs. Doug Unger, Mrs. C.L. Walters III, Mrs. Carlton Walton, Mrs. Jack Watson, Mrs. George Williams, Mrs. John Williams, Mrs. Burton Thomas and Mrs. Roy Young. Mrs. Jimmy Carter was an honorary member.

Current members are Richelle Bivins, Tiffany Buchanan, Tracy Campbell, Allison Clark, Shelly Godwin, Audra Jennings, Debra Mims, Eve Yarbrough and Stephanie Young. Richelle Bivins will assume the role of president in April 2003.

—*Submitted by Stephanie Young and Steve Short*

Corn Shuckers Association

The Corn Shuckers Association was a non-profit organization that began in 1977. Seven friends got together for a fish fry and decided to meet monthly on Mondays. They decided to call themselves the corn shuckers since everything around Plains involved peanuts. The charter members included: Bobby Salter, Walter Guy Spann, Billy Ratliff, James Dozier, Eddie Revell, Walter Dozier, and Norman Murray.

The only way to become a member of the club was to be invited by a member. The club was incorporated, issued membership cards and a certificate. By 1987, the membership for the club had grown to 96 members. After Bobby Salter sold the restaurant were members met, the club disbanded.

—*Submitted by Bobby Salter*

Plains PALS Club

On January 13, 1987, Maxine Reese invited 50 widows from Plains to an organizational meeting for a widows' club. Those who attended formed the first widows' club and the name PALS (Plains Association of Lady Survivors) was selected. The charter members were Carol Anderson, Betty Carter, Doris Downer, Dot Gardner, Eunice Griggs, Marjorie Hobgood, Nellie Jennings, Maxine Reese, Lilloise Sheffield, Allie Smith, Louise Smith, Loease Speegle, Mattie Beth Spires, Annie Mae Vaughn, Beth Waters, and Irma Wise.

Past presidents include Maxine Reese, Louise Smith, Beth Waters, Jerri Bailey, Ruby Watson, Fannie Wiggins, and Hazel Hobgood Smith.

The PALS Club serves a dual purpose for our members. We get together once a month and go out for dinner. Each member is paired with a special PAL who is responsible for keeping in touch, sending birthday cards, calling, and serving as a support system.

In 1997 we compiled a cookbook called "Sharing Our Best." All money made from the sales of these cookbooks goes to projects benefiting the city of Plains and its citizens.

—Submitted by PALS Club

Gallery of Plains Mayors

*Edwin Timmerman
(term 1905-1906)*

*Rodolphus Silas Oliver
(term 1908-1916) Evidence
that his years as mayor may
have been longer, but City
Council minutes are missing.*

*George W. Montgomery
(term unknown)
City Council minutes missing.*

*Charlie Lunsford
(term unknown)
City Council minutes missing.*

*Emmett E. Cook
(term 1938-1940)*

*Edgar Timmerman
(term 1940-1941)*

Chapter 10: Mayors

In September 1997 Plains sponsored its first "Peanut Festival." It was on this occasion that pictures of our city fathers were displayed publicly in City Hall. Mrs. C.G. (Allene Timmerman) Haugabook collected these pictures.

Burr Thomas Wise
(term 1897-1902)

Though Plains was chartered in 1885, the first mayor on record was Burr Thomas Wise, a prominent area physician who served from 1897 to 1902. Mayor Wise served during the exciting times of the turn of the century. In the United States, the Gay Nineties were just over and the country was finally recovering from the War Between the States. On the international scene, the dominant powers were in Europe, and all eyes were on the recently unified powers of Germany and Italy.

From 1903 to 1918, the mayors in respective order were: James Graham, Edwin Timmerman, James E. Chappell, George W. Montgomery, and R.S. Oliver. During this time the Plains government passed a law prohibiting persons from riding bicycles on the sidewalks in the Town of Plains. Another law prohibited gambling of any kind within the town limits, and the town council hired our first night watchman for $30 a month.

In early 1905, a disastrous smallpox epidemic hit Plains, and it was noted in the council minutes that all houses infected with the disease had to be quarantined for eighteen days. On the first anniversary of the disease, in its April meeting, the council, remembering the time of trouble, ordered that all hog pens be torn down and none be allowed in the town until October 1. The thinking was that disease spreads more readily during the summer months, and hog pens could be dangerous to city inhabitants.

It was at this time that Dr. George A. Harper, a Plains physician who had earlier attended Confederate troops in the War Between the States, was appointed by the council to be sanitary inspector. His job was to survey each house in town and report any conditions that could cause sickness.

On October 4, 1911, Dr. Harper reported that he had visited every home and found many sites in poor sanitary condition. Those in noncompliance of the town's code were ordered to clean up their premises by a specified time.

On June 3, 1912, it is interesting to note that the town prohibited citizens from tying their horses or other livestock on the downtown street posts, at the schoolhouse, and on church grounds. A year later the council prohibited hogs from being allowed to randomly roam the streets. After April 1913, "any hog caught on the streets will be put in the pound for 24 hours and the hog's owner will be required to pay one dollar. Half the money would go to the city treasurer, the other half to the town marshal."

Then in April 1917, the council passed a resolution that each family could keep at least one hog in the back yard for food purposes. This would enhance the family's food supply, plus the hog would be a good agent for leftover food disposal. At the same council meeting, Plains made its contribution to area "Blue Laws." A law was passed that the sale of gasoline be forbidden on Sunday without permission from the mayor. Council members also resolved that no "shoe shining activities" could be performed on the downtown streets on the Sabbath.

As Plainsites recovered from their bout with the plague and began to be concerned with other problems, a greater and worse scourge was threatening on the international scene. The Europeans had divided themselves into two armed camps, and crisis after crisis was menacing world peace. A chance spark could set off a Great War, and indeed it did. On June 28, 1914, the heir to the Austro-Hungarian throne, Archduke Francis Ferdinand, was assassinated in Sarajevo, Bosnia. Out of the pursuing antagonisms the central powers were pitted against the allies. The First World War had begun and Plains' young men went to defend their country.

For the years 1918 to 1944, no city records exist. However, from other sources it has been gathered that the mayors included Jim E. Chappell, George W. Montgomery, Charlie Lunsford, Emmett Cook, and Edgar Timmerman. These were crucial years including post war recovery, economic boom, and then war again.

Soon Plains and the rest of the country rushed into the Roaring Twenties. Americans were tired of war, disillusioned with Europeans whom we thought dragged us into the war, let us win it for them, and then left the bill for us to pay. The Twenties was a decade in which we did a lot of new and wonderful things. For starters, the United States had emerged from the war a very powerful country. We would become isolationists and enjoy our newfound wealth and power. New clothing and lifestyles were tried. We danced the Charleston, enjoyed the "flapper craze;" women bobbed their hair, used rouge and lipstick. Men changed from pocket to wrist watches. It was also a time of conspicuous consumption. As we danced and

played, we spent money, quite a lot of it. Times were good, credit was plentiful, and jobs could be had for the looking. For about 10 years we lived so, and the bust came.

In the fall of 1929, the economic system of the United States collapsed. Many economically secure Plains folks found that their money had vanished.

As the situation required, the United States political system did a turnaround. After years of Republican ascendancy, voters chose a Democrat for President to lead the country out of trouble. In 1932, Franklin Delano Roosevelt of New York entered the White House. He was a man of action. He won a personal bout with polio and now, with the same gumption, offered us a new deal and recovery seemed possible.

As we recovered, however, trouble threatened again. The Europeans, apparently not content with peace, decided to fight again. Hitler in Germany, Mussolini in Italy, and the war party in Japan became aggressive. War seemed inevitable, and it came in September 1939, when Germany invaded Poland. America remained neutral, however, and hoped for the best. Then on December 7, 1941, the Japanese attacked Pearl Harbor, Hawaii, and the United States entered a war the Europeans had started; it ended in 1945 with the defeat of Germany and Japan.

From 1941 to 1953, Alton Carter served as mayor. He owned Plains Mercantile Company and kept a bank for the convenience of the Plains people. "Miss" Marilou (Mrs. Floyd) Burnette worked in the store that sold everything from shoes and clothes to bubble gum and "funny books."

In January 1944, the council made A.B. Moore night watchman and paid him $70 per month. In 1947, council minutes show that the following salaries were agreed upon:

Police .... $120 per month
Night watchman .... $80 per month
Clerk .... $30 per month

Garbage collector .... $5.75 per week

In 1951, the mayor and council decided to transfer the Plains telephone franchise from Thad Jones of Plains to Tommie Smith of Leslie. Also in 1951, the Americus Housing Authority proposed to build "10 white units and 14 colored units" in Plains. Mayor Carter and C.L. Walters, Jr. were asked to serve as the committee to pick the most desirable sites.

P.B. Jones was elected mayor in December 1953. The new mayor died in 1954 and a special election was called. Dr. J.C. Logan, a noted Plains physician, was elected and served until 1965. These were years of growth. Plains received a new four-lane road through the center of town, all the streets in town were paved and the new housing projects were built by 1955. In addition, the downtown park called the Grove was changed into a state roadside rest area.

Plains moved into the present era with mayors in order being: G.F. Williams, 1965-1971; L.E. Godwin, Jr., 1971-1975; A.L. Blanton, 1975-1979; L.E. Godwin III, 1979-1984; Jimmy Bagwell, 1984-1985; R.W. McDonald 1985-1988; and L.E. Godwin III, 1988 to present.

This period was dominated by the presidential election of 1976, when one of our very own natives, Jimmy Carter, was elevated to the nation's highest office. At once, Plains came alive with news reporters, TV cameramen, and tourists. This was a most important time for Plains and interest in national affairs skyrocketed. Our eyes turned with pride toward Washington.

—Submitted by Dr. James E. Bagwell

Mayors whose pictures could not be obtained:

J. Graham 1903-1905
D.I. Hite 1907-1908
Jim E. Chappell .... record missing
P.B. Jones 1953-1954

Gallery of Plains Mayors

*William Alton Carter
(term 1941-1953)*
Also served during period of missing City Council minutes.

*J. Colquitt (Col) Logan
(term 1954-1965)*

Gallery of Plains Mayors

George Frank Williams, Sr.
(term 1965-1971)

L.E. (Pete) Godwin, Jr.
(term 1971-1975)

A. Loren Blanton
(term 1975-1979)

Ralph W. McDonald
(term 1985-1988)

James Emmett Bagwell
(term 1984-1985)

L.E. (Boze) Godwin III
(terms 1979-1984; 1988-
through writing of this book)

Chapter 11: Postmasters

Plains of Dura was located at an intersecting point of two well-traveled routes. One was known as Bond's Trail,[1] which connected sites between the Flint River south of Montezuma and two creeks – Chokeeligee Creek and Kinchafoonee Creek. The other intersecting route known as the Old Americus-Preston Road followed part of a former Indian route connecting the Hawkinsville area to former Indian settlements on the Chattahoochee River.[2]

Postmasters: Plains of Dura

The United States Post Office lists the following people appointed as postmasters.

David W. Robinett 8/17/1839
Ebenezer Curry 12/11/1841
John Coker 3/25/1843
Thomas Simpson 3/25/1856
William B.C. Coker 9/20/1856
Josiah Howell 3/20/1858
Newnan McBain 10/27/1858
Bedford J. Head 6/10/1859
Alton B. Hawks 12/19/1859

Alton B. Hawks may not have served. The post office was discontinued on January 19, 1860. It was reestablished on January 26, 1860.

J. Harper Black 1/26/1860
Athern B. Hawkes 1/05/1861
Hawkins H. Nunn 8/13/1866
Samuel B. Glass 2/26/1868
Milton L. Hudson 4/13/1886

The Post Office Department required towns to plot locations of a post office on a map and to complete a detailed description of the location. The earliest document located for Plains of Dura is dated 1886. M.L. Hudson completed this form requesting to change the location of the post office at Plains of Dura on April 6, 1886, to the present location. Mr. Hudson stated the closest route for the new post office was on Route No. 1550 from Americus to Lumpkin. The contractor's name was listed as S.H. Hawkins. The name of the nearest office to the proposed new site was listed as Plains of Dura stated as being 3 miles in a northern direction from the new location. The name of the most prominent river was the Flint, located 30 miles away, and the nearest creek was the Choctawhatchee located 5 miles to the west. The nearest railroad, A.P.&L., was 100 feet from the new post office site with the station name being listed as Milton. The village was listed as having 50 inhabitants with a population of 300. This document was signed by M.L. Hudson.

Another document was recorded by the Post Office Department on April 12, 1890, and was signed by the postmaster, M.L. Hudson. This document was updating the topographer's office of the post office location. The document is interesting, listing Bottsford as the nearest post office 5 miles southwest of the route, Providence 8 miles to the south, Tropic 8 miles to the southeast, Roney 8 miles northeast, and Friendship located 10 miles to the north. This form lists the post office's name as Plains with the S.A.M. being the railroad serving the community.

Postmasters: Plains

The post office moved to Plains on March 8, 1890. The official record lists the following postmasters for Plains.[3]

Milton L. Hudson 3/08/1890

William H. Forrester 2/26/1900

Sarah F. Jones 2/19/1902

Samuel H. Timmerman 1/15/1909

Jessimae McGill (Acting) 12/01/1923

Jessimae McGill Glenn 3/18/1925

Mary H. Campbell 3/15/1934

J. Robert McGarrah 7/28/1945

Thomas E. Harris 6/30/1978

•Claude L. Walters III 6/28/1979

Millard Simmons 12/01/1979

•Clarence O. Johnson Jr. 6/01/1990

Vera Elizabeth White 11/03/1990

•Officer in charge

—Submitted by Annette Wise

Endnotes

[1] *The Map of Sumter County, Georgia* (Atlanta: Hudgins Co., circa 1910)

[2] Goff, John H., *Place Names of Georgia,* pages 35-36

[3] Records of Appointments of the Post Master-Georgia, Records of the Post Office Department, 1839-2002

(No. 1113, New Series.)

Post Office Department,

OFFICE OF THE FIRST ASSISTANT P. M. GENERAL,

WASHINGTON, D. C., *Mch 29*, 188 *6*

Sir:

Before the Postmaster General decides upon the application for a change of *the* site of the post office at *Plains of Dura*, County of *Sumter*, State of *Georgia* No. — *Milton* he requires that the blanks in the following statement be filled, and the questions carefully and correctly answered, verified by your signature, certified by a neighboring postmaster, and returned to this Department, addressed to me. The contractor should be informed of this application; and if the site proposed be off the mail route, you will forward his certificate as to the practicability of supplying it, and also as to the increase of distance.

Be careful to designate the post offices by their true official names; and answer the subjoined queries fully and accurately, *or the case will not be acted upon.*

Very respectfully,

FRANK HATTON,
First Assistant Postmaster General.

To Mr. *M. L. Hudson*

care of the Postmaster of *Americus*, who will please forward to him *at once*

STATEMENT.

The office to be called *Milton   Plains of Dura*

Select a short name for the proposed office, which, when written, will not resemble the name of any other post office in the United States.

The new site will be situated on the _____ quarter of Section _____, Township _____
Range _____, in the County of *Sumter*, State of *Ga.*

It will be on or near route No. *15.850*, being the route from *Americus*
to *Lumpkin*, on which the mail is now carried *Daily* — _____
The contractor's name is *S. H. Harris   for A. Pt. & L. R. R.*
Will it be *directly on this route*?—Ans. *Yes* —
If not, how far from, and on which side of it?—Ans. _____
Х How much will it INCREASE the travel of the mail one way each trip?—Ans. *None*
Where will the mail leave the present route to supply the proposed site?—Ans. *Not at all*
Where intersect the route again?—Ans. _____
What post office will be left out by this change?—Ans. *None at all*
Х The name of the nearest office to the proposed site, *on the same route*, is *Preston*
its distance is *10 4/4* miles, in a *Western* direction.
Х The name of the nearest office on the same route, on the other side, is *Hurricane*
its distance is *13 1/2* miles, in a *Eastern* direction from the proposed site.
Х The name of the nearest office to the proposed site, not on this route, is *Plains of Dura Ga*
distance by the most direct road *3* miles, in a *Northern* direction.
The name of the most prominent river near it is *Flint*
The name of the nearest creek is *Choctawhatchee*
The proposed site will be *3 0* miles from said river, on the *Western*
side of it, and will be *5* miles from said nearest creek, on the *Eastern* — side of it.
The name of the nearest railroad is *A. Pt. & L. R. R.*
If on the line of or near a railroad, on which side the office be located; how far from the track, and what is, or will be, the name of the station?—Ans. *On South Side about 100 ft. Milton*
What will be the distance from the proposed site to the nearest flag station?—Ans. _____
State name of station: _____
What will be the distance from the proposed site to the nearest station at which *mail trains make regular stops*?—Ans. *None*
State name of station: *Preston*
If the proposed office is located where it can be supplied from a crane or flag station, or located over 80 rods from the station where mail trains make regular stops, will the mail be carried to and from the proposed office without expense to the Department?—Ans. *Yes*
Х If it is a village, state the number of inhabitants.—Ans. *Fifty Three hundred*
Х Also, the population to be supplied by proposed office.—Ans. *F. & three hundred*

A diagram, or sketch from a map, showing the position of the proposed new office, with neighboring river or creek, roads, and other post offices, towns, or villages near it, will be useful, and is therefore desired.

A correct map of the locality might be furnished by the county surveyor, but this must be without expense to the Post Office Department.

ALL WHICH I CERTIFY to be correct and true, according to the best of my knowledge and belief, this *6th* day of *April*, 188 *6*
(Ɂ Ɂ. Sign full name.) *M L Hudson*, Proposed P. M.

I CERTIFY that I have examined the foregoing statement, and that it is correct and true, to the best of my knowledge and belief.

J C Roney
Postmaster at *Americus*
Ga

(OVER.)

Part 1 of the Post Office Department, Topographer's Office, request to furnish information on the location of the Plains Post Office, 1886.

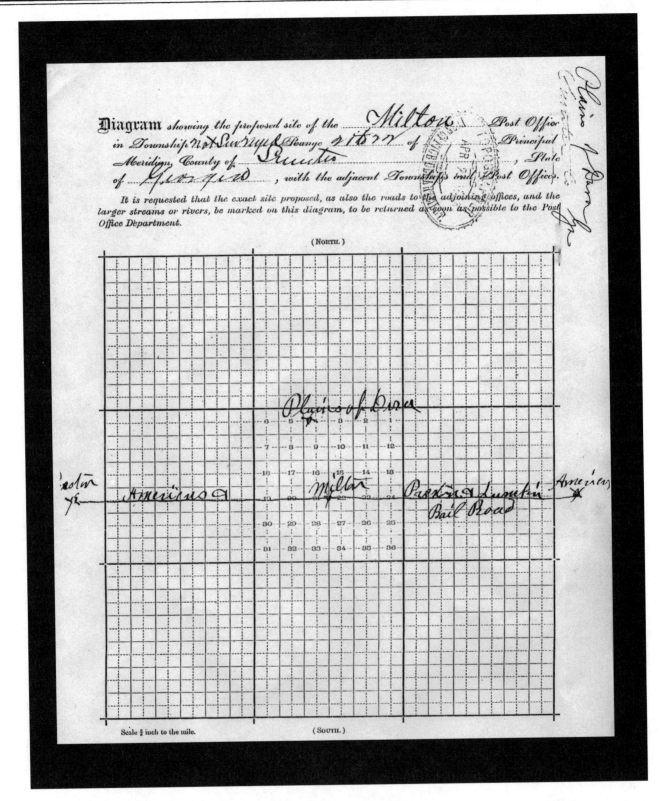

Part 2 of the Post Office Department, Topographer's Office, request 1886.

(101.)

Post Office Department,
TOPOGRAPHER'S OFFICE

Washington, *April 2,*

Sir:

To enable the Topographer of this Department to determine, with as much accuracy as possible, the relative positions of Post Offices, so that they may be correctly delineated on its maps, the Postmaster General requests you to fill up the spaces below, and the diagram on fourth page, returning the same, verified by your signature and dated, under cover to this Office.

Respectfully, &c.,

C Roeser

Topographer P. O. Dept.

To POSTMASTER AT *Plains (late Plains of Dura)*
Sumter Co.
Ga

The (P. O. Dept.) name of my Office is *Plains*
*Its *local name* is *Plains*
It is situated in the _____ quarter of Section No. _____, in *Township* _____ (north or south), Range *_____* (east or west), County of *Sumter*, State of *Georgia*

The name of the most prominent *river* near it is *Flint.*
The name of the nearest *creek* is *Choctawhatchie*
This Office is *30* miles from said *river*, on the *West* side of it, and is *2½* miles from said nearest *creek*, on the *East* side of it.
The name of the nearest Office on route No. _____ is *Americus*, and its distance is *10* miles, by the traveled road, in a *East* direction from this my Office.
The name of the nearest Office, *on the same route*, on the other side, is *Preston* and its distance is *11* miles in a *West* direction from this my Office.
The name of the nearest Office off the route is *Bottsford*, and its distance by the most direct road is *5* miles in a *S. West* direction from this my Office.
This office is at a distance of *100 ft.* from the *Plains* Station of the *S. A. & M.* Railroad, on the *South* side of the railroad.
State, under this, the names of other Offices near your Office, in different directions from it, and their distances from it by the most direct roads. *Providence 8 mi. S. — Tropic 8 mi. S. Roney 8 mi. N.E. — Friendship 10 mi. N.*

*If the town, village, or site of the Post Office be known by *another name* than that of the Post Office, state that other name here, that it may be identified on the map of the State (or Territory).

☞ A *diagram* of the township and sections (or, where the land is not so divided, a sketch map), showing the precise location of your Office, together with the adjoining Post Offices, towns, or villages, the roads, *railroads*, and larger streams or creeks, in addition to the above, will be useful, and is desired.—(*See diagram blank accompanying this, to be filled up.*)

(Signature of Postmaster.) *M L Hudson*

ELECTRO'S.

(Date.) *4 – 9 – 90*

Part 1 of the Post Office Department, Topographer's Office, request to furnish information on the location of the Plains Post Office, 1890.

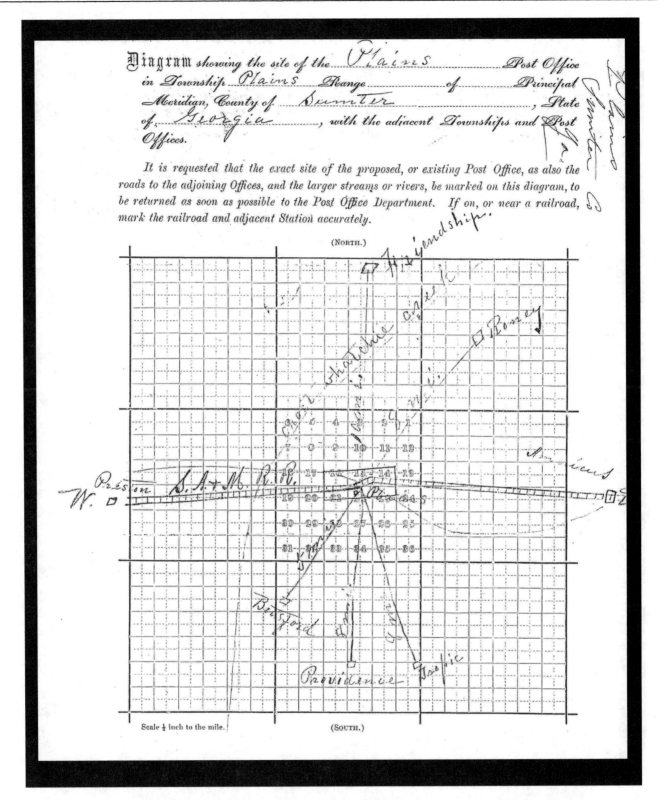

Part 2 of the Post Office Department, Topographer's Office, request 1890.

Chapter 12: Farming

Plains was a successful, thriving agricultural community in the 1920s and early 1930s. Surplus agricultural products were shipped by the railroad to other markets. The main products shipped were cotton, peaches, watermelons, hogs and cattle. Wheat was grown for grain to be ground into flour and the straw was used for packing watermelons. A large peach packing shed was located here until diseases and insects became major problems with no solutions at the time; therefore, the product could not be sold.

The impact of the Depression forced many changes due to low prices for surplus products – if a market could be found. Money was scarce and a survival type farming system was the predominant type of farming in the 1930s. This system used high labor input with mules used for pulling plows, planters, wagons and syrup mills as well as many other uses. Horses were used by some for pulling buggies and riding. The census reported Sumter County had 4,128 mules in 1930. The Plains area certainly had its share of this number.

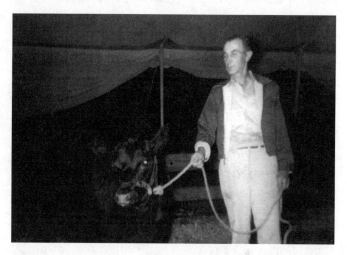

Ernest W. Harris with one of his prize-winning Angus cattle. He won many ribbons for his cattle. Photo credit: Frank Williams

Each farmstead usually had its own milk cows, hogs, chickens, and vegetable gardens to supply food requirements. Corn was grown for livestock feed, eaten by families and grinding into meal for making bread. Any surplus production was sold or traded for clothing, shoes and household products such as sugar, coffee, and kerosene. Only small quantities of fertilizer and other items were purchased at this time for the farming operation. Manure produced by the farm animals was used as a source of fertilizer for the crops and gardens. One report shows that the value of manure produced from one mule in one year was $10. This helped offset its cost for feed and housing.

Horses were enjoyed and widely used in Plains

Left: Bubba Chambliss, his horse and friend at the Chambliss home circa 1930. Right: O.A. Williams, Sr. on horse and buggy in Plains during the early 1900s. Photo credits: Wynell Chambliss and Frank Williams

John William Fulwood Murray on family farm outside of Plains. Photo Credit: Eunice Griggs

Large farms also had stores called commissaries for the convenience of the community and their sharecroppers or tenants. Many families living on farms did not have automobiles, any source of electrical power and only manual hand methods to get water supplies for their families and livestock. Cotton was the major commodity that could be produced and warehoused for sale. Peanuts were planted primarily for hogs to harvest as a source of food. Some were roasted and boiled for eating by the farm families.

Millard Simmons in 1940s driving a tractor on the James M. Howard farm. Photo credit: Millard Simmons

During the late 30s and early 40s, a significant change was made in the farming communities around Plains as well as most other farming communities in Georgia. Peanuts were beginning to be used for oil purposes. Small tractors became available to replace mules. Job opportunities other than farming began to surface and the World War II draft for the military took most of the young men from farms. Consequently, tractors were used to make labor more efficient, and the demand for peanuts for oil purposes made this crop more profitable than cotton. The expense of trying to control the cotton boll weevil also contributed to peanuts being more profitable.

The peanut acreage in Sumter County changed from 13,973 acres planted in 1930 (mostly for hog food) to 37,216 acres harvested for nuts in 1945. Cotton acreage dropped from 48,916 acres in the county in 1930 to 12,232 acres in 1945. Peanut and cotton production still required many hours of labor per acre. During these years, school-age children were paid to help meet seasonal labor peaks. With many men away from home because of the war, the government allowed World War II prisoners of war to be used as farm laborers. Plains was no exception to this. Many residents of Plains remember the German prisoners of war being brought to the local farms to do the fieldwork. After World War II, change in farming was continuous. Some veterans of the war returned to farm for a livelihood. Educational programs were stressed to learn better ways and how to use new technology with increased mechanization.

Farmers in this area of the state had a convenient location for observing some of these practices when the Agricultural Experiment Station was located and developed near Plains in the 1950s by the University of Georgia. Larger and more efficient equipment, new chemicals for controlling insects and diseases, chemicals for weed control, seeds of new varieties, the use of irrigation and many other factors have contributed to fewer farmers and larger farms since the 1960s. These factors helped to increase farm profits in the 1970s and 80s. However, many young people from this agricultural area chose to select other vocations or jobs for a livelihood.

O.A. Williams, Sr. farm near Plains in 1939. Frank Williams looking at pine seedling bed. This was a F.F.A. school project. A mule barn and corn crib are in the backgroud. Photo credit: Frank Williams

Governmental programs, because of surplus production, encouraged land to be planted in pine trees and other conservation practices. Consequently, farms have been sold, combined with others and leased to a few large operators, which reduced row crop farming, as it was known in the past. Plains has also seen many changes in the agribusinesses that were established in the late 1800s and early 1900s to meet the needs of the farming community. There is no longer a cotton gin located in Plains, only one full farm supply store, one grain buying point, and two peanut buying points now exist.

Viewing the fields from the roads and highways, you can still see some beautiful crops grow-

Luther David Wise, first person on the right side, standing in a wheat field outside of Plains in the early 1900s. Photo credit: Charlene Mallard

ing, especially peanuts. Other crops commonly grown in this area include corn, soybeans, wheat and cotton. However, many fields now are planted in pine trees that were row crops a few years ago. Hog farms and cattle farms have been reduced significantly and now there are no dairy farms in the area.

The area around Plains has the climate, soils and topography that are good for growing vegetables, pastures, trees, peaches, pecans and practically all row crops that can be grown in the Southeast. The question for the future is whether farmers in this area can make a reasonable profit in an open world market from producers who have cost and regulation advantages.

Frank Spann standing in front of a peanut combine in 1950s. The combine was used in the Sumter County Fair. Photo credit: Steve Short

Farming today is a high-risk business requiring huge sums of investment capital and potentially low profits rather than a way of life for survival with the high labor requirements in the 1930s and 1940s or the more profitable times of the '60s, '70s, '80s and early '90s.

—*Submitted by Robert B. Moss*

Chapter 13: Railroads

A History of the Railroad in Plains, Georgia

As told by Mrs. Hugh A. Carter, Sr.
July 26, 1986

President and Mrs. Jimmy Carter, Congressman Richard Ray, Mr. Ray Bullard, Mr. John Snow, Mr. John Walker, Peanut Brigade, 1980 Club, friends of the Depot, and fellow citizens:

July 26, 1986, will go down in the history books as a RED LETTER DAY in Plains. For this is the day of dedication of the little Railroad Depot which has been deeded to the Plains Historical Preservation Trust, a historic spot that has played one of the most important roles in the history of Plains, and made a tremendous impact on the welfare of its people.

Our town of Plains existed in the 1840s but was not established on its present site until 1885 when the railroad moved into the area. Under the General Railroad Incorporation Act of Georgia, a charter was issued June 17, 1884, incorporating the Americus, Preston and Lumpkin Railroad Company (AP&L) to construct and operate a railroad from Americus, Georgia, to Lumpkin, Georgia. The thirty-seven mile narrow gauge road was completed March 1, 1886. The name was changed on December 26, 1888 to the Savannah, Americus, Montgomery Railway (SAM).

The SAM entered receivership on November 30, 1892, and on July 27, 1895, the property and franchise, which had been sold at public auctions, were conveyed to the newly formed Georgia and Alabama Railway (G&A). The then already existing Seaboard Air Line Railway gained control of the G & A on July 1, 1900, through stock ownership; and on February 20, 1902, the property and franchises were sold to the Seaboard Air Line Railway.

A consolidation on November 16, 1915, resulted in a surviving cooperation to be known as the Seaboard Air Line Railway Company. The merger on July 1, 1967, of the Seaboard Air Line and the Atlantic Coast Line Railroads created the Seaboard Coast Line Railroad Company. The line was later known as the Seaboard Family Lines, then the Seaboard System Railroad, and at present is the Chessie Seaboard Corporation (CSX).

This station building dates back to 1888 when the line was in operation by its originator, A.P.L. The frame building with a tin roof (later replaced by slate) was a combination freight and passenger station until the passenger end was removed in 1951 with the discontinuance of passenger service through Plains.

At one time there were four day and two night passenger trains. The Shoofly came through at 10 A.M. going to Columbus and returned at 5 P.M. The trip back from Columbus took longer because the train had to run the "Y" in Richland. Other trains came through at Noon and 3 P.M. There was one at midnight and another in the wee hours. Of course, these trains were locomotives run by steam engines. There were wood yards and water tanks all along the rail line.

Eventually there were only two passenger trains through Plains – one at noon going east toward Americus, and then one at 3 P.M. going west toward Montgomery. The eastbound train was No. 12 and the westbound train was No. 11. It is interesting to note that all eastbound trains had even numbers and westbound trains had odd numbers. These two trains were powered by diesel engines and became known as the "Butthead." One day the "Butthead" ran out of fuel and was stalled at the crossing just west of the depot. Everybody in town flocked to the stalled train to see what had happened. They all had a big laugh because a train "ran out of gas." A crew had to be sent to Richland to get fuel because that was the closest railroad shop at the time. That occurrence was just one among many that drew the townspeople to the railroad and depot. The train was the highlight of almost every day in Plains.

Mr. E.H. Watson, who was a section foreman for the railroad, was remembered by my generation as a basketball fan even more than a section foreman. However, his record as a foreman was near perfect. His eight miles of track to keep in good repair was from Plains west, toward Preston, and the work was done by hand labor. I must report that his section never allowed a wreck. Today a section foreman keeps fifty or sixty miles of track, the difference being the use of large machinery.

Foreman E.H. Watson and crew at Archery. Photo credit: Ruby Watson and Annie Mae Vaughn

My grandfather, William Harrison Sanborn, was an engineer on the Seaboard Air line, and after fifty years service he retired in 1938 with a certificate of merit. I'm sure the president of this railroad, Mr. Richard D. Sanborn, is a cousin of mine. The first Sanborns came from England to America in the early 1600s. There were three brothers and today all the Sanborns in America are descendants of John, William, and Joseph Sanborn.

As a child I remember my mother waving a large white towel from our back yard to my grandfather as he passed through Plains. She knew his runs and he knew the location of our house. When she waved, he tooted the train whistle. What a big thrill!

"Papa's" engine turned over once on the sharp curve east of Plains. He jumped and fortunately was not hurt. Incidentally, his favorite song was "Life's Railroad to Heaven."

A fireman, Jeffey Lewis, also had to jump from the train. Both of Jeffey's legs got broken and he was no longer able to work for the railroad. He did, however, start cooking barbeque for a living. Everyone in Plains loved Jeffey's barbeque.

In the late 1920s the Wise Sanitarium, which was built in 1921, served as the S.A.L. Hospital. Following a train wreck at Savannah some 10 to 15 patients were brought. All ambulances, pickup trucks and other available conveyances met the train as it rolled into Plains that night. Two of the patients remained in the hospital a year but everyone was able to return to their home.

Plains was the most profitable of farming markets in the state. She was first in the state, second in the South and third in the United States in agricultural products in the late 1800s and early 1900s. Trains pulled out of town hauling more than they had brought.

What wonderful mail service we had when the passenger trains ran through our town! We could send and receive mail twice a day when the "Butthead" ran. Mr. Robert McGarrah, postmaster then, and Mrs. Allie Smith (Rosalynn Carter's mother) tell how fast they would work along with Miss Annie Mae Brannen to get the mail to the train on time. My father, Dr. L.E. Godwin, Sr., was the druggist then and his porter, Tobe, met the train twice a day to get drugs and ice cream from the express car. The train was met with a large two-wheel cart that my brother still has today. The station agent had to be paid for shipments that came C.O.D. Barrels of fresh fish came in every Friday. A hoop of cheese could be shipped from Americus for 25 cents in those years.

The crowds at the train station were both happy and sad at times but what a paradox one day in 1913 – they were both happy and sad at the precise same moment. It took a generation for the town to get over the incident. It seems that Mrs. Uriah McTyier, the wife of a prominent farmer in nearby Bottsford, received a very important telephone call for the Laster family who were tenant farmers for the McTyiers. The family was to meet the train at 3:00 because Roscoe, their son who had gone to Florida to seek fame and fortune, would be arriving. In her excitement, Mrs. McTyier told the Lasters that Roscoe had died and his body was coming in on the train. Why would someone else have done the phoning for him? So the Lasters had Mr. Ross Dean, the local undertaker, there at the station with a funeral hearse drawn by two gray horses all ready to take the body off the train. People from far and wide – about 150 strong, were there to see Roscoe's body arrive in a box. President Carter's father along with Hugh's father were among the crowd. The train pulled in, smoke puffing out of the smoke-stack, coal cinders flying everywhere and steam blowing off under the engine. The ladies were holding their handkerchiefs to their eyes and the gentlemen had removed their hats. The door of the baggage car opened slowly, but instead of Roscoe in a box, out he stepped from the coach with a suitcase in hand. He was a picture of success in new suit, tie, and celluloid collar. An hour had passed before the young "adventurer" knew what all the cheering and whooping was all about and why the people were hugging and kissing him or just trying

to touch him. A sad occasion quickly changed to a happy melee.

Although the depot was closed in 1951, it was reopened April 18, 1976, to serve as President Carter's campaign headquarters for the Democratic nomination and eventually the presidential election. Many volunteers worked here for months and many happy homecomings were held whenever President and Mrs. Carter came home.

The Plains Depot was the campaign headquarters for Jimmy Carter when he ran for the Democratic nomination for the presidency of the United States. Photo credit: Georgia Department of Archives and History

It served as the official gathering place for reporters from all over the world to interview the Carters before and after the election. In fact, so many pictures were taken at this spot the superintendent called from Jacksonville giving instructions for (1) to put a Railroad Decal on every side of the station so there would be one in every picture taken, and (2) to get a Southern Railway car off the side track – it was in too many pictures at a Seaboard station, and (3) to get a wreck out of the way because it was being shown too much.

A special train called the Peanut Special left the depot January 19, 1976, made up of eighteen cars – filled to capacity with over 300 people headed to Washington, D.C. and the inauguration

Peanut Special
This train carried over 300 Carter supporters to Washington for the January 20, 1977, presidential inauguration. Photo credit: Allene T. Haugabook

of the 39th president of the United States, Jimmy Carter. Maxine Reese had reserved the train even before President Carter received the Democratic nomination. What confidence! Of course the press from all over the world was here to cover the story from start to finish. BBC did a documentary of the trip and it was shown in England, the Scandinavian countries and all of Western Europe.

This very dear little railroad depot may seem just a small shack to the world but it means every-thing to the people in our town. It stands today as a memorial to those early settlers, to historical events, and most of all to the everyday life of the people in Plains for nearly a century.

Local People Who Have Worked For the Railroad

M.L. Hudson (first depot agent), P.O. Allen, Edward H. Watson, William Harrison Sanborn, Raymond Lamb, Charlie Lewis, Fletcher Chambliss, Simeon Wakefield, W.P. Booker, Seig Holmes, Mr. Sellards, Grey Blacksheare, W.L. Alford, Bill Arnold, Gurley Davis, A.L. Blanton, Sr., Homer Bankston, Ruby Watson, Sara B. Paradise, Mrs. Hugh S. Burnam, Cody Timmerman, Lummie Smith, Norman C. Murray, Charlie Vaughn, Dan Smith, Charles "Charlie" W. Smith, Sr., Homer Chambliss, Wilburn Smith, Virgil Chambliss, Henry Jackson, Louis Brown, Timothy Jackson, Clinton Jackson, Rail McGarrah, Joe Franklin, Clayton "Kit" Watson, Curtis Evans, Jack Smith, Eck Everett, Thomas Wakefield, Sr., Joe Hill, Willie Wilson, Eddie Pryer, Johnny Raven, Sr., Dock Sims, Martin Luther King, Sr., Louis King, Hollis Slade, Curtis Evans, Carl Scott, Wade Wilson, Charlie Lewis, Floyd Tullis, Floyd Jackson, Robert Jackson, Cullis Tullis, Jr., Charlie Whitfield, Fletcher McHolmes, Joe Jarden, T.R. Wakefield, Sr. David Henry, Johnnie Dudley, Otis Denson, Morgan Wise, and Charles Cummings "Baby Shep" Sheppard.

—Submitted by Amy Wise and Ruth Carter

Chapter 14: Jimmy Carter National Historic Site

Preserving the homes of our presidents has long been an American tradition. Roughly, one-half of all the former president's homes or similar structures are preserved by the National Park Service. Many others have been preserved either by private organizations or by state governments. In a few tragic cases, some of these homes, along with their rich history, have been lost forever. Visiting the home of a president and his family helps millions of Americans yearly to understand these people who have done extraordinary things with their lives. These places are where one can learn what influences shaped our leaders in their youth, and ultimately influenced policies and programs on a national and world scale.

The plans to establish the Jimmy Carter National Historic Site began in 1981 around the time that President Carter left office and returned to his home in Plains. Initially, the National Park Service held a meeting with President and Mrs. Carter in January 1981 to discuss the possibility of a historic site. This meeting led to discussions with people in the local community, primarily through the Plains Historical Preservation Trust. A critical step was developing a feasibility study where the National Park Service examines what resources would be appropriate to preserve. The feasibility study produced in 1983 was also a critical step to the development of legislation that created the Jimmy Carter National Historic Site.

An Act of Congress is required to authorize a National Park Service area. The Jimmy Carter National Historic Site legislation proved to be controversial for several reasons. The new Secretary of the Interior, James Watt, had placed a moratorium on additional Park Service areas. There was

also a concern in establishing a presidential site for a living president. Within some circles, it was thought to be appropriate that a president should be dead 50 years to first determine the significance of the site. Another concern was that the administration was opposed to the bill because it included Plains High School, which was seen as too costly a restoration project. There was a strong feeling among local residents that Plains High School should be included in the National Historic Site.

Thanks to the skillful negotiating skills of Congressman Richard Ray, sponsor of the bill, a compromise was reached and the bill was passed. The compromise stated that, "Not more than 60% of the aggregate cost of restoring Plains High School may be provided by Federal funds. The remaining non-Federal shares such costs may be in the form of cash, goods, or services fairly valued." The compromise language was enough to ensure the bill was passed and signed into law by President Reagan. The legislation included four resources for the National Park Service to acquire, preserve, and interpret. They were the Plains Depot, Plains High School, the Carter Boyhood Farm, and the Carters' residence on Woodland Drive.

On February 13, 1988, the Depot was opened as the park's primary visitor contact facility. It operated in that capacity until October 1996. The National Park Service acquired an exhibition, which had been developed by local citizens to share the Carter story. Although the Depot had some structural problems and lacked many creature comforts, it served the park well as a Visitor Center for eight years.

In the early 1990s, two major projects moved ahead simultaneously. First was the development of the General Management Plan as required by the park's legislation. A General Management Plan takes the wishes of Congress as outlined in the legislation and determines how the park will be preserved, what key stories will be told, and how they will be told to the visiting public. The General Management Plan required two years to complete and was developed by a planning team from the Denver Service Center of the National Park Service in Colorado. The planning team held several public meetings to solicit input from local citizens and took steps to gather input from a larger audience throughout the country. The results were a plan that continues to serve the Park Service in providing management direction for all park operations.

The restoration of Plains High School was an enormous and challenging undertaking. Immediate steps were taken to assess the structure to see what had to be done to prevent further deterioration. The school had been vacant for 10 years and was in extremely bad condition. The roof had leaked, the auditorium tresses were rotten, and asbestos was present throughout the building. The Division of Historic Architecture of the National Park Service's Southeast Region went to work to develop a stabilization plan. This plan simply listed what steps were needed to halt deterioration and ensure that the building would not deteriorate further. The price tag to complete the plan was $5 million. The plan was presented at a community meeting in June 1989 to seek support for the project and to discuss funding needs.

As presented, the plan was not well received. The cost of 40 percent share of stabilization of the plan was $2 million, an unrealistic amount in the small town of Plains where city funds are very restricted. There were also questions about how cost estimates were developed by the National Park Service. Upon close examination, the estimates seemed extremely high by Plains' standards. However, they were federal estimates developed under rigid contracting rules that often tend to increase

prices. The end result of this meeting was that the community would not commit to the restoration plan.

This initial presentation led to the formation of the Plains High School Liaison Committee that would work with the National Park Service on restoration of the building and in raising the necessary funds to complete the project. The committee included local residents P.J. Wise, John Pope, Maxine Reese, and Millard Simmons. Later, Ms. A.B. Jackson replaced Millard Simmons on the committee.

Federal funds were secured in 1990 for the replacement of the roof, the removal of asbestos, and to repair the sagging auditorium ceiling. The Park Service was able to secure a waiver from an Executive Order that prevented the use of prison labor on federal projects. This allowed for the use of inmate labor from the Sumter County Correctional Institution, which began that same year. Their work was highly defined and closely supervised as they began to replace the entire termite infested roof and floor joists.

The community began raising necessary funds for the project. Two grants totaling $20,000 were secured from the state of Georgia. Another highly successful program was the donation of building materials needed for the restoration. These donations were made directly from companies that produced these products. Altogether, more than $270,000 worth of building products were donated to the high school project. The city of Plains sponsored several large events to raise money for the high school project. One was "Trains in Plains," held in March 1991, where 12-vintage Pullman train cars were brought into Plains for display. The Plains Peanut Harvest Picnic in October 1993 on the grounds of Plains High School brought in $15,000 for the project. President Carter also held several fund-raisers and book signings that raised significant funds for the project.

The General Management Plan called for Plains High School to be developed as the park's primary visitor contact station and museum. This required the production of a 25-minute film about the life of Jimmy Carter and the history of Plains. Private funds were raised to pay for this film project produced by Ray DeTournay. Another major step was to develop exhibits for the high school. The planning and designing of exhibits was arranged through a contract with Jeff Kennedy & Associates from Boston, Massachusetts.

Once the design plan was completed, it was time to implement it. The estimates for exhibit fabrication were more than $500,000. This large amount of money was not available from federal sources so the community turned to a local company that manufactured components for the mobile home industry. Plains Products stepped in and offered to fabricate all the exhibit cabinets. It is difficult to estimate the savings from this donation; however, it is believed to have been in excess of $120,000.

Plains High School opened as the park's primary visitor facility on October 1, 1996, Jimmy Carter's 72nd birthday. The event was attended by approximately 1,000 people including Governor Zell Miller. The work of the partners on the restoration of Plains High School was affirmed when the National Park Foundation awarded the Plains High School project the National Partnership-Leadership Award for 1996. The award was presented at a ceremony at the United States Capitol on April 24, 1997.

The opening of Plains High School launched the Education Program at the site. This is a cooperative program between the Georgia Department of Education, Sumter County Schools, and the National Park Service. An instructional specialist provides programs to school students based on the Georgia Quality Core Curriculum. Since the establishment, the program has brought thousands of school students to the park for an educational experience at the school where the 39th president of the United States and first lady were educated.

The 1992 General Management Plan of the Carter Historic Site called for the Depot to house an exhibit devoted to the 1976 presidential campaign. However, the high cost of exhibits and the time involved in getting projects such as this funded made the likelihood of the Depot being developed very remote.

In 1995, President Carter suggested that the Carter Political Items Collectors (CPIC) assist the National Park Service in this endeavor. CPIC is an organization of approximately 80 members who collect memorabilia concerning Jimmy Carter's political career. This group is a subsidiary of the American Political Items Collectors organization. CPIC quickly formed the Depot committee and began work raising money and planning the exhibits.

The volunteer committee made many trips to Plains to develop exhibits. The group designed exhibit panels, donated historic objects, wrote exhibit text and selected graphics. Charles Plant, a photographer from Americus, developed a short video about the 1976 campaign to be shown in the Depot. The staff of the Jimmy Carter National Historic Site supervised the project as well as contributed their talents in exhibit design, layout, and fabrication. Members of the Plains Historical Preservation Trust also assisted with the project. The overall mission at the Depot was to display the historic campaign as an example of democracy in America.

The 1976 presidential campaign was unique in American political history and one that will be studied by political scientists well into the future. The Depot, which had been closed after Plains High School opened, was reopened to the public on September 27, 1997, at a ceremony where President and Mrs. Carter welcomed their close friends Bert and LaBelle Lance. Mr. Lance was the director of the Office of Management and Budget during the Carter administration.

Another key resource of the historic site is President and Mrs. Carter's home on Woodland Drive. Built in 1961-1962, it has been their primary residence since that time with the exception of the Georgia Governor's Mansion and the White House. The home includes a rich collection of personal items that reflect the Carters' love of family, home, and faith. The legislation that created the site called for the property to be acquired by donation with which the Carters complied in late 1994. The donation included a life estate agreement that allows President and Mrs. Carter to reside there until their passing. This was the same agreement the National Park Service had with the Truman, Eisenhower, and Johnson families. The property is a national historic treasure that will be preserved for future generations.

Without a doubt, one of the prime resources associated with Jimmy Carter's early life is the Boyhood Farm. Jimmy Carter had moved to the site in 1928 when he was four years old. It was on this farm where he learned first-hand the values of family, work, stewardship, and community that shaped his character. Jimmy's father, Earl, was a hardworking businessman who exposed his children to nearly all areas of work on the farm. Like any other small boy, Jimmy Carter enjoyed playing with friends, fishing, hunting, games, and contests. Living in close proximity to the African-American community of Archery, most of his playmates were black. It was in this setting that he learned first-hand the effects of segregation and racism.

The greatest difficulty in developing this site, just two miles west of Plains, was acquiring the property. After a long and difficult negotiation and court case, a representative piece of the farm was acquired in September 1994. The Park Service had decided early on to acquire only 15 acres of the original 360 acre farm. Once the property was acquired, the park went about stabilizing the structures.

In 1996, a restoration contract was awarded that restored the home and store to its appearance in the 1930s. Full funding to restore the farm to its 1930s pre-electricity appearance was included in the fiscal year 1999 Interior Department budget. This funding was secured thanks to the efforts of a dedicated group of local citizens who traveled to Washington, D.C., to lobby hard for the project. Work to restore the farm began in late 1999 by David Elliott & Associates of Columbus, under the direction of the Denver Service Center of the National Park Service. This group restored the historic landscape, restored or reconstructed seven historic buildings, built an entrance road, parking lot, and a comfort station. Other projects included the removal of non-historic utility lines and the reconstruction of the 1930s windmill.

Outdoor wayside exhibits were designed and fabricated and placed along the walking trail. Several audio stations were placed so that visitors could hear Jimmy Carter personally describing life on the farm during the Depression.

The Boyhood Farm opened on November 17, 2000, with a ceremony attended by approximately 2,000 people on hand to hear President Carter and Secretary of Agriculture Daniel Glickman formally open the historic farm. The opening of the Boyhood Farm coincided with the release of President Carter's most popular book ever, *An Hour Before Daylight*, which achieved best-seller status within a few months of the farm's opening.

In the 15 years that the National Park Service has worked in Plains to preserve and tell the story of Jimmy Carter's life and presidency, the park has enjoyed widespread public support within the local community. Much of the development of the park would not have been possible had it not been for the volunteers, contributions, and support from the people of Plains and Sumter County. Without the efforts of the people of Plains and Sumter County, the Jimmy Carter National Historic Site's 57,000 visitors in 2001 would not have enjoyed their visit to Southwest Georgia.

—*Sumitted by Fred Boyles*

Chapter 15: The Secret Service in Plains

Plains, while similar to many other small communities, is unique in that it is one of the few towns to have been a birthplace of an American president. This distinction brings with it a unique form of citizenry in the form of the U.S. Secret Service. While in the past there has been general stability in the Plains population with little "turnover," since 1981 there has been a continuous rotation of special agents reporting to or departing from the Carter Protective Division. These agents have in reality become de facto, although transient, citizens of Plains since 1976.

When Jimmy Carter became a major presidential candidate in 1976, he was assigned Secret Service protection. When the directive to begin protection for him was issued, agents traveled to Plains to form his 24 hour-a-day candidate security detail. This detail was responsible for his safety both at home and anywhere in the country (or world) he traveled. Agents also had to assess the security situation from intelligence and physical security perspectives, including his home and geographic surroundings.

A law enforcement command post for agents and Georgia State Patrol officers was established in the form of a single-wide trailer situated on the north end of Woodland Drive. During the remainder of the presidential campaign, rotating teams of special agents from USSS field offices all over the country (including myself) were assigned to temporary duty in Plains to provide security for the Carters and their residence.

While the agents worked in Plains, due to the lack of rental housing they commuted first from the Ramada Inn in Americus, and then later the Ramada Inn in Albany.

President Carter's rise on the political scene from a relative unknown to becoming the Democratic Party's presidential candidate brought some abrupt changes to both the citizens and the demeanor of Plains. As the national spotlight began to focus on both the Carters and the small town of Plains (approximately 700 residents), almost overnight the town changed from being a quiet rural community to being a unique center of attention by hordes of tourists, state and national press media, and of course, the Secret Service. In a December 17, 2000, interview with Jason Embry of Cox News Service, former Plains City Clerk Penny Smith remarked that "it's almost like you've been invaded. The Secret Service is going to be the most frightening thing for the community to get used to. They don't play around when it comes to securing the president."

She also noted that since Plains was Jimmy Carter's hometown, local residents were used to chatting with him when they saw him. Plains' citizens quickly realized that their normal, neighborly access to Jimmy Carter had changed as he was constantly flanked by his Secret Service Detail. While the agents were professionals in both their protection of former President and Mrs. Carter and in their public demeanor, they found it quite an adjustment to be spending most of their time working in a small-town environment. They were also well aware of the unintentional difficulties they imposed on local citizens simply by their presence.

One of the frequent events attended by candidate Carter and the Secret Service were serious softball games in Plains. These games normally featured Mr. Carter and the Secret Service playing as a team against the news media. These games usually drew a crowd and, while they were a change from the normal protection activities at campaign events, they were for the agents a different but just-as-serious protection environment. After President Carter left office, these softball games (with President Carter pitching for the Secret Service against the alumni of Plains High School) were to become one of the highlights of the annual Plains Peanut Festival.

When President Carter took office, the Secret Service Presidential Protective Division (PPD) was in charge of his security. During the 1977-1978 time frame, the Secret Service began renting, and moved into, the gray house on the corner of Woodland Drive and Highway 280 as their command post. This frame house, located next door to the Carters, was built by Jesse and Emma Timmerman in 1923.

Above: Before Remodeling

Below: After Remodeling

Secret Service compound before and after remodeling. Photo credits: Before, Jan Timmerman Abbott; after, Todd Kreisher

They in turn sold it to their daughter and son-in-law, Maybelle and Rees Andrews, who later sold it to the Gnann family and it became known as the Gnann house. The location of the Gnann house was perfect for the CPD Command Post; Secret Service agents and officers could work out of the house and be in close proximity to the Carters, and the support staff could fulfill their responsibilities to the detail. The detail later added a trailer in back of the house that acted as an ad hoc gym and storage area. When President Carter left office, the Carter Protective Division (CPD) of the Secret Service assumed responsibility for President and Mrs. Carter's security, and they continue to use the Gnann house as their command post.

In 2001, under the leadership of Special Agent in Charge (SAIC) Rick Kerr, a major and long overdue renovation was undertaken. It has to be remembered that the Gnann house was simply that – a family house. It was not built for a business, much less as a law enforcement command post. Thus, while it was fine for a family's needs, it was inadequate for the detail's requirements. SAIC Kerr consulted with the Plains Historical Society and other responsible agencies to determine what they could do while still remaining within legal historical guidelines.

The resulting renovations, which included the construction of a new building attached to the back of the house, provided additional offices and restrooms, a workout gym to enable agents and officers to stay in shape (as required by their job descriptions), an enclosed two-car garage, and a new carport for their vehicles.

While the physical surroundings of CPD have been updated and modernized, the Secret Service mission in Plains remains the same. The detail is composed of special agents, special officers, and an administrative support staff. Secret Service agents are first and foremost federal criminal investigators. Having a bachelor's degree, agents undergo a rigorous and lengthy application procedure and background investigation and, if selected, then attend a lengthy training program at the Federal Law Enforcement Training Center (FLETC) in Glynco, Georgia, near Brunswick. Afterward, they attend a lengthy Secret Service training academy to obtain expertise in both criminal investigations and protection skills. They normally spend several years in one or more field offices throughout the United States before being assigned to a protective detail. The agents assigned to CPD are almost always individuals who have expressed a strong desire to be on the Carters' protective detail. Some of them may have roots in Georgia, some may desire to live in a different part of the United States for a portion of their career, and some may also be enthusiastic hunters and fishermen. They will generally spend three to five years on the detail before being reassigned to another USSS field office, or to a headquarters assignment in Washington, D.C.

Special officers' backgrounds, requirements, and duties differ from agents, and they provide a unique expertise to the detail. Most officers have roots in this area, and their extensive knowledge of the local area is often coupled with a specialized background (such as military or weapons training). They are not subject to the extensive transfer requirements of agents, and they provide a continuity to the detail as agents transfer in and out of the detail.

The CPD administrative support staff is the "glue" that holds the detail together. The majority of the detail works 24-hour-a-day rotating shifts, and are often on the road, either in the United States or elsewhere in the world. The staff ensures that all Secret Service requirements are met, resolve administrative problems that may arise from time to time, and perhaps most importantly, ensure that everyone on the detail is paid in an accurate and timely manner.

As previously mentioned, CPD's mission has not changed. The detail is responsible for the safety and security of former President and Mrs. Carter at all times and in all places. Both of our protectees are highly active individuals who travel extensively. During my five years on the detail, both as an agent and as a supervisor, I added 22 countries on four continents to my "have traveled to" list (and I wasn't on all of the trips). The agents and officers who accompany the Carters on these trips are continually working to ensure that their safety and security are never compromised, whether it is spending one day in downtown Atlanta or two weeks in a jungle or remote village in Africa.

One of the joys of an assignment to CPD was alluded to in my opening remarks. Upon assignment to the detail, we do in fact become de facto citizens of Plains. While we may not reside in Plains, we do spend at least five days a week here. The agents and officers accompany former President or Mrs. Carter everywhere they go locally, whether it's to the high school for a speech, a local restaurant for a meal, or church on Sunday. We often become acquainted with local residents to such an extent that both they and we regard the relationships as something more – they become friendships. On our own we also frequent local restaurants and businesses on a regular basis, and in time both the permanent Plains citizenry and we temporary "citizens" start to recognize each other on the street and in the shops. It's quite a change from the "big-city" environments most of us have worked in, and indeed, a welcome one.

—Submitted by Richard W. Hayden
Assistant Special Agent in Charge (Retired)
U.S. Secret Service - Carter Protective Division
(1997-2002)

Chapter 16: Carter Political Item Collectors

The Carter Political Items Collectors

After the 1980 election when Jimmy Carter was defeated by Ronald Reagan, there was a lot of ridicule of Carter and anything related to him. A. Neil LeDock of Tucker, Georgia, became interested in collecting political memorabilia about Jimmy Carter and the Carter administration. He soon found out because Jimmy was not particularly popular at this time, that Jimmy Carter memorabilia was selling very affordable. He kept on collecting campaign buttons, 3-D items, and paper items until his collection included more than 500 pieces. Neil had always admired and respected Jimmy Carter because he was from his home state of Georgia. During this time the idea of starting a group that would collect and preserve Carter memorabilia became a burning desire of his. Neil thought that a group would be a way of returning and restoring Jimmy Carter to a place of dignity, honor and respect. Neil felt that as the years went by, Carter would be placed in history with the dignity and honor he deserved.

Neil heard of an international group called the American Political Items Collectors. He contacted them and found out that he could charter a subchapter of this organization. They had to have the magic number of 10 members to apply. They would name their group The Carter Political Items Collectors. The group was founded on January 1, 1984, by A. Neil LeDock.

The CPIC chapter was officially granted on May 1, 1984. Neil's wife, Meg, was also instrumental in establishing this group. The CPIC is a chapter of the American Political Items Collectors. Neil served as the first president and newsletter editor and his wife served as the first secretary and treasurer. Greg Lines served as the first vice president of the group. The CPIC chapter is the only one of APIC that has had a former president and first lady attend its annual meeting.

The first Carter Political Item Collectors meeting was held in Plains on July 10, 1988. Photo credit: Bob Linzey

The CPIC charter membership roll is as follows: A. Neil LeDock, Meg G. LeDock, George E. Jones, Kenneth Kline, Captain Norbert Melnick, David Grand, Rev. Oscar A. Guinn, Herb Hennings, Bruce Hilliard, John McLane, John Steven Prag, Stuart Rubin, Roger M. Van Sickle, and James D. Warlick.

As President Carter's popularity was at a low ebb in 1984, it was not easy to build or increase the membership. Neil LeDock did all he knew to expose and advertise the new group. One thing he did was to exhibit his collection anywhere he could.

He exhibited his collection at the 1985 Plains Centennial Celebration, which was viewed by President and Mrs. Carter. A news item about his collection was sent throughout the United States and published in the newsletter of the American Political Items Collectors. This exposure helped build the membership. Later, at a book signing for Rosalynn Carter's first book, Neil approached Mrs. Carter and gave her information about CPIC. Mrs. Carter seemed to appreciate the idea that the group had been formed.

On July 3, 1984, Meg, Neil's wife, received a handwritten letter from President Carter in which President Carter noted the information of CPIC and invited Neil to come to Plains for a personal visit. President Carter also asked to receive the CPIC newsletters. Neil and Meg went to Plains and had a private meeting with Jimmy and Rosalynn Carter at their church.

Neil's private collection of Carter memorabilia had grown to 8,000 items, of which 2,400 were campaign buttons. He was trying to do everything himself to keep the group going and working a full-time job. Unfortunately, Neil became ill and had to resign as president of CPIC. After Neil resigned, Roger Van Sickle of Delaware, Ohio, became the

Roger Van Sickle, Bob Linzey and Neil LeDuck have served as presidents of CPIC. Photo credit: Bob Linzey

president of the group. He was followed by Bobby Linzey of Lawrencesville, Georgia, as the third president. As the years have passed Roger Van Sickle has served as president several times as has Bob Linzey. Mitch Kuhn of Michigan has also served as president of the group for a short period.

In 1988, Bob Linzey and Roger Van Sickle along with Ken Barfield of Columbus came up with the idea of having a national convention in Plains. The first several years, we met in Plains and displayed our memorabilia on the city block of downtown Plains. President and Mrs. Carter would always come by and view our displays. The convention in those days was held in connection with the Plains Country Days Festival. After a few years, the town of Plains decided to change its annual festival to the Plains Peanut Festival, which would be held in September each year.

The Carter Political Items Collectors became involved as much as they could in the community of Plains. One way they became involved was to hold a yearly auction that includes three personal items from Jimmy and Rosalynn Carter. The proceeds are divided between the CPIC group and Maranatha Baptist Church, where the Carters are members. This event continues today. A lot of the Carters' items have brought large amounts of money. For example a Bible belonging to President Carter brought $800 and Mrs. Carter's dresses have brought large sums of money, also.

Later, Bob Linzey and Roger Van Sickle came up with the idea of a Saturday night banquet during the weekend of the national convention. The group has had as guests a number of people who were involved with the Carter campaign and administration. In 2001, Rosalynn Carter was the main speaker. It was a very emotional time coming just days after the World Trade Center disaster of 9-11-01 as President Carter led the group in the Pledge of Allegiance. Rosalynn spoke of the World Trade Center disaster and attending the prayer meeting at the National Cathedral with other presidents and their wives. Through the years we have had many outstanding speakers at the annual banquet such as Maxine Reese, Phil Wise, Gerald Rafshoon, Bert Lance, Susan Clough, Dot Padgett and others of the Carter campaign years and administration.

The CPIC worked diligently to help raise funds for the restoration of Plains High School museum. At a fish fry to raise funds for the school, President

The Carter Political Items Collectors held a fish fry on May 20, 1995, to assist with fund raising for the restoration of Plains High School. Photo credit: Bob Linzey

Carter asked Bob Linzey if the group would be interested in working on a project to put a museum in the old Plains Depot. Linzey and members of the group were happy to take on this project. After two years of hard work the display in the Depot was dedicated by President Carter. Linzey and Ken Barfield were the co-chairmen of this group.

Members of the Carter Political Items Collectors have become close friends of many of the members of the Plains community. As of 2002, the membership of the Carter Political Items Collectors has grown to 146 members from 38 states. The 2002 officers include: Bob Linzey, president; Mike Brooks, vice president; Vivian Ekberg, secretary; and Roger Van Sickle, treasurer.

The members of the Depot Committee who assisted the National Park Service in funding and designing the panels for the Depot museum included co-chairmen Bob Linzey and Ken Barfield, and committee members Roger Van Sickle, Ronald Ekberg, Douglas Kelley, Kenneth Klein, Mitch Kuhn, and Kenneth McClure.

—Submitted by Bob Linzey

Section III: Families

Chapter 17: Family History A–D

George Addy and Allied Families: Etheredge, Jennings and Wise

The progenitor of the Addy family was Solomon Addy. He, his wife Margaretha, and son Johann Heinrich (John Henry) arrived in Savannah, Georgia, from Germany aboard the ship "Two Brothers" in 1738. The Derrick family was transported on the same vessel. Over a century later, along with the Addys, their descendants would move to Plains, Georgia, and surrounding areas. While living in the Salzburger settlement of Ebenezer, Georgia, another son, Freidrich, was born to Solomon and Margaretha Addy. By 1748 the family had migrated to Saxe-Gotha Township, South Carolina, where Solomon received a land grant on the Saluda River. Solomon faded from the records about 1754. Simon (Simeon) Adey appeared in 1787 as a petitioner for the incorporation of the German Lutheran Church of St. Martin, located in the lower fork of the Broad and Saluda Rivers near Wyse Ferry. Whether Simeon was a son or grandson of Solomon has not been determined.

Simeon had four sons and two daughters: George, Henry, Jacob, John Simeon, Barbara, and an unknown daughter. Simeon's son John Simeon (1779-1841) married Catherine Taylor (1789-1857). She was the daughter of William and Elizabeth Taylor. John Simeon Addy and Catherine Taylor are buried in a family plot outside of what is now known as Leesville-Batesburg, South Carolina. They were the parents of at least thirteen children.

George Addy, son of John Simeon and Catherine Taylor, settled between Plains and Preston near Bottsford, Georgia, by 1866. Many relatives accompanied or later joined him. Among the early settlers of Plains and surrounding areas were a number of interrelated families from Edgefield, Fairfield, and Lexington Districts, South Carolina: Addy, Derrick, Etheredge, Hiller, Jennings, Timmerman, and Wise. The interrelationships among these families became even more intricate as they continued to intermarry after migrating to Georgia. These families were instrumental in establishing St. Mark's Lutheran Church at Bottsford.

George Addy, born February 25, 1814, in Lexington County, South Carolina, and died August 5, 1877, married 1st Jemima Wise, born November 24, 1815, daughter of John Wise and Elizabeth Kelly. Jemima was a sister of David (1809-1882) Joel, Jesse, and Jeremiah Wise. George and Jemima Wise Addy had three children, all born in Lexington County, S.C: (1) Levi Wilson Addy, born July 28, 1837, married his first cousin Julia Elizabeth Wise, daughter of David Wise and Rosa Elizabeth Etheredge. (2) John Calvin Addy (1838-1864). (3) Amanda Elizabeth Addy (1840-1909) married 1st Guilford Etheredge, son of Lucy Jennings and William Etheredge. Guilford was a brother of Rosa Elizabeth Etheredge who married David Wise. Amanda Addy married 2nd Allen Etheredge. (See Wise Family.)

Jemima's brother, Jesse Wise, married 1st Martha Etheredge and 2nd Jensie Etheredge. George Hiller married Jesse's daughter Harriet Wise. Jesse's daughter Mary E. Wise (1842-1898) married William Jennings "One-Armed Billy" (1836-1909), son of William Jennings and his 2nd wife Eleanor Etheredge.

After the death of his first wife in 1855, George Addy married 2nd Frances "Fanny" Jennings, born in Edgefield County, South Carolina, November 16, 1834, and died May 18, 1916, in Sumter County, Georgia. She was the daughter of William Jennings and his second wife, Eleanor Etheredge. (See Jennings: South Carolina to Plains.) Frances was a half sister to Lucy Jennings whose son Guilford Etheredge married Amanda E. Addy.

George Addy and Frances Jennings had four children, all born in Edgefield County, S.C: (1) Ellen Catherine Camilla Addy (1857-1947) married Samuel Pickens Wise (1851-1881). (2) Mary Rosanna Addy (1859-1976) married Josie L. Wells (1856-1918). (3) William Philip Addy (1861-1936) married 1st Josie Stephens (1862-1893) and 2nd Rosa Lula Addy (1866-1949) his first cousin once removed. (See William Philip Addy Family.) (4) Laura Rachel Addy (1864-1943) married Burr Thomas Wise (1858-1910). (See Wise Family.) Burr Thomas and Samuel Pickens were sons of Joel Wise. Joel's daughter Mary Melissa married Philip Jennings, brother of Frances Jennings. Joel's brother, Jeremiah Wise, married 1st Letitia Jennings, another half sister of Frances.

George Addy and Frances Jennings, along with a number of their relatives, are buried at St. Mark's Lutheran Church Cemetery at Bottsford near Plains. The Old Record Book includes the following resolution: Resolved, that in the death of Brother Addy, St. Mark's Church has lost a most active member, the Council an able advisor, the Sunday school a zealous advocate, and the community in which he lived a most valuable citizen. A stained glass window in St. Andrew's Lutheran Church in Plains honors his memory.

—*Submitted by Sandra Perry Wellons, Americus, Georgia, english@sowega.net*

William Philip Addy Family

William Philip Addy, son of George Addy and Frances Jennings, was born August 25, 1861, in Edgefield County, South Carolina, and died October 21, 1936. William Philip Addy was a landowner and farmer. The German stock from which he came placed a great emphasis on education and religion. He served on the Webster County Board of Education. As a child he was a member of St. Mark's Lutheran Church at Bottsford. Later, he, his wife and children were active members of St. Andrew's in Plains. He married Josie Stephens on December 18, 1881. They had four children: I) George Stafford Addy (1882- 1940) married Ophie Markette. II) Fannie Florence Addy (1884-1957) married J. Fanin Tillman. III) Max Gordon Addy (1888-1953) married Edna Golden. IV) Annie Will Addy (1890-1968) married Eamest Wellons.

After the death of his first wife, William Philip Addy married his first cousin, once removed, Rosa Lula Addy, born November 24, 1866, in Coweta County, Georgia, and died June 25, 1949, in Sumter County, Georgia. She was the daughter of Wesley William Addy and Margaret Bernhard. Wesley was a son of Jacob Addy (brother of George Addy) and Mary Rawls. Margaret Bernhard was the daughter of Jacob Bernhard and Ester Lites of Henry County, Georgia. Margaret Bernhard's grandfather, Christopher Bernhard, was brought from Germany to Savannah in the early 1770's to teach the children at the German settlement of Ebenezer, Georgia. He later became a noted Lutheran pastor in North and South Carolina. All of these families were German Lutherans who had settled in the "Dutch Fork" section around Lexington, South Carolina. Just as George Addy was a founding father of St. Mark's Lutheran Church at Bottsford, his brother Jacob was a founding father of Mt. Pilgrim Lutheran Church in Coweta, County. Rosa's parents and paternal grandparents are buried at Mt. Pilgrim Lutheran Church Cemetery in Harrelson, Georgia.

William Philip and Rosa are buried at St. Mark's Lutheran Church Cemetery at Bottsford

William Philip and Rosa Addy had five children: I) Margaret Lucile Addy, born March 19,1895, and died November 26, 1936, married Herschel Thomas Johnson. They had fifteen children. II) Wesley Philip Addy (1898-1966) married Effie Lee Drew. They had two children. III) Laura Loreen Addy, born (1900-1973) married Joseph Herlovich. They had eight children. (See History of Webster County. Georgia.) IV) Grace Caroline Addy (December 27, 1903-June 13, 1959) married Edwin "Dick" Kitchens English (1896-1956), son of Samuel Sampson English and Minnie Julia Kitchens of Andersonville, Georgia. (See Macon County Life.). They had eleven children:

A) Louise English, born June 22, 1922, and died May 27,2000, married Tommie Brown Perry, son of Jimmie Lee Perry and Ida Brown Perry-Children: Sandra Kay Perry married Taurence Wellons, Jr.; Barbara Lee Perry married Larry Miller; Tommie Brown Perry, Jr. married Sherry Lettelier .

B) James Edwin English, born November 5, 1924, married Doris Maroney-Children: Judith Ellen English married George Arrendale; Linda Mae English married William Parry; James Edwin English, Jr.; Nancy Doris English married Bob DeBord.

C) Doris Elizabeth English, born August 15, 1926, married James Kennedy "Buck" Sproull-Children: James Kennedy "Kenny" Sproull, Jr. married Tina Rae Briscoe; Sara Elizabeth "Beth" Sproull married Michael Wallace Wheeler.

D) Betty Felicia English, born November 28, 1927, married Bernard Clifford Inlow-Children: Carol Ann Inlow married Sidney David Wiggins; Royce Bernard Inlow married Patricia "Patty" Pruitt; Martha Louise Inlow married Don Wayne Lyon; Gary Steven Inlow married Catherine "Beth" Roberts.

E) Samuel Anthony English, born April 28, 1930, married Zigi Cedarbaum of Latvia.

F) William Addy English, born June 8, 1932, married Jean Stone-Children: Carolyn Frances "Fran" English married Michael Christopher Rust; Kathleen Grace "Kitty" married Jimmy Paul; Billie Jean English married Michael McCracken; Samuel Edwin "Sam" married Dana Tillman.

G) Martha Ann English, born March 6, 1934, married Johnny Roy Studstill-Children: Johnny Roy Studstill, Jr.; Martha Susan Studstill married Nicholas Allen Davis; Sherry Lynn married Marcus John Lyon.

H) Alice Eugenia English, died as an infant.

I) Eleanor Henietta English, born November 16, 1939, married Harold Leon Davis-Children: Derrick Leon Davis married Mary Kathryn Horne; Glenda Grace married Mark Edward Holloway; Douglas Harold Davis.

J) Gloria English, born March 27, 1943, married Kenneth Earl Dunmon-Children: Marri Kay Dunmon married George Haggerty; Lauren Paige Dunmoo married Anthony Clinton Long; Heidi Grace Dunmon married Kerman Douglas Goodin.

K) Donald Maurice "Donnie" English, born March 5, 1945, married Barbara Calloway- Children: William Chandler "Chan" English married Kimberly Daniels.

V) Herman Tillman Addy (1906-1937) married Carrie Nicholson. Herman, the youngest son of William Philip and Rosa Addy, was killed in a logging accident. He had no children.

—*Submitted by Sandra Perry Wellons, Americus, Georgia, english@Sowega.net*

The Anderson Family

Thomas Garland Anderson (1855-1898) married October 29, 1884 to Margaret Elizabeth (Lizzie) Murray (1866-1940).

Children: Garland Durelle (1886-1968); Eola Vira (1888-1972); Irwin Fulwood (1893-1972)

Garland Durelle Anderson (September 12, 1886-June 2, 1968) married October 29, 1919 to Alethea Josephine (Allie) Adams (January 11, 1891-February 10, 1977)

Children: Elliott Fulwood; Eola Mae; Thomas Durelle; Allie Florine; Eunice; Mattie Beth

I. Elliott Fulwood Anderson (November 14, 1921-February 12, 1972) married Bobbie Carroll Mims, (born January 23, 1934).

Children: Susan Anderson (September 8, 1958) and Jill Anderson (September 2, 1966) Jill Anderson married July 18, 1992 to Samuel Keith Simmons(born October 15, 1961).

Children: Lily Anderson Simmons (born December 26, 1999)

II. Eola Mae Anderson (November 25, 1922-May 27, 2002) married January 28, 1942 to John William (Jack) Jennings (March 26, 1917)

Children: Jacquelyn (Jackie); David Anderson; Debra Jean; Jacquelyn (Jackie) Jennings (September 4, 1942) married August 20, 1961 to Leonard Larkin (Lynn) Dupree (September 29, 1941) Children: Leonard Larkin, Jr. and Elizabeth Louise (Beth)

Leonard Larkin Dupree, Jr. (April 30, 1963) married January 1982 to Janet Leigh Brooks, (born April 25, 1963) Div. Children: Suzanna Leigh Dupree (August 16, 1982); Leonard Larkin (Lee) Dupree (September 27, 1983); Leonard Larkin Dupree, Jr. married November 28, 1992 to Carol Dahlene Franklin (July 25, 1962)

Children: Abigail Laurin Dupree (June 4, 1995) and Brant Jackson Dupree (November 30, 1996)

Elizabeth Louise (Beth) Dupree (December 11, 1964) married March 15, 1986 to Donald Stephens Powers (November 2, 1953) Children: Jacob Stephens Powers (May 8, 1989)

Claire Elizabeth Powers (April 24, 1991-April 24, 1991); Leah Elizabeth Powers (August 5, 1992); Carl Mitchell Powers (January 20, 1996); Alec Dupree Powers (June 10, 1997)

David Anderson Jennings (June 23, 1944) married June 11, 1966 to Brenda Rodgers (September 27, 1946) Children: Mitzi Gaynelle Jennings (February 25, 1971) and Jarrett David Jennings (July 5, 1973)

Mitzi Gaynelle Jennings, born Feb. 25, 1971, married May 27, 1994 Barney Dwayne Sapp (August 2, 1967) children: Palmer Harrison Sapp (October 22, 1999) and Hudson Jennings Sapp (June 17, 2001)

David Jarrett Jennings (July 5, 1973) married May 22, 1999 Mary Lynn Thielemann (February 2, 1973) Children: Jack William Jennings (January 2, 2002)

Debra Jean Jennings (August 31, 1955) married November 28, 1987 Dr. Glyn Edward Lewis (January 4, 952) Children: Iliana Jennings Lewis (October 8, 1996)

III. Thomas Durelle Anderson, Sr., born January 8, 1924-died January 16, 2000

Married 1st: Helen Ann Scaglione December 1, 1945 (Born April 8, 1925 Died March 6, 1948)

Married 2nd: Dorothy Jane Whiteley May 15, 1949 (Born August 29, 1926)

Children: Thomas Durelle Anderson, Jr., born March 6, 1948

Married: Virginia "Ginny" Crudo August 6, 1977 (Born: October 22, 195?)

Children: Thomas Durelle Anderson III, born June 8, 1979 and Christine Ann Anderson, born June 16, 1985

Charles Elliott Anderson, born March 18, 1950
Betty Josephine Anderson, born August 11, 1952

Married: Jesse Floyd Reynolds June 12, 1971-divorced: September 1, 1981 Born June 17, 1952

Children: Christopher Whiteley Reynolds, born May 9, 1972

Married: Jennifer Henry on September 24, 1994-divorced in 1997(Born January, 1975)

Married: Shelia Cooper December 1, 2001(Born January 3, 1967)

Children: Chase Cooper, born October 26, 1988 and Chad Cooper, born November 16, 1993

Karen Elizabeth Reynolds, born February 20, 1974 Married: Ling Chen on February 17, 2001 (born August 23, 197?)

Mary Catherine Reynolds, born November 19, 1976 Married: William Blare Ten Eyck on March 16, 1995 divorced-1997

Children: Zamemian Blare Ten Eyck, born August 26, 1995; Anna Elizabeth Roberson, born October 9, 1999; and Brandon Paul Roberson, born October 1, 2001

Stephen Whiteley Anderson, born September 30, 1956 Married: Clare Butler Ogletree on January 14, 1978 (divorced) Born on August 19, 1956 Children: Elizabeth Butler Anderson, born September 7, 1978 and Mary Clare Ogletree Anderson, born December 30, 1979

IV. Allie Florine Anderson, born October 28, 1925 and married Arthur Page Bailey, Jr.(May 14, 1921-October 16, 1999) on May 29, 1943.

Children: Linda Florine Bailey(November 27, 1946) first married to Virgil Eugene Goodin (born March 26,1945) on September 4, 1970 and later divorced. Then married Harry Wade Bartlett (born July 24, 1935) on August 29, 1992 Children: Jason Merritt Goodin, born September 14, 1971 Married: Emily

Ann Shoemaker(born April 10, 1978) on November 6, 1999

Children: Anna Katherine Wells Goodin, born July 9, 2001. Children:Lesley Suzanne Goodin, born May 23, 1975 Married: Harold D. Martin on April 19, 1997 Born September 30, 1968 Children: Zachary William Martin, born October 5, 2001

Sherrell Ann Bailey, born October 13, 1948 Married: Kenneth Wesley McKinnon on September 23, 1967 (divorced) Born January 11, 1948 Married Ralph Edward Brown on October 12, 1979 (divorced) Born January 14, 1947

Children: Lisa Ann Harry, born February 5, 1968 and married Hank Allen Harry on June 13, 1993 (Born May 12, 1974)

Children: Allie Mishelle McKinnon, born August 8, 1988; Kaitlan Belle McKinnon, born May 24, 1990; Aaron Ty Harry, born May 8, 1995

Kenneth Wesley McKinnon III, born March 14, 1970

Married: Krissy Ann Harbuck on September 23, 1989 Born July 6, 1972

Children: Kenneth Wesley McKinnon IV, born May 23, 1991

Lyndsey Alexis McKinnon, born February 23, 1994

James Arthur Bailey, June 28, 1952-July 5, 1988 Married: Jackie Ann Murray on October 28, 1977 (divorced) Born January 5, 1958

Married: Cherry Lynn Greenway on June 27, 1981 (divorced) Born December 16, 1956

Jerry Page Bailey, born November 6, 1953 Married: Carol Lynn Mclemore on June 28, 1980 Born July 31, 1958

Children: Diane Page Bailey, born August 16, 1984 and Arthur James (A.J.) Bailey, born September 25, 1990

V. Eunice Anderson, born September 25, 1927 Married on January 13, 1951 to James Marvin Griggs (November 7, 1921 - August 26, 1985) Children:Maxine Eunice; James Marvin, Jr.; Gail Alethea

Maxine Eunice Griggs, born December 20, 1951 Married on January 14, 1972 to John Dargon Wells, Jr. June 24, 1953 (divorced 1989) Married January 20, 2001 to Leon Luther Beall (May 20, 1945) Children:Kimberly Nicole (Niki) Wells, born July 12, 1972 Married May 12, 1994 to Jeffrey Scott McGee, born April 28, 1969 Children: Miranda Nicole McGee, born September 23, 1995 Joel Alexandra McGee, born March 19, 2001

James Marvin Griggs, Jr., born December 23, 1952 Married April 11, 1979 to Carol Lynn Bozeman, born December 5, 1956 Children: Wesley Adam Griggs, born November 4, 1979 Kimberly Ashley Griggs, born July 6, 1983

Gail Alethea Griggs, born December 9, 1958 Married January 15, 1978 to Robert Brinson Alston, born April 4, 1956 Children: Shonna Marie Alston, born August 19, 1950

VI. Mattie Beth Anderson (August 25, 1928-April 21, 1988) Married September 2, 1972 to William Arthur Spires (May 11, 1909-July 16, 1982)
—*Submitted by Eunice Griggs*

Rees Mahone Andrews History

The name Andrews is Scotch, the surname being taken from the baptismal name, Andrew.

Somewhere in the history of almost every prominent family esteemed in the community for public service and Christian character, there appears a time of trial. During those dark periods the family may falter and fail, dropping forever from the public eye; or they may be rallied by a new leader, a "Foundation Rock," and regain an even higher position of prominence. Such a time of trial occurred for the Andrews family in the 1890's, and such a "Foundation Rock" was Rees Mahone Andrews.

In 1890 Rees' father died suddenly from a ruptured appendix at the age of 33, leaving his wife with four young children.

In the fall of 1893, Rees' mother married Mr. Thomas J. Stapleton and a daughter, Martha Rebecca, was born to them the following year. Rees' mother and Mr. Stapleton soon agreed to separation without a divorce.

In 1906 Rees Mahone Andrews and his mother, Mrs. Rebecca Anne Stapleton, moved to Plains from Terrell County, Georgia. They bought the house on Church Street which is now occupied by C.L. Walters, III. With them was another brother, Robert Lee Andrews, and a half-sister, Martha Rebecca. The other two sisters, Carrie Joe and Nannie Crittenden Andrews were married. Rees came to Plains to go in the lumber business with his brother-in-law, J.R. Logan.

Rees Andrews was first made a Steward in the Enterprise Methodist Church in Terrell County when he was only 17. Shortly after moving to Plains he was named Steward of the Methodist church there. He served on the Sumter county Board of Education for 16 years and was chairman of the Board for 10 years. He was a Mason for many years.

I will start my Andrews history with Rees Andrew's father, Robert Crittenden Andrews, born March 4, 1857, died May 2, 1890, married Rebecca Ann Rees, born December 8, 1859, died October 16, 1930. She was the daughter of Joel Jordan Rees, Jr. and Caroline E. Mahone. There were four children born to this union and one child born to Rebecca Anne Rees Andrews Stapleton and Thomas J. Stapleton.

I. Rees Mahone Andrews, born October 11, 1879, died August 25, 1958, married Maybelle Timmerman, born November 8, 1887, died November 14, 1980. Both are buried at Lebanon Cemetery in Plains, Sumter County, Georgia. There were five children born to this union.

A. Rees Mahone Andrews, Jr., born March 20, 1909, married September 15, 1935 to Helen Reddick, born September 15, 1908.

1. Annabel Andrews, born January 28, 1947, married John Erick Stadig, September 13, 1975.

a. Elizabeth Ann Stadig, born February 25, 1977.

b. Katherine Christine Stadig, born March 2, 1980.

B. Harold Stinson Andrews, Jr. born February 13, 1911, married December 21, 1940 to Mildred Scruggs.

1. Harold Stinson Andrews, Jr. born December 23, 1943, died July 23, 1960. Buried at Oak Grove Cemetery in Americus, Sumter County, Georgia.

2. Patricia Eileen Andrews, born December 22, 1948, married James Staub in 1970, divorced 1982.

a. James Edgar Staub, Jr., born March 7, 1973.

3. Frances Carolyn Andrews, born June 28, 1950, died February 16, 1969, buried at Oak Grove Cemetery in Americus, Sumter County, Georgia.

4. John Stephen Andrews, born September 2, 1951, married Cynthia Louise Connell November 30, 197?. a. April Frances Andrews, born April 7, 1977.

C. Marjorie Andrews, born April 21, 1912, died March 25, 1969, married E.E. Summerford March 17, 1936, buried Oak Grove Cemetery, Americus, Sumter County, Georgia. E.E. Summerford was born August 25, 1891, died June 19, 1972

1. Harold Andrews Summerford, born April 6, 1937, married Patricia (Patsy) Ethel Davis.

a. Harold Andrews Summerford, Jr., born November 18, 1960, married Theresa Ann Crawford November 1, 1977.

1a. Brandi Dawn Summerford, born June 12, 1978.

b. Julie Anne Summerford, born June 25, 1962.

c. William Eugene Summerford, born May 1, 1964.

d. Peter Craig Summerford, born March 25, 1966.

2. Virginia Ruth Summerford, born July 21, 1938, married Guy Pollard York.

a. George Woltz Pollard York, born February 3, 1964.

b. Marjorie Timmerman York, born November 12, 1970.

3. Nancy Belle Summerford, born January 27, 1944, married January 15, 1966 to Charles Thomas Mitchell (divorced) married 2nd to Joseph Hudson Sadler, November 10, 1977.

a. Rees Timmerman Mitchell, born July 27, 1967.

b. Amanda Kathryn Mitchell, born September 14, 1970.

4. Rees Mahone Summerford, born January 1, 1948, married Brooke Barnett.

D. Dorothy Andrews, born August 23, 1914, married December 27, 1935 to Pinckney M. Sullivan.

1. Mary Ann Sullivan, born January 8, 1940, married Douglas Armistead (divorced) married 2nd Frank Bonrey.

a. Michael Douglas Armistead.

2. Sandra Sullivan, born June 24, 1945, married Benny Morris (divorced), married Norman Hays, died May 1972, buried at Roswell, Georgia.

3. James Pinckney Sullivan, born August 5, 1950, married Ellen Cobleigh, 1970, divorced 1981.

a. James Blair, born February 11, 1979.

E. Virginia Andrews, born June 19, 1916, married June 13, 1941 to Zera Littlejohn Hair, born August 31, 1916, died May 18, 1979, buried Oak Grove Cemetery, Americus, Georgia.

1. Zera Littlejohn Hair, Jr., born February 17, 1945.

2. Rees Andrews Hair, born November 26, 1947.

3. Virginia Clotilde Hair, born April 12, 1950, married Delmar George Huffman, (divorced).

II. Carrie Joe Andrews, born June 5, 1881, died December 5, 1947, married John Randolph Logan, born 1874, died 1932, both buried at Rylander Cemetery in Sumter County, Georgia.

A. Geraldine Logan, born 15, 1901, married December 24, 1921 to James Soule Pope, born September 14, 1900.

1. James Soule Pope, Jr. born June 17, 1924, married June 6, 1949 to Anne Louise LeCompte, born January 29, 1928.

2. Jerry Logan Pope, born May 29, 1930.

3. Logan Merritt Pope, born July 20, 1933.

B. Ernestine Logan, born September 13, 1902, married February 15, 1923 to William Harrison Brimberry, born 1897, died August 9, 1931, married Robert Crittendon Lane, divorced June, 1948.

1. Frances Anne Brimberry, born November 12, 1923, married December 22, 1942 to Alexander Peter Vaky, born February 28, 1919.

a. Diane Brimberry Vakey, born November 16, 1945.

b. Carolyn Virginia Brimberry, born October 23, 1925, married August 18, 1947 to George Eadie Orr, II, born April 11, 1924.

2. William Harrison Brimberry, III, born August 2, 1931.

3. Robert Crittendon Lane, Jr., born September 15, 1937.

C. Robert Mitchell Logan, born Febuary 1, 1905, died July 27, 1988, married first Frances Martha Lowrey, married second to Ruth Howell. Children by first marriage:

1. Robert Mitchell Logan, Jr., born April 27, 1924.

a. Robert Mitchell Logan, III.

2. Roxie Joe, born December 31, 1927, married Clyde Roach.

a. Stephen Wade, born October 8, 1949.

3. Jane Russell, born December 23, 1929, married Hugh Harrison, Jr.

a. Bobby

D. Gladys Mahone Logan, born June 1, 1907, married June 21, 1932 to Hubert Allan Horne, born April 23, 1903.

1. Hubert Allan Horne, Jr., born October 7, 1938.

2. John Randolph Horne, born December 28, 1941.

E. Kathryn Logan, born October 14, 1909, married October 12, 1930 to Archie Edgar Parks, born July 7, 1908.

1. Archie Edgar Parks, Jr., born January 8, 1934.

2. Kay Elizabeth Parks, born April 1, 1938.

3. Mary Jo Parks, born August 22, 1944.

F. John Randolph Logan, born December 25, 1911, married February 24, 1948 to Ossie Lane Mathis Adams.

III. Nannie Crittenden Andrews (see Daniel Reese Smith history).

IV. Robert Lee Andrews, born October 31, 1888, in 1910 married first Alice Williams, born October 3, 1891, died November 15, 1912; in 1914 second marriage to Effie Smith, born September 19, 1896.

A. <u>George Raymond Andrews</u>, born July 14, 1911, married December 22, 1934 to Eugenia Anne Elizabeth Hough, born December 16, 1913.

1. George Raymond Andrews, Jr., born January 15, 1936.

2. Sylvia Elaine Andrews, born January 12, 1940, died 1976.

3. Robert Hough Andrews, born July 19, 1951.

B. <u>Sarah Alice Andrews</u>, born October 22, 1912, married February 14, 1932 to B.F. Young, born April 3, 1909.

1. Robert Edward Young, born November 17, 1932, married Gloria Faye Landry December 5, 1959.

a. Robert Edward Young, Jr., born June 22, 1960.

b. Paul Andrew Young, born September 21, 1964.

c. Laura Rebecca Young, born April 18, 1966.

2. Barbara Alice Young, born November 14, 1934, married June 16, 1956 to Harry Leon Howell, III (divorced), married Walter Moye Colquitt, January 14, 1966.

a. Walter Moye Colquitt, born September 24, 1968.

3. B.F. Young, Jr., born August 20, 1936, married October 5, 1936, to Anita Brown.

a. Stephen Colin Young, born April 10, 1970.

b. Elizabeth Ann Young, born April 10, 1970.

4. Elizabeth Ann Young, born March 21, 1940, married December 24, 1963 to Haskell Leo May (divorced), married Rudolph Thomas June 3, 1977.

a. Haskell Leo May, born January 18, 1965.

Children of Robert Lee Andrews, Sr. and second wife Effie May Smith;

1. Marian Edith Andrews, born July 18, 1915, married May 30, 1941 to James Robertson Angel, born February 24, 1910, died February 9, 1975, buried at Smithville, Georgia.

a. Susan, born December 25, 1942, married July 17, 1965 to Randall Lee Copeland. Their children: (1) Kelly Copeland, born March 9, 1966; (2) Randal Lee Copeland, Jr., born July 3, 1968.

b. Sally, born October 5, 1944, married January 16, 1971 to Paul Cole. Their child: Geoffery Cole, born December 29, 1974.

c. James Robertson, Jr., born March 16, 1947.

d. Richard Andrews, born December 7, 1948, married March 1, 1969 to Carol Napier (divorced). Their child: Richard Andrews Angel, Jr., born July 20, 1969.

2. Robert Lee Andrews, Jr., born July 3, 1920, married December 26, 1949 to June Davis.

a. Robert Erle, born December 5, 1953, died.

b. Erle Beunion, born June 10, 1955.

c. Jenny Lea, born March 22, 1958, married January 29, 1980 to Edward Bryan Smith.

d. Robert Riley, born July 20, 1960 (twin).

e. Roslyn June, born July 20, 1960 (twin).

f. Betty Jane, born May 4, 1963, married April 25, 1981 to Jimmie Cowan.

V. Martha Rebecca Stapleton, born November 4, 1894, married May 30, 1916 to Iverson Harris Hall, born June 3, 1894, died August 13, 1963, buried at Milledgeville, Georgia.

A. Louis Harris Hall, born January 2, 1921, married April 21, 1942 to Sara Ouida Smith, born March 7, 1921.

1. Carolyn Harriett, born November 6, 1947, married August, 1968 to Lester Marvin Rowland, Jr., (Pete) (divorced November, 1976).

a. Lester Marvin Rowland, III.

b. Audrea Hall Rowland.

c. Stephanie Ellen Rowland, born ?, died October 20, 1972.

B. Thomas Hartley Hall, born October 20, 1926, married October 8, 1950 to Haywood Deane (divorced) married June 16, 1973 to Martha Janice Snow. Children of Thomas Hartley Hall and Haywood Deane Hall:

1. Mary Virginia, born July 9, 1957, married February 5, 1980 to Gregory Gene Stanley, born September 14, 1956.

2. Rebecca Louise Hall, born July 11, 1952, married September 21, 1974 to Willie Elbert Sweat, born March 24, 1977.

3. Linda Jane Hall, born May 23, 1955, married July 26, 1975 to Gerney Quinters (divorced).

a. Michael Thomas Quinters, born August 11, 1977.

4. Martha Deane Hall, born March 24, 1961.

Child of Thomas Hartley Hall and Martha Janice Snow: Catherine Anne Hall, born June 27, 1976.

—*Submitted by Grace Smith Medlock (1983)*

Ariail Family

Rev. and Mrs. Daniel Gilbert Ariail moved to Plains in October of 1982 when he assumed the pastorate of Maranatha Baptist Church. They purchased the Timmerman house from G. Frank Williams, Sr., where they still live at 213 Walters St., Plains.

Both Dan and Nelle Ariail grew up in the town of Maysville, GA. He was born on Aug. 24, 1938 and she on Feb. 28, 1939. He is the son of late Omer Gilbert Ariail and Marion (Payne) Ariail of Maysville, and she is the daughter of the late Clarence Enoch Wood and the late Alma Smith Wood, also of Maysville. They were married on Dec. 20, 1959, and have two children:

Robin Elizabeth Ariail (born Nov. 15, 1960) works for Rail America in San Antonio, TX.

Daniel Gilbert Ariail, Jr. (born Sept. 18, 1962). Married Christine Tietjen on June 14, 1986 and make their home on Shaban Subdivision Rd, Plains. He works with Treibacher Corporation in Andersonville. Their children are Hannah Elizabeth (born Oct. 28, 1988) and Nicholas William (born Oct. 28, 1992).

Dr. Ariail holds the Bachelor of Arts degree from Mercer University and the Master of Divinity and Doctor of Ministry degrees from Southern Baptist Theological Seminary in Louisville, KY. He has served as pastor in Jefferson, GA; Hull, GA; Owenton, KY; as Associate Pastor of First Baptist Church, Macon, GA; and served nine years as pastor of First Baptist Church, Perry, GA.

He is author of The Carpenter's Apprentice: A Spiritual Biography of Jimmy Carter (Zondervan, 1996), writes music for the folk play "If These Sidewalks Could Talk," serves on the board of directors of the Plains Historical Preservation Trust, and serves as chairman of the Plains Zoning Board.

—*Submitted by Dan Ariail*

Bacon History

Joseph Edmund and Leila Katherine Wells Bacon
1902-1940

Joseph Edmund Bacon was born on October 29, 1856 in Marion County, Georgia in the Red Bone Community to Edmund Bacon and Nellie Catherine Cranford Bacon. Leila Katherine Wells was born on May 1, 1861 to David Bony Wells and Charity Donnan Wells of the same community. Joseph Edmund and Leila Katherine were married December 20, 1881. Their early years of marriage were spent in the Red Bone Community of Marion County, Georgia.

Early one spring morning in the year of 1902, Joseph Edmund, his wife, Leila Katherine (Katie) and their seven children, Ida Lenora, Edmund David, Jennie Lind, Bony Wells, Leila Adella, Charity Eleanor, and Joseph Abner, traveled by wagons and buggy from their home in Marion County, Georgia to make their new home on a farm Joseph Edmund had bought earlier in Sumter County outside the community known as Plains, Georgia.

The moving was very difficult, furniture was loaded onto wagons and some of the animals were tied behind. Chickens were caged and loaded onto wagons. Cows and hogs were driven from behind. Each child had a certain job to do if old enough and after some time traveling and camping along the way they finally arrived at their destination weary, sore and tired. A major feat accomplished, and now Katie would have better schools for her children.

The years ahead were busy years with much to do. Building a new life was not easy or convenient. When home remedies did not work, the country doctor was called. Leila Katherine (Katie) had many home remedies of her own - one which was mold which she would apply to sores for both children and animals.

The farm had a pond where the children along with friends enjoyed swimming during the summer months and also was used as a baptismal site. The farm grew cotton, peanuts, tobacco, corn, wheat, oats, sorgham, watermelons, sugar cane, and always a garden with vegetables year round. In addition, there were pear, apples, pecans, black walnut trees, a Japanese walnut tree, figs, quince, scuppernongs, wild plums, peaches, and various kinds of berries. These all added to the farm's bounty. Horses, cows, mules, pigs and chickens were also a vital part of the farm. Water was supplied by a windmill and during summer and early fall months when wind was still, water was pumped by hand. The farm bell played an impor-

tant part of farm life. It was used to toll hands to work in the fields, break for dinner and then tolled again for the afternoon work at the end of the day. The farm bell was also used for emergencies in between the working hours and on days when field work was not done. Children did not ring the bell unless told to ring it.

The shop was a vital part of Joseph Edmunds farm life. It was here that he made his family shoes, some furniture, mended the farm tools and implements, shoed the horses, did carpentry work. Syrup was made in the fall from the juice ground from the cane in a big open kettle with a fire underneath.

Hog killing was another vital part of farm life. Together Joseph Edmund and Leila Katherine along with the negro families living on the farm would participate in this chore. Everyone was willing to help as this meant fresh meat was shared with all, and also neighbors since there was limited refrigeration. The hams, shoulders, and sides were cured with salt and later other seasonings. Sausage both fresh and later (as next day) were ground and stuffed. Souse meat, liver pudding also were enjoyed. Lard was cooked from skins and put into five gallon cans for keeping. The smokehouse was used to share the curing and cured meat. Sausage and other meats were kept in an ice box.

There were other facets of farm life. The fields had to be worked, soap was made, wild game killed, chickens raised, cows milked, hogs, mules, and pigs to be tended and taken care of. There was always new life on the farm. Plows and implements, collars for mules, trace chains, leather strips that were used to guide the mules, wagons and the general maintenance and other chores that were required of the farm life.

In the meantime Leila Katherine did the housework, sewed, cared for the children and her house and yard. The family grew and matured. Leila Katherine encouraged all of her children to seek higher education and music. All of the children graduated from college and taught school with the exception of two, and they later educated themselves equivalent to a college education and beyond.

Five children later married and three moved away. Edmund David died in 1915 from Pneumonia. Jennie Lind died in February 1942 of cancer. Both unmarried and buried in Lebanon Cemetery, Plains, Georgia. Joseph Edmund died on October 29, 1939 at the age of 84. Leila Katherine died on February 8, 1940 at the age of 78, both buried in Lebanon Cemetery, Plains, Sumter County, Georgia just a few steps from their farm and home place, their long struggle in the family of man completed.

—*Submitted by Sara B. Paradise*

Boney Wells Bacon and Celestia Morgan Bacon

Wells Bacon born May 2, 1887 died December 6, 1936. Married Celestia Morgan born January 3, 1889 died December 6, 1967. They are both buried in Dawson, Ga.

Children: Adrianna born January 20, 1914, died January 4, 1981 married Ernest Settles of Shellman. There children are:

Lenora born November 18, 1916, died June 4, 1981 married Charles Crutchfield of Americus

Boney Wells born August 12, 1919, died October 23, 1971 married Norma England (Boney and Norma were both killed in a car wreck near Boston, Massachusetts).

Edmund born 1922 died 1925 at the age of three. Buried in Dawson, Ga.

Adrian Sidney born May 8, 1924 died June 3, 2001. Arian married Charlotte Sullivan on August 25, 1950.

For a number of years Mrs. Celestia Bacon ran the Swannee Store in one of the small wooden buildings in downtown Plains. Wells Bacon lost one of his arms in a bread machine sometime in his younger days.

—*Submitted by (no name given)*

Bagwell Family

The Bagwells came to Jamestown Virginia in 1608, just one year after the founding of the colony. The progenitor of the American line was Henry Bagwell who came over from England in the above mentioned year. He was born in 1589 and died between 1659 and 1663. He was elected to the Virginia House of Burgesses in 1629. In 1636 he married Alice Hawkins Stratton. About 200 years passed and a wide gap in the Bagwell genealogy occurred furnishing fertile ground for additional family research.

Chester Bagwell married Sally Nabors or Neighbors. They moved to Bartow County, Georgia from South Carolina. Their children included: William Henry who married Ella Butler; George, married Lee Hubbard; John, married Lou Bradford; Willard, marrie Fannie Stephens; Harley, married Lula Findley; Elgin, married Mary Neal; Mollie, married Marion Fuller; Lou, married Mack Higgins; and Evie never married.

William Henry Bagwell, born December 8, 1848, died August 13, 1922, married Ella Butler born December 6, 1851 and died December 3, 1929. Their children included: Oliver Taylor, Essie, Eula, Cora, Maude, Belle, Louella, and John Henry.

Oliver Taylor Bagwell born August 18, 1875, died June 15, 1955, married Mattie Lou Vaughn, born December 16, 1878, died December 1, 1958. Oliver and Mattie Bagwell moved from Monroe, Georgia to Sumter County as a young couple in the first years of the twentieth century. They settled in the Concord Community and lived in a large white frame house in a grove of oak trees. (The house burned in the 1960's.) Oliver became a farmer owning some 500 acres. Their children included Madge, Henry, Freeman and Magella.

Marriages of these:

Madge married Pete Castleberry, no children. Magella Married John Harris. They had one daughter, Sina Kay Harris. Freeman married Mae Smith. Their children were Ephraim Freeman (E.P.), Betty Blue and Jack Wayne. Henry Lafayette Bagwell, born March 9, 1900, died April 17, 1980, married Floy Howell, born December 18, 1901, on May 23, 1924. Their children were Anne Howell Bagwell born August 17, 1925, and James Emmett Bagwell born March 16,1941.

Anne Howell Bagwell married Millard Franklin Simmons March 18, 1946. They had one son Millard Franklin Simmons, Jr. called "Mill." Mill married Gloria Chavers on June 20, 1970. Mill and Gloria Simmons have two children: Millard Rhett Simmons called "Rhett" and Paige Simmons.

James Emmett Bagwell, Ph.D., a professor at Georgia Southwestern College, married Cynthia Faye Baker of Abbeville, Ga., on June 8, 1980. They have two children James Bradford Bagwell, called "Brad." born May 19, 1981, and Victoria Floy Bagwell, born January 11, 1985.

—*Submitted by Jimmy Bagwell, Plains, Ga.*

The Blanton Family

The Blanton family tradition has taught us that three Blanton brothers came from England to America about the time the Civil War broke out in England in 1642. They migrated from Lancashire, England.

Aaron Morgan was born in Lee, Florida in 1884, died in 1950 in Plains, Georgia. Mr. Blanton and his family moved to Plains in 1940. He was sent here for railroad depot agent.

His wife, Ruby Pearl Rhodes, was born in 1892 in Cuthbert, Georgia and died in 1966 in Plains, Georgia.

They had two children. 1. Sarah Pauline was born in Cuthbert and finished high school in Parrott, Georgia. She had six children. 2. A son, Aaron Loren Blanton was in the 7th grade when his family moved to Plains. He graduated in the class of 1944 with Rosalynn Carter. He enlisted in the Navy and retired with twenty years as an air traffic controller. During his service, he met and married Florence Harris of Webster County. Her parents, William Henry Harris and Willie Lee Cooper of Webster County.

Florence and Loren had two children; a son, James Ellis Blanton II, Ph.D., a professor at the University of South Florida in Tampa, Florida. Ellis was born in Argentina, Newfoundland in 1949. Ellis has one son, Joseph Shawn, and one daughter, Yvonne Faye, born in 1954 in Pensacola, Florida. She graduated from Plains High School in Plains, Georgia in 1972, Medical University in Charleston, South Carolina in medical records. She married Craig Mackey in Buena Vista, Georgia. They have two daughters, Melody and Ginger.

After Loren retired from the Navy, he went to school to be a barber in Columbus for two years. He then moved his family to Plains in 1967 to his parent's home. He bought a building (which is now City Hall) for his barbar shop. He also did work for FAA as an air traffic controller at Albany Airport for twelve years where he retired in 1980. He was on town council. He was Mayor of Plains 1975-1979. After retiring from FAA, he worked for the city. He went to school in Carrollton for water and waste water.

The Blantons are members of Plains Baptist Church. Lorin died in 1989 with cancer at 61. Florence, his wife, has done volunteer work at Palmyra Medical Center for twelve years in Albany, Georgia. She received the Dr. Frist Award of 1999 (volunteer of the year). The family home is located on North Hudson Street In Plains, Georgia.

—*Submitted by Florence Blanton*

Miss Annie Mae Brannen

Miss Annie Mae was an unusual person. Though she never married, she had many children.

She "adopted" you might say, all the town's children and loved them dearly. She worked for the Wise doctors, Sam, Bowman, and Thad. However, when the Plains hospital burned in 1936, and the Wise doctors moved their practice to Americus, Miss Annie Mae took a job in the Plains Post Office as a clerk.

She devoted much of her time, effort and money to the Plains United Methodist Church. For years, she directed the children's program, including Bible school and teaching Sunday school. Many a child learned under her direction and is better for it. She influenced many minds for good.

Miss Annie Mae's parents were Cad Brannen and Victoria Caroline Lassiter Brannen. Miss Annie Mae had one brother, Roy David Brannen who married Bertha Howell. They married in the parlor of the Howell house in 1918 after Roy came home from World War I. Miss Annie Mae lived in the Brannen home place on Paschall Street, now owned by Pat and James Conger who are in the process of restoring it to its former beauty.

—Submitted by Jimmy Bagwell

The Ira Brown Family

Ira Brown moved to Plains in 1940, from Ellaville, Georgia. In June 1942, he married Miss Exie Angry, a native of Plains. During their sixty year marriage, they have seen many changes and are proud of their accomplishments. They farmed from 1942-1970. Then they moved to town and Ira began a thirty year career as a highly successful carpenter. Today, Ira is retired but enjoys good health. Though he is in his eighties, he still leads an active life, finding time to kill hogs and cure meat in the winter and do carpenter work on occasion. Plains people appreciate the Brown family for their leadership in the area and Ira in particular for his sterling character. The Brown children include Fannie, Tom, Albert, Clydie Lee, Nathaniel, Sid, Judy and Gwen. Ira is a legend in his own time. Ira

was famous for saying when giving advice, "Now that's just me talking." but the wise knew that they had better do what he said.

—Submitted by Jimmy Bagwell

The Buchanan Family

Benjamin Buchanan was born about 1754 in South Carolina and died August 1, 1821 in Jasper County, Georgia. His wife was Mary Woods. Benjamin enlisted in the Sixth Regiment South Carolina troops in the American Revolution. On April 6, 1778 he was a corporal. In February 1780 he enlisted in the First Regiment, South Carolina Troops. He was the father of 12 children, the youngest of whom was:

Micajah Buchanan who was born September 29, 1804 in Georgia and died 1873, Sumter County, Georgia. He married Sarah Hamilton Alewine September 13, 1829 in Jasper County Georgia. She was born March 19, 1805 in Georgia and died ca. 1875, Sumter County, Georgia. He came to Sumter County in 1836 and settled on a farm approximately 3 miles west of Plains on Bonds Trail Road (state hwy. 25). He later sold this farm because, according to family tales, the land was heavy clay and difficult to cultivate with the implements of that time. He died at his farm on Myrtle Springs Road and is buried there in an unmarked grave. He was the father of six children, the eldest of whom was:

Anderson Benjamin Buchanan who was born in Jasper County, Georgia June 16, 1832 and died February 13, 1898 in Sumter County Georgia. He married Nancy Amanda Williams, daughter of Judge Andrew J. and Elizabeth Darden Williams September 20, 1855. She was born in Sumter County January 26, 1838 and died May 14, 1909. Both are buried in Concord United Methodist Church Cemetery, Highway 45, Sumter County, Georgia. Anderson Benjamin and his three brothers were enlisted in the "Zollicofer Rifles", Co. B. 10 Battalion

Georgia Infantry, enlisting at Americus, Georgia on May 15, 1862. He served until the end of the war and is shown on a Roll of Prisoners of War May 8, 1865, Athens, Georgia. While he was serving in the Confederate Army, in 1863, he lost 3 children to dyptheria, in the space of one month. In 1877 he lost 2 daughters to dyptheria. Surviving children were Anderson Washington, who taught school at Concord and Shiloh and served as Justice of the Peace for the Concord district for many years; Lillian R.; Jefferson Clay; India Hill; Minnie Gordon and:

Joseph Micajah Buchanan was born April 20, 1866 in Sumter County and died March 6, 1928 in Sumter County, Georgia. He married Martha A. Powell January 7, 1890 at the "haunted house" on the road to Lebanon Cemetery, which was the home of her sister, Mrs. Ed Stewart. Martha A. Powell was born February 11, 1868 in Marion County, Georgia and died May 10, 1945. She was the daughter of Confederate veteran John Edward Powell and Nancy A. Dodson (see Dodson family). Joseph and Martha Buchanan are buried in Concord United Methodist Cemetery. Their children were: Nannie Ruth, born December 13, 1891, died November 28, 1942; married Earl Bass Sr. of Leslie. Buried at Mt. Zion Cemetery, Sumter County, Georgia.

Benjamin Powell, born March 5, 1898; died December 2, 1965 and

Brooks Edward Buchanan was born April 16, 1891 in Sumter County and died November 28, 1942 in Sumter County, Georgia. He married Johnnie Ethel Woods May 2, 1913 in Crisp County, Georgia. She was the daughter of John Woods and Etna Mozell Hall and was born May 9, 1893 in Dooly County, Georgia and died May 20, 1980 in Sumter County, Georgia. Both are buried in Concord United Methodist Cemetery. They had the following children:

Robert Lee born January 11, 1916; died December 22, 1979. He married Sarah L. Countryman and they had six children.

Brooks Edward born February 17, 1917. He married Susie Bell Halstead and they had 4 children.

Marion Stewart Buchanan born January 23, 1920; died October 21, 1983. He married Virginia Mae Brock. They had 4 children.

David Clay Buchanan born March 4, 1924; died August 9, 1988. He Married Eva Mae Stewart. They had one child.

Joe Monroe Buchanan Sr. was born February 9, 1914 and died February 10, 1960. He married Ruby Texas Lamb (see Lamb family) November 21, 1932 in Sumter County, Georgia. She was born November 14, 1912 in Dooly County Georgia and died November 11, 1982 in Americus. She attended Plains High School. She was the daughter of Bill Hubbard Lamb and Dora Holloway. Both are buried at Concord United Methodist Cemetery. They had the following children:

Albert Maynard born September 22, 1934; died May 19, 1936.

Carrie Earline, born April 4, 1937. She was valedictorian of Plains High School class of 1955. She attended Georgia Southwestern College and received her B.S. from West Georgia College and her M.S. from Georgia Southern College. She received her Ed.S. from Georgia Southwestern College. She taught school for 39 ½ years, 36 ½ of which were in the Americus City system. She was married, on June 3, 1973, at Calvary Episcopal Church in Americus to Jack F. Cox (see Cox family). They have 1 child, a son, Carey Buchanan Cox born September 14, 1975 in Americus. He was valedictorian of the class of 1993 at Americus High School and graduated from the University of Georgia with the degree of Doctor of Pharmacy in May 2002.

Joe Monroe Jr., born July 3, 1939. He graduated from Plains High School. He married Brenda Iris Toms, daughter of Claude and Effie Wellons Toms. They have the following children:

Tammy Sue born April 1, 1965. She married David Philip White, born September 20, 1960. They have the following children:

Donna Lynn, born August 10, 1968. Married Jamie Compton, born January 27, 1974.

Joseph Colquitt Buchanan born April 20, 1942. He married Frances Lucille Hubbard. She was born May 7, 1944. Joseph graduated from Plains High School. They have the following children: Sherri Layne, born February 20, 1963 and Terri Jayne, born February 20, 1963.

—Submitted by Earline Cox

William Alton Carter Family

William Alton Carter was married to Annie Laurie Gay. They had two sons, Hugh Alton and Donnel. Annie Laurie died in 1940, and he married Mabel Elizabeth (Betty) Jennings.

Hugh Alton Carter (b. 13 Aug. 1920, d. 24 June 1999) married Ruth Godwin (b. 25 Jan 1921) on Dec. 25, 1941. Their children were:

I. Hugh Alton Carter, Jr. (b. Sept. 29, 1942) in Americus, GA. He married Glenna Garrett on May 19, 1979. Their children were:
a. Mary Elise Ruth Carter, b. Dec. 22, 1982.
b. Kathleen Elizabeth Carter, b. June 2, 1987.
c. Emily Garret Carter, b. Sept. 7, 1988.

II. Laurie Gay Carter, b. Oct. 23, 1946. She married Thomas Edwin Tharpe on June 30, 1968 at Plains Baptist Church. Their children were:
a. Carter Edwin Tharpe, b. Sept. 1, 1972. He married Joy Purvis of Valdosta, June 12, 1999.

b. Ansley Sanborn Tharpe, b. Jan. 9, 1976.
c. Katherine Warren Tharpe, b. July 18, 1977.

III. Connie Carter, b. Dec. 28, 1952. She married Clarence Leon Collins, Jr., on June 26, 1976 at Plains Baptist Church. Their child was:
a. Carolyn Jennings Collins, b. Aug. 18, 1978.
—Submitted by Connie Carter Collins

Carter Family

Wiley Carter (1798-1864) moved to a farm north of Plains of Dura from what had been a Quaker community called Wrightsboro, about 30 miles west of Augusta. He was a descendant of Thomas Carter, Sr. who settled in Virginia in 1637, and Wiley's wife was the granddaughter of Thomas Ansley, who built the Old Rock House near Thomson, Georgia.

Wiley's fourth son, Littleberry Walker Carter, farmed the land that later became the Souther Field airport. His second son was William Archibald Carter, who moved to Rowena, Georgia, where he owned and operated a farm, sawmills, and a cotton gin. When he was killed in 1903, his wife Nina moved to Plains with her children, Ethel, Alton, Lula, Earl, and Jeanette. They lived in the house just south of the Methodist Church, and bought land in Webster County after selling the Rowena property.

Ethel married veterinarian Jack Slappey, had two sons, Linton and Willard, and moved into the Carter home after the death of Nina in 1939. Willard became a veterinarian and moved to Fayetteville, N.C. He married Helene Mayo, and their four sons were Jack Mays, James Willard, Donnel Carter, and William Fleming. Lula married Will Fleming and lived in Birmingham, Alabama, where her husband published the Southern Baptist Convention literature. Jeanette's husband was Wade Lowery, who was a farmer and managed large dairies in Florida. They had one daughter, Nina Pratt.

Alton was 16 years old when the family moved to Plains and, as sole breadwinner for the family, got a job as clerk for Oliver-McDonald Co. for $25 a month. In 1909 he started his own business, Plains Mercantile Co., which expanded rapidly. Alton was elected to the town council in 1918 and became mayor two years later. Except for six years as county commissioner, he served as mayor until 1954, during which time his monthly salary increased from $1.50 to $2. The Plains Bank failed in 1926, and Alton provided banking services to the community until 1965. He began trading mules and horses in 1938, and eventually became one of the largest dealers in Georgia. Alton married Annie Laurie Gay, from Cuthbert, and they had two sons, Donnel and Hugh.

As a widower, Alton married Betty Jennings. Donnel was a graduate of Georgia Southwestern College and the University of Georgia and a life long newspaper editor and publisher. He married Carolyn McKenzie, and was a U. S. Army officer in World War II, serving overseas in India and China. He was city editor of the Atlanta Journal, joined Dow Jones & Company in 1959 for assignments in New York and Washington, and in 1971 became executive editor of the Macon Telegraph and News. He was next publisher of the Lexington (Ky.)Herald-Leader and later corporate vice president of Knight-Ridder Newspapers, supervising 18 of its daily newspapers throughout the United States.

After being educated at Riverside Academy near Gainesville, Earl served as a grocery clerk, operated the family's farm in Webster County, and then established his own grocery business on the east end of Main Street. He moved to the Archery community in 1928, and concentrated on agriculture. Earl served on the county school board, the hospital authority, and in the state legislature.

Earl married Lillian Gordy, from Richland, who came to Plains to train as a registered nurse and, late in life, served in the Peace Corps in India. They had four children, Jimmy, Gloria, Ruth, and Billy. Jimmy attended the U.S. Naval Academy, served in the submarine force, and returned to Plains after his father's death. He operated Carter's Warehouse, was elected to the Georgia Senate in 1962, as governor in 1970, and as President of the United States in 1976. He married Rosalynn Smith, and their children were John William, James Earl III, Donnel Jeffrey, and Amy Lynn.

Gloria married Walter Guy Spann, from Webster County, and lived on a farm near Plains. They were avid motorcyclists. Gloria had one son, William Hardy.

Ruth married Robert Stapleton, a veterinarian, who joined Willard Slappey as a partner in Fayetteville, N.C. Their children were Lynn, Scott, Patti, and Michael.

Billy served in the U.S. Marines, operated Carter's Warehouse and his famous service station on Church Street, and was later involved in the manufacture and sale of modular homes. He married Sybil Spires, and their children were Kim, Jana, William (Buddy), Marle, Mandy, and Earl.
—*Submitted by Jimmy Carter*

Chambliss Family

The Chamblisses of Sumter County are apparently all descendants of Jesse Chambliss, born 1793 in North Carolina, died 1878 and buried at Shiloh Church cemetery.

Residing in Jones County, on April 4, 1835, he purchased 202 ½ acres in Sumter County, formerly the 26th District of Lee County. According to 1840 census records he was a resident of Sumter County with a wife and nine minor children, six being male offspring.

After carefully checking ages of Jesse's children on census records of 1830, 1840, 1850, and 1860, and locating marked graves in Shiloh Church

Cemetery, it appears the lineage of Jesse and wife Nancy include the following:

1. William 1822-1901, married Eliza 1843-1922. Children: Joseph, William, Melissa Ann, Jesse, Nancy Ann, Needham, Lurafay.

2. John 1820-1873, married Lucy Chappell 1828-1882. Children: A.) Mary, B.) John Jr. 1852-1883, children: 1). Dr. John Wade Chambliss children: a) J.W. and b) Ross and 2). Floyd Chambliss; C) Joseph, D) Hardin, E) Mark, F)Rollin, children: 1) Florrie, 2) Louis, 3) Rollin, Jr., 4) Nadine, G)Charlie, H) Ben, I)Homer,children: 1)Mark, children a) Everett, b) Valerie, 2) Virgil, children, a)Faye, b)Homer, 3) Lucy, 4) Eleanor married Estes Forrest, children a) Bill and b) John; J) Mary.

3. Andrew 1832-?, married Millie 1828-? Children: John, Lucinda, James, Thomas, Frances, Amanda, Paschal, Adam.

4. Jesse 1820-? married Matilda 1835-? Children: Vanne, Frances, Sarah.

5. Wiley 1833-?, married Mary Ann. Children: Nancy Ann, Wiley, Isaiah. Sometime between 1860-1865 the elder of Jesse Chambliss married Eliza Gamage Griffin, widow of Thomas Griffin with two sons, Fletcher and William.

My grandfather, Jesse L. Chambliss was born to this union February 17, 1865. In 1885 Jesse L. Chambliss married Julia Franklin Stubbs of Macon County. He had inherited the home place located in the 28th District of Sumter County upon the death of his father in 1878. Children of Jesse L. and Julia were:

1. Anne Elizabeth married Dr. W.H. Houston. Children: Elizabeth married Felix Davis, Carl, Billy, Julia married Charles Grow.

2. Jesse married Eunie Story. Children: Jesse George, Jr. married Dolly Mitchell.

3. William Lee married Ethel Henderson. Children: Children: Mildred married Palmer Cheves.

4. Clifford married Jewel Jordan. Children: Cliff, Jr., Davis, Lorraine and Floraine (twins).

From all records the Chambliss men living in the 1800's were farmers. At the time of his death in 1911 my grandfather owned several thousand acres of farm and woodlands in the northeast area of Sumter County adjacent to Flint River.

The homeplace remained in the Chambliss family until 1950 or thereabouts when Mildred's uncle, Jesse G. Chambliss, sold to Floyd Frazier. The original home is at least 100 years old and was the birthplace of the children of Jesse L. and Julia. I was born and reared in this home and have many happy memories of her life in Sumter County.

—*Submitted by Mildred Chambliss Cheves*

James E. A. Channell Family

James Edwin Augustus Channell was born September 23, 1871 in Barbour County, Alabama. His parents were James Turner Channell (1825-1897) and Caroline O'Connor (1846-1885). James was of English and French descent. Caroline was from Country Kerry Ireland and descended from the early kings of Ireland. James Turner traced his line to his great-great grandfather who was the Archbishop of Canterbury.

Prior to the outbreak of the Civil War, James Turner was a planter of wealth and influence on a large plantation near Lumpkin, Georgia. At the outbreak of the war he enlisted and fought for 4 years. He was Captain under Stonewall Jackson, later under Major General Hooker. After the war, on account of certain losses due to the war, he returned to his old home in Texas, settled on a large ranch in Cass County and continued farming until his death.

James T. and Caroline had six children, three were born in Barbour County, Alabama: George (1867-1924), Anna (1869-1948), and James Edwin (1871-August 24, 1939). When Ed was three years old, they moved by covered wagon to Texas. Here James became a farmer and rancher to be near other relatives. After settling in Texas three more children were born: Robert (1878-1971), Eugenia (1882), Caroline Sophronia (1885).

When Edwin grew to manhood, he was educated at Texas University. On January 8, 1908, he married Eva Rainey from Ellaville, (Schley County) Georgia. Eva was the daughter of Charlie M. Rainey and Henrietta Battle Rainey. Edwin had met Eva six years earlier while she was on a visit to Texas.

James Edwin was ordained as a Methodist minister in Quitman, Georgia, December 1908 and served with loyal devotion for 29 years to many churches including Plains, Concord, Rylander and New Point. He retired to live in Ellaville among friends and relatives. He died August 24, 1939 and is buried in the Ellaville cemetery.

One child was born to Ed and Eva, a daughter, Henrietta Caroline who married James Caraway Webb on December 30, 1937. Their children were James Channell Webb (J. C. III born September 3, 1939) and Warner Baxter Webb (born September 7, 1942).

J. C. III married Donna Tanner on October 6, 1962. Their children were Helena born September 21, 1964; Veronica born March 4, 1966; and Patricia born October 11, 1970. They were later divorced in 1975. On February 26, 1977, J.C. III married Linda Reedy from Tupelo, Mississippi, who had two daughters: Lisa born September 17, 1964 and Lori born November 29, 1971. Lisa was killed in an accident on April 5, 1988.

Warner married Patricia Hoyal from Thomaston, Georgia on May 5, 1967. They had two sons: Warner Baxter Webb II (born August 24, 1981) and James Clark Webb (J.C.IV) born December 2, 1982. This couple was divorced August 24, 1987. Warner later married Debra Castleberry on December 30, 1988. Debra had two sons Christopher Castleberry born December 9, 1976 and Nicholas Castleberry born September 1, 1978. Warner and Debra had three sons, William born October 15, 1990; Robert born February 5, 1992, and Travis born June 15, 1993.

The greatest tribute to Ed Channell was an editorial in the newspaper after his death entitled, "His Life Literally Introduced People to God".
—*Submitted by Caroline Channell Webb*

The Family of Thomas Chappell

THOMAS CHAPPELL: eldest son of John and Nanny Chappell was born in Sussex County, Va. on January 23, 1761. Between 1770 and 1785 he removed with his father and brothers from Granville Co., N.C. to the state of Georgia and settled in what was then, probably, Washington County, but in that part which afterward became Hancock County. In 1797 he married Lavinia Wheelus, a widow, whose maiden name was Cox. He moved to Twiggs County, Ga. Where he died September 1, 1836 at the age of seventy-five. He was the father of five children: Nancy, Bethena, Mahala, Joseph John, and Thomas Simmons.

THOMAS SIMMONS CHAPPELL: was born in Hancock Co., Ga. June 24, 1801. He married Ruth Nelson in 1821 in Hancock County and died in Twiggs County, Ga. On July 29, 1861 and his wife died on May 24, 1874. They had the following children: Susan E., Alexander, Sarah Jane, William, Nancy, Roxie Ann, and Louise Matilda.

ALEXANDER CHAPPELL: was born December 28, 1823 and died February 28, 1905. He is buried in Lebanon Cemetery, Plains, Ga. He was an early member of Plains Baptist Church. He was married 3 times. His first wife was Eliza Bragg and they had 2 children Rufus and Thomas. His second wife was Georgia Ann Hawkins who was born September 22, 1829 and died May 21, 1891. They were married in Sumter County, Ga. On October 23, 1849. They had the following children: Sallie married Armsted Dodson (see Dodson family); John Alexander (more later);

William, Joseph, Fanny, Edwin, Ida, Lon, Homer, and Georgia.

His third wife was Emma E. Mays, a widow and they had no children

JOHN ALEXADER CHAPPELL: child of Alexander Chappell and Georgia Ann Hawkins was born April 4, 1852 and died July 13, 1913. He was married February 24, 1876 to Eliza Caroline Dodson (see Dodson family) who was born February 28, 1856 and died May 31, 1942.

RUFUS CHAPPELL: child of John Alexander and Eliza Carolina Dodson was born June 20, 1896 in Marion Co., Ga. He married Callie Bertha Israel on December 25, 1928. She was born August 17, 1904 in Sumter Co., Ga. Their children were: Mary Jane and Sandra Bertha Chappell.

MARY JANE CHAPPELL: was born September 9, 1934. She was married August 2, 1953 to James William Short who was born September 19, 1930. Their children are:

RUFUS WILLIAM SHORT: born October 7, 1957; married November 14, 1975 to Debra Ann Cochran. Children: Rufus William Short Jr., born March 9, 1979; Andrea Jane Short born October 27, 1985.

JAMES GLENN SHORT: born September 24, 1962.

SHIRLEY JANE SHORT: born December 7, 1963; died June 13, 1972.

SANDRA BERTHA CHAPPELL: second child of Rufus Chappell and Callie Bertha Israel was born April 25, 1939; married June 1963 to James Oscar Lloyd, born May 1, 1938 (divorced). Their children are:

JAMES ALAN LLOYD: born December 8, 1969

GREGORY STUART LLOYD: born August 3, 1974.

—Submitted by Jane Chappell Short

John Bartow Clark Family

John Bartow Clark (sometimes spelled Clarke) was born in Webster County, Ga., on Oct. 11, 1861. His sisters were Kate, Mattie, Penelope, Ellie and Mariah. His brothers were Thomas, Lewis, William Henry and Ed.

Mary Eliza Spann also was born in Webster County on Sept. 1, 1864. She had four sisters – Bettie, Josephine, Della and Nannie. She had three brothers – John, William and George.

John Bartow Clark and Mary Eliza Spann were married on Dec. 19, 1886. They began their home living in the country outside of Plains. After the first four children were born they moved to Plains and lived on the corner of Main and Church streets. The last two children were born here. The family was supported by income from farming and the buying and selling of horses and mules. Of special importance in rearing their family were spiritual development and education. All the children were members of Plains Baptist Church.

Mary died on Nov. 13, 1920 after an illness which at that time was undiagnosed, but later medical knowledge has analyzed her symptoms as those of diabetes.

John lived 10 more years. In 1927, he married Mrs. Charles Phillips, sold the family home in Plains and moved to Columbus. He died of complications from a gall bladder attack and pneumonia on Sept. 13, 1930.

John and Mary Spann Clark are buried at Lebanon Cemetery in Plains.

Their six children were:

1) Amise Elizabeth Clark (b. July 1, 1888 d. March 17, 1969)
2) Berta Will Clark (b. Aug. 27, 1890 d. July 7, 1963)
3) Carol Delevan Clark (b. Sept. 1, 1893 d. Jan. 17, 1975)
4) Lucy Kate Clark (b. April 15, 1896 d. Dec. 28, 1957)

5) Mary Clark (b. Aug. 24, 1899 d. Jan. 4, 1992)

6) John Bartow Clark, Jr. (b. March 18, 1905 d. Jan. 4, 1970)

Amise, the oldest child, attended Monroe College. She later took a position teaching school. She married William Edgar Carter on June 29, 1911 and joined him in farming the Carter family land outside Americus. After rearing three children there, she and Ed gave up farming and retired to live in Panama City, Fla. Ed died in Panama City in 1964 and Amise in 1969 after she had a brief hospitalization for cancer of the liver. Amise and Ed are buried at Oak Grove Cemetery in Americus. Their three children:

A) William Edgar Carter, Jr. (b. Sept. 4, 1912 d. Sept. 1992). He married Ruth Kauffman on March 28, 1945. One child: 1A) Elsie Marie Carter (b. June 15, 1948)

B) John Clark Carter (b. April 9, 1915 d. Jan. 25, 1994). He married Bessie Mathews on March 29, 1946. Two children: 1A) Wayne Clark Carter (b. Oct. 30, 1949) and 2A) John Ronald Carter (b. Sept. 26, 1951)

C) Martha Carter (b. Dec. 18, 1916). She married William Archie Hargrove, Jr. on June 12, 1947. Two children: 1A) William A. Hargrove III (b. June 5, 1949) and 2A) James Edgar Hargrove (b. Dec. 9, 1950)

Berta Will, the second child, also attended Bessie Tift College (formerly Monroe) to study music. Since her interest was music, she discontinued her study at Tift and studied piano privately in Americus. Later she taught piano in Plains and kept the family home during her mother's illness and after her death. When the family home was sold, she went to Macon and took a business training course. She then took a job with Dessau Realty Co. where she worked until her retirement. After a lengthy struggle with Parkinson's disease, she died. Berta Will is buried next to her parents at Lebanon Cemetery in Plains.

Carol, the third daughter, wanted to study nursing, but gave in to her parents' wish she study something else. She attended Bessie Tift College for her first year and then transferred to Shorter College. The summer after her sophomore year she married Charles Elmo Crook, on July 29, 1912. They lived in Macon. Elmo died in 1939 of a heart attack. Carol remained in Macon and shared her home with Berta Will. Carol died from injuries received when she was struck by a car as she crossed the street in front of her home on Hardeman Avenue. She is buried next to Elmo at Macon Memorial Park in Macon. They had one child:

A) Mary Clark Crook (b. March 11, 1914 d. April 26, 1998). She married Arthur Griffith, Jr. on Feb. 9, 1940. Five children:

1A) Carol Barnes Griffith (b. March 9, 1941)

2A) Arthur Griffith III (b. April 24, 1943 d. Dec. 6, 1996)

3A) Derrelle Barnes Griffith (b. Jan. 23, 1947)

4A) Mary Ann Griffith (b. May 20, 1952)

5A) Marcella Louise Griffith (b. Feb. 1, 1955)

Lucy Kate, the fourth daughter, graduated from Bessie Tift College and taught school. She married Harper Butterworth, a pharmacist, and went to live in Atlanta. When Harper contracted TB, she continued to run the family drugstore for a while with the help of their two sons. She was diagnosed as having cancer, and after years of fighting and 13 operations she became its victim in 1957. She is buried at Westview Cemetery in Atlanta. Their two children:

A) Henry Harper Butterworth, Jr. (b. Dec. 17, 1927). He married first Raymond Patricia Byrd. Three children:

1A) Susan Kay Butterworth (b. 1957)

2A) Henry Harper Butterworth III (b. 1958)

3A) Pamela Ann Butterworth (b. 1962)

He married second Evelyn Ghetty. No children.

B) John Clark Butterworth (b. April 6, 1930). He married Elizabeth Ann Pope on Aug. 25, 1951. Two children:

1A) John Clark Butterworth, Jr. (b. Nov. 29, 1956)

2A) Sherri Lynn Butterworth (b. May 22, 1964)

Mary, the youngest of the five daughters, graduated from Bessie Tift College and also taught. She married Judson Byard West, a pharmacist, on July 13, 1924 and soon moved to Florida. After living in Rockledge, Fla., they settled in St. Augustine. Later they bought the St. George Pharmacy and operated it until Judson's death and her retirement. She died in 1992 at age 92. They are buried at Evergreen Cemetery in St. Augustine. They had two children:

A) Judson Byard West, Jr. (b. May 29, 1928). He married Annelle McCartha on June 23, 1951. Five children:

1A) Samuel Judson West (b. May 9, 1952)

2A) George Timothy West (b. July 27, 1953)

3A) Carol Rozanne West (b. July 24, 1955)

4A) Paul Vernon West (b. Jan. 17, 1958)

5A) Deborah Lee West (b. March 8, 1963)

B) Mary Carol West (b. April 1, 1932). She married Benjamin Prince Bagwell on Aug. 17, 1957. No children.

John Bartow Clark, Jr. attended Auburn University after graduating from Plains High School. He graduated as an electrical engineer and got a job with General Electric. He married Eleanor "Nellie" Boston on Sept. 18, 1926. After working in several different cities for G.E., he was hired by the city of Jacksonville, Fla., to work with its power company. After completing 26 years in this position, he retired and organized his own Clark Electrical Co. Five years after surviving a severe heart attack and developing diabetes, he died of a second heart attack while piloting his boat on a Sunday afternoon. He is buried in Oaklawn Cemetery in Jacksonville. He and Nellie had four children:

A) Shirley A. Clark (b. April 28, 1928). She married Arthur H. Peck. Three children:

1A) Arthur Hubert Peck, Jr. (b. Sept. 8, 1948)

2A) Brenda Sue Peck (b. Feb. 15, 1951)

3A) Warren Bartow Peck (b. June 14, 1955)

B) Mary Elizabeth Clark (b. Oct. 7, 1929). She married Wilbur Edmund "Bill" Daly. Two children:

1A) Robert Clark Daly (b. Aug. 16, 1955)

2A) Mary Ann Daly (b. May 30, 1958)

C) Eleanor Clark (b. April 1934). She married first Jim Crutchfield. Three children:

1A) Mark Crutchfield

2A) Dan Crutchfield

3A) Carol Crutchfield

She married second Paul Rosselle. No children.

D) John Boston Clark (b. Feb. 9, 1940). He married Constance Mae Pabst on Feb. 20, 1965. Two children:

1A) John Bartow Clark III (b. July 14, 1968)

2A) Judson Boston Pabst Clark (b. Dec. 30, 1972)

—*Submitted by Mary Carol Bagwell of St. Augustine, Fla.*

Rachel Idlette Clark

Rachel Idlette Clark was born April 2, 1890 and died March 9, 1986. She was a member of New Lebanon Baptist Church and is buried at the New Lebanon Cemetery south of Plains. She was born in Sumter County, Georgia to the parentage of Tamer Holt and John Idlette. Rachel lived her entire life in Sumter County. At an early age, Rachel joined New Lebanon Baptist Church serving the church faithfully until her death. Due to this, she was given the honor of being named as the "Mother of the church".

Rachel's first husband was Sonny Boy Williams and they had a daughter, Bertha Mae Williams. Bertha was born November 2, 1907, died February 25, 1989 and was married to Nannie Ross. Bertha and Nannie did not have any birth children but had one godson, George Angry of Smithville,

Georgia. They raised George as one of their own. Bertha was a member of Bethlehem Baptist Church serving actively for many years. She is buried next to her beloved church in the Bethlehem Cemetery.

Rachel later married Jack Clark. They lived and worked on the Earl Carter farm in Archery. The house they lived in is now part of the Jimmy Carter National Historic Site's Boyhood Farm. Jimmy Carter has fond memories of Jack and Rachel and has written about the Clarks in several books explaining how they helped shape his life. Today, as you visit the Clark home, you can sense the love and admiration the community had for this hard working couple. A taped message by Jimmy Carter plays in the small, sparsely furnished Clark house, telling of the lifestyles of farm life during the 1930's and the special memories he has of time spent with the Clarks.

After Earl Carter sold the farm in Archery in the 1940's, the Clarks would eventually move to Plains living in a public housing unit in Plains. Rachel is strongly remembered by those in the community as a strong Christian lady who instilled goodness in those who had the pleasure of knowing her.

—*Submitted by Annette Wise*

Coker Family

In 1843, brothers Henry, John and William Coker moved to Sumter County, Georgia from Upson County. They purchased adjoining farms at Plains of Dura, near the intersection of the Ellaville Road (Route 45) and Green Store (Bob Dodson) Road (just north of the current town of Plains). They were among the first settlers of the community.

These brothers were the sons of Issac Coker and Nancy Daniel Coker, who had moved from North Carolina to Elbert County, Georgia prior to 1790. Issac was a Revolutionary War veteran from Chatham County, NC, the son of Joseph and Mildred

Coker. Issac Coker's family moved from Elbert County to Henry County, Georgia in the late 1820's. Following Issac's death in 1833, two of his sons - James and Elisha - remained in Henry County, while younger sons Henry, John and William left to seek their fortune in South Georgia.

Henry Coker, born in Elbert County in 1797, was the oldest of the Coker brothers that settled in Plains. He married Nepsey Wilson, and together they had six daughters - Nancy, Rebecca, Wiley, Elizabeth, Orphy Jane, and Louisa - and three sons - Issac P., James F., and William H. Coker. Henry Coker died in 1863 and Nepsey Coker died sometime after 1879. They are probably buried in a Coker graveyard that appears to be located within the 2 acres of land ceded by John Coker to the New Hope Universalist Church in 1855—later known as the "Devil's Half Acre."

John Coker, born in Elbert County in 1800, was married to Nancy Ballenger. They had one daughter, Martha Ann, and six sons - Charles W., William B.C., Francis M., Andrew J., John M. and David G. "Tink" Coker. John Coker died in 1855, and is buried in Oak Grove Cemetery in Americus. His house still stands today, having been wonderfully restored and maintained by Clarence and Ann Dodson.

William Coker, born in Elbert County in 1805, was married to Sarah Buckner. They had two daughters - Elizabeth and Lucy - and three sons - John W., Francis M. and Pleasant H. Coker. William Coker was a Justice of the Peace for Sumter County, and died in 1891.

The Coker families were among those that helped to establish the Plains Methodist Church. Ten sons of the Coker brothers served in the Confederate Army, most enlisting in the 11th Georgia (Sumter) Artillery Battalion. Two of these sons — Henry's son William Henry Coker and John's son Andrew Jackson Coker — died of disease in Virginia during the war. Another of Henry's sons, Issac Paul Coker, was in a Confederate hospital on sick roll near end the war and appears to have died shortly after his return home. John M. Coker, another son of the elder John Coker, was wounded at Kennesaw Mountain.

John Coker's son Francis Marion Coker served as Senior Lieutenant/Adjutant in the 11th Georgia Artillery Battalion. Highly educated, he was among Sumter County's leading citizens before and after the Civil War. A resident of Americus, he was one of the county's first bankers, serving as the local agent for the Bank of Savannah. He died in 1905, and is buried in Oak Grove Cemetery.

James Franklin Coker was the only son of Henry Coker to survive the Civil War. Born March 12, 1836 in Upson County, Georgia, he first married Martha Butler in Sumter County on December 23, 1858. Their only child, James Anderson Coker was born October 25, 1859. Martha, however, died just two weeks later on November 8 and the infant child survived less than nine months, dying on July 9, 1860.

Having lost a wife and child, a 25-year-old James F. Coker enlisted as a private in the "Sumter Flying Artillery" in July 1861. He served for the duration of the war, working as a teamster and seeing action in the unit's major battles: Dranesville, South Mountain, Sharpsburg, Fredericksburg, Salem Church, Gettysburg, Spotsylvania, North Anna River, Petersburg and Appomattox Station.

After the war, he returned home to Plains. His father and brothers all dead, he assumed responsibility for the family farm which occupied the balance of his life. On December 12, 1866 he married Sarah Ann Jane Walters, the oldest daughter of Seaborn and Sarah Pullen Walters. This marriage produced seven children - Willis Barnum (b 1867), William Bartow (b 1868), Dora Joline (b 1870), Thaddeus Bee (b 1871), Belle Boyd (b 1874), Maggie Louise (b 1876) and Effie Dessolee Coker (b 1878).

On November 9, 1883, Sarah Walters Coker died. Just over five years later, on January 28, 1889,

James F. Coker took a third wife, Mary Emma Belew Cosby. Born in 1860, she was from Schley County and the widow of J. B. Cosby who had died in 1881. She had two sons from her first marriage, Willam Belew (b 1878) and James Franklin Cosby (b 1879). After their marriage, James and Mary Emma Coker resided on the original Coker farm north of Plains, and parented four additional children, Ethel Velona (b 1889), Janie Mabel (b 1891), James Bradford (b 1894) and Mary Ida (b 1897). The final child, Mary Ida Coker, died February 27, 1898 at the age of only five months, and is buried in the family plot at Magnolia Springs.

James Franklin Coker died on June 15, 1899. He was buried next to his second wife Sarah in Magnolia Springs Cemetery outside Plains. Within a few years of his death, his widow Mary Emma sold the Coker farm and moved to Mitchell County along with her children. The older children of James F. Coker (from his marriage to Sarah Walters) were adults at the time of their father's death.

The second son, William Bartow Coker had died of typhoid fever in June 1889 at the age of 21. At the time, he was working as a clerk in the store of his cousin John Coker, and lived in the home of his Uncle John Walters. He is buried in Magnolia Springs Cemetery.

The other sons both left Sumter County, choosing to seek a better way of life. Willis Barnum Coker moved to Jacksonville, Florida, and worked in the printing business. He married Jessie Clara leBoeuf Davis in 1887, and they had four children - Lura, Nellie, Frank Vickery and Willis Beta Coker. He died in 1956. Thaddeus Bee "Beta" Coker trained as a typesetter in Macon before moving on to Pittsburgh and eventually settled in Baltimore, Maryland. He married Rachel Weeks, and they had two children - Robert W. and Margaret Jane Coker. He also died in 1956.

The four daughters of the Coker-Walters marriage, however, all married local Sumter County men. Dora Coker married Henry Williams in 1886 and had two sons (Robert and Lewis), but moved to Oklahoma shortly after son Robert died as a child in 1892. Effie Coker married William White Argo in 1897. They had several children, but she died in childbirth in 1905. She is buried in Coker family plot at Magnolia Springs.

Belle Coker married Ross Eugene Pilcher in 1892. They had seven children — Clifford, Harvey Lee, Milton, Ross, Bertha Mae, Lura and Dora Belle Pilcher. Belle Coker Pilcher died in 1938. Maggie Coker married Thomas M. Jones in 1893. They had four children - Arthur, Linwood, Thaddeus and Bertha. Maggie Coker Jones died in 1956. The Pilcher and Jones children grew up in Sumter County, and many of their descendants continue to live there today.

The youngest son of James Franklin Coker - James Bradford Coker ("J.B." or "Jim Brad") - was my grandfather. Although he left Plains at a very young age, he returned often to visit his older half-brothers and half-sisters and their families. Raised by his widowed mother in Camilla, Georgia, he, like his older brothers, eschewed the tough farming life of rural South Georgia. Enlisting in the U.S. Navy in 1916, he served for 30 years. A veteran of both World War I and World War II, he also participated in various naval actions in Central America in the 1920's. He married Maria Elizabeth Sanchez in 1929 and had three children - Louise, James B. Jr. and William. He retired from the Navy in 1946 and settled in Jacksonville, Florida. He died September 1, 1961.

—*Submitted by J. Bradford Coker III Columbia, Maryland*

Coker History

It is thought that the Cokers came from Oxford, Devonshire, England to Virginia in the late 1600's, then to Charleston, South Carolina, then to North Carolina. Henry Coker arrived in Plains of Dura with brothers John and William Coker in 1842.

They lived on Highway 45 originally. Ann Dodson moved the house to the Bob Dodson Road which was her country home. Henry Coker, born and died some time between 1862 and 1868, married Nepsey Coker, born 1811. They had nine children including:

(a.) James Franklin Coker, born March 12, 1836 and died June 15, 1899, married Sarah Ann Walters December 12, 1866, born January 24, 1836 and died November 9, 1883.

One of seven children was:

(a.) Maggie Louise Coker, born May 4, 1876 and died April 8, 1956, married Thomas Marion Jones January 15, 1893, born February 22, 1858 and died August 9, 1934.

Second of their four children was:

(a.) Walter Linwood Jones, born August 21, 1895 and died November 30, 1975, married Zera Alberta Smith, born April 8, 1896 and died March 11, 1980.

Third of their four children:

(a.) Morgan Howard Jones, born August 28, 1929 and married Dollie Rae Bridges September 13, 1952, born March 31, 1934. Their only child: Lynn Jones, born April 9, 1957, married Ricky Leon Hudson September 29, 1957, born March 29, 1957. Their only child: Jennifer Lynn Hudson, born November 1, 1980.

James Franklin Coker served in Sumter Battalion Confederate Army through the whole war without being wounded, but never received a promotion. He returned to Plains, Georgia as the only son who survived the war. He inherited the farm of his father, Henry.

—*Submitted by (no name given)*

"Miss Julia" Coleman

"Miss Julia", as Plainsites fondly knew her, was a lady of inordinate grace, charm, and intellect. As Superintendent of Plains High School, she had many noteworthy accomplishments. She served on the first statewide textbook selection committee. Also, in the mid 1950s, she served on a statewide committee to plan the adding of the twelfth grade. She was also named State Teacher of the Year in 1956. Miss Julia was proudest, perhaps, of her work in developing commencement programs in which all students took part. She also produced plays each spring, many of which she wrote. In addition, she was an accomplished artist who delighted her students with colored chalk scenes depicting novel under study. A poet in her own right, "A Song of Sumter," being one of her best, Miss Julia held poetry contests with prizes for the best entries. One of the major compliments paid for her work in education was when President Franklin Roosevelt invited her to a White House reception honoring outstanding educators from across the country. Being physically handicapped, it just so happened that she went to meet the President, she fell flat on her face, got up, brushed herself off and said, "Hello, Mr. President I came all the way from Plains, Georgia to see you."

Miss Julia has left an indelible mark on the lives on the people of Plains. Invariably, even today as people gather at church, school or civic functions the name of Miss Julia is likely to be invoked.

Miss Julia Coleman, the daughter of a Baptist minister, was born in Nacogdoches, Texas. She came to Plains as a small child and attended school there. She graduated from Bessie Tift College at Forsyth, Georgia. She began her teaching career in 1908 in Friendship, Sumter County, Georgia, where she taught in a one–teacher school of ten grades.

In 1912, she moved to Plains where she taught English. In 1920, she was appointed Principal; in 1927, she was promoted to Superintendent. In that same year, she hired Mr. Y. T. Sheffield as coach and math teacher.

In 1949, Miss Julia resigned as Superintendent, but remained at Plains to teach English until

1958. She taught all high school English classes, grades eight through twelve, at Plains High School.

During her tenure at Plains, Miss Julia was responsible for many outstanding accomplishments in the field of education. Plains High, under Miss Julia's leadership, was designated by the Georgia State Department of Education as one of three model or laboratory schools in Georgia. For years, it did experimental work, which was later adopted into the State's program of education.

While under Miss Julia's direction, Plains High School received national recognition on two occasions. The first occasion was from the Junior Garden Clubs of America. The second was national recognition for work in the area of citizenship.

When Miss Julia stepped down as Superintendent after twenty–one years in that position, a day of great festivity, celebration, and honor was given to her. Weeks went into the planning and on May 17, 1949, the auspicious event was held. The whole town participated and paid respect to their beloved mentor and friend. During the day, the campus was given the name of Julialand. This honor was bestowed due to her long interest in campus landscaping. For example, one of the most beautiful spots on campus was the Friendship Garden. Here students, in their leisure time, could meet and enjoy both fellowship and appreciation of beauty in the delightfully landscaped garden in which all types of shrubs and flowers indigenous to the region grew.

Across from Friendship Garden was Rose Point, a smaller but equally appreciated garden spot. The principle flower in this spill–over of the Friendship Garden was the rose.

Another division of the landscape design was "Baby Row". At the birth of each future student of the school, a tree of the parents' choice was given to the school to be planted in "Baby Row".

Miss Julia, due to failing health, retired at Christmas in 1958. She continued to live in Plains until health reasons forced her to move to Buena Vista to live with her niece, Mrs. L. K. (Anne) Moss. Miss Julia died in 1973 and was buried in Lebanon Cemetery in Plains.

Recently, a great honor has been added to Miss Julia's list of accomplishments. Posthumously, she has been awarded the Georgia Women of Achievement Award for the year 2001. This is indeed an honor she so richly deserves. [1]

—*Submitted by Dr. James Bagwell*

Endnotes:

[1] Bagwell, Dr. James Bagwell, *Plains Echoes*, Volume 8, Number 4, p. 1.

Cox Family Record

I. Cary Cox, Sr.-born ca. 1736, died March 24, 1814 in Putnam Co., Ga. He was reputed to be a soldier in the American Revolution. He was in Halifax Co., N. C. as early as 1764 and was in Edgefield Co., S. C. before 1790. He is listed on the 1790 U.S. census of the [...] Co., S. C. In 1796 his family moved to Warren Co., Ga. and joined the Williams Creek Baptist Church. [...] After [...] Putnam Co., Ga. [...] he is buried on the Cary Cox, Jr. plantation in Putnam Co., Ga.

II. Cary Cox, Jr. - [...] C., probably Ha[...] died June 02, 1871 at his hom[...] County, Ga. He married Martha [...] Rountree on Jan[...]. She was the daughte[...] Revolutionary War [...] Richardson Rou[...] acre plantation in[...] wife are buried [...] plantation. He w[...] of [...] children, the eldest of whom [...]

III. Chappell Cox - [...]as born [...] 18[...] probably in Warren Count[...]. Ga. He died in 1864 at his plantation in Web[...]ter Co., Ga. and is buried in an unmarked grave in Lebanon Cemetery, Plains, Ga. He served as a state representative from

Talbot Co., Ga. in 1837. He was married to Martha Mathis, daughter of Revolutionary War veteran Thomas Mathis and his wife Mary Rutherford, in Hancock Co., Ga. on Dec. 22, 1819. He bought the land, some 400 acres, where the town of Plains is now located, in 1839 from his first cousin Eli Glover. Some years later he sold this property to his two sons, Carey Thomas Cox and John Mathis Cox. He bought a 1000 acre plantation in Webster County, Ga. where the town of Archery later was sited, in 1856, and lived there until his death in 1863. He was the father of 2 sons and 4 daughters. He was the 1st cousin, once removed, of Confederate General John B. Gordan who was later governor and U. S. Senator from Georgia. Chappell's sister, Frances Cox Holt, was the sister-in-law of U. S. Senator Walter Colquitt and the aunt of Confederate General Alfred Holt Colquitt who was later governor and U. S. Senator from Georgia. Chappell's uncle, Ichabod Cox, was the first state senator from Talbot Co., Ga. when the county was created in 1828.

IV. Carey Thomas Cox - was born ca. 1812 in Georgia and died on the Cox Plantation in Webster Co., Ga. in 1856. He bought land from his father where the town of Plains is presently located. When Kinchafoonee, now Webster County was created, he moved to his father's plantation in Kinchafoonee County and was elected the first sheriff of the county. He was married to Martha Davis, daughter of William and Priscilla Davis Daniel of Talbot County, Ga. They were the parents of two children, Martha who died very young and John Augustus. Carey Thomas and his wife are buried in unmarked graves in Lebanon Cemetery, Plains, Ga.

John Augustus Cox - was born on the plantation of his grandmother, Priscilla Davis Daniel in Talbot Co., Ga. while his parents were visiting, on June 25, 1845. He served as a private in the Confederate Army in the Schley County Cavalry which was commanded by his uncle, Captain Jeremiah Lasiter. He married Sarah Missouri Hixson, daughter of Seaborn and Mary Stallings Hixon of Schley Co. Her father, Seaborn Hixon was a county commissioner in Marion County in 1849 and the first state senator from Schley County when the county was created. John and Sarah were the parents of 10 children who grew up in the Plains area. John Augustus Cox died December 31, 1918. Sarah was born March 10, 1850 in Marion (now Schley) County, Ga. and died September 01, 1908. Both are buried in Lebanon Cemetery, Plains, Ga. Mr. Alton Carter lived with the Cox family when he first came to Plains as a young man and said that Sarah Cox was the best cook he had ever seen. Children of John and Sarah buried in Lebanon Cemetery are: Mary Cox Whaley and her children; William (Willie) Daniel Cox; John Morgan Cox; Charles Crisp Cox; Annie Cox Hale; Sallie Cox Stubbs.

VI. Thomas Mathew Cox - was born in Webster County, Ga. August 14, 1882 and died in Americus, Ga. February 05, 1940. He was buried in Lebanon Cemetery and in 1965 his body was moved to Sunset Memorial Cemetery, Americus, Ga. He lived in the Plains area most of his life as a farmer. He was married to Laura Emma Fulbright October 16, 1918 in Preston, Ga. She was the daughter of William Wesley and Sallie Whatley Fulbright who came to Sumter Co., Ga. in 1914 from Heyward Co., N. C. Thomas and Laura Cox were the parents of eight children: Sally, Martha, William Augustus, Alma, Lorena, Dorothy, Rosa and Jack F. Cox.

VII. Jack F. Cox - was born in Sumter County, Ga. on February 21, 1936. He graduated from Americus High School and attended Furman University in Greenville, S. C. He received a B. S. and M. S. degree in education from Georgia Southwestern State University and a Ed. S. from the University of Georgia. He was the manager of the Georgia Dept. of Labor in Americus for ten

years and then served as assistant principal of Sumter County Comprehensive High School and Americus High School. He married Carrie Earline Buchanan (see Buchanan and Lamb families) on June 3, 1973 at Calvary Episcopal Church in Americus. She was the daughter of Joe Monroe and Ruby Texas Lamb Buchanan. They are the parents of one son:

VIII. Carey Buchanan Cox - was born September 14, 1975 at the Americus Hospital. He was the valedictorian of the class of 1974 Americus High School. He was Star Student and selected for the Governors Honors Program. He attended Georgia Institute of Technology as a Deans Scholar for 3 years in chemical engineering before transferring to the School of Pharmachy at the University of Georgia. He received a degree of Doctor of Pharmacy at the graduation exercises in May of 2002.

—*Submitted by Jack F. Cox*

The Family of L.J. Cranford

Luther J. Cranford (b. 1872-d.1957) Born in Marion County, Georgia, later moved to Plains where he ran a cotton gin. The gin was located just off South Hudson Street about where the housing units are now located. He also had farming interests, and served many years on the local school board.

Mr. Cranford was married first to Bessie McGarrah. By this marriage he had one son, Joseph Cranford (b. 1908-d.1939). Upon the death of his first wife, Mr. Cranford married Mary Willie Hagerson (b.1886-d.1968) The children of Luther and Mary Willie Cranford are:

(1.)James William (b. Oct. 15, 1915-d. Sept. 8, 1944) James worked as a young man with Mr. Ross Dean in the mortuary business. He died serving his country in World War II while stationed in New Guinea. His body was returned and he is buried in Lebanon Cemetery along with his parents and half-brother, Joseph.

(2.) Marianne (b. May 21, 1926). Marianne married S.R. (Dick) Stevens, Jr. on April 9, 1947. They live in Americus, Ga. They have no children

(3.) Elizabeth Currie (Betty) (b. April 13, 1928). Betty married Charles S. Carter, Jr. of Camilla, Georgia on April, 13, 1948. They later moved to Cordele. Charlie died in 1973. Their children are: (a.) James William (Jimmy) (b. Feb. 25, 1950) (b.) Deborah (Debbie) (b. Feb. 9, 1952) (c.) Charles S. III, (b. March 22, 1955)

—*Submitted by Allene T. Haugabook*

Hon. William H. Davidson

William Hardison Davidson was born in Jones County, Georgia, April 2, 1820, His forebears came from Ireland through North Carolina to Jones County. His parents were Talbot Davidson and Lenora Hardison Davidson, who moved to Upson County where he received his education. Talbot, b. 2-2-1800 and d. 10-4-1875, was the son of Nancy Childree and William Davidson who was born around 1770 and died 11-7-1815. Nancy and William Davidson's children were Richard, John, William, Talbot, Green, James and Nancy. Nancy Childree's parents were William and Sarah Childree (d. 1899).

William Hardison first married Finn R. Boseman of Crawford County on May 6, 1840, and their children were Jimmy, T. Alfred (who was a Confederate soldier), Ira, Elizabeth, Talbot, Samuel E., and W.H. Davidson, Jr. Mr. Davidson moved to Sumter County in 1848 and built a log house which burned the day it was completed. He rescued only his safe, and the family said this was the only time in his life he was ever excited! He rebuilt the house and eventually owned several thousand acres of land in the 17th District of Sumter County. Mr. Davidson engaged in farming, merchandising, and in the milling business. He built a millhouse called Davidson's Mill, later known as Thomas' Mill. He went to Columbus to purchase a mill rock. He found that one could be secured which would be imported from Germany, but he was informed that there was no way to transport it from the dock in Columbus to the mill in Sumter County. However, Mr. Bond heard this conversation and approached Mr. Davidson with the offer to deliver the mill rock with a team of oxen "even if he had to blaze a trail." The rock was ordered and the trail was blazed by Mr. Bond, avoiding streams from Columbus to the 17th District millhouse. This is the road now called Bond's Trail.

On January 8, 1865, William Hardison married Lucretia C. Malone of Gordon County who was b. 1-14-1844 and d. 11-3-1911. She was the daughter of Doctor R. Malone and Celestia B. Williams. Their children were Annie Laurie Davidson who married LaFayette A. Thomas (children: Mamie Evelyn, Annie Mae, Katie Belle, Charles Harrison, Burrell Wise, Lillian Lucille, William LaFayette, Alice Louise, and Woodrow Wilson), Henrietta Davidson who married Rolin Chambliss (children: Rolin, Lois, and Nadine), Willie Davidson who married Felix Boswell (children: two sons and a daughter, Ula), and Naomi Davidson who married John Feagan (children: Willie, Mary Lou, Leila and Nettie).

Mr. Davidson was elected to the Georgia Legislature in 1876 and re-elected without opposition in 1877.

He was a member of the Providence Baptist Church and was a Baptist layman for 40 years. He died 1-19-1899 and was buried at Providence Cemetery in the 17th District where many of his family are also buried.

—*Submitted by Marian Mitchell Harris*

Henry Rufus Dean Family

I. Henry Rufus DEAN b 13 Nov 1828 In Edgefield SC s/o Col. William DEAN d 25 Dec 1900 in Plains GA buried in Lebanon Cemetery. He married 9 Jul 1868 in Bottsford Church, Plains GA to Georgia E. MCTYIER b 16 Jun 1852 in GA, d 3 Feb 1917 in Plains GA buried in Lebanon Cemetery. Rufus & Georgia had the following children:

(1) Lilla DEAN b 9 Jul 1869 d 12 Sept 1899 buried in Lebanon Cemetery, Married Luther David WISE b 21 Mar 1863 d 14 Feb 1926 buried in Lebanon Cemetery. They had one daughter:

(a) Ethel WISE b 1 Jun 1890 d 12 Jun 1964 buried in Lebanon Cemetery m Charles C. LUNSFORD 6 May 1886 d 31 Mar 1947 buried in Lebanon Cemetery. They had one daughter:

1) Lilloise LUNSFORD b 13 Dec 1912 married Young Thomas SHEFFIELD b 24 Jun 1904 d 21 Sep 1967 buried in Lebanon Cemetery. Their children:

a) daughter Charlene SHEFFIELD

b) son Young Thomas SHEFFIED Jr.

(2) Henry Rufus DEAN b 26 Jul 1870 d 5 May 1896 buried in Lebanon Cemetery married Mamie Lou HAMPTON

(3) Mary L. DEAN b about 1872 d 27 Jul 1946 Orlando Fla buried in Lebanon Cemetery married Rutherford ROSS no dates. They had one son:

(a) Dean ROSS b about 1900 married Rebecca FERGUSON no dates. Their children were:

1) Louise

2) Claire

3) Dean ROSS Jr "Bubba"

(4) Ernest M DEAN b 22 Nov 1875 d 25 Aug 1944 Miami, Fla buried Lebanon Cemetery married Rosa M COBB b 17 Nov 1880 d 23 Mar 1956 Miami, Fla buried Lebanon Cemetery. Their children:

(a) Ernest Dessi DEAN b 17 Mar 1901 d 31 Dec 1943 Miami, Fla m Edna May DARLOW b 27 Jun 1901 d 27 Jan 1988 Miami, Fla. Their daughter:

1) Gloria Lillian DEAN

(b) Lillie Ruth DEAN b 11 Mar 1905 d 4 Jun 1907

(c) William Ross DEAN b 28 Mar 1907 d 11 Jun 1946 Miami Fla

(d) Lillian Doris DEAN 18 Feb 1916 d 12 Dec 1967 Miami Fla married Tillman Thomas ROLAND "Buddy" no dates. Their daughter:

1) Rosalie ROLAND

(5) William Ross DEAN b about 1876 d 5 Feb 1941 m Carrie TURNER b aboutt 1869 d 26 Jul 1939 buried Lebanon Cemetery.

(6) K. Eloise DEAN "Ella" b 22 Oct 1878 d 12 Feb 1960 m Rufus Michael MONTS b 1 Jan 1871 d no date. Their children:

(a) Rufus Michael MONTS Jr b 15 Jul 1900 d 12 Mar 1976

(b) Julia Kathleen MONTS b 4 Nov 1906 d no date married Ed RAST no date.

(7) Oscar Howard DEAN b Dec 1880-1882 d 31 Mar 1947 Miami, Fla married Ellen Theresa SCULLY "Nellie" b 1886 d 11 Nov 1918 Savannah GA. Their Children:

(a) Dorothy Theresa DEAN b 5 May 1909 d 30 Jun 1979 Sav m Reginald Calvin HAUPT no date. Their children:

(1) Dorothy Dean HAUPT

(2) Ellen Maureen HAUPT

(b) Rosemary DEAN 11 Nov 1910 d 16 Feb 1945 married Thomas John BURKE 26 Apr 1906 d 10 Dec 1978. Their son:

(1) Thomas John BURKE Jr

(c) infant DEAN b 1918 d 1918

(8) <u>James Crawford DEAN</u> b 22 Oct 1885 d 22 Aug 1903 buried Lebanon Cemetery
—*Submitted by Gloria Dean Ellison*

Armistid Dodson

1849-1942

Armistid Dodson was the youngest son of Joel and Jamima Henderson Dodson. He was born September 18, 1849 in Jasper County, Georgia. He married Miss Sallie Chappell, a life long resident of Sumter County in 1873. She was a most faithful wife, mother, and friend, and a devoted Christian. She died November 20, 1922, at the age of 72.

Mr. Dodson had lived in Sumter County for many years. He built a large, two story house on College Street in Americus, and lived there from 1887-1901.

He was a charter member of Central Baptist Church, which was first known as Furlow Lawn Baptist Church. Dodson Street in Americus was named for him.

Mr. Dodson was manager of four plantations for the Americus Investment Company and handled their real estate interests in several towns along the SAM railroad. He was a businessman of excellent judgement and ability.

Armstid owned a plantation in DeSoto consisting of 5,125 acres of splendid land. He was one of Sumter's most successful and progressive planters.

In search of more good farm land, he purchased 1,200 acres from S.H. Hawkins on June 7, 1882. It was all in one tract, 3 ½ miles north of Plains on which he built his second house, presently the home of Mrs. Louise Whitten.

Later, Mr. Dodson sold his country home with a tract of land and deeded five of his children 150 acres of land each. Armstid Chappell Dodson, a son of Armstid was deeded his portion of land earlier in 1906.

Mr. Dodson moved to Plains to his newly constructed home at the corner of Bond and Paschal Street, which was later owned by his grandson, Clarence Dodson. The last thirty years of Mr. Dodson's life was spent in Plain. He had tow daughters, Mrs. J.R. Britton and Mrs. J.H. Williams; four sons: Clarence, Henderson, Pleman, and Chappell. Chappell Dodson had preceded his father in death in 1923.

Mr. Dodson built his fourth house next door on Paschal Street, presently the home of Chappell and Anita Dodson. It is identical to the one he was living in and gave it to his daughter, Mrs. J.H. Williams. By this time, he was experiencing declining health and moved in with her.

Armstid Dodson died September 30, 1942 at the home of his daughter. The funeral was held there and he was buried beside his wife in Lebanon Cemetery.
—*Submitted by (no name given)*

Robert Emanuel Dodson

"Bobby" Dodson, son of Bob Wells Dodson and Susie Lansford Dodson was born November 4, 1938. He grew up on the family farm, graduated from Plains High School in 1956 and served 6 ½ years with the Georgia National Guard. Following graduation, Dodson persued a career in farming, had a large hog operation and became a rural mail carrier in 1958.

Dodson purchased 150 acres in 1960 from the heirs of his great uncle, Henderson Dodson. Later, he purchased an additional 200 acres of Dodson land. In March 1962, Bobby had a brick house built on his farm.

On June 16, 1962, he married Barbara O'Neal, and once again, history repeated itself, as he brought his bride to the new house which they continue to reside in 40 years later.

Dodson was honored by the Georgia Department of Natural Resources in Perry on October 4, 1996, by designating the R.E. Dodson Farm on Bob Dodson Road near Plains as a "Centennial Family Farm." He is proud of his heritage and is happy that the farm has been in continuous operation by members of the Dodson family for 125 years.

In 1990, Dodson felt the need to slow down, so he rented out the most of the farm, but he continues to grow wheat and soybeanws. He still carries the mail and has served to date, 44 years and still has not set a retirement date.

Dodson's wife, Barbara, is a graduate of Plains High School, The Woman's College (now Georgia College) and a former Sumter County school teacher. She helped run the farm, but now takes care of their rental property and other invenstments. Both are active members of Central Baptist Church.

Their son, Robert Wade Dodson, was born October 20, 1966. He graduated from Southland Academy in 1985. "Rob" farmed a few years before pursuing a career with Caravelle Boats. He is proud to be the 5th consecutive Dodson generation to be a member of Central Baptist Church.

—*Submitted by (no name given)*

Bob Wells Dodson

August 2, 1909-October 23, 1988

Bob Wells Dodson, a son of Armstid Chappell Dodson and Maude Wells Dodson was born August 2, 1909. He grew up on the family farm located 2 ½ miles north of Plains with his four brothers and one sister. He was educated at Plains High School and was a member of Plains Baptist Church. Due to the early death of his father at age 44, Bob felt the responsibility of his family and assumed the task of farming at an early age.

On November 9, 1929, he married Susie Mae Lansford. Dodson continued farming, along with raising livestock. He served as an ordained deacon at Plains Baptist Church for many years and later at Central Baptist Church. He was a mason and a member of M.B. Council Lodge in Americus.

Dodson was a successful farmer and businessman. He served for many years on the Sumter County Tax Assessors Board and was a member of Sumter EMC's Board of Directors for over 34 years. He was a dedicated director serving with distinction continuously from 1954 until the time of his death.

Perhaps Dodson's greatest honor was when Sumter County named the connecting road from Highway 280 to Highway 45, the Bob Dodson Road. He died quietly at his country home near Plains on October 23, 1988.

—*Submitted by (no name given)*

Chappell Dodson

1879-1923

Chappell Dodson, a native of Marion County was born April 11, 1879. His parents were Armstid and Sallie Chappell Dodson. He had two sisters; Mrs. J.R. Britton and Mrs. J.H. Williams and three brothers; Clarence, Henderson, and Pleamon.

Chappell was a prominent Sumter County farmer and was outstanding in the affairs of the community. Like his father, he was also a charter member of Central Baptist Church.

He built a large house on his farm located on Bob Dodson Road, which is presently owned by a grandson, Walter Mathews. He married Miss Maude Wells of Friendship. The wedding was at the home of the bride's parents and was performed by Rev. R.L. Bivins of Americus. Immediately after the ceremony, the bridal party left for the home of the groom where an elegant reception was given them.

As time went on, they were blessed with seven children: Cecil, Elizabeth, Bob, Joel, Mary (who died as a child), Clarence and Chappell.

Unfortunately, Chappell had a brief illness and died November 22, 1923 at the age of 44.

—*Submitted by (no name given)*

Maude Wells Dodson

Maude Wells was born February 9, 1884; died 1986. Her parents were Sally Dodson Wells and Robert C. Wells. She had two sisters: Pearl and Carrie and a brother, Robert Wells. They lived in the Friendship community.

As mentioned earlier, she married Chappell Dodson, but with his untimely death, she was left alone to rear their six children: Cecil, Elizabeth, Bob, Joel, Clarence and Chappell.

Times were really hard, but with Maude's faith and stamina, she reared a fine family. The children all learned to work at a very young age. They sold milk, butter, and eggs in order to keep food on the table and clothes on their backs. Cecil was away at college when his father died and he didn't have the money to come home for the funeral.

Bob and Joel both students at Plains school would alternate the farming chores. During the busy farm season, each one would go to school every other week. Elizabeth and Clarence were college graduates.

Mrs. Dodson was a devoted Christian and faithful member of Plains Baptist Church. On April 26, 1981, special recognition was given to her as a Real Daughter at a Confederate Memorial Day ceremony in Americus. She was presented with a plaque and a medal.

Another outstanding event in her life was February 9, 1984 when she celebrated her one hundredth birthday. The occasion was hosted by her children at her home with many friends and relatives attending.

Mrs. Dodson was blessed with good health and a clear mind. She and her daughter Elizabeth continued to live in the same house her husband had built and brought her to as a bride. She passed away July 27, 1986 at the age of 102. She is buried at Lebanon Cemetery.

—*Submitted by (no name given)*

Susie Mae Lansford Dodson

1910-1998

Bob's wife, Susie Lansford, a native of Sumter County was born September 30, 1910, a daughter of Emanuel Britton Lansford and Lula Virginia Morrell Lansford. She was the third of six children.

She received her education at Shiloh School in Sumter County and later graduated from Patterson Business School in Americus. Upon her marriage in 1929 to Bob W. Dodson of Plains, she became a homemaker. Nine years later, on November 4, 1938, a son Robert Emanuel Dodson was born.

Mrs. Dodson joined Plains Baptist Church where she taught Sunday school for 40 years in the primary department and served 37 years as a prayer leader in the Woman's Missionary Society.

At the time of her death, November 23, 1998, Mrs. Dodson was a member of Central Baptist Church. She served as secretary and card chairman of the Kathleen Gardner Sunday School Class, was a member of "Super Seniors" and was a member of Chapter 63, Order of the Easter Star. Mrs. Dodson was a refined, loving lady, and a devout Christian who served her Lord as long as her health permitted.

—*Submitted by (no name given)*

The Dominick Family

The first members of the Dominick family to move to the Plains area were Henry Clarence and Minnie Gertrude Dominick. Henry Clarence was born November 5, 1878 and died January 15, 1958. Minnie Gertrude was born July 9, 1882 and died September 10, 1961. They moved to Plains in December of 1914. They moved from Newberry, Saluda County, South Carolina to purchase a farm in the Mossey Dell community near Botsford and were instrumental in building the Mossey Dell School which also served as a Sunday school and a type of Civic Center and in 1920 consolidated with

Plains school. Mossey Dell community is now the Salters Mill Road.

Clarence and Minnie Dominick had the following children:

1. Bertha Elizabeth Dominick born January 23, 1902 and died in 1990. Bertha married Burr Wishard. They had the following child:
   (a.) B.T. Wishard

2. Bonnie Louise Dominick born June 6, 1903 and died December 31, 1974. Bonnie married Jay Webb. They had the following children:
   (a.) J. Gordy Webb
   (b.) Bill Webb
   (c.) Martha Webb
   (d.) Elizabeth Webb
   (e.) James Webb
   (f.) Hugh Webb

3. George Theron Dominick born November 1, 1905 and died November 6, 1999. George Theron married Jewel Smith. They had the following children:
   (a.) Barbara Dominick
   (b) George Dominick, Jr.
   (c.) Thomas Dominick

4. Mary Esther Dominick born April 7, 1907 and died March 12, 1952. Mary married Lumas Smith. They had the following children:
   (a.) Wilburn Smith
   (b.) Emily Smith

5. James Guy Dominick born October 1, 1909 and died March 27, 1986. Guy married Helen Walters. They had the following children:
   (a..) Polly Dominick
   (b.) Glenda Dominick

6. Vera Una Dominck born November 28, 1913 died August 16, 1981. Vera married Clyde Butts. They had the following children:
   (a..) Robert Butts
   (b.) Tom Butts
   (c.) Bunyan Butts
   (d.) Judy Butts

7. Abbie Francis Dominick born April 23, 1918 died in 2001. Abbie married Charles Hale. They had the following child:
   (a.) Charlene Hale

Descendants of Bertha and Burr Wishard:
1. B.T. Wishard married Gloria Burton. They had the following children:
   (a.) Sally Wishard
   (b.) Bonnie Wishard

Descendants of Bonnie and Jay Webb:
1. Bill Webb married Francis Cayon. They had the following children:
   (a.) Jan Webb
   (b.) Sally Webb

2. Elizabeth Webb married Hershal French. They had the following children:
   (a.) Ricky French
   (b.) Butch French

3. Jimmy Webb married Dorothy Bush. They had the following children:
   (a.) Marion Webb
   (b.) Martha Webb
   (c.) Jim Webb

4. Hugh (Don) Webb married Jane Feeney. The had the following children:
   (a.) Bonnie Webb
   (b.) Elizabeth Webb
   (c.) Tammy Webb
   (d.) Kimberly Webb
   (e.) Gary Webb

Descendants of George and Jewel Dominick:
1. Barbara Dominick married George Hollinshead, Jr. They had the following children:
   (a.) George Hollinshead III

(b.) John Hollinshead

(c.) Patty Hollinshead

2. George Dominick, Jr. married Sue Blankenship. They had the following children:

(a.) Jeff Dominck

(b.) Rhonda Dominick

(c.) Michael Dominick

(d.) Dana Dominick

(e.) Kim Dominick

3. Thomas H. Dominick married Rose Tarrance. They had the following child:

(a.) Chris Dominick

Descendants of George and Sue Dominick:

Michael S. Dominick, Sr. married Pam Johnson. They have the following children:

(a.) Michael (Slade) Dominick, Jr.

(b.) Lauren B. Dominick

—*Submitted by Pam Dominick*

The Downer Family

The John Downer family moved to Sumter County in December, 1941. The family bought land adjoining the Earl Carter farm approximately three miles west of Plains and was engaged in sawmilling and farming. The family consisted of the father, John Thomas Downer, Sr., his wife, Lena Ginn Downer, four sons, Doyle, Tom Richard (Dick), Andrew and Colley, a daughter, Fannie Belle Paradise and a granddaughter, LaVilla Paradise. Two sons, Oliver Downer and J. T. Downer, Jr. were serving in the army and a grandson, Dewey Wright Paradise, was serving in the Air Corp.

The family owned numerous cars and trucks and due to their occupations were not affected by rationing during the war years as much as most families.

When the Earl Carters built a home in Plains in 1949 and moved, Thomas Richard Downer bought the Carter farm which is now part of the National Historic Park Service as the childhood home of Jimmy Carter. Dick Downer did not wish to sell the Carter farm. He wanted to leave it to some of his heirs. The government did not consider his wishes, condemned the land, and bought it at a price they set. Stating it had no historic value, they only paid the heirs what the governments' agents said was a fair price. This price was based on what they determined was the value of other farms in the area. The house on the farm has been renovated and is now a tourist attraction and billed as the childhood home of Jimmy Carter, 39th president.

August, 2002 - Only two survivors remain of the original family, J.T. Downer, Jr. who lives at the old home site, and LaVilla Paradise Bryan, who resides in Americus.

Births and deaths of the family are as follows:

John Thomas Downer, Sr. - August 18, 1875 - July 3, 1955. Lena Ginn Downer - April 18, 1878 - February 4, 1961. Doyle Downer - October 14, 1899 - Fall of 1972.

Fannie Belle Paradise - September 13, 1901 - October 8, 1998.

Andrew Downer - September 5, 1912 - September 8, 1951. Colley Downer - October 6, 1914 - January 27, 1959. Oliver Downer - June 31, 1919 - February 27, 1947.

Dewey Wright Paradise - January 28, 1922 - March 15, 2000.

—*Sumitted by LaVilla Paradise Bryan- 2002*

John Russell Durham and Carolyn Harris Durham

John Russell Durham was born October 3, 1925 in Crisp County, Ga., and Carolyn Harris was born December 12, 1928 in Quitman County, Ga. They were married January 9, 1949 at Plains Baptist Church. Their children are John Russell Durham, Jr., born December 23, 1949 in Albany, Dougherty County, Ga., and Susan Carole Durham born May 18, 1954 in Decatur, Morgan County, Alabama.

John Russell Durham was the seventh child born to Laura Love Hall born March 8, 1884 in Dooly County, Ga., died November 1, 1969 in Sumter County, Ga., married June 3, 1908 to Arnold Enoch Durham born January 22, 1878 in Baker Co., Ga. Died March 5, 1963 in Sumter County, Ga. John's family moved from Crisp County to Americus in 1933. John attended Furlow Grammar School and graduated from Americus High School in 1943. He volunteered for service in the U.S. Navy on September 30, 1943 and served as Storekeeper, Second Class, in Hawaii and on Samar in the Philippines until he was discharged on March 15, 1946. His mother and father had five of their six sons to serve in World War II. The youngest was too young to enlist. John attended Georgia Southwestern College. In March 1948, John began his career with J.C. Penney Company and served in management positions for thirty-two and a half years. His work with Penney's took him and his family to Alabama and Louisiana. In 1969 the family returned to Albany, Ga., where John retired in October 1980.

Carolyn Harris was the fourth child born to Ernest Willie and Ouida Murphy Harris. She moved with her family at Christmas time in 1934 to a farm about a mile from Plains that her father had rented. (See Ernest W. and Ouida Murphy Harris history in this book.) Carolyn had attended Concord School, about 8 miles from Plains before she enrolled in the first grade at Plains High School. One of her first memories at Plains was of her teacher, Miss Eleanor Chambliss, and the little store that stood in the first grade classroom that students would go into and "purchase" sample products of soaps, cereals, etc…a teaching tool for reading and arithmetic. This was the first time that Carolyn knew there was a breakfast cereal other than grits. It was years after graduating from Plains that Carolyn realized that students there had been privileged to have books,

art, and music that other small schools did not have. Carolyn graduated in a class of eleven students in June 1945 and enrolled in the secretarial science program at Bessie Tift College in Forsyth, Georgia in September 1945. Carolyn retired in 1990 after thirty years service with the University System of Georgia. She was employed at Darton College for almost twenty years as Secretary to the President.

John and Carolyn started an antique business as a hobby in 1982 in the house previously owned by her parents. This hobby turned into a business that operated for fifteen years. In 1999, they were commissioned to liquidate the contents of a 22-room house in Braselton, Ga., the estate of one of the founders of Braselton.

John and Carolyn own and operate a tree farm on Highway 45 North, Plains. Genealogy has been a hobby of John and Carolyn for thirty-plus years. They have traced some of their Harris and Durham lines to the Revolutionary War and earlier. Carolyn became interested in genealogy as a small child when she would spend time with her grandmother Murphy and listened to stories of the family.

John Russell Durham, Jr., married June 10, 1972 Janet Marie Candy born March 4, 1953 in Tulsa, Oklahoma to John and Lydia Candy. Children of Russell and Janet are Jennifer Marie born December 7, 1975 in Atlanta, Fulton Co., Ga., employed with the Dekalb/Tucker Young Men's Christian Association in Atlanta and Kelly Lynn born October 21, 1978 employed with Fresh Beginnings in Valdosta, Georgia. Russell graduated from Cedartown High School in 1968 and attended West Georgia College. He holds the designation of Chartered Life Underwriter and owns Durham Insurance Agency in Albany, Ga. Janet received the Bachelors Degree in Business Administration from Georgia Southwestern College, Americus and is a Certified Public Accountant.

Susan Carole Durham married September 3, 1995 James Alan Knapp born February 22, 1959 in

Rochester, New York to Theresa Marie Burgess and Roger Easton Knapp. Susan graduated from Westover High School, Albany, Ga., in 1972. She received the Bachelor of Arts Degree, cum laude, in Philosophy from Kenyon College at Gambier, Ohio in 1976; the Juris doctor Degree from The Ohio State University in 1981; and a Dual Masters in Social Work and Public Policy and Management from The Ohio State University in 1995 at which time she was inducted in Phi Kappa Phi, an honor society. She also holds the designation of Chartered Property and casualty Underwriter. Susan holds the position of Counsel-Litigation in the Corporate Offices of American Electric Power Company, Columbus, Ohio. James received the Bachelors of History Degree and the Bachelors of Theater Degree from State University of New York at Brockport, New York in 1983. He received the Masters of Fine Arts Degree from the University of Wisconsin at Madison in 1990 and is Production Coordinator in the college of the Arts, The Ohio State University in Columbus, Ohio.

—*Submitted by Carolyn Harris Durham*

Chapter 18: Family History E–H

Edge-Jackson Family

The history of black people is a story of a struggle, the hope for a better life and a brighter future. It's a story of our past, a bitter past that is a mixed story of the bondage of slavery and the shattered hopes of true freedom. The history of Black America goes back to the riverbanks of West Africa- from the area south of the Sahara Desert. These natives called Black Africans and Negroes were characterized by beautiful dark skin, brown eyes, dark woolly or curly hair and thick lips. This area was ruled by 3 wealthy empires: Ghana, Mali, and Songhai. Their civilizations thrived on trade. Trade which meant exchanging one good for another good allowed tribes to gain valuables, as well as, the things they needed in order to live. Through warfare, one of those goods became human servitude— and was later referred to as that "necessary evil" in American society.

The history of our forefathers and all other Black Americans is largely a story of their struggles for freedom and equality. Slaves were goods that were sold at the town markets particularly in the Southern states—Georgia, Alabama, and the Carolinas. During the 1500's, European nations began to trade rum, and cloth and other items for war captives imprisoned during tribal wars in West Africa. For the next 300 years, millions of enslaved Black persons were shipped across the Atlantic Ocean to what are now known as the United States and Latin America for profit. These slaves were labeled and treated as cargo. They were bound and packed on slave ships. Some captains used the system called "loose packing" to insure delivery. Under this system, few slaves died from disease, illness, or accidents. From the 1500's to the 1800's about 10 million slaves were transported to the Americas. A total of 600,000 were received in North America. The remaining died aboard ship or were sent to Latin America.

The history of the Edge-Jackson family, evidently, is one that is unique in its lineage. This collection of historical entries is the result of some research, collective memories of loved ones, and stories passed on from one generation to another. There are few black family names that are original in respect to origin of racial background. The origin of the name Edge seems to be England. The name Edge was given, as were many names, by a particular characteristic of their person or their original geographic location. The name Edge was derived from a location. It seems that for identification purposes surnames or last names were given. So, if you lived near the edge of a hill or hillside you were given the name Edge, or if you were the son of Jack you may have been given the surname Jackson. There are many variations of the spelling of Edge, such as Eg, Egg, or Eggen. The Jackson spelling is pretty constant. A small percentage of families in the world use the old distinguished English spelling of Edge. There may be a large number of direct relatives in the world who still use other variations of other spellings of Edge. The surname Jackson is a name that is widely used in the United States. Many Jackson descendants originated from Scotland and Ireland.

It is recorded in history that one of our earliest white ancestors arrived in the United States in 1682. His name was John Edge and his family settled in Pennsylvania. There are numerous accounts of white families who also settled in this general area from 1682 to 1635. According to my grandfather John Claude Edge, second known generation of Edge-Jackson offspring, our family moved from the Carolinas by way of covered wagon to Andersonville, GA.

Records further reveal that the first Edge immigrant, Thomas Edge, entered the Carolinas in 1724. So then, what is the connection between these white settlers and us? Further evidence shows that our black ancestry derives from the riverbanks of West Africa aboard slave ships. Our ancestors were sold on town markets in the Carolinas, Georgia, and Alabama. Slaves were bred or mated to produce stronger slaves. The women were used for the master's pleasure. All were required to work hard for the master in the fields or the big houses. The children were sold to other masters like common livestock. It was by these means that our heritage has become a mixture of Caucasian and African blood. There is little evidence of the parentage of the first known generation of this family.

It seems that some time between the years 1865 and 1900, the family moved by way of covered wagon from the Carolinas to Andersonville to the Lacross Community. Claude Edge, Arthur Edge, Lawsie Edge and Whitfield Jackson were the brothers in that family. Little information is known about the parents of these children. There is no mention of the father and minor incidences of insignificant details of the mother. It appears that the four grew up in a single parent home. The boys grew up and began their own lives in different directions.

Claude married Mary Lou Williams on July 14, 1907. Mary Lou lived to see her children born. She died of malaria fever in 1922 and left Claude to raise 8 children: Albert, John Claude, Judson, Grady, Annie Kate, Nona, Edna Ella. They moved to Plains, GA. Claude then remarried Nancy Jones February 25,1923. The children eventually started to grow up. The girls stayed off and on with their older brothers, Claude and Judson. Claude passed away on October 22,1929, and Nancy went back to

live with her family. There is only one living survivor —Edna Edge Burroughs who resides in Tifton, GA.

Lawsie Edge moved to Atlanta, GA and eventually became a Pullman porter on the Santa Fe. He married Daisy Lee Perkins and they had five children: Frank, Lawsie,Jr, Jesse, Gwendolyn, and James. The boys joined the military and later ventured into other careers. Gwendolyn died at an early age. Lawsie Sr. died December 1964. The only remaining survivor is James Edge and he resides in Richmond, VA.

Whitfield Jackson was the town's barber. He moved from Andersonville to Americus where he and his sons cut hair. Whitfield's life was filled with the tragic loss of 3 wives. On September 20, 1901, he married Mary Wade. From this marriage, two children, Theotis Jackson and Willie Jackson were born. On, August 22, 1907 he married Mattie Hargrove. From this marriage, Ben Hargrove was born. On April 18, 1908, he married Sallie Waters and from this marriage Josephine Jackson was born. Josephine Jackson died as a teenager. All of his wives preceded him in death. The only survivor is Ben Hargrove who resides in Americus, GA.

No information has been located on the fourth son, Arthur Edge. We are still searching.

—*Submitted by Eugene Edge*

Richard Neal English Family

Richard Neal English born in Macon County March 7, 1926. Evelyn Louise Fowler born in Worth County April 21. 1929. They married May 30, 1947 and have three children:

I. Brenda Susan English born in Sumter County March 13. 1949 married Wesley Wells Taylor February 11, 1972 They have two children:

1. Julie Denise Taylor born in Sumter County February 9, 1974

2. Evelyn Elizabeth Taylor (born in Sumter County November 27, 1977) married Eduardo

Ramon Torres July 22, 2000 has one son and one step son:

   a. Michael A. Torres born January 9, 1992

   b. Jaden Elijah Torres born December 28, 2000

II. Richard Neal English II born Sumter County December 30, 1950 married August 15, 1973 to Norma Ruth Law. They have two children:

   1. Richard Quincey English born in Sumter County June 16, 1978 married Courtney Alford December 28, 1996 one son 1. Colten Schuyler English born April 13, 1997. They divorced and Richard married Amanda Buckley November 21, 1999, one daughter., Hannah Rae English born August 25, 2000

   2. David Neal English born in Sumter County March 24, 1983

III. Jerry Bradford English born in Sumter County August 15, 1954 married Teresa Maria Jackson August 4, 1973 Two children:

   1. Jerry Bradford English II born in Sumter County Mar. 22, 1974; married Amanda Satterfield Dec. 10, 1994. One child: Jordan Olivia English born October 24,1997

   2. Brandon Keith English born in Sumter County September 15,1981

—*Submitted by Evelyn English*

Everett Family

Mary Helen Paul Everett's mother, Virgise Coggins lived in Plains before she married Robert Paul. They lived in a big house at the corner of Highway 308 and Thrasher Rd. She worked for the telephone company about 1928 to 1930. They moved to Shiloh and Mary Helen went to school there through 6th or 7th grade. They moved to Plains and have been there since then. Mary Helen graduated from Plains High School in 1947 and went to Georgia Southwestern for one year.

In 1948 she married Edward (Eck) C. Everett. They had 3 daughters: Carol, Elaine, and Donna Everett. Mary Helen still lives on South Bond Street. "Eck" worked with the Seaboard Coach Line Railroad for 40 years. He worked the track through Plains on his job until he retired in 1988.

Mary Helen had 2 brothers that also went to Plains High School. Fred Lamar Paul and Ferrell Paul, now deceased. Lanar lived on the Hospital Street. He had 5 children, but they moved to Rome, Georgia.

—*Submitted by Mary Helen Evertt*

The Fletchers of Plains Georgia

Susan Idella Fletcher was the daughter of Will and Lucy Ellen Spann of Webster County. She married Harden Stewart Fletcher on April 10, 1893 Harden Stewart Fletcher was accidentally killed returning from a bird shoot near Preston, Georgia in February 1899. Della Fletcher and Harden Fletcher had two children. Carme Ruth who was born in March 1894 and died of an unexplained illness on June 10,1905 in Webster County. Royl Harden Fletcher was born in Webster County in September 1896,and died in Molena Georgia in May, 1970. Della Fletcher, after the loss of her husband and daughter, was unable to run the family farm that she and her husband owned, and she moved to Plains after 1901. Shortly after that Mr. Alton Carter offered her a job in the Plains Mercantile Co. store, where she worked until her death in May 1937. Her principle duties were to sell cloth goods, sewing material, ladies clothes including millenary, various gifts, dress patterns, and in addition helped with the grocery department.. "Miss Della" lived on the same street as the Plains High School and her home was 3 houses north of the Plains Baptist Church. Della Spann Fletcher also made a home for her sister Josephine Spann who moved to Plains following the death of their parents. Miss Joe kept house and gardened, while Della worked in the Carter Store.

Royl Harden Fletcher grew up in Plains, and graduated from Plains High School. He attended Auburn University for a short while, but became homesick for Plains and returned there. He served in WWI in the Army as a machine gunner. Upon returning to Plains from the Army, he worked for Railway Express in Columbus for awhile, and then began training in the field of banking. He worked for the Bank of Commerce in Americus until 1926 when he moved to Molena, Georgia to be cashier of the bank there. He returned to Plains in 1928 and again worked for the Bank of Commerce, but in 1929 returned to the Bank of Molena where he worked until retiring as its' President.

While living in Plains following WWI Royl Harden Fletcher Married Mary Lou Kennedy in June of 1921. Mary Lou was the daughter of James Walter Kennedy and Mary Lou Harling also of Plains. Royl and Mary Lou had two Children Born in Plains. Carme Ruth born August 1922, lived in Plains until 1926, then moved to Molena, Georgia. She moved back to Plains for a year in 1928 when the family moved permanently to Molena. Carme Ruth was a graduate of the University of Georgia, and was a buyer for the Rich's Store for Homes in Atlanta. Carme Ruth loved Plains and spent many summers there with her grandmother and Aunt Joe.

James Harden was born on January, 1928, and lived in Plains for only a year. He grew up in Molena, Georgia, served in the Navy at the close of WWII and attended Georgia Tech. He later owned and operated Pasley-Fletcher Funeral Home in Thomaston, Georgia and at the time of this printing is Chairman of the Board of First Bank of Pike with branches in Concord, Georgia end Zebulon, Georgia. An interesting fact is that the active management of the Firm Bank of Pike consisted of J. P. Barker, Jr., president, and J.P Barker III, vice president and CEO; they are the grandson and great grandson of Jeff and Jessie Sproull of Plains.

After moving to Molena, Georgia the Fletchers kept close ties to Plains as their parents on both sides still lived in Plains and because they were raised there, they had many close friends there. The names of Price, Timmerman, Wise, Abrams, Howard, Wellons, Spann, Harris, Carter, Forest, Chambliss, Sproull, and others were constantly in our conversation. Mary Lou Fletcher was a contemporary of "Miss Abrams" and Miss Lillian Carter. The kindness and care that was given to Mrs. Della Fletcher by Mr. Alton Carter will always be remembered by the Fletcher family.

—*Submitted by (no name given)*

James E. Forrest, Jr. Family

Jim Forrest and Leila Mae Wishard Forrest had five children. One child was James E. Forrest, Jr. who married and lived in Plains. Mr. and Mrs. J.E. Forrest had a son, James who was born in 1920. At the age of 35 in 1931, J.E. Forrest was killed in a tragic accident. John Nicholson, William Thomas and J.E. Forrest were cutting down a tree on the Kinchafoonee Creek to obtain honey which a swarm of bees had stored in a hollow cavity. The tree began to fall before the men expected it to fall and in running to safety, J.E. became entangled in vines. The 4 foot diameter tree landed on him, crushing him to death. J.E. Forrest had one brother, Cleveland Forrest, and three sisters: Mrs. Will Fletcher, Mrs. Mollie Daniels and Mrs. Abner Wright all of Jacksonville, Florida. J.E. Forrest's wife and young son James who was eleven years old when his father died, continued to live in Plains.

J.E. Forrest, Jr. was a veteran of World War I and was buried with military honors. A firing squad commanded by W.A. Hart, fired three salutes over the casket at the Lebanon Cemetery as C.A. Ames sounded taps softly while friends and family stood around the casket, which was draped with an American flag. Pall bearers at the funeral included: J.E. Carter, W.O. Williams, R.D. Brannen, Bart Glenn, Robert Ratliff, and Andrews Moore.

Later, J.E. Forrest's son, James Forrest, would graduate from Plains High School in 1937 and enter the Army Air Corps. James continued his education receiving a B.S. and M.S. degree. In 1942, he would follow the path of his father by serving his country. James advanced to the rank of an Air Force Colonel retiring as a navigator of the Strategic Air Command's B-36 bombers. James and his wife, Augusta Powell Forrest, live in Montgomery, Alabama.

—*Submitted by Annette Wise*

Estes Forrest Family

Estes Forrest was a prominent farmer of Plains, Georgia in the early 1900's. He was born July 26, 1894 in Virginia. He had two brothers, Robert and Arnold. Two sisters, Kate and Kathleen, graduated from the old original Plains High School and both turned to teaching school. Estes made his way from Virginia by the way of North and South Carolina before settling in Plains.

Estes was married to Clara Holly. After her death he married Eleanor Chambliss, who lived in Plains and taught school for many years at Plains High School. Estes had several children, Rembert who was born in 1925, then Charlotte. After marrying Eleanor, Bill and John Forrest joined the family. Rembert now resides in Melbourne, Florida with his wife, Hilda. Bill is a farmer in Webster County, Georgia, and Charlotte lives in Alabama. Estes passed away July 26, 1946 on his farm just south of Magnolia Springs.

—*Submitted by (no name given)*

Ernest Grover Foster Family

Our father "E.G." Foster came to Sumter County, Friendship Community from Milltown, AL, where he was born May 11, 1885. His brother Dr. John Foster and wife Eunice were living in the Friendship village later moving to Preston. My Dad and Uncle John were very close as brothers so he soon followed them to Friendship to make his home in 1912. He later met my mother, Myrtice Mashburn, daughter of John and Ella Haynie Mashburn. They were married February 8, 1914. To this union 5 children were born – John, Henry, Mary, Fred, and Jimmy.

My parents moved to Plains in 1918. John and Henry were born by this time. A house on Walters Street was purchased and later sold this house and bought another on Walters Street north of the Cody Timmerman home. It was renovated to some extent and the Foster family were living there until their death. My Mom came up to Macon to live with my husband and me during her last declining years and passed away in Macon. My dad had passed away in 1967 at the Americus Hospital. Brother John was living at the home place in Plains during our parents last years.

Dad or "Papa" as we lovingly called him had a thriving business as a blacksmith working and making all types of iron products and was very talented with his hands. He also sold farm equipment and repaired them which was a good source of income. His place of business was a large wooden structure at the end of a lane off Bonds Trail Street between Mr. Edgar Smith's Auto Repair Shop and the Telephone Exchange Building. Several Plains people worked for may father including Eli Wilcox, brother of Mrs. Pantall. The wooden structure is no longer there and no trace of it left. Through the years many changes were made.

In 1929 the decision was made for our family to move to the beloved "Lowery Place" and it was our home for many years. It was a lovely, big home with a wrap around porch and picket fenced front yard, one mile from Plains with a grand view of the whole little town. It had a rather large acreage with large barns, a pasture and lake, an ideal and perfect place for raising cattle, horses and other farm animals. My father did some farming along with his other business. We loved it there and had hopes of buying it. We still had the house in Plains and it was rental property. In the meantime the Great Depression came along. The Plains Bank failed in 1926 and the stock market crashed in New York. It created "hard times" for most everyone in Plains. But we as children were unable to realize the significance of it all. After all we had a car, nice home and plenty of food. My Dad, being a member of a beef club helped. Approximately 15 families were in this club. We were very fortunate in many ways but my father and mother with 5 children were struggling.

Brother Jimmy was born in June of 1933. He was a precious, blue-eyed, blonde headed baby and at around that time the decision was made to move 3 miles west of Plains to a farm adjoining the Earl Carter farm.

Many people were unable to pay bills that they owed my father so he was ready to make a change knowing the purchase of the "Lowery Place" was very slim.

We soon realized that the move we made was almost a total disaster. The cattle and horses and other animals did not have the wonderful pasture or lake they were accustomed to. Most of them were sold or were diseased one way or another. We all missed our home "the Lowery Place". However, we enjoyed living by the Carters for 3 years. Little did we know how famous their family would become with Jimmy being elected President of the United States and the fame he brought to our wonderful little town of Plains! As children and teenagers we all played together, walked to and from school many times and shared happy times! Our parents drove us to school often. There was no school bus out our way.

Our main source of fun and pleasure was school and church activities. My mother was a sweet, wonderful Christian and we were always at all church activities where we attended Plains Baptist Church. My dad did not enter in church services as often but was right there helping all of us get ready

and helping us be on time! Then there was Magnolia Springs, a type of summer resort a short distance from Plains – the coldest mineral water spring around! We look forward to swimming, picnicing and dancing at the pavilion there. What fun for children and adults. It is no longer there and sad to me in many ways!

There were so many people influencing our young lives –too numerous to name. Mrs. Harrell, a friend of my mother's , died when I was a senior in Plains High School and willed to me and two other girls a college education. She was indeed a very unselfish and lovable person and I am so grateful to her. I graduated from the University of Georgia. Mrs. Harrell was kind to me as a child and I loved spending nights with her.

My brother Henry attended Georgia Southwestern College. Fred attended Berry College in Rome, Jimmy attended Columbus College, John stayed home and married late in life. We were all a very closely knitted family. Our mother passed away in 1971. Our father passed away in 1967. Both were buried in Friendship Baptist Cemetery in the Haynie Mashburn family plot where our loved ones of 4 generations are interred. My husband, Ray Crawford, is there and I will be buried there.

We were all wonderfully blessed for having lived and growing up in the famous town of Plains where caring and kindness existed and loving friends meant so much. This account is dedicated to my Mother and Father, Ernest and Myrtice Foster to whom I owe so much.

—*Submitted by Mary F. Crawford*

Gardner

James Gardner, born April 1, 1919, died January 13, 2000 and Vera Mae Gardner, born April 17, 1923 and died may 25, 1997 moved to Plains in 1940. James lived in Marion County; Vera lived in Archery community. They met, fell in love and were married. They decided to make Plains their home. The old home place is 123 Georgia Highway 308 - South Bond's Trail. The family church is St. Mark A.M.E. located in Archery community. James retired from Champion Home Builders, Plains; Vera retired from manhattan Shirt Company, Americus, Georgia. James and Vera Gardner had twelve children. Grandchildren are listed under their names.

A. Vera Wakefield-Gardner - deceased (James) deceased

1. Adeline G. Terry (Otis)
  *Jeffrey Terry (Donna)
     *Amber Terry
     *Angel Terry
     *Aja Terry
     *Alia Terry
  *Vertis Lamont Terry (Eileen)
     *Bimini Ilea Terry
     *Belize Terry
     *Vertis Terry, Jr.
     *Vashon Xavier Terry
  *LaDon Renee Terry
  *Kennard Terry, Sr.
     *Kennard Terry, Jr.
     * Devon Terry
  *Frederick Terry, Sr. (Elizabeth)
     *Frederick Terry, Jr.

2. Olivia Williams (Earnest Aaron, Sr.)
  * Earnest Aaron Williams, Jr. (Donna)
     * Kiara Marie Williams
     * Kameron Williams
  * Michael Bernard Williams (Nicolle)

3. Oscar Charles Johnson (Elwin)
  *Veronica McElroy-Johnson (Thomas)
     * Thomas Johnson, Jr.
     * Tyshon Johnson
  *Armon Scott
     * Aromone' J. Scott

  * Aren J. Scott
  * Alicia Scott Walton (Tervon)
     * Aje'Shylin Walton

4. Theodore Roosevelt Gardner (Jacqueline)
  *Kim Wright
     * Shakendra Wright
     * Nicole Palmer
     * Nicholas Palmer
  * Shanita Wright
  *Teddy Rashaud Gardner
  * Johnathon Gardner

5. Dozier Mack Gardner (Joyce)
  * Cedric Gardner
  * Damien Gardner

6. Sidney Wade Gardner (Dorothy)
  * Brandon Gardner

7. Josephine Gardner-Thomas (Jeremiah)
  * Keisha DeVonn Coley (Donavon)
  * Gregory Omar Thomas (Lenekia)
     *Braylon Thomas

8. Edna Lois Gardner-Laster (Clarence)
  * Tiffany LaWanda Laster Lusane (Marcus)
     * Marcus Lusane
     * Joshua Lusane
  * Ashley Jamison Laster (Natalie)
     * Demetrius Denson
     *Jordan Alexis Laster

9. Clifford Jerome Gardner
  * Terry Lynn Tatum
  * Erika Janelle Gardner

10. Debbie Gardner-Waller (Charles)
  *Brandi Latrice Waller
  * Chelsee Alexandria Waller

11. Willie Lee Gardner (Joyce)
  *Colby Jashad Gardner

* Calia Janise Gardner

12. Rusha Bell Gardner

* Spencer James McDowell

—*Submitted by (no name given)*

James Monroe Gaston Family

James Monroe Gaston, World War I veteran, was born in Carroll County, Ga. December 4, 1898, married Mary Louesa English, January 25, 1935, born August 15, 1910 in Sumter County. James Monroe Gaston was the son of Robert Barker Gaston, born in Randolph County, Alabama, June 24, 1867, died December 31, 1925, and Ida Rosanie Hesterlee, born April 23, 1875, died September 9, 1970. All four are buried in Friendship Baptist Church Cemetery, Sumter County.

Robert B. Gaston and family moved from their farm in Carroll County to a large farm he purchased in Monroe Co., Ga. In 1911. In 1918 he bought the Crawford Plantation in Concord Community from the Oliver-McDonald Company in Plains, and farmed until his death. The house was built in 1856 by Mr. and Mrs. Shadrach Crawford, and is presently used as a hunting lodge. He and Ida had eight children:

1. James Monroe (Monroe)

2. Robert Benton, born February 4, 1900, died May 24, 1972, married Marjorie Smith of Terrell County

3. George Washington, born April 21, 1901, died September 7, 1982, married Nellie Mae Gunn of Crisp County.

4. Paul Jones, born July 4, 1903, died October 29, 1982, married Polly Whitehead of Fulton County.

5. Florence Lenora (Nora), born December 19, 1907, died May 29, 1957, married Leroy Sewell Stevens.

6. Otis Lee, WWII veteran, born July 28, 1909, died January 12, 1992, married Catherine Clardy of Randolph Co., Alabama.

7. Ida Louise, born August 17, 1911, married George Washington Mosely.

8. Ruth Elizabeth, born February 16, 1916, died November 30, 1961. Never married.

Robert and Ida's children attended Concord School. While in high school, George and some other students caught some pigs outside the school yard, and he cut off the pigs' tails. George was suspended from school, and this upset his father (he felt the penalty too severe) who withdrew his three older children from Concord School and sent them to Plains High School. Paul and Nora graduated from Plains High on June 5, 1923. Nora was the class President. Otis was Valedictorian of the Plains High School class of 1925.

Robert purchased additional land joining his farm in April 1923, from Mrs. Mary Harper Dozier. James Monroe returned to the family farm in 1926 to take over the management of it. Following WWI, he had worked in Florida, and in numerous other states up North and out West. He farmed the land until his retirement in 1959, living on the farm until his death. During the years he and his wife tended the farm, Monroe was very active in Concord Methodist Church, civic organizations and political affairs. He was very proud of his Southern heritage, and a Confederate flag and a U.S. flag flew beside his casket in Concord Methodist Church. He grew up with a strong work ethic, and believed that a man's word was his bond. His tombstone bears the Proverb, "A good name is rather to be chosen than great riches."

Monroe and Louesa Gaston had three children:

1. Dorothy Louesa, born August 22, 1941, married Verron Wilson Lee of Baldwin County, Alabama June 27, 1965. The have lived for many years in Lee County, Alabama. They have two sons and 3 daughters.

2. James Monroe, Jr., born January 2, 1945, married Nancy Carol Wesson of Haywood County, Tennessee, November 24, 1973.

3. Corrie Ida, born April 22, 1946, married Thomas Harold Richburg, of Muscogee County Georgia August 12, 1972. They have lived for many years in LaGrange, Georgia. They have 3 daughters.

Dorothy was an honor graduate at Plains High in the Class of 1959, and Corrie was an honor graduate of the Plains High School Class of 1964. James was Valedictorian of the Class of 1963. All three received four year degrees from Auburn University after attending Georgia Southwestern College in Americus for two years.

James was a charter teacher at Southland Academy in September 1967, and taught there for 5 years. He began full time farming in 1972 on the family farm, and presently continues that vocation. In 1970 he was elected to the Sumter County Board of Education as a write-in candidate (the first person in Sumter County in many years to be elected to any office as a write-in). In 1972 he was elected by the other Board members to be the Chairman. He was elected to his second four year term in 1974, and did not offer for re-election in 1978. He and his wife have been active in Concord Methodist Church, historical groups, civic organizations, and political affairs.

James and Nancy have two sons:

1. James Monroe III, born September 4, 1976 (a graduate of Bob Jones University)
2. Wesson Dalton, born December 5, 1980 (a student at Bob Jones University, to graduate May 9, 2003)

—*Submitted by James Gaston*

Godwin Family

Godwin is an old English name meaning "good-friend."

I. Arnold Godwin, Sr, born 7 May 1776 in N.C. died 27 July 1859 in Sumter Co., Ga. Wife Barbary born 19 July 1773 died 2 April 1815. married ca. 1802-4. Children were:

1. Elizabeth born 5 Dec. 1805 in S.C. married Amos Smith 1 Jan. 1824
2. Margaret born 12 Mar, 1808 in S.C. married Thos. L. Smith, 2 Feb. 1824
3. Rhoda born 24 May 1809 in S.C. married Smith Haymon
4. Arnold Jr. born 26 Oct. 1810 in S.C. died 1844
5. Barbary born 2 Jan. 1813 in S.C. died 29 Nov. 1868
6. Rufus S. born 26 Mar. 1815 in Ga. died 1883-4

Arnold Godwin, Sr. was given a land grant for 500 a. in the Dist. of George, S.C., which was surveyed for him 13 Aug. 1798. He was in the 1820 and 1830 census of Wilkinson Co., Ga. He came to Sumter County, Ga., in 1831. He was listed in the 1840 census.

II. Rufus S. Godwin born 26 Mar. 1815 died 1883-4 1st. wife Martha Cunningham, dau. of Col. John Cunningham, Rev. soldier, was born 1817 in S.C. died 1798-9 in Ga. married ca. 1840-1. married 2nd Sarah Jowers; married 3rd Henrietta Chandler, 1845. Children were:

1. Mary born 14 Oct. 1842 died 21 Nov. 1917 married Reid
2. Fannie Lieutisha born 4 Sept. 1844 died 28 May. 1905 married G. Logan
3. Margaret born 17 Aug. 1846 died 10 May 1926 married 1st Mask 2nd Mohrman
4. John born 29 Nov. 1847 died 13 Mar. 1908 married Willie Z. Murray
5. Arnold III born 29 Nov. 1847 died Aug. 1 1907

6. Zenobia born 12 Nov. 1853
   died 8 June 1924

7. Josephine born ? died 22 Jan. 1934

8. Rufus Bramwell born 1858
   died 1 Aug. 1907 married Mary Sims

9. Ada born ? c. ?
   married William Mathis Holland

Rufus and Martha lived on their farm several miles w. of Kidd's Mill, now Young's Mill pond.

III. John Godwin born 25 Nov. 1847 died 13 Mar. 1908. Wife Willie Z. Murray born 19 Sept. 1861 died 31 July 1953 married 13 Nov. 1878. (He was a confederate veteran.) Children were:

1. Arnold IV born 8 Sept. 1879 died Sept. 1905
   married 18 Oct. 1904 Eddith Harte

2. Nona Gertrnde born 13 Feb. 1882
   died 4 May 1883

3. John Rufus born 12 July 1884
   died 2 May 1887

4. Baby boy born & died 18 Aug. 1886

5. Willlie Lee born 22 June 1888
   died 1 April 1964
   married Dr. A.J. Odom 23 Dec. 1905

6. Theron Erquette born 28 Jan. 1891
   died 21 Sept 1891

7. Lynton Earl Godwin born 8 Sept. 1892
   died 13 Oct. 1954
   married Mar. 1917 Ruth Sanborn.

8. Mary Ellen born 14 Oct. 1895
   died 21 Jan. 1911

9. Martha Allethea born 17 June 1899
   married Geo E. Wise June 1916

John and Willie lived on their farm near Plains which included the farms, later owned by Rosa Fussell, Frank Spann and Crawford Wise.

Lynton Earl Godwin, Sr. born 8 Sept. 1892, died 13 Oct. 1954, wife Ruth Sanborn Godwin, born 26 June 1897, married 14 March 1917. died 2

Dec. 1995. Ruth Sanborn was the daughter of William Harrison Sanborn, whose ancestry has been traced to England as early as 1320.

The children of Lynton and Ruth Godwin are:

1. L.E. Godwin, Jr. born 14 Sept. 1918
   married Dorothy Oliphant
   born 15 April 1922 married 30 May 1942.

2. Ruth born 25 Jan. 1921
   married Hugh A. Carter, Sr.
   born 13 Aug. 1920 married 25 Dec. 1941.
   He died 24 June 1999.

3. Virginia born 3 Dec. 1923
   married Albert L. Bostwick
   born Nov. 1916 married 27 Dec. 1944.
   He died June 1963.

—*Submitted by Virginia Bostwick*

Joseph Milton Hagerson

Joseph Milton Hagerson, b. 2-17-1924 in Sumter Co., son of Charlie Neal Hagerson and Annie Vera Darden, m. 5-9-1948 to Betty Lou Williams b. 10-16 1928. Children:

(A) Thomas Neil b. 5-17-1950, m. 1-17-1970 to Linda Sue Athon b. 7-8-1949, Children: (1) Tracey Elizabeth, b. 7-23-1971, m. April 1, 2000) to Warren Walter Campbell b.8-16-1973 Children: (a) Mary Emily b. Nov. 10, 2000 (2) Christopher Neil "Chris" b. 8-17-1974 Married June 30, 2001 Kathryn Ashley Cole "Katy" b. 1-31-1977

(B) Boyd Milton b. 3-25-1952, m. 8-25-1973 to Margaret Irene Shivers b. 8-16-1953, children: (1) Kevin Boyd b. 1-5-1975, (2) Joseph Andrew b. 9-12-1977, (3) Bradley Tilden b. 5-19-1980..

(C) Marsha Kay b. 3-23-1957, m. 1-8-1977 to Larry Chris Spann, b. 2-18-1957 in Marion County. Children: (1) Larry Chris, Jr. "Chip" b. 8-17-1980. (2) Charles Joseph "Chad" b. Oct. 25, 1983

Milton and family are living on same homesite where Scott Hagerson and Mary Ann Morgan lived when married. Their son, Charlie Neal was born and raised and died here; also, his son Milton was born on same homesite. Milton, with help from friends and relatives tore down the old building and built a new one on the same corner where he now resides. He served 3 months in the Army before World War II ended.

—*Submitted by Hazel Hagerson Smith*

George Robert Harper Family

George Robert Harper born February 26, 1810 near Gladys Creek, Jones County, Georgia, died November 14, 1877, married Margaret Ponder birth and death unknown. The family came to Sumter County, Georgia in 1839, and was one of the main founders of the Plains of Dura (now called Plains). The name of the Plains of Dura came from the book of Daniel where it says, "And Nebuchodneggar set up a brazen bull upon the Plains of Dura." For some unknown reason, a number of Universalists settled in Plains, the other major Christian denomination was Methodist led by Rev. James Glass. G.R. Harper, Esq. Became an ordained universalist minister and led the universalists flock. He also served as pastor of the Universalist Church, Camp Hill, Alabama. Moreover, his family gave the land on which Auburn University, Auburn Alabama was built. A stone marker in downtown Auburn, Alabama tells of the donation. Universalists were free thinkers whose theological doctrine held that all souls would eventually find salvation in the grace of God and that there was no place as hell. The children of his granddaughter, Annie Leona Harper Howell were the last of his descendants to embrace this theology. The Columbus Enquirer in 1842, quoted that, "George R. Harper was the only educated man, and his strength rested more upon his natural and moral forces than his literary attainments." He became the school master for the

fledging settlement. Later, from 1850-1870 he served as legislator for the area in the Georgia Legislature.

Their children were: (A) William J. birth (unknown), death unknown, married Malissa Kendrick. (B) Dr. Lewis Agustus, born June 8, 1833, died May 27, 1908, married Amelia Harvey. (C) Lavinia born January 2, 1835 and died July 27, 1908, married Dr. Jesse Havis Pickett. (D) Dr. George Amos born March 31, 1837, died January 12, 1917, married Martha Evaline Simmons. (E) Micajah born March 29, 1839, died 1893 (unmarried). (F) Sarah born May 8, 1841, died April 5, 1930, married B.F. Toole. (G) Mary Elizabeth born April 18, 1843, died March 30, 1905, married Benjamin F. Todd. (H) James M. born 1846, death (unknown), married (unknown). (I) Samuel C. born 1849, death (unknown), married 1st Lillie Vanover; married 2nd Mattie Vanover. (J) Frances birth (unknown), death (unknown), married Charles H. Clark. (K) Daniel Delaney b. (unknown), d. (unknown), m. Mary Willie Collier. (L) Robert Harper b. (unknown), d. (unknown).

George Amos Harper b. 31 Mar. 1837, d.,12 Jan. 1917, was fourth child of George R. and Margaret Harper, m. Martha Evaline Simmons b. 25 Oct. 1841, d. 29 Apr. 1899. In March 1860 he received his diploma from Eclectic Medical College Philadelphia Penn Dr George Amos Harper served the Confederacy in Company B, 11 Battalion, Georgia Artillery as a physician. After the Civil War, Dr. Harper returned to his farm near Plains, Ga. Their children were: (A) John Lewis b.18 Nov. 1861, d. 23 June 1906. (B) Annie Leona b. 25 Feb. 1866, d. 17 Apr. 1924, m. James Ira Howell, Jr. (See Howell)(C) James Emmette b.19 Jan. 1872, d 7 Apr. 1954, m Jewell Kidd. (D) Bernice b. 29 Jan. 1881, d. 1 Sept. 1968, m. Claude L. Walters.

James Emmette Harper b. 19 Jan. 1872, d. 7 Apr. 1954 was the third child of Dr. George Amos and Martha Evaline Simmons Harper; m. Jewell Kidd b. 11 Apr. 1889, d. 8 Apr. 1980. James Emmette owned and farmed the family farm near Plains, Ga. Their children are: (A) George Amos b. 21 Aug. 1920, m. Georgia Elizabeth Brightwell b. 6 Aug. 1923. Their children are: (1) Faye (twin) b. 7 July 1946, m. 1st Eddie Smith, their child Debra Ann b. 1 Mar. 1964; m. 2nd Millard Farr, their children (a) Lana Kaye b. 21 Aug. 1970 (b) Millard Cameron b. 22 Apr. 1975; m. 3rd Richard Long, no children. (2) Kaye (twin) b. 7 July 1946, m. Linward Ishmael Morris. Their children; (a) Linward Lance b. 14 June 1970 (b) Georgia Lanette b. 28 May 1974 (c) Chad Harper b. and d. 2 Mar. 1976. (3) James Samuel b. I 1 June 1952, in. 1st Vickie Kitchen, no children; m. 2nd Linda Karen Handley, their child (a) Shauna Marie b. 30 Oct. 1979. (4) George William b. 1 Oct. 1956, m. Jeanne Thrasher, their children: (a) George Edward b. 4 Apr. 1977 (b) Audrey Lynn b. 18 Nov. 1979. (5) Robert Louis b. 27 Mar. 1959. (B) Frances b. 21 Aug. 1923, m. George Wilbur Dillard b. 15 Jan. 1921. Their children: (1) Daniel David b. 25 Dec. 1944. (2) George Cary b. 28 May 1948. (3) Robert Marvin b. 28 Sept. 1950, m. Nancy Susan Chambliss, their child (a) Robert Jason b. 21 Dec. 1979.

—*Submitted by Dr. James Bagwell*

Ernest W. Harris and Ouida L. Murphy Harris

Ernest Willie Harris was born December 12, 1898 died May 21, 1980 in Albany, Georgia married January 17, 1920 Ouida Lucile Murphy born December 27, 1900 died August 27, 1969 at home near Plains. Their children are Margaret born February 8, 1921 in Schley Co., Ernest Rastus born February 1, 1922 in Marion Co., Virginia born November 25, 1923 in Marion Co., and Carolyn born December 12, 1928 in Quitman Co., Georgia.

Ernest W. Harris was born in Marion County near Friendship, the first of eleven children of Willie Marie Tharpe born February 17, 1881 in Marion County died August 27, 1949 in Americus, Ga., married Blake Ernest Harris born February 28, 1881 in Marion County and died July 7, 1939 in Marion County, Ga. The Harris family and thirteen Tharpe related lines have been accepted by the Daughters of the American Revolution to have served in the Revolutionary War and several lines have been traced to the early 1600's. Ernest Harris attended school in the small building now used for Sunday school at Friendship Baptist Church. His teacher was Miss Julia Coleman, and in a letter he received from her soon after his wife's death in 1969, Miss Julia said, "It gives me such delight to recall you as one of my beloved *school boys!* How *gallant* and *kind* you were to *this teacher!* And again how you could *dismay* this teacher when you *hardened* your *head!* You have remained in my heart all these years with such pleasure and affection." It was at this school that on a dare Ernest lost two fingers in a wood chopping accident while a group of boys were gathering wood for the school stove. In the early 1940's he served on the Plains High School Board of Education.

Ouida Lucile Murphy was born in the Ebenezer Community of Schley County, Ga., the first of eleven children of Car Lee Hutto born March 7, 1880 in Henry County, Alabama died March 14, 1949 at home in Schley County, Ga., and William Thomas Murphy born March 14, 1880 and died April 4, 1951 at home in Schley County, Ga. They married on April 2, 1900 in Ft. Gaines, Ga. Cora Hutto and Thomas Murphy were descendants of the Pilchers, Murphys, and Johnsons, pioneer families of Sumter and Schley Counties. The Pilcher line has been proven to 1770s and although there is a monument in Warren County, Ga., to William Pilcher, II, for his service in the Revolutionary War, no official record has been found. Ouida and three of her sisters were boarded and schooled in

Ellaville since the Ebenezer School was too far for four little girls to walk to. Ouida remembered spending lots of time with her grandmother, Minerva Pilcher Murphy, who among other things taught her to fish, something she enjoyed all her life. This Harris family visited their Murphy kin every Sunday or two for lunch or the afternoon. Writer remembers the "sings" when the family gathered in the living room where the piano was played and the group was led in singing by Thomas Murphy, her grandfather, who had a beautiful baritone voice. Ouida's faith in God, love of her family, friends and home were most important to her. Ernest and Ouida attended Plains Baptist Church.

Ernest W. Harris and his family moved to Plains at Christmas time in December of 1934 from Marion County to a small farm which he rented from Mr. Jack Slappey. In about two years the family moved to a farm on the Magnolia Springs Road known as the Cowart Place that Ernest had bought. Magnolia Springs was about a mile from this house and was a great source of recreation for this family. Here Ernest was engaged simultaneously in farming, in a logging business, in land terracing, and he owned a bus which transported passengers to Americus in the morning and returned to Plains in the afternoon.

In 1944, Ernest Harris bought at public auction approximately 525 acres of land and a house built about 1854 by the McGarrah family on what is now Highway 45 North. The family moved to this house in 1947 and the farm was named Plains Plantation. Ernest started his first cattle farm here when he purchased breeding stock from Mr. John Hitch of Maryville, Tennessee. He was one of the first men in the state of Georgia to own, breed, and show Aberdeen Angus cattle. In March, 1951 at the Aberdeen Angus Show and Sale held in Atlanta, he entered the grand champion female, Queen of Plains 4th, which was sold to A.R. Lovvorn of Shandra Farms, in Rome, Ga., for $2,200. County Agent J.K. Luck stated in the newspaper that "This is the highest price ever paid for a Georgia-raised Angus at a Georgia Show." Ernest Harris continued in the cattle business for almost twenty-five years. During this time, he owned one of the first self-propelled grain combines in the state and did custom combining in Sumter and surrounding counties and as far north as Upson County. As a retirement project, he built layer houses and was in the egg production business for several years.

Ernest W. Harris and Ouida Murphy Harris are buried at Sunset Memorial Gardens in Americus, Ga.

—*Submitted by Carolyn Harris Durham*

Martha Tidd Harris

Edgar Graves Tidd born November 1, 1901 and died July 26, 1977 is buried at Oak Grove Cemetery in Americus. He married on December 13, 1938, Martha Elizabeth Raines, daughter of James and Myrtice Raines who was born December 8, 1919. Martha had a son, James Henry Rushin by a former marriage.

James Henry Rushin was born September 9, 1937 and married October 19, 1957 to Mary O'Reily who was born on February 4, 1937. Their children are: James Reily Ruskin born July 24, 1959, Patricia Michelle Rushin born February 13, 1962, Richard Glenn Rushin born July 13, 1962, Sheene Marie Rushin born September 21, 1965.

Edgar Lee Tidd born May 2, 1940 and married September 21, 1962 to Ernestine Bailey who was born February 22, 1944. Their children are: Susan Lynn Tidd born June 11, 1963, Karen Leigh Tidd born November 30, 1965, Amy Marie Tidd born December 7, 1967.

William Earl Tidd born July 30, 1943 and married March 7, 1970 to Nancy Cleverdon who was born May 25, 1943. Their children are: Julia Cleverdon Tidd born September 11, 1973, Susann Drew Tidd born December 14, 1976, William Graves Tidd born August 13, 1980.

Myrtice Ann Tidd born September 1, 1946 and married August 17, 1969 to Thomas Cecil Allgood, Jr., who was born October 30, 1945. Their children are: Thomas Cecil Allgood III born June 18, 1973 and Elizabeth Wynn born June 13, 1976.

Martha Tidd married on December 8, 1979 to Jack Edward Terry who was born March 24, 1918 and died April 16, 1992. He is buried in Oak Grove Cemetery.

Martha Tidd Terry married on October 9, 1993 to Ernest R. Harris who was born February 1, 1922 and died August 23, 2002. He is buried in the Andersonville Historic Site.

—Submitted by Martha Tidd Harris

Lark Carthan Hobgood, Sr.

Lark Carthan Hobgood, Sr. moved to Sumter County the first time in 1913 from Bartow County, Ga. He moved to Colquit County, Ga. in 1918 and back to Sumter County near Plains in 1928. He was a man of many talents. In addition to his occupation of farming, he was a carpenter, gins man, saw miller and well digger. When he was not busy with these professions, he could usually be found hunting the sly old fox along with his fellow fox hunting friends and their fox hounds.

Lark Carthan Hobgood Sr. b. 4-26-1884 d. 1-24-1950. son of Lewis Monroe and Victoria Covington Hobgood, m. 1st Laura Greene b. 1890, d 6-16-1916, one son Thomas Lewis b 8-21-1914, d 8-21-1987; m. 2nd Rosa Lee Greene b 10-24-1902, d. 12-13-1990. All of the children of Lark Carthan Hobgood, Sr. and Rosa Lee Greene Hobgood graduated from Plains High School. Their children:

I. **Theron Hobgood** b. 5-20-1921 Colquitt County, Ga., d. 5-30-1986 buried at Lebanon Cemetery, Plains, Ga., m. 6-17-1949 Marjorie Slocumb b. 11-7-1930, daughter of Ruric Nevel and Anice Cole Slocumb of Webster County, Ga. Theron graduated from Georgia Southwestern College.

Like his father he enjoyed farming. He worked 20 years with the Department of Agriculture (ASCS). Their children:

1) Karen Hobgood b. 6-21-1950, m. 3-17-1972 Roland Sloan "Steve" Broadhurst son of Frank and Jane Broadhurst of Americus. Steve is a contractor. Their children: A) Stephanie Karen Broadhurst b. 10-22-74, m. 7-10-1999 Chad Eugene Offenbacker b. 9-28-1972 son of Arthur and Janice Offenbacker of Elkton, VA. Stephanie graduated from Georgia Southern University, Statesboro, Ga. and is a teacher. Chad is a computer scientist at the Naval Surface Warfare Center in Dahlgren, Va. B) Lisa Jan Broadhurst b. 8-18-1979, graduated with a BS in Biology from Georgia Southwestern State University and is enrolled at Emory School of Public Health working on a masters in Public Health. C) Michael Sloan Broadhurst b. 4-14-1981 currently serving in the United States Marines at Camp Lejeune, Jacksonville, NC.

2) Marlene Hobgood b. 8-30-1952, m. Jimmie Hobbs son of James and Frankie Hobbs, his son Jeremie b. 9-30-1978, their daughter, Annah Faith Hobbs b. 7-8-1993. Jimmie serves as pastor of Cusseta First Baptist Church, Cusseta, Ga.

3) Darrell Theron Hobgood b. 8-31-1958, m 5-23-1981 Jan Hobbs b. 11-8-1956 daughter of Carl and Frances Hobbs, Butler, Ga., their sons, A) Lijah Darrell b. 3-5-1985, B) Carl Landon b. 4-3-1992. Darrell works with Georgia Farm Bureau and sod farms.

II. **Lark Carthan Hobgood, Jr.**, b 4-10-1924 Colquitt County, Ga., d 5-22-2002, served in the U. S. Army during World War II (3-3-1943 to 12-29-45), member of the 79th Infantry Division Headquarters Company. He was active in Normandy, Northern France, Rhineland and Central Europe Campaigns, m. 11-16-1948 Barbara Jean Hogg b. 4-23-1930 Randolph County,

Ga daughter of Ernest and Annie Lura Hogg. Their children

1) Lynda Marie Hobgood b 4-8-1950, m Joseph Maxwell Respess 8-20-1977 of Fulton County, Ga b. 6-16-1948 son of James L. and Barbara Ann Respess. Their children A) Erin Marie Respess b. 4-18-1980, m. William Daniel Howell, Jr. 8-17-2001 b. 9-15-1975 son of William Daniel and Billie Jean Howell, Jr. of Oglethorpe, Ga. B) Lindsey Marshall Respess b 6-1-1982, m. Jonathan Lee Belcher b 6-6-1982. Their child Johnathan Cameron Belcher b. 9-17-1999.

2) Eugene Carthan Hobgood b. 12-28-1954, m. Debbie Rae Halliwell b 2-20-1962 daughter of Russell and Elizabeth Halliwell. Children A) Elisia Michelle Hobgood b. 2-5-1979, m 1st Gus Brunson, their children a) MaKayla Rae Brunson b. 11-23-1995, b) Jacob Earl Brunson b. 1-31-1997 m. 2nd Ronald Corey Ingle, b. 8-6-1977 son of Robert and Lynn Ingle of Americus, their child Ronald Corey, Jr. b. 3-1-2002. B) Lark Russell Hobgood b. 10-29-1981

III. Ollie Bell Hobgood b. 2-12-1926 Colquitt County, Ga. A bookkeeper by profession and Treasurer and Sunday school Teacher at Plains Baptist Church.

IV. Elma Hazel Hobgood b. 5-14-1929 Sumter County, Ga., m. Joseph Harrison Smith, Jr. son of Joseph Harrison and Mildred Booker Smith, Sr. b. 4-26-1929. Their children:

1) Joseph Harrison Smith, III b. 3-26-1951, m 1st Sheila Ann Hillock b. 3-22-1955, daughter of James W. and Shirley Hillock, Kokomo, Indiana. Their children; A) Brandy Lee Smith b. 6-2-1976, her son Chance Warren Smith b. 7-27-1994; B). Chadwick Warren Smith b. 2-20-1978 m. Jennifer Williams, one daughter, Nicole, b 12-4-1997. m. 2nd Joyce S. Bloodworth, Macon, GA. Her son Wesley Bloodworth.

2) Thomas Richmond Smith b. 7-18-1954, m. 1st Donna Sue Everett b. 2-20-1956 daughter of E. C. and Mary Helen Everett of Plains, Ga. Their children, A) Jennifer Dawn Smith b. 10-12-1972 m.9 15-2001 Jamie Crosby, Hilton Head, SC B) Julie Kendall Smith b. 8-20-1977. m. 2nd Robin Hummel, daughter of Jerry and Gail Hummel, Pamana City, Fla. Her sons Jacob Glen Engle and Jonathan Holt.

3) Wesley Sherwin Smith, b 8–30-1955, m. Janice Elaine Roberts b. 12-2-1957 daughter of Janice and Carlton Roberts. Their children A) Tonia Marie Smith b 8-20-1974, m. Todd Williams, Albany Ga. Their children: a) Isaiah James Williams b 4-17-1998 b) Isabell Grace Williams b. 11-2000. B) Joshua Adam Smith b. 10-18-1977 m. 1st Julie Duke of Albany, Ga. Their child Adrianna Smth b. 4-17-1997; m. 2nd Cassandra Taylor, Albany, Ga. C) Daniel Troy Smith b. 6-16-1980 D) Gabrielle Laine Smith b. 6-6-1982

V. Heyward Walton Hobgood b 7-7-1937 m. 1st Gay McRainey. Their child;

1) Agnes Rosalyn b. 12-25-1955; m 2nd Lorraine Clark, Peach County, Ga. Their child;

2) Hal Clark Hobgood b 10-23-1957 . 3-14-1974. m. 3rd Mattie Lavonia Hamilton Radford b 6-11-1935. Her children A) Margaret Lucille born 4-1-1955 m. 1st Joe Hill. Their child: Christopher Hamilton Hill b 12-15-1972 m. 2nd Bill Linder. Their children: (a) Davis, (b) Jordan. B) Richard Hamilton b. 1-29-1957. Childen of Heyward and Lavonia;

3) Heyward Walton Hobgood, Jr. b. 2-13-1963,.

4) Roger Thomas Hobgood b 6-23-1965, m. Rochelle, their children: a) Melissa, b) LaRue.

—*Submitted by Broadhurst Development Co., Inc.*

Hogg Family

Ernest Randle Hogg (born Sept. 15, 1906) married Annie Laura Garrett (born Jan. 6, 1908) on Dec. 29, 1928. They moved to Sumter County in 1938 to a place near Plains. They were the parents of two daughters and three sons. All were graduated from Plains High School. Their children:

I. **Barbara Jean** (born Apr. 23, 1930). Married Lark Carthan Hobgood, Jr. (Apr. 10, 1924) on November 6, 1948. See Lark C. Hobgood, Jr., history.

II. **Ernest Malcolm** (born Jan. 14, 1933) married Mary Ann Hardy on Feb. 6, 1955. One son, Dale Warren (born June 2, 1960), who married Melinda Cay Thompson (born July 21, 1961). Three children:

1. Alyzander Cay, born Apr. 12, 1990
2. Caitlyn Marie, born June 29, 1993
3. Sean Lanier, born Oct. 12, 2000.

III. **Elizabeth Ann** (born Mar. 6, 1941) married Larry Riley Dillard (born June 20, 1941) on Feb. 12, 1961. Three children:

A. Laurie Ann (born Jan. 13, 1962). Married Clifford E. Pilcher III (born Sept. 15, 1959) on Aug. 28, 1983. Children:

1. Alexander Kyle, born April 10, 1989
2. Mallory Brooke, born May 3, 1990
3. Megan Rae, born June 23, 1992

B. Sharon Denise (born June 8, 1964). Married Fredrick Brinson (born Jan. 1, 1964) on Sept. 24, 1983. Children:

1. Sharon Ann, born Apr. 5, 1986
2. Kellie Elizabeth, born May 30, 1990
3. Fredrick Casey, born Sept. 9, 1992.

C. Randall Vern (born Feb. 7, 1966). Married Marsha Lynn Downer (born Jan. 13, 1967) on June 16, 1989. Two daughters:

1. Jennifer Krista, born Apr. 21, 1992
2. Erika Kate, born Mar. 4, 1994

IV. **James Erle** (born Nov. 12, 1943). Married Duane Cruchens (born Sept. 10, 1946) on Oct. 9, 1995. Two daughters:

A. Emily Durene (born May 31, 1970). Married Adam Douglas Smith (born Feb. 26, 1971) on Dec. 29, 2001.

B. Allison Lorine (born July 9, 1975). Married Daniel C. Prudehomme (born Feb. 24, 1974) March 29, 1999. Daughter Claire Noel born Nov. 4, 2000.

V. **Thomas Lynn** (born July 28, 1946). Married Andrea Lee Jensen (born Jan. 1948) on Jan. 13, 1976. Two children:

A. Andrew Thomas born Dec. 7, 1977

B. Kristina Lea born Feb. 24, 1980

—*Submitted by Barbara Hobgood*

Clinton Max Holloway, Sr. Family

I had heard, during childhood, that two Holloway brothers came to Schley/Sumter area from S.C. When I started my genealogical research, I found Martin Maston Holloway and most of his children settled here. Maston was the son of Jordan b. ca. 1765 Va. - 1815 S.C. and Rebecca unknown b. ca. 1770 Va. d. ca. 1828 S.C. Jordan may be a son of Martin, R.S. but the King & Queen Va. courthouse burned. When Maston left Edgefield Co. S.C. he was married with three or more children. He is listed as Martin in his father's estate settlement. He is also listed as Martin a few other times but usually is listed as Maston. His second marriage occurred in Clark Co. Ga. to Mary Henson. They settled in Sunter/Schley area by 1850.

Simpson Jordan 1815 S.C.-1813, Ga. and Harrison H. 1827 Ga. - 1912 Ga., both had large families. My GGGrandfather Simpson Jordan married 3-29-1842 in Butts Co. Ga. Martha Delene Crabtree 1818 S.C. - 1908 Ga. She was Cherokee but percent and history remains unknown. They both are buried in the old Bethel Cemetery in Schley Co. near the Sumter Co. line. Part of their original farm is now owned by a descendant, Frank Bivins. My GGrandfather Maston VanBuren 1847-1918 married 1873 Sarah (Sal) Oliver 1850 - 1927. They raised 5 sons and 2 daughters. He farmed near Andersonville in the Cut-off Community. Sal was the daughter of Sarah Youngblood ca. 1810-after 1850 and (? John McDonald) Oliver died before 1850 census.

My grandfather, William Harvey Holloway 1874-1964 married Elizabeth Ellen Methvin 1879-1960 and raised three sons and one daughter. He was the overseer of Benjamin James Methvin's farm and sawmill. In later years he rented a farm. He drove the first school bus in the Chambliss Community. He was the county bailiff in the 28th district for nearly 50 years. He also did blacksmithing, carpentry and syrupmaking. He lost one eye when a nail bounced back. He lost his second eye due to shingles around 1955. They raised 4 children. They are both buried in the Leslie City Cemetery.

My father, Burtram Ernest Holloway 1910-1983, married 1931 Mary Alice McCarty b. 1913. She is the daughter of James Edward McCarty 1871-1945 and Beulah Benton Brooks 1875-1963. Four sons: (1) Ernest Alfred b. 1933 lives in Wichata Falls, Tx.- two sons, one daughter and nine grandchildren; (2) Thomas Erwin b. 1935 and lives near Americus, several marriages, no natural children; (3) Clinton Max (continued later); (4) Donald

Bertrum b. 1942, three marriages, two sons and two grandchildren. All my brothers graduated from Plains High School.

I was born 3-4-1937 on the east side of Sumter Co. and raised on the north side of Sumter Co. in the Shiloh Community. I was an honor graduate of Plains High School in 1955. I attended GSW for two years, ABAC for one summer and UGA for five years. I received a BSA in 1959 and a DVM in 1962 from UGA. I married 6-11-1960 Marianna Belle Spann of Preston b. 11-26-1938, daughter of Clayton J. Spann and Katie Belle Brightwell. Marianna now lives in Americus and is the Probate Court Clerk.

Our children are: (1) Denise Ann b. 5-8-1962 married 10-21-1982 Richard Lynn Burgess b. 8-11-1956, children Heather Lynn b. 6-27-1986 and R. Scott b. 8-1-1990; Denise is a medical technologist and the assistant director of the clinical lab at Sumter Regional Hospital. They live in Americus. (2) Laura (n) b. 8-6-1963, married 7-2-1981, Jimmy Allen Faircloth b. 6-1-1961, children Christina Belle b. 12-19-1981 and Garrett Taylor b. 9-29-1987. Laura owns "A Cut Above" in Americus and lives just east of Americus; (3) Lynn (n) b. 8-6-1963 married 12-3-1983 Michael Harold Farmer b. 7-18-1960, children M. Brandon b. 12-23-1989 and Phillip Chad b. 9-12-1991. Lynn is now the Columbia Co. Delinquent Tax Officer. and lives near Appling, Ga., west of Augusta; (4) Clint M. Jr. b. 1-28-1966 m. 12-19-1987 Lisa Cornelia Bailey b. 8-22-1966, children C. Max III b. 6-2-1992 and Mitchell John b. 6-15-1995. Clint is a diesel mechanic at J and M Trucking and lives east of Plains.

After receiving my DVM in June of 1962, I ran Dr. R.L. Meeks practice at Eatonton for three weeks. We moved to Plains 7-18-1962. I have practiced vetenrinary medicine in Sumter Co. and surrounding area every since. I purchased a farm east of Plains and built a house. We moved 7-18-1973. I had a large herd of Charolais cattle but sold most in 1988. I sold my clinic in Americus in 1989 due to highway construction. I practice now out of my house and truck.

I joined the Plains Lions Club in 1962 and have held every office in the club, including President three times for three and one half years. I have also held several offices in the district, including District Governor. I was Scout Master for several years. I joined the Methodist Church as a teenager. I joined the Plains Baptist in 1977. I served as Minister of Music at Brooklyn Heights Baptist Church for six months. I grew up singing in a family group. I was in the high school glee club and a member of the school and FFA quartet for two years. In 1983 I became involved again in gospel singing, convention style. I have served as President of the Georgia State Gospel Singing Convention in 1990, 1996 and 2002. I emcee several all day gospel singings in Worth, Turner and Crisp Counties.

Other Holloway descendants are Lambs, Buchannans, Coxs. Bivins, Wells, Whites and others. Other ancestors include Methvin, Murphy, Mitchell, Norvell, Bulloch, McCarty, Raiford, Brooks, Turner, Law, Maxey, Burton, Curry, Pope and others.

—*Submitted by Dr. Clinton M. Holloway*
1460 US Hwy. 280 W. Plains, Ga. 31780

Howell Family

John Howell, Sr., American progenitor of the line, arrived in Virginia in 1637, and was given a land grant by Governor Sir John Harvey of the Colony of Virginia. He received the grant for transporting three persons to the colony. The land grant was dated January 10, 1639. Years later he received an additional 212 acres in land grant from the Royal Governor Sir William Berkeley. Both tracts were located in Henrico County, Virginia. Children of John Howell, Sr. were two boys, John Jr. and William.

John Jr. inherited his father's land and in April, 1664 added to it with another land grant from Sir Edmund Andros, Lt. Governor of Virginia, amounting to 100 acres in Isle of Wight County, Virginia. He later moved to Bertie County, North Carolina where he bought land. At this time he owned eight black slaves and seven whites (indentured servant). John Howell married Elizabeth. Children included: John, Joseph, Thomas, Robert, Hopkins, and William.

Joseph Howell, son of John Howell Jr., prospered in Edgecombe County, North Carolina. He married Margaret. At his death in 1750, an inventory of his estate showed that he owned three plantations, possessed a large number of slaves, 129 head of cattle, a large number of other farm animals and a great variety of personal property. Joseph was also elected to the North Carolina Assembly as representative from Edgecombe County in 1746. Children of Joseph Howell and Margaret include: Joseph, Jr., Mary, Marphrey, Thomas and Martha.

Joseph Howell, Jr., son of Margaret and Joseph Howell, was born in Edgecombe County, North Carolina in 1733 and died in DeKalb County, Georgia, in 1835, aged 102. Joseph Howell, who was 43 years old when the Revolutionary War broke out, saw active service in the Militia of Macklenburg County, North Carolina, in Captain Adam Alexander's Company, having enlisted June 6, 1766. He fought in the Battles of Guilford Court House and Kings' Mountain. His service is recorded in the collection of the North Carolina Historical Commission, Book C. He also furnished supplies and money to the continental army. Children of Joseph Howell, Jr., and Margaret Eleanor Garmon include: John, Joseph, Elizabeth, Henry, Eli, Margaret, William, Isaac, Evan, Michael, and Eleanor.

William Howell, Jr., son of Joseph Howell, Jr. and Margaret Eleanor Garmon was born in Anson County, North Carolina and died in 1822 in Georgia. He married Elizabeth Sides on Feb. 12, 1801.

The son of the above union was James Ira Howell. He was b. Oct. 24, 1802 and d. June 30, 1875. He m. Elizabeth Pearce Jan. 14, 1830.

James Ira Howell immigrated to Sumter County, GA from Twiggs County, GA., in 1835 when he was 33 years of age. He settled on this land as the Creek Indians were being driven out and cleared land which was in Virgin Pine Forest. He built a home which is still in possession of the family. It is now owned by John Wilson's brother, Claude Wilson, and his sister, Mrs. Rubye McIlwraith, also shared in the division of the land properties. James Ira and his wife, Elizabeth, are both buried in the Howell Family Cemetery which is about ¼ mile from the original house.

Children of James Ira and Elizabeth: (1) Edmond Granberry b. July 28, 1831, d. June 5, 1853, never married. (2) Mary Anne P. b. Sept. 19, 1833, d. June 13, 1898, m. Joseph McMath. (3) Layrons E.P. b. Dec. 6, 1835, d. Sept. 12, 1892, m. Mollie Rylander. (4) John Wm. Talley b. June 30, 1838, d. Jan. 15, 1921 at Pavo, GA, bur. In Howell Cemetery Sumter Co., GA, m. Jane Elizabeth Stallings. (5) Nancy L.A.K. b. Nov. 27, 1840, d. Dec. 9, 1911, m. Alonzo Josephus. (6) Emily Evie E. b. Oct. 3, 1843, d. Jan. 4, 1927, m. Benjamin Rooks. (7) William Taylor b. Dec. 2, 1846, killed in battle May 4, 1864. (8) Sarah Anne Laura b. Nov. 14, 1848, d. Mar. 16, 1886. (9) James Ira Jr. b. Oct. 11, 1853, d. Oct. 30, 1910.

James Ira Howell, Jr. m. Laura A Parker. They had two children, but Laura and the two children died with a contagious fever at about the same time. Then James Ira married his second wife, Annie Leona Harper on June 14, 1893. They were married in a double wedding ceremony in the Windsor Hotel, Americus, GA.

James Ira Howell was a graduate of Mercer University. After graduation he taught school for a year at Magnolia Springs, but quit to operate a grocery store on Cotton Avenue in Americus. After a year or so he sold out and moved to Sasser, GA, where he bought another grocery store. In Sasser he and his wife prospered. He became a wealthy merchant, so much so, that he was able to purchase a 4,000-acre plantation and pay cash for it. Thus, he added planting to his mercantile interest. His success continued as he amassed holdings in Alabama and Florida. He was an avid reader and collected a large private library. However, in 1905 he suffered a stroke that paralyzed his brain. When this happened his wife put the plantation in the care of the overseer, Miles Jordan, and she asked Charlie Anthony to look after the mercantile business. Then Mrs. Howell moved with her sick husband and five children to Sumter County, GA, so her father, Dr George A. Harper, a prominent Sumter County physician, could help her look after her family. Mrs. Howell bought a wooded area in Plains, had it cleared and had a house built which was completed in 1908. The house, which is still in possession of the family, was built from timber cut from the plantation and hauled from Terrell County to Plains in mule-drawn wagons.

Children of James Ira and Annie Harper Howell include: (1) James Harper Howell (Harper); (2) Bertha Howell; (3) Bernard Dewitt Howell (Dewitt); (4) Floy Howell; (5) John Emmette Howell.

Marriages of these: James Harper Howell m. Grace Kornegay Aug. 30, 1924. They had three children: Louise Howell, Cotton Howell, and Ruby Lee Howell.

Bertha Howell m. Roy David Brannen June 7, 1918, no children.

Bernard Dewitt Howell m. Gussie Abrams Oct. 30, 1924. They had one child, Dee Howell. Dee Howell m. Frank Worthy, Jr., of Americus in the 1950's. Dee and Frank moved to Austell, GA. They have two boys, Johnny and Brad.

Floy Howell b. Dec. 18, 1901, m. Henry Lafayette Bagwell May 23, 1924. They had two children, Anne Howell Bagwell b. Aug. 17, 1925 and James Emmett Bagwell b. Mar. 16, 1941.

Anne Howell Bagwell m. Millard Franklin Simmons Mar. 18, 1946. They had one son, Millard Franklin Simmons, Jr. called "Mill." Mill m. Gloria Chavers on June 20, 1970. Mill and Gloria Simmons have two children, Millard Rhett Simmons called "Rhett" and Paige Simmons.

James Emmett Bagwell, Ph.D., a professor at Georgia Southwestern State University m. Cynthia Faye Baker of Abbeville, GA, June 8, 1980. They have two children, James Bradford Bagwell, called "Brad." He was born May 19, 1981. Another child, Victoria Floy Bagwell, was born Jan. 11, 1985. She is called "Victoria."

—Submitted by Jimmy Bagwell

M.L. Hudson Family

Milton Leander Hudson, regarded as the founder of Plains, was born 10 June 1853 in Sumter County. He was the son of Thomas Green Hudson and Martha Frances Stewart Hudson, who were married 5 Oct. 1852. His father was born in Laurens County in Middle Georgia. M.L.'s sister was Florence Hudson Alston. M.L.'s father died at age 30 before M.L. was 3 years old. The grave of Thomas Green Hudson, dated 30 April 1856, is believed to be the oldest marked grave at Lebanon Cemetery in Plains.

After her husband's death, M.L.'s mother remarried Dr. Joseph T. Turner, an itinerate Methodist minister. They had four children, two of whom lived to adulthood. They were Effie Turner Oliver and Carrie Turner Dean, both half-sisters of M.L. Hudson and among Plains' most prominent people.

M.L. Hudson married Julia Cassandra "Cassie" Clark on 20 Oct. 1878. She was the daughter of Edward Clark and Mary E. Watts Clark. M.L. and Cassie Clark Hudson were the parents of eight children: Stewart C. Hudson, Florence Lucile Hudson, Mary Frances Hudson, Douglas Clifford Hudson, Milton Leander Hudson, Jr., Lewis M. Hudson, Marguerite "Tot" Hudson, and Edward T. Hudson. Only four of the eight children lived to adulthood. Seven of the eight, including the last surviving child, who died in 1969, are buried at Lebanon Cemetery.

Cassie Clark Hudson died on 29 Dec. 1896, only 11 days after the birth of her youngest child, Edward. She was 39. Edward died five months later.

M.L. Hudson remarried Willie M. Cato on 21 Dec. 1902. He, Cassie and Willie are all buried at Lebanon Cemetery. The inscription on his tombstone reads "An honest man's the noblest work of God." M.L. Hudson served as Plains' first postmaster and first railroad agent. He gave the land for the town itself, and also the land on which the depot was built in 1888. He built the first house in what would become the town, and his daughter, Mary, was born in this house at the corner of Church Street and Bond's Trail Road in 1884.

A devout Methodist, M.L. Hudson deeded land for the Methodist church in town in 1888. He also deeded the land on which the 1921 Plains school sits. He was one of the town's most prominent merchants and was long associated with the Oliver-McDonald Co. He also carried on large farming operations. He died unexpectedly at his Plains home on a Sunday afternoon, 30 June 1912 at age 59. His obituary stated the "end came quite suddenly and followed an illness of a day only." Some acute stomach trouble was believed to have been the cause of death. The malady baffled "the skill of physicians called to attend him."

The children, grandchildren, great-grandchildren and great-great-grandchildren of M.L. and Cassie Hudson:

1) **Stewart C. Hudson** (b. 24 July 1879 d. 11 Jan. 1900). Stewart died in a freak horse accident in his father's yard in Plains. He was straddling two horses that ran under a big oak tree and he was hit by a low-lying limb and killed. He was 20 years old.

2) Florence Lucile Hudson (b. 6 March 1881 d. 7 Aug. 1884). Florence, named for her father's sister, died tragically when she fell into a pot of lye soap. She was 3.

3) Mary Frances Hudson (b. 9 Feb. 1884 d. 28 July 1965). Mary, the first white child born in the town of Plains, married Karl Clarence Campbell (1880-1916) on 9 April 1903. He was a native of Monticello who had attended the University of Georgia and came to Plains to teach. Mary was educated at Brenau College and taught school several years. After her husband's death, she went to Emory University in Atlanta to become a medical technician. She returned to Plains and served as a laboratory technician at the Wise Sanitarium for many years. She also was a Plains postmistress. A devout member of the Plains Methodist Church, she taught a Bible class for many years. In 1954-55, she was the first appointed female lay speaker of the South Georgia Conference. She also was a member of the Sumter County Board of Education. In Plains, she was lovingly called "Miss Mary" by all who knew her. She died at age 81 at Magnolia Manor in Americus. She and Karl had three children:

A) Milton Lucius Campbell (b. 14 June 1904 d. 15 Nov. 1965). Milton attended Marion Institute and was the president of the first Peoples Bank and Trust (now Central Bank) in Montgomery, Ala. He is buried at Greenwood Cemetery in Montgomery. He married Marguerite Miller on 14 June 1927 in Miami. They had one daughter:

1A) Mary Marguerite Campbell (b. 24 Jan. 1932) married Webber Van Hudson on 8 June 1951. One child: Webber Van Hudson, Jr. (b. 8 May 1952)

B) Karl Clarence Campbell (b. 30 Aug. 1908 d. 10 Feb. 1996). Karl graduated from Georgia Tech in 1930 and worked many years as an accountant. He entered the ministry of the United Methodist Church in 1955 and served churches in Crestview, Panama City and Gonzalez, Fla., and Montgomery, Dothan, Ashford, Mobile and Union Springs, Ala. He married Rachel Q. Winn on 30 March 1935 in Miami. They had three children:

1B) Mary Jo Campbell (b. 7 Sept. 1936) married first Roger Post Enzor on 15 April 1954. Three children: Opal Winn Enzor (b. 20 May 1956); Rachel Lois Enzor (b. 17 Oct. 1957); Olin Oliver Enzor III (b. 22 June 1961). Mary Jo married second Charles Dean Stout on 19 April 1969.

2B) Cassandra "Sandra" Campbell (b. 18 Aug. 1943) married James Cecil Faust on 6 Oct. 1962. Three children: James C. "Jimbo" Faust, Jr. (b. 6 Jan. 1964); Dedra Dyan Faust (b. 22 Sept. 1969); Matthew Ryan Faust (b. 30 Sept. 1972).

3B) Karlene Campbell (b. 13 March 1950) married James Walter Polk, Jr. on 30 Aug. 1970. Two children: Karla Michelle Polk (b. 13 June 1977); Susan Marie Polk (b. 8 Dec. 1983).

C) Stewart Hudson Campbell (b. 9 April 1911 d. 18 Feb. 1990). Stewart owned and operated Stewart Campbell Funeral Home in Richland for many years. After retiring, he traveled the state of Georgia as funeral home inspector. He married Edith Hodges on 20 June 1939 in Langley, S.C. They had three children:

1C) Martha Joane Campbell (b. 13 March 1940 d. 3 Aug. 1955). She died following a car wreck and is buried in Richland.

2C) Caroline "Carol" Campbell (b. 1 Aug. 1944) married William Earl Smith on 15 July 1967. Two children: Martha Joane Smith (b. 6 Jan. 1969); Jennifer Lynn Smith (b. 7 May 1973).

3C) Dorothy Campbell (b. 11 Sept. 1949 d. 12 Sept. 1949). She is buried in Richland.

4) Douglas Clifford Hudson (b. 4 Feb. 1886 d. 21 March 1956). Douglas moved to southern California early in life and was living there when his father died in 1912. He later lived in New York. He married May Elizabeth Henderson (1886-1932) on 28 July 1913 in New York City. She died on 1 Sept. 1932 at age 36 and is buried in Brooklyn, N.Y. Douglas died at age 70. He and May had two children:

A) Dorothy Hazel Hudson (b. 9 May 1914 d. 6 Nov. 1996). Dorothy for many years worked for Cosmopolitan magazine. She married Robert Clayton Fay on 29 July 1954 in New York City and lived in East Berne, N.Y. They had one child:

1A) Robert Hudson Fay (b. 17 Oct. 1957)

B) Douglas Clifford Hudson, Jr. (b. 10 May 1916 d. 9 Jan. 1984). He married first Ethel Watson; married second Valerie Eaten in 1956. They lived in Las Vegas, and at the time of his death lived in Knox, N.Y. He and Ethel had one child:

1B) Douglas C. Hudson III (b. 29 March 1944).

5) Milton Leander Hudson, Jr. (b. 5 April 1888 d. 29 March 1952). M.L. was an accountant who once owned his own accounting firm. He later worked for many years as an accountant for A.G. Rhodes and Son. He later owned and operated a furniture business in Norcross. M.L. married Pearl Reynolds (1887-1973) on 22 Jan. 1909. He died at age 63. They are buried at Westview Abbey in Atlanta. They had two children:

A) Hendrik Reynolds Hudson (b. 6 June 1911 d. 19 Nov. 1973). Reynolds graduated from Georgia Tech in 1934 and served in the U.S. Navy 1941-45. He was a research engineer at Georgia Tech and a lecturer for NASA's science program in Washington. He married Sally Potts in May 1944. They had five children:

1A) Celia Graham Hudson (b. 25 Feb. 1945) married first James Dixon Wright, Jr.; married second Jerome Chandler. Two children: Anne Wright Chandler (b. 9 Aug. 1976); Paul Theodore Chandler (b. 28 Nov. 1977)

2A) Dorothy Ruth Hudson (b. 4 June 1946) married Michael Hardy.

3A) Hendrik Reynolds "Rey" Hudson, Jr. (b. 20 April 1948) married Eva. Three children: David Hudson; Daniel Christian Hudson; Carol Hudson

4A) Milton Leander Hudson (b. 16 Aug. 1949) married Linda Ann Bliss. Three children: Milton Leander "Andy" Hudson, Jr. (the fourth M.L. Hudson) (b. 25 Feb. 1976); Heidi Hudson; Sterling Hudson. He also adopted Linda Ann's children from a previous marriage: Lisa; Jay; Cindy; Jeffrey.

5A) Martha Lucille "Lucy" Hudson (b. 17 Aug. 1955) married William Frank Stembridge III on 1 May 1982. One child: Gwendolyn Eve Stembridge (b. 18 April 1988)

B) Allen Clark Hudson (b. 9 Dec. 1913 d. 20 Oct. 1988). Clark graduated from Georgia Tech in 1939. An architect, he worked primarily on hospital and medical projects. He married Dorothy Dent on 28 Feb. 1942 in Atlanta. They had two children:

1B) Harriet Elizabeth Hudson (b. 14 July 1949) married first John L. Carr 24 Aug. 1973; married second Richard Knittle. One child: Clark Knittle (b. 28 Aug. 1987)

2B) Thomas Allen "Tom" Hudson (b. 19 Nov. 1951) married Renee Ruppersberg on 24 June 1980. Three children: Emily Catherine Hudson (b. 12 July 1981); Margaret Leigh "Meg" Hudson (16 Oct. 1983); Camille Elizabeth Hudson (b. 1 Oct. 1986)

6) Lewis M. Hudson (b. 26 Oct. 1890 d. 28 Feb. 1898). Lewis died at age 7.

7) Marguerite "Tot" Hudson (b. 24 Aug. 1894 d. 8 Jan. 1969). Tot, who never married, was a graduate of Plains High School and Georgia Southwestern College in Americus. She also attended the

University of California and Columbia University. She taught school in Plains for 43 years and traveled extensively. During her career, her students sometimes included three generations of the same family. In a 1965 newspaper article noting her upcoming retirement, she was quoted as saying "I am grateful to the people of this community for having given me the rare privilege of teaching children whose parents had similar ideals for a good school as my own parents. It has been a great privilege and pleasure for me to have been associated with so many fine patrons and children." She died unexpectedly at age 74 at Piedmont Hospital in Atlanta, the last of her generation.

8) Edward T. Hudson (b. 18 Dec. 1896 d. 18 May 1897). Edward was only 11 days old when his mother died. Tragically, he died at the age of 5 months the following spring.

Today, descendants of M.L. Hudson's four children who reached adulthood live in Georgia, Florida, Alabama, Louisiana and other states.

In Plains, the road leading in front of City Hall and the 1888 depot remains named M.L. Hudson Street, a fitting tribute to the man and the town he created.

—Submitted by Steve Short
(includes extensive research done by Rachel Winn Campbell in 1983)

Jackson

Henry E. Jackson
July 27, 1916-August 21, 1983
Nozie B. Jackson
May 7, 1913-August 15,2001

Henry E. Jackson was born in Webster County Georgia. In 1938, he met and married the former Nozie B. Mason. They had one child, Mae Frances. They later moved to Sumter County. In 1942, Mr. Jackson joined the U.S. Navy during World War II and served in Japan and the South Pacific. He was honorably discharged in 1944. That same year, they moved to Plains, Georgia where he served as a deacon at St. Luke Baptist Church and he was very active in his community. Mr. Jackson also was a barber. He worked on the railroad and with B&L Steel Company of Americus. In 1972, Mr. Jackson was elected the first black city councilman of Plains. In 1972, he was instrumental in obtaining grants to build a community center and swimming pool for the black citizens in Plains. In 1975, he served on the campaign committee for former President Jimmy Carter.

Mrs. Nozie B. Jackson was a hairdresser for a number of years in the Plains community. She also started a daycare in the new Plains Community Center where she served a number of children for almost 10 years. Mrs. Jackson was a secretary at St. John A.M.E. Church for over 50 years.

In 1965, after the death of their only child, Mae Frances, they took in their five grandchildren to raise. The children ranged in age from two years to sixteen years old. Mr. and Mrs. Henry Jackson are true heroes of the Plains community.

—*Submitted by Mike Coley*

Jennings Family

From South Carolina to Plains

Before migrating to Plains many of the descendants of the Jennings family had already intermarried with Addys, Etheredges, Wises, and Timmermans. All were families from Edgefield, Fairfield, and Lexington Districts, South Carolina.

John Jennings (1740/45-1819) was the father of seven known children: (1) James Jennings (1765/70-1830/40); (2) Lucy Jennings (1765/70-before 1840); (3) John Jennings (1765/70-1839/40); (4) William Jennings (1771/72-1842); (5) Philip Jennings (1775/82-1848); (6) Jesse Jennings (1782-1854); and (7) Mary Jennings (1780/90-before 1848). Most were Baptist with many being members of the Red Bank Baptist Church in Saluda, along with the Etheredges with whom they intermarried. Some of their descendants who married German Lutherans and moved to Plains converted to the Lutheran faith.

William Jennings (1771-1842) and his 1st Nancy Dove, with whom he had ten children, never left South Carolina, but their descendants are numerous in Plains: Their son, John B. Jennings (1797-1878), married Barbara Allen Clark; John B. Jennings' daughter, Milbrey Jennings, married John Timmerman (See Timmerman Family); Their daughter Lucy Jennings (1795-1841) married William Etheredge. Lucy and William Etheredge were the parents of Rosa Elizabeth Etheredge (1821-1900) who married David Wise (See Wise Family); William Etheredge and Lucy Jennings' son Guilford Etheredge married Amanda Addy. Amanda was the daughter of George Addy and his 1st wife Jemima Wise who was the sister of David Wise. George

Addy's 2nd wife was Frances Jennings, daughter of William Jennings and his 2nd wife Eleanor Etheredge. (See George Addy and Allied Families).

After the death of Nancy Dove, William Jennings (1771-1842) married 2nd Eleanor Etheredge (1795-July 13,1846), the daughter of Lott Etheredge and Rachel Spencer. Rachel Spencer's sister, Mary, married William Bell. (See History of Stewart County. Georgia. Vol. II, for Bell/Spencer descendants who settled in neighboring areas.) In Edgefield County, South Carolina, William Jennings predeceased his wife Eleanor Etheredge, leaving her with six young children. She survived him only by a few years. Both are buried in South Carolina in unmarked graves. Her brother, Mark Etheredge, petitioned the court and received guardianship of her children. He and his wife, Caroline Jennings, daughter of Jesse Jennings who was the brother of William Jennings, reared them in South Carolina.

By 1866 all of the children of William Jennings and Eleanor Etheredge, except Rachel who died in 1848 in South Carolina, were living in Plains: (1) Lott Jennings (1828-1899) married Mary Mathews Dozier. (2) Eleanor (Ellen) Jennings (1832-1869) married Davis Crapps. (3) Frances (Fannie) Jennings (1834-1916) married George Addy. (4) William Jennings (1836-1909) married Mary E. Wise. (5) Philip Jennings (1840-1894) married Mary Melissa Wise. It is not known where Ellen Jennings and Davis Crapps (Kreps) are buried. The rest of the siblings and their spouses are buried at St. Mark's Lutheran Church Cemetery at Bottsford, Sumter County, Georgia.

The pioneer spirit remained strong in these families for generations. A descendant of Benjamin Etheredge (first cousin of Eleanor Etheredge who married William Jennings) and his wife Elizabeth Jennings (niece of William Jennings), Caroline Etheredge, along with her husband Les Hemble, trained pilots from the University of South Carolina at Owen's Field in Columbia, South Carolina, during World War II.

—*Submitted by Sandra Perry Wellons, Americus, Georgia 31709 (english@sowega.net)*

Millard Margart Jennings Family

M.M. Jennings Sr. grandfather, John Jennings born in 1740, came from South Carolina. Philip Jennings, his father, was married to Malissa Wise. They had eight children, Millard M., Lott, Sam, Philip, Fannie and John. One other Joseph Edgar died as an infant. Burr Thomas moved away to Florida.

Millard M. married Irma Brown who came from Early Co. to teach school in Plains. They had two children, Philip Brown born 1904, and Millard M. Jr. born 1909.

M.M. Jennings, Jr. married Nellie Phillips in 1932. They had three Children, Millie born 1937, Phyllis born 1940, and Gail born 1944.

Phyllis was married to Kenneth R. Naves and had a son, K.R Jr. They divorced and she married J.L. Murray had one son, Brett Jennings Murray.

Gail Married Bo Bo Short, they had a daughter Tanya. They were divorced and she married Charles Cresswell.

M. M. Jennings, Jr. (Mill) and Nellie bought the house on 219 N. Hudson St. in 1940 from Miss Maria Walters. Nellie continues to live there with her daughter Millie. Mill died in 1972.

The Phillips family came to Sumter Co. in 1924 from Marion Co. W.S. Phillips and Essie Stringfellow Phillips had eight children: Etta Walters, Lorice Hammond, Nellie Jennings, Estelle Smith, Raymond Phillips, Marie Griffin, Doris Christian, and Calvin Phillips.

—*Submitted by Nellie Jennings*

Phillip Jennings Family

John Jennings b. 1779 moved to Plains, Georgia from Edgefield District in South Carolina. His son William m. Eleanor Etheridge.

I. Phillip Jennings (b. 2/19/1840 d. 5/14/1894). Married 7/25/1865 Mary Melissa Wise "Little Granny" (b. 2/25/1843 d. 6/14/1917. Both are buried at Bottsford Lutheran Church Cemetery. Their children are:

A. **John William Jennings** (b. 11/10/1866 d. 11/21/1931) Married Ella Addy (b. 5/5/1858 d. 8/13/1936. Both buried in Lebanon Cemetery, Plains GA. No Children.

B. **Joseph Edgar Jennings** (b. 10/9/1870 d. 11/24/1871) Buried at Bottsford Lutheran Church Cemetery.

C. **George Samuel Jennings "Sam"** (b. 8/29/1872 d. 1919) Married Lillian McGarrah (Lilly) (b. 1876 d. 1960) Both buried in Lebanon Cemetery, Plains GA. Children:

1. Phillip McGarrah Jennings "Mac" (b. 1898 d. 1951) Married Agnes Salter (b. Year ? d. Year ?) Children: (a). Charles Phillip, (b). Alice; (c). Betty, (d) Barbara, (e) Shirley.

2. Samuel Ross Jennings (b. 3/18/1900 d. 11/13/1955)

3. Mary Edna Jennings (b. 4/28/1902 d. 10/4/1947) Married Dr. Hershel Bray. Chidren: (a). Mary Frances (b. 3/5/1925), (b) Hershel, (c) Dee Ann.

4. William Lott Jennings (b. 7/3/1904 d. 8/13/1927). Buried in Lebanon Cemetery, Plains GA.

5. Ethel Lolita Jennings (b. 12/18/1907 d. 2/14/1966) Buried in Lebanon Cemetery, Plains GA.

6. Minnie Lillian Jennings (b. 5/16/1914 d. Year ?) Buried in Preston Cemetery.

D. **Fannie Gertrude Jennings** (b. 8/20/1874 d. 3/26/1913) Married Claude Forest. Buried in Lebanon Cemetery, Plains GA.

E. **Mlillard Margart Jennings "Bill"** (b. 10/13/1876 d. 10/20/1936) Married Irma Brown (b. 2/13/1880 d. 8/5/1962) Children:

1. Phillip Brown Jennings "Skeebo" (b. 5/10/1904 d. 12/14/1962) Married Ethel Yaughn "Droopy" (b. 5/3/1905 d. 1998) Both buried in Lebanon Cemetery, Plains GA.

2. Millard Margart Jennings, Jr. "Mill" (b. 2/27/1909 d. 9/27/1972) Married Nellie Phillips (b. 6/12/1915) Mill buried in Lebanon Cemetery, Plains GA. Children: (a). Millie, (b. 10/11/1937), (b). Phyllis (b. 3/26/1940), (c). Gail (b. 12/7/1944).

F. **Lott Elmore Jennings** (b. 6/25/1879 d. 1942) Married Eula Hiller (b. 1884 d. 1969) Both buried in Lebanon Cemetery, Plains GA. Children:

1. Hugh Jennings Married Jane Graves

2. Paul Jennings

3. Martha Jennings Married Lt. Col. James Kennedy. Both buried at Andersonville Cemetery. Children: (a) Martha Ann, (b) Robin.

G. **Phillip David Jennings "Phid"** (b. 11/4/1881 d. 1956) Married (6/7/1911) Mamie Evelyn Thomas (b. 12/3/1892 d. Year ?) Both buried at Hebron Baptist Church Cemetery. Children:

1. Thomas Alfred Jennings, Sr. (b. 6/21/1914 d. 3/3/1995) Married (3/10/1943) Lula Barnette McCleod (b. 8/9/1920 d. 1/8/1991) Children:

(a) Thomas Alfred, Jr. (b. 8/26/1944) Married Elaine Doyle Bartlett (b. 1/5/1943) Children:

(a1) Catherine Elaine. (b. 11/5/1968), (a2) Trent Jeffery (b. 4/15/1971), (a3) Beth Ann (b. 8/18/1972, (a4) Kevin Lynn (b. 6/16/1975.).

(b) Mamie Ruth (b. 8/4/1946) Married Jerry Jerome Harper, Sr. (b.1/29/1946) Children:

(b1) Jerry Jerome Harper, Jr. (b. 5/3/1967), (b2) Christy Renee Harper (b. 2/11/1970).

(c) Cynthia Sue Jennings (b. 4/17/1960)

2. Evelyn Jennings "Sit" (b. 12/3/1915) Married (12/23/1934) Morris Broughton Smith, Sr. (b. 10/2/1909) Children:

(a) Morris Broughton Smith, Jr. (b. 1/6/1937) Married (12/23/1958) Willene Stuckey (b. 7/15/1940) Children:

(a1) Marcia Alane Smith (b. 1/1/1960), (a2) Morris Broughton Smith III (b. 1/11/1961), (a3) Hazel Amanda Smith (b. 8/22/1965)

(b) Pete Pruitt Smith (b. 1/8/1948) Married (3/16/1972) Dorothy Robinson (b. 1/13/1953) Children:

(b1) Stephanie Hope Smith (b. 2/21/1973), (b2) Amy Michele Smith (b. 2/25/1974), (b3) Kerri Leigh Smith (b. Year ?)

3. John William Jennings "Jack" (b. 3/26/1917) Married (1/28/1942) Eola Mae Anderson (b. 11/25/1922 d. 5/27/2002) Children:

(a) Jacquelyn Jennings (b. 9/4/1942) Married Leonard Larkin Dupree, Sr. (b. 9/29/1941) Children:

(a1) Leonard Larkin Dupree, Jr. (b. 4/30/1963), (a2) Elizabeth Louise Dupree (b. 12/11/1964)

(b) David Anderson Jennings (b. 6/23/1944) Married (6/11/1966) Brenda Rodgers (b. 9/27/1947) Children:

(b1) Mitzie Gaynelle Jennings (b. 2/25/1971), (b2) Jarrett David Jennings (b. 7/5/1973)

(c) Debra Jean Jennings (b. 8/31/1955).

4. Annie Laurie Jennings "Pie" (b. 3/14/1920) Married (10/1/1949) George L. Moore (b. 9/14/1917 d. 6/?/1979) Children:

(a) John Wesley Moore (11/17/1951).

5. Phillip Lafayette Jennings (b. 11/14/1921 d. 8/27/1974) Married (6/20/1948) Mary June Powell. Children:

(a) Phillip David Jennings (b. 3/4/1957)

(b) Michael Patrick Jennings (b. 4/16/1959.

6. Hortense Jennings "Tense" (b. 7/23/1924) Married (11/17/1943) James David Williams (b. 8/14/1920). Children:

(a) Edra Elaine Williams (b. 9/21/1944) Married (6/12/1963) Richard Stuart (Divorced). Children:

(a1) Lauren Lee Stuart (b. 1/9/1963), (a2) Mandi Elaine Stuart (b. 9/24/1965)

(b) Phillip Levere Williams (b. 7/18/1946) Married (1968) Linda K. Rodgers (b. 4/14/1947). Children:

(b1) Tracie Leigh Williams (b. 3/13/1959)

(c) Donald Terry Williams (b. 8/30/1947) Married (3/16/1968) Marjorie Vogal (b. 5/11/1946) Children:

(c1) Melissia Anne Williams (b. 12/14/1970), (c2) Christine Nicole Williams (b. 7/25/1976)

7. Betty Jane Jennings (b. 7/9/1927) Married (6/24/1944) Hubert Olin Windham (b. 10/12/1919). Children:

(a) Lauren Windham (b. 7/19/1945) Married (11/7/1964) Carl Wilson Ryals, Sr. (b. 6/10/1945). Children:

(a1) Terry Lane Ryals (b. 6/20/1965) (a2) Carl Wilson Ryals, Jr. (b. 10/19/1968).

8. Margaret Millicent Jennings (b. 3/6/1930) Married (9/20/1947) Lucius Battle Johnson (b. 6/9/1917). Children:

(a) Bobby Gerald Johnson (b. 1/22/1950)

(b) Wanda Gail Johnson (b. 8/7/1951) Married (8/16/1970) Jere Lee McClendon (b. 10/12/1949) Children:

(b1) Teresa Gail McClendon (b. 6/11/1971) (b2) Jennifer Lee McClendon (b. 10/31/1975).

9. Franklin Eugene Jennings "Gene" (b. 7/11/1934) Married (6/7/1953) Mary Barbara Stevenson (b. 1/20/1935). Children:

(a) Gena Sue Jennings (b. 11/5/1956)

(b) Mark Tyler Jennings (b. 8/16/1958)

(c) Christopher Jay Jennings (b. 1/13/1961).

10. Burr Wise Jennings (b. 2/11/1935) Married (2/2/1956) Emogene Price (b. 12/25/1937). Children:

(a) Floyd Lee Jennings (b. 1/19/1957)

(b) Tammie Marie Jennings (b. 6/1/1960)

(c) William Conner Jennings (b. 9/14/1963).

H. Burr Thomas Jennings "Pet" (b. 5/11/1885 d. 8/14/1934) Married (4/13/1913) Mellie Mae Wise (b. 5/4/1893. They moved to Polk Co. Florida. Buried in Forrest Hills Cemetery, Haines City, FL.

—Submitted by Audra Jennings

Dr. Francis Marion Jones

Dr. Francis Marion Jones moved to western Sumter County in the mid 1800s from Twiggs County, Ga. He served in the Confederacy as a medical doctor during the War Between the States. He married, 12/19/1848, Juliann Amelia Elizabeth Morgan, 10/3/1829, daughter of Charles W. Morgan, b.2/12/1792 and Charlotte Gibbons b. 12/11/1794, m. 03/01/1821. Three children-Thomas Marion Jones, Alice Jones, Laura Faye Jones.

I. Thomas Marion Jones, carpenter, farmer, b. 12/22/1858, d. 8/4/1934, m.1/15/1893 Maggie Louise Coker, b. 5/4/1876, d. 4/8/1956. They had four children.

A. Arthur G. Jones 1/10/1894-12/13/1975 m. Beatrice Griffin. One daughter,

1. Marian Louise Jones Elliott

B. Walter Linwood Jones, 8/21/1895-11/30/1975, m. 1/22/1922 Zera Alberta Smith, 4/8/1896-3/11/1980, Four Children.

1. Edith Lynn Jones b. 11/8/1922, m. 4/11/1945, Boude Bowman Leavel, b. 5/12/1919. Two Children. 1. Linda Carole Leavel, b.10/28/1947, m. 6/24/1967 Norman Howard Bassett, Jr. b. 10/11/1946. One child. Elizabeth Dianne Bassett, 9/1/1978. 2. Cynthia Boude Leavel, b. 12/5/1953,

m. 11/10/1994, Morris Scott Roddenberry, b. 4/4/1950. One child. Sawyer Austin Roddenberry, 7/19/1985.

2. Walter L. Jones Jr. b. 3/13/1925 d. 8/17/1935.

3. Morgan Howard Jones, b. 8/28/1927, d. 11/3/2001, m. 9/13/1952, Dollie Rae Bridges, 3/31/1934-11/3-2001. One Child. Lynn Jones, b.4/9/1957, m. 9/29/1979, Ricky Leon Hudson, b. 3/29/1957. One child. Jennifer Lynn Hudson, 11/1/1980.

4. Jack Burton Jones, 3/20/1929-11/20/1951.

C. Thaddeus Marion Jones, 11/17/1901-1/24/1972, m. Irene Murray, 6/5/1904-7/3/1979. Two Children.

1. Thaddeus Marion Jones, Jr., 11/17/1924-2/21/1945.

2. Irene "Rene" Jones, 7/1937, m. William Ronald Smith, 5/30/1934-12/14/1975. Four Children, a. Juliann Smith, b. William Ronald Smith, Jr., c. Thaddeus Smith, d. Scott Smith.

D. Bertha Jones, 4/30/1907-9/1/1992, m. 10/11/1931, Caleb Fred Comer, 7/24/1907-12/13/1983. One Child.

1.Oscar Lawrence Comer II, 6/18/33, m. 10/29-196, Jane Marian Little, 5/14/1935. Three Children. a. Brandon Jones Comer, 6/2/1970, m. 11/27/1993 Kimberly Harper, 6/15/1968. One Child, Davis Campbell Comer, 7/12/1999. b. Lauren Little Comer, 8/21/1973, m. 12/21/1997, Martin Spann Stovall, 3/13/1970. Two Children. Andrew Martin Stovall, 7/20/1998, Sarah Elizabeth Stovall, 3/26/2000. c. Sarah Elizabeth Comer, 4/6/1979.

—Submitted by Larry (Oscar Lawrence) Comer

Kennedy Family

James Walter Kennedy and Mary Lou Harling Kennedy were natives of Bartow County, Georgia. They lived near Taylorsville, Georgia where Mr. Kennedy ran a general store and grew cotton on the farm. Their Family consisted of eight children six girls and 2 boys. From oldest to youngest the children were: Sarah Jessie, married to William Jefferson Sproull; Jolly Harling Kennedy, married to Alma Ramona King- Katheryn Beddingfield-Irene Duke; Mary Lou, Married to Royl Harden Fletcher; Violet Kennedy, died at birth; Elsie Christine, married to Mr. Pitman- William Edward Connally; James Walter Kennedy, Jr., Willie Kate Kennedy; Lura Neill, Married to Maurice Jones Mobley. One item of interest is that all of the Kennedy girls that were old enough received some college education prior to moving to Plains. Lura and Willie Kate attended Plains High School, with Lura Graduating in 1926. Willie Kate met an untimely death in April, 1923. It was thought that she mistakenly took poison thinking is was a quinine. She was a senior at the Plains High School at the time of her death.

According to the Americus Times-Recorder, "Mr. Kennedy was one of the most successful merchants and farmers in Bartow County". Drawn by the beautiful flat, fertile land in Plains the family sold the Taylorsville property, bought a large farm and home near Plains and moved the entire family to Plains in 1919. Mr. Kennedy at one time served on the Bartow County Board of Education. Mr. Kennedy had two brothers who migrated to Plains - Mr. Gill Kennedy and Mr. Will Kennedy who operated a meat market in Plains in the early 1920's.

The Kennedy family became very active in the community affairs of Plains. They all joined the Plains Baptist Church. Mr. Kennedy was a Sunday school teacher, a deacon and a member of the Plains Evangelistic Club. Mrs. Kennedy and Mrs. Sproull also taught Sunday school, and played the piano for services when needed. Mrs. Sproull served the Church in almost all areas including WMU, Training Union, youth classes and departmental units of the church until she moved from Plains due to failing health. Mrs. Kennedy never had a permanent home following the loss of the farm. She lived

with her daughters, moving from time to time to be with a daughter and their family. She died in Plains in April 23, 1944 and is buried in Lebanon Cemetery with her husband, her sons, her daughter Willie Kate and Jessie and Jeff Sproull.

On moving to Plains Mr. Kennedy began to operate the farm, and purchased tractors to till the soil. It was reported that he had one of the first "Delco" light plants in his home. The economy was not kind to the Kennedy's. With WWI over the demand for goods slumped and the boll weevil devastated the cotton crops. All of this and the untimely death of his daughter took its toll on Mr. Kennedy's health and he died on May 11, 1925 following a "stroke" on May 10 which was Mothers Day. With the death of its leader, the Kennedy family fell apart, and eventually lost all of the farm and the home.

Most of the family stayed in Plains for a while. Jolly Kennedy moved to Brunswick, Georgia and worked in a bank there. Walter Kennedy joined the merchant marine and died of an unknown cause in New York City in July 1942.

Jessie Kennedy who married Jeff Sproull continued to live in Plains and reared her family there. The Sproulls had 5 children: Kathryn S. Barker who later moved to Concord, Georgia and retired as Post Master of the Concord Post Office; Charles Sproull who moved to Milwaukee, WS, played some professional baseball, and retired as a machinist: Gladwin S. Barfield was a school teacher and retired in Perry, Ga. Kennedy (Buck) Sproull lived in Plains for many years and then moved to Colbert, Georgia, was a rural mail carrier and retired there. Harold Sproull joined the Navy and became a Navy Pilot rising to the rank of Commander. He retired from the navy due to a heart problem, taught school in Eustis, Florida, for a while and retired in LaFayette, Georgia.

Mary Lou Kennedy married Royl Fletcher also of Plains. They moved to Molena, Georgia where Royl eventually retired as President of The Bank of

Molena. Mary Lou taught school and retired as the "Visiting Teacher" for Pike County. Royl and Mary Lou had two children, Carme Ruth and Jimmy. Carme Ruth worked as a buyer for Rich's Store for Homes. She moved to Huntsville, AL. where her husband worked as a chemist for the Redstone Arsenal. Carme Ruth retired as a homemaker in Huntsville: Carme Ruth loved Plains and spent many summers with her Grandmother Fletcher and other relatives there. Jimmy served in the Navy, attended Georgia Tech, and operated the Pasley-Fletcher Funeral Home in Thomaston, Georgia. He also continued the family interest in banking. At the time this article was submitted he was Chairman of the Board of the First Bank of Pike County (formerly Bank of Molena). Jimmy died in November 2002.

Elsie Kennedy first married Mr. Pitman and lived in Carrollton, Georgia. Mr. Pitman died and she later married Ed Connolly of Molena, and moved there. She taught school until retirement and was killed in an automobile accident in Molena, Georgia in November, 1972. Mr. and Mrs. Connally had one daughter, Sue Connally Pruett.

Lura Kennedy graduated from Plains High School. She moved to Rome, Georgia for nurses training and became a Registered Nurse. She later married Maurice Mobley of Rome. The Mobleys had no children. They were very successful in the furniture and the real estate business. At her death Mrs. Mobley left in trust a sizable sum to the Plains Baptist Church, Shorter College and Rome First Baptist Church.

—*Submitted by Jimmy Fletcher of Thomaston*

Kitchen Family

Joe Kitchen, Sr. (deceased) and Annie Lee Clark (deceased) had 13 children:

I. George Clark Kitchen Sr. (deceased)
II. Rosa Lee Kitchen Raven (deceased)
III. Annie Mae Kitchen (Sugar) (deceased)
IV. Willie Kitchen (deceased)
V. Lucy Mae Kitchen Laster Berry (deceased)
VI. Ola B. Kitchen Wilson (deceased)
VII. Addie Kitchen Wright
VIII. Lora Bell Kitchen (deceased)
IX. Nella Kitchen (deceased)
X. Joe Kitchen Jr. (deceased)
XI. John Kitchen (deceased)
XII. Mozelle Kitchen Wakefield
XIII. Homer Kitchen

I. George Clark Kitchen Sr. (deceased) Ethel Lee Holley
    George Kitchen Jr. (deceased)
        Linda Kitchen Hurley
            Justin Kitchen
            Chasty Kitchen
    Evelyn Kitchen
        Joe Kimbrough Jr.
        Deion Glover
        Ronkeyious Glover
    Willie Clyde Kitchen "C-Baby" (deceased).
    Doris Kitchen
        Daryl Kitchen
        Deron Kitchen

II. Rosa Lee Kitchen Raven (deceased) Francis Marion Raven Sr. (deceased)
    Nancy Bell Raven Tommie
    Bloomie Tommie (deceased)
        Josie Lee Raven Williams
        Johnny Williams (Deceased)
            Sheila S. Raven
            Christy A. Williams
        Evelyn Tommie
        Flora Mae Tommie
        Freddie James Tommie

Francis Marion Raven Jr. "Brother" (deceased)
Mary Ann Raven
   Gloria Raven Montgomery
   Roland Montgomery
Dorothy Raven Merritt
Gene Merritt
Baldwin Schley
   Betty Merritt
   Mack Merritt
   Erma Jean Merritt
   Laverne Schley
   Gwen Schley

III. WillieKitchen
Shirley Sheppard Gary
"Rabbit" Gary
   Tiffany Gary
   Shannon Gary
   Sheun Gary

IV. Annie Mae Kitchen "Sugar" (deceased)

V. Lucy Mae Kitchen Laster Berry (Deceased)
John Laster (deceased) Fred Berry(deceased)
   Mary Lee Laster Sally
   Leroy Sally
     Larry Sally
     Ronald Sally
   Georgia Lee Laster King
     Mary Louise King
       Oscar Wendell King
         Darius Antwan King
       Kenya Niele Collier
         Chakera Jynelle Bateman
     Irene King Edge
       Desmond Edge
         Lacountess Edge
       Tanesha Edge
       Renaldo Edge
       Rory Edge

       Virgilia Edge
     Shirley Ann King Wilson Waymon
       Ronquillo Wilson
       Chauncey Waymon
       Chisa Waymon
     Maverick King   Debra King
       Michael Bridges
       Tyrone Bridges
       Toenisha King
     William Spann Jr.
       Dominique Spann
       William Spann III
       Malcolm Jamal Spann
Freddie Mae Berry Polk Roberts
Mack Polk Sr.
John L. Roberts
   Brenda Ann Polk Hall   Jeffrey Hall
     Zerrick J. Hollis
       Matisha "TT"
Reginald Polk   Jackie Polk
   Candice Polk
   Reneka Polk
Stephanie Polk
   Damion Burns
Gregory Polk
   Mark Polk
   Gregory K. Polk
   Brandon M. Polk
   Brittany Nicole Polk
Mack Polk Jr. Tammy P. Polk
   Tracy F. Polk
   Mack Arthur Polk III
Fred Berry(deceased)
   Wayne Whitehead
John Ed Berry
   Michael Jerome Hollis
   Robert F. Berry

Johnny Hollis
Catherine Berry Perry   Andrew Perry
   Alexander Berry (deceased)
      Brandon Covin
  Efrem Berry
Florene Berry
  Vincent Berry   Anita Berry
     Vernecia Berry "Miss Lucy"
     Vincent Berry Jr.
Lorene Berry Champion Tony Champion
Eddie Mack Berry
Luther James Berry

VI. Ola B. Kitchen (deceased)
Lawrence Wilson(deceased)
  Gene Wilson   Rosa Mae Wilson
   Eric Wilson
      Eric Jermone Wilson
   Diane Wilson
      Petoyria L Wilson
      Brittany R. Wilson
   David Wilson
      David Wilson Jr.
   Dale Wilson
      Talethia Wilson
   Jeannie Wilson
      Jasmyne A. Wilson
  Virginia Wilson
   Willie Bell Wilson Duden
   Leroy Wilson
   Beatrice Wilson Goldstein
     Martin Goldstein
   Eleanor Wilson
     Athena Wilson
     Levar Wilson
  Harold Wilson Sr.
     Harold Wilson Jr.
  Lawrence Wilson

     Isaiah Wilson
Ann Wilson
  Priscilla Willson
      Darren Patrick Wilson
      Capri Galberth
Lena Mae Wilson Laney Raymond Laney Sr.
  Gwenevier Laney
  Tracy Ann Laney (deceased)
  Raymond Laney Jr.
Laura Ruth Wilson
  Michelle Wilson
  Asiah
Wade Wilson   Christine Mansfield Wilson
  Calvin Eugene Colbert
  Bruce Bridges
  Diane Bridges
John Henry Wilson Sr. Juanita Freeman Wilson
  Otis Jerome Wilson
  John Henry Wilson Jr.
Ola Mae Wilson
Marvin Wilson
  Ferrell
Mae Francis Lampkin Merritt   James Merritt
  Annette Wilson
     Anthony B. Wilson
     Corralus C. Wilson
     Javis Jamell Wilson
  Julie Lampkin Leverett Xavier Leverett
     Jamie Bernard Lampkin
     Jeffrey Antonio Lampkin
     Courtney Lakeshia Lampkin
  Christine Lampkin (deceased)
     Shanda Marie Murphy (deceased)
Nathaneil Wilson
Alabert Wilson (deceased)
Willie James Wilson (deceased)
VII. Addie Kitchen Wright

Ernest Wright (deceased)
   Ernestine Wright Martin Melvin Martin Jr.
      Amer Martin
      Andre Demetrius Martin
VIII. Lora Bell Kitchen (deceased)
   Pauline Kitchen
      Elizabeth Kitchen Angry   Eugene Angry
         Lenekia Angry Thomas
         Greg Thomas
         Braylon Thomas
         Eugenia "Gina" Angry Cooper
         Jamie Cooper
         Kolbie Cooper
      Annie Lora K. Harris
         Matisha Kitchen
         Marquailis Kitchen
         Tonya Harris
         Renae Harris
      Wayne Kitchen
      Cornelius Kitchen
      Janice Kitchen Pless
         Terrance Cantrell Kitchen
         Davarus Kitchen
         Xavious Jakese Pless
   Annie Bell Kitchen Pitts
      Darryl Kitchen
   Ruby Jean Kitchen Willoughby
      Lynette Willoughby
      Qwarhdariyah Shabre Willoughby
      Mark Willoughby
   Clara Mae Kitchen Thomas
      Donnell Kitchen Sr.
      Donnell Kitchen Jr.
      Patrick Thomas
IX. Nella Kitchen
X. Joe Kitchen Jr.
   Joann Kitchen Green

      Alfred Kitchen
      Joe Kitchen III
      Annie Lee Kitchen "Nick"
XI. John Kitchen
   Anthony Kitchen
   Pepper
XII. Mozelle Kitchen Wakefield
Sammie Wakefield (deceased)
   Rena Mae Wakefield
      Wilma Wakefield   Wiley Richardson
         Kelia Shanta Tullis
         Lakesha W. Tulus
         Eddie Tulus
   Dannie Mae Kitchen
      Tameca Lawanda Kitchen
         Brent Dontavious Monts
      Sheree Jamilla Kitchen
         Froggie
      Mikos Jawan Kitchen
   Loretta Kitchen
   Dorothy Jean Kitchen
      Shaquena Mack
      Sekiethia Mack
   Barbara Kitchen
XIII. Homer Kitchen
Celestine Kitchen
   Alverta Kitchen Smith
      Deidra Smith
      Buster Smith Jr.
   Darwin Kitchen
   Marcia Kitchen Diggs

Lamb Family

I. Hardy Lamb was living in Wayne Co., N.C. in 1790 and his will which was probated in that county in 1810 names a son Miles.

II. Miles Lamb was born in N.C. in 1786. His obituary in the Americus Weekly Republican of 15 June 1883 states that he died on 8 June 1883 and that he was the father of 23 children. It further states that he was a member of the Primitive Baptist Church. He bought land in Sumter Co. 1843. He was a veteran of the War of 1812. Four of his sons served in the Sumter Flying Artillery during the War Between the States.

III. David Crockett Lamb was born in Georgia in May of 1834. He m. Sarah (Sallie) Rouse Andrews (b. Sept. 1835 in Georgia), a widow of a Confederate soldier, on 23 Aug. 1866, in Sumter Co. She had one child, Lucy, by her first marriage. They had the following children: Dollie, Dorie, Bill Hubbard, Dolan, Sallie & Maud. They are both buried in Wilcox Co., Ga.

IV. Bill Hubbard Lamb was born 2 Dec. 1875 in Sumter Co. He d. 19 Nov. 1938 and is buried at Concord United Methodist Church cemetery on Hwy. 30, Americus. He was m. to Dora Holloway (b. 15 Dec. 1886, d. 1 Sept. 1962), daughter of James Holloway (see Holloway family) and Texanna Lamb. They had three sons and one daughter, Ruby Texas who was b. 14 Nov. 1912 in Dooly Co., Ga. She m. Joe Monroe Buchanan (see Buchanan family) on 21 Nov. 1932 and had the following children: Maynard; Carrie Earline; Joe Monroe, Jr.; and Joseph Colquitt. Carrie Earlene Buchanan m. Jack Frank Cox (see Cox family) and has one child, Carey Buchanan Cox.

—*Submitted by Earline Buchanan Cox*

The John A. McDonald Family

John A. McDonald was born in 1848 in Sumter County, Georgia in the area between Highway 19 South and the Lee Street Road south from Americus, Georgia. In the early 1870's, he married Cornelia Page from the same area; and they later moved to Plains, Georgia. Their house is located on Church Street in Plains and at the present time is painted yellow!

John A. McDonald was a prominent landowner in Sumter County, as well as co-owner of the Oliver-McDonald Company in Plains in the early 1900's. It is reported that this was the most patronized store in the area, with items ranging from food to furniture. Carolyn and John Durham have in their possession a bedroom suite originally purchased from the Oliver-McDonald Company by her father.

Mrs. John McDonald, the former Cornelia Page, was born in 1851 and died in 1923 at Plains, Georgia. From this marriage a daughter, Mamie, was born in 1876 and died in 1967. On December 26, 1900, she married Horry T. Bradley, who was born in 1870 and died in 1918. They had no children and Cousin Mamie never remarried.

The John McDonald family was very active in the Plains Methodist Church. Cousin Mamie reportedly financed the annex to the church building in 1937, according to the plaque in the foyer, in memory of her parents, John A. and Cornelia Page McDonald. I, Cornelia Harris Greene, attended Cousin Mamie's funeral at the Plains Methodist Church in 1967. Jimmy Carter, later President of the United States, was one of her pallbearers.

Cornelia Page McDonald and my grandmother, Mary Ann "Mollie" Page, were sisters. My grandfather, Samuel Amos Harris, married Mary Ann Page on March 15, 1867. They lived in the Friendship Community of Sumter County and were the parents of four children, Lula, John, James, and Blake. I am the daughter of John and Sina Jones Harris and was named "Cornelia" for my great aunt, Cornelia Page McDonald. According to my mother, she was very pleased to have a namesake and at my birth presented me with a one hundred-dollar gold piece on November 20, 1921. She died in 1923 and that ended my inheritance from her. However, in 1967 Cousin Mamie died and in her will left to me a share of her estate, including her mother's gold watch and chain.

In recalling the love and friendship between the families of Cornelia Page McDonald and Mary Ann "Mollie" Harris, my mother shared this experience of God's love, compassion, and protection. In 1913, his doctor told my father, John Harris, that he must have stomach surgery in order to live. Money was very scarce, and his responsibility to my mother and four children was great. The McDonalds invited my father, mother, and baby to come to their home in Plains so that the doctors could perform the surgery in their living room. The dining room table was moved into the living room to be the operating table. Five doctors were present to assist in the surgery; perhaps including the Wise brothers and Dr. Colquitt Logan. The surgery was successful and, after a six-week recovery period, my father and his family returned to their home in the Friendship Community. In the years ahead they had five more children, of which I was the eighth. According to my mother, my father outlived all of the attending doctors.

This gracious act of the McDonalds was a Christian witness to the community. I am now 80 years of age, and I never knew John or Cornelia McDonald; but I greatly appreciate their kindness to my family and their Christian witness to the community of Plains.

—*Submitted by Mrs. Hubert Greene (Cornelia Harris), 305 Wildwood Circle, Americus, 31709*

Ralph McDonald

Ralph McDonald born October 5, 1924 in Pierce County, son of the Samuel E. McDonald and Elizabeth Aldridge McDonald, married Evelynn Jacobs born December 11, 1928 daughter of Clara Altman and Bill Ebenezer Jacobs of Brantley County, Georgia. Ralph and Evelynn married March 19, 1948.

The McDonalds moved to Plains and he began a teaching career at Plains High School retiring after 33 years of teaching. During his years as a teacher of Plains High School he was selected STAR Teacher twice. In 1962, the Plains High School annual was dedicated to him. He taught math, science, drivers education as well as coaching B-team basketball, baseball and track. The family home of the McDonalds' is located just off South Bond St. at 308 Sumter St. The first person know to live in this house was Mrs. Sam (Lillie) Jennings. Then, Mr. Toms lived there for several years. J. W. Sewell bought it from Mr. Toms and sold it to Ralph McDonald in 1959.

Ralph was appointed by U.S. Congressman Richard Ray as a member of the Task Force for the Historic Preservation Trust of Plains. He also served on the Plains City Council for fifteen years and as Mayor of Plains until the time of his death in 1988.

The children of Ralph and Evelyn McDonald are: (1) Angela Althea McDonald married Wendell Alfors and live in Monroe, NC. (2) Gail McDonald who married Richard Lowery - daughters, Hannah and Madeleane lives in Atlanta (3)Dale McDonald who married Cathie Justice -two daughters, Christie and Lindsay and they live in Charlotte, NC.

—*Submitted by Evelynn McDonald*

Medlock

My earliest records indicate the name is English, and early records show that Isham Medlock was born to John Medlock, Jr. and wife Catherine in 1777 in Virginia. The brothers from this marriage settle in Kentucky, Missouri, South Carolina, and Alabama.

My Great Great Grandfather was John Williams Medlock (wife was Sarah Jamerson Ware) born April 4, 1803 in Greenville County, South Carolina and was brought to Georgia some time before 1811. He had a large farm located on both sides of Ponce De Leon from Piedmont, including Piedmont Park, and old Sears Roebuck store and Cracker Ball Park. His home was where Grace

Medthodist Church now stands. They had 13 children. My Great Grandaddy, William Parks, was the 7th child born June 6, 1837. He married Velenah Antonette Mason on August 7, 1861. There were 7 children born to this marriage. My Grandfather was second, Charles Oscar Medlock, born June 2, 1869 married Mollie Hudgins on June 4, 1893. From this marriage came my father, William Verlyn (Mose) Medlock, Sr., born November 6, 1902 and died February 8, 1968. He was buried at Enterprise Methodist Church Cemetary in Terrell County, Georgia. He was married to Elizabeth Grace Smith, January 14, 1924, who died November 14, 1991. She also is burried at Enterprise Methodist Church Cemetary. Grace Smith was the daughter of Daniel Reese Smith and Nannie Andrews Smith who were long time residents of Plains, Georgia. The children of Mose and Grace Medlock were:

A. Charles Reese Medlock, born December 21, 1924, married Alice Josephine Dupree on July 15, 1951.

1. Elizabeth Corine Medlock, born January 21, 1958, married Gregory Clyde Alford, born August 20, 1956, married on April 16, 1975. They had the following children:

1. Courtney Mechell Alford, born November 6, 1978, married Richard Quency English, December 28, 1996. One child was born of their marriage, Colton Schuyler English, born April 13, 1997. They were then divorced. A second child was born to Courtney and Zachariah Stephens, Gavyn Sebastian Reese Stephens, born September 26, 2001.

2. Jeremy Reese Alford, born November 24, 1979.

3. Bryan Patrick Alford, born May 29, 1983.

2. Mary Evelyn Medlock, born May 29, 1961, married Julian Keith Moncus on August 2, 1980. Julian Keith Moncus is the son of Betty Bruce and stepson of William E. Wise. The children are:

1. Julian Michael Moncus born August 28, 1984.

2. Lindsay Marie Moncus born October 5, 1987.

3. William Charles Moncus born October 17, 1990.

B. Mary Rebecca Medlock, born August 4, 1927, married Lucius Earl Dale on January 18, 1947. Earl died on November 26, 1989 at Palmayra Hospital in Albany, Georgia and buried at Cedar Hill in Dawson, Georgia. They had the following children:

1. Phillip Earl Dale

2. Mary Janice Dale

3. Theresa Lynn Dale

4. Willard Verlyn Dale

5. Tammy Jo Dale

1. Phillip Earl Dale, born December 22, 1947, in Americus, Georgia, Sumter County, married Mary Katherine Nicholson on May 28, 1971 in South Carolina. They were divorced, then he married Janice Melton on August 9, 1983. Janice Melton was born on May 2, 1950. Phillip Earl and Mary Katherine Dale had the following children:

1. April English Dale

2. Amy Rebecca Dale

1. April English Dale, born December 1, 1971 in Charleston, South Carolina, married April 20, 1996 to Joseph Asway from Albany, Georgia. They had the following children:

(1.) Phillip Jacob Asway, born October 18, 2000, at Kailua,

(2.) Amy Rebecca Dale, born October 3, 1976, in Americus, Georgia, Sumter County.

2. Mary Janice Dale, born June 27, 1949 in Americus, Georgia, Sumter County married David Clifford Gause on December 27, 1968 in Terrell County. They divorced. Mary Janice Dale and David Clifford Gause had the following children:

(1.) David Eric Gause

(2.) Gregory Dale Gause

(3.) Jana Dale Gause

(1) David Eric Gause, born September 30, 1969 in Americus, Georgia, Sumter County married on June 27, 1991 at Panama City Beach, Florida. They had the following children:

(a.) Megan Nichole Gause, born November 5, 1993 in Americus, Georgia, Sumter County.

(b.) Gregory Chase Gause, born March 9, 1996 in Albany, Georgia.

(2.) Gregory Walton Gause, born June 9, 1972 in Americus, Georgia, Sumter County. He had the following children:

(a.) Anthony Eric Gause, born May 23, 2001 in Americus, Georgia, Sumter County.

Mary Janice Dale married Donald Glenn Jones on February 29, 1992 in Panama City Beach, Florida.

(3.) Jana Dale Gause, born August 25, 1974 in Columbus, Georgia, died August 7, 1978, buried at Cedar Hill Cemetary in Dawson, Georgia.

3. Theresa Lynn Dale (Terry), born October 11, 1978, in Americus, Georgia, Sumter County, married Theo Harris Peddy, Jr. at Enterprise Methodist Church. They had the following children:

(a.) Virginia Lynn Peddy, born April 25, 1978 in Albany, Georgia

(b.) Hillary Harriett, born April 14, 1981.

Theresa Lynn Dale was then divorced and married George Monroe Roberts

4. Willard Verlyn Dale, born September 20, 1953 in Americus, Georgia, Sumter County, married Vickie Barfield in Byronville, Georgia. They had the following child:

(a.) Anthony Earl Dale (Tony), born December 16, 1974. He married Cherrish Daniel in Albany, Georgia. They had the following child:

(a.) Anthony Logan Dale, born February 18, 1991, in Americus, Georgia, Sumter County, married Melanie Elaine King in Albany, Georgia.

5. Tammy Jo Dale, born March 12, 1960, in Americus, Georgia, Sumter County, married Wesley Steven Brown on April 12, 1980 at Pleasant Hill Baptist Church in Terrell County. They had the following children:

(a.) Jana India Brown, born February 25, 1982, in Jacksonville, Florida, married Jessie Music on September 16, 2001. They had the following children:

(a.) Jessie Tyler Music, born May 29, 1999

(b.) Sally Rebecca Brown, born August 4, 1985 in Jacksonville, Florida.

(c.) Stephen Phillip Brown, born March 17, 1988 in Bath, Maine .

C. William Verlyn Medlock (Bill), born May 1, 1930, married Betty Ruth Raybon, born January 18, 1929. Betty Medlock, died April 15, 1985. Bill married Sandra McKinnon on September 1, 1985. Bill and Betty had the following children:

1. Elizabeth Ellen Medlock, born May 13, 1957.

2. Cynthia Ruth Medlock, born April 17, 1963.

3. Pamela Jane Medlock, born May 27, 1964.

Elizabeth Ellen Medlock married Preston Scott Harris June 20, 1981. Ellen and Preston had the following children:

1. William Chad Harris, born August 4, 1983.

2. Patrick Scott Harris, born May 27, 1987.

Cynthia Ruth Medlock married Robert Mitchell Harris July 2, 1994. They have the following children:

1. Robert Mitchell Harris, II, born January 2, 1997.
2. Logan William Harris, born March 23, 2002.

Pamela Jane Medlock married David Cole February 1, 1987. They later divorced. Pam and David had the following children:

1. Damian Vincent Cole, born March 25, 1988.
2. Elizabeth Danielle Cole, born October 16, 1989.

Pam married Timothy Green August 9, 1997. They have one child.   1. Miranda Raye Green, born April 29, 2002.

D. Georgia Ann Medlock, born July 23, 1934, died February 3, 1935 and was buried at Enterprise Methodist Church in Terrell County.

E. Pat Smith Medlock was born on August 21, 1936 to Grace Smith Medlock and William Verlyn Medlock in Sumter County, Georgia. He wed Patsy Ruth Short at Hebron Baptist Church (Sumter County) on June 4, 1955. They had the following children:

Kenneth William Medlock - born July 25, 1960 in Sumter County, Georgia.

Molly Eugenia Medlock - born June 14, 1964in Sumter County, Georgia. She wed Gregory Lavonne Speir on July 21, 1984 at Hebron Baptist Church. They had the following children:

Molly Amanda Speir - born April 14, 1987 in Sumter County, Georgia

Joshua Medlock Speir - born February 28, 1990 in Sumter County, Georgia

Polly Grace Medlock - born June 14, 1964 in Sumter County, Georgia. She wed Arthur Floyd Martin on June 4, 1983 at Hebron Baptist Church. They had the following children:

Benjamin Verlyn Martin - born November 16, 1984 in Sumter County, Georgia.

Cassie Lee Martin - born March 22, 1988 in Sumter County, Georgia.

Callie Ruth Martin - born September 15, 1992 in Sumter County, Georgia.

Patty Ruth Medlock - born November 10, 1965 in Sumter County, Georgia. She wed Jonathan Bond Webb August 6, 1988 at Hebron Baptist Church. They had the following children:

William Medlock Webb - born February 28, 1990 in Sumter County, Georgia.

Sara Ruth Webb - born October 5, 1992 in Sumter County, Georgia.

F. Wade Parks Medlock, Sr. married Mary Katherine Cape September 2, 1960. They had the following children:

1. Shelia Ruth Medlock (stillborn) March 29, 1964.
2. Mary Ann Medlock, born December 8, 1965
3. Wade Parks Medlock, Jr., born August 25, 1967.

Mary Ann Medlock married Leo Frank Pouliot August 23, 1986 and divorced 1996. They had the following children:

1. A'Leigha Katherine Pouliot, born September 19, 1987.
2. Abigail Frances Pouliot,

born October 16, 1989.
3. Zachery Leo Pouliot,
   born March 1, 1992.

Wade Parks Medlock, Jr. married Kimberly Gayle Doane August 2, 1993. They had the following children:
1. Zoe Kate Medlock, born April 7, 2000.
2. Emma Grace Medlock, born May 10, 2001.
3. Elise Angelee Medlock, born May 10, 2001.

G. Nancy Jo Medlock, born April 12, 1944, married John D. Alston, Jr., born February 20, 1943, on April 24, 1964. They had the following children:
1. Mary Rebecca Alston,
   born February 4, 1968.
2. John Scott Alston, born July 4, 1969, married Mitzi Kay Bopp, born April 21, 1968, on August 5, 2000.
—*Submitted Charles R. Medlock*

Mims Family History

William Wright was born in June 1736 in Washington County, Georgia He fought in the Revolutionary War from 1777 to 1782, while living in Virginia and serving in the Virginia Militia. He married Mary Philpott (1740-1801). He died in Wilkes County, Georgia in 1795.

William and Mary Wright had a daughter, Mary Wright (1756-1812) who married William Mims (1757-1817). Their son Wright Mims (1796-1852) married Elizabeth Kendall (1799-1850). Their son Peyton Mims was born in 1812 at Lee-Sumter County, Georgia and died in Sumter County in 1890. He married Sara Brady (1810-1893), also born in Lee-Sumter County, in 1832.

Martin Hamilton Mims was born to Peyton and Sara Mims on January 27, 1842 at Drayton, Georgia. Martin served in the Civil War and fought at Chickamauga. He died in Sumter County, Georgia on December 17, 1908. On January 25, 1872, he married Sarah Amanda Lassiter, born March 28, 1846, in Sumter County. They had two sons and three daughters. Their youngest son, George Thomas Mims was born August 21,1886 in Sumter County, GA and died February 9, 1955.

On June 30, 1920, George Thomas Mims, Sr. married Minnie Louise Carroll, born May 18, 1899 in Twiggs County, GA. They settled in Mossy Dell and Bosford Community, south of Plains, in 1920 following his discharge from the military (army). They resided in and around Plains for the rest of their lives. George T. Mims, Sr. died Feb.9, 1955, and Minnie Carroll Mims died January 14, 1989.

George and Minnie Mims had three children:
Sara Helen Mims, born October 25, 1921, married David Bozeman (born March 10, 1919) on September 4, 1955. They have 2 children and reside in Plains. Their children are:
1. Carol Lynn Bozeman (born December 5, 1956 in Effingham County, Georgia). Married James Marvin Griggs (born December 23, 1952) on April 21, 1979 Their children are Wesley Adam Griggs (born November 4, 1979) and Kimberly Ashley Griggs (born July 6, 1983). The Griggs reside in Preston, Georgia.
2. Diane Bozeman (born August 3, 1959) in Effingham County, Georgia. Married Roy Munn Worrell (born December 17,1957) on May 5, 1977. Their children are Mamie Meagan Worrell (Born December 3,1977) and Jessica Diane Worrell (born March 20, 1981) Mamie Meagan Worrell married Richard Adam Tate (born November 7, 1976) on May 15, 1999. Diane and Roy reside in Americus, Georgia.

George Thomas Mims, Jr., born July 10, 1929, married Helen Jeanette Phelps (born July 16, 1931) on August 11, 1956. They have 4 children and reside in Marietta, Cobb County, Georgia. Their children are:

1. George Thomas Mims, III (born March 29, 1958) married Elaine Pope and resides in Marietta, Georgia. Children are Danita Pope, Delores Pope and Travis Pope (deceased). Delores Pope married Randy Montgomery and they are parents of Amanda Rose Montgomery (Born 2000)

2. Jennifer Mims Slagel (born April 20, 1960). Resides in Allison Park, Pennsylvania with children Emily Elizabeth and Mary Katherine.

3. Julie Lois Mims (born November 24, 1961), married Michael Zajac and resides in Marietta, Georgia They have 2 children, Sydney Leanne and Abigail Rae

4. Mary Janice Mims (born May 5, 1965), married Michael Hostetter and resides in Marietta, Georgia They have 2 children, Erica Lynn and Clayton Thomas.

Bobbie Carroll Mims, born January 23, 1934, married Elliott Fulwood Anderson (Nov.14,1921- Feb. 12, 1972) on September 22, 1957. They had 2 children and Carol Anderson still resides in Plains. Their children are:

1. Susan Anderson (born September 8, 1958) in Sumter County, Georgia. Resides in Columbus, Georgia.

2. Jill Anderson (born September 2, 1966) in Sumter County, Georgia. Married Samuel Keith Simmons (born October 15, 1963) on July 18, 1992. They are parents of Lily Anderson Simmons, born December 26, 1999. They reside in Columbus, Georgia.

—*Submitted by Carol Anderson, Sara Helen Bozeman, and George Mims, Jr.*

Robert B. Moss

Robert B. (Bob) Moss of Lincolnton, Ga., and Betty Miriam Horne of Albany, Ga. were married in Albany in 1954. After living in Albany, Lincolnton, Elberton and Athens, they and their two children,
Robert, Jr. and Linda, moved to the University of Georgia's Southwest Georgia Branch Experiment Station in Plains in 1962. Bob was Assistant-Superintendent at the time, but was promoted to Superintendent when Mr. N. C. McRainey retired in 1963.

Bob remained in that position until his retirement in 1992. In 1964, their third child, Jeffrey, was born. On Jeff's ninth birthday, the Moss family moved into their home on Ga. Hwy. 45 North, and the Sr. Mosses still live there.

Robert, Jr. married the former Marianne Chastain, and they and their three daughters, Courtney, Ashley, and Catharine live in Leesburg, Ga. Robert is as Orthodontist in Albany, Ga.

Linda also lives in Leesburg, Ga. She is Assistant-principal at the middle school in Lee County.

Jeff is married to the former Camille Morton, and they and their two children, Mallory and Jay live in Alpheretta, Ga. He is a drug representative for Pfizer Pharmaceuticals.

The Mosses have been active members of the Plains United Methodist Church since 1962, and other community clubs and activities.

— *Submitted by Robert B. Moss, Sr.*

Murray Family

Drury (Drewry) Murray (1787-1862), the first of this line, came to Sumter County, Georgia, in 1833. Son of Nathan Murray (1756-c.1808), a Revolutionary Soldier, he moved 6 miles south of Plains in the early 1830s shortly after the area was opened for settlement. A farmer, he amassed an acreage of 1360 acres by 1860, growing wheat, corn, cotton and vegetables. At his death in 1862, he was buried on the home place in the Murray Family Cemetery on land that is still in possession of his descendants.

Drury's son, John Fulwood Murray, one of four children, enlisted in the Georgia Volunteer Infantry in 1862 and was present at the surrender at Appomattox. He married Alethea Josephine Parker and farmed the same land as his father. To this union, which lasted 50 years, were born eight children:

1. Willie Zuella married John Godwin, and lived in Plains

2. Margaret Elizabeth married Thomas G. Anderson and lived in Plains.

3. Drury Parker married Maude E. Jennings and lived in Plains.

4. John William. More below.

5. Susan Alethea married Ichabod L. Balkcom and lived in Georgetown, Georgia.

6. Almer Clyde, married Florrie Stevens and began the first telephone company in Plains. Their children were: Norman Clyde, Annola, Gladys Estelle, Florrie Elizabeth (Beth), and Sara Eva.

7. Anna Josephine married Wm. T. Mackey and lived in Florida.

8. Nathan Fulwood married Kathleen McGarrah and lived in Americus.

John William Murray, (1871-1966), known as "Captain Murray," continued farming the home place. He was a member of the Plains Baptist Church and a Justice of the Peace. In 1904, he married Rosa Nettie Wise and they had one child to live to maturity: Frances Allethea "Allie" Murray. Allie graduated from Georgia State College for Women in 1926, married Edgar Smith (see Smith Family) and lived in Plains. After her husband's death in 1940, she worked in the Plains Post Office, retiring after 29 years. Edgar and Allie Smith had four children: Eleanor Rosalynn, William Jerrold, Murray Lee, and Lillian Allethea.

—*Submitted by Rosalynn Smith Carter*

Family of Rodolphus Silas Oliver

The Oliver family in England goes back for centuries and there seems to have been three main branches: the oldest settled in Southwestern England, another in Southern England, and the third, off-shoots from these older families, in Scotland and Ireland. The possession of a coat of arms by the family demonstrates the fact that they held an honorable position in the old country.

The Oliver family in Georgia was founded by one James Oliver, grandfather of R.S. Oliver. James came from South Carolina and settled near East Point, Georgia.

John J. (probably James) Oliver was born in Webster County on February 29, 1825 (?). He was a farmer and served in the War Between the States, in Company C-5th Battalion of Georgia Infantry (State Guard). He was Lieutenant, possibly 3rd, in the summer of 1864.

Later he married Miss Carrie McGrady. They had four children: John Wesley (born June 27, 1874; died April 21, 1888); Rodolphus Silas (born December 2, 1859; died May 30, 1928); Emma and George McGrady.

This is the line of Rodolphus Silas Oliver known as R.S. or Dolph.

He lived his early years in Webster County and attended school in Preston, Georgia. He then went to the University of Georgia and finished his junior year.

In 1882 Dolph married Miss Aughtry Rylander. She was the daughter of Matthew Edward Rylander and Catherine Brown Rylander of Sumter County. They had a large farm and a nice country home one-mile west of Plains, Georgia.

Miss Aughtry was born March 27, 1864 and died November 16, 1899.

Dolph farmed until 1885. They lived in a small community, three miles from the present site of Plains, near Magnolia Springs in Sumter County. He started a one-room store to meet the needs of the people. This settlement was called "The Plains of Dura" (from the Bible: Book of Daniel: Chapter 3: 1st Verse).

Some years later the railroad came to a section three miles from Magnolia Springs, so the town moved to a site on the railroad and called it 'Plains'.

In 1885, Dolph established himself in the mercantile business there. It was called the "Oliver-McDonald Company" and became one of the largest and most successful in Sumter County.

In 1901 he organized the Plains Bank and was president as long as it was in existence. He was a member of the Methodist Church of Plains, was a member of the Board of Steards and was very active in all phases of the church work.

He was mayor of the town for many years. He belonged to the Knights of Pythias, and the various Masonic bodies from the Blue Lodge to the Shrine. He was also a member of the Americus Kiwanis Club. He was a successful banker, merchant and farmer, and was very effective in the building of Plains and Sumter County.

There were nine children born to this couple: Walter Harney, Jessie, Clifford Rylander, Edmund Matthew, Floy, John Wesley, Carrie McGrady, and Catherine Brown (twins) and Annie Laura.

In December 1899 Dolph married Annie (called Effie) Stewart Turner (born April 1, 1868; died October 28, 1958). Her father was Dr. Josephus Tarpley Turner, a Methodist Preacher, who served many churches in South Georgia. Her mother was Martha Frances Turner. Two children were born of this marriage: Frances Aughtry and Rodolph Stewart.

R.S. Oliver died May 30, 1928.

—Submitted by Frances Oliver Adams and Aughtry Oliver Averill. Frances was R.S.'s daughter. Aughtry was R.S.'s granddaughter

From The Notes of Harriett Rylander Ansley:

The first Rheinlander I have a record of joined the Salzburger Colony at Ebenezer, Georgia near Savannah in 1734, going there from Charleston, South Carolina. He was a glazier and animal husbandman, and for the help he could give in these lines was allowed to join the Salzburgers. I have never been able to find his first name or that of his wife. His son, John Martin, was born after they came to Georgia.

John Martin Rheinlander's first wife was Mary Kalsher. She died in Savannah, March 15, 1760 at age 21.

The first time the name was found spelled RYLANDER was in records concerning Matthew Edmund Rylander. He and his second wife are buried at Oak Grove Cemetery in Americus. His son, John Emory Rylander was killed in the Civil War at Cold Harbor, Virginia. A son, by his second marriage to Sara Catherine Brown, died in Richmond, Virginia from wounds received in a Civil War Battle. He is buried in Oak Grove Cemetery in the same grave with his half brother, Major John Emory Rylander.

Matthew and Sara Catherine are buried in Oak Grove Cemetery. Ann Gamble Rylander is buried in Rose Hill Cemetery in Macon on the lot of Matthew's second wife's family (Brown).

—Submitted by Joyce Oliver Bergman

Family of Pacie L. Pickett, Sr. and Lillian Pickett

Pacie L. Pickett Sr. and Lillian J. Pickett moved to Plains in the year of 1958. They were born and lived in Sumter County all their life. They have 8 children: 6 boys and 2 girls. The boys are: Pacie Jr., Willie Freeman, Raymon, Buster, Chester, and Norman. The girls are Alice Ruth and Wilma Jean. Pacie Jr. never married. Willie Freeman married Pearlean Bridges and they have 5 children and he had 3. Raymon married Emmer J. Snipes they had 2 children Kimble and Raymon Christopher; Chester married Brender Oats(died July 14, 2002) they had 2 children; Buster never married; Norman married but had no children; Alice Ruth married Leonard Muff they had 5 children; Wilma Jean married Billie McCorey and have two children Chrystul and Williman Axlendar. Lillian and Pacie have 20 grandchildren and 10 great grand children.

Pacie served in World War II. He served 3 years 3 months and 26 days.
—*Submitted by Lillian Pickett*

Jack Pugh Family

Jack Pugh (b. 5-9-1900/ d.12-18-1981) married Esther Ketchum (b. 5-10-1904/ d.4-1 0-1999) on Oct.8, 1927 in Clayton AL. Moved to Plains, GA. in 1944 with their 7 children.

I. Jeannette Pugh (b. 8-1-1928 / d. 10-9-1994) married Fred M. Chavers (b. 9-22-1926 /d.10-25-1989) on Dec.21, 1946. They had 3 children: Patricia Ann (b. 5-1-1948), Linda Marie (b. 11-20-1949), and Beverly Sue (b. 4-27-1954).

A) Patricia Ann Chavers married 1st Johnny L. Stewart (b. 7-15-1944 / d.12-31-1966) from Ellaville, GA. on Aug. 28,1964. They had one son, Charles D. Stewart (b. 6-28-1965) married Kellie Peeples (b. 10-7-1966) from Americus, GA. on June 22,1985. They reside in Ellaville, GA. They have one son, Preston Leroy Stewart (b. .2-13-1993).

Pat married 2nd James D. Conger (b. 2-23-1944) from Albany, GA on Nov. 13,1970. James brought a son to the marriage: James D. Conger, Jr. (b. 5-31-1965). James married Pollyanne Simpson (b. 9-28-1968) from Americus, GA. on Nov. 20, 1993. They reside in Americus, GA. They have two children, Hannah Lauren (b. 9-25-1994) and Chase Baker (b. 5-23-1997)

Patricia and James had one son, Benjamin Daryl (b. 4-24-1973), who married Kelly Ann Horne(b. 8-28-1974) from Americus, GA. on June 19,1993. They reside in Americus, GA. They have two children, Savannah Nicole (b. 11-28-1996) and Alyssa Ann (b. 4-17-2001).

Patricia works at the Plains Post Office as a clerk. James and son Jamie own and operate C & C Construction Co. They reside in Plains, GA.

B) Linda Marie Chavers married Thomas L. Pilcher (b. 4-1-1949) from Americus, GA on Mar. 1, 1968. They reside in Americus, GA. They have three children: Freddie M. (b. 7-12-1968), Robert E. (b. 1-19-1970), and Wendy Kaye (b. 6-8-1979).

Freddie M. married Mindy Renee Morgan (b. 10-23-1968) from Cobb, GA. on May 23, 1993. They reside in Cobb, GA. They have two children: Patrick McDuffie (b. 1-12-1994) and Morgan Danielle (b. 7-25-1998).

Robert married Kimberly Benner Ray (b. 6-11-1971) from Jesup, GA. on Oct. 28, 1995. Kim brought one son into the marriage, Brandon Garrett Ray (b. 10-18-1991). Robert and Kim have one child, Lyndsie Marie (b. 5-29-1996), and they reside in Americus, GA.

Wendy Kaye (b. 6-8-1979) married Adam Morris Winters (b. 3-19-1976) from Americus, GA. on Aug. 3, 1996. They have two children, Katelyn Nicole (b. 10-1-1997) and Adam Morris Jr. (b. 7-31-2001). They reside in Americus, GA.

C) Beverly Sue Chavers (b. 4-27-1954) married David Law of Leslie, GA. in 1975 and the marriage dissolved in divorce in 1980. Married Edgar Gilbert of Blakely, GA. on June 17, 1983 and marriage dissolved in divorce in March of 1998. Sue presently lives in Panama City, FL.

II. Billie Jean Pugh (b. 4-27-1930) married A.F. (Bo) Cosby (b. 8-10-1918/d. 6-29-1999) of Preston, GA. on Jan. 18, 1946. They had one son, Robert Terry (b. 2-13-1947/d. 3-15-1947).

Billie and Bo were married 53 yrs. before his death. He served 8 yrs. in the Army Retired from Civil Service at the Marine Base in Albany, GA., served as Probate Judge of Webster County. Cosby Family buried in Preston City Cemetery. Billie worked as Manhattan Shirt Co. in Americus, GA. for 28 yrs. She presently lives in Preston.

III. Vivian Grace Pugh (b. 3-30-1933) married James Harold Bankston (b. 6-17-1928) from Preston, GA. on June 3, 1950. They have two children.

A) James Harold Bankston. Jr. (Jimmy) (b. 3-15-1952) married Kathy Elaine McKinnon on Aug. 22, 1971. Marriage dissolved in divorce. They had one child, Leslie Suzanne (b. 5-14-1973) who married Keith Seymour in 1996. Marriage dissolved in divorce. They had one child, . Hunter Bankston Seymour (b. 10-2-1996).

B) Micheal LaDon Bankston (b. 3-14-1956) married Nan Taylor Dunn (b. 7-15-1956) from Richland, GA on June 11, 1977. They have 4 children.

1. Maggie Anderson (b. 5-28-1985)
2. Michael LaDon, Jr. (Sonny Buck) (b. 7-13-1988)
3. William Jackson (b. 11-17-1994)
4. Susan Dunn (2-19-1998)

Vivian and Harold are retired and are presently living in Preston, GA. Jimmy is a Deputy Sheriff in Webster County and lives in Preston. Mike is an Attorney and State Court Judge. Mike, Taylor, and children live in Camilla, GA.

IV. Jack Pugh, Jr. (8-1-1934) married Jean Smith (2-20-1934) of Plains on May 25,1955. Marriage dissolved in divorce. They had one son, Robert Allen (b. 3-4-1959).

Jack married Elaine Powell Drew (1-15-1945) from Preston, GA. on Nov. 3, 1996. Jack retired from Ga. Power Co. after 32 years and is presently living in Preston, GA.

V. Hazel Margarite (b. 4-10-1939) married Joe Nowlen Kinnett (b. 5-20-1941/d4-6-1982). from Preston, GA. on May 22, 1964. They had one child, Kelli Lynn (b. 6-21-1979).

Hazel has been employed with Redman Homes for the past 43 years, and presently lives in Preston, GA. Kelli graduated from the University of Georgia in Dec. 2001, and is presently living in Athens, GA.

VI. Cecil Milton Pugh (b. 4-8-1942) Information withheld upon request of person.

VII. Bertram Lee "Butch" Pugh (b. 1-10-1944) married 1st Gail Robinson from Americus, GA in 1964. Marriage dissolved in divorce. They had two children:

A) Devonya Zan (Dee) Pugh (b. 12-4-1964) married Bruce Bivins from Americus. They had two children. Marriage dissolved in divorce. Their children were: Chamera Nicole Bivins (b. 11-30-1983) and Jake Landon Bivins (b. 7-17-1989).

B) Shawna Fran Pugh (b. 12-26-1965) married Ken Nobles (b. 12-19-1963) from Americus, GA. on June 29, 1989. They have two children: Kenneth Levi (b. 10-9-1987) and Lenzee Gail (b. 10-13-1990).

Butch married 2nd Dianne Cromer (b. 2-11-1956) from Americus, GA. on Feb. 7, 1976 They have one child, Dawn Michelle (b. 3-2-1976) who married Denver Scott Justus from Gainesville, GA on July 15, 2000. Butch and Dianne presently reside in Andersonville, GA.

Jack and Esther Pugh, their daughter Jeannette, and her husband Fred are all buried at Lebanon Cemetery, Plains, GA.

—*Submitted by Patricia Chavers Conger*

Chapter 20: Family History Q–T

Robert S. Ratliff Family

The house known as 219 West Main Street was built by Griff Eldridge in the year 1901. Bruce Hall lived there until the year 1926 when Mr. Eldridge's widow sold the house and 100 acres of land to Robert S. Ratliff who then moved his wife Herman and their three daughters who were Sara born 1921, Lorraine born 1922 and Eloise born in 1924 from where they were living in a house on South Bond Street where Miss Allie Smith and her family later lived.

Robert and his family lived on one side of the house and his brother Bernard and his family lived on the other side. Robert and his brother Bernard operated a garage on the south side of Hudson Street behind the stores downtown.

After Robert and family moved to Main Street, he started a fish route. He would go to Florida buy fish and bring back to sell. He also farmed and was a substitute mail carrier. He and Herman had one son Robert (Bobbie) Jr. born in 1936 after moving to Main Street.

Robert S. Ratliff, Sr. born 1893 died 1978 married Herman Johnson born 1896 died 1961. There children:

1. Sara Ratliff Howard Leuty born 1921 died 1983 married Oscar E. Howard born 1913 died 1961. Their children were a) Robert Isacs (Bob) Howard born 1943 died 1997 had one son Greg Howard born 1971 who married Wendy Sorrenson in 1996 and they live in Columbus, Georgia. Bob married Annette Oliner O'Neal in 1983 and brought her to live on Main Street. Annette has 3 children Brenda Wise, Buddy O'Neal and Jim O'Neal, Annette still lives in the house today. b)Linda Howard born 1948 married George Pritchard born 1948. They live in Riverdale, Georgia.

2. Lorraine Rafliff Paradise was born in 1922 died 1948 was married to Dewey W. Paradise.

3. Eloise Ratliff Taylor was born 1924 died 1948 married Lonnie Taylor and had 2 children. Lonnie Taylor, Jr. born 1946 and died 1948. Patricia Taylor born 1947 died 1948.

4. Robert (Bobbie) S. Ratliff, Jr., born 1936 died 1948.

Lorraine, Eloise and Lonnie and their two children and Bobbie Ratliff were all killed in a private airplane crash on their way home to Plains from Tennessee. Their plane crashed near Junction City, Georgia in 1948.

Sara Ratliff that day lost her sister and her brother and their families. When Sara's mother Herman died in 1961 she moved with her children, Bob and Linda, back to the homeplace to look after her father Robert.

Sara went back to college in 1964 to Georgia Southwestern and became a Registered Nurse working at Plains Nursing Home and later as a Health Care Nurse for the Americus Health Department. Sara married Neal Leuty around 1969 and they were charter members of Maranatha Baptist Church where they attended until their death. Robert S. Ratliff's family have continually lived in their house since it was bought in 1926.

—Submitted by Annette Howard

Levie Simeon Raven

Levi Simeon Raven was born 1865 in Webster County, Georgia. In the 1870 U.S. census taken in Webster County on the 22nd day of July, Levi Raven was living in the home of Chas Raven. He was five (5) years old. According to family history his father, William Raven, was born a slave and later became an itinerant elder in the African Methodist Episcopal Church. Rev. William Raven had already moved away to take a pastoral assignment somewhere near Savannah Georgia. In 1881 Rev. Raven was elected a Trustee for the founding of Morris Brown College (noted on page 13 in the book 'Morris Brown College A Century of Pride and Strength. The First 100 Years 1881-1981).

By the time of the 1880 U.S. Census, Levi Raven was living in the home of Charles and Elizia Marshall. The Marshalls were living in Georgia Militia District 978 of Webster County. Elizia was Levi's older sister. Another sister Margrett Raven (two years older than Levi) was also living in the home. Levi's age was listed as fourteen years.

There was no U.S. Census taken in 1890 due to the French and Indian war. The U.S. Census of 1900 was taken, but the file copy of the census is not legible enough to identify the names recorded in Webster County.

For the next 20 years after the census of 1880, Levi Raven grew into manhood in Webster County. During that period he met and married the former Miss Emma Hill. He started a family that eventually grew to consist of ten children.

According to family history, he was a caretaker of the "Old Dudley Plantation". He also became a local minister with his home church being the Saint Mark A.M.E. Church, still thriving in the Archery community. He was a founder and treasurer of the "Sublime Order of Archery". The Sublime Order was established to aid area farmers when they had a bad crop year.

In the U.S. Census of 1910, Levi Raven (age 43 according to the census) was listed as the head of household. Once again his residence was listed in Georgia Militia District 978 of Webster County. Included in the household were his wife, Emma Hill, age 38, and 8 children. Their oldest daughter, Georgia, had already moved out of the home. She was living next door with her husband, Will Laster.

The names of the eight children living in the home were as follows: Johnnie (father of five children: Clinton, Johnnie, Jr. Samuel Lee, Floyd and Milton); Rosa (Dunning); Bessie(Bryant); Willie; Carrie (Willis); Arena (Wakefield); Clifford and William.

Levi Raven's daughter Bessie Raven Bryant lived to be 102 years old. According to her account of her early childhood, she grew up on the "Old Dudley place" approximately seven miles from Plains, Georgia. A few years after her birth, the Johnson family moved to the Dudley place. Soon thereafter a school was opened on the Dudley Place site.

Levi Raven was one of the founders of the school that came to be known as "The Johnson Home Industrial College." The school operated a sawmill and a farm to help cover expenses.

According to Bessie Raven Bryant, the school changed the status of the community and the minds of the people. Before long, the name of the community was changed from Dudley to Archery.

By the time of the 1920 U.S. Census, Levi Raven was again listed as the head of household in Georgia Mililitia District 978. He was also listed as widowed. His wife Emma died in November of 1918.

The dwelling listed just before the home of Levi Raven was identified as the Archery School. This was the Industrial College of which Levi Raven was a founder along with the Johnson family.

The dwelling listed after the home of Levi Raven was identified as the home of a white family headed by Marshall Minick.

The children living in the home in 1920 were Carrie (Wiltis), Arena (Wakefield), Cliffiord and Francis.

Levi Simeon Raven was a lifelong resident of Webster County. He died July 4, 1925 and is buried in the Saint Mark A.M.E Church cemetery near where he grew up and lived. He dedicated his life to providing opportunities for his family and others in the community. According to family history, his motto was "kick at the moon." To "kick at the moon" was his way of telling his children: "You can be whatever you want to be."

—*Submitted by (no name given)*

Buford Reese Family

Maxine Reese was born one of five children to Ben Newberry and Laura Tyner Newberry on June 10, 1931 in Miller County, Georgia. She grew up doing farm chores and was involved in many school activities. As a student in Colquitt, her favorite subjects were reading and history. In high school she played varsity basketball, sang in a quartet, was active in junior and senior plays, and was secretary and president of her chapter of the Future Home-makers of America. In 1948, she was voted the "Prettiest Girl" in her class and graduated with honors from Jakin High School.

In school, Maxine met her future husband, Buford Henry Reese. They started dating seriously when Maxine was a senior in high school and Buford was a freshman at Abraham-Baldwin College. They were married on Maxine's birthday in 1948. Soon afterward, Maxine and Buford moved to Athens, Georgia, where Maxine worked as a waitress and cashier while Buford attended the University of Georgia. On February 26, 1951, their first daughter, Sherry Maxine Reese was born.

After Buford graduated from the University of Georgia, the Reeses returned to Colquitt. Buford was a teacher of Vocational Agriculture at Miller County High School. Their son, Larry Buford Reese was born on September 25, 1955.

In 1956, Buford accepted a job as the Vocational Education teacher at Plains High School. Principal Y.T. Sheffield and Jimmy Carter, school board member, interviewed Mr. Reese for the position. The Reeses then moved to Plains.

In Plains, Maxine pursued her dream of obtaining a college degree. As a freshman, Maxine attended Georgia Southern College. By the fall of 1962, Maxine would graduate from the University of Georgia with a double major in English and Social Studies. Maxine soon began teaching several subjects at Plains High School and served as the school's secretary, handling many administrative duties. A few years later, Maxine left teaching to run the family business, managing a mobile home community between Plains and Americus. At the height of a successful business, Buford and Maxine experienced a very unexpected major event in their lives. The happy event was the arrival of their third child, Theresa Ann Reese, who was born on August 3, 1966.

In 1975, when Jimmy Carter told his neighbors in Plains that he was running for President, Maxine and Buford agreed that Maxine would help Jimmy Carter win the election. During the frenzied campaign years, Maxine performed many tasks. The most important of these included organizing the million-dollar fun raising dinner and managing the campaign headquarters at the Plains Depot. When Jimmy Carter was elected, Maxine organized an Amtrak Train named "The Peanut Special" to carry the people of Plains to the inauguration in Washington, D.C. When President Carter returned to Plains from the White House in 1981, Maxine organized another major event: the world's largest covered dish dinner to honor his return home.

In the late 1980's Maxine was busier than ever. In 1985, she chaired the Plains Centennial Celebration, which culminated with a Willie Nelson concert at Plains High School. She also began working towards legislation to designate the Jimmy Carter National Historic Site. However, the 1980's also brought great sorrow to Maxine's life when in 1987, her beloved husband, Buford died. With the help of many other women in similar situations, she helped establish the Plains Association of Lady Survivors (PALS), which remains active today.

During the 1990s, she worked with other Plains residents to restore Plains High School. Maxine's role in the restoration was to raise over $1 million dollars in contributions and building materials. The National Park Foundation honored her and other members of the Plains High School Liaison Committee with the National Park Partnership-Leadership Award in 1996. That same year, she chaired the first Plains Peanut Festival. In 1997, she joined the effort to see Plains High School designated the State School of Georgia. Finally in 1999, Maxine arranged an event to honor former President Jimmy Carter on his 75th birthday. This gala all-star celebration would help to open the beautifully restored Rylander Theatre in Americus, as well as pay special tribute to President Jimmy Carter. Maxine served as a Trustee of the Maranatha Baptist Church in Plains and was an active member in several notable organizations including the City of Plains Historical Preservation Trust and as a board member for the Plains Better Hometown Program. The downtown City Park located behind the depot was named Maxine Reese Park in honor of her dedication to the community on March 18, 2000. Maxine died May 25, 2000.

—*Submitted by Dan Ariail*

Rogers Family

In late 1954 Mr. Edgar Rogers and his wife Pearl (of New York state), returning from a stay in Florida, stopped in the small town of Plains. They both found it so charming that they decided to rent a room from Miss Annie Mae Brannen. They rented a room for almost six months and after that purchased a home and farm a mile outside of the city limits. In 1956, their son Everett Lloyd Rogers came from New York to help his parents due to their failing health. Mr. E.L. later purchased the farm from his parents. In the summer of 1959, his wife Margaret Rogers and their daughters Peggy, Mary Jean, and Hope moved from New York to the home in Plains.

Margaret Rogers taught in the local Plains High School from the years of 1959 to 1971. Mr. and Mrs. E. . Rogers sold the farm site in 1975 but purchased and built a home on land south of Plains. The couple remained in the friendly area of the town of Plains until their deaths in 1994 and 2000.

—*Submitted by Hope Rogers Buchanan*

Salter Family

Bobby Salter (born August 6, 1939), son of Virgil (Shorty) and Beulah Salter married on April 24, 1960 to Jean Hall(born July 23, 1940), daughter of Roy and Bular Hall. Bobby and Jean have one daughter Angela (born August 24, 1962) who on September 11, 1983 married Mark Pitts (born December 23, 1963). Their children are: Christopher born August 26, 1986, Jeremy born May 12, 1988, and Ashley born August 13, 1990.

Bobby and Jean decided to open a business in Plains in 1975. The business was named Kountry Korner Krafts and was located on the corner of Hudson and Highway 280. In June 1976, a restaurant was added to the shop. The building was remodeled and expanded several times during the Presidential years. Then in 1981, they relocated the Kountry Korner Restaurant down to the building where Mom's Kitchen is located. At that time they started offering seafood suppers on Friday and

Saturday nights. The business was located there until February 1987 under the Salters ownership

Then a business called BJ's Pitt Stop in the old Billy Carter Service Station. B stood for Bobby – J stood for Jean – Pitt was for our grandchildren. The shop serviced cars, sold gas, etc. It was in this building, they started frying peanuts. There was such a great response the business moved over to their other building, the Old Carter Warehouse and added candy making. The business has been in operation since 1992 as Plain Peanuts selling peanuts and candies in their shop on main street in Plains and shipping peanuts and candies all over the U.S.A.. Bobby and Jean's three grandchildren have helped with the business since 1989.

—*Submitted by Jean Salter*

Hanson and Mary Jane Schley

Little is known about the Schley family before 1871. It is lost in the nightmare that was slavery. Most of the history that is known is through the history of the Lebanon Baptist Church.

After the Emancipation we know of two members of the family. Hanson Schley and Adam Prince. These two brothers proceeded to raise their families and establish their lives. Adam Prince refused to take the name of his slave master. His grandfather had told him that they were royalty in Africa, so he chose the name Prince to reflect the lost heritage. Hanson Schley was a minister.

As slaves, the African-Americans of Plains Georgia had attended the Plains Baptist Church. They were not allowed to attend services at the same time as the Caucasian members of the congregation. In 1871, the African-American member of the congregation were given their letter of dismissal from the Plains Baptist Church founded the Lebanon Baptist Church.

Among the founding members were Hanson Schley and his wife Mary Jane Schley. Hanson and Jane Schley had a son, Baldwin Dowdell Schley.

He was also a minister. He was the founder and pastor of the New Lebanon Baptist Church. He married Levonia Biggins and together they had nine children. The third child of their union was Booker Biggins Schley.

Booker Schley was very active in the church and the local community. He was a Ward Captain, president of the Progressive Missonary Sunday School Convention, President of the International Benevolence Society, the Independent Fraternal Union Local Lodge and founder of the Ushers Union. He was ordained as a deacon of the Lebanon Baptist Church and served as chairman of the deacon board for 15 years.

Although he had a minimal education, Booker Schley was a fervent believer in the education as a means of self-improvement. He served as chairman of the local school board and worked tirelessly with the civic organizations he was involved with to insure that local students were provided with scholarships. He was instrumental in getting a transportation allowance for students attending Staley High School in Americus Ga.

Until the transportation allowance was granted, African-American parents had to pay for their children to be transported to the high school, which was about 15 miles away. In a struggling community this was a significant hardship that resulted in some students being unable to finish high school. He served as president of the International Benevolence Society and the Independent Fraternal Union. He was also active in the local politics and remained a pillar of the African-American community in Plains until his death in 1984.

—*Submitted by Clara Franklin*

Seaborn and Lessie Schley Family

Seaborn was born in Plains in the late 19th Century to the parentage of Lucy and Wiley Schley, who were born into slavery and descended from

West Africa. He married Lessie Williams from neighboring Webster County on May 20, 1920. . Her parents John and Lavenia Williams were also former slaves descending from West Africa. There were fourteen children derived from this union, which were Seaborn Jr, William, Effie, Joseph, Betty Jean, Dorothy, Annette, Francis, Edward, Paul, Saul, Samuel, Chester & Robert. At this writing, five of the children are deceased. Paul, Saul & Betty Jean died at birth. Francis died in 1962 in a Massachusetts car accident. Chester was killed tragically in Atlanta in the late 70's. A grandchild, Cynthia was also raised by Seaborn and Lessie. She graduated from Plains High School in 1976. Seaborn died in the early 70's and Lessie passed in 1998.

The family house is located at 114 Carter Street. Seaborn Jr., Joseph, and Edward reside in Toledo, Ohio. William, Annette, Dorothy and Samuel reside in Bloomfield, Connecticut. Robert resides at the family house in Plains and Cynthia resides in metro Atlanta.

—*Submitted by Robert Schley*

Troy Sellards Family

Troy Sellards was born June 6, 1942, the son of James and Flora Collins Sellards. Troy had one brother, James Robert, and five sisters. These were Madeline, Ruby, Geraldine, Bobbie, and Carol. All of these still reside in Floyd County, Kentucky. Troy left home at eighteen to join the Army. He was stationed at Fort Benning in Columbus, GA. This is when he met his wife, Ethel Cooper Sellards. They were married August 3, 1963 and resided in Columbus during the time he was in service. After discharge from the Army in 1964, they moved to Kentucky for a short time. They returned to Center Point which is a small community out from Preston, Georgia.

In 1982, they moved to Plains, Georgia at 315 Walters Street where they still live. During this time, they had two daughters to join the family.

Marie was born in 1964 and Barbara arrived in 1966. Marie graduated from Greenfield Academy in Weston, Georgia, and Barbara graduated there also.

Marie married Michael Wills in 1983, and Barbara married Stan Lowell in 1984. Marie and Michael have three boys, Brantley, Stanton, and Sydney. Barbara and Stan have six children; Kelly, Ted, Christopher, Justin, Cassie and Casey are twins.

Troy is employed at Webster County High School and he and his wife Ethel have an upholstery business at their home in Plains.

Ethel's parents, Walter Ed Cooper and Sarah Lou Slocumb lived in Webster County where Ethel was born. Walter Ed was a farmer, and Sarah was a homemaker. Their family was comprised of one boy, Logan, and five girls; Ethel, Joyce, Irene, Mattie Edith, and Annell.

—*Submitted by Ethel Sellards*

Sewell Family

Richard Clarence Sewell of Newnan, Ga. married Ruth May Lane of Newnan, Ga. and together had 5 children.

1. Agnes Lucille
2. John William (J. W.)
3. Charles Robert
4. Roy
5. Sara Jane

Clarence owned and operated a logging business and moved about the country cutting timber. After the death of his wife and son Roy, Clarence and remaining family moved from Newnan, Ga. to Clayton, Al. where the family continued the logging business.

In 1942 son J. W. moved the business and his family to Plains, Ga. Working with J. W. and moving also to Plains was a first cousin M. H. Sewell and his wife Annella and children Barbara, Lee and Janelle.

In 1946 Clarence, being in poor health with a heart condition, moved to Plains to be near the famous Wise doctors and their clinic. Years before as a young man Clarence had been in the area of Plains logging and had lost a leg due to an accident at the mill. He was taken to the Wise Clinic and had never lost touch with the doctors there. One of his nurses was Lillian Gordy Carter.

Clarence purchased a farm outside Plains on Cow Pen Road, now owned by Pat Medlock. Moving with him to Plains were his widowed sister Agnes and his daughter Lucille and her family. Son, Robert later bought a farm on Bob Dodson Rd., now owned by the Dozier family. He farmed for a few years and then moved back to Clayton, Alabama, and started a logging business there.

Around that same time, Al Sewell, brother to Clarence moved to Plains with his wife Bessie Sprayberry of Newnan, Ga. Al and Bessie's son Lester, his wife Myrtle Leroy and son William also came to Plains. Al bought a farm on Highway 308 and lived there until his death. The farm is now owned by L. E. Godwin, Jr.

Clarence lived the balance of his life in Plains, Ga. farming the land on Cow Pen Road.

Listed Below is his family:

1. Agnes Lucille married Louis Harrison of Eufaula, AL, who died after 3 years.

1 son- Louis Patrick Harrison -Married Shirley Hunicke, St .Louis, MO. Their Children: Louis Patrick (Rick) and Larry Allen.

Lucille later married William Spires of Clayton, Al. Daughter- Lila Ruth- married Billy Mack Howard- Plains, Ga. Their children- Michael Alan, James Arthur, Steven Douglas.

Daughter- Sybil Lenora- married Billy Carter of Plains, Ga. Their Children: Katherine Kim, Jana Kae, William Alton IV (Buddy), Marle Leah, Sara Amanda and Earl Gordy.

2. John William (J. W.) married Martha Johns of Clayton, AL. Their children:

John William- Deceased, died as a child.

Ruth Lane- married Marvin Nation, Americus, Ga.- Ruth now deceased. 1 child- Heather Lane.

Martha Ann- married Michael Fennessy, Americus, Ga. Their Children: Allison, Dana and John.

James Wesley- married Lucy Waters of Arabi, Ga. 1 son- Robby.

Charles Ross- Deceased, died as a child.

3. Charles Robert married Betty Teal, Clayton, AL. Their children:

Charles Robert (Bobby)- married Martha Clyde Warr of Clayton, AL. Their children: Lisa and Bob

Another child, Pam was later born to Bobby's second marriage.

Clarence Richard (Dicky)- married Theresa McGoo- Plains, Ga. Their Children- Rick and Pam

4. Roy died at 17 in a logging accident.

5. Sara Jane married Tommy Jernigan (Preacher), Eufaula, AL. No children- Both now deceased.

Descendants of Clarence Sewell married people in the area and now live in and around Sumter County and also other parts of Southwest Georgia. —*Submitted By Sybil Carter*

Sheffield Family

In 1797 West Sheffield, as a young boy, left Duplin County North Carolina for the Georgia frontier. His father, John Sheffield, had died there in 1791. His mother, the widow Elizabeth Grady Sheffield, purchased a 350 acre plantation near Brewton Creek in present-day Laurens County. Her family, consisting of West, brothers Isham, Arthur, Wright, Bryant and sister Tabitha; all settled nearby in the Laurens County area. When ceded Indian lands became available for settlement in Southwest Georgia in 1820, West, Arthur, Bryant, Wright, Isham, and Tabitha Sheffield Feagan were among the first settlers. All moved to Early County in the vicinity of Bainbridge and Colquitt, Georgia.

West acquired a sizable plantation in the vicinity of Spring Creek, just north of present-day Colquitt in Miller County. He had married Susannah Clark in 1810 in Montgomery County, Georgia. Children of this marriage were Isham, Katy, Betsy, and Bryan. He married Mary Renfro in Pulaski County May 9, 1818. Children of this marriage were John C., Rebecca, Samuel S., Arthur, Thomas W., Mary Ann, and Louisa. He died about 1860. He is buried beside wife Mary in Shepherd Cemetery north of Colquitt, GA.

Thomas W. Sheffield, youngest son of West Sheffield, was born 21 November 1839. He married Lucy C. Thompson on May 7, 1862. During the civil war, Thomas was 2nd Lieutenant in the Miller County Wildcats, was captured near Lookout Mountain Tennessee, and remained prisoner of War in Ohio until Appomattox. After the war, he farmed and ran a saw-mill in Miller County for several years, later moving to Dooly county to manage the plantation of his Father-in-law William Thompson. Children of Thomas W. and Lucy Thompson Sheffield were: Young Thompson, Carrie Tallulah, Julius Edward, Mary Loucinda, William West, Alice Trudie, twins Minnie and Mittie, John, Lucy Pearl, and Annie Irene. Thomas died 6 December 1891. He and wife Lucy Sheffield are buried in the Thompson family Cemetery near Unadilla, Georgia.

Young Thompson Sheffield, son of Thomas W. Sheffield, was born 11 March 1866, in Miller County GA. As a young man he spent a few years in Texas employed in the Postal Service before returning to Dooly County Georgia, where he married Cora Eva Murray. He managed a farm, and in later life he moved to the town of Pinehurst where he was RFD Postman. He was a member of Pinehurst Baptist Church and Unadilla Masonic Lodge. Children of Young Thompson and Cora Thompson Sheffield were: Julius Onis, William Alfred, Mary Loucinda, Columbus Hyman, twins Eva Mae, Young Thompson Jr., and Murray Lee. All of his children except Y. T. Jr. eventually moved to Texas. Young

Sheffield died 21 October 1932. He is buried in the Pinehurst Cemetery.

Young Thompson Sheffield Jr., son of Young Thompson Sheffield., was born June 24, 1904, in Pinehurst GA. He attended the public elementary schools in Pinehurst, and high school at Locust Grove Institute, a military preparatory school. He attended college at Mercer University, Macon Georgia, and Carson Newman College, Jefferson, Tennessee. He later received the Degree of Masters of Education from Mercer University.

After teaching school in Jackson County Georgia, he came to Plains to teach under Superintendent Julia L. Coleman, in 1927. He served Plains school as teacher, assistant superintendent, principal, and coach until his retirement in 1966. He also was active in Georgia High School Athletic Association. He was an active member and deacon of Plains Baptist Church.

Mr. Sheffield married Lilloise Lunsford of Plains, on 29 June 1934. Their children were Young Thompson Sheffield III and Charlene Sheffield Mallard. Mr. Sheffield died 21 September 1967 and is buried in Lebanon Cemetery, Plains Georgia.
—*Submitted by Tommy Sheffield*

Descendants of C.B. and Ruth Turner Short

Clarence Belvy Short (b. 19 Feb. 1908 at Shiloh in Sumter County) and Ruth Lee Turner (b. 7 Jan. 1913 in Polk County) were married on 23 Feb. 1929 in Plains at the home of Clarence's great-uncle, Rev. Augustus C. Wellons. The Victorian home, built in 1910, is today the Plains Bed and Breakfast Inn.

C.B. Short was the oldest of eight children of William Leonard Short, Sr. (1876-1951) and Laura Eugenia Wellons Short (1876-1956). His grandfather, Larkin T. Wellons, was a brother of A.C. Wellons.

Ruth Turner Short was the youngest of 12 children of Rev. David Moton Turner and his second wife, Nancy Matilda Smith Turner, who moved their family to Plains in 1919 (See David Moton Turner Family). Both are buried at Lebanon Cemetery in Plains.

Ruth Turner Short received much of her education in the Plains school, having begun first grade in the old wooden building that preceded the current brick structure built in 1921.

After their marriage, C.B. and Ruth Turner Short lived throughout Sumter County, primarily in the 17th District about seven miles southeast of Plains. They were longtime members of Hebron Baptist Church, which was founded in 1894 and first pastored by A.C. Wellons.

All four of their children graduated from Plains High School, in the classes of 1946, 1948, 1955 and 1962, and excelled in athletics. Their oldest son, Jack Short, served in the Army National Guard for six years, receiving an honorable discharge in 1954. Their youngest son, Bobo Short, who graduated from Florida State University and later earned a master's degree from Georgia Southwestern College, served in the U.S. Army from September 1970 through February 1972. He was a light infantryman specialist stationed in Friedberg, Germany, for a year.

C.B. Short, an esteemed farmer, died 4 Aug. 1973 at age 65. Ruth Turner Short survived him for 25 years before her death on 19 Dec. 1998 at age 85. She was the last surviving child of Rev. David M. Turner. Both she and C.B. Short are buried at Hebron Baptist Church Cemetery.

Their four children:

I. Lawrence Lee "Jack" Short, Sr. (b. 23 Nov. 1929) married Anna Frances Spann (b. 29 Aug. 1936), daughter of Walter Franklin Spann and Ada Brooks Spann, on 11 Jan. 1953 at Plains Baptist Church. Four children:

1. Lawrence Lee "Jackie" Short, Jr. (b. 14 Oct. 1953). Jackie married first Catherine Elaine "Cathy" Cook on 11 June 1972. Two children:

A.) Michael Shane Short (b. 19 Jan. 1973). Shane married Alesha Paige Dunaway on 27 June 1998. One child: 1A.) Katherine Mackenzie Short (b. 22 April 2001)

B.) Brian Lee Short (b. 13 Feb. 1975). Brian married Ginny Leigh Reeves on 4 April 1998.

Jackie married second Pharis Davis Lewis on 2 Dec. 1988.

2. Frances Anne Short (b. 27 Nov. 1956)

3. Walter Randall "Randy" Short (b. 27 June 1961). Randy married Jennifer Denise "Jenny" Durham on 8 Oct. 1988. Two children:

A.) Erica Anne Short (b. 26 April 1991)

B.) Jake Randall Short (b. 14 March 1996)

4. Steve Clarence Short (b. 8 May 1964)

II. Peggy Ann Short (b. 22 Dec. 1931) married Harold James Israel, Sr. (b. 30 June 1926), son of Charlie Lee Israel and Ruth McCoy Israel Carden, and a World War II veteran, on 2 Dec. 1951 at Hebron Baptist Church. Five children:

1. Beverly Ruth Israel (b. 3 Oct. 1952). Beverly married Alan Bruce Johnson on 14 July 1974. Three children:

A.) Justin Israel Johnson (b. 9 Aug. 1977). Justin married Susan A. Newberry on 20 April 2002.

B.) Alan Ryan Johnson (b. 12 Aug. 1981) (twin)

C.) Allison Ruth Johnson (b. 12 Aug. 1981) (twin)

2. Charles Lee Israel (b. 22 May 1955). Charles married Tracy Elizabeth Johnson on 16 Feb. 1980. Three children:

A.) Trevor Lee Israel (b. 3 Dec. 1989) (adopted)

B.) Chance Johnson Israel (b. 22 Aug. 1992) (adopted)

C.) Delanie Michael Israel (25 Oct. 1994) (adopted)

3. Harold James "Hal" Israel, Jr. (b. 17 Sept. 1957). Hal married Dawn Rebecca Miller on 8 Nov. 1980. Three children:

A.) Kelly Dawn Israel (b. 16 Jan. 1983)

B.) Harold James Israel III (b. 24 April 1984)

C.) Eric Charles Israel (11 Sept. 1987)

4. Peggy Marie Israel (b. 19 Jan. 1959). Peggy married first Kenneth Dalrymple on 4 April 1981. Peggy married second Richard Martin "Rick" Urash on 9 May 1999.

5. Mark Wendell Israel (b. 24 Nov. 1962). Mark married Sharon Denise Barhold on 4 Oct. 1986. Two children:

A.) Kayla Sharon Israel (b. 15 Sept. 1988)

B.) Peggy Claire Israel (b. 19 June 1993)

III. Patsy Ruth Short (b. 21 Jan. 1938) married Pat Smith Medlock (b. 21 Aug. 1936), son of William Verlyn Medlock and Grace Smith Medlock, and an eight-year member of the Army National Guard, on 4 June 1955 at Hebron Baptist Church. Four children:

1. Kenneth William Medlock (b. 25 July 1960)

2. Molly Eugenia Medlock (b. 14 June 1964) (twin). Molly married Gregory L. Speir on 21 July 1984. Two children:

A.) Molly Amanda "Mandy" Speir (14 April 1987)

B.) Joshua Medlock "Josh" Speir (28 Feb. 1990)

3. Polly Grace Medlock (b. 14 June 1964) (twin). Polly married Arthur Floyd Martin, Jr. on 4 June 1983. Three children:

A.) Benjamin Verlyn Martin (b. 16 Nov. 1984)

B.) Cassie Lee Martin (b. 22 March 1988)

C.) Callie Ruth Martin (b. 15 Sept. 1992)

4. Patty Ruth Medlock (b. 10 Nov. 1965). Patty married Jonathan Bond Webb on 6 Aug. 1988. Two children:

A.) William Medlock "Will" Webb (b. 28 Feb. 1990)

B.) Sara Ruth Webb (b. 5 Oct. 1992)

IV. Clarence William "Bobo" Short (b. 9 June 1944) married first Gail Jennings, daughter of Millard Margart Jennings, Jr. and Nellie K. Phillips Jennings, on 3 Oct. 1964 at St. Andrews Lutheran Church. One child:

1. Tanya Gail Short (b. 12 Jan. 1969) (adopted by C.W. Cresswell). Tanya married John Peter Zehnder on 30 Dec. 1998. Two children:

A). Jack Millard Zehnder (b. 14 Dec. 1999)

B). Matthew Frederick Zehnder (b. 7 Nov. 2001)

Bobo married second Nancy Ann Howells (b. 19 May 1951), daughter of James August Howells and Lois Schoen Howells, on 28 Aug. 1971 at St. Andrew United Church of Christ in Louisville, Ky. Two children:

1. Laura Schoen Short (b. 30 June 1978). Laura married William Curtis Rooks on 29 June 2002.

2. Chandler William "Chan" Short (b. 10 Feb. 1981)

—*Submitted by Steve Short*

Simmons Family

Martin Pardae Simmons and Verda Ruth Tyson Simmons lived in Sumter County, Georgia. They had 8 children. They were: Arrie, M.P. Jr., Dealva, Millard Franklin, Bonnie, Vida Ruth, Martin John, and Inez - 5 girls and 3 boys.

Millard and De Alva are the only ones in Sumter County. De Alva was married to James M. Howard who lived and farmed in the 17th District of Sumter County. He was Chairman of the Plains High School Board in the early 1960's. Millard was

Chairman of the Plains High School Board in 1966. Millard married his classmate Anne Bagwell in 1946. They have one child, Millard, Jr. who graduated from Plains High School in 1966, college in 1970. Millard Jr. owns a Cotton States Insurance Agency in Americus, Georgia but lives in Plains and is very active in community affairs. He married a schoolmate, Gloria Chavers, and they have two children. One boy, Rhett, who owns an insurance agency in Thomasville, Georgia and Paige who works and lives in Columbus, Georgia. They both are single at the present time.

After graduation from Plains High, Millard Sr. went into the Navy and participated in the Normandy invasion; then went through the Iwo Jima and Okinawa invasions. After Japan surrendered, Millard went in with the occupation forces in Japan and then blew up mines off the coast of Formosa (now Taiwan). After leaving the Navy, Millard came back to Plains, married Anne, and became a permanent resident of Plains. He was a half partner with Roy Brannen in a freezer locker after coming home; later being a rural letter carrier for 21 ½ years; then Postmaster for 11 years before retiring in 1990. Millard and Anne are members of the Plains United Methodist Church and live at 211 Thomas Street. Millard is 77 years old and Anne is 76.

—*Submitted by Millard Simmons*

Charles Phillip Smith Family

Charles Phillip Smith was born in Terrell County, Georgia, Octobr 22, 1914, the son of Daniel Reese Smith and Nannie Crittendin Andrews Smith; graduated from high school in Plains, Georgia; worked for Sheppard Construction Company of Atlanta; served with the U.S. Navy in the Pacific during World War II; married Jessie Merle Smith Johnson of Blakely, Georgia, March 8, 1946. Children:

(A) Richard Wooten Johnson (step son), born April 28, 1944, married December 23, 1975 to Angelina Spearman Howard of Clemson, South Carolina.

(B) Stephen Charles Smith (twin) born October 22, 1947, married Lisa McKee Dotson of Mobile, Alabama, on October 19, 1979. Child: Anna.

(C) Jeffrey Phillip Smith (twin) born October 22, 1947, married Lynn Hall of Forsyth, Georgia, March 20, 1976, child: (1) Emily Elizabeth Smith born Macon, Georgia, September 6, 1981.

(D) Elizabeth Grier Smith born May 15, 1955, married Edward Jean (Mickey) Wise, Americus, Georgia, July 29, 1978, later divorced.

—*Submitted by (no name given)*

Smith Family

The Smiths came from England in 1620 when Captain John Smith brought his three first cousins with him to America. Captain John Smith, born in England in 1579. He was 92 when he died. He was one of the founders of the English colony in Virginia. After many adventures as a soldier of fortune in Europe, Asia and Africa, he went out with the first expedition of the London Company to America in 1606. Dissensions broke out before the destination was reached, and Captain Smith was condemned to be hanged; but he escaped this fate and became the most influential member of the colony.

In 1609, according to his account, was captured by Powhatan, and was saved by Pocahontas from being killed. In the same year he was injured by an explosion of gunpowder, shortly afterwards he returned to England. Some years later he came back to America, and explored the coast of New England.

On this second voyage to this country in 1620, he brought his three first cousins over with him. They were George, Adam and James Smith. The grandfather of these cousins was Adam Smith.

James Smith, first cousin of Captain John Smith, was born in 1588 in England. He was the first line immigrant of our family in this country.

James Smith was 22 when he came to America in 1620 to teach school and to help his cousin Captain John Smith survey land on the eastern coast. In 1652 he was married to Miss Rebecca Whitmore. Their first child, George Smith, born in 1665. He was second in line in our family. He was a doctor and a dentist.

He married Miss Elizabeth Chesley in 1696. He was 31 years old. Their oldest child was a girl named Amelia, their next child was a son named James. He was a minister and a schoolteacher born in 1701. He is third in line in our family.

He was married to Miss Teressa Daily in 1724. They had a son also named James II, born in 1727. He was a schoolteacher. He was fourth in line in our family.

He married Miss Mary Lynch in 1760.

They had a son George Lynch Smith born in 1767. He was fifth in line in our family. He married a Miss Delannah Peddy. They were the parents of 12 children. Their fifth child Walter Tenderson Smith born in (date not known). He was sixth in line in our family. He married Frances (Frankie) Thomas Smith. They had nine children. Their seventh child Wilburn Smith born 1853. He is seventh in line in our family. He married Sarah Eleanor Bell Smith 1893. (To everyone here in Plains she was "Mama Sallie", even to the black porter boys. They had eight children. Their oldest child Lela Teressa Smith born 1894. She married Evan Thomas Smith in 1914. They had seven children. Their oldest son Charles Wilburn Smith was born March 25, 1916. He married Louise Everett October 22, 1948.

Louise was born Aug 9, 1920 the daughter of James Will Everett (1893-1982) and Bertha Mae Witt (1893-1943).

They had three children.

1. Charles Wilburn Smith Jr. Born August 16, 1950. He married Bonnie Brown, later divorced. They had one son Charles (Tripp) Wilburn Smith III. born February 11, 1970. Charles Jr. later married Penny Mitchell September 17, 1977. Penny had a son Jason Alan Mitchell born February 22, 1975. Charles and Penny had twin boys Branden James Smith and Justin Haywood Smith born April 9, 1986. Charles' oldest son Tripp married Cindy Cook they have one son, Charles (Chase) Wilburn Smith III born September 5, 1997. Penny's son Jason married Holly Palmer Nov 6, 1999. They have 1 daughter, Hannah Reese Mitchell born Apr. 25, 2002

2. Charla Sue Smith born March 10, 1952, married Ken Williams Apr.24,1993. Charla had no children of her own, She has one-step daughter Nicki Williams.

3. Janet Lea Smith born July 13, 1961, married Johnny Porch Oct. 1,1994. They have no Children.

—*Submitted by Charles and Penny Smith*

Daniel Reese Smith Family

Daniel Reese Smith came to Sumter County from Bronwood, Terrell County, Georgia, in the summer of 1915. He was a farmer and also had a meat market in Plains, Georgia. Later he sold his market and went into the lumber business with Logan and Andrews. The Smiths were Methodists. Daniel Reese Smith was born June 28, 1877, died March 17, 1947, married Nannie Crittenden Andrews born February 23, 1887, died March 2, 1919; both are buried at Enterprise Cemetery in Terrell County. To this union 10 children were born.

(A) Elizabeth Grace Smith Medlock born August 30, 1903, married William Verlyn Medlock, Sr., January 14, 1924. (See William Verlyn Medlock, Sr. history).

(B) Daniel Reese Smith, Jr. died an infant, buried Enterprise Cemetery, Terrell County.

(C) Patrick Henry Smith died an infant, buried Enterprise Cemetery, Terrell County.

(D) Florrie Ellen Smith born July 24, 1907, married 1st James C. Wimberly, divorced; married 2nd Joseph F. Von Bokern December 21, 1946, died August 30, 1981. After his death Ellen moved back to Plains.

(E) Carrie Rebecca Smith born 1909, died 1911, buried Enterprise Cemetery, Terrell County.

(F) Robert Crittenden Smith born January 7, 1911, married Mary Lou Burnett December 21, 1930 (see R.C. Smith history).

(G) Flournoy Marshal Smith died an infant, buried Enterprise Cemetery, Terrell County.

(H) Charles Phillip Smith born October 22, 1914, died September 4, 1981, buried Enterprise Cemetery, Terrell County, Georgia, married Jessie Merle Smith March 8, 1946. (See Charles Phillip Smith history.) He served with U.S. Navy in Pacific during World War II.

(I) Richard Easter Smith born April 8, 1917, married Hazel Scott Hagerson July 3, 1943. (See R.E. Smith history.)

(J) Joel Stinson (Logan) Smith born December 16, 1918, died May 7, 1977, buried at Orleander Memorial Garden, Wilmington, North Carolina, married Edith Lee December 13, 1945.

After the death of Nannie C. Smith, Reese Smith married 2nd to Mary Antoinette Medlock on November 1, 1923. There were four children born to this union.

(A) Doris Antoinette born March 23, 1925, died March 19, 1969, buried Friendship Cemetery in Sumter County, married Samuel O'Neal McLeod. Two children: (1) Samuel O'Neal McLeod born July 15, 1948, married Martha Bridges, two children: (a) Sandy Annette McLeod born January 21, 1976; (b) Wesley O'Neal McLeod born December 16, 1979. (2) Annetta Ruth McLeod Moss born September 3, 1952, married Robert Moss September-

ber 1, 1973, one child: (a) R. Tarrod Moss born March 1, 1979.

(B) Michael Winnifred Smith born December 30, 1926 died January 14, 2003. Married Grace Taylor.

(C) Samuel Reese Smith born April 13, 1932, married Shirley Bowers, three children: (1) Amelia Lynn Smith born February 5, 1957, married Edgar Patterson hart April 30, 1977, one child: (a) Amelia Paige Hart born October 7, 1981. (2) Mary Joye Smith born May 25, 1960, married Kenneth Y. Stanaland August 11, 1979, one child: (a) Robert Blake Stanaland born February 19, 1981. (3) Samuel Reese Smith, Jr., born February 8, 1964.

(D) Malcolm Mason Smith born September 20, 1941, married Margaret Ann Kitchens born October 8, 1941, three children: (1) Katherine Antionette Smith born March 11, 1962. (2) Michael Ashley Smith born September 8, 1964. (3) Stephen Gregory Smith born September.

—*Submitted by (no name given)*

Smith Family

The first of the Smith family line to come to Georgia was Rev. George Lynch Smith (1775-1868). He first appeared in Georgia around 1807. Rev. Smith was a frontier missionary—a true circuit riding preacher—who moved throughout the state with his family. In 1833, he was a delegate to the State Constitutional Convention.

Rev. Smith married Delanna Peddy (1786-1874), and they had 12 children, many of whom were given Christian names: Palestine, Jubilee, Paul, John, Apollas, Rachel.

Among the children was Tenderson, the father of Wilburn Juriston Smith, who grew up on his parents' farm in Marion County, Georgia. Wilburn recalled the devastation of their land by Yankee soldiers in 1865. Due to an injury at age 9, he learned different trades other than farming. He became a Justice of the Peace and wanted to become a doctor, constantly reading medical books. Since there were so few doctors in the area, sick people often came to his home. He took care of them and his prescriptions were honored by local druggists.

In 1893, he married Sarah "Sallie" Eleanor Bell, and in 1903, they moved about 2 miles north of Plains so the children could attend school. Several years later, after his death, his widow moved into Plains.

Wilburn and Sallie had 8 children: Teressa, Edgar, Elder, Tennyson, Lumas, Oliver, George and a daughter who died in infancy.

Wilburn Edgar Smith, the oldest son, assumed responsibility for the family at age 21 when his father died. Edgar and his younger brothers ran the school bus system. He also worked in one of the town's mercantile stores on week-ends, ran a small farm on the outskirts of town, and established in Plains the first garage for "motor machines" in Sumter County. In 1926, he married Frances Allethea "Allie" Murray (See Murray Family). At the time of his early death at age 44, he was a steward in the Plains Methodist Church, a member of the Plains City Council, and a Mason.

Edgar and Allie Smith had four children: Eleanor Rosalynn, William Jerrold, Murray Lee, and Lillian Allethea. Allethea, who lives in McDonough, Ga., married Lee Wall from Ellaville, and they have 3 children: Henry Clate, John William, and Julie Keith. Jerrold (Jerry) moved out of the state soon after graduating from Georgia Tech, married and divorced. He has 2 children: Jerrold Alan and Kevin Christopher. Murray always lived in Plains. He and his first wife, Frances McLendon, had 3 children: LeAnne, Charles "Chuck" Edgar, and Steven Randall. He and his 2nd wife, Helen Donnan, have 1 child: Edgar Murray. Rosalynn attended Georgia Southwestern College and in 1946 married Jimmy Carter, who would become president of the United States. She and her husband have

4 children: John William, James Earl "Chip," III, Donnel Jeffrey, and Amy Lynn.
—*Submitted by Rosalynn Smith Carter*

Richard Easter Smith Family

Richard Easter Smith (son of Daniel Reese and Nancy (Nanie) Andrews Smith) (b. April 8. 1917-d. 1985), Plains, Ga., Sumter County, (m. July 3, 1943) Hazel Scott Hagerson (daughter of Charlie Neil and Vera Darden Hagerson) (b. Nov. 22, 1922) Sumter Co. Ga. Children of this union:

(1) **Jennifer Scott Smith** (b. 1950) married March 18, 1972, Fred Newton Buchanan, Jr. (b. Jan. 7, 1947) Their children: (a) Cathy Lee Buchanan (b. May 14, 1974) married (Dec. 4, 1999) Joshua (Josh) Adam Schwart, (b. July 2, 1975) (b) Benjamin Scott Buchanan (b. Oct. 16, 1977)

(2) **Merle Easter Smith** (b. Oct. 11, 1952) married Patricia Ann Easton (b. Nov. 26, 1952). Children: (a) Mitchell Easter Smith (b. July 13, 1976) (b.) Mary Kathryn (Katie) (b. June 26, 1979) (c.) Jeri Ann Smith (b. March 4, 1988).

(3) **Elizabeth Ellen** (Beth) (b. June 18, 1956) married April 5, 1986 William Raymond (Bill) Cochran (b. July 26, 1953. Children(a) William Caleb Cochran)b. Feb. 28, 1990.

—*Submitted by Hazel Hagerson Smith*

Henry Wilburn Smith Family

Lumas Leonidus Smith 7/13/1903 - 11/22/1969
Married Mary Ester Dominick
4/7/1907 - 3/12/1952
Henry Wilburn Smith 10/2/1924
Married Ruby Mae Parker 10/31/1923
    Dan Parker Smith 3/5/1951
        Rodney Wilburn Smith
        11/13/1977
    James Wilburn Smith 1/1/1956

Married Ladelle Preston 8/10/1955
Justin James Smith 4/21/1984
Kelli Meghan Smith 1/15/1988

Henry Wilburn Smith of Plains married Ruby Mae Parker of Buena Vista, GA. Miss Parker is the daughter of Mr. William Reese Parker (12/22/1889 - 3/23/1971) and Mrs. Pearl Highnote Parker (12/22/1893 - 3/17/1964).

Henry Wilburn Smith served as a Staff Sergeant in the U. S. Army - Armored Force in the European Theater during World War II during 1943-1945. He later retired from the Seaboard Railroad after 42 years of service. Ruby Mae Parker Smith taught elementary school in Plains before their two children were born. Dan Parker Smith was born on March 5, 1951 and James Wilburn Smith was born on January 1, 1956.
—*Submitted by Wilburn Smith*

Walter Franklin Spann Family

Walter Franklin Spann (b. 15 July 1902) was born in Webster County, fifth son of John Griffin Spann (1871-1925) and Anna George Ball Spann (1873-1956). He was the namesake of Walter F. George, a relative and Preston native who served as a U.S. senator for more than 30 years.

Frank Spann was married to Ada Susie Irena Brooks (b. 7 July 1904) on 21 Oct. 1923 in Parrott. She was the oldest daughter of Charlie Monroe Brooks (1879-1918) and Fannie Fredonia Goare Brooks (1879-1945) of Weston, where she was reared. Her father was an overseer. Both of her grandfathers and both of Frank's grandfathers were military veterans, having fought for the Confederacy during the Civil War.

Following their marriage, Frank and Ada Spann lived in Webster County for 25 years, where he was a prominent farmer, extending a family tradition.

They moved to Plains in January 1949, where he continued farming in a partnership with his son, Walter Spann.

Among his earliest relatives with ties to Plains were Phillip Henry Spann (1844-1908), a great-uncle; William Henry Spann (1859-1933), an uncle; and Mary Spann Clark (1864-1920), an aunt, all of whom are buried at Lebanon Cemetery.

Two of the children of Frank and Ada Spann graduated from high school in Webster County, and the other two finished studying at Plains High School. Their youngest daughter, Frances Spann, was both a cheerleader and varsity basketball player at Plains High School. Three of their four children were either valedictorian or salutatorian of their respective classes. Walter Spann also studied electronics at the Coyne American Institute in Chicago.

Frank and Ada Spann lived in two Plains homes before purchasing and moving into their last home, known originally as the Lowery Place, in 1952. The home sits on picturesque farmland on Spann Drive about six-tenths of a mile from the Plains city limits. The home, now occupied by their grandson Jackie Short, was seen worldwide from an aerial view during the 1996 Summer Olympic Games in Atlanta.

Frank and Ada Spann were members of Plains Baptist Church, and members of the Plains Supper Club in the 1950s. In succeeding years, their family also has been active in the community. Their oldest great-grandchild, Stephanie Young, has held numerous leadership offices in the Plains Jr. Woman's Club. She was awarded Woman of the Year honors three times in a recent eight-year period.

Frank and Ada Spann celebrated their 50th, 55th and 60th wedding anniversaries at parties at their home in 1973, 1978 and 1983.

Ada Brooks Spann died on 5 June 1987 at age 82. Frank Spann died 23 July 1992 at age 90. At the time, he was the oldest male member of Plains Baptist Church. They are buried at Lebanon Cemetery in Plains.

Their four children:

1. Walter Guy Spann (b. 5 May 1925). Walter married Gloria Carter Hardy (b. 22 Oct. 1926), daughter of James Earl Carter, Sr. and Bessie Lillian Gordy Carter, on 14 Dec. 1950 in Plains. Gloria was an artist, teacher, bookkeeper and avid motorcyclist. She was co-author of "Away From Home: Letters to My Family," which chronicled her mother's two-year stay in India as a Peace Corps volunteer from 1966-68.

Walter and Gloria had no children. She had one son by a previous marriage:

A) William Carter "Tody" Hardy (b. 10 Oct. 1946). (Tody was adopted by Walter Spann.) Tody, a U.S. Air Force veteran, died 2 Feb. 1997 at age 50. He is buried at Chico Cemetery in Chico, Calif., where his children live.

Gloria Spann, the last surviving sibling of former President Carter, died 5 March 1990 at age 63. She is buried at Lebanon Cemetery in Plains. Walter lives in Plains.

2. Anita Louise Spann (b. 29 Aug. 1932). Anita married Julian Pierce Dillard (b. 9 Dec. 1928), son of Marvin Wilbur Dillard and Mervin Ada Davis Dillard, on 19 June 1949 at Weston Baptist Church in Weston. Julian served in the U.S. Army for two years. He was first stationed at Fort Hood in Killeen, Texas, and later at Fort Sill in Lawton, Okla. He and Anita moved back to Georgia in early 1954. Anita and Julian had two children:

A) Karen Faye Dillard (b. 19 Dec. 1952). Karen married first Robert Thomas "Bobby" McNeilly in 1971. One child: 1) Tina Michele McNeilly (b. 8 Nov. 1972) (adopted by John Sheffield). Michele married Gerald Ashley Reddick in 2000. Karen married second John West Sheffield III in 1977. Karen married third Dr. Harold Earl Holloway in 1989.

B) Lisa Gayle Dillard (b. 22 Feb. 1958). Lisa married Dr. Robert Franklin "Bobby" Turner in 1980. Two children: 1) Julianna Christine Turner (b. 15 April 1996) (adopted) 2) Christopher Alexander Turner (b. 29 April 2002) (adopted)

Julian Dillard died 17 Sept. 1969 at age 40. He is buried at Oak Grove Cemetery in Americus. Anita lives in Americus.

3. Melba Eugenia Spann (b. 14 Oct. 1933). Melba married John David Clements, Jr. (b. 13 Feb. 1928), son of J.D. Clements, Sr. and Hazel Ruth Moore Clements, on 11 June 1950 at Plains Baptist Church in Plains. J.D., a graduate of North Georgia College, was a U.S. Army veteran, having served 1½ years before their marriage. He was stationed in Varadera, Cuba. Melba and J.D. had three children:

A) Donna Lynne Clements (b. 17 May 1951). Donna married first William Wayman "Billy" Sawyer, Jr. in 1968. Two children: 1) Starling Brooke Sawyer (b. 24 Nov. 1975) 2) Benjamin Clements Sawyer (b. 26 Jan. 1978). Donna married second Gerardo Cisneros in 1986.

B) Susan Ruth Clements (b. 29 Oct. 1953). Susan married first Roy R. Jackson, Jr. in 1971. One child: 1) Stephanie Lynn Jackson (b. 21 Dec. 1971). Stephanie married George William Young, Jr. in 1990. Two children: 1A) Jake Austin Young (b. 4 Jan. 1992), and 2A) George Tyler Young (b. 27 Aug. 1994). Susan married second Steve Ricks in 1984. Susan married third David "Dave" Webb in 1994. Susan died 12 Jan. 2000 at age 46 and is buried at Lebanon Cemetery in Plains.

C) John David Clements III (b. 17 May 1957). David married first Mildred Ella "Middy" Chappell in 1976. One child: 1) Caron Nicole Clements (b. 19 Feb. 1977). Caron married first Walter Williams in 1995. One child: 1A) Walt Williams (b. 3 June 1995). Caron married second Douglas Raymond Hodgins, Jr. in 2001.

David married second Laurie A. Swinson in 1982. One child: 1) John David Clements IV (b. 5 Oct. 1985).

J.D. Clements, Jr. died 25 Feb. 1984 at age 56. He is buried at Lebanon Cemetery in Plains. Melba lives in Americus.

4. Anna Frances Spann (b. 29 Aug. 1936). Frances married Lawrence Lee "Jack" Short, Sr. (b. 23 Nov. 1929), son of Clarence Belvy Short and Ruth Lee Turner Short, on 11 Jan. 1953 at Plains Baptist Church. Jack served in the Army National Guard for six years, receiving an honorable discharge in 1954. Frances and Jack had four children:

A) Lawrence Lee "Jackie" Short, Jr. (b. 14 Oct. 1953). Jackie married first Catherine Elaine "Cathy" Cook in 1972. Two children: 1) Michael Shane Short (b. 19 Jan. 1973). Shane married Alesha Paige Dunaway in 1998. One child: 1A) Katherine Mackenzie Short (b. 22 April 2001). 2) Brian Lee Short (b. 13 Feb. 1975). Brian married Ginny Leigh Reeves in 1998.

Jackie married second Pharis Davis Lewis in 1988.

B) Frances Anne Short (b. 27 Nov. 1956)

C) Walter Randall "Randy" Short (b. 27 June 1961). Randy married Jennifer Denise "Jenny" Durham in 1988. Two children: 1) Erica Anne Short (b. 26 April 1991) 2) Jake Randall Short (b. 14 March 1996)

D) Steve Clarence Short (b 8 May 1964).

Frances and Jack live near Americus.

—Submitted by Steve Short

William Henry Spann Family

William Henry Spann was born Jan. 30, 1859 in Webster County. He was the oldest son of William Francis Spann (1832-1899) and Lucy Ellen Spears Spann (1833-1906). His paternal grandparents were natives of Jefferson County, Ga., who moved to Lee (now Webster) County about 1837. They settled within a few miles of where William Henry Spann spent most of his life.

On Dec. 22, 1881, William H. Spann married Theodosia Ernest Nicholson (b. Nov. 20, 1858). She was the daughter of Archibald Nicholson and Mary Elizabeth Hall Nicholson, pioneer settlers of Webster County. Her father moved to Georgia from Alabama about 1830.

William H. and Theodosia Spann had four children, one of whom died as an infant. They spent most of their lives in their native Webster County near Weston, and lived in a two-story home on Ga. Highway 41 known as the Spann-Bryson House. The Spanns lived in Plains from about 1900 until 1915 and were among the town's older families after its founding. Three of William's sisters – Josephine Spann, Della Fletcher, and Mary Clark – lived in Plains for many years.

William H. Spann was a prominent resident and, according to his obituary, was "one of the leading farmers of this section of the state." He had begun farming on his own account in 1881, the year he was married.

His life was chronicled in "Memoirs of Georgia," published in 1895. At that time, as a resident of Webster County, he owned 1,000 acres of land, "the result of his own labor and good management." He also owned a great number of head of livestock, a gin of large capacity and a sawmill. An "uncompromising Democrat," he was active in politics but never sought an office.

William H. Spann died on Aug. 28, 1933 at his home near Weston. He was 74. His obituary read that the "state has lost a noble citizen." It referred to him as a man who stood for "honor, principle and character and was always found advocating the things that meant most for the welfare and uplift of his people and community."

Theodosia Spann died Jan. 2, 1948 at age 89. They both are buried at Lebanon Cemetery in Plains, as are three of their children.

Their children were:

I.) Lizzie May Spann (b. 1888 d. 1906). Lizzie May died of tuberculosis as a teenager when the family lived in Plains. She is buried beside her parents.

II.) Ernest Linwood Spann (b. Sept. 17, 1892 d. July 24, 1984). Ernest was a graduate of Mercer University in Macon. He married Carrie Oliver of Plains, a twin daughter of R.S. Oliver and Aughtry Rylander Oliver. Ernest ran the hardware department for the Oliver-McDonald Company in Plains. In the 1930s, he built and operated Spann's Service Station at the corner of Church and Hudson streets in what is now the Plains City Hall building.

Ernest and Carrie had one son:

A) Oliver William Spann (b. June 14, 1917). Oliver attended Gordon College in Barnesville and was a World War II veteran. He married Eva M. Martin of Arlington on April 8, 1937. They live in Americus. In the 1940s, Oliver operated a bowling alley at the corner of Church and Hudson streets. He also once operated a grocery store in Plains. Eva, a 1937 University of Georgia graduate, was a schoolteacher who taught home economics at Plains High School and at Americus High School for many years. Four children:

1) Evangeline "Vangie" Spann (b. March 3, 1938). Vangie married John Homer. Four children: Lauren, Jack, Aimee, Heath

2) Jerry Ernest Spann (b. Oct. 3, 1941 d. Oct. 13, 1943)

3) Patricia Spann (b. March 5, 1943). Patricia married William J. Stovall, Jr. on March 20, 1965. Two children: Bill, Martin

4) Oliver William Spann, Jr. (b. April 16, 1953 d. April 20, 1953)

III.) Frances Christine Spann (b. Nov. 25, 1898 d. Nov. 6, 1987). Christine attended Bessie Tift College in Forsyth and studied music and art. She married Clifton Emerson Bryson in 1924. He was a son of John Humes Bryson and Cynthia Catherine Wade Bryson. Clifton served in World War I and graduated from Mercer University in 1923. He was a Mason, minister and a principal of Weston School. Christine and Clifton had two children:

A) William Emerson Bryson (b. Sept. 28, 1926). Emerson married Eunice Holton on Sept. 15, 1950. He is a World War II veteran. They live in Shellman.

Two children:

1) Mary Eunice Bryson (b. March 16, 1952). Mary married John Hampton Reese in 1975.

2) Emmy Joy Bryson (b. March 25, 1954). Joy married first William Mizelle "Zan" Tracy (b. 1948 d. 1999) on Aug. 16, 1975. Two children:

Julie Holton (b. Aug. 13, 1978), Mary Beth (b. Feb. 12, 1983). Joy married second Michael Lumpkin on July 6, 2001.

B) John Francis Bryson (b. Jan. 9, 1932 d. July 20, 1932)

—*Submitted by Steve Short*

Sproull Family

William Jeff Sproull was born August 31, 1890 and died May 12, 1968. He married Sallie Jessie Kennedy Sproull who was born March 4, 1893 and died February 14, 1973. Jeff and Jessie were married on December 4, 1913. They moved to Plains about 1919 and lived in the house just north of Plains Baptist Church.

Their children were: Kathryn S. Barker born Dec. 8, 1914 and died October 23, 1994; Charles W. Sproull, born January 7, 1919 and died January 13, 1980; Gladwyn Kennedy S. Barfield born October 13, 1920; James Kennedy Sproull born Septmber 28, 1923 and died April 13, 1997; and Harold Harling Sproul born April 5, 1928 and died September 22, 1996.

—Submitted by (no name given)

L. A. Thomas

LaFayette Anderson "Fate" Thomas, born at Cussetta, Ga., on March 31, 1858, was the son of Harrison Thomas, planter, landowner, school patron, and fortunate drawer in the 1827 land lottery in Upson County. Harrison Thomas was born in 1812 in Virginia. Evidence seems to point to Harrison Thomas of Upson County as his father; b. 1779 N.C., m. Apr. 3, 1806 to Silvey Wallace in Hancock County, Ga.

Fate's father, Harrison Thomas, was m. on May 3, 1843, to Sarah Angeline House who was b. in 1822 in Lincoln County. She was the daughter of William House who was b. in 1796 in Lincoln County, and Mariah Grimsley House, who was b. in Virginia in 1802 and was the daughter of Zachariah Grimsley, resident of Lincoln County. William House was the son of Lott House, who was b. in 1767 in North Carolina. Lott was a Revolutionary soldier and a dedicated Baptist layman, serving as a messenger from Union Baptist Church in Lincoln County to the Georgia Baptist Association for well over a decade. For many of those same years, Zachariah Grimsley was also a messenger from Union Baptist Church.

The Harrison Thomas family and the William House family migrated before 1850 to the Harris District of Muscogee County which was later to become Chattahoochee County. Harrison and Sarah had nine children. William W. was b. in 1845 and was a Confederate soldier who served in the 31st Regiment, Company G, of Georgia, Volunteer Infantry, Evans Brigade, Gordon's Division, Army of Northern Virginia. He was severely wounded and died in the Soldiers Home at Columbus, Geor-

gia, on July 31, 1862. He was buried in the family cemetery, now a part of the Fort Benning Reservation and numbered Cemetery 33. John Wiley Thomas was b. in 1847. James Malcolm was b. in 1849; his wife's name was Lucy Stokes Thomas. Their son was Robert Thomas who moved to Plains. His children were Ellen and Hazel.

Palmer was b. in 1851. As a young man he entered military service. He moved, later to Crowell, Texas. He had three daughters. Alva D. was b. in 1855; he was buried at Americus, Ga. His daughter "Cousin Minnie" m. George White of Columbus, Ga. Mary E. was b. in 1856 and died at about 14 years of age. She was buried at Cusseta. R.K. Jackson, b. 1861, moved to Frisco, Texas, then back to Webster County and later returned to Frisco. He had four children: John, Ernest, Mary, and "Fate." He was named for his uncle, LaFayette Anderson, called "Fate" by his friends, b. on Mar. 31, 1858, at Cusseta. His father, Harrison Thomas, died when Fate was only 5 years of age. Fate 1st m. Ella Sears of Stewart County, and she died soon thereafter. On Jan. 25, 1892, he m. Annie Laurie Davidson of Sumter County, daughter of Hon. William H. Davidson and Sarah House Davidson. Annie Laurie was b. 1-8-1868, and d. 11-17-1930. She attended Mossy Dell School and graduated from Dawson College. In the very early 1890's, they operated a drygoods strore in Plains.

They went to live on Fate's farm in Terrell County, but in 1901 they agreed to put both farms up for sale and regardless of which sold first, they would live on the other. Fate's sold Jan. 24, 1901 and the family moved to 17th district Sumter County. Fate used his money to buy adjoining land, and as the farms prospered, he bought one at a time the inheritance of the other Davidson heirs.

Their children were: Mamie Evelyn b. 12-3-1892; Annie Mae b, 9-17-1894; Katie Belle b. 8-13-1896; Charles Harrison b. 3-2-1899; Burrell Wise b. 2-2-1901; Lilliam Lucille b. 2-23-1903; William Lafayette b. 3-4-1905; Alice Louise b. 8-7-1907;

Woodrow Wilson b. 1-17-1912. All the children attended the Plains school.

Fate was a dedicated Baptist layman for all of his adult life. He served as the first clerk of Richland Baptist Church when it was organized. Later he was a member of Plains Baptist Church, and then Hebron Baptist Church. He was a farmer and a miller. Fate built the concrete dam and spillway at the Thomas' Mill, the only mill dam in the county to survive subsequent floods. He died on March 20, 1952, at age 94. He was buried at Hebron Baptist Church. Friends will remember his wife Annie Laurie for her excellent cooking and will remember Fate for his jolly good humor and ever cheerful nature. They both will be remembered for their bountiful hospitality and interest in civic affairs.

—*Submitted by Marian Mitchell Harris*

William Lang Thomas Family

The W.L. Thomas family was such a prominent part of the beginnings of Plains that it seemed important to include them in the History of Plains. There being no family members to write about them, what is included is from Lebanon Cemetery and things remembered by Plains citizens still living.

Mr. William Lang Thomas, better known as Mr. Will, was born July 23, 1859 and died July 8, 1943. He married Lavonia Shropshire according to the name on her grave. She was called "Miss Daisy". It is not known if this was part of her name or if it was a nick-name. She was born September 27, 1867 and died February 3, 1953. There are many Shropshires and Davenports buried near the Thomases. It is assumed these are members of her family.

Mr. Will and Miss Daisy had one daughter, Agnes, who married James W. (Jimmy) Lott from Americus. The Lotts also had one daughter, Constance who married and lives in Florida.

I never knew of another child of the Thomas family. However, in looking in the cemetery a small grave was found marked Little Ruth, born March 9, 1892 and died May 8, 1893

Since Agnes is not buried in Lebanon Cemetery we have no dates on her birth and death. She is probably buried in Oak Grove Cemetery in Americus, Ga. with her husband Jimmy Lott. Since she was a close friend of my Aunt Alice Ruth Timmerman who was born in 1895, it would be assumed that this was about the time of Agnes' birth.

W.L. Thomas built the two story house directly across from the Lutheran Church on Bond's Trail. He was a member of the first school board in Plains, a cashier for Plains Bank, a prominent member of Plains Baptist Church and had an insurance business here. Upon Mr. Thomas' death, the insurance business was bought by Mr. Earl Carter, father of President Jimmy Carter. Miss Nelle Walters was secretary for this business.

On Mr. Will's grave is the inscription, "Lord, who shall dwell in thy tabernacle? Who shall dwell in thy holy hill? He that walketh uprightly, and worketh righteousness, and speaketh the truth in his heart." Psalm 15. No finer words could be attributed to a person than these.

On Miss Daisy's grave is written "To live in the hearts of those we love is not to die."

—*Submitted by Allene T. Haugabook*

Timmerman Family History

Wherever the Timmerman name is found, it can be accurately assumed that they sprang from the German immigrant who settled in Edgefield County, South Carolina, shortly after the Revolutionary War.

The years following the Civil War saw an influx of South Carolinians to Georgia. Among those who came seeking a new start was the John Jennings family. Coming with John and Barbary

Jennings, was their daughter Mylbrie (Mrs. John Bartlett) Timmerman, whose husband had been killed in a railroad accident in Mississippi, while serving in the war. Settling in Webster County, she brought with her four young sons and one daughter, namely, Edwin, Tyre, J. Will, Jesse, and Carrie. The two sons who remained in Plains were Edwin and Jesse. It is these two whose family histories will follow.

I. Edwin Timmerman (b.1854-d.1922) m. Alice Forth (b.1856-d.1937) and moved to Plains when the town was settled, from his farm on Kinchafoonee Creek in the southwestern part of the county. This farm is now known as the Joel Thomas place. Upon moving to Plains, the Ed Timmerman home was built on Walters Street, being one of the first homes constructed in Plains. Soon after settling there, he became co-owner and operator of Timmerman and Wise Cotton Warehouse. This business later became Timmerman and Williams and in 1940 became O.A. Williams and Sons Plains Cotton Warehouse. Ed Timmerman was one of the five original city councilmen of Plains, the third mayor of Plains, serving during 1905-1906, and was elected to the state legislature from Sumter County in 1917, serving for two terms and not offering for re-election. Children of Alice and Edwin Timmerman were: Edgar (b.1882-d.1941); Frank Forth (b.1885-d.1939); Samuel Herbert (Kitty) (b.1886-d.1951); Alvin Jennings (b.1890-d.1927); Louie (Brownie) (b.1892-d.1961); and Alice Ruth (b.1895-d.1926). Four other children were born to this union but died in childhood. All living children settled in Plains.

(1) Edgar Timmerman m. Lillie French (b.1886-d.1957) of Richland and served as mayor of Plains while operating the family farm. Their children are:

(a) Hazel (b.1908-d.1982) Hazel m. H.M. (Bill)Herin and their only daughter is Alice Ruth.

(b) James Edwin (b.1913-d.1964) James married Marty Fish and their children are Susan and James Edwin Jr.

(2) Frank Forth Timmerman (b.1885 d.1939) m.(1920) Ida Lee Pritchard of Parrott (b.1990-d.1986) and built the brick home next door to the Ed Timmerman home on Walters Street in 1923. Educated at Mercer University, he was a pharmacist at Plains Pharmacy, later being associated with his father, Edwin, in the warehouse business. Upon the death of his father, he took as his partner, O. A. Williams, Sr. Upon Frank's death in 1939, his interest in the business was sold to O. A. Williams, Sr. Frank's and Ida Lee's children are:

(a) Allene, (b. 1929) m.(1955) C.G. Haugabook Jr. (b.1928) of Montezuma The children of Allene and C.G. are (1)Elizabeth (Beth) (b.1956), m.(1983) William Dallas NeSmith III (b.1957)of Macon They have one daughter, Dallas,(b.1996). (2) Amy (b.1958), m.(1983) Thomas Lockwood(b.1959) of Decatur. Their two sons are Thomas Ryerson (b.1988) and Daniel Hanson (b.1990).

(b) Edwin,(b.1932) m.(1963) Sarah Minter of Cairo (b.1943). Their children are: (1) Edwin Frank (b.1965) and (2) Sarah Miriam (b.1968) They both live in Atlanta and neither are married at the time of this writing.

(3) Samuel Herbert (Kitty) Timmerman (b.1887-d.1951)m. Effie McArthur They have one daughter, Bettie Jean,(b.1926) (m.1951)Tom Lorentzson of Palatka, Fl. They have one son, Tom Lorentzson, Jr whose only son is Ezra Lorentzson.

(4) Alvin Jennings Timmennan (b.1894-d.1980) m.(1917) Alice Cody (b.1894-d.1980) of Columbus. Their children are

(a) Miriam Ruth b.(b.1918-d.1995)m. Ward Saylor of Iowa. Their children are Hal, Tim and Mary Alice.

(b) Edwin Cody (b.1920-d.1988)m.(1954) Joyce Fuller of Reynolds Their children are: (1) Terry Dawn (b.1955) m. Wayne Smith of Butler. The children of Terry and Wayne are Colby (b.1985) Ansley (b.1988) and Sydney (b.1989). (2) Jerry Cody (b.1957) m. Rita Richardson. Their children are Fuller (b.1989) and Callie (b.1994) (3) David Wayne (b.1959) m 1st. (1981) Mary Kathryn Horne. Their childrren are: Cody (b.1984) and Kathryn Lee (b.1988) m.-2nd Teresa Scott. The children of David and Teresa are: Jade (b.1995) and Brooke (b.1998) 4.Daniel Kevin (b.1968) At the writing of this history Kevin is unmarried.

(c) Margaret Irma (b.1926) m. Gordon Pyle. Their two daughters are Cindy and Cheryl.

Alice was widowed in 1926. Alice had a son, Robert Harvey Burns,(b.1931-d.1995) by a second marriage. Robert (Bobby) later took the name of Timmerman. He married Betty Ann Fulford of Dawson and their children are Robert Harvey and David Cody.

(5).Louie (Brownie) Timmerman (b.1892-d.1961)m.(1932) Lillian Templeton (b.1906-d.1996) of Blythe. Lillian was teacher of home economics and history at Plains High School for many years, later becoming visiting teacher for the Sumter County School System until her retirement. "Brownie", a registered pharmacist, was for years associated with Clinic Drug Store in Americus, continuing to live in the old Timmerman home in Plains They had no children and later moved to their home on Burke Street in Americus. His widow retained this home for many years after his death, later moving to Atlanta to live with a niece.

(6) Alice Ruth Timmerman (b.1895-d.1926) the youngest child and only daughter of Ed and Alice Forth Timmerman to reach adulthood, was educated at Shorter College, and taught school in Richland and Dawson for several years before being killed in an automobile accident between Plains and Americus in 1926. She never married.

II. Jesse Timmerman (b.1859-d.1934) married Emma Woodham (b.1862-d.1933) After living in Macedonia Community of Webster County for many years, this family settled in Plains. The house now occupied by Secret Service for President Carter was built by Jesse and Emma Timmerman in 1923. Their children were:

(1) J. Clinton Timmerman (b.1883-d.1943) m.1st (1907) Rosa May Phillips (b.1884-d.1910) m.2nd Leo Virginia Randolph (b.1888-d.1973) Clint's only child by Rosa May Phillips was John Clinton (b.1908) Children by Leo Virginia Randolph were Jesse R. (b.1912-d.2001) and Emily (b.1915)

(2) Warren Timmerman (b.1885-d.1964) m. (1914). Marie E. Adams children Evelyn (b.1918) and Mary (b.1921)

(3) Maybelle Timmerman (b.1887-d.1980)m. (1908) Rees Mahone Andrews Their children are listed in a later paragraph.

(4) Tom Timmerman (b.1890-d.1952) m. (1921) Marie Hicks (d. 1975) Children: Thomas W. Jr. (b. 1923 d. 1975) Emily (b. 1925 d. 1994).

(5) Ruby Timmerman (b.1892-d.1991) m. Mattauer E. Davidson (d.1956) Children: Mettauer E. Jr. (b. ? d. in England World War II) Elisabeth (b. 1915 d. 1996) Ruth (b. 1921)

(6). Ernest W.(Billy) Timmerman (b.1895-d.1952))m.1927).Cleora Freeman. Their only child is Cleora Terry (b.1929)

The only child from the union of Jesse and Emma to remain in Sumter County was Maybelle, who married Rees M. Andrews and reared her family here. The Andrews children were Rees Jr., who married Helen Reddick of Sylvania. Harold, who married Mildred Scruggs of Americus; Marjorie, who married Eugene Summerford of the New Era Community near Americus; Dorothy, who married Pinkney Sullivan of Zebulon; and Virginia, who married Zera Littlejohn Hair of Columbus. Virginia owned the land on which The Boys and Girls Club in Plains is built. It was donated by her heirs for the building of that complex.

The Timmerman family has, through the years, contributed greatly to the civic, educational, cultural and religious life of Sumter County and Plains in particular. They were all active leaders in Plains Baptist Church from the time it was moved to Plains and its name changed from Lebanon Baptist

Church. Most graves of five generations of the Jennings and Timmerman families mentioned in this history may be found in Lebanon Cemetery west of Plains.

—*Submitted by Allene T. Haugabook*

David Moton Turner Family

Rev. David Moton Turner (also spelled Moten) was a native North Georgian who moved his family to Plains when he was 60 years old. He was born 23 July 1859 in Cherokee County, the second son of Rev. Henry Green Berry Turner (1836-1923) and his first wife, Nancy Ann Susan Carney Turner (1838-1903).

H.G.B. Turner, a native of Pickens County, S.C., moved with his father to Cherokee County, Ga., in 1846. H.G.B. and Annie Turner had one of the largest family connections in the state.

David M. Turner was married twice, first to Katie Smith (b. 1 Dec. 1859 d. 24 Jan. 1891), who died at age 31. She is buried at Olive Vine Baptist Church Cemetery in Pine Log, northeast of Cartersville in Bartow County. He and Katie had five children, the youngest of whom was only 2½ years old when her mother died.

David M. Turner was married second to Nancy Matilda Smith (b. 21 Oct. 1872), the daughter of James Benson Smith (1836-1914) and Nancy Matilda Alexander Smith (1843-1923). She and David M. Turner were married at her parents' Cherokee County home on 6 Dec. 1891 by Rev. Bragwell Harris. She and David had 12 children.

David M. Turner was a prominent minister, farmer and businessman. He was ordained into the ministry in October 1887 at age 28 at Olive Vine Baptist Church, which was founded by his father. He and his father, who was a Civil War veteran, preached at many North Georgia churches, and on occasion would succeed each other as pastor of the same church.

David M. Turner owned hundreds of acres of land in Polk County near the Flint Hill Baptist Church in neighboring Floyd County, where he was called to preach in 1907. It was from Polk County that he and

Nancy Turner "sold out" and moved their extended family to Plains in November 1919. His brother, James H. Turner, had moved his family to Sumter County about seven years earlier.

The Turners left the train station in the Seney community, coming to Plains on a chartered freight train with three boxcars. Their first home in Plains, on Main Street, was occupied years later by the Spires family.

David M. Turner owned land and houses in Sumter, Webster and Terrell counties, and was a prosperous resident. He spent all the time after his move south in Sumter County, except for three years in Terrell County, where he was pastor at Pleasant Hill Baptist Church. He worked in partnerships on fertile cotton farms throughout the region.

Like many others in the South, his holdings were devastated by the boll weevil in the late 1920s. He continued ministering, however, until his death. He died at his home south of Plains on 21 May 1934 at age 74.

His wife, Nancy, survived him for nearly 12 years. She died at the Prather Clinic in Americus on 14 March 1946 at age 73. Both are buried at Lebanon Cemetery in Plains.

Like his father, David M. Turner had an extended family connection. By his two wives, he had 17 children, 73 grandchildrern, and at least 166 great-grandchildren. Two grandsons, Dennis Turner and Watson Turner, once served as policemen in Plains. Dennis Turner also operated a grocery store in Plains for many years. Another grandson, Bennie Turner, ran a used furniture store in Plains in the 1950s and '60s.

Other grandsons with unique ties to Plains were Auston Turner and Ernest Turner. Auston Turner was ordained as a minister at Plains Baptist Church. Ernest Turner, who once was in a five-way fertilizer business partnership that included former President Carter, owned and operated a hardware store on Main Street from 1973-78. He later sold the hardware store's inventory, but reopened Turner's Store, selling new and used odds and ends and antiques from the early 1980s until 1996.

Today, several descendants of David M. Turner continue to call Plains home. Others live throughout Georgia, Florida, Alabama, Oklahoma and beyond.

Children of David M. Turner and Katie Turner:

1) Arthur Vance Turner, Sr. (b. 21 April 1881) married Mamie Lee Popham (b. 7 Sept. 1887 d. 14 Jan. 1973) in January 1903. Arthur Turner died 19 Jan. 1938 at age 56 and is buried at Lebanon Cemetery in Plains. Eleven children:

A) William Dennis Turner (b. 9 Oct. 1904 d. 16 Sept. 1972) married Jewel Sears. One child: Melanie

B) Allie Inez Turner (b. 15 March 1906 d. 29 April 1991) married Robert F. Thompson, Sr. Two children: Robert Jr., Anna Belle

C) Benjamin Franklin "Bennie" Turner (b. 17 Oct. 1907 d. 18 Sept. 1994)

D) Henry Watson Turner (b. 6 May 1910 d. 21 Nov. 1995) married Grace Weaver. One child: Iris

E) David Auston Turner (b. 26 May 1912) married Cora Harvey

F) Anna Lenora Turner (b. 13 Oct. 1913 d. 4 Sept. 1991) married Victor Padgett. Two children: Wanda, Janet

G) Arthur Vance Turner, Jr. (b. 13 Aug. 1916)

H) Ernest Conley Turner (b. 9 June 1919) married Betty June Harris

H) Joel Vinson Turner (b. 25 Oct. 1921 d. 21 July 1984) married Sara Hughes. Two children: Cheryl, Patricia

I) Alvin Lavon "Von" Turner (b. 7 June 1925 d. 13 April 1995)

J) Alice Ruth Turner (b. 4 Nov. 1931) married Guy B. Gunnels. One child: Cindy

2) Zona Turner (b. 1884) married Charles M. "Charlie" Pendley (b. 31 July 1882 d. 27 Dec. 1950). Zona Pendley died 5 May 1920 at age 36 and is buried at Live Oak Baptist Church Cemetery near Aragon. Eight children:

A) Edith Mae Pendley (b. 30 Dec. 1901 d. 14 May 1987) married Benson L. Hulsey. Eight children: Arnel, Virnel, Dorothy, Van Scott, Edward R., Willard, Wilburn, Mary Jane

B) infant son Pendley

C) Mattie Grace Pendley (b. 6 April 1907 d. 31 Jan. 1919 at age 11)

D) Samuel Turner Pendley (b. 28 Oct. 1910 d. 2 Dec. 1974) married Bessie A. Landers. Twelve children: Zona Lou, Betty, Shelby, Billy T., Bobby Arthur, Linda Ann, Sandra, Travis, Sherry, Deborah, Gary W., Cynthia

E) Leola Catherine Pendley (b. 13 May 1913 d. 20 Aug. 2000) married Leo S. Fainn. Three children: Charles, Thomas, David

F) Herbert William Pendley (b. 8 May 1915 d. 9 May 1976) married Inez Baker. One child: Nicky

G) Beuna Elizabeth Pendley (b. 26 July 1917 d. 8 Dec. 1999) married James Mims. Four children: Patsy, Jerry, Arthur, Polly

H) Charles Rufus Pendley (adopted by John Harvey Turner after his mother's death)

3) Carlton Leroy "Carl" Turner (b. 24 Jan. 1885). Carl Turner died 8 Jan. 1923 at age 37 and is buried at Lebanon Cemetery in Plains.

4) Fannie Mae Turner (b. 8 Feb. 1887) married Columbus Decatur "Lum" Bishop (b. 27 Feb. 1877 d. 15 April 1948) in 1903. Fannie Bishop died 21 Dec. 1967 at age 80 and is buried at I.O.O.F. Cemetery in Norman, Okla. Eight children:

A) Agnes Gertrude Bishop (b. 3 March 1904 d. 1 May 1973) married Arnold T. 'Pat" Willingham. Two children: Patsy Jean, Bob

B) Nettie Ann Bishop (b. 24 July 1905 d. 25 Jan. 1976) married John Wesley Grotts. Four children: John Jr., Oren, Don E., Phillip

C) Warren Mason Bishop (b. 1 Feb. 1907 d. 16 June 1975) married first Ellen Helman; married second "Saraphine Stratiger. One child: Virginia

D) Frances Arizona "Zona" Bishop (b. 6 April 1909 d. 23 Jan. 1999) married Sylvan Taylor. Two children: Sue, Ramona

E) Selma Beatrice "Dutch" Bishop (b. 2 May 1911 d. 28 Jan. 1982) married Harvey Bruce. Eight children: Jimmy Joe, Joy, Vandle, J.M., Wanda, Paulene, Larry (twin), Jerry (twin)

F) Henry Grady Bishop (b. 20 Dec. 1914 d. 10 Jan. 1967) married Juanita Scott. One child: Patsy June

G) Violet Mae Bishop (b. 13 March 1918 d. at age 6 months)

H) Jack Joel Bishop (b. 8 May 1930) married Lorene Grizzle

5) Ethel Gertrude Turner (b. 10 July 1888) married George Mason "Mace" Bishop (b. 8 June 1873 d. 26 Nov. 1947). Ethel Bishop died 22 June 1961 at age 72 and is buried at I.O.O.F. Cemetery in Norman, Okla. Two children:

A) Lizzie Lucile Bishop (b. 29 Nov. 1908 d. 12 Jan. 1993) married John Lawrence Jones. Four children: W. Lawrence, Betty, Glenn, Katie

B) infant son Bishop

Children of David M. Turner and Nancy Turner:

1) Alice Pearl Turner (b. 20 March 1893) married Merritt Ernest Scoggins, Sr. (b. 17 March 1890 d. 14 April 1971) on 21 Aug. 1910. Pearl Scoggins died 10 June 1958 at age 65 and is buried at Oaklawn Cemetery in Jacksonville, Fla. Four children:

A) Gladys Ann Scoggins (b. 11 Aug. 1912 d. 18 April 1961) married first Bob Bennett; married second Paul Kendrick. Two children: J. Larry, Bobby

B) David Martin "D.M." Scoggins (b. 5 June 1915 d. 3 Feb. 1973) married Helen Gunn. Two children: David, Danny

C) Robert Charles Scoggins (b. 14 July 1917 d. 11 May 1982) married first Frances Creel; married second Kathryn Wilson. One child: Kaye (adopted)

D) Merritt Ernest Scoggins, Jr. (b. 5 Sept. 1927) married Juanita Sims. Two children: Kendall, Sandy

2) Rilla Edna Turner (b. 2 Jan. 1895) married John Thomas Williams (b. 13 Oct. 1890 d. 11 June 1952) on 2 June 1912. Edna Williams died 16 Sept. 1967 at age 72 and is buried at Rehobeth Baptist Church Cemetery near Americus. Eight children:

A) David Thomas Williams (b. 25 April 1913 d. 1919 at age 6)

B) Derrell Grady Williams (b. 26 Oct. 1916 d. 10 May 1959) married Charlotte Preskitt

C) Annie Matilda Williams (b. 11 Oct. 1917 d. 15 Feb. 1990) married first A.C. Short, Sr.; married second Charles "Chuck" Klages; married third Jack Beardsley; married fourth Kenneth Seibert. Three children: Carolyn, A.C. Jr.; Tommy

D) Margaret Sarah Williams (b. 29 April 1920 d. 10 May 1998) married M. Herschel Frost. One child: Mac

E) Stanley Boyd Williams (b. 29 Dec. 1923 d. 6 Sept. 1947) married Agnes Parker

F) Dewey Lee Williams (b. 14 July 1926 d. 30 April 1968) married Daisy Worthington. Four children: Jessica, Lisa, Leslie, LeAnne

G) Betty Lou Williams (b. 16 Oct. 1928) married Joseph Milton Hagerson. Three children: Neil, Boyd, Kay

H) John Robert "Bobby" Williams (b. 5 June 1931 d. 8 May 1998) married Donna L. Smith. Seven children: Robby, Vicki, Vangie, Terri, Jill, Jeffery (twin), Jenny (twin)

3) Henry Turner (b. 19 Sept. 1896 d. 14 Nov. 1896 at age 2 months). Henry Turner is buried at Olive Vine Baptist Church Cemetery in Pine Log, just outside his grandfather H.G.B.'s lot. The inscription on his tombstone reads "Budded on earth to bloom in Heaven."

4) Grady Andrew Turner (b. 13 Dec. 1897) married Fannie Elizabeth Popham (b. 17 May 1899 d. 15 May 1985) on 28 Jan. 1917. Grady Turner died 30 March 1938 at age 40. He is buried at Taylorsville Cemetery in Taylorsville in Bartow County. Eight children:

A) David Harrison Turner, Sr. (b. 7 April 1918) married Fannie D. Moor. Three children: David Jr., Diane, Phillip

B) Grady Wallace Turner, Sr. (6 Aug. 1919) married Ruth McCoy. Two children: Wallace Jr., Wanda

C) Ralph Winfred Turner (b. 26 April 1921 d. 1 Feb. 1998) married Martha L. Nelson. Three children: Charlotte, Sharon, Gary

D) Houston Lee Turner (b. 29 March 1924 d. 23 Jan. 1970) married first Helen Graves; married second Mary Lee Phillips. Six children: Patricia; Ronnie, Calvin, Andrea (twin), Sandra (twin), Shelia

E) Daniel Webster Turner, Sr. (b. 8 June 1926) married Magdalene Lyle. Three children: Daniel Jr., Theresa, Keith

F) Virginia Elizabeth Turner (b. 2 Aug. 1929) married first Horace L. Brookshire; married second Carl Fulton. Three children: Jere, Deborah, Joy

G) Wayne Popham Turner, Sr. (b. 9 Sept. 1931) married Bette Carol Davis. Two children: Carolyn, Wayne Jr.

H) Wilma Mozelle Turner (b. 3 Nov. 1933) married Clifford Lloyd Towe

5) Ruby Matilda Turner (b. 16 Feb. 1900) married Curtis Samuel Formby (b. 25 Dec. 1895 d. 19 March 1942) in 1915. Ruby Formby died 20 Aug. 1986 at age 86 and is buried at Live Oak Baptist Church Cemetery near Aragon. Seven children:

A) D.L. Formby (b. and d. 31 Jan. 1916)

B) Glenn Moaten Formby (b. 20 June 1917) married Jewel Hall. Two children: Glennis, Douglas

C) Hugh Dorsey Formby (b. 8 June 1919) married Ruby Raiford. One child: Larry

D) Doyle Martin Formby (b. 21 Aug. 1921) married Edna Kay. Two children: Daniel, Ken

E) Milton Hoyt Formby (b. 31 Dec. 1923) married Mickie Selman. Three children: Vickie, Nancy, Carol

F) Mable Evelyn Formby (b. 20 July 1927) married Roy L. Brumbelow. Two children: Tony, Sandra

G) Mavis Jeanette Formby (b. 15 Oct. 1930) married David R. Edge. Three children: Melinda, Stephen, Brian

6) James Conley Turner (b. 21 Jan. 1902) married Minnie Lee Williams (b. 19 Oct. 1921 d. 30 Oct. 1999) in 1939. Conley Turner died 28 July 1962 at age 60 and is buried at Oak Grove Cemetery in Americus. Six children:

A) Connie Lee Turner (b. 3 March 1940 d. 7 Aug. 1999) married Charles Wayne Heath. Four children: infant son, Dawn, Millette, Virginia

B) John David Turner (b. 23 May 1941) married Mary E. Turner. Three children: Clayton, Hugh, Tonya

C) Nancy Lou Turner (b. 24 April 1942 d. 14 Sept. 1992) married Robert J. "Bobby" Hamilton. Two children: Kimberly, Kathy

D) Flora Susie "Sue" Turner (b. 22 June 1944) married first Robert A. Perry, Sr.; married second Mickey Henry Pityer; married third Homer Chambliss. Three children: Robby; Michael; Casey

E) James Thomas "Tommy" Turner (b. 9 Oct. 1946) married first Josephine "Jody" Thomas; married second Rhonda Tucker. Three children: Leah; Lori, Lindsey

F) James Conley "Jimmy" Turner, Jr. (b. 3 May 1948 d. 5 Jan. 1965 at age 16)

7) Lula Mable Turner (b. 15 Oct. 1903) married William Leroy Bailey (b. 2 Nov. 1897 d. 13 Feb. 1949) on 27 Sept. 1943. Lula Bailey died 27 Dec. 1991 at age 88 and is buried at Hebron Baptist Church Cemetery near Americus. No children.

8) David Winfred Turner (b. 27 Oct. 1905) married Marguerite Irvine Rowe (b. 22 Dec. 1916 d. 16 July 1998) on 30 May 1937. Winfred Turner died 9 May 1944 at age 38 and is buried at Edgewood Cemetery in Jacksonville, Fla. Two children:

A) Infant son Turner

B) David Fred Turner (b. 12 Nov. 1940) married Sandra Mosley. Two children: Yvette, David

9) Winnie Jane Turner (b. 12 Nov. 1907 d. 17 Feb. 1908 of pneumonia at age 3 months). Winnie Turner

is buried at Pleasant Hope Baptist Church Cemetery near Silver Creek in Floyd County. The inscription on her tombstone reads "Sweet babe, thy shield now hath rest."

10) <u>Patrick Rhodes Turner</u> (b. 16 Sept. 1909) married Janie Kate Hall (b. 11 Oct. 1921) on 3 Sept. 1938. Pat Turner died 15 March 1975 at age 65 and is buried at Oak Grove Cemetery in Americus. Five children:

A) Patrick Rhodes "Teddy" Turner, Jr. (b. 18 Feb. 1940) married first Gloria Howard; married second Carolyn Kinnebrew Riccardi. Three children: Mike, Michelle, Ted

B) Gerald Warren Turner (b. 25 Feb. 1943 d. 8 April 2001) married first Charlene Dunmon; married second Inez Johnson. Two children: Lisa, Erikka

C) Donnie Motten Turner (b. 11 Nov. 1947) married Patricia Miller. Three children: Todd, Angie, Brian

D) Winfred Pat Turner (b. 4 Nov. 1951) married Debbie Kendrick. Three children: Deanna, Kristy, Patrick D.

E) Janie Patricia "Jane" Turner (b. 16 Dec. 1957) married first Mickey Dennard; married second David Austin. Three children: Brittney; Chealsea, Cullen

11) <u>Audrey Turner</u> (also spelled Audra) (b. 4 Dec. 1911 d. 24 Dec. 1911 at age 20 days). Her death marked one of the saddest days in the family's history.

She was found dead in her crib on Christmas Eve. The older children remembered being told by David M. Turner that "Santa Claus would have to come another day." Her funeral was held on Dec. 26. Audrey Turner is buried at Live Oak Baptist Church Cemetery near Aragon. The inscription on her tombstone reads "Darling we miss thee."

12) <u>Ruth Lee Turner</u> (b. 7 Jan. 1913) married Clarence Belvy Short (b. 19 Feb. 1908 d. 4 Aug. 1973) on 23 Feb. 1929. (See Descendants of C.B. and Ruth Turner Short). Ruth Short died 19 Dec. 1998 at age 85 and is buried at Hebron Baptist Church Cemetery near Americus. Four children:

A) Lawrence Lee "Jack" Short, Sr. (b. 23 Nov. 1929) married Frances Spann. Four children: Jackie, Anne, Randy, Steve

B) Peggy Ann Short (b. 22 Dec. 1931) married Harold J. Israel, Sr. Five children: Beverly, Charles, Hal, Peggy, Mark

C) Patsy Ruth Short (b. 21 Jan. 1938) married Pat S. Medlock. Four children: Ken, Molly (twin), Polly (twin), Patty

D) Clarence William "Bobo" Short (b. 9 June 1944) married first Gail Jennings; married second Nancy A. Howells. Three children: Tanya; Laura, Chan

—Submitted by Steve Short

Chapter 21: Family History U–Z

Rev. Theodore Roosevelt Wakefield, Sr.

Theodore Roosevelt Wakefield, Sr. (known as T.R.) was born April 23, 1901 in Calhoun County, Dickey, Georgia to Zenobia and Rev. Sidney Wakefield. He was their eighth child.

In the year 1919, he came to Archery, Georgia (near Plains, Georgia) to the home of Bishop William Decker Johnson, Sr. There he and his younger brother, Alfonso, attended Johnson's Home Industrial College at night and worked on the farm during the day. T.R. completed his education at Johnson's Home Industrial College that was founded by the late Bishop William Decker Johnson, Sr. This College was located in Archery, Georgia for educating Negro youth in that section of the country.

In 1922, he was united in marriage to Miss Arrena Raven. They were married for fourteen years before her untimely death on April 16, 1936 at the age of 30. Ten children were born: Vera, Daisy, Naomi, Thomas, Samuel, Willie, Mary, Theodore, Jr., Franklin and Herman.

Not long after the death of the children's mother, the Lord blessed T.R. with another wife and mother for the ten children. Bertha Schley Wakefield was that very, very special woman. Although Bertha never gave birth to a child of her own, she was a special gift as wife and mother to the Wakefield family. She and T.R. shared 35 wonderful years together. In May 1970 Bertha suffered a stroke and a heart attack that left her paralyzed all over and without her voice. On February 2, 1972 Bertha went to be with the Lord at the age of 70 years. Bertha spent her last days in the Plains Convales-cent Home (known earlier as the Wise Hospital) where she worked as a registered nurse.

On October 9, 1972, T.R. was married to Mrs. Jewel McLendon, whom he preceded in death. At the age of 76, T.R., Sr. died in the Americus and Sumter County Hospital on August 20, 1977. He left a legacy of ten children, fifty-eight grandchildren, 116 great-grandchildren and 53 great, great grandchildren.

—*Submitted by (no name given)*

Rev. Theodore Roosevelt Wakefield, Jr.

June 16, 1932 marks the birth of the eighth child of Theodore and Arena Wakefield. It was only fitting that this boy child bear the sir name of the leader of this great family, thus he was named Theodore Roosevelt Jr. He was a quiet, gentle child who showed signs early of his future destiny.

Junior, as he was called, grew up on the farm in the Archery Community with his nine other brothers and sisters. Junior was almost 4 years old when his mother passed, but he remembers the soft sound of her voice and the loving touch of her hand at night when she checked on her babies.

While growing up on the farm helping with the chores, Junior was educated in the Archery community where he found a love for math and a unique ability to work with numbers in his head. Even to today, it is uncanny his ability to "figure in his head", to the amazement of his grandchildren.

The Archery community did not hold many activities for the children of the community, so they all looked forward to the weekend trip to Plains to spend time with the city children and visit the picture shows and occasionally went to a dance in town. It was on one of these trips, when the young lanky teenager saw a brown skinned, attractive young lady with long ponytails. This young lady, Mary Nellie Polk, was a close friend of Junior's sister Mary, who introduced him to his future bride.

Junior and Mary courted for a few years before marrying on Jan. 12, 1952. To this union, five children were born. Mary and Theodore were very concerned for their family and made sure they grew up in a loving, Christian family. To support his family, Junior had several jobs over the years. He worked at the Dumas Saw Mill for several years processing lumber while the family remained in the Archery Community.

In the late 50's, Mary and Junior moved their three babies, Erma, Arthur, and Simeon, from Archery to Plains, Georgia and located in the small community called South Plains. While living here, Junior worked on several work crews who were instrumental in the completion of bridgework and interstate construction. He amazed his babies by showing work involved in the construction of the two bridges going into and out of Americus on Meadowbrook as well as the work on Interstate 75. There were times that he had to live away from home during the week because of the distance of his jobs, but he would always make a point of making a trip to the location with his family to let them know where he was staying and to see the work he was doing.

The next year the family moved to, Plains, Georgia. While living in Plains another child, Mary Jean was born to the family. Erma was especially excited to finally have a little sister, even though she was born nine years after Erma, it was wonderful to have this little baby to take care of and to mother.

It was here that the last child, Vivian was born. This birth was difficult for Mary and it helped Junior decide that he could no longer afford to be away from home but needed to seek work closer by so that he could also be near to help with the raising of five children.

He was able to find employment with the Metalux Corporation in Americus, Georgia as a printer in the finishing department. He worked here for several years and became a supervisor of the painting department of the Lighting Division. Mary remained at home, as a housewife and taking small odd jobs of cleaning, cooking and ironing to help support the family while the older children were young.

The early 60s were trying times for all; the economy was not doing very good and especially not for the black communities of Georgia. It was during this time that Junior found another path for his life and the lives of his family. The family was spiritually based in the Methodist church and God saw fit to call Junior into the ministry. Junior was not sure that this was what he wanted to do, and resisted the calling for some time. However, after many discussions with his Father, Mary, and his pastor, Rev. W.B. Brown, he knew this was what God wanted him to do and it was what he had to do.

In November 1963 T.R. Wakefield, Jr. became Rev. T. R. Wakefield Jr. Starting in small churches, the family served many communities. The first church was Fountain Chapel A.M.E. in Leslie, Georgia. There was a very small congregation at this church, in fact, there was only one Steward at the church and it met in an old schoolhouse. The first thing Jr. did was to invite the community into worship and worked to improve the condition of the sanctuary. The family became emerged in the small community of Leslie and the church.

Because of the hard work exhibited by Rev. Wakefield and his family, the Presiding Elder, at that time, decided to add other churches to T.R.'s leadership. Rev. Wakefield and his family were introduced to the New Hope A.M.E. church family in Smithville, Georgia and the St. Luke A.M.E. Church near Plains. Many souls were brought to

Christ' during the years T .R. served in these communities.

During these years, the late 60's and early 70's his little family was growing up. Erma, Arthur and Simeon grew up and attended elementary school in Plains at the Westside Elementary School. Erma and Arthur were bused to Americus to the Sumter County High School in ninth grade even though there was "freedom of choice" at that time to attend the all white high school in Plains. Education was very important to both T.R. and Mary. They were determined that their children would receive a better education than each of them. Their children had no doubt they would attend high school and go on to further their education. Erma graduated in 1970 from Sumter County High School, and went on to Fort Valley State College. She planned to major in business administration, when she packed up and the family moved her to Fort Valley, Georgia. This was Erma's first time away from home and it was a little scary, but frequent trips home helped make the transition smoother. It was during one of these trips home that T.R. had a discussion with Erma about her major.

While the family was in Smithville, with the New Hope A.M.E. church, Erma developed a desire to play piano during church after hearing the melodic sounds made by a cousin who played during service for the choir. Mary had insisted that she received piano lessons earlier, but she did not really get serious with it until she had an opportunity to observe Ronald Dismuke's talent. He showed her some simple chords and that opened a new world of adventure to her.

Erma's parents wanted a teacher in the family. They discussed the options with Erma, who decided that maybe teaching would not be so bad. It was at this time that Erma changed her major to Music Education. Arthur also decided to attend Fort Valley State College and major in Music, where he played trombone in the Marching Wildcat Band.

While Erma was at Fort Valley, she met Donald Kenneth Jenkins, who became her husband. Donald was also a music major at FVSC so they had a lot in common.

While Erma and Arthur were at Fort Valley, T.R. was moved to the Blakely-Donaldsonville District where he was called to the Wesley Chapel A.M.E. Church. For nearly 10 years, the family drove the 70-mile trip to Blakely every Sunday. Under, T .R.' s leadership, Wesley Chapel became the lead church in the district. Many activities were formed in the church to help the young people of the Blakely area. This leadership ability was rewarded in the early 80's when T. R. became Presiding Elder of the Blakely District, which was later renamed the Southern District.

Under the leadership of Presiding Elder Wakefield, the district quickly became the envy of the state. An example of this energy was in his ability to tackle problems others would think insurmountable because of the limitations man puts on himself when he does not truly depend and lean on the grace of God to take care of our wants and needs.

The district purchased a used school bus to provide transportation for the parishioners and young people of the district. While the young people of the district were visiting Atlanta for a leadership conference, the bus broke down on the way home. Elder Wakefield made sure all of the young people got home okay but this sparked an effort to make sure this did not happen again. The district went to the Blue Bird Bus Company and ordered an air-conditioned 80-passenger bus. They were not concerned about the cost because they knew their leader would work as hard as each of them to make sure the note was paid off. The Southern District was the first in the state to have a bus of this magnitude due to the leadership and guidance of the eighth child of T .R. and Arena Wakefield. After many years in the ministry, T.R. was rewarded with a retirement celebration in October 2001.

This courage and leadership ability was instilled in each of Mary and T .R.' s children. Each have always been encouraged to do their best and not let anything or anybody stand in your way. "With good will doing service, as to the Lord, and not to men", Ephesians 6:7. Briefly, the children grew up to be examples of their parent's hard work.

Erma Faye Wakefield Jenkins graduated from Fort Valley with honors with a B.S. Music Education and worked as a music teacher for one year in Montgomery County Elementary and High School. Earned additional certification in Elementary Education in 1975 from Georgia Southern College and taught second grade for 10 years at Swainsboro Primary School in Swainsboro, Georgia. In 1986 Erma moved from the classroom to become Lead Teacher moving into administration as Asst. Principal in 1986. In 1989, Erma became Principal of Swainsboro Primary School where she served until 2001. In Aug. 2001, Erma became Director of Elementary Curriculum and Instructional Technology for Emanuel County Schools. Erma married Donald Jenkins in 1972 and is the mother of three children: Dorna Demetrus Jenkins, Graduated from University of Georgia and John Marshall School of Law-Attorney At Law-Rushing Firm in East Point, Georgia specializing in real estate Litigation and Entertainment Law. She is also a songwriter and music producer.

Donald Kenneth Jenkins, Graduated from Fort Valley State University majored in Criminal Justice and is presently seeking enrollment into Law School. Robert Theodore Jenkins- eighth grade student at Swainsboro Middle School.

Arthur James Wakefield, upon graduation from Plains High School, attended Fort Valley State College and later graduated from South Georgia Tech with a diploma in Machine Tool Technology. Served in the United States Navy stationed in San Diego, California and Norfolk, Va. Upon leaving the Navy was in the Naval Reserves and is presently a Machinist at the Norfolk Naval Shipyard in Norfolk, Va.

Simeon Herman Wakefield, upon graduation from Plains High School, attended South Georgia Tech with a diploma in Electronic Technology. Upon completion of this program, Simeon started employment with the CSX Railroad. Presently he is Signal Inspector for CSX Transportation. He is married to Gloria Ann Battle Wakefield in 1987 and is father of four children: Sanekia Stewart Grier of Decatur, Georgia employed in Home Health with Menders, Inc.; Antonio Kentrell Battle a student at Sumter County Comprehensive High school; Sheketta Shanta Wakefield, a student at Sumter County Middle School; Chelsea Symone Wakefield, a student at Sumter County Primary School.

Mary Jean Wakefield Harden graduated from Plains High School with honors and attended and graduated from Georgia Southwestern College in Americus, as a Registered Nurse. Attended Medical College of Georgia in Augusta and graduated as a Respiratory Therapist and a Bachelors Degree from Southern Illinois University in Health Care Administration. She is currently pursuing her Masters of Science Degree in Health Administration from Kennedy Western University. Mary has been employed at Augusta Regional Hospital and is presently at University Hospital where she serves as the Administrator of their North Augusta Division Home Health Agency. Married to Michael Harden in 1986 and has one daughter, Rachel Michelle Harden

Vivian Ann Wakefield Singleton graduated Valedictorian Plains High School and attended the University of Georgia, School of Journalism. Upon graduation, Vivian moved to Wilmington, North Carolina to pursue a career in television production. Next Vivian moved to Augusta, Georgia to work at television station WFFIF as news producer before moving to Jacksonville, Fla. where she has worked with both mediums of media in television and print as a news reporter for the Florida Times-Union. Presently, Vivian is taking a leave from work as she pursues a degree in Law. She is presently attending The Law School at Florida Community College. Married to Walter Singleton in 2000 and has one daughter, Faith Maria Singleton.

As we look at the challenges facing the black community, we must understand that love is the only power that will save us. God's love can look at the worst situation and see hope. God's love can stand in the midst of hate and poverty and speak a word of deliverance; God's love can transform communities and transform minds. "The fruit of the Spirit of love...against such there is no law" (Galatians 5:22-23).

—*Submitted by (no name given)*

The Walters Family

Seaborn Walters moved to the Plains area around 1850, living in several locations in close proximity to Plains. His son, Thomas Gordon Walters, lived in a house on the hill just north of Rabbit Branch on what is now Rabbit Branch Road. One of Thomas Gordon Walters sons, Claude Walters Sr., moved into the house now occupied by Jack Watson, on Paschal Street in Plains. In later years, the Thomas Gordon Walters family moved to Plains into what is commonly called the Nelle Walters house, on the western edge of Plains. This was where Nelle and Pearl Walters lived until Pearl died and Nelle went to a nursing home. This house was moved into the pecan orchard next to the house occupied by C.L. Walters III. Claude Walters Sr. later moved to a house on U.S. 280, currently occupied by C.L. Walters III, and lived there until his death, at which time C.L. Walters Jr. bought the house and resold it ot C.L. III. C.L. Walters Jr. moved his family into the house on the east side of the Plains United Methodist Church, and his house is currently occupied by his granddaughter, Cathy Walters Young, and her family.

Richard R. Walters, progenitor of the line, had five sons: Thomas, Gordon, Richard, Simeon, and Seaborn.

Seaborn Walters born January 12, 1809 in Laurens County Georgia, died June 24, 1867, Sumter County, Georgia married Sarah Elizabeth Pullen, born December 6, 1816, died July 21, 1896, Sumter County, Georgia. Fifteen children were born to the union.

Thomas Gordon Walters, son of Seaborn, born September 20, 1841, died May 20, 1914, married Mary Emily Forth, born November 9, 1847, died March 15, 1887. Twelve children were born to this union including Pearl and Nelle.

I. **Claude Leonard Walters, Sr.** son of Thomas Gordon, born January 31, 1878, died February 4, 1955, married Bernice Irene Harper, born January 29, 1881, died September 1, 1968. (See Harper geneology.) The children of this union were Inman (Inky), Mary Evaline (Polly), Ray, Hugh (Bud), Helen, and C.L. Jr., born October 6, 1904, died November 25, 1980.

A. Claude Leonard Walters, Jr. married Florrie Elizabeth Murray (Beth) who served faithfully as pianist and organist for some 40 years at the Plains Methodist Church. She was born May 7, 1913, and died June 2001. To this union were born three children:

1. Claude Leonard III born December 27, 1938, married Sandra Helen Harrell, born October 9, 1939. Children of this union include:

a. Cathy Lynn born October 31, 1963, married on December 18, 1981 to Walter Fred Young who was born November 9, 1961. Children: (1) Lauretta Jane Young born July 9, 1982 (2) Charles Walter Young born September 24, 1984 (3) Walter Leroy born August 9, 1990, died April 26, 2001

b. Carol Lane born April 21, 1966, married Kyle Ray Kennon. Children: (1) Katherene Elizabeth (Kate) born April 30, 1996 (2) Jacob Galloway (Jake) born September 18, 2001

c. Craig Harrell Walters born February 27, 1969

2. Elizabeth Claudette born January 29, 1942, married John Elliott Strickland born June 6, 1942. Children:

a. John Elliott, Jr. born March 2, 1971, married Carolyn Lee Riechart June 19, 1999

b. Leah Beth born May 5, 1973, married Brett Jason Nazworth September 16, 2000

3. Almer Murray born February 14, 1948, married Claudia Marie Cochran born December 4, 1948. Children:

a. Adam Murray born September 28, 1974

b. David Cochran born January 28, 1977

c. Stephen Claude born October 1, 1980

—*Submitted by Dr. James Bagwell*

Francis Marion Webb Family

Francis Marion Webb was a descendant of William Green Webb, a native Virginian, farmer, teacher, minister, and was in the War of 1776. His grandson, John, settled in Georgia and had four wives and thirteen children, one of whom was Edward B. Webb, father of Francis Marion Webb B.1868 (D.1953) who married Georgia Frances Finch B.1878 (D.1944). They had seven children:

1) Louise B. 1897 married Perry K. Countryman who had Francis Kirk married Lois Cramer who had Perry, Patty, Bruce, and Carol.

And Kenneth who married Marjorie Davis and had Julie, Scott, and Mark.

2) Floyd Benton born 1900 married Betty Ferree Rusmiselle and had Betty

Carolyn married Edwin Wagnon who had Betty Alicia; Floyd Filmore (not married) and Sara Frances married Lewis Williams who had Lewis Dave. 2nd wife Elizabeth Sawyer (no children).

3) Maty B.1901 married Fred Wayne (no children).

4) Willie Clifford born 1903 married Wilbur Giddings who had Anne married Babe Walker Webb who had Susan, Wayne, and Lynn; James Irwin married Kay who had Paige, Jim, and Dan; Margaret (not married)

5) Francis born 1908 married Kitty (no children)

6) Eva Laura born 1910 married James Crawford (no children)

7) James Robert born 1913 married Mary Baugh (no children)

Francis Marion and Georgia Frances Finch Webb lived in the Thalean community and were members of Rehoboth Baptist Church where he was clerk for many years. As the older Webb siblings reached high school age, they lived in Smithville with their Aunt Eva and Uncle Wade Turner to attend school there. But in the 1920's the family moved to Plains so their youngest, and later a granddaughter, could attend Plains High School. Eva taught at Plains Elementary and Mary completed Nurse's training at Wise Sanitarium. The family was active in Plains Baptist Church.

In the 70's when they retired Floyd and Elizabeth Webb bought the Carter/Slappey home next to the Methodist church—the quietest, most peaceful place they'd found. The quiet didn't last long when the now-Webb home became a stop on the tourist tour of Plains during the Carter era.

None of our Webbs reside currently in Plains, but the Plains influence will forever impact the lives of all the descendants of Francis Marion and Georgia Frances Finch Webb.

—*Submitted by Carolyn Webb Wagnon*

Rev. A.C. Wellons Family

Joseph A. John Wellons was born June 19, 1822 in Jones County near Macon. He was a descendant of John Wellons, who was born in England about 1706 and came to America as a sea captain. John Wellons settled on a large plantation, Mount Round Hill, in Southampton County, Va. He died in 1778 in York County, Va.

Joseph A.J. Wellons married Eleanor Murcheson (also spelled Murchison) on July 2, 1846 in Crawford County. Joseph A.J. Wellons and Eleanor Wellons had six children: John T. Wellons (b. about 1848); Laura E. Wellons; Larkin T. Wellons (b. Feb. 23, 1852); Augustus Caesar Wellons (b. 1854); Mary Ella Wellons (b. 1857); and Joseph Brown Wellons (b. March 4, 1858). Joseph J.A. Wellons was in the Confederate Army, Co. D 87th Battalion, in July 1863.

Augustus Caesar Wellons, the fourth child, was born June 16, 1854 in Crawford County. He was a farmer, contractor and ordained Baptist minister. He married Anna B. Murcheson (b. Sept. 22, 1855 d. Jan. 3, 1942) and they spent most of their married life in Plains. Her father was a physician who practiced in both Crawford County and Monroe County in west-central Georgia.

Rev. A.C. Wellons built many homes in Plains as well as the Plains Baptist Church building in 1906. He built his Victorian home that is now the Plains Bed and Breakfast Inn in 1910.

He served as pastor of Plains Baptist Church in the 1890s. He was one of the founders of the nearby Hebron Baptist Church in 1894. His photograph hangs on a plaque inside the church today.

Rev. A.C. Wellons also was pastor of Bethel, County Line, Friendship, Shiloh, Preston and Weston Baptist churches during his career. He died at his Plains home on March 20, 1932 at age 77. His wife died in 1942 at age 86.

Rev. A.C. Wellons and Anna Wellons had two daughters who died young – Mary Anna and Blanche. Their family also included the following six children and descendants:

I. Aletus B. Wellons (b. about 1876 d. March 11, 1958). Aletus married Camilla Boyd. They had no children. He was a carpenter and lived in Plains. He and Camilla are buried at Lebanon Cemetery in Plains.

II. Notrice Ernest Wellons (b. Nov. 9, 1882 d. 1974). Ernest was born in Barnesville in Lamar County. He married Annie Will Addy (1890-1968) of Preston on Dec. 28,1909. He was a contractor and lived in Portsmouth, Va., after 1918. He and Annie Will are buried at Evergreen Cemetery in Portsmouth. He and Annie Will had three children:

A) Ernest William Wellons (b. 1910). William attended William and Mary College and the University of Virginia. He is a teacher and artist and lives in Portsmouth.

B) Marie Wellons (b. 1912 d. 1984). Marie married Quinton Butler. They had one son: 1) James Ernest "Jimmy" Butler. Jimmy and his wife had two daughters: 1A) Melissa Butler Graves and 2A) Jamie Butler Philpott

C) Edwin Lavon Wellons (b. 1915 d. 2001). Lavon was born in Plains. He was an inventor. He married first Josephine Snellings. They had one son: 1) Edwin Wellons (b. 1943). Edwin married Marsha Caskey. They had two children: 1A) Edwin Ross Wellons (b. 1967) and 2A) Neal Franklin Wellons (b. 1971). Lavon married second Dorothy Gwynn. They had one son: 1) William Rick Wellons (b. 1949). Rick married Connie Stevens. They had one son: 1A) William Rick Wellons, Jr. (b. 1970)

III. Broadus Augustus Wellons (b. March 9, 1889 d. Sept. 3, 1952). Broadus was born in Barnesville. He was a barber in Plains. Broadus married Mary Ella Mills (1897-1991) of Sumter County. They are buried at Lebanon Cemetery in Plains. They had three children:

A) Grady Mills Wellons (b. Oct. 6, 1919 d. Sept. 5, 1988). Grady was a sergeant in World War II. He never married. He is buried at Lebanon Cemetery.

B) Virginia Dare Wellons (b. 1918 d. 1980). Virginia, a teacher, married John W. Wingate, Sr. (1917-1988). They had two children:

1) John W. Wingate, Jr. (b. 1943 d. 1998). He married Linda Kaye Davis and was a lawyer and lived in Macon. He has two children: 1A) Elizabeth Louise Wingate (b. 1964), who married Charles Wayne Veal in 1989; and 2A) John W. Wingate III (b. 1971).

2) Mary Virginia "Ginger" Wingate (b. 1948). Ginger, a teacher, married Glynn Thompson in 1967. They had three daughters: 1A) Jacquelyn Doan Thompson (b. Sept. 3, 1968); 2A) Stacy Suzanne Thompson (b. Aug. 20, 1973), who married Dr. Paul Jason Hyler in 1998; and 3A) Kristin Lynn Thompson (b. Aug. 4, 1975), who married Brennen Hicks in 2000.

C) Winifred Jacquelyn "Jackie" Wellons (b. 1921). Jackie, a nurse who served in World War II, married John G. Binns, Sr. (1917-1993) of Pennsylvania. He served in World War II and the Korean War. Jackie lives in Charlotte, N.C. They had two sons:

1) John George Binns, Jr. (b. 1947). He married first Mary Jeanne Gerz in 1966. They had one son: 1A) John George Binns III (b. 1967). John George Binns, Jr. married second Constance Dale Burger on Jan. 25, 1969 in Pennsylvania. He married third Saralyn JoAnn Miller in 1982 in Charlotte. They have four children: 1A) Beau Christopher Binns (b. 1975) (adopted); 2A) Rob Julian Binns (b. 1978) (adopted); 3A) Lauren Ann Binns (b. 1984); 4A) Megan Saralyn Binns (b. June 27, 1989)

2) Charles Grady Binns (b. 1957) married Ann Seabolt on May 10, 1980 in Decatur. Two children: 1A) Mary Kaitlyn Binns (b. May 8, 1988); and 2A) Melissa Ann Binns (b. June 28, 1993)

IV. Otis Olin Wellons (b. July 1, 1893 d. Dec. 23, 1930). Otis was a barber in Plains and a World War I veteran. He married Ethel McGarrah (1899-1971) of Friendship. They are buried at Lebanon Cemetery in Plains. They had three daughters:

A) Hilda Elizabeth Wellons (b. 1921). Hilda married Ben Sims Moore. She lives in Americus. They had one child: 1) Ben Sims Moore, Jr. Ben and his wife Barbara had one child: 1A) Christopher Alan Moore (b. March 8, 1980)

B) Mildred Wellons (b. 1923). Mildred married Ralph Tyler. She lives in Americus. They had three children: 1) Dr. Pamela Tyler (b. 1949), a professor in Raleigh, N.C. 2) Elizabeth "Beth" Tyler (b. 1954 d. 1994). Beth married Danny Sandock. 3) Sally Tyler (b. 1963)

C) Lois Wellons (b. May 9, 1926 d. June 3, 1946). Lois married C. Gordon Saxton. She is buried at Lebanon Cemetery in Plains. They had one son: 1) Gordon Saxton, Jr. (b. 1944)

V. Ulon Victor Wellons (b. Aug. 22, 1896 d. Nov. 28, 1970). Ulon was an engineer and a graduate of Auburn University. He married Bonnie Gross (1901-1989), and lived in Trenton, Atlanta, Waukegan, Ill., and St. Louis during his career. He worked for Hartford Insurance Co. for 25 years. They had no children. He died at his St. Louis home in 1970. He and Bonnie are buried at Trenton Baptist Church Cemetery in northwest Georgia.

VI. Bessie Wellons (b. 1900 d. Aug. 17, 1961). Bessie married Arthur Hood Crozier (1898-1965) and lived in Plains. They are buried at Lebanon Cemetery in Plains. They had one son:

A) Arthur Hood Crozier, Jr. (b. Oct. 19, 1925 d. July 28, 1976). He was a Navy veteran and served in World War II. He died in Alabama and also is buried at Lebanon Cemetery.

—Submitted by Jackie W. Binns of Charlotte, N.C., and Steve Short

Ralph and Fannie Wiggins Family

Ralph Carlton Wiggins was born June 3, 1917, in Preston, Georgia. Fannie Ethel Hand was born November 19, 1914, in Wilcox County, in the country near Abbeville, Georgia. They married April 5, 1941, and settled in Plains in 1943. Ralph was employed by Sullivan Lumber Company. Later, he became a civilian airplane mechanic at Southerfield. He then became a building contractor and built many of the homes around Plains. He then retired and worked as a carpenter for Plains Convalescent Home. Jimmy and Rosalynn Carter asked him to build a home for them on Woodland Drive in Plains.

Miss Fannie worked for Manhatten Shirt Company in Americus for 34 years. She retired from this and then went to work for Lee Manufacturing Company in Leesburg. At length, she moved from this to become manager of Middle Flint Council on Aging.

Mr. Ralph died April 9, 1993, but Miss Fannie still enjoys excellent health and continues to be active in civic and religious activities in Plains. She is an active member of the Plains United Methodist Church.

They have two daughters, Ouida Norrine born 1943, and Marian Elizabeth, born 1945. Norrine married Eddie Lowell and the couple have three sons, Edward Stanley Lowell, Jr., David Carlton, and Stephen Phillip. Stan married Barbara Sellards. They have six children: Kelly, Ted, Christopher, Justin and twins Cassy and Cassie. Carl married Dana Driver; they have two children, Cory and Courtney.

—Submitted by Jimmy Bagwell

The Family of Henry Williams

The lineal descent of Henry Williams, son of Drury Williams and his wife, Alethia Hood, has been traced back to 1668 in Bertie County, N.C.; John Barrow married Sarah Sutton 1668. Their daughter, Joanna Barrow, married Jenkin Williams, 1690. Their son, Rueben, married in 17?? and moved to old Washington County, Georgia. Their son, Drury, married Alethia Hood and settled in Leon County, Florida. Their two sons were Williams Williams and Henry Williams.

Born May 1, 1800, Henry Williams was married August 11, 1839, to Charlotte Bryon, born November 2, 1823, daughter of Thomas Bryon and wife, Dorothy, and settled in Stewart County where he was a farmer, a Mason, and active in the affairs of Lumpkin, Georgia. He moved his family to Sumter County during the late 1860's where he died April 8, 1874, and Charlotte October 15, 1899. They had seven children: Mary Ann born November 28, 1840; Joseph Monroe born July 23, 1841; Martha Catherine born June 27, 1846; Sarah Jane born April 5, 1849; Henry George Washington born October 17, 1853; Charles McDonald born January 30, 1855; and James Buchanen born December 5, 1857, died October 10, 1866.

Mary Ann married Martin Burke April 24, 1861, in Stewart County and settled in Americus. Joseph Monroe married Mary Ellen Glass in 1866, settled in Sumter County and finally moved to Greensboro, N.C. Henry George Washington married Fannie Moore February 28, 1877, and lived on a farm about 3 miles west of Plains. Charles McDonald married Mary Jessie Hardy December 16, 1879, and lived on a farm about 6 miles from Americus near Kidd's Mill. From there he moved to Americus where he died.

James Buchanen died in his youth. Further research is needed regarding lives of Martha Catherine and Sarah Jane.

—Submitted by G. Frank Williams, Sr.

The Family of Joseph Henry Williams

I. Joseph Henry Williams, b. July 21, 1889 d.Feb.24, 1936 in Sumter County Georgia. Buried at Lebanon Cemetery in Plains, Georgia. Married Bertha Hawkins Dodson, Sept. 12, 1907. Bertha Dodson, b. Oct. 27, 1884 d. April 2, 1958 Buried at Lebanon Cemetery in Plains, Georgia.

Joe and Bertha lived all their married life in Plains in the house just across the street from Plains Baptist Church. Joe owned a mercantile store in downtown Plains. After Joe's death Bertha continued to live in Plains until sometime during WW II. She then went to live with her daughter Harriet W. Sumpter in Jacksonville, Florida. Upon her death in Florida her body was brought back to Plains for the funeral at Plains Baptist Church and burial in Lebanon Cemetery. The children of Joe and Bertha Williams are:

I. Joseph Henry Williams Jr. born October 15, 1908 Died and buried in Denmark, S.C. Married Martha Willis, October 19, 1934. Martha left her body to a Medical Lab. Their children are: 1. Joseph Henry Williams, III and 2. Martha(Markee) Williams

II. Harriet Williams, born 1913 in Plains. Married James G. Sumpter in 1937. James Sumpter was born Oct. 23, 1912 and died Oct. 15, 1976 He was a Retired Civil Service worker. No children were born to this union

III. Rachel Williams, born 1917 in Plains. Died March 15, 1986. Buried in DeSoto Cemetery in DeSoto Georgia. Rachel married Woodrow Wilson (Billy) Ferguson, in 1934 in Seal, Alabama. Billy is the son of John Edward Ferguson Sr. and Mary Elizabeth Pursley. Billy was born in 1916 in DeSoto, Georgia. He was Mayor of DeSoto from 1947-1969 where he owned and operated DeSoto Mercantile Company. He served as a member of the Sumter County Commission for 37 years, most of the time as Chairman of the Board. He served in WWII. Their children are 1. Beth Ferguson born in 1935 in DeSoto Georgia. And 2. John Williams Ferguson, born in 1947 in Americus,Georgia.

IV. Armstead Dodson Williams, b. 1919 in Plains, Georgia. 1970 in Leslie Georgia. Buried in Leslie, Georgia. Married Pauline Howard Royal in 1946. Died in Americus, Georgia. And is buried in Leslie, Georgia. She and Armstead were divorced. Their children were 1. James Williams and 2. Susan Williams.

V. Mary Rebecca Williams b. 1923 in Plains, Georgia. Married Irwin Karr in 1944. He died April 1, 1999, Their children are 1. Anna Karr and 2. Bertha (Beth) Karr Rebecca lived all her married life in New Jersey.

(See III. above) Beth Ferguson, daughter of Rachel and Billy Ferguson, born in 1935 married Robert Stanley Holman in 1951 in Georgetown, Georgia. He was born in 1932 and died in 1997. Buried December 30, 1997 in Leslie, Georgia. He and Beth were divorced. They had the following children:

1. Harriet Lee Holman b. 1953 She married Kenneth Larry McSpadden. Their children are: 1. Kenneth Larry McSpadden, Jr. and 2. Aimee Michelle McSpadden

2. Billie Rachel Holman b. 1956 m. Raymond Lewis Lee, Jr. There child is Raymond Lewis Lee, III They were divorced and she later married Dwight Underwood.

3. Robert Stanley Holman b. 1957 m.Loretta Brantley. They were divorced. Their children are:1. Tammy Cheyenne Holman 2. Robert Stanley Holman III, 3. Clayton Hudson Holman 4. Melissa Ann Holman. He married 2ⁿᵈ time Angie R. Ricks They were divorced. He mar-

ried 3rd time Miriam Bass in 1990. Their only child is Ashley Nicole Holman

Beth Ferguson Holman married the second time Thomas William Usry in 1960 in Kingsland, Camden County, Georgia. Their four children are:
1. Thomas Dwayne Usry born 1959. Thomas has no children
2. Barry Deon Usry born 1961. One son, Michael Allen Usry born 1998
3. Cheryl Usry born 1965. Married Steve Bowen, divorced. One son, Thomas James Bowen, born1986
4. Mary Beth Usry born 1967. Married Freddie Cooper, divorced. One son, Christopher Thomas Cooper, born 1997

John Williams Ferguson, son of Billy and Rachel Ferguson b. 1947 in Americus, Georgia. He married 1st Gwen Ellen Hyman in 1968 and 2nd. Mikki Kay Saliba in 1977 Their children are: 1. John Williams Ferguson, Jr. born 1982; 2. Joseph Michael (Joey) Ferguson born 1986; 3. James Chester(Jimmy) Ferguson born 1988
—*Submitted by Beth Usry*

Oscar Albert Williams, Jr.

Henry Williams, born May 1, 1800, married Charlotte Bryon on August 11, 1839. On August 27, 1853, George Henry Williams was born to this couple. George Henry married Fannie Moore on February 28, 1877, and they lived on a farm about three miles Northwest of Plains in the Magnolia Springs area, the birthplace of O.A. Williams, Sr. and O.A. Williams, Jr.

This marriage produced Oscar A. Williams, Sr., born December 19, 1884 along with other children: Oscar Albert Williams, Sr. married Leila Earl from Clayton, Georgia, Rabun County, on

May 21, 1916, after she moved to Plains to teach school. They had Henry Earl, born May 14, 1918; George Franklin born December 12, 1919 and Oscar Albert Williams, Jr., born October 22, 1921.

Oscar A. Williams, Jr. attended Plains High School. After graduation, he attended the University of Georgia and graduated in 1942 with a degree in Agriculture. After nine days, he reported to Officers Candidate School at Ft. Riley, Kansas. He served in Reconniance in 3rd Army, being wounded on November 29, 1944. After recovery, he was discharged and came to Plains and worked as rural mail carrier for 34 years. He also worked with Plains Cotton Warehouse and Williams Warehouse. During these years, he served as President of State Rural Carrier Association, school board member for 12 years, member of the Atlanta Postal Credit Union now with assets over one billion. He served as treasurer of Plains Baptist Church 25 years plus and deacon.

In 1948, Oscar A. Jr. married Marlys Tripp Porter in MN and had Peggy Ann, born December 22, 1948. Peggy married Charles F. Rumsey from Buchanan, Michigan on December 22, 1973 and had David Charles on June 18, 1978, and Daniel James born on August 1, 1980. Oscar A. Williams III, born May 30, 1950, married Cathy Cook from Leesburg, Georgia, Lee County on July 20, 1980 and had Oscar A. Williams, III on September 21, 1981; Larry Tripp Williams married Sharon Shannon, from Preston, Georgia, Webster County on June 15, 1974 and had Kelly Ann, born December 3, 1975; Nicholas Tripp born June 24, 1980; and Dustin Williams born November 13, 1984.
—*Submitted by Albert Williams*

Oscar A. Williams, Sr. Family

The first of this family in this area was Henry Williams, born May 1, 1800, married August 11, 1839, to Charlotte Bryon. On August 27, 1853, Henry George Washington Williams was born to this couple. Henry George Washington married Fannie Moore February 28, 1877, and they lived on a farm about 3 miles northwest of Plains in the Magnolia Springs area. This marriage produced Willie T. Williams, born March 10, 1878; Joseph Henry Williams, born July 21, 1880; Oscar Albert Williams, born December 19, 1884; Lucy Williams, born October 10, 1889; Alice Sarah Williams, born October 3, 1891; and also twin boys born sometime between 1880 and 1884, and died at birth.

Willie T. Williams, after growing up, moved to Jackson, Mississippi, having his family of two boys and a daughter, Will Tom, B.J., and Lucile.

Lucy, married Seig Holmes and moved to Denmark, S.C., having Seig Jr. and Ann.

Joseph Henry remained in Plains, married Bertha Dodson and had Joe Jr., Armstid, Harriet, Rachel, and Rebekah. He farmed and operated a grocery store.

Alice married Robert Andrews in 1910 and had Alice and Raymond and died at the early age of 21 on November 15, 1912. She is buried in the Methodist Cemetery near Magnolia Springs in Sumter County.

Oscar Albert, born December 19, 1884, and died March 29, 1976, married Leila Earl, born April 28, 1892, and died March 8, 1975, from Clayton , Georgia, Rabun County, May 21, 1916, after she moved to Plains to teach school, and they had Henry Earl, born May 14, 1918; George Franklin, born December 21, 1919; and Oscar Albert, Jr., born October 22, 1921.

From 1926 to 1939 Frank Timmerman and Oscar Williams, Sr., owned and operated the Timmerman and Williams Warehouse (formerly Timmerman and Wise Warehouse). The warehouse handled seed, fertilizers, cotton, and bricks. The bricks were, presumably, made at the nearby Tan and Brick Yard. Following the death of Mr. Timmerman in 1939, Mrs. Timmerman retained half ownership until 1941, when Mr. Williams became sole owner, and the name was changed to Plains Cotton Warehouse.

Henry Earl Williams (born May 14, 1918 in Plains) married Beatrice Lang Colson (born October 2, 1926 in Savannah, Georgia) on August 23, 1942. They live in Woodbine, Camden County, Georgia. Born to them was Henry Earl Williams, Jr. (born July 1, 1943 in Woodbine, Georgia) and married August 30, 1969 in Athens, Georgia, to Linda Margaret Prince (born June 20, 1947 in Athens, Georgia), and they live in St. Mary's, Georgia. Born to Henry, Jr. and Linda: Allison Prince Williams (born May 24, 1974 in Brunswick, Georgia), Henry Earl Williams, III (born September 3, 1976 in Dhahran, Saudi Arabia), and Robert Samuel Williams (born October 31, 1981 in Dhahran, Saudi Arabia). Their second son, Joel Colson Williams (born August 1, 1948 in Woodbine, Georgia) married July 31, 1971 in Brunswick, Georgia, to Margaret Doris Stuckey (born December 16, 1945 in Brunswick Georgia). They had one child, Leila Caroline Williams (born November 20, 1980 in Atlanta, Georgia), and now live in Woodbine, Georgia.

Oscar Albert, Jr., married Marlys Tripp, Porter, MN, March 27, 1948, and had Peggy Ann, born December 22, 1948; Oscar Albert III, born May 30, 1950; and Larry Tripp, born October 4, 1954.

George Franklin married Virginia Harris, third child of Ernest Willie and Ouida Lucile Murphy Harris. Virginia was born in Marion County, Georgia, on a farm known as the "Rees Place" on November 25, 1923. She graduated from Plains High School in the class of 1941, attended Georgia Southwestern College, Americus, Georgia, and married January 14, 1943, in the Plains Baptist Church.

George Franklin, called "Frank," graduated from Plains High School and the University of Georgia with a BS degree in Agriculture. He served in the US Army during World War II, attaining the rank of captain. He served on the Plains City

Council 1948-1965 and was mayor of Plains from 1965 to 1971. He is President of Williams Warehouse (formerly Plains Cotton Warehouse), an agri-business owned by the family for almost eighty years. Frank and Virginia are active members of Plains Baptist Church, where he has served as deacon for over sixty years. The Williams have three children:

George Franklin Williams, Jr., born November 6, 1943, in Americus, Georgia, and on June 12, 1971, married Janet Ann "Jan" Bailey, born September 29, 1949, in Athens, Georgia. They were married at the Leslie United Methodist Church. Jan is the daughter of the late Edward Norwood Bailey and Betty Hawkes Bailey Todd, Cobb, Georgia. Jan graduated from Leslie High School, Berry College, with a BS in Physical Education, and received a MS degree in elementary education from Georgia Southwestern College. She is employed by the Citizens Bank of Americus. George graduated from Plains High School, attended Abraham Baldwin Agricultural college, Tifton, Georgia, and the University of Georgia and is associated with Williams Warehouse. Their children are Christie Lynn, born April 10, 1978, in Columbus, Georgia, and Jason Frank, born April 17, 1981, in Columbus, Georgia.

John Oscar Williams, born December 7, 1947, in Americus, Georgia, married on June 9, 1972, Cynthia Leigh "Cindy" Legg, born April 14, 1948, in Tampa, Florida. They were married at the First Baptist Church, Albany, Georgia. Cindy is the daughter of James Robert and Lillian Mae Legg, Columbus, Georgia. Cindy graduated from Lyman High School, Longwood, Florida, and Florida State University, Tallahassee, Florida, where she received her BS and MS in Education. She teaches at Southland Academy in Americus, Georgia. John graduated from Plains High School, Abraham Baldwin Agricultural College and the University of Georgia, where he received a BS degree in Agronomy. John is associated with Williams Ware-

house. Their children are Leigh Anne, born January 3, 1978, in Americus, Georgia, and John Oscar "Jay" Jr., born July 11, 1980, in Columbus, Georgia.

Virginia "Ginny" Williams was born May 29, 1951, in Americus, Georgia. She first married December 18, 1971, in the Plains Baptist Church to William Garey Callis, Jr., born August 5, 1947, in Terrell County, Georgia, son of the late William Garey Callis and Doris Mobley Callis. Garey was a dentist in Moultrie, Georgia, and was lost at sea on October 27, 1984. Their children are William Garey "Bill" Callis, III, born December 18, 1975, in Atlanta, Georgia, and Thomas Earl "Tom" Callis, born June 5, 1980, in Moultrie, Georgia. Ginny graduated from Plains High School and Georgia State University, Atlanta, Georgia, where she received a BS degree in early childhood education. She teaches kindergarten at Cunningham Creek Elementary School near Jacksonville, Florida. Ginny's second marriage was March 30, 1990, at the Rock United Methodist Church, Tallahassee, Florida, to Martin Richard "Marty" Leopold, born December 2, 1949, in Cleveland, Ohio, son of the late Richard Charles Leopold and Mrs. Alice Welch of Stow, Ohio. Marty received a BS degree in business from Kent State University and is employed by General Motors Corporation. He has a son, Bryan, born March 22, 1976, who lives in Stow, Ohio.

—Submitted by Cindy Legg Williams, wife of John Oscar Williams

David Wise and Joel Wise Families

The Wises of Plains descended from two brothers, David Wise and Joel Wise, who moved to Plains from South Carolina in 1869. They were looking for a fresh start after the Civil War brought much destruction to their native Newberry County, South Carolina. The two brothers followed other

South Carolina families who had relocated to the Plains area. They came to Plains with their wives, grown children and their children's spouses. David had 14 family members with him. Joel brought his wife and children. They settled about 5 miles west of Plains in the edge of Webster County near the village Bottsford.

Joel Wise and his second wife, Mary Jane Moore, had two sons and three daughters. Their two sons were Samuel and Burr Thaddeous. Samuel, known as Professor Sam, operated a school for boys near Plains. He died at age 36. The other son, Burr Thaddeous, was a medical doctor who had three sons, all graduates of Tulane Medical School in New Orleans. The sons were Dr. Thad, Dr. Sam, and Dr. Bowman. The four Wises built the Wise Sanitarium in Plains and later the Wise Clinic in Americus. They enjoyed good medical reputations and had patients come to them from throughout the state. Over the years this branch of the Wise family has continued to produce members of medical profession.

David's family was farmers. He and his wife, Rosannah Elizabeth Ethridge, had four daughters and seven sons. Their daughters were Julia, Nancy, Clara and Frances. Their sons were William (died in the Civil War), George Calhoun, Tyre (died in the Civil War), Joseph Patrick, Jeremiah Pickens (settled in Haleysville, Alabama), Philip and David Luther. Most of the eleven children moved to Plains, married and had children. The Wises from these first generations are buried at either St. Mark's Lutheran Church, Bottsford or Lebenon Cemetery.

When the railroad was built, the town of Bottsford lost out to nearby Plains. Today the only remaining building from Bottsford is St. Mark's Lutheran Church, which the Wises helped found and build. This church is a replica of the St. Mark's Lutheran Church near Pomaria, South Carolina. When the families moved to Plains they wanted to bring "the church of the Reformation" with them. David was on the original church council. Church members donated lumber and assisted with construction. G. Calhoun helped plane the lumber because he had lost a leg in the war. The original church had two doors with a short wall in the middle. Women and men entered the doors separately and sat on opposite sides of the church. This partition was removed when the church was remodeled in the early 1950's. Also, the church had African-American members until they built churches of their own. The original church records contained two lists of baptisms, one noted by "colored." St. Mark's Bottsford still meets for "homecoming" on the fourth Sunday in July each year. All are welcome.

The full lineage of the Wise is documented in the book, "The Wise and Wyse Families of South Caroline." For our discussion we will follow the lineage of on of David's sons, George Calhoun Wise. G. Calhoun was born in Newberry County, South Caroline. He served in Company B, 14th Infantry in the Civil War. He was wounded at the Battle of the Wilderness and lost a leg. Family tradition says his brothers found him injured on the battlefield and moved him to safety in a cotton house. When the battle receded that night, his brothers came back for him and, with the help of a military doctor but no anesthesia, amputated his leg. G. Calhoun married Adella Ethridge and had a son, Allen. After her death, he met his second wife Frances "Fannie" Coogle of Oglethorpe at a Lutheran Convention in Oglethorpe, Georgia. Fannie Coogle's family had moved to Oglethorpe from the South Carolina Dutch Fork area before 1850. Three stained glass windows in St. Andrew's Lutheran Church in Plains have the names of G. Calhoun and his parents, David and Rosannah Elizabeth.

G. Calhoun and Fannie had eight children. Likely their children were fully German given their ancestors only married within the German Lutheran community in South Carolina. The oldest was William who married Alma Clark. Next, Rosa

Nettie who married Captain J.W. Murray. They had one child, Allie, who is the mother of Rosalynn Smith Carter. John Calhoun married Eola Anderson, Walter married Myrtle Crawford, Hattie Bell married Frank McGill, Melly Mae married Burr Thomas Jennings, George married "Allie" Godwin and Daniel married Corinne.

We will follow the descendent of two of the sons listed above, William and John Calhoun. William married Alma Clark and worked at a store in Plains. He was renowned for knowing the names of every family member of his customers. The children of William and Alma were Annie Bell, Calvin, Ray, Clark, David, Doris, Alma, and Miram. Of these children, David married Irma Linton, and they had two children, Beverly Wise Buchanan and David. Both graduated from Plains High School. Beverly Ann Wise, born November 1, 1942, married Brooks Edward Buchanan, III, born October 23, 1938. They had two sons, Timothy Edward Buchanan, born July 18, 1963, and Kelly Wise Buchanan, born October 7, 1965. Kelly married Jennifer Lynn Glasscock September 27, 1968. They had two sons, Cody Wise Buchanan, born December 22, 1994 and Cory Brooks Buchanan, born February 15, 1999. David Thomas Wise, Jr., born April 30, 1947, married Jane Ann Knowles, born November 19, 1949. They had two sons, Andrew David Wise, born September 26, 1975 and Scott Thomas Wise, born August 12, 1978.

John Calhoun Wise, Sr. married Eola Anderson. They lived 10 miles from Plains near Sumter City. Their children were Elizabeth, John Calhoun, Jr. (J.C.), Loris, Margaret, allie Mae, Hilda and Thomas. All graduated from Plains High School. Five of the children graduated from the University of Georgia and the youngest, Thomas, from Auburn. Grandchildren of John, Sr. and Eola are a) Roy and Frank, sons of J.C. and Virginia Easterlin, b) Hardie Jo, Woody and Elaine, children of Hardy Cornwell and Allie Mae, c) LaVeverne, John, Rhoda and David, children of LeRoy Walker and Loris, d)

Craig and Beth, children of Thomas and Oreta Brazier.

—*Submitted by Roy Wise*

Phillip Joseph Wise, Sr. (P.J.)

The first records of the Wise family place them in Germany. The first to arrive in the U.S. was Ernst Friedrich Weiss, who docked in Charleston aboard the ship Snow Rowand on October 2, 1752. The family first settled in the Dutch Fork Territory of South Carolina, on a 300 acres land grant by King George II of England, about 1870.

David Wise, who was born in 1809 and his wife Rosa Elizabeth Etheridge moved with eleven other families to the area around Plains. Their children were Nancy, Julia Elizabeth, Fanny Susanna, Clara Camilla, Tyre, William, Phillip Johnson, Joseph Patrick, George Calhoun, Daivd Luther, and Jeremiah, the only one of them who didn't move to Plains.

Phillip Johnson Wise (1861-1907) married Lou Etta Chappell (1866-1953). Their children were Luther Alonzo who married May Shirley, Elma Clair who married William Stovall, Phillip Chappell who married Vivian McMichael, Georgia Frances who married Fred Stasts, Arnold Alexander who married Pellie Doyal, and after her death, married Elizabeth Camp, and Leland Etheridge who married Marie Ellis.

Luther Alonzo Wise (1888-1940) was born in Plains (probably Magnolia Springs). He married Ella May Shirley (1896-1991) on January 2, 1916. The following children were born to Luther Alonzo Wise and May Shirley Wise. Phillip Joseph (P.J.), Sarah Jeanette, Luther Alonzo (Morgan), Edna Mae, and twins William Dan and Betty Ann. All graduated from Plains High School.

Phillip Joseph (P.J.) was born at Magnolia Springs April 10, 1917. He married Mary George Wynn on September 5, 1942. She was born on December 1, 1920 in Walnut Grove, Alabama. Her parents were Frank Newton Wynn and Jessie Dalton Wynn.

Three children were born to P.J. and Mary Wise-Marilyn, Phillip Joseph, Jr., and Gwendolyn.

Marilyn was born August 17, 1946. She married Dr. Paul V. Phibbs (born July 24, 1942) on August 11, 1968. Their children are Heather (born October 1, 1972) and Elizabeth (June 25, 1974).

Phillip Joseph (Phil) was born March 12, 1951. He was the Appointment Secretary at The White House for President Jimmy Carter from 1977-1981. He married Allison Rainey (born November 3, 1964) on April 23, 1994.

Gwen was born on August 26, 1954.

All three children were born in Plains and all graduated from Plains High School.

P.J. served in the U.S. Navy Seabees, stationed in South Pacific during WWII.

—Submitted by Mary Wise

The Wises from Germany to Georgia

The Wises lived in the region of Baden in Germany before immigrating to South Carolina in 1752 and later to Plains in 1869. The family can be traced to Johann Georg Weiss, born in 1715, who married Anna Maria. Their son, Ernst Friedrick Weiss, was the immigrant ancestor. He married Maria Barbara Ruff on December 2, 1732 in the Evangelical (Lutheran) Church of Nottingen, Baden, Germany. Like other American immigrants, they left Germany because of religious persecution, unbearable taxes and constant wars. An agent of the British government spread the word that all German citizens of the Protestant faith were welcome in America. Each family member would be given 50 acres of land, farm tools and transportation to their land once they arrived in America. On March 21, 1752, Ernest Frederick applied for a "manumission" which is a document freeing a person from

ties in Germany. The church records at Nottingen have "gone to the new land" inserted in the margin beside the names of Frederick and Maria Barbara and their children. The two older boys, Johann Martin and Jacob, likely came to America before their parents. The third child, Maria Barbara, died as a child in Germany. The next four were aged 11 to 3 when they came to America with their parents. They were Marie Salome, Johann Georg, Johann Phillip and Ernest Frederich II.

Travel from Germany to America took six months and was filled with peril and inflated prices at each step of the way. They arrived in Charleston on October 3, 1752. Ernest Frederick and his family were given 300 acres of land, provisions for one year and transportation via wagon to the frontier. The grant of land to Ernest Frederick from King George II of England was certified on September 4, 1753. The land given to the Germans served as a buffer between the British in South Carolina and the Cherokee Indians. The Weiss's land grant was located between the Broad and Saluda Rivers west of Columbia, South Carolina. The Wises lived in this area for over 100 years before David and Joel Wise moved to Plains in 1869.

Johann Georg Weiss (1742-1821), son of Ernest Frederick, is the direct ancestor of the Plains Wises. He was 10 years old when he arrived in Charleston. He married Anna Barbara Buckle. Georg was 33 years old when the Revolutionary War began. Oral family tradition says Georg participated in the Revolutionary War in the Battle of King's Mountain in South Carolina. Georg was a founder of Bethel Lutheran Church. He and Anna Barbara had thirteen children. This was the first generation born in America. Three of their sons, George, John (ancestor of Plains Wises) and Frederick, married three Kelly sisters. The three sisters were German as their father's name was "Kolle," not "Kelly." When Anna Barbara died at age 88, she had 64 grandchildren and 100 great grandchildren with a total posterity of 182 souls.

John Wise (1779-1860), the second son of Georg and Anna Barbara Weiss, is the ancestor of the Plains Wises. His life is well documented. John and his brothers helped found St. Michael's Lutheran Church as an English speaking church. John married Anna Mary M. Kelly. John and Anna Mary had six boys and six girls, all born in the Lexington District, South Carolina. Anna Mary died in 1830 and is buried in the Wise Cemetery on John's plantation. This cemetery is on Newberry Shores Road in Newberry County on a hill just above the waters of Lake Murray. Later John remarried and moved. He and his second wife were the principal founders of St. Mark's Lutheran Church near Pomaria, South Carolina where he is buried. This is the mother church of St. Mark's, Bottsford.

Two sons of John and Anna Mary were David and Joel. They moved to Plains in 1868. This brings us back full circle to the beginning of our story of the Wise family of Plains. Founders of five Lutheran churches, the many descendants of David and Joel now live throughout Georgia and other parts of the United States.

—Submitted by Roy Wise

The Family of Joseph Patrick Wise

Joseph Patrick Wise was the first owner of the home located on North Bond Street, where Mr. and Mrs. Luther A. (Morgan) Wise now live. Joseph Patrick Wise was born December 26, 1847. He married Anna Josephine Derrick. She was born on March 2, 1852 and died November 6, 1918. Joseph died January 4, 1926. Joseph and Anna raised 9 children. *I. Tyre Patrick Wise* born on January 5, 1874 died December 8, 1960; *II. Samuel D. Wise* born October 23, 1869 died June 30, 1891; *III. Frances Wise* born 1871 died 1954; *IV. Mary Irene Wise* born October 10, 1876 died 1954; *V. Florence*

Dallas Wise born January 11, 1880 died November 5, 1956; *VI. Annie Wise* born 1882 died 1948; *VII. Minnie Clara Wise* born October 17, 1884 died October 17, 1956; *VIII. Luther Wise* born September 8, 1988 died October 21, 1922; *IX. Carrie Wise* born 1893 died January 29, 1948

Tyre Patrick Wise married John Armenia Livingston born September 14, 1875 died November 3, 1965. Tyre and Armenia raised 6 children: I. Samuel Joseph Wise born 1897 died 1948; II. Catherine Mae Wise born 1899 died December 16, 1982; **III. Tyre Phillip Wise** born October 24, 1901 died September 17, 1969; IV. John Clifford Wise born 1903 died 1957; V. Maude Vernon Wise born 1905 died 1976; VI. Frances Josephine Wise born 1907 died 1976

III. Tyre Philip Wise, the only one who never moved away from Plains, married Lottie Thomas Meadows in 1923. There children are:

A) Lottie Vivion Wise born March 13, 1924

B) Armenia Eloise Wise born April 28, 1925 died February 26, 1926

C) Annie Byrdie Wise born February 9, 1927

D) Luther Elmore Wise born April 19, 1930 died May 9, 1997

E) Tulula Phillip Wise born May 20, 1933

F) Joseph Meadows Wise born December 12, 1935

All of Tyre Phillip and Lottie M. Wise's children and most of their grand children graduated from Plains High School.

A) Lottie Vivian Wise born March 13, 1924 married Donald Tanner January 7, 1943 Donald born April 11, 1917. Children:

1) Donna Victoria Tanner born July 19, 1944 married James Channelle Webb. Children:

a) Helena Marcia Webb born September 21, 1964 married Terry Marshall December 31, 1988.

Children: 1a) Madisyn Ranea Marshall born February 11, 1999

b) Veronica Vivian Webb born March 4, 1966 married Robert Sylvester: Children: 1a) Channelle Lee Sylvester born May 2, 1983

c) Patricia Lara Webb born October 11, 1970 married Michael Mauldin. Children: 1a) Michael Alan Mauldin born February 4, 1990

2) <u>John Phillip Tanner</u> born September 8, 1946 married Patricia Louise Darrah. Children:

a) Diane Michelle Tanner born October 26, 1968 married Kelly Moles March 10, 1992. Children: 1a) Ashton Patton Moles born August 26, 1993

b) Donald Phillip Tanner born April 9, 1973

c) Stephen Darrah Tanner born May 5, 1976 married Catherine Thrasher January 21, 1995. Children: 1a) Harold Darrah Tanner born September 3, 1997

3) <u>Louise Carolyn Tanner</u> born July 23, 1948 married Luther Alvin Pilcher. Children:

a) Zonda Victoria Pilcher born Aug. 8, 1967, married Daniel Petty October 28, 2000

b) Luther Alvin Pilcher, Jr. born March 24, 1971 married Cassandra Ann Morgan October 29, 1994. Children: 1a) Donald Shaw Pilcher born December 4, 1997; 1b)William Seth Pilcher born February 15, 2002

B) Armenia Eloise Wise born April 28, 1925 died February 26, 1926

C) Annie Burdie Wise born February 9, 1927 married 1st John Kenneth Bradley 2nd Harry Lee Gilbreath

1) <u>Priscilla Ann B. Gilbreath</u> born April 10, 1947 married Frank Boyette Bivins on December 11, 1965, who was born on August 10, 1939

a) Frank Tyre Bivins, born January 26, 1970 married 1st Angie Sutton born October 20, 1972 2nd Richelle Dawn Irwin born January 23, 1971.

Children: 1a) Justin Cody Bivins born September 30, 1990; 1b) Zachary Logan Bivins born July 24, 1996; 1c) Grace Sharon Makenzie Bivins born March 11, 2002

b) Donna Jacquelyn Bivins born August 24, 1973 married Shane Joel Adkinson. Children: 1a) Kristen Leigh Adkinson born December 18, 1992; 1b) Amber Kaitlyn Adkinson born May 26, 1995

c) Elizabeth Ann Bivins born April 20, 1977 married Chad Thomas Masters born December 22, 1976. Children: 1a) Joshua Ryan Masters born November 21, 1998; 1b Chamler Blake Masters born July 2, 2000

2) <u>Georgia Lee Gilbreath</u> born September 5, 1954 married David E. Ronningon born September 12, 1947

a) Kelly Ann Ronningon born July 13, 1981

b) Scott Nicholi Ronningon born May 29, 1984

D) Luther Elmore Wise born April 19, 1930 died May 9, 1997 married Martha Holcombe born December 9, 1936

1) <u>Debra Wise Pena</u> born November 23, 1954

a) Lucas Jared Pena born July 21, 1983

b) Thomas Wise Pena born May 28, 1986

2) <u>Sherry Wise</u> born December 28, 1959 married Billy Ratliff born April 1, 1943

a) William Phillip Wise born September 10, 1975

b) Pierce Usry born December 9, 1988

c) Jesse Luther Ratliff born June 24, 1995

3) <u>Sonya Wise</u> born January 6, 1965 married Joseph Earl Recker II born May 13, 1964

a) Joseph Earl Recker III born July 9, 1987

b) Sarah Katherine Recker born January 24, 1990

c) Jessica Martha Recker born January 24, 1991

E) Tulula Phillip Wise born May 20, 1933 married July 21, 1950 Julian Fletcher Cosby born November 12, 1926. Julian died July 6, 1972.

1) Julian Fletcher Cosby Jr. born May 20, 1951 married June 11, 1972 Brenda Kay Chitwood born March 1, 1954

a) Aaron Fletcher Cosby born September 17, 1975 married March 25, 1995 Jennie Goodin born September 26, 1976. Children: 1a) Bryce Fletcher Cosby born November 3, 1996; 1b) Megan Kiley Cosby born January 23, 1998

b) Wendy Diane Cosby born May 1, 1977 married September 11, 1999 David Brandon Mills born March 8, 1975. Children: 1a) David Chandler Mills born July 11, 2002

2) Phyllis Ann Cosby born April 29, 1957 married December 13, 1975 Michael Glenn Harvin born February 14, 1955

a) Michael Glenn Harvin Jr. born October 35, 1977 married June 3, 1998 Jennifer Leigh King born January 29, 1979. Children: 1a) Michael Glenn Harvin, III born May 24, 1999

b) Jillian Kay Harvin born April 15, 1985

3) Betsy Lou Cosby born March 2, 1967 married December 13, 1975 Norman Lee Reeves born April 24, 1951

F) Joseph Meadows Wise born December 12, 1935 married December 12, 1957 Betty Gladys Snider born April 8, 1931

1) Betty Jo Wise born October 10, 1961 married August 18, 1984 (1) James Buck Woods Jr. born March 3, 1952 died June 9, 1999. Children: a) Joseph Byron Woods (son of James Buck Woods by 1st marriage) born September 24, 1976; b) James Matthew Woods born April 5, 1987; c) Christin Nicole Woods born February 18, 1989 2nd married December 29, 2001 Terry Michael Songer born June 15, 1958. Step-children: a) Jacob Grant Songer born January 25, 1991; b) Zachery Layton Songer born August 9, 1993; c) Mary Micah Songer born December 5, 1995

2) Lottie Foy Wise born December 27, 1963 married August 2, 1986 Donnie Ray Lamb Sr. born January 3, 1951. Children: a) Angela Foy Lamb born January 24, 1988; b) Donnie Ray Lamb Jr. born October 20, 1990

3) Mary Carleen Wise born August 23, 1968

—*Submitted by Ann Gilbreath*

The Luther Alonzo Wise, Jr. Family

The Wise ancestry is traced back to the ancestor, Johann Georg Weiss and his wife Anna Maria who resided in Obermutschelbach, Germany. Their son Ernst Friedrich became the first immigrant ancestor to the Wises' in America when he and his wife, Maria Barbara Ruff Weiss, and four of their children sailed from Rottedam, Holland on the ship, *Snow Rowland*. They arrived in Charleston, South Carolina on October 2, 1752. The family of Ernst Friedrich Weiss was granted 300 acres of land in the wilderness north of where Columbia, South Carolina now stands. Their partial of land was located on the Saluda River near the location where the Lake Murray dam was later built. It was determined much later that King George was using these German settlers as buffers between the English settlements and the Indians.

Johann Georg Weiss (1742-1821) son of Ernst Friedrich and Maria Barbara Weiss is considered the first generation of Americans in this family as he arrived in America at young age of ten. Johann Georg married Anna Barbara Buckle (1749-1837) in 1768. They were the parents of thirteen children. Their second son, John Wise (1779-1860) married Anna Mary Kelly (1779-1830) and had twelve children of which David Wise (1809-1882) was the fifth. David, his wife Rosannah Elizabeth Etheridge (1821-1900), with their children and David's younger brother Joel (1820-1895) moved to Sumter County, Georgia after the Civil War as times were hard in South Carolina. Joel married Melissa Schumpert and later Mary Jane Moore when his first wife died. From these two brothers, David and

Joel, came all of the Wise descendents in Plains, Georgia.

David and Rosannah had eleven children. They were Francis "Fanny", Julia, William, George Calhoun, Tyre, Joseph Patrick, Jeremiah Pickens, Nancy, Clara, Phillip Johnson, and Luther David.

Phillip Johnson Wise (1861-1907) married Lou Chappell (1866-1953) and were the parents of Luther Alonzo (1888-1940), Leland (1905-?), Elmer (1891-?), Phillip (1894-?), Georgia Francis (1899-) and Arnold (1903-?). Their son Luther Alonzo Wise Sr. married Ella May Shirley (1896-1991) on January 2, 1915. This was not long after May had arrived from Townville, South Carolina with her brothers and sisters and their father, Joseph Woodward Shirley (1859-1956) on a horse drawn wagon. May's mother, Sarah Jeanette Giles Shirley (1873-1910) had died on October 11, 1910 in South Carolina prior to their journey to Georgia.

The children of Lon and May Wise are Phillip Johnson (PJ) (1917-), Sarah Jeanette (1919-), Luther Jr. (1922-), Edna Mae (1925-), and twins Betty Ann and William Dan (1929-). PJ married Mary George Wynn (1920-) and their children are Marilyn (1946-), Phillip Jr. (1951-) and Gwendolyn (1954-). Sarah married Blake Harris and their children are Patsy and Jeanette. Luther Jr. married Ann Elizabeth Slocumb (1927-) and children are Lonnie Morgan (1950-), Shirley Ann Knapp (1952-) and Amy Elizabeth (1957-). Edna Mae married Reese Hendricks and their child is Jimmy. Betty married Luther L. Albritton and their children are Luther Jr.(1951-) and Dale (1953-). William married Linah Hutto and their child is Tommy.

Luther known locally as 'Morgan', married Ann from Webster County, Georgia on December 12, 1948. They lived in Americus for a few years before returning to Plains where they have called home since the early 1950's. All of their children graduated from Plains High School, as did their father and all of his brothers and sisters. Morgan retired from the Marine Corps Supply Base in 1986.

Lonnie married Annette Lockerman (1954-) from Montezuma, Georgia and they have one child, Rebecca Elizabeth Wise (1986-). They now reside in Plains after living in several locations around the State of Georgia. Shirley Ann first married James Ellis Blanton II (1949-) and they had two sons, James Ellis (Jamie) Blanton III (1970-1983) and Joseph Shawn Blanton (1975-). Next she married Marc Knapp (1950-) who had a son, Christopher (1988-), from a previous marriage. The Knapp's reside in Land O'Lakes, Florida. Amy Elizabeth (1957-) the third child of Luther and Ann is not married and lives in the home her dad lived in from the age of eleven until he entered the U.S. Army Air Force.

Morgan served his country with distinction like so many of his ancestors before him. He was an aerial gunner on a B-17 bomber crew with the 100th Bomb Group of the Eighth Air Force in Europe during World War II. His son, Lonnie, also served his country as a Non Commissioned Officer in the US Army Infantry during the Vietnam War with the Seventh Cavalry, 1st Cavalry Division (Airmobile). Both were decorated for their actions in combat.

—*Submitted by Lonnie Wise*

Samuel and Camilla Wise Family

Camilla is my (Horace Walton Seymour, Jr.) grandmother and lived in the same household with me, Fleeta Leola (her daughter and my grandmother), my father, Horace, Sr., and mother, Fleeta Kathryn Smith (Fleeta's only child),in Desoto, Georgia. From about 1943 until her death. She came to live with us after her sister, Laura Rachel Addy Wise, died in 1943. Camilla had lived with Laura for some years after she sold her home at Magnolia Springs. She told me of many of her experiences, probably the most important for these purposes is of the family's resettlement south of the present village of Plains. To wit: [portions come directly form her writings and those of her Sister Laura Rachel Addy Wise the rest from my memory of her teachings.]

Camilla was born in 1857 in Lexington County South Carolina on Big Hollow Creek on the homestead of her father George Addy and her mother Fanny Jennings Addy, a German Lutheran family.

At the end of the Civil War, Sherman and his army were approaching from the south after having burned their way across Georgia to Savannah (10/16-12/22 1864), then turned North and captured Charleston, South Carolina early in 1865. Of course the family was very much aware of his actions and were in great fear of his arrival. Camilla was 8 years old at the time but remembered the events vividly for the rest of her life.

Her father, George Addy, to save his family and property from destruction, built a cabin in the swamp behind their fine home. He used a different way each time he went to build and stock the cabin so that he would not leave a trail for Sherman's soldiers to follow.

When he learned of the approach of the union army he took his family and their most valuable possessions and lived in the cabin until the vengeance-seeking hoard had gone. When they returned to where their home had stood there was nothing but the ashes of the house, smokehouse, and barn but the slave houses were intact. The army had carried off the slaves who had remained faithful until the end and had not told of the family cabin.

The family set up housekeeping in the larger of the slave cabins and tried to decide what to do next. They managed to round up some cattle and horses that had escaped the union army and they had some food that they had buried but they had no money except confederate which was worthless. Some of the faithful slaves returned and were an additional burden on the family's limited resources.

Camilla remembered that winter to be the worst of her long life. Her father needed to cure meat and

preserve vegetables for the winter but they had no salt nor could any be bought for the economy in the ravaged south had ceased to exist.

They were sitting by the open fire in the old slave cabin one cold October morning. Her mother was busily making a fire screen out of $100 confederate notes (their current best use). Her father suddenly jumped up and exclaimed "salt does not burn". They thought that his mind had snapped under the strain. When he grabbed the washtub and ran to the ashes of the smokehouse yelling "Bring me water." He shoveled the ashes into the tub and poured in 2 buckets of water. Nearby he built a fire. The ashes floated to the top and were removed. The murky water was poured through several thicknesses of cloth and then boiled away over the fire in their big iron wash pot. When the water boiled away, in the bottom of the pot was salt. Now they could preserve food for the coming winter.

In the spring the men gathered. The land they owned here in South Carolina was rocky and heavy with clay. They did not see how they could farm it without slaves They had no concept of hiring labor and if they had they had no money to do so. One of the group, probably John Jennings, had fought with Andrew Jackson in the Indian wars in south west Georgia, Alabama and Florida. He remembered land that was light and sandy in south west Georgia. There was already a Lutheran settlement in Macon County about 30 miles north of the area in question and many residents were from South Carolina and personally known to the men.

After verifying the existence and availability of the land several families loaded their possessions into wagons and started out on the 300 mile trip. Among the families that moved were George Addy, John Jennings, Philip Jennings, and Joel Wise.

They arrived in Webster/Sumter County, Georgia in summer of 1866 and, since there was no Lutheran church within a day's ride, they put their letters in Bottsford Methodist Church until a proper

Lutheran church could be built. More friends and relatives followed until a large Lutheran colony was located in the southwest corner of Sumter and the adjoining parts of Webster and Terrell counties. Among the first settlers were: Lott, William, John and Philip Jennings; David and Joel Wise; George and Joe Hiller; George Addy; and D. S. Derrick and all their families.

The Methodist congregation was very kind and understanding and allowed them to hold Lutheran services in the Methodist church. They obtained services of Rev. John Phillips Margart of Eufaula, Alabama as pastor. The congregation soon elected George Addy as building advisor and bought land for a new church. They bought lumber in Dawson and hauled it to Bottsford. Soon the dear old mother church was completed, for the entire congregation assisted in its construction, each doing what he or she could do best.

The church now stands as a monument to their untiring energy and devotion, while they sleep in the peaceful cemetery to await the resurrection morning.

In 1877 Rev. Margart resigned and Rev. J. S. Elmore became pastor and served for 14 years [until 1891]. Rev. H. E. H. Sloop, Dr. Tyler, Rev. Nease, and Rev. W. H. Hiller served as pastor in that order. Then came our dear brother Phillips who served for 17 years [1902 to 1919], building the churches in Plains and in Oglethorpe. Brother Wingard served from May 1919 to 1923, then came Dr. Bowers, Rev. Lefstead, and other young ministers from the seminary. Now we have pastor Seckinger who has been here for almost 4 years. The band of Lutherans were loyal to the faith of their fathers. Mrs. Kate Hiller, 84 years is still living and is one of the charter members and truly a Saint in Israel. So many of our young members have moved to other states and lands far distant, but we hope to meet them on another shore.

[Note: as I write this in 1989 "mother church" at Bottsford, Sumter County, Georgia. No longer has regular services nor has it for many years. I believe the foregoing references to Mrs. Hiller and Pastor Seckinger to be from the early 1940s. The church and grave yard is being kept up by the surrounding community and is in reasonably good condition.]

Camilla met and fell in love with Samuel Pickins Wise at an early age. He returned her affection but would not propose marriage until he went to and finished college. [I have many letters written by the two lovers during this period.] After Sammy graduated from Mercer University in Macon, Georgia they married (1877). She was then 20 and he was 26. He bought land and a house north of Plains. Plains (originally called Plains of Dura) was established several miles north of Bottsford to be on the new railroad and became the nearest town.

Their new home was named Magnolia Springs after the pure, cold, mineral spring that erupted from the ground behind the house. Here they established their home and here also Sammy set up a boys preparatory boarding school where he prepared boys for college. Camilla was a tiny woman small boned and less than 5 feet tall and it was very difficult for her to have children. However, she presented him with two fine healthy children. Then disaster struck – Sammy died after just 4 years of marriage.

Camilla was prostrate with grief. She "took to the bed and turned her face to the wall for 2 years, asking God to take her too." That was not to be and her loving family and deep abiding faith finally pulled her through.

She still had the house and she started taking in boarders to make enough money to raise her children. Her belief in God and the teaching "God will provide" came true. The waters of the spring became rumored to have mystical healing powers and there was no lack of business for the boarding house. The children grew up and Fleeta, her daughter and eldest child, became determined to follow in the footsteps of her father as a teacher.

When Fleeta graduated from Washington Seminary she returned to Plains and set up a boarding school much like Sammy's. Here she taught privately for several years and later was paid by Sumter County and at the end, making as much as $25 per month.

Meanwhile across the county in DeSoto lived a fellow Lutheran, Dr. William Jackson Smith who was having problems.

Dr. Smith had grown up in the Macon County Lutheran settlement. His father, James William Smith and mother Mary Catherine Kleckley Smith owned a large farm north of Andersonville, Georgia in Macon County and were descended from German Lutherans who originally settled in the same area of South Carolina as had Camilla's family.

Dr. Smith was destined, everyone thought, to be a farmer like his father. One hot summer day he was plowing the field close to the house using a two horse hitch. As the heat waves rose from the field he looked at the house shimmering in the sun. The longer he plowed the longer the rows seemed to become. He stopped the horses, dropped the reigns and walked to the house. Upon entering he found his father and mother in the kitchen. He said to his father, "Life is too short to spend looking at a field through a mule's ears. I want to go to collage and become a Medical Doctor. Will you send me?" The answer was "yes."

So off he went to the Academy of Medicine of Kentucky in Louisville. Upon graduation he asked "what is the most unhealthy place in Georgia?" The answer was DeSoto. DeSoto had long been plagued with malaria and yellow fever. No one knew why then, but it was because of the extensive swamps to the south and southeast, both diseases being carried by mosquitoes.

He first moved to Leslie, a more civilized town, one mile west of DeSoto and set up his practice. DeSoto, at that time, was known for its 14 saloons and almost daily street shoot-outs. Its repu-

tation rivaled the worst towns of the west. All this with a population that never topped 500. In 1899 Dr. Smith bought a home in DeSoto and moved his family there. Although there were as many as seven doctors in DeSoto at one time there was enough sick and injured to provide all with patients. Dr. Smith became nationally known for his innovative treatment of malaria and yellow fever.

Dr. Smith's first wife, Emma Adams Smith died leaving him without a mother for his three young children. His wife's sister, "Sissy," was living with them before his wife's death and, from accounts, expected him to marry her, but he was not of a mind to do so.

Because he was from the Lutheran settlement in Macon County, Georgia, he was familiar with the residents of the Bottsford Community and had probably already met Fleeta Wise.

Dr. Smith was instantly attracted to the tall (5'10") school teacher. He called on her twice and then asked her to marry him "for the sake of my poor motherless children" [I have the letter of proposal]. Camilla refused for her daughter giving as her reason that she did not want Fleeta to have to go through childbirth.

Dr. Smith appealed to another physician, Dr. Burr Thomas Wise, Sammy's brother, a very respected and close friend of Camilla's. Burr told her that she should not attempt to run her daughter's life, and that since she was almost 30 and considered by most an "old maid" this might be her last chance for a husband. Camilla relented and Fleeta and Dr. Smith were married. This just began other complications.

Sissy must have been irate. Dr. Smith asked Fleeta to accept the continued presence of Sissy and she readily agreed to do so. Sissy, however, had no such intentions. She informed Fleeta that it was her (Sissy's) house and that she had no better than a grudging welcome.

Fleeta was a statuesque woman about 5 feet 10 inches and at that height 2 inches taller than Dr.

Smith. She had no trouble having Fleeta Kathryn Smith (1908), my mother. They all lived there in DeSoto with Dr. Smith practicing medicine and Sissy caring for the three older children, Henry, William, and Ruth, pointedly ignoring Fleeta and Kathryn. Kathryn grew up very repressed from constantly being shushed for fear of disturbing Sissy and the other children.

This was the era of beginning understanding of germs and Dr. Smith would remark often on recent germ theories instilling the fear of germs in Kathryn albeit unintentionally. Dr. Smith had a very successful practice and invested his money well – in land. He said to his children, "there is only two safe investments that can not be taken from you – education and land". He advised his children to acquire as much as they could of each. They listened to him.

Henry became a physician like his father but caught a strep infection from a patient and died at an early age.

William became a lawyer and ran for the office of city judge. His campaign did not go well until Fleeta made some calls on former students and asked for their support. He was elected and served until he retired well up in years. He kept his land and his wife, Julia, still has enough income to live comfortably [1989].

Emma Ruth graduated from college and married Emmett Ferguson, Sr. They lived all their lives in DeSoto. He inherited a general store and they kept and added to their share of Dr. Smith's land. Mr. Emmett being up in years was diagnosed with incurable cancer and was thus certain that he would not live much longer. He therefore proceeded to deed all his property to Ruth, who was in good health, to avoid probate and taxes. She proceeded to nurse him for months providing all the love and comfort a good wife and friend should to the terminally ill. Then about two weeks before Emmett died Ruth suffered a massive heart attack and died. Thus the property passed through both estates before

reaching his son Dr. Emmett Ferguson, Jr. and his daughter Frances "Spooks" Ferguson Stuart. I do not know how much of Dr. Smith's property survived in tact but I would wager some did.

My mother Fleeta Kathryn being the youngest lived at home with her mother and father.

As I have noted Kathryn had a mixed childhood. On the one hand was Sissy who rejected Kathryn and her mother. On the other was a father that adored and spoiled her. She rebelled early against her father. Sneaking her brother's pants to go riding. No proper girl wore pants in 1925. She would hide under the lap robes in the back of Dr. Smith's buggy to be taken on house calls. This continued and became more pronounced after Dr. Smith bought his first automobile. In the early days of cars the brakes were not very reliable. After Dr. Smith drove his car through the back wall of the garage several times he had an oak beam cut and placed across the back wall. This beam was about 2 feet square and 30 feet long. Needless to say nobody crashed through the back wall of that garage again.

Dr. Smith had a small group of friends who met regularly to debate the news. They were Dr. W.J. Smith, L.L. Wiggins, lld., Cobb Summerford, Alex Duncan, Frank Ferguson, E.A. Luke, A.S. Johnson, and others. They called themselves "The Guardians of Our Country Committee" and this was their drill.

Each morning about eight-thirty the train arrived from Savannah having traveled overnight. Its arrival was greeted with much anticipation for it carried fresh seafood and more importantly newspapers. I do not know which excited Dr. Smith more the fresh mullet or the newspapers for he loved his mullet for breakfast. I suspect the newspapers would win out in a vote.

The men would all meet at the depot each morning, get their newspapers and mullet and go home for breakfast and the news. After they absorbed and interpreted the news they would meet on the benches outside the downtown stores and debate world affairs. There were some really hot debates and most found Dr. Smith on the winning side. One that he lost has been passed down to me.

Prior to our entrance into World War I, Dr. Smith, being of German ancestry, was convinced of the rightness of the German cause. He had to eat a considerable amount of crow when we declared war on Germany.

One day as the men were sitting on the benches in downtown DeSoto Kathryn came driving up in Dr. Smith's car. She stopped in front of her uncle-in-law Emmett Ferguson's general store and had the car filled up with gas, charged it to her father and drove away. Dr. Smith then launched into a tirade to all those assembled on how she spent too much money and drove the car too much. The men quietly listened and when Dr. Smith finished Mr. Duncan said, "If she were my daughter I would take the car away from her." Dr. Smith turned on him with a vengeance saying "Alex Duncan I'll raise my daughter the way I want to," all the while shaking the middle finger of his right hand at Duncan, "and don't you try to tell me how."

Kathryn continued to rebel when she was sent to college. Every few weeks she would show up at home and Dr. Smith would put her in the car and take her back to school. She eventually graduated from Agnes Scott and Wesleyan Colleges and married (1932) my father Horace Walton Seymour, Sr. Who attended Howard University but did not graduate, having only one quarter remaining when depression finances forced him to quit.

Dr. Smith died in 1930. I (Horace W. Seymour, Jr.) was born in 1935 and Camilla moved in about 1942 or 43. They lived with Fleeta, called by everyone "Mrs. Smith", and Camilla, called "Mrs. Wise" or "Aunt Milla", in Dr. Smith's big house in DeSoto. My father, "Seymour" as he was called, managed the estates inherited by Mrs. Smith and Kathryn.

—*Submitted by Horace Seymour, Jr.*

Walter Wise Family

Walter James Wise was born November 25, 1890, son of George Calhoun Wise and Fannie Coogle Wise. Walter married Myrtle Ruth Crawford in 1912. Myrtle was born August 1, 1893 and died December 30, 1978. His grandfather was David Wise, the first Wise to settle in Plains, Georgia. Walter died March 9, 1964. The children of Walter and Myrtle were James Harrison, Ida Ruth, Dorothy Blanche, Rosa Kathryn, Mildred Lucille, Charles Crawford, William Edward, Carlton Hiller and Harold Joe. James was born June 20, 1913 and died January 29, 1983. Dorothy was born September 2, 1916 and married Buehler. Kathryn was born March 19, 1918 and married Alton Murrah. She died July 2, 1990. Mildred was born January 14, 1920. Charles Crawford was born May 14, 1922. He married Carrie Hampton and they had the following children: Jerry, Brenda, Cheryl and Helen. Crawford died December 7, 1996. William was born June 24, 1924 and died April 13, 1992. Carlton was born in 1925 and Harold was born in 1929. Harold had the following children: Harold Jr., Mike and Jane Ellen. He died in 1964. For additional information on the Wise family see "The Wises from Germany to Georgia".

—*Submitted by Mildred Wise*

Leonard Wright, Sr. Family

Leonard Wright, Sr. and Mary Elizabeth Wakefield were united in marriage on February 19, 1950. To this union five children were born.

Mary Elizabeth Wakefield Wright Minion was born July 23, 1930 the seventh child and youngest daughter of Rev. Theodore Roosevelt Wakefield, Sr. and Arena Raven Wakefield in Plains, Georgia. She enjoyed the many things that the children her age enjoyed. When old enough she worked on the farm for several years.

She attended elementary school at the Archery School, the Plains Rosenwald and her high school years took her to Staley High School. She went as far as the eleventh grade and became ill the school year of 1947-48. At that time the eleventh grade was the last grade. Mary did not return to school after recovering from her illness, therefore did not march with her graduating class. Her desire for learning, though halted, did not cease.

Mary met and dated Leonard Wright, Sr. for about three years (3) and on February 19, 1950 they were married. This union produced five beautiful children, all of whom were delivered by a midwife. The midwife was Bertha Schley Wakefield, her stepmother. Mary and Leonard reared their five wonderful children on the farm where they picked cotton, shook peanuts and did many farm chores.

Mary's life was and is very involved in a close walk with the Lord. This involvement dates back to her young years at St. Mark A.M.E. Church in the Archery Community where she was actively involved in the Sunday school and Young People's Department. In August of 1959 she joined the Lebanon Baptist Church with her husband and children.

Mary was married to Leonard for thirty-three years. On April 18, 1983 Leonard went to be with the Lord. He was a hard worker and an excellent provider for his family. On August 27, 1992 Mary was married to Robert Minion for three years. On June 18, 1995 the Lord called Rev. Robert Minion home.

This full of life, energetic, blessed and happy lady continues to serve her Lord, her community, mankind as a whole and most dedicated to her family. She is also a walking miracle! Since October of 1995 she is a Breast Cancer survivor (To God we give glory!!!). In 1996 she was trained and became a Hospice Volunteer and is currently in that role. Mary continues to fulfill her quest for learning, loving and serving.

April Dee Wright Wyatt was born October 21, 1950 in Preston (Webster County), Georgia the oldest of the five siblings. Others are Susie Bell, Charlie Will, Bernstine and Leonard, Jr. all of who were born in Webster County on the Carter Farm except Leonard was born in Plains. When April was seven years old the family moved to Plains and she continued her elementary education in a frame structured house school until the Westside Elementary School was built for the black students in the Plains area. April attended Staley Junior High School in Americus, Georgia. Mrs. Annie B. Floyd served as Principal of Westside during the education of all five children.

In 1965 as history would dictate in the life and history of Plains, Georgia the integration of the one and only high school in Plains which was an all white school took place. April was in the first group of blacks to break the walls of segregation in Plains, Georgia. She experienced one good year academically at Plains High School. Due to the relationship, Leonard, Sr., her father, was a sharecropper with the Carters. The Carters experienced racism pressure tactics. She did not complete her high school education at Plains High School but she did graduate from the Sumter County High School in 1968 in Americus, Georgia.

After graduation from high school, April attended Fort Valley State College now Fort Valley State University and earned a degree in Home Economics Education. She began her career with the University of Georgia Cooperative Extension Service as a County Extension Agent in July 1972 and she retired after twenty-seven years of service in 1999. She presently resides in College Park, Georgia with her husband Tommie Lee Wyatt and their son Roderick Toure'. April is a licensed and ordained minister with Christ Discipleship Ministries in Tyrone, Georgia.

Susie Bell Wright Henderson was born September 30, 1952 and educated at Westside Elementary School and graduated from Sumter County

High School in 1970. Susie is the only child that did not attend Plains High School. After graduation from Sumter High she attended South Georgia Technical and Vocational School in Americus, Georgia where she earned a degree in Business Education in 1971.

After graduation she began her work career in the city of Plains working with a group called Southern Rural Action (SRA). This organization built homes for the low-income families within the Plains community. During this time SRA made their own bricks, which were used to build the homes. In 1976 Susie changed careers and began working with the Department of Family and Children Services (DFACS) and later transferred to the Sumter County Health Department where she is currently employed as a Clerk II. Susie still resides in Plains, Georgia, and her one daughter, LaSonja Renee Henderson Harris lives in Griffin, Georgia.

Charlie Will Wright, was born August 12, 1954 is the first son. He attended Westside Elementary School and Sumter County High School but he did not complete high school. He proceeded on to attend South Georgia Technical and Vocational School where he earned a degree in Automotive Mechanics. After our father's death in 1983 Charlie quit his job at Davidson's to work the farms but as economy would have it, the farms were dying out due to drought. After Charlie sold out the farm he pursued a career at Cooper Lightning where he is currently working as a Fork Lift Operator. Charlie has four children and resides in Americus, Georgia.

Bernstine Wright Hollis, was born June 5, 1956 attended Westside Elementary School thru the eighth grade. She was the only child to receive all her education in Plains, Georgia. Just as Bernstine was ready to attend Junior High School the Sumter County Board of Education made history once again when they ruled that the school system would be integrated. Therefore, she went from Westside to Plains High School graduating in 1974.

After graduation she attended South Georgia Technical and Vocational School in Americus, Georgia where she earned a degree in Business Education. She then pursued a career - jobs were frozen for a while. She took a job at the Plains Community Center as a cook and teacher. In 1976 she began a life long career working with the Carters. She served as an office assistant to the Director of the Carter/Mondale Headquarters based in Plains. In 1977 after the election of Jimmy Carter as President of the United States she served as a Presidential Appointee to the White House during his administration. While in Washington, D.C., she worked for the Director of Correspondence. When President Carter lost the second term in Washington, Bernstine was a part of the transition team from Washington to Atlanta. Bernstine is currently working at The Carter Center as a Senior Accountant in the Finance Office.

Bernstine indicated that she is very happy and blessed to be a product of Plains, Georgia. She currently resides in Ellenwood, Georgia with her husband Charles B. Hollis.

Leonard, Jr., the second son was born August 30, 1958. He is the only one born in Sumter County and grew up in the same house he was born in until he left home, still on the Carter's Farm.

He attended Westside Elementary School, then Central Junior High School in Americus, Georgia. From 1972 -1976 he attended Plains High School and was part of the Bicentennial graduating class.

Upon graduation he entered the United States Air Force where he spent 20 years of his life and retired from the military in 1996. Earlier years spent on the farm was preparing Leonard for the things to come with the military life. After retiring from the military Leonard began another career where he is currently working with All State Insurance as a Claims writer.

During his tenure in the military he met his wife Vickie of more than twenty years of marriage. They have four children, who presently developing careers of their own. God has truly been good to Leonard and his family. They continue to praise and honor God for the family values our parents and grandparents instilled in all of us. We are thankful for the love and respect shown by our family member one for another. It was deeply engrained in us all that God must be first in our lives. Leonard and his wife and children live in Charleston, South Carolina.

During harvest time each year we were all excused from school at lunchtime to return home to work in the fields. We all experienced the farm life and are grateful for those experiences. Today, each Thanksgiving Season, it is a Family Custom to gather together at one of our homes on rotating basis for FAMILY FELLOWSHIP, FOOD and FUN to give praise and thanks for the many, many blessings the Almighty God has bestowed upon us all.

—*Submitted by Bernstine Wright Hollis*

Section IV: Remembering

Jimmy Carter
Photo credit: The Carter Center

Chapter 22: Articles of Interest

Jimmy Carter

Brief Biography

Jimmy Carter (James Earl Carter, Jr.), thirty-ninth president of the United States, was born October 1, 1924, in the small farming town of Plains and grew up in the nearby community of Archery. His father, James Earl Carter, Sr., was a farmer and businessman; his mother, Lillian Gordy Carter, a registered nurse.

He was educated in the Plains public schools, attended Georgia Southwestern College and the Georgia Institute of Technology, and received a B.S. degree from the United States Naval Academy in 1946. In the Navy he became a submariner, serving in both the Atlantic and Pacific fleets and rising to the rank of lieutenant. Chosen by Admiral Hyman Rickover for the nuclear submarine program, he was assigned to Schenectady, N.Y., where he took graduate work at Union College in reactor technology and nuclear physics, and served as senior officer of the pre-commissioning crew of the *Seawolf*.

On July 7, 1946, he married Rosalynn Smith of Plains. When his father died in 1953, he resigned his naval commission and returned with his family to Georgia. He took over the Carter farms, and he and Rosalynn operated Carter's Warehouse in Plains, a general-purpose seed and farm supply company. He quickly became a leader of the community, serving on county boards supervising education, the hospital authority, and the library. In 1962 he won election to the Georgia Senate. He lost his first gubernatorial campaign in 1966, but won the next election, becoming Georgia's 76th governor on January 12, 1971. He was the Demo-cratic National Committee campaign chairman for the 1974 congressional and gubernatorial elections.

On December 12, 1974, he announced his candidacy for president of the United States. He won his party's nomination on the first ballot at the 1976 Democratic National Convention, and was elected president on November 2, 1976.

Jimmy Carter served as president from January 20, 1977 to January 20, 1981. Significant foreign policy accomplishments of his administration included the Panama Canal treaties, the Camp David Accords, the treaty of peace between Egypt and Israel, the SALT II treaty with the Soviet Union, and the establishment of U.S. diplomatic relations with the People's Republic of China. He championed human rights throughout the world. On the domestic side, the administration's achievements included a comprehensive energy program conducted by a new Department of Energy; deregulation in energy, transportation, communications, and finance; major educational programs under a new Department of Education; and major environmental protection legislation, including the Alaska National Interest Lands Conservation Act.

Mr. Carter is the author of 17 books, many of which are now in revised editions: *Why Not the Best?* 1975, 1996; *A Government as Good as Its People*, 1977, 1996; *Keeping Faith: Memoirs of a President*, 1982, 1995; *Negotiation: The Alternative to Hostility*, 1984; *The Blood of Abraham*, 1985, 1993; *Everything to Gain: Making the Most of the Rest of Your Life*, written with Rosalynn Carter, 1987, 1995; *An Outdoor Journal*, 1988, 1994; *Turning Point: A Candidate, a State, and a Nation Come of Age*, 1992; *Talking Peace: A*

Vision for the Next Generation, 1993, 1995; *Always a Reckoning,* 1995; *The Little Baby Snoogle-Fleejer,* illustrated by Amy Carter, 1995; *Living Faith,* 1996; *Sources of Strength: Meditations on Scripture for a Living Faith,* 1997; *The Virtues of Aging,* 1998; *An Hour Before Daylight: Memoirs of a Rural Boyhood,* 2001; *Christmas in Plains: Memories,* 2001; and *The Nobel Peace Prize Lecture,* 2002.

In 1982, he became University Distinguished Professor at Emory University in Atlanta, and founded The Carter Center. Actively guided by President Carter, the nonpartisan and nonprofit Center addresses national and international issues of public policy. Carter Center fellows, associates, and staff join with President Carter in efforts to resolve conflict, promote democracy, protect human rights, and prevent disease and other afflictions. Through the Global 2000 program, the Center advances health and agriculture in the developing world.

The permanent facilities of the Carter Presidential Center were dedicated in October 1986, and include the Jimmy Carter Library and Museum, administered by the National Archives. Also open to visitors is the Jimmy Carter National Historic Site in Plains, administered by the National Park Service.

Jimmy and Rosalynn Carter volunteer one week a year for Habitat for Humanity, a nonprofit organization that helps needy people in the United States and in other countries renovate and build homes for themselves. He also teaches Sunday school and is a deacon in the Maranatha Baptist Church of Plains. For recreation, he enjoys fly-fishing, woodworking, jogging, cycling, tennis, and skiing.

On December 10, 2002, the Norwegian Nobel Committee awarded the Nobel Peace Prize for 2002 to Mr. Carter "for his decades of untiring effort to find peaceful solutions to international conflicts, to advance democracy and human rights, and to promote economic and social development."

FAMILY

Parents: James Earl Carter, born 1894, Arlington, Georgia; died 1953. Lillian Gordy Carter, born 1898, Richland, Georgia; died 1983. They married September 27, 1923.

Sisters and Brother: Ruth Carter Stapleton (Mrs. Robert T.), died 1983. Gloria Carter Spann (Mrs. Walter G.), died 1990. William Alton (Billy) Carter III, died 1988.

Wife: Rosalynn Smith Carter, born August 18, 1927, Plains, Georgia.

Children and Grandchildren:

John William (Jack) Carter, born July 3, 1947, Portsmouth, Virginia. His son, Jason James Carter, was born August 7, 1975, and his daughter, Sarah Rosemary Carter, was born December 19, 1978. Jack is married to Elizabeth Brasfield of Chagrin Falls, Ohio. Her children are John and Sarah Chuldenko.

James Earl (Chip) Carter III, born April 12, 1950, Honolulu, Hawaii. His son, James Earl Carter IV, was born February 25, 1977, and his daughter, Margaret Alicia Carter, was born September 23, 1987. Chip is married to Becky Payne.

Donnel Jeffrey (Jeff) Carter, born August 18, 1952, New London, Connecticut. Married Annette Jene Davis of Arlington, Georgia. Their children are: Joshua Jeffrey Carter, born May 8, 1984, Jeremy Davis Carter, born June 25, 1987, and James Carlton Carter, born April 24, 1991.

Amy Lynn Carter, born October 19, 1967, Plains, Georgia. Married James Gregory Wentzel of Herndon, Virginia. Their son, Hugo James Wentzel, was born July 29, 1999.

—*Submitted by Steven H. Hochman, The Carter Center*

Jimmy Carter

Who's Who Information

Carter, Jimmy (James Earl, Jr.), thirty-ninth president of the United States of America.

Born: Plains, Georgia, October 1, 1924, the son of James Earl and Lillian (Gordy) Carter. Married: Rosalynn Smith, July 7, 1946. Children: John William, James Earl III, Donnel Jeffrey, Amy Lynn.

Student, Georgia Southwestern College, 1941-42, Georgia Institute of Technology, 1942-43; B.S., U.S. Naval Academy, 1946 (class of 1947); postgraduate, Union College, 1952-53; LL.D. (hon.), Morehouse College, 1972, Morris Brown College, 1972, University of Notre Dame, 1977, Emory University, 1979, Kwansei Gakuin University, 1981, Georgia Southwestern College, 1981, New York Law School, 1985, Bates College, 1985, Centre College, 1987, Creighton University, 1987, University of Pennsylvania, 1998; D.E. (hon.), Georgia Institute of Technology, 1979; Ph.D. (hon.) Weizmann Institute of Science, 1980, Tel Aviv University, 1983, Haifa University, 1987; D.H.L. (hon.) Central Connecticut State University, 1985, Trinity College, 1998; Hoseo University, 2001; Doctor (hon.) G.O.C. Universite, 1995, University of Juba, 2002.

Served in U.S. Navy to rank of lieutenant, 1946-53; farmer, warehouseman, Plains, Georgia, 1953-1977; member, Georgia Senate, 1963-67; Governor of Georgia, 1971-75; President of the United States, 1977-81; University Distinguished Professor, Emory University, 1982-.

Author: *Why Not the Best?* 1975; *A Government as Good as Its People*, 1977; *Keeping Faith: Memoirs of a President*, 1982; *Negotiation: The Alternative to Hostility*, 1984; *The Blood of Abraham*, 1985; (with Rosalynn Carter) *Everything to Gain: Making the Most of the Rest of Your Life*, 1987; *An Outdoor Journal*, 1988; *Turning Point: A Candidate, a State, and a Nation Come of Age*, 1992; *Talking Peace: A Vision for the Next Generation*, 1993; *Always a Reckoning*, 1994; *The Little Baby Snoogle-Fleejer*, 1995, *Living Faith*, 1996; *Sources of Strength: Meditations on Scripture for a Living Faith*, 1997; *The Virtues of Aging*, 1998; *An Hour Before Daylight: Memoirs of a Rural Boyhood*, 2001; *Christmas in Plains: Memories*, 2001; *The Nobel Peace Prize Lecture*, 2002.

Member, Sumter County (Ga.) School Board, 1955-62, chair, 1960-62; member, Americus and Sumter County Hospital Authority, 1956-70; member, Sumter County Library Board, 1961; president, Georgia Planning Association, 1968; district governor, Lions Clubs International, 1968-69; chair, congressional and gubernatorial campaign committee, Democratic National Committee, 1973-74; founder, The Carter Center, 1982; board of directors, Habitat for Humanity, 1984-87; chair, board of trustees, The Carter Center, Inc., 1986-; chair, Council of Presidents and Prime Ministers of the Americas, 1986-; chair, International Council for Conflict Resolution, 2001-

Recipient, Conservationist of the Year Award for 1978, National Wildlife Foundation, 1979; Gold medal, International Institute for Human Rights, 1979; International Mediation medal, American Arbitration Association, 1979; Martin Luther King, Jr. Nonviolent Peace Prize, 1979; International Human Rights Award, Synagogue Council of America, 1979; Harry S Truman Public Service Award, 1981; Ansel Adams Conservation Award, Wilderness Society, 1982; Distinguished Service Award, Southern Baptist Convention, 1982; Human Rights Award, International League for Human Rights, 1983; World Methodist Peace Award, 1985; Albert Schweitzer Prize for Humanitarianism, 1987; Edwin C. Whitehead Award, National Center for Health Education, 1989; Jefferson Award,

American Institute of Public Service, 1990; Philadelphia Liberty Medal, 1990; Spirit of America Award, National Council for the Social Studies, 1990; Physicians for Social Responsibility Award, 1991; Aristotle Prize, Alexander S. Onassis Foundation, 1991; W. Averell Harriman Democracy Award, National Democratic Institute for International Affairs, 1992; Spark M. Matsunaga Medal of Peace, US Institute of Peace, 1993; Humanitarian Award, CARE International, 1993; Conservationist of the Year Medal, National Wildlife Federation, 1993; Audubon Medal, 1994; Rotary Award for World Understanding, 1994; J. William Fulbright Prize for International Understanding, 1994; National Civil Rights Museum Freedom Award, 1994; UNESCO Félix Houphouët-Boigny Peace Prize, 1994; Great Cross of the Order of Vasco Nunéz de Balboa, 1995; Bishop John T. Walker Distinguished Humanitarian Award, Africare, 1996; Humanitarian of the Year, GQ Awards, 1996; Kiwanis International Humanitarian Award, 1996; Indira Gandhi Prize for Peace, Disarmament and Development, 1997; Jimmy and Rosalynn Carter Award for Humanitarian Contributions to the Health of Humankind, National Foundation for Infectious Diseases, 1997; United Nations Human Rights Award, 1998; The Hoover Medal, 1998; International Child Survival Award, UNICEF Atlanta, 1999; Presidential Medal of Freedom, 1999; William Penn Mott, Jr., Park Leadership Award, National Parks Conservation Association, 2000; Zayed International Prize for the Environment, 2001; Jonathan M. Daniels Humanitarian Award, VMI, 2001; Herbert Hoover Humanitarian Award, Boys & Girls Clubs of America, 2001; Christopher Award, 2002; Nobel Peace Prize, 2002.

Democrat. Baptist. Home: Plains, Georgia. Office: The Carter Center, One Copenhill, Atlanta, Georgia 30307.

—*Submitted by Steven H. Hochman, The Carter Center*

Nobel acceptance speech in Plains
Photo credit: Lawrence Smith

2002 Nobel Peace Prize Awarded to President Carter

October 11, 2002

The Norwegian Nobel Committee has decided to award the Nobel Peace Prize for 2002 to Jimmy Carter, for his decades of untiring effort to find peaceful solutions to international conflicts, to advance democracy and human rights, and to promote economic and social development.

During his presidency (1977-1981), Carter's mediation was a vital contribution to the Camp David Accords between Israel and Egypt, in itself a great enough achievement to qualify for the Nobel Peace Prize. At a time when the cold war between East and West was still predominant, he placed renewed emphasis on the place of human rights in international politics.

Through his Carter Center, which celebrates its 20th anniversary in 2002, Carter has since his presidency undertaken very extensive and persevering conflict resolution on several continents. He has shown outstanding commitment to human rights, and has served as an observer at countless elections all over the world. He has worked hard on many fronts to fight tropical diseases and to bring about growth and progress in developing countries. Carter has thus been active in several of the problem areas that have figured prominently in the over one hundred years of Peace Prize history.

In a situation currently marked by threats of the use of power, Carter has stood by the principles that conflicts must as far as possible be resolved through mediation and international co-operation based on international law, respect for human rights, and economic development.

—*Oslo, October 11, 2002, Norwegian Nobel Committee's announcement*

Rosalynn Carter Vice Chair The Carter Center

Former first lady Rosalynn Carter has worked for more than two decades to improve the quality of life for people around the world. Today, she is an advocate for mental health, early childhood immunization, human rights, and conflict resolution through her work at The Carter Center in Atlanta. The Center is a private, nonprofit institution founded by former President and Mrs. Jimmy Carter in 1982.

Rosalynn Carter
Photo credit: The Carter Center

A full partner with the president in all the Center's activities, the former first lady is vice chair of the Center's Board of Trustees. She created and chairs The Carter Center's Mental Health Task Force, an advisory body of experts, consumers, and advocates promoting positive change in the mental health field. Each year, she hosts the Rosalynn Carter Symposium on Mental Health Policy, bringing together leaders of the nation's mental health organizations to address critical issues. Mrs. Carter emerged as a driving force for mental health when, during the Carter administration, she became active honorary chair of the President's Commission on Mental Health, which resulted in passage of the Mental Health Systems Act of 1980.

Mother of four, Mrs. Carter has maintained a lifelong dedication to issues affecting women and children. In 1991, she launched with Betty Bumpers, wife of U.S. Sen. Dale Bumpers of Arkansas, "Every Child By Two," a nationwide campaign to publicize the need for early childhood immunizations. She served on the Policy Advisory Board of The Atlanta Project (TAP), a program of The Carter Center addressing the social ills associated with poverty and quality of life citywide, from the program's inception in 1991 until its transfer to Georgia State University in 1999. In 1988, she convened with three other former first ladies the "Women and the Constitution" conference at the Center to assess that document's impact on women.

Outside the Center, Mrs. Carter is president of the board of directors for the Rosalynn Carter Institute of Georgia Southwestern State University (RCI), which was established in her honor on the campus of her alma mater in Americus. The mission of the RCI is to help family and professional caregivers. In 1996 she became honorary chair of the call-to-action campaign, Last Acts: Care and Caring at the End of Life, a national coalition of individuals and organizations advocating more compassionate care for those who are dying. She also works for Habitat for Humanity, a network of volunteers who build homes for the needy, Project Interconnections, a public/private nonprofit partnership to provide housing for homeless people who are mentally ill, and Friendship Force International, a citizens exchange program in more than 55 countries. She served as distinguished centennial lecturer at Agnes Scott College in Decatur from 1988-92 and is currently a distinguished fellow at the Emory University Institute for Women's Studies in Atlanta.

Since graduating from Georgia Southwestern College in 1946, Mrs. Carter has received many honors, among them the Volunteer of the Decade and "Into the Light" awards from the National Mental Health Association; the Award of Merit for Support of the Equal Rights Amendment from the National Organization for Women; the Notre Dame Award for International Service; the Eleanor Roosevelt Living World Award from Peace Links; the Kiwanis World Service Medal from Kiwanis International Foundation; the Jefferson Award from the American Institute for Public Service; the Georgia Woman of the Year Award from the Georgia Commission on Women; the Rhoda and Bernard Sarnat International Prize in Mental Health from the Institute of Medicine; the United States Surgeon General's Medallion; and the Presidential Medal of Freedom, America's highest civilian honor.

She has written four books: her autobiography *First Lady from Plains; Everything To Gain: Making the Most of the Rest of Your Life*, a book about life after the White House co-authored with President Carter; *Helping Yourself Help Others: A Book For Caregivers* (with Susan K. Golant); and *Helping Someone with Mental Illness: A Compassionate Guide for Family, Friends, and Caregivers* (with Susan K. Golant), which was selected as the winner of the 1999 American Society of Journalists and Authors Outstanding Book Award in the service category. She continues to travel and speak throughout the world and enjoys fly-fishing, bird-watching, biking, and jogging in her free time.

—*Submitted by Steven H. Hochman, The Carter Center*

Rosalynn Carter

Personal

Eleanor Rosalynn Smith Carter, wife of the 39th president of the United States, Jimmy Carter
Born: Plains, Georgia, August 18, 1927
Parents: Edgar and Allie (Murray) Smith
Married: July 7, 1946
Children: John William, 1947; James Earl III, 1950; Donnel Jeffrey, 1952; Amy Lynn, 1967
Religion: Baptist
Politics: Democrat

Home Address: Plains, Georgia 31780

Business Address: The Carter Center, One Copenhill, 453 Freedom Parkway, Atlanta, GA 30307

Academic

Graduated Georgia Southwestern College, 1946

H.H.D. (Honorary) Till College, 1979

L.H.D. (Honorary) Morehouse College, 1980

D.P.S. (Honorary) Wesleyan College, 1986

LL.D. (Honorary) University of Notre Dame, 1987

D.Litt. (Honorary) Emory University, 1991

L.H.D. (Honorary) Georgia Southwestern State University, 2001

LL.D. (Honorary) Regis College, 2002

Professional

Vice Chair, Board of Trustees, The Carter Center, Inc., 1986-Chair, Carter Center Mental Health Task Force, 1991-

President, Board of Directors, Rosalynn Carter Institute of Georgia Southwestern State University, 1988-

President and Co-Founder, EVERY CHILD BY TWO Campaign for Early Immunization, 1991

Chair, International Women Leaders for Mental Health, World Federation for Mental Health, 1992-

Distinguished Fellow, Emory University Institute for Women's Studies, 1990-

Board of Directors, Friendship Force International, 1981-

Board of Advisors, Habitat for Humanity, 1984-

Board of Trustees, The Menninger Foundation, 1986-

Honorary Chair, Last Acts: Care and Caring at the End of Life, 1996-

Honorary Chair, Project Interconnections, 1987-

Honorary Fellow, American Psychiatric Association

Past Professional

Member, Georgia Governor's Commission to Improve Services for the Mentally and Emotionally Handicapped, 1971

Honorary Chairperson, Georgia Special Olympics, 1971-75

Active Honorary Chair, President's Commission on Mental Health, 1977-78

Honorary Chair, Board of Trustees, John F. Kennedy Center for the Performing Arts, 1977-80 Board Member Emeritus, National Mental Health Association

Distinguished Centennial Lecturer, Agnes Scott College, 1988-1992

Board of Directors, Gannett Company, Inc., 1983-1997

Policy Advisory Board, The Atlanta Project (TAP), 1991-1999

Awards/Honors include:

Volunteer of the Year Award, Southeastern Association of Volunteer Services, 1976;

Award of Merit for Support of the Equal Rights Amendment, National Organization for Women, 1976;

Humanitarian Award, Save the Refugees Fund, 1980;

Volunteer of the Decade Award, National Mental Health Association, 1980 Presidential Citation, American Psychological Association, 1982

Nathan S. Kline Medal of Merit, International Committee Against Mental Illness, 1984 Leadership Award, Georgia Friends of the Mentally Ill, 1985

Distinguished Service Award, National Association of Secondary School Principals, 1985;

Distinguished Alumnus Award, American Association of State Colleges & Universities, 1987;

Dorothea Dix Award, Mental Illness Foundation, 1988;

Centennial Award of Distinction, Agnes Scott College, 1989;

Camille Cosby World of Children Award, Judge Baker Children's Center, Boston, 1991;

Columbia University College of Physicians and Surgeons Dean's Award, 1991;

Notre Dame Award for International Humanitarian Service, 1992;

Eleanor Roosevelt Living World Award, Peace Links, 1992;

Howard Safar Memorial Award for Distinguished National Service, National Council of Community Mental Health Centers, 1993;

Lifetime Achievement Award, Foundation for Hospice and Homecare, 1993 Kiwanis World Service Medal;

Kiwanis International Foundation, 1995;

National Caring Award, The Caring Institute, 1995;

Georgia Woman of the Year Award, 1996;

Jefferson Award, American Institute for Public Service, 1996;

"Into the Light" Award, National Mental Health Association, 1997;

United Nations Children's Fund International Child Survival Award, 1999;

United States Presidential Medal of Freedom, 1999;

Rhoda and Bernard Sarnat International Prize in Mental Health, Institute of Medicine, 2000;

United States Surgeon General's Medallion, 2000.

Books Published

First Lady From Plains, an autobiography, 1984.

Everything to Gain: Making the Most of the Rest of Your Life, 1987, Co-authored with Jimmy Carter.

Helping Yourself Help Others: A Book for Caregivers (with Susan K. Golant), 1994.

Helping Someone With Mental Illness: A Compassionate Guide for Family, Friends, and Caregivers (with Susan K. Golant), 1998.

—Submitted by Steven H. Hochman, The Carter Center

Rosalynn Carter

Mental Health Activities

Former first lady Rosalynn Carter has been a driving force in the field of mental health throughout her public service career. She was a member of the Governor's Commission to Improve Services to the Mentally and Emotionally Handicapped when her husband was governor of Georgia. As active honorary chair of the President's Commission on Mental Health during President Carter's administration, she helped bring about passage of the Mental Health Systems Act of 1980.

Today, she continues her leadership through The Carter Center in Atlanta. Founded by President and Mrs. Carter in 1982, the Center is dedicated to improving the quality of life for people at home and in the developing world through programs in health, democracy and development, and urban revitalization. Mrs. Carter is vice chair of The Carter Center Board of Trustees.

In 1985, she initiated the Rosalynn Carter Symposium on Mental Health Policy, which brings together representatives of mental health organizations nationwide to focus and coordinate their efforts on key issues. Since then, annual symposia held at The Carter Center have investigated such topics as mental illness and the elderly, child and adolescent illness, family coping, financing mental health services and research, treating mental illness in the primary care setting, and stigma and mental illness. Responding to the need for local collaboration, she instituted in 1996 an annual Georgia Mental Health Forum for professionals and consumers statewide.

The Carter Center Mental Health Task Force, chaired by Mrs. Carter and comprised of individuals in a position to affect public policy, meets quarterly to identify policy initiatives and set the agenda for The Carter Center Mental Health Program and annual symposia. Program staff work year-round to sustain the momentum of the symposia and to unify professionals in various mental health disciplines.

Mrs. Carter also chairs the World Federation for Mental Health committee of International Women Leaders for Mental Health, a global coalition of first ladies, royalty, and heads of state. Formed as a catalyst through which the expertise and influence of these prominent women could be channeled, the committee's goals are to raise awareness about mental health issues, to identify and prioritize related needs in individual countries, and to implement appropriate actions. Under Mrs. Carter's leadership, this prestigious group meets periodically to continue its work to improve mental health worldwide.

Through the Rosalynn Carter Institute (RCI) at Georgia Southwestern State University, established in her honor at her alma mater, Mrs. Carter addresses the concerns of those who take care of people suffering from mental illnesses and other chronic illnesses and long-term disabilities. Both professional and family caregivers benefit from RCI programs to improve coping skills and foster greater emotional and physical well-being. As a result of research conducted at the RCI, Mrs. Carter published in 1994 *Helping Yourself Help Others: A Book for Caregivers,* co-authored with Susan Golant.

Following on the success of her caregiving book, Mrs. Carter teamed up again with Susan Golant to write *Helping Someone With Mental Illness: A Compassionate Guide for Family, Friends, and Caregivers.* Building on her 25 years' experience in the field, Mrs. Carter discusses the latest treatments and research generated from her symposia and in consultation with the major mental health organizations in the United States. She also addresses how best to help those with illnesses such as depression, schizophrenia, manic depression, panic attacks, and obsessive-compulsive disorders by being an effective, compassionate caregiver and advocate. *Helping Someone With Mental Illness* was selected as the winner of the 1999 American Society of Journalists and Authors Outstanding Book Award in the service category.

Mrs. Carter has received many honors and awards for her support of mental health causes including the Volunteer of the Decade and "Into the Light" awards from the National Mental Health Association, the Dorothea Dix Award from the Mental Illness Foundation, the Nathan S. Kline Medal of Merit from the International Committee Against Mental Illness, the Rhoda and Bernard Sarnat International Prize in Mental Health from the Institute of Medicine, the United States Surgeon General's Medallion, and the Presidential Medal of Freedom, America's highest civilian honor. She is an Honorary Fellow of the American Psychiatric Association.

—*Submitted by Steven H. Hochman, The Carter Center*

Earl Carter

My father, Earl Carter, was elected in 1950 to serve in the state House of Representatives, after a close and heated contest against the incumbent. Earl had a close personal relationship with Governor Herman Talmadge, who had spent the night with my parents when he came to

Earl Carter. Photo credit: Jimmy Carter Library

give the graduation address at Plains High School. Since governors had great control over the Legislature in those days, Earl was able to get choice assignments dealing with agriculture and education. He quickly became a champion of vocational-technical schools, and helped to elevate greatly their status throughout the state. Because of these accomplishments, the Board of Regents voted to honor him at Georgia Southwestern College by giving the library his name.

Earl Carter was so interested and knowledgeable about vocational technical education due to the years he served on the Sumter County Board of Education.

—*Submitted by Jimmy Carter*

James Earl Carter Library

The new Georgia Southwestern College Library, in use since June 1971, has been named the James Earl Carter Library by request of the college "In appreciation of his loyal support for this institution and the University System."

Mr. Carter was a Sumter County farmer and businessman, civic leader, strong supporter of education, and representative from Sumter County to the General Assembly of Georgia. Mr. Carter served on the Sumter County Board of Education for 17 years and was chairman of that board at the time of his death. He was dedicated to the ideal that all young people should have an education and to that end he sponsored the construction of an adequate modern building for negroes 20 years ago before "equal opportunity" ever became a major social issue.

As might be expected in the case of a man of his stature, members of his own family are among the most dependable and constructive citizens of Georgia. His immediate family includes his wife, Lillian Gordy Carter, who is the mother of his four children and who recently completed a tour as a Peace Corps worker in India; two daughters: Ruth (Mrs.

Bobby) Stapleton of Fayetteville, N.C., and Gloria (Mrs. Walter) Spann, a Georgia Southwestern alumnus who is a Sumter County homemaker and civic leader; and two sons: William Alton (Billy) Carter II, Sumter County farmer and businessman, and James Earl Carter, Jr., a Georgia Southwestern alumnus now governor of Georgia. Rosalynn Smith Carter, Georgia's reigning first lady is a graduate of Georgia Southwestern.

Mr. Carter served in the United Sates Army with the rank of lieutenant during World War I. In the Georgia Legislature, James Earl Carter served on the following committees: Academy for the Blind,

The Carter family, 1944. Front row, seated: Lillian Gordy Carter, Lula Carter Fleming, Jeanette Carter Lowery, Ethel Carter Slappey, Ruth Carter Stapleton (holding Nina Pratt's baby), Nina Pratt Lowery, Gloria Carter, Ruth Godwin Carter (holding Hugh, Jr.). Standing: Wade Lowery, Alton Carter, Will Fleming, Donnel Carter, Jimmy Carter, Willard Slappey, Earl Carter, Jack Slappey. Kneeling in front: Billy Carter. Missing: Hugh Carter, serving in Army. Photo credit: Jimmy Carter

Aviation Commerce, Municipal Government, Public Highways and University System of Georgia.

His service to this county and to education throughout the state, which was so well begun, was cut short by his death in July 1953. However, "his influence is still effective toward constructive citizenship and improved education. In appreciation for these qualities and achievements and for his loyal support for this institution and the University System," Georgia Southwestern requested authorization to name this facility the James Earl Carter Library.

—*"Americus Times-Recorder," 1971*

State Officials from Plains

Two State Senators from Plains

James Earl Carter, Jr. Born October 1, 1924, in Plains, son of Lillian Gordy Carter and James Earl Carter, Sr. Married Rosalynn Smith July, 7, 1946. Served in the Georgia State Senate from 1963-1967.

Hugh Alton Carter, Sr. Born in Plains, Sumter County, August 13, 1920. Son of William Alton Carter and Annie Laurie Gay Carter. Married Ruth Godwin December 25, 1941. Served in the Georgia State Senate from 1967-1981. He died June 24, 1999.

Sen. Hugh Carter
Photo credit: Georgia Department of Archives and History

Three State Representatives from Plains

Edwin Timmerman: Born October 14, 1854, in Edgefield County, S.C. He moved with his grandparents, John and Barbary Jennings, and his mother, Milbry Jennings Timmerman, to the Plains area in 1866. His father, John Bartlett Timmerman, had been killed in Mississippi during the Civil War. He married Alice Ruth Forth December 24, 1879, near Magnolia Springs. He was co-owner of Timmerman and Wise Cotton Warehouse. Before serving in the State Legislature, he had served on the City Council and as mayor of Plains. His term of office in the Legislature was 1918-1920. He did not seek a second term. He died June 12, 1922.

James Earl Carter, Sr.: Born September 12, 1894, in Arlington, Georgia. He moved to Plains with his mother, Nina Pratt Carter, and four siblings, at an early age after the death of his father, William Archibald Carter. He was married September 27, 1923, to Lillian Gordy of Richland. He was an Insurance broker, farmer, and fertilizer dealer. Before serving in the State Legislature, he served on the Sumter County School Board. His term of office in the Legislature was 1953-54, cut short by his untimely death on July 22, 1953.

Thaddeus Marion Jones, Sr.: Born November 17, 1901, in Plains, the son of Thomas Marion Jones and Maggie Coker Jones. He was owner and president of Jones Automatic Sprinkler Co. He married Irene Murray, daughter of Drew P. and Maude Jennings Murray, on December 31, 1922. He followed James Earl Carter, Sr. in the House of Representatives, serving from 1954 until 1962. He died January 24, 1972.

State Auditor with Plains Connections

B.E. Thrasher, Jr.: Born June 29, 1904, in Fulton County, Georgia. The Thrasher family lived in Plains during his teenage years and part of his education was at Plains High School. The family lived in a house at the junction of Highway 308 and Thrasher Road, the road having been named for the Thrasher family. He served as state auditor from January 14, 1941, until January 8, 1964.

A quote from his obituary states, "The auditor had been in the state's employ for nearly 37 years. He worked his way up from an examiner to assistant auditor to become auditor in 1941."

Tributes came from high officials. It was Gov. Carl Sanders who said, "Thrasher spent a lifetime in the service of Georgia." Sanders added, "Few men in the history of our state have ever worked as diligently or as hard as did Ed Thrasher, Jr. He devoted every available moment to his position of public trust, and he did so with intelligence and honest application."

Secretary of State Ben W. Fortson, a longtime official, said, "He was the finest state and public official I have ever known. He left his mark on state government far beyond the public recognition of it. Many of Georgia's finest programs were the result of his untiring efforts."

His obituary also states that he was instrumental in building many new office buildings, supervising the modernization program and developing the idea of authorities to keep the state from being tied directly to debts.

He also was a moving force in the development of Jekyll Island. He served on the University System Building Authority, State School Building Authority and Capitol Square Improvement Authority.

Mr. Thrasher died January 8. 1964.

—*Submitted by Allene T. Haugabook*

Men of Mark in Georgia

Two men who were very instrumental in establishing the town of Plains were John Archibald McDonald and Rodolphus Silas Oliver. Together they established Oliver-McDonald Company. This was a mercantile business that was reputed to be the largest retail store south of Macon. Most all necessities could be bought at Oliver-McDonald Company, even furniture. The following articles are taken from a 1912 book, "Men of Mark in Georgia," which was sent to Allene T. Haugabook by Mr. Oliver's granddaughter, Joyce Oliver Bergman.

John Archibald McDonald

John A. McDonald, of Sumter County, who makes his home at Plains, is a veteran both in war and peace. He was born in Sumter County on September 17, 1848. His father, John Bethune McDonald, was a hatter by trade, who later became a farmer and married Catherine Worthy. John B. McDonald came from North Carolina to Crawford County in 1836 and to Sumter County in 1839. His father, Angus McDonald, came from Scotland to North Carolina. Some of Mr. McDonald's uncles migrated to New South Wales, Australia.

Mr. McDonald comes from that great Scottish clan which for hundreds of years disputed the place of supremacy among the Scottish clans with the Campbells. The MacDonald clan was divided into four great branches: Clans Ronald, Glengarry, Sleet, and Staff. There is some little doubt as to which was the parent family of these four great divisions of the clan, but there weight of evidence seems to be in favor of the MacDonalds of the Isles and Sleat, for they can be traced back to the year 1135, and the clan is known to have existed even prior to that. It is one of the most interesting histories of all the clans of Scotland, and there is no more interesting history in the world than that of these Scottish clans. From 1135 down to the present time the MacDonalds have been conspicuous, both in war in peace, wherever Scottish or British people have penetrated. In 1745 they adhered to the Stuarts and were able to put two thousand fighting men in the field. After the destruction of the Stuart cause an enormous number of the MacDonald clan emigrated to North Carolina, and there as a condition of being allowed to take up lands they were compelled to take the oath of allegiance to the British crown. They had fought the House of Hanover until fighting was hopeless. Their loyalty to pledged word may be judged by the fact that having taken the oath of allegiance to the House of Hanover in order to secure their lands, when the Revolutionary War came on, although in full sympathy with the

Colonists, a large number of them took up arms for the Royal cause on the ground that they could not break their plighted work. Deserted in the first year of war by the Royal leaders, the majority of them returned to their homes and remained quietly during the war, while a minority, feeling that they had sufficient provocation to renounce their allegiance, joined themselves in the Colonists and some of them made notable records as soldiers; and it is from this strong stock that John McDonald is descended.

He was educated in the Sumter County Schools, and though a mere lad on the outbreak of the Civil War he became, during that struggle, attached to the Eleventh Regiment of the Reserves, and after five days' service, before he had ever had an opportunity even to be drilled, was too severely wounded (at Griswoldville) for further service. After the war he farmed for a time, conducted a woodyard and wood supply business for the Central of Georgia Railroad from 1874 on for some years, and in 1895, 1896, and 1897 ran a planning mill. In 1896 he finally moved from Sumter to Plains, which has since been his home.

Mr. McDonald's business ventures, backed by industry and sound judgment, have been very largely successful. He is now vice president of the Oliver-McDonald Company, the largest mercantile concern of his section, and a director and vice president of the Bank of Plains. He is a man of much public spirit, and takes an active hand in everything that will contribute to the improvement of his community. In the Grange and Alliance movements he was a conspicuous member, and though he had always declined public office, when in 1890, the Alliance insisted on his serving on the committees of Agriculture and Blind Asylum in the General Assembly, he accepted and served for one term. He have fourteen years of service as a member of the School Board of Sumter County, six years as a Jury Commissioner, served on the Town Council of Plains, declining to be Mayor; is a member of the various

Masonic bodies, from Blue Lodge to Shrine, and has been Master of his local lodge for many years. He has given thirty years of service as a steward of the Methodist Church and did not miss a quarterly meeting for fourteen years. In the old Reconstruction days he was a member of the noted Ku Klux Klan which did more to clear up the atmosphere in the South than any institution ever organized. The record shows that he has been helpful and useful in every direction, and has well earned the prosperity which has come to him.

His preferred reading through life has been the Bible, coupled with biographical and historical works, and he is a man of sound information. While he was in the General Assembly, the *Constitution* of that period, which was not altogether in sympa-

R.S. Oliver and J.A. McDonald
Photo credit: "Men of Mark in Georgia," 1912

thy with his political convictions, stated that he was a man of generous actions, clear head, and altogether one of the soundest members of the House.

Rodolphus Silas Oliver

R.S. Oliver, of Plains, Sumter County, president of the Oliver-McDonald Company, the largest mercantile concern of that section, President of the Bank of Plains, and the owner of large farming interests, is a native of Webster County, born on December 2, 1859. Mr. Oliver's parents were J.J. and Carrie (McGrady) Oliver. His father was a farmer and Confederate soldier. His family in Georgia was founded by his grandfather, James Oliver, who came from South Carolina and settled near East Point, Georgia.

The Oliver family in England goes back for centuries and there seems to have been three main branches; the oldest apparently settled in South-western England, another in Southern England, and the third, offshoots from these older families, in Scotland and Ireland. The possession of coat armor by the family demonstrates the fact that they held an honorable position in the old country.

R.S. Oliver had good educational advantages. After attendance upon the Webster County schools he went to the University of Georgia, remaining through the sophomore and junior years. He then turned his attention to farming and followed that pursuit until 1885, when, without abandoning his farming interests he established himself in the mercantile business at Plains. He speedily demonstrated his ablity as a merchant; was soon recognized as a sound financier, and in 1901 was the principal organizer of the Bank of Plains, of which he has been president since its organization. His business success has been of such a character that he may be fairly called the most prominent businessman of his community. He also possesses a sufficient measure of public spirit and is now serving as Mayor of his town. He is a member of the Methodist Church, the Knights of Pythias, and the various Masonic bodies from the Blue Lodge to the Shrine.

Mr. Oliver has been twice married: In 1882 he married Miss Awtrey Rylander, daughter of Matthew and Kate (Brown) Rylander, of Sumter County. Subsequent to her death he married Miss Effie Turner, daughter of the Rev. Joseph and Tanne Stewart Turner, of Sumter County. Rev. Joseph Turner, father of Mrs. Oliver, was a Methodist minister. Of Mr. Oliver's marriages there are eight children: Clifford, Edmond, Floy, John, Carrie, Catherine, Francis, and R.S. Oliver, Junior.

Mr. Oliver's preferred reading has been found in the press, which in these later days affords a liberal education to the intelligent man. Like many other thoughtful men of our time, he has come to the conclusion that compulsory education is necessary. He sees, as many others do, that we have a vast number of people who are either too poor or too lacking in intelligence to make the necessary effort to give their children the rudiments of an education unless forced to do so by the strong arm of the law. He sees also that if this Republic is to endure, we must have in the future a more intelligent electorate than we have had in the past. Recognizing these facts, Mr. Oliver as a good citizen is in favor of spending the public money freely to give everybody an opportunity for an education and then force them to take it. He would back this up with a system of good roads, believing that both the moral and material welfare of the community would be greatly added to by putting a splendid system of good roads into every nook and corner of the State. This has too long been deferred on the pleas of poverty. We are now well able to undertake it, and if we do our duty wisely in that direction the State will be far richer when the job is concluded than it is now. It is to the credit of Mr. Oliver that he has not allowed himself to become so completely immersed in his won affairs as to lose sight of these great needs.

Reprint from *Men of Mark in Georgia*, by A.B. Caldwell, publisher, Volume VI, 1912, pages 315-317 and 321-322.

—*Submitted by Joyce Oliver Bergman*

Cassandra Pickett Durham

1824 – 1885

Imagine the scene. A woman, age 46, stands before an audience, largely male, to make a speech. It is 1870, and the place is Macon, Georgia, at the corner of Mulberry Street and Broadway, next to the Federal Building. The students and faculty of the Reform Medical College are gathered for the awarding of degrees. The speaker is Cassandra Pickett Durham.

"Ladies and Gentlemen: ... In order to properly appreciate the difficulties that surround me, you have but to view me as a woman, alone and helpless, but determined to inaugurate a New Era in the medical profession for the benefit of my sex. From time immemorial we have by the powers that be, and the prejudice of man, been denied the right to minister to the wants of our own sex as practicing physicians. ... The female sex has, in the past, from false notions of propriety and refinement, been denied their rightful privilege of entering the medical profession. ... "

Cassandra Pickett Durham is about to be the first woman in Georgia to receive the degree of Doctor of Medicine. How did she come to this point? Hailing originally from South Carolina, where she was born in 1824, she moved to Georgia well before the Civil War. We don't know when or why. By the time she was thirty, she had lost two husbands to illness. Then in 1855, she married Dr. John Tapley Durham in Preston, Georgia. He was a successful physician with an extensive practice in Sumter, Dooly and Webster Counties. The Durhams had five children. In the last years of the Civil War, Cassandra experienced the wrenching hunger and deprivation that afflicted the land. She was most affected by the plight of women and their lack of adequate health care.

"The thousands of emaciated forms of womanhood that today are breathing out a lingering existence on earth is no evidence of incompetency on the part of male physicians. It does prove, however, that the refined and long cultivated modesty that adorns a woman must be blunted, or a physician of her own sex must be supplied — a physician whose

sympathy for her patient will ensure that degree of confidence that will enable her to arrive at a true diagnosis of the disease to be treated. ... "

Something else she had seen in those terrible times was the part that women could play in emergency treatment of the sick.

"I call your attention to the results achieved by the Sisters of Charity. Without the right to practice as physicians, they have, as mere attendants upon the sick, and through the sympathy existing for other women, been able to learn acts which, when imparted to the attending physician, gave him the power to diagnose and treat successfully the disease."

In the terribly lean years that followed the war, Cassandra's life was to become more difficult. She lost her husband, Dr. Durham, in 1869. His estate was a trunk full of Confederate money, completely useless as a resource for feeding her children, but she also had $200 in gold, inherited from an ancestor. Only a woman who has known widowhood can appreciate the courage of the decision she made then. She sent her children to live with relatives and friends, and she moved to Macon to live in a boarding house and attend the Reform Medical College. She received support and encouragement from churches in Americus. Now she stands ready to receive her medical degree, the first woman in Georgia to do so. She has no illusions about the difficulty of the task that awaits her.

"Ladies and Gentlemen, such are the facts which prompt me willingly to encounter the trials and difficulties which I know must follow my feeble efforts to inaugurate a new era in the medical profession. Even a failure on my part will not call forth one regret in regard to this undertaking. Success may not bring forth one approving smile to encourage me in my lone labors. Yet I have the greatest encouragement in a pure and exalted desire

to confer a benefit upon my own sex. My failure would not be the last effort made in this great reform. More brilliant intellects, with superior advantages, will rise up in the future and consummate the great and noble work commenced in 1870."

She returned to Americus and practiced from home, next door to Brown's Shoe Store. She offered all that was in her power in prenatal care, safe delivery, and nutrition to the women she could reach. She was a woman with a mission.

"God has not made women to live lives of ease, but has endowed them with powers and capabilities which, when fully developed and properly directed, present them to the world as women of full stature in knowledge and wisdom, and capable of discharging the many duties which devolve upon them as helpmeets of men."

We honor Cassandra Pickett Durham as a Georgia Woman of Achievement.

—Georgia Women of Achievement
Second Induction Ceremony
Macon, Georgia
March 11, 1993

Georgia's First Woman Doctor Is From Sumter County

On March 7, 1993, at Wesleyan College, five Georgia Women of Achievement were honored: D.B. Bandy, M.M.M. Bosomworth, V.R. Napier, G.P. Rainey and Cassandra Pickett Durham. I immediately seized on Dr. Durham, for she is one of my favorite personalities in our local history.

You see, gentle reader, Cassandra Durham, of the Plains of Dura, was the first woman licensed as a doctor by the state of Georgia, perhaps in the entire South! Cassandra Pickett was born May 21, 1824, in Fairfield District, South Carolina, the daughter of John J. Pickett and Nancy Boulware.

She was known affectionately to her family as Kisannah. She reached adulthood in Stewart County and married first a Pickett cousin, then second a member of the Windsor family (yes, the ones the hotel is named after in Americus). She outlived both of them. Women were tough in those days, they had to be.

Cassandra's third husband, Dr. John Pryor Durham, set the stage for her historic claim to fame. For over a decade and a half, she accompanied her husband and his ministrations to the sick, all the while developing an affinity for the healing arts. When Dr. J.P. Durham died at Bottsford, on the Sumter-Webster line, on December 9, 1869(he reposes in an unmarked grave at that former community's cemetery), she and her family were left with a trunkful of worthless Confederate money and $200 in gold. Bottsford and the Plains of Dura were bereft of a doctor and Cassandra only had about a year's income. The Baptist, Methodist, and Universalist churches in that section took care of her children while she went to the Reform Medical College at Macon and earned her diploma there in 1871.

Returning to Sumter and taking up residence on the north side of Lamar, between Cotton and Jackson Street, she began the practice of botanic eclectic medicine often gathering her own herbs in the swamps near Americus. Unfortunately, a disastrous fire in 1878 destroyed that block of Americus and with it, Dr. Durham's pictures and her prized diploma.

On October 18, 1885, while attending a patient at Ward's Station, now Shellman, in Randolph County, she died suddenly from an attack of apoplexy and was buried there. Ironically, like her husband, her final resting place is unmarked.

In her graduation speech, Dr. Durham, an ardent feminist, had noted "that God has not made women to live lives of ease, but that he has endowed them with powers and capabilities which, when fully developed and properly directed, present them to the world women of full stature in knowledge and wisdom, and capable of discharging the many duties which devolve upon them ... no marble column may mark (my) resting place, but in the ... South infirmaries and homes for the destitute sick will be found and recognized as standing monuments to the ultimate success of the reform now begun."

—*Written by Alan Anderson, columnist for "Americus Times-Recorder," March 20, 1993*

Julia L. Coleman

1889-1973

Julia L. Coleman is best known for her contributions to the people of Plains, Georgia, though she was born in Nacogdoches, Texas, the daughter of a Baptist minister. She came to Plains as a small child, attending school there and then at Bessie Tift College in Forsyth. After graduating with her teaching certificate, she began her teaching career and returned to Plains in 1912, where she would become the most beloved educator in the region.

Miss Julia on work day in Friendship Garden Plains High School, Jack Short in background. Photo credit: Allene T. Haugabook

"Miss Julia," as she was known by everyone in Plains, was a lady of inordinate grace, charm and intellect. Growing up visually impaired and lame, she was not able to drive a car and had to read with a magnifying glass, but her physical handicaps didn't slow her down. This remarkable woman began teaching English at Plains High School and would subsequently become principal. After 15 years in that position, she was named superintendent of Plains High School, a role normally given to a male. It was her outstanding and innovative teaching skills that made her the perfect choice for the job.

As one of the first female superintendents in Georgia, Miss Julia embraced the position with passion. In 1937, Plains High School was named one of three model schools in Georgia, primarily because of the innovative curriculum developed through her leadership. Because of this designation, graduates of teaching institutions statewide were eager to come to Plains to teach in the model school. Many of Miss Julia's experimental programs were later adapted by the state school system.

This amazing woman never stopped moving ahead. Beginning in 1941, she began one of the first "soup kitchens" in Georgia, which grew into what is now the school lunch program. She started the "Friendship Garden" to beautify the school campus, adding a new plant each time a baby was born in the community. In 1950, she served on the state committee to investigate adding the 12th grade to the school system. She also directed plays, coached the debate and literary teams and spent her own money for school supplies and for the needs of various individual students. Her students were always her primary interest and Miss Julia kept in touch with them after graduation through beautifully written letters of encouragement.

In 1935, Miss Julia was invited to the White House by Eleanor Roosevelt, where she was recognized for her contribution to education. Mrs. Roosevelt was not the only White House occupant to notice her extraordinary talents. Former President Jimmy Carter, one of Miss Julia's many students, says, "Of all the teachers I have ever had, including those for my studies at four different colleges and universities, Miss Julia has been the one who has done the most for me and made the most beneficial and lasting impression on my life." Carter began his 1977 inaugural address with Miss

Julia's words: "We must adjust to changing times and still hold to unchanging principles."

In 1949, Miss Julia retired as superintendent, but continued to teach English in her beloved school. She continued to garner local, regional and national awards and honors. She retired after 50 years of teaching. She considered the community of Plains as her family and expressed her gratitude to the citizens for allowing her to teach their children. With her strong moral character, work ethic and dedication to her profession, Miss Julia Coleman left an indelible mark on the lives of the people of Plains, the residents of Georgia and through a former student who became president, the world. We are proud to honor Julia L. Coleman as a Georgia Woman of Achievement.

—*Georgia Women of Achievement, Induction Ceremony, March 29. 2001*

The Establishment of Plains

The "Columbus Enquirer" of September 4,1839, carried the notice of the establishment of a post office at the Plains of Dura in Sumter County, with D.W. Robinet as Post Master. Such was the beginning of the town we call Plains.

On February 24,1842, Micajah B. Pickett met Dave Robinet when Pickett "halted his team in front of a log cabin, then known as the Plains of Dura." Robinet welcomed Pickett to the place he characterized as "the furnace of Nebuchadnezzar." When Pickett inquired as to the unusual name, Robinet replied that he chose that name in reference to the story in the Book of Daniel about Shadrach, Meshach and Abednego being thrown into the furnace for not bowing down to the Babylonians' idol. He was making an analogy wherein he, Hon. George R. Harper, then our state representative, and Reuben B. Pickett, all Universalists, were being pressured by "a determined host of other followers of Christ," basically the Methodists. That denomination had already erected a church

named Tabernacle on what is now Young's Mill Road, west of Highway 45. They sold it to an A.M.E. congregation after the Civil War, but in the middle of the cemetery are the graves of Seaborn Walters and two of his sons, along with the woman who would play a key role in the final dissolution of the union school, a fact presaged by David W. Robinet's selection of the community's name.

For those unfamiliar with the term, Universalists were free thinkers whose theological doctrine held that all souls will eventually find salvation in the grace of God. This did not sit well with the more dogmatic Baptists, Methodists and Presbyterians at the Plains of Dura.

M.B. Pickett identified the first settlers of the Plains of Dura as "Father Pullin, Rufus Godwin, Simmons, Curry, Wm. P. Jones, Jeptha Pickett, Jesse Barnes, Joseph G. Porter and R.B. Pickett" (the 1840 census of the 884th G.M.D. listed Moses Pullin, James and Mary Simmons, James and Whitmill Curry).

Of the acknowledged leaders of the two competing religious factions, "Geo. R. Harper was the only educated man, and his strength rested more upon his natural and moral forces than his literary attainments." Rev. James Glass, the local Methodist preacher, was "a man of fine intellect, sustained by unquestionable morals, energy and perseverance." He had earlier served as Sumter County's third sheriff in 1836-37.

Although G.R. Harper had taught a school in an unroofed log cabin in 1841, the need for an academy supported by both factions soon became apparent to even the most zealous followers of Glass and Harper. Consequently, in 1843, the children of the Methodist and Universalist families were jointly educated in a school in the Providence community, near Pessell Creek on Salter's Mill Road. Key to its implementation was the enlistment of Joseph J. Chappell and Ezekiel Hawkins, both Baptists.

When Chappell heard of the proposition ... he became somewhat alarmed for the morals of their children and lost no time in obtaining a consultation with brother Hawkins, who replied,

"Well, Brother Joe, I am not going to let no such foolishness keep me from giving little Sammy his education. I want him to take care of me in my old age. If Geo. Harper and Pickett and Joe Porter wants to huddle together in heaven among a parcel of Christian women and children, why just let them do it. Heaven is a mighty big place ... there will be room enough for us all at the Father's house ... and I am not going to spend any time building up fire works for my neighbors, there is enough of that below. Sammy must be educated."

Ezekiel Hawkins' son Sammy is better known as Samuel Hugh Hawkins, who would some forty years later build the only privately capitalized railroad in state history. Ironically, that railroad would move Plains to its present location and result in the shortened version of the name.

With the arrival of brothers Henry, John and William Coker at the Plains of Dura in 1843-44, as well as Henry Davenport about the same time, the stage was set for two competing schools within a mile of each other. John Cox, " a worthy son of Baptist parents," supervised the one located where Lebanon Cemetery is now, "the other on a beautiful hill," taught by Rev. George R. Harper, who had become an ordained Universalist minister. The Baptist effort only lasted one year.

Rev. Glass yielded the palm to Henry Davenport, while the Universalists called to their aid Rev. James C. Kendrick, "a tower of strength physically, morally and intellectually."

Despite strong philosophical differences, peace was kept among families in the community by the wives of the active co-workers in these rival schools. These sainted women were Mrs. Sarah Glass, Mrs. Mary Kendrick, Mrs. Margaret Harper, Mrs. Caroline Davenport, Mrs. Jane Stewart, Mrs. Sarah C. Rylander, Mrs. Nancy Coker, Mrs. Sarah Black and Mrs. Wm. Simmons.

To avoid any sectarian strife from becoming a serious detriment to the Plains of Dura, James Stewart, James H. Black and Newnan McBain led a union movement and, with the assistance of the Masonic fraternity, erected a school at Magnolia Springs, the town's original site. The first teacher, William Wallace, was so popular the school's burgeoning enrollment required a lady assistant, Miss Caroline Guerry, daughter of Judge James P. Guerry. Wallace wooed and married her, read for the law, "removed to Tennessee, became a brigadier General in the Union Army and died a renegade son of the South."

With the departure of Prof. Wallace at the end of 1852, the Mineral Spring Academy at Plains of Dura came under the supervision of Uriah A. Ransome, principal, and Miss Mariah E. Shivers, of Macon. Prof. Ransome was described as "a man of great force of character, with mental power far above an average." Students were taught to analyze a problem, "which effort developed the powers and capabilities, and prepared them for higher efforts."

No teacher was employed who taught upon any other principle. Acting as references for the academy were Dr. Wm. J. Reese, J.H. Black, G.R. Harper, Esq., A.F. Burke, Col. P.H. Wooten, Thomas Simpson and George Torbert.

Unfortunately, in his zeal to maintain a nonsectarian literary institution, in the spring of 1854 Prof. Ransome discreetly requested Rev. Glass' daughter to refrain from doing her Bible lessons at the school. Reaction was swift and strong. Rev. Glass withdrew his children from the academy, Prof. Ransome called a meeting to explain his actions and a resolution supporting him was published in the "Sumter Republican" on August 3,1854. Support came from members of all four denominations, but there were two strong minded opponents.

In a series of essays over the next few months, Rev. Glass and Henry Davenport excoriated U.A. Ransome in particular and the Universalists in general. It is no accident that New Hope Universalist Church's location, on the south side of Slappey Road, immediately east of Highway 45, is labeled on maps as "Devil's" or "Hell's Half Acre." All that remains is a small cemetery.

The election of George R. Harper once again to the state Legislature from 1857 to 1860 removed one of the Universalists' most valuable supporters (George Robert Harper also represented Sumter from 1868 to 1870). Prof. U.A. Ransome went on to enlist in the Sumter Light Guards and died in Richmond, Virginia, in December 1861.

By 1855, advertisements appeared in local papers for the Magnolia Male and Female Institutes, the two schools occupying houses about a quarter mile apart, within a few hundred yards of the spring. John Emory Rylander, who would later have his own academy on Rees Park, was principal of the male department, with Wm. C. Dodd for the female department and Mrs. J.E. Rylander over the primary department. The trustees were M.E. Rylander, Robert Russell, Moses Pullin, H.L. Whitehurst and T.J. Shinholster.

According to M.B. Pickett, the schools at the Plains of Dura, despite their ups and downs, contributed "thirty teachers, 3 editors, 12 attorneys, 17 physicians, 4 commercial drummers (salesmen), 5 clerks, 7 Confederate officers, 10 merchants, 8 Representatives, 2 bankers, 12 ministers and 1 author, and many of the ablest farmers in South Georgia." His 12-part series of discourses, published in the "Sumter Republican" in the summer and early fall of 1884, was the source of most of this column's quotes.

—*Submitted by Alan Anderson*

Reminiscences of the Plains of Dura

From The Sumter Republican 1842 To 1860
By M.B. Pickett

The Plains of Dura was the name of the Post Office, located in the old 26th District of Sumter County, west of the city of Americus, which extended to the line of Webster. This office, I think, was established in 1840 or '41 and is near the place now known as Magnolia Springs.

In response to the many importunities of the public, I propose, in a series of letters, to put upon record a few reminiscences of the great struggle at the Plains of Dura, Sumter County, between the two branches of the Christian Church, known as the Evangelical Church and the Universalists, with a true and correct statement of the result ... I know that I tread upon delicate ground ... As a Christian writer my whole duty is to do good, "deal justly and walk humble before God." The struggle, of which I am now to write lasted 18 years... (*Sumter Republican* June 6, 1884).

On the morning of the 25th of February, 1842, I reviewed the conversations at the Plains of Dura ...On the right I saw three firm, unyielding and determined Universalists. On the left a determined host of other followers of Christ, who claimed to be the only depositories of Gospel truth. In view of my dwelling, stood an unroofed log cabin in which the Honorable Geo. R. Harper had taught school in the year 1841, and in the distance a single church as evidence of a religious public and the only index to the moral and intellectual status of the people of the old 26th District of Sumter.

That the people among whom I had cast my lot were religiously inclined, I had the highest evidence. That they had religious zeal, I was satisfied, but that they were educated I had my doubts. The people seemed to me a wilderness of ruff ashlars, with a single workman without the ability to polish them ... I looked upon my young and confiding wife and helpless daughters, and rested my hope upon assurance that the Lord would provide.

Geo. R. Harper was the only educated man, and his strength rested more upon his natural and moral forces than his literary attainments ... Rev. James Glass, the local preacher, was a man of fine intellect, sustained by unquestionable morals, energy and perseverance. These two men were the acknowledged leaders in the great struggle soon to follow.

I cannot resist the temptation at this point to relate an incident, illustrative of the peculiarities, of these two rival friends and leaders of the two parties. The Honorable G.R. Harper had a man by the name of Bill Jefferson with him, who lost no opportunity to make himself merry at the expense of another. Rev. Joseph Glass had with him an inveterate jester by the name of John Forrest. Very early on Sabbath morning the preacher was seen rambling through the fields accompanied by John, over to his friend Harper's with the intention (as it was supposed), to return in time to attend his appointment at the church. Upon their arrival at the house, John told Bill that the Lord would be cheated out of a Sabbath in less than twenty-four hours. The friends spent the morning chatting until breakfast. The appointment was forgotten, a good dinner was prepared, eaten and just as they took their seats at the supper table the preacher said to Harper that he admired his yoke of oxens very much, but he supposed that nothing short of fifty dollars would buy them? Here John gave Bill a wink, calling his attention to the progress. Harper remarked that he would not like to sell the oxens, but being in need of a little cash just at that time he should be tempted to take that sum. The preacher was as keen as a fox in money matters, and very wisely said no more at that time. After tea the preacher extended the hand of friendship to George saying in a low voice that he should send for the oxens in the morning. On the day appointed the preacher's memory served him

much better than on the Sunday's appointments, and John Forrest was busily engaged with the oxens in removing a widow lady and children into a more pleasant home upon the farm of Rev. James Glass, presented to her free of rent. George got the fifty dollars, the preacher got the oxens, the poor woman a pleasant home, and John and Bill a good laugh, but the Lord was minus the Sabbath. We suppose the end justified the means. John said to Bill that the oxens were in the ditch and had to be lifted out (*Sumter Republican* June 13, 1884).

About the year 1843 or 1844, the three Coker brothers, Henry, John and William arrived at the Plains. These men were progressive in a very high degree which gave an impetus to the cause of education far beyond that which might have been expected from men of limited means and who had made no pretentions to literary attainments. They seemed ready to devote their whole time and last cent for the propagation of the doctrines of Universalism and the diffusion of knowledge. At or near the same period, Mr. Henry Davenport, a zealous member of the Baptist Church and a man far above mediocre attainment in literary attainment, jealous of any innovations upon that which he claimed to be the doctrines of Christ. With these two proud, conscientious, high toned, and Christian men, the conflict was sure and desperate. The result was two schools like Jonah's goard, sprung into existence within a mile of each other. The one on the site upon which Lebanon church now stands, under the control and supervision of Mr. Davenport, the other on a beautiful hill in view of the writer's dwelling, taught by the Hon. George R. Harper (*Sumter Republican* June 20, 1884).

Our children like lambs of a common fold were all gathered together under Professor Ransom and Miss Shiver, who had been put at the head of the school by the unanimous vote of the patrons. But all is not gold that glitters, away down in these waters of strife there rested the germ of sectarian and religious antagonism. The minds of the patrons were not quiet. They were like the ocean whose waters were not at rest, but casting up mire and dirt. We all become propagandist of conflicting creeds. In the defense of the Bible we violated the first principles of the Gospel.

At this time the Methodist church, located at the old camp ground, was in a flourishing condition, with a membership of near or over one hundred ... at the end of the struggle this useful society of Christians was by deaths and removals reduced to a mere fraction of its former numbers, yet not a single renegade from the Wesleyan faith was found upon record. Mt. Zion, the only Universalist church in the county, was closed up, and New Hope church erected at the Plains. This church had about ninety members, and enjoyed the ministerial labors of Rev. J.C. Kendrick whose intellectual powers were sustained by a degree of holiness, energy and perserverance that has over characterized the pioneer minister from the days of Paul to present.

It was at this crisis that Rev. John C. Burruss of Alabama, Dr. L.F.W. Andrews, D.B. Clayton and Rev. C.F.R. Shehane were called into the state to sustain the struggling church at the Plains.

How painfully pleasing the recollections of the past. Forty summers have come and gone since the beginning of the great struggle at the Plains of Dura, and yet how clearly and indelibly impressed upon the mind are the features, the eccentricities, the foibles and virtues of the friends and co-workers in the great task that had been assumed.

But few of them now live to share with the writer and the readers of the Republican the joys of a triumph over the obstacles that lay in our way.

J.H. Black and his wife, Smith Davenport, Mrs. M.E. Rylander, Mrs. Henry Davenport and the writer and his wife, are all that live in Sumter County of that long list of true women and determined men to read the reminiscences of the Plains. Pullen, Harper, Cheeks, Porter, Glass, the three Coker brothers, and Ezekial Hawkins and Henry Davenport have long since past over where the

wicked cease from troubling and the weary are at rest. Like the Apostle, they fought a good fight and kept their faith and we have an abiding faith that henceforth there is laid up for them a crown of righteousness and glory. Their crown may chance to differ in splendor, brightness and glory, like the angels in the morning of the resurrection. Their warfare on earth is over and the joys of heaven begun. This may be all a delusion, but it is a happy one, and leads to higher efforts and exalted virtues in the christian's life.

Though silent at the Plains, our voices are gone out into the world as educators in the ministry and for the diffusion of knowledge. There can be no higher evidence that we yet live and speak and that God in His wisdom has governed and kept within due bounds the elements of strife at the Plains and from a local and temporary evil evolves a general and permanent good (*Sumter Republican* September 5, 1884).

Excerts from "Sumter Republican Newspapers from 1884"

—*Submitted by Amy Wise*

Plains of Dura, Sumter County

Frequently called Magnolia Springs and Magnolia Village. Is on Chocotawhatchee Creek, eleven and one-half miles west of Americus, county seat, depot, bank, telegraph and express office, by which it is 181 to Atlanta. Population 100, with Methodist church, an academy, and two grist mills, one by steam and the other by water power. The Magnolia Springs are well patronized. Cotton, the chief interest. Mail daily. Black Brothers general store, tanners and shoe mnfrs.

Cato F., teacher

Chappel A., general store

Coker James F., carpenter

Forth F.W., general store

Glass S.P., P.M.

Green James, machinist

Johnson R.E., wheelwright and carriage maker

Littlejohn J.R. Rev., Methodist

Ragesdale P.R., carpenter

Rawson L.S., general store

Wise S.P. Mrs., hotel

FARMERS

J.H. Black	S. Davenport
A. Dodson	F.W. Forth
M. Hudson	C.C. Jernigan
Y.F. Market	R.S. Oliver
J.E. Powell	J.A. Reid
W.H. Reid	G.J. Slappy

—Reprint from WM. KEHOE & CO., Founders and Blacksmiths, Savannah, Georgia, 1883-1884, page 657.

First Pharmacy Opened in 1890s

Plains' first pharmacy was founded in the late 1890s and was located in a brick building, built by Edwin Timmerman and Jesse Timmerman, at the north end of South Bond Street. The pharmacy was owned by Dr. J.C. Logan and Randolph Logan and managed by David Jennings. Harris Hall was the pharmacist.

Several years later the pharmacy moved into a location on the ground floor of the hospital building on Main Street.

In 1910 Plains Pharmacy was located on the ground floor of a two story-brick building, built by the Wise brothers for their first hospital and located at the corner of Hudson and Main streets. M.M. Jennings was manager with Dr. L.E. Godwin and Dr. J.H. Monts pharmacists. In 1917, these two pharmacists bought into the store as partners.

During these years, the drug store was a center of community life, with a Victrola providing musical entertainment, a soda fountain for refreshments, three soda tables with chairs for seating, and a ceiling fan provided cool breezes.

Having a volume of business from the hospital, cascara and mineral oil was purchased in 50-gallon barrels, castor oil in five-gallon cans, epsom salts, sulphur and borax in 100-pound bags. Three pharmacists were employed full time. Robert McGarrah served as a pharmacist there from 1928 to 1945.

In 1928 Dr. Godwin and Dr. Monts bought Plains Pharmacy and also opened the Wise Clinic Drug Store on the ground floor of the Wise Clinic in Americus. When the Plains Wise Sanitarium was damaged by fire in 1935, the doctors moved their pharmacy practice to Americus.

For a short time, Dr. Godwin was at the Americus Drug Store and Dr. Monts in Plains, but they dissolved their partnership some few years later, with Godwin retaining the Plains Pharmacy, and Monts moving to Americus. His son, Jody Monts, has Clinic Drug Store in Americus today. Dr. Brownie Timmerman, a lifelong resident of Plains, was assistant to Dr. Monts at the Clinic Drug Store in Americus.

L.E. Godwin, Jr. became owner of Plains Pharmacy in 1954 upon the death of his father. Godwin, Jr. retired in 1968 and his son L.E. Godwin III assumed ownership and continues to operate the pharmacy today. The top story of the building was removed in 1967 and the pharmacy moved into the west section. The section previously occupied by the pharmacy became a grocery store.

—Reprint from "Americus Times-Recorder," May 15, 1985

Mercantile and Industrial Review

The Seaboard Air Line Railway printed Mercantile and Industrial Reviews concerning communities on their route. The purpose was to develop and utilize the natural resources and raw materials located on their line. It was the desire of the railway to promote businesses and encourage people to settle along their lines. The following information was published in the Mercantile and Industrial Review of Americus and Sumter County, Issued by the Industrial Department of the Seaboard Air Line Railway, Portsmouth, Virginia, published about 1907.

Plains, Sumter County, Georgia

Plains is the largest city in Sumter County outside of Americus. It has 550 inhabitants. Plains is reached from Americus by the Seaboard Air Line Railway, a distance of ten miles and is also connected to Americus by a splendid hard road of which Sumter County has many. The city is located in a very fertile farming country, is surrounded by splendid farms in a high state of cultivation, the cotton production of the region amounting to 7,500 bales per year. Situated on a tableland as it is makes Plains one of the very healthiest places in the county. The drainage is perfect, and the water supply is abundant, pure and healthy.

Plains has a fine two-story high school building, three teachers and a music teacher. The enrollment for the past year was 125 and there were 30 music pupils. The school is free, there are ten grades and the term covers seven months.

Plains has one bank, three churches, one high school, two cotton warehouses, nine commercial houses, one fresh meat market, one livery stable, one planning mill and lumber yard, two blacksmith and wood working shops, telegraph, telephone, express and railroad office.

Much interest is being manifested in and around Plains in commercial peach culture. There are already some 50,000 trees and the number is being added to constantly. Fruit growers say that the soil around Plains is splendidly adapted to the culture of peaches, as it contains sufficient iron to give the peach the proper flavor and color. The peach crop of Plains is ready for the market fully two weeks sooner than that of Fort Valley and North Georgia. This is a point in its favor, as it is enabled to place its crop on the market before the competition of the districts named becomes apparent.

The land around Plains is splendid for agricultural purposes. On a tract of ten acres a crop of oats amounting to 850 bushels was produced last year. The land is owned by L.D. Wise. Cotton crop of T.L. McLendon for 1906 averaged 55 bales to 60 acres, which is far above the average; corn will also run 30 bushels to the acre, as was demonstrated by E. Timmerman, on 50 acres. Fine crops of wheat are also grown. There is very little necessity for a farmer around Plains having to go into the market for any of his supplies. They all can be grown right on the place. Corn, oats, wheat, cane, vegetables, fruits, cattle and hogs, and many other items.

The roads leading to Plains are fine, level and well kept. The Bond's Trail road, running north and south through the town, crosses water only once in 30 miles, automobiling and driving are all enjoyable pleasures.

PUBLIC SCHOOL, PLAINS, GA.

Plains High School circa 1900
Photo credit: Mercantile and Industrial Review of
Americus and Sumter County

Above: Timmerman and Wise Warehouse. Below: Timmerman and Wise cotton gin. Photo credit: "Mercantile and Industrial Review of Americus and Sumter County"

Spann and Montgomery Warehouse. Photo credit: "Mercantile and Industrial Review of Americus and Sumter County"

Timmerman & Wise

For several years this firm of warehouses has been building up a large business in the several lines they represent, and are now among the leaders in the sales of buggies, harness, lime, brick, and farm implements, fertilizers, etc. They are also agents for the McCormick Machines, and are managers of the Plains Warehouse & Ginning Co., operating a ginnery of 480 saws which has a capacity of 3,000 bales per season. Messrs. Timmerman & Wise employ 12 people in the operation of their interests, and have done much for the building of their section.

Spann & Montgomery

The above firm of cotton factors was started here four years ago with Mr. W.H. Spann and G.W. Montgomery as proprietors. They are among the largest cotton dealers in the county, and handled last year about 3,500 bales, and they also operate a planning mill of 15,000 feet per day capacity. They employ several men regularly and their yard and warehouse cover about three-fourths of an acre.

Oliver-McDonald Co.

This firm deals in general merchandise having, it is said, the largest retail business in this section. They handle large quantities of fertilizer, about five thousand bales of cotton per season, and deal extensively in cotton seed and cotton seed products. They were established and incorporated in 1906, for $20,000 capital, with such officers as R.S. Oliver, president; J.A. McDonald, vice presi-

Oliver-McDonald Co. store and cash register from the store shown to Dallas NeSmith by Nellie Jennings, both descendants of early Plains settlers. Photo credit: "Mercantile and Industrial Review of Americus and Sumter County" and Allene T. Haugabook

dent; and M.L. Hudson, secretary and treasurer, and give employment to ten people.

Plains Bank

Though not as large as some of the banks of this section, this is one of the strongest and is engineered by some of the most reliable men in the community, who have had charge of financing some of the most important moves of the community. Plains Bank was organized in 1902 with capital stock of $25,000, and the deposits in round figures are $100,000 in the cotton season, and undivided profits are $12,000. They are located in their fire-proof brick building with specially constructed burglar proof vault, and the officers are Mr. R.S. Oliver, president; B.T. Wise, vice president, and W.L. Thomas, cashier. All the capital stock with the exception of $1,000 is owned by local men.

Stephens & Murray Brothers

This is the only livery and feed stable in Plains, and was established September 1, 1906, by Mr. A.C. Stephens and the Murray Brothers. They employ three men, and have special facilities for arranging funeral outfits, together with nine other modern neat turnouts.

Thomas & Clark

This in one of the best known sales stables in the county, and they handle on an average of 200 head of horses and mules per season, the majority of these being high class mules. They give steady employment during the season to eight men and own one of the largest peach farms in the county, containing twenty-five thousand trees.

Lunsford-French-Timmerman Co.

This firm was incorporated in 1902 at a capital of $10,000 with Mr. Jno. E. French, president;

G.P. Lunsford, vice president; and J.W. Timmerman, secretary and treasurer. They employ four men, and carry on a general merchandise business, carrying a large stock of ladies' and gents' furnishing goods, hardware, furniture, farm supplies, etc., and occupy their own two-story brick structure on the main thoroughfare of Plains.

Chappell's drugstore. Photo credit: "Mercantile and Industrial Review of Americus and Sumter County"

J.E. Chappell Drugstore

There is nothing so important to any town as the careful dispensation of drugs, and Plains is fortunate in its choice of druggists. Mr. J.E. Chappell has for several years been building up a large business, and his stock of drugs, rubber goods, cigars, etc., is displayed in such a manner as would give credit to a much larger establishment.

"Mercantile and Industrial Review of Americus and Sumter County," issued by the Industrial Department of the Seaboard Air Line Railway, Portsmouth, Virginia. Published about 1907.

—Submitted by Annette Wise

Plains Hospital
Once Had National Reputation

Plains Hospital was opened in 1913 by Dr. Burr Thaddeus Wise, joined later by his two brothers, Dr. Sam Wise and Dr. Bowman Wise, in the upstairs 10 to 15-bed floor of the building on West Hudson Street. A smaller frame clinic was built on the west side to care for the black patients. Their first patient was Mrs. Almer C. Murray (mother of Beth M. Walters, Gladys Murray, Norman Murray and Annola M. Perry – all of Plains) for whom nurse Effie McArthur (later Mrs. S. H. Timmerman) was brought in to care for her. Because of the overflow of patients, when improved but not able to return home, Mrs. D.C. (Victoria Lassiter) Brannen took them into their home, applying treatments under the supervision of the doctor.

Her daughter, Miss Annie Mae Brannen, assisted her mother with this service, and continued this career with the Wise Brothers until the hospital burned and the doctors moved to Americus in 1936. In 1915 when Dr. Joseph H. and Mrs. Rosalee Douglas Monts moved to Plains, she became the first superintendent of nurses at Wise Sanitarium. She died in 1983, preceded by her husband.

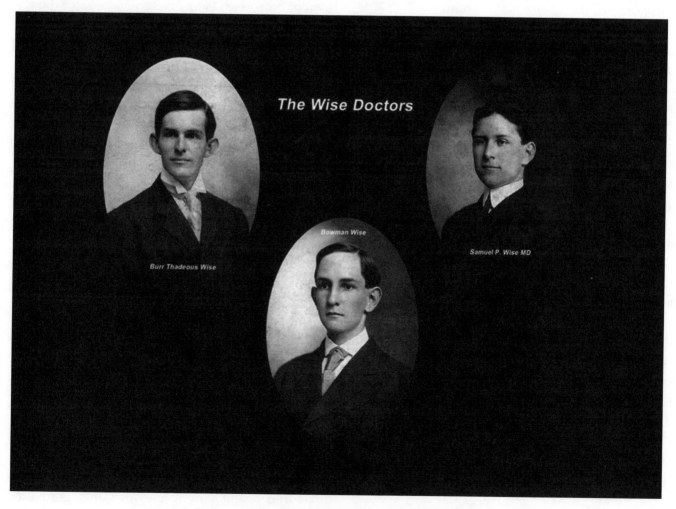

Left to right: Thad, Bowman, and Sam Wise
Photo credit: Horace Seymour, Jr.

To increase bed space, the hospital was moved in 1916 to the upstairs area of their new building on Main Street, having been constructed by a local contractor, Rev. A.C. Wellons, a Baptist minister.

In 1921, the $75,000 new brick hospital building was ready for occupancy, accommodating sixty beds with an X-ray and Radium Department. It was chartered "Wise Sanitarium" and was one of the first "less than 100 bed" hospitals to be accredited. An accredited training school for nurses was operated from 1917-1936 with a Plains residence called "The Nurses Home," where the out-of-town nurses boarded with their house mother, Mrs. Sam (Lillie McGarrah) Jennings.

Some of the young ladies coming to get R.N. training and who married the young Plains men, causing jealousy among the local ladies, were Bessoe Lillian Gordy (Mrs. James Earl Carter, Sr.), Lottie Thomas Meadows, a twin (Mrs. Tyre Phillip Wise), Jewel Sears (Mrs. Dennis Turner), Gussie Abrams (Mrs. DeWitt Howell), Betty Pennington (Mrs. Joe Bacon), Ethel Yaughn (Mrs. Phillip Brown Jennings), Grace McConnell (Mrs. John Cato Murray) and Effie McArthur (Mrs. S.H. Timmerman).

In the late 1920s, the Wise Sanitarium served as the S.A.L. hospital. Following a train wreck at Savannah, some ten to fifteen patients were brought in. All ambulances, pickup trucks and other available conveyances met the train as it rolled into Plains that night. Two of the patients remained in the hospital a year but everyone was able to return to their home.

Doctors who were associated with Wise Sanitarium were Dr. Sam Wise and Dr. Bowman Wise. They served in the United States Army during World War I, leaving Dr. Thad Wise to care for the patients. The 1917-18 flu epidemic kept the doctor busy night and day. When the two doctors returned from the war, Dr. Thad limited his practice to surgery and hospital; Dr. Sam did general practice and some surgery, and Dr. Bowman practiced obstetrics and anesthesia.

Dr. Henry Smith, after finishing his internship and residency in medicine at Grady Memorial Hospital in Atlanta, came to Wise Sanitarium as a staff member. Developing a rare blood disease, his untimely death came in 1929.

Dr. Sylvester Cain graduated from Oglethorpe and Emory universities, Atlanta, serving internship and residency in the Emory Division at Grady Memorial Hospital before coming to Plains in July 1927. At Grady, he was chief of the Internal Medicine Service. After several years at Plains, he went to Greer, South Carolina, then to his hometown of Norcross, Georgia, where he later died.

Dr. Robert C. Pendergrass joined the Wise Sanitarium in 1927, after having an internship and residency training in radiology. He played an important role as a hospital staff member. During World War II, he was assigned as radiologist at Ashford General Hospital at White Sulphur Springs, West Virginia. At the conclusion of the war Dr. Pendergrass opened his office in Americus, where he died a few years later.

Dr. John B. Thompson came to Plains in July 1928 after graduating from Emory University, to serve his internship. He had further ambition to specialize in ear, eye, nose and throat, so he went to Columbus where he practiced until his death in the late 1960s.

Dr. J.D. Martin came to Plains in July 1928 after three years as an intern and house officer in surgery at Grady Memorial Hospital, the last year of which he was chief resident in surgery. His plans were to remain a short while before going to Europe to study pathology before returning to Atlanta. After his return to Atlanta in 1930, he married the former Elosie McLaughlin from Macon.

Dr. George Mims, Jr., reared in Plains, the son of George T. and Minnie Carroll Mims, graduated from Plains High School and Georgia Southwestern College in Americus, the University of Georgia in Athens, medical school in Augusta and interned in St. Louis. He did work at Charity Hospital in New Orleans. He then served in the U.S. Army for two years stationed at Newfoundland. He is associated with Kennestone Hospital, Marietta, Georgia. He married the former Helen Phelps and their children are George T. III, Jennifer, Julie and Jan.

Dr. Robert Lavender became associated with the clinic after his graduation from Emory following a year's internship but did not complete his residency. While here, he married a young lady from Americus and remained at the sanitarium for several years before retuning to his native state of Mississippi.

Dr. James Hardaway from Edison, Georgia, graduated from Emory University in 1926, and at one time was associated with Wise Sanitarium for a few years.

Some student doctors who spent summer months under the Drs. Wise were Dr. Douglas B. Kendrick, Dr. Russell B. Thomas, Dr. Emmett Ferguson, and Dr. Leslie.

Other very capable hospital staff member:

Mrs. DeWitt (Gussie Abrams) Howell, for several years was the director of nursing and the nurse anesthetic contributing to the day-by-day operation of the hospital. There was no function of requirement in which she was not involved in the completely adequate and dedicated manner.

Mrs. K.C. (Mary Hudson) Campbell served as laboratory technician to the hospital soon after it opened until it closed in 1936. She had trained at Grady Memorial in Atlanta and contributed superb assistance to the patients. She also assisted in some of the book work.

Miss Annie Mae Brannen maintained the business office for the doctors and the hospital location above the Plains Pharmacy where Dr. B.J. Wise continued to maintain an office for patients for the Plains area after the hospital had moved to Americus.

Damaged by fire in 1936, the patients and doctors moved to the Americus hospital.

—Reprinted from "Americus Times-Recorder," May 15, 1985, pp. 13-15.

"Loveliest Village of the Plain"

Miss Julia Coleman, superintendent of the Plains School, gave a beautiful word picture of the little city of Plains in an address over radio station WSB recently, upon invitation of Rich's Atlanta department store. Following is a copy of Miss Coleman's address.

If you are interested in making a pleasant little visit, come to southwest Georgia to Sumter County, call by Americus, its capital – that "city set on a hill" – follow the Crisp Military Highway running like a gray ribbon through areas of level land, from Fort Benning to the sea. Drive on through woodland doorway, until you see before you in the words of Oliver Goldsmith – "the loveliest village of the plain." Enter the town – Plains!

On the left, a proud little Main Street where the busiest and kindliest of people come and go, buying and selling goods and gas, furnishing and supplies for farms and houses – all intermingled with a generous amount of good will. Turn to the right and Plains public school greets you. The students are gone, for it is the close of day, but as you drive through the "Friendship Garden," you receive the greeting of the school and community, in the fragrance of tea-olive. Enter the school office, and observe upon a pedestal, a silver cup. It seems a veritable "bride of quietness, a foster child of silence and slow time" a silver historian. For you read the inscription:

Ga. State College of Agriculture
American Farming
Best Community Contest
Second Prize
Won By Plains Community
Georgia 1927

Across the street from the school, in his quiet home, sits our eldest citizen, Mr. A. Dodson, who has reached the very crown of the years. As a faithful historian, he would know the story of men and women who had built a community receiving this modest recognition of a silver cup, for the work of their hands.

Long ago, Creek Indians roamed over this good land, and tradition tells romantic tales of warriors and queens, Spanish adventures in this, Georgia's noblest region.

Between two streams, bearing the Indian names "Muckalee" and Choctawatchee," white men made their homes and as the days of many years passed, they established a community which they might have given a name from the Indians, noblest of heathen. Again there was a bold and beautiful spring nearby, called "Magnolia," whose name they might have chosen. The spring attracted many visitors and during the days of Southern chivalry, it was a place of resort for youth and beauty. But these early settlers turned to the Bible, and, from Old Testament lore, named their community "Plains of Dura."

It was an event when the first railroad was built – the A.P. and L., now the Seaboard Air Line.

The planters from "Plains of Dura" built new and spacious homes near the railroad, set up a Post Office, built stores, established a bank, in fact in 1884 founded the town of Plains.

The people who founded the town had high ideals in many ways. In industry and trade, they expressed them by establishing modern stores and shops and places of business, warehouses and a gin, for the community was a growing cotton market; finally gas stations, electric lights, a good telephone system, and a pure water supply.

They loved education and built a school to meet changing needs, in which teachers have a fair opportunity to serve youth, truly by carrying out a vital program of education. There are three churches whose men worship and where, on every Sabbath

day, devoted Christian women carry from their own home gardens, flowers, offerings of love, whose richness is rivaled only by the colors of the stained glass windows.

Come to Plains. See the homes on friendly streets where children play. See the red soil, which makes the rarest roses grow. Observe the abundant harvest of wheat and oats, cotton, corn, peanuts and pecans.

Come to Plains, a town of 600 people, meet a genial and progressive mayor, Honorable E. Timmerman. Share in civic problems. Right now the people are striving sacrificially to build an addition to the school, for they have the spirit of their forefathers. Revel in the beauty and goodness of the fertile plains, which Sidney Lanier says "publish themselves to the sea." Or, we may say in fanciful mood – Plains is a jewel – worn by the Lady Sumter – in her sunny hair.

This article was taken from a scrapbook belonging to Mary Jo Campbell Stout, (great-granddaugter of M.L. Hudson). Speech was made in the 1930s.
—Submitted by Allene T. Haugabook

New Homes Are Going Up At Plains

The thriving town of Plains continues to expand with every year. Never a season passes that does not find some addition to its large number of comfortable and attractive homes. Year after year the compactly built section of the town has increased until it presents an appearance that few towns of its size in Georgia can offer. On all sides there are the unmistakable signs of comfort, of thrift, of prosperity, and of an appreciation of beauty as applied to home surroundings.

Four houses are now nearing completion, the finishing touches being put to them, that would ornament any town, and that are a decided addition to the beauty of Plains. Mr. W.L. Thomas has a fine two-story residence nearly completed, a large, attractive home that will have pretty grounds to set it off. Mr. Tom Lawson, Mr. Edmund Oliver, and Mr. Ernest Wellons are also watching with pleasure the completion of homes that represent good taste in architecture, and that appeal to the lover of large rooms and ample space.

W.L. Thomas House
Photo credit: Allene T. Haugabook

These four houses will be followed by other new structures in the near future. A number of building lots have been sold on the Bond's Trail road, and plans are being made for the building of several homes during the spring and summer. The outlook is that the current year will find Plains increased by fully a dozen new homes. The citizens of the bright, enterprising little city to the west are naturally proud of the development the town is making and look forward with satisfaction to further expansion of the population and business.

—From "Americus Daily Times-Recorder," March 20, 1912

New Building at Plains

The large brick building which is being erected by Drs. Thad and Sam Wise, on the lot just south of the Seaboard depot, formerly owned by Mr. Mize of Americus, is steadily growing. Constructor T.O. Lawson expects to complete it by the first of August.

Down stairs, facing Main Street, on the corner to the left will be a drug store where a new business will be opened by Mr. M.M. Jennings. Back of this, opening toward the business part of town, will be the doctors' office. That portion on the right, fronting Main Street, will be rented for a store, while the entire back of the first floor will be arranged as a private garage. On the second floor to the left, an operating room will be at the back, with the three front rooms as reception, examination, and consultation rooms, while the fourth will be for medicine. The other nine rooms will be fitted up as a hospital.

The building will be fully equipped with acetyline gas lights, baths, and all modern appliances.

—From "Americus Daily Times-Recorder," July 5, 1912

Citizens Bank

Opens Doors on Monday
Plains has Second Bank

The Citizens Bank of Plains, the second bank to be established in that thrifty town and the ninth bank in Sumter County, opened its doors for business Monday morning, and under conditions that insure long posterity for the new institution. The capital stock is $25,000, all subscribed and paid.

In fact, such was the demand for stock in the new bank that the capital stock might easily have been doubled, had it been deemed desirable by the officers to do so.

The officers of the Citizens Bank are: L.O. Benton, president; T.W. Timmerman, cashier. The directors are: J.E. Harper, A.C. Wellons, J.E. Chappell, J.M. Cook, G.E. Hiller, Dr. J.C. Logan, J.W. Timmerman, R.M. Andrews, and L.O. Benton.

In such a prosperous community, and directed by a corps of efficient officers, the new bank will be accorded a full share of business, and begins its career under very flattering auspices.

—*Reprint from "Americus Daily-Times Recorder," November 19, 1912*

Building Boom

Is Now On At Plains

Plains, Ga., May 13 — This season is being marked by much construction work in Plains, and the ring of the hammer is heard here every day. Several new buildings are going up now, while there will be others later.

The Oliver-McDonald Company is engaged in adding and has just about completed a two-story brick annex, which will be used for the furniture department of that well known firm. This will give this large firm excellent facilities for handling its large and varied trade.

J.E. Chappell has recently moved into new quarters, and he has his modern drugstore fully equipped. After having completed four tenant houses, A.C. Wellons is now engaged in laying the foundations for a two-story residence.

Taken altogether this is one of the busiest building seasons that has been known here in some time. The building will continue through summer.

—*Reprint from "Americus Daily Times-Recorder," May 14, 1913*

Modern New Building Is Completed At Plains

Messrs. Edwin Timmerman and L.D. Wise, who have for eighteen years been identified with the cotton trade at Plains, having conducted during these years a warehouse business there, will soon be at home to their many customers in new quarters, a modern and substantial brick warehouse now nearing completion.

The building is constructed of brick throughout, with concrete floors, and is fully equipped with water connections and chemical fire apparatus, thus insuring protection against possible fire.

Every care has been given the construction of this building, and it will be completed and made ready for occupancy by or before September 1st. As a safe and conveniently arranged cotton warehouse this is one of Messrs. Timmerman and Wise is unsurpassed in south Georgia.

Mr. Timmerman will give his personal attention to the sales department of the business, while Mr. Wise will preside at the scales, and in looking after the interests of patrons generally.

—*Reprint from "Daily Time Recorder," August 14, 1913*

New Wise Hospital to Be Built at Plains

$75,000 Structure Planned As Result of Stock Company Offer

PLAINS, December 11 — It is stated definitely by the Drs. Wise that they have decided to remain in Plains and that they will build their new hospital here. The subject of location has been under consideration for some time by the Drs. Wise and they have had various offers from different towns and cities made them. The citizens of Plains and the community have been greatly interested in the question of their removal and the citizens have made every effort to keep them in the town.

Some time ago a stock company was formed and funds were offered for the erection of a new $75,000 hospital building that would meet the needs of the doctors for their practice. But it has not been known until this week whether the offer would be accepted or not.

The site for the new building lies almost behind the Lutheran church, very near the Plains-Americus highway and in plain view from the

S.A.L. Railroad. The location is considered advantageous since it will be quiet and at the same time easily accessible.

The Drs. Wise have not stated when work will begin on the new building but it is thought that its erection will be started just as soon as arrangements can be be made, since the building in present use is entirely inadequate.

The people of Plains and the community are rejoiced over the decision of the doctors to remain in the town. These physicians are greatly beloved, personally and professionally. The citizens of the town and community feel a genuine pride in the success that the doctors have made and they consider it a great fortune that they all remain in Plains and locate their hospital here.

—Reprint from "Americus Daily Times-Recorder," December 11, 1919

A.C. Murray House showing gas light in 1910. Photo credit: Georgia Department of Archives and History

Centennial Articles

Kerosene lamps in the homes and gas lights on the streets were replaced with electricity when Plains installed a light system in 1919 that was operated by a diesel engine driven generator. A large celebration was held the night the lights were turned on.

Snow Bowers was manager of the new light system, and his job included reading the meters and making out the monthly statements. In 1935, Leonard Newton Evans, Sr. assumed managership of the light plant located on the east side of town.

The first city well pump was dug in 1906 and located between the Plains Baptist Pastorium and the home of Mrs. Alice Green. A small well with a tank was on the north side of the A.C. Murray home on South Bond Street, and in 1919 the Scholfield Iron Works, Macon, erected a 50,000-gallon water tank on the west corner of Logan Park.

Water mains were installed, but citizens had the responsibility of connecting pipes to their homes. The story goes that a citizen said he would gladly dig the trench with his hands to save hauling water on wash day, according to a history compiled by Beth Walters.

An auxiliary well was dug some years later.

In 1956, a $7,500 water filter was installed to help remove iron contents from the city water system during the leadership of Mayor Dr. J. "Col" Logan.

And in 1965, a 200,000 capacity tank was erected on the east side of Plains off of U.S. 280, and during the 1976 presidential campaign the United States flag was painted on the tank by a man from Tampa, Florida as a tribute to then Democratic presidential candidate Jimmy Carter. And the old water tank was repainted in 1984 with another U.S. flag.

According to Mrs. Walters' history, Plains has had a Volunteer Fire Department from "since the beginning" when everyone rallied with buckets after being notified by the telephone operator during the day or gunshot at night.

The city of Plains purchased a used fire truck in the late 1940s which was sold in the mid-1960s and another newer model purchased. C.L. Walters, III returned home to Plains and became the first fire chief, having had experience in the fire inspection field with Southeastern Underwriters where he had been employed.

A new fire truck was purchased in 1972 with a 750 gallon-per-minute pump, making Plains have a fleet of two fire trucks. A fire phone line has been added, comprised of 12-phone direct call when the fire number is dialed. The 12 connecting phones continually ring until answered and phone receiver replaced on the stand.

—*Reprint from the Americus-Times Recorder, May 15, 1985.*

Plains Digging Itself Out of Storm Debris

New Twister Hits Town Doing Widespread Damage

The town of Plains is still busy today, and will continue busy for several days, attempting to bring order out of the chaos wrought by a terrific wind, rain and hail storm, taking on much of the nature of a twisting tornado, which struck the town Tuesday afternoon, doing much damage to property of many kinds and filling the streets with a tangle of trees, poles and wires, as well as other debris.

Telephone communication with Plains from Americus was still interrupted today, the damage both to toll lines and local exchanges not having been repaired. The news of the extent of the storm did not begin reaching the Times-Recorder, brought in by person who came by auto from the neighboring city, until shortly after Wednesday's editions had gone to press and it continued to come today.

The storm struck somewhere between the home of Jack Slappey just to the northeast of the town and, sweeping through the town proper, continued in a southwesterly direction through Old Bottsford, across Kinchafoonee Creek and into the vicinity of the intersection of Sumter, Terrell and Webster Counties, swerving there and sweeping to the farm of Jack Goss a mile to the eastward. The storm was accompanied by heavy hail for a stretch about half a mile which stripped crops of all kinds.

The Plains electric light and pumping station, a steam plant recently erected by a bond issue, was unroofed and the walls demolished, putting the plant out of commission for a time. The Montgomery cotton warehouse was unroofed and partially blown in. Houses were damaged, and flooded and havoc generally produced. A remarkable feature was that in Plains, despite the heavy damage, not a person was injured.

A party of Americus people, including Mrs. W.T. Lane, were calling that afternoon at the home of Mrs. Randolph Logan in Plains. So severe was the storm damage that they were unable to return until Wednesday.

Mrs. Lane told the extent of the storm damage as she had observed it, reciting the following details of which she learned before leaving there:

Thirteen chimneys were blown down and nearly every home in Plains damaged by the water which fell in torrents for forty-five minutes. The city power house, nearly new, was struck by the full force of the storm, the building unroofed and the machinery being almost submerged by the water. The plant was put out of commission during that night and the next day, the city being in darkness and lamps and candles being brought into service in the stores and homes.

The roof of the Montgomery cotton warehouse was completely torn off with one end of the building blown in and considerable damage done by the rain to the cotton stored in the warehouse.

The home of Jack Dorsey situated about two miles from Plains was badly damaged and his two children painfully but not seriously hurt. Two mules standing in the barn were struck by flying timbers and their legs broken so they had to be killed Wednesday morning.

The handsome large stained art glass window in the front of the Baptist Church in Plains was lifted from its casing and blown about 50 feet, it being undamaged except for a small corner chipped from the glass.

Almost every residence in the town sustained such damage by the water as to render the occupants unable to use their beds during the night, nearly everyone in town remaining up all night. Wednesday morning nearly every mattress in the town was carried outside into the sunshine to dry.

A chicken coop was blown from the yard of one neighbor into that of another with no damage to the two chickens therein. A washtub, which was bottom up in one yard, as blown fifty feet distant and seen shortly after, right side up, nearly full of water. All about the vicinity of Plains the hail fell with such force that the cotton, corn, and other crops were stripped in the fields, many of the cotton stalks standing leafless.

—Reprinted from "Americus Times-Recorder," July 14, 1921

Plains People Still in Dark

Weather Delays Rebuilding of Store Wrecked Power Plant

Plains, July 20 — Indications are that Plains will be dark for some time. The heavy rains which continue to fall daily are materially hindering the work of rebuilding the power house, demolished by the recent storm and making the changes decided upon in some of the electrical works.

The rains also greatly retard the work of repairing the telephone system, and the damage to the roads. All telephone lines to the south of wires and replacing many poles broken by the storm. Some of the roads below town are still impassable. The convicts are working on bridges and washouts, as weather conditions permit, but the rural mail carrier on Route No. 1 is finding it difficult to deliver the mail.

—Reprint from "Americus Times-Recorder," July 29, 1921

First School of Plains

In recent months, something of special interest near and dear to us all is the restoration of the Plains High School building. It seems proper that we might be interested in knowing something of the history of the building that preceded the present one.

The town of Plains did not exist until 1885. It was the magnet of the railroad that drew the outlying communities to what is now our little town of Plains. As the people moved in from these outlying areas to what was to become the Plains of Dura, their interest in education for their children came with them. There was a school three miles north of Plains named Magnolia Springs and one three miles to the south named Planters Academy. In 1891 these schools joined forces and a public subscription for funds to construct a new building was begun. Plains citizens contributed $1,800 toward a two-story building with four rooms on the lower floor. The Masonic Lodge paid part of the expenses and in turn was given the upper floor to use as a lodge room. This building was located on the same lot as the present school building but faced the Plains Baptist Church.

Education was an integral part of the community from its inception. A Professor Jarrell, graduate of Mercer University, was hired as superintendent of the school under the direction of six trustees consisting of R.B. Evans, M.L. Hudson, C.C. Jernigan, R.S. Oliver, W.L. Thomas and E. Timmerman.

At first pupils attending the school had to pay tuition. In 1900 the county began supporting the rural schools with tax money.

This building served well to educate the boys and girls of the Plains community. Then in 1921 the present building was built and the old wooden structure sold for $500. It was moved to the Archery Community and used as a school for the black children of that area. The bell was loaded on a wagon and moved down the streets of Plains. As it tolled its way through the village, tears came to the eyes of many of the citizens. It was the end of one era but the beginning of another.

—*Reprint from "Plains Echoes," Allene T. Haugabook, Volume 1, Number 2*

Stories About Friendship Garden

A Story in Each Plant in Plains Garden

It is twilight. A man and woman walk slowly along the hedge of bridal wreath and turn in among the shrubs and flowers of the garden. They pause before one golden tipped arbor vitae. To the casual eye it is not unlike others in the garden, but to them it is different.

Years ago a chubby youngster planted it. He watched it grow from year to year, proudly caring for "his" tree. Now as the woman picks a dying branch from it she is thinking of that boy — far away on a beachhead in the Pacific. All about her are other flowers and shrubs, rich in beauty and in sentiment. Each with its own story of someone who planted it and cared for it.

It is the Friendship Garden of Plains school, one of the unique beauty spots of south Georgia.

Once Was a Barren Waste

Eight years ago the garden was a barren ugly waste of sand and clay and weeds. Then teachers of the school enlisted the interest of the children to convert their campus into a place of beauty, a project in which each individual and each group would have a part. Soon the garden became more than just a school enterprise. Garden clubs and citizens of the community became interested. Today the garden represents the entire countryside.

Every shrub has been planted in honor or in memory of some person. Even the white concrete posts that mark the driveway have sentiment. Boys of the vocational training department erected them and carved their initials on the posts.

Inside the enclosure flowers and shrubs of every variety are growing. From early spring through the year the garden is a beauty spot with daffodils, tulips, lilacs, roses. When the garden first was started the school spelled the letters "P.H.S." in a bed of iris.

Many varieties of the cedar family have been planted, azaleas, forsythia, junipers, japonicas. Because of its brightness and durability, the golden tipped arbor vitae has become one of the features of the garden.

As the garden grew many parents would bring their babies to it and from this custom grew a unique feature known as "Baby Row." Babies and small children are invited to have a part in the garden. Parents and friends plant shrubs or flowers for them. From the oldest to the youngest, the community all have a part in the garden. Baby Row is now a lovely array of golden-tipped arbor vitae bordering a long wall and one side of the campus.

The garden is a school and community center. Classes are often held there during the summer; garden clubs and other organizations meet there; chapel exercises and May Day celebrations find the garden an ideal spot. Graduating classes have their pictures taken with the garden as a background.

No Acts of Vandalism

The garden is guarded and cared for by every child in the community. There are no acts of vandalism. On the annual "Garden Day" the entire school cooperates in cleaning and improving the garden – pruning and trimming the shrubbery.

Miss Julia Coleman, superintendent of Plains schools, and Y.T. Sheffield, principal, were responsible for starting the project.

"It was school and community spirit which developed the project," Miss Coleman insists. Everyone helped, she says — children, teachers, friends.

An illustrated record book is kept of the garden, giving the names of all who have had a part in its growth.

The school and community take pride in the garden, but to some the garden is a place of sentiment as well. One mother whose son died his first year in school planted an arbor vitae in his memory the year he would have graduated. It stands there along with those of other members of his class.

To her and others "Friendship Garden" is more than a mere garden. It is a sacred spot.

—By Lester R. Ruth (Taken from Scrapbook of Mary Jo Campbell Stout, great-granddaughter of M.L. Hudson)

Will Dedicate New Negro School Soon

Col. J.E.D. Shipp today accepted an invitation to deliver an oration at the dedication of a new Rosenwald Negro Industrial School at Plains on January 2, 1923, it is announced.

This school, erected almost entirely through the patronage of the Julius Rosenwald fund, is the largest and finest of several similar school buildings built in the county through cooperation between the school authorities and managers of the funds. In addition to a limited literary course the students there will receive instruction in many industrial branches, including farming in accordance with the policy of the county school board to advance industrial education among negroes here.

Besides Col. Shipp, it is expected that E.W. Dupree, county school superintendent, and a number of other white citizens interested in education of the negro will attend the dedicatory exercises.

—Reprint from "Americus Times-Recorder," December 18, 1923

Schools Open for Colored

Six Rosenwald Institutes Plan Pre–Session Friday

The six Rosenwald schools for colored in Sumter County will open for registration Friday morning, Ocotber 9 at 8:30 o'clock. All pupils will be enrolled and given book lists by noon.

The pre-session will enable parents to purchase needed books on Saturday and will equip students to begin full-time class work Monday.

On Friday afternoon, teachers of the six schools are requested to attend the dedication of the new Shady Grove school building, a Rosenwald structure, where officials of the county board of education will speak.

Schools opening Friday, with principals are: Shipp Training, C.H. McLeod; Nunn Industrial, J.A. Coachman; Plains Industrial, B.M. Hedge; Shady Grove, W.L. Littleton; Gatewood, Anna Wimbush; Seay, Eleanor Fuse.

—Reprint from "Americus-Times Recorder," October 7, 1931

Gymnasium Is Dedicated By Plains High School

Hundreds Enjoy Joyous Celebration Wednesday Night

PLAINS, Ga., February 15—Last night marked a joyous occasion in Plains, as the citizens of the community, young and old, turned out by the hundreds to enjoy a Valentine Day party and to dedicate the Plains school's fine new gymnasium and vocational training building. Many guests from Americus and other communities joined with the local residents in the celebration.

The evening's program opened in the high school auditorium, where an interesting entertainment was given, and was concluded in the new gymnasium, where dedication exercises were held and a basketball game played by the girls teams from Plains and Anthony high schools. Plains won the game, making the evening's program a complete success.

Wooden floor used for basketball prior to the building of Sheffield Stadium. Photo credit: Lilloise Sheffield

Dr. Bowman Wise, of the school board, opened the program with a short talk in which he explained how the new building was made possible through the splendid cooperation of the school faculty, Parent-Teachers Association, the community in general, the county commissioners, and the CWA officials.

Miss Julia Coleman, superintendent of the Plains schools, made a short talk explaining the evening's program. Miss Coleman and Y.T. Sheffield, principal of the high school, then read the names of several members of the Plains school alumni who had sent messages by letter and telegram. A telegram of congratulations from Gov. Eugene Talmadge was read also. A letter from M.D. Collins, state superintendent of schools, was received by the school also.

The next feature of the program was the introduction of H.S. Simpson, new vocational training instructor of the school, and several members of his classes. Mr. Simpson explained the work to be done by himself and his department. Mrs. Mamie McDonald Bradley has donated many valuable tools that once belonged to her father, the late John McDonald, to the vocational training department's workshop. The gift, valued at approximately $100, was accepted in behalf of the department by Phillip Smith, president of the local chapter of Future Farmers of America, and announced that the shop would by named the John McDonald shop.

A Valentine Day number was then presented on the stage. Several young couples, dressed in appropriate Valentine costumes, presented a pantomine while Eli Wilcox sang, "I Love You Truly."

A clever little play, entitled "The Old Spinning Wheel," was then presented by a cast of Plains young people.

At the conclusion of the play, the audience moved to the new gymnasium.

—Reprint from "Daily Times-Recorder," February 15, 1934

Plains Woman Invited To Luncheon At White House

PLAINS, Ga., January 17 — Miss Julia Coleman, superintendent of Plains High School, has been invited to attend a buffet luncheon at the White House in Washington on January 21.

This unique honor comes to Miss Coleman as a recognition of her devoted interest to education. For several summers in the past Miss Coleman has attended lecture courses at the famous Lake Chautauqua Institute in New York State.

During this time she has become connected with the Chautauqua Club, an organization of women interested in social work, education, international relations, and other current political problems.

Mrs. Franklin D. Roosevelt is also a member of the club, and it is she who is entertaining the body on January 21.

The gist of the invitation is as follows: "Mrs. Roosevelt requests the pleasure of the company of Miss Coleman at a buffet luncheon on Monday, January twenty-first at one o'clock." In another corner are the instructions, "Please present this card at the East Entrance."

Miss Coleman has been superintendent of the Plains School for seven years. Previous to this time she had served as principal of the local school, besides teaching one term in the Newnan schools at Newnan, Georgia.

She has not decided whether or not she will accept the invitation.

—Reprint from "Americus Times Recorder," February 17, 1935

Note: Miss Julia corresponded with Mrs. Roosevelt about this trip and followed up with an invitation to Mrs. Roosevelt to visit Plains High School. This correspondence follows this article.

Coleman – Roosevelt Correspondence

The source for these letters: Franklin D. Roosevelt Library in Hyde Park, New York.

Copies of correspondence between Julia L. Coleman and Mrs. Franklin D. Roosevelt regarding Miss Coleman's visit to the White House in January 1935 and inviting Eleanor Roosevelt to visit Miss Coleman's school in Plains, Georgia in 1934 and 1935.

The typed letter of January 24, 1935 is from Eleanor Roosevelt. Mrs. Roosevelt's handwritten notes from that letter are in the upper right hand corner of the first page of Miss Coleman's letter of January 17, 1935. They read: "Had not read her letter when she spoke to me. Am so glad she came. Will try sometime to drop in on her."

Why This Correspondence Is Included

It is hoped that these letters give some insight into the type teacher Miss Julia Coleman was, the concern she had for her students, school, and community, as well as the influence she had on each. She often challenged her classes with the words "some young person in this class could become president of the United States." She even had some boys in high school make a replica of the White House that was used for display in the classrooms. The reader might well understand why one of her students did become president of the United States and quoted Miss Julia Coleman in both his inaugural address and in his acceptance speech of the Nobel Peace Prize.

Letter 1 Pages 1-2

Sumter County Teachers Association
Americus, Georgia

Plains, Ga.
Jan. 11, 1934
Mrs. F. D. Roosevelt,
Washington, D.C.
Dear Mrs. Roosevelt,
    I am an obscure
teacher in South Georgia.
Plains is in Sumter
County, ten miles west
of Americus, seventy miles
South of Macon. I am
Superintendent of a
rural consolidated
school, located in

Sumter County Teachers Association
Americus, Georgia

the village of Plains.
    I am daring to write
you and make a re-
quest. Would it be
possible for you to
be our guest speaker
at Commencement
June 11, 1934?
    Commencement is
a beautiful season
and occasion in our
community. We have

Letter 1 Pages 3-4

Sumter County Teachers Association
Americus, Georgia

a splendid class of
graduates, twenty two
this year. Our audi-
torium is spacious
and large audiences
attend the annual
Commencement, which
is a beloved event.
    The problem of edu-
cation in Georgia is
a great one. It is

Sumter County Teachers Association
Americus, Georgia

with heroic sacrifice
that we have kept
our school open. The
spirit of the people
has been indeed - won-
derful. With your great
heart, you must know
something of the strug-
gle of the masses of
humanity. My life is
dedicated to the youth

Coleman-Roosevelt Correspondence

Letter 1 Pages 5-6

MISS JULIA L. COLEMAN, Pres.   L. C. LANFORD, Vice-Pres.   MRS. C. J. DANIEL, Sec'y.

Sumter County Teachers Association
Americus, Georgia

of this community, wholly I have faith in them and hope for them. I am asking this most gracious courtesy of you, in their behalf.

You have ideals. I know you have. Catch this beautiful vision of service. Come to our obscure rural school.

MISS JULIA L. COLEMAN, Pres.   L. C. LANFORD, Vice-Pres.   MRS. C. J. DANIEL, Sec'y.

Sumter County Teachers Association
Americus, Georgia

Let the youth of this state and nation witness a lovely courtesy to the plain boys and girls of a rural school.

Let us hear you speak fine strong words of encouragement and cheer and it will be to the people of Georgia

Letter 1 Pages 7-8

MISS JULIA L. COLEMAN, Pres.   L. C. LANFORD, Vice-Pres.   MRS. C. J. DANIEL, Sec'y.

Sumter County Teachers Association
Americus, Georgia

a veritable "breath of life". Consider our request before you decline It would mean much to countless thousands, the very graciousness and sweetness and idealism of your acceptance — if it only could be possible.

Pardon my

MISS JULIA L. COLEMAN, Pres.   L. C. LANFORD, Vice-Pres.   MRS. C. J. DANIEL, Sec'y.

Sumter County Teachers Association
Americus, Georgia

boldness. I realize my letter is an appealing one. But I beg of you to consider what a contribution you could make to village life, ours being typical of villages all over our great country

Our Commencement

Coleman-Roosevelt Correspondence

Letter 1 Pages 9-10

MISS JULIA L. COLEMAN, Pres.   L. C. LANFORD, Vice-Pres.   MRS. C. J. DANIEL, Sec'y.

Sumter County Teachers Association
Americus, Georgia

is scheduled for Monday evening, 8 o'clock, June 11, 1934. — Could a dream come true? Like the apostles of old, "silver and gold have we none" — "but such as we have — loyalty, faith, friendship" — only these could we offer

MISS JULIA L. COLEMAN, Pres.   L. C. LANFORD, Vice-Pres.   MRS. C. J. DANIEL, Sec'y.

Sumter County Teachers Association
Americus, Georgia

you. Is it possible — for a dream to come true? Sincerely, Julia L. Coleman, Supt. Plains Public School

Mrs Roosevelt's Reply to Letter 1

January 17, 1934

My dear Miss Coleman:

Mrs. Roosevelt asks me to thank you for your letter of January 11. She deeply regrets that so many schools have asked her to speak at their commencement exercises that she has had to refuse them all.

With appreciation of your thought of her, I am

Very sincerely yours,

Secretary to
Mrs. Roosevelt

Miss Julia L. Coleman   RWM
Plains
Georgia

Coleman-Roosevelt Correspondence

Letter 2 Pages 1-2

Plains, Ga.
Jan. 17, 1935

Mrs. Franklin D. Roosevelt,
Washington, D.C.

Dear Mrs. Roosevelt,

Your invitation to me, as a member of the Chautauqua Womans' Club, to luncheon, Jan. 21, 1935, one o'clock has been received.

I am writing you this personal note to express my joy and appreciation.

Your kindness and graciousness to me is a blessing, the extent of which you can not realize.

I am an obscure teacher in South Georgia, a day's ride from Warm Springs. I am Supt. of a Consolidated Rural School. My work is my ruling passion. I wish you knew something of it and that it were possible

Letter 2 Pages 3-4

for you to visit us, at some time when you are in Warm Springs.

Imagine my joy, if you can, when I write you that I shall be present at your luncheon. I consider it the event of a lifetime. My School Board will permit me to be absent from my work and

they are pleased and grateful for your courtesy.

I shall be the most obscure guest, but you must have the consciousness that you are giving one lady, of a handicapped life, the adventure, only a real gentlewoman could have bestowed.

Coleman-Roosevelt Correspondence

Letter 2 Page 5 and Roosevelt Reply

Would you consider it vulgar if I reminded you of this when I see you?

If your secretary will see that you read this letter, it may at least give you pleasure, that you have given me such transcendent joy.

Sincerely

Julia L. Coleman.
Plains, Ga.

January 24, 1935

My dear Miss Coleman:

I had not read your letter when you spoke to me on Monday, as my mail is so heavy it does not reach me as promptly as it really should. I am so glad that you came and really enjoyed your trip.

I will keep your letter in mind and try some time when I am in Georgia to drop in on you.

Very sincerely yours,

Miss Julia L. Coleman
Plains
Georgia

Letter 3 Pages 1-2

Plains, Ga
Feb. 14, 1937
Dear Mrs. Roosevelt,

I am writing you informally to express to you my great appreciation of your Kindness.

I was a guest at the luncheon, given to the Chautauqua Woman's Club.

I believe that you will enjoy knowing that your invitation to me was a blessing of unusual

proportions.

My visit to the White House as your guest is the cherished event of my life. I feel sure that you will be glad to know that you have so irradiated another life.

Since my return, you have written kindly to me, saying that when you come to Georgia at some convenient time you may

Coleman-Roosevelt Correspondence

Chapter 22: Articles of Interest

Letter 3 Pages 3-4

be able to "drop in".

I am Superintendent of a Village School — an Accredited Rural School. The children and young people come in on school buses. Plains is a village of 600 inhabitants — very fine people.

If you can give me just a little "niche" in your memory — if you could really "drop in" — it would

be an inspiration to the youth of this community, not to be estimated.

I have delayed writing even a note of thanks to you after the wonderful occasion you gave so many. I knew your correspondence was enormous. I wanted you to really know how much joy and inspiration you

Letter 3 Pages 5-6

brought to an obscure life.

Your cordiality, your naturalness, your ideas endear you to a nation.

I am laying aside all reserve and telling you how very, very much we Georgians love you. May I call you my friend?

Again let me express my gratitude

for your graciousness at the lovely luncheon; and may we really hope that some day you will "drop in —".

Sincerely,
Julia L. Coleman.

Coleman-Roosevelt Correspondence

Letter 4 Pages 1-2

Plains, Ga.,
Nov. 29, 1935.

Mrs. F. D. Roosevelt,
Warm Springs, Ga.

Dear Mrs. Roosevelt,

I am writing you from my home in Plains, a little town ten miles west of Americus, Ga., Sumter County.

May I write that I was entertained in the White House, as a member of the Chautauqua Woman's Club last year. I can never forget that great occasion and your gracious

hospitality.

I am an obscure Georgia teacher, Superintendent of a Consolidated School, which has been my life work.

I am one of those who have had to overcome a greatly handicapped life. I rejoice greatly that Warm Springs, and all that it means, saves many others from what I have had to endure. Therefore, from a personal

Letter 4 Pages 3-4

viewpoint, I love the ideal of the great work in which you and your noble companion are interested.

I am writing you to make an earnest request. Would it be possible for you to call on our school and talk to our children and young people?

May I remind you

that you wrote me after the Chautauqua reception that it might be possible for you to call by when you were in Georgia.

I talked with you for a few moments in the White House, and I can never forget your kind words, nor the gracious note you wrote me afterward.

Coleman-Roosevelt Correspondence

Letter 4 Pages 5-6

A ride of less than two hours would bring you to our School. May I say that we would not worry you with great clamor and parade. If you could come for a lovely call, talk to our students for a short while, have tea or lunch in my Temple home, it would ~~be~~

a great event in our town and community.

May I say that I am not attempting to secure personal _glory_. Instead, we _want_ you to come as an inspiration to the youth of our community. It has been my policy for years, as a part of our system, to invite _good_ _people_ and

Letter 4 Pages 7-8

great _people_ to our school. The results of these visits are not to be estimated. It is a case of "casting bread on waters".

Mrs. Roosevelt, _could_ you find time to come? I believe that the courtesy would be appreciated by _all_ the people of Georgia for it would be taken as an evidence of

your good will and your interest in the _masses_ of _children_ and young people in Georgia. It would mean more than a visit to _us_; it would be a visit to the _rural_ _schools_ of the whole _state_.

Could a dream come true? May we dare hope ~~that~~ you

Coleman-Roosevelt Correspondence

Letter 4 Pages 9-10

can come?

I do not wish to worry you; to be too urgent, or too familiar. But if you *can* come, as you wrote that some day you *might*, it would mean a great deal to the youth of our community. You would receive our deepest gratitude. Our loyalty,

our friendship, our sincere appreciation of your life and its ideals — these simple tributes, we offer you, hoping that you can find time to grant our request.

Sincerely,

Julia L. Coleman,
Supt. Plains Public Schl.
Plains, Ga.

Letter 4 Roosevelt Reply

December 5, 1935

My dear Miss Coleman:

Mrs. Roosevelt is sorry that your letter of the 29th did not reach her before she left Washington for Warm Springs. In any case she could not have accepted your kind invitation as her stay in Georgia was very brief and her time was completely filled.

Very sincerely yours,

Malvina T. Scheider
Secretary to
Mrs. Roosevelt.

Miss Julia L. Coleman
Plains
Georgia

Coleman-Roosevelt Correspondence

Plains Church Badly Burned

Heavy Loss Estimated At Baptist Church 1936

PLAINS, Ga., December 21.— Fire swept Plains Baptist Church last night, causing a loss estimated at several hundred dollars.

Rev. Auston Turner, of Plains, returning home after filling an appointment at a rural church near here, discovered the fire shortly before 10 o'clock. The local volunteer unit mobilized and an alarm was sent to Americus fire department, four firemen from there bringing a truck here.

The fire started between the annex and auditorium. Chief John Monahan, of Americus, said a defect in the heating plant of the frame building started the fire.

An evening service was held at the church at 7 o'clock.

—Reprint from "Americus Times-Recorder," December 21, 1936

Plains Rosenwald School Graduation on Friday Evening

Plains, Georgia – May 2, 1945

Commencement exercises of the Plains Rosenwald School will be held Friday evening, May 4. The following program will be given. Processional chorus, "Sweet Hour of Prayer"; scripture, by Rev. W.T. Hicks; invocation, Rev. B.D. Schley: selection, by the chorus; salutatorian, Joshuah Morgan; valedictorian, Elizabeth Wilson; introduction of speaker; address, A.W. Lash, principal of Staley High School, Americus; selection by the chorus; remarks by B.B. Schley, chariman of the Community School Club.

—Reprint from "Americus-Times Recorder," May 2, 1945

Stitch-n-Chat Club over 50 years old

For more than 50 years, there has been a unique organization in Plains called the Stitch-n-Chat Club. Though the club name implies that members sit and visit over their needlework, this is not necessarily true.

Meeting twice each month, members bring their handwork, enjoy refreshments, visit with one another, and also perform many civic duties, contributing to good causes. Organized in the spring of 1933 by Mrs. Royal Calloway, a young bride of the pastor of Plains Baptist Church, who invited ten ladies to the Baptist pastorium for the purpose of establishing a club.

Plains was a thriving business community enjoying the friendliness and worships from its churches, but there seemed to be something missing – a social group. Originally, it was intended to be more or less a sewing group, but of course, as there would be only women members naturally there would be much chatting; so it was suggested that the name of the club be called the Stitch-n-Chat, according to a history complied by Mrs. J.C. Webb II, a charter member.

As there were no civic organizations in Plains at this time the Stitch-n-Chat Club performed many civic duties. Among these, the financing of an outdoor recreation center, tennis courts, landscaping, operating a concession stand at the swimming pool for years and buying benches and tables. The club also gave money and books to the school library and carried baskets of food and clothing to the needy several times a year. When a family lost a home by fire, a check along with articles of clothing or household supplies were sent.

Before it was popular for high school seniors to wear a cap and gown for graduation exercises, the Stitch-n-Chat bought graduating outfits for seniors who could not afford them. They also bought basketball uniforms for the boys and girls teams for three years and a "time clock" scoreboard for the gym. They bought playground equipment for the elementary school. The Stitch-n-Chat furnished and maintained a skating rink and croquet court in Dean Park downtown until the State Department made a tourist rest center in this location. The club has also contributed in many other areas over the years.

Membership is limited to 15 members and all new proposals are voted on by secret ballot. All minister's wives in the town are invited to be honorary members. Meetings are held every other Wednesday at 3 p.m. in the homes of the members. Members pay minimal dues of 25 cents a meeting, and a member is fined five cents if she fails to bring her needlework to a meeting.

There are three charter members who are still active: Grace Young (Mrs. Leroy); Allie Smith (Mrs. Edgar), and Carolyn Webb (Mrs. J.C. II). The late Lillian Carter (Mrs. Earl) was a charter member.

Members include Mrs. Carol Anderson, Mrs. David Bozeman, Mrs. Alton Carter, secretary-treasurer, Mrs. Hugh Carter, Mrs. Dick Downer, Mrs. Everette Chambliss, the current president, Mrs. Howard Leroy, Mrs. Bob Moss, Mrs. Walter Spann, Mrs. Edgar Smith, Mrs. Charlie Vaughn, Mrs. J.C. Webb II, Mrs. Frank Williams, and Mrs. Leroy Young. Honorary members are Mrs. Dan Arial and Mrs. Ralph Hoffmeyer.

According to Mrs. Webb's history, "this unique little club has weathered all criticism, misunderstanding, and questioning from outsiders as it continues to meet together with warm fellowship and love for each other."

—Reprint from "Americus Times-Recorder," Wednesday, May 15, 1985

Iris Garden Club began in 1959

The Iris Garden Club of Plains was organized in May 1959 and is an outgrowth of the Plains Garden Club. Mrs. Hugh Carter served as first club president, and Mrs. L.C. Hobgood, Jr. is the current president.

The 15 charter members included Mrs. Jimmy Carter, Mrs. Hugh Carter, Mrs. Billy Carter, Mrs. Virgil Chambliss, Mrs. Frank Chappell, Jr., Mrs. Clarence Dodson, Mrs. Woodrow Hair, Mrs. Phillip Jennings, Mrs. Buford Reese, Mrs. J.W. Sewell, Mrs. Y.T. Shefield, Mrs. Walter Spann, Mrs. Joel Thomas, Mrs. J.C. Webb II, and Mrs. J.C. Wise, Jr.

Along with the Plains Garden Club, the Iris Garden Club received a national award for the 1962 Camellia Show in Plains. The framed award hangs in the Sumter County Garden Center.

During the presidential inauguration of Jimmy Carter, club president Betty Lou Hagerson served on the White House Decorating Committee, along with others from the Garden Club of Georgia, Inc. She was invited to return to the White House and assisted with floral decorations when the vice premier of China visited. Camellias from Georgia were used in profusion at that occasion.

Two Iris Garden Club members served as chairman and co-chairman for table arrangements used at the awards banquet at the State Garden Club Convention in Albany in 1984.

The main project of the club over the years has been Logan Park, a triangular area in the center of Plains. Before beautification of this one-half acre, it was covered with weeds growing waist high and littered with trash.

Although the Iris Garden Club initiated the park project, many others, including the Plains Garden Club, joined in and helped promote this work.

The club has participated in many other local, state, and national projects. Club membership today totals 22, and three of the members – Mrs.

Hugh Carter, Mrs. Joel Thomas, and Mrs. J.C. Webb II – have been active all 25 years. Six of the members have served as district chairmen in many different capacities. One member has served as a co-director and has been on the State Board in several chairmanships for eight years. When she was legislation chairman billboards were regulated by getting Senate Bill No. 501 passed in the 1980 legislative session. Trees were saved on Georgia state right of ways when she led the fight to defeat Senate Bill No. 513 during the 1982 session. The Garden Club of Georgia, Inc. had been trying to accomplish this for 50 years.

Those serving as president have been: Mrs. Hugh Carter, Mrs. J.W. Sewell, Mrs. Easter Smith, Mrs. Billy Carter, Mrs. Harold Israel, Mrs. Joel Thomas, Mrs. Theron Hobgood, Mrs. Milton Hagerson, Mrs. Jack Jones, Mrs. Dewitt Webb, Mrs. Jimmy Jones, and Mrs. L.C. Hobgood.

—*Reprint from "Americus Times-Recorder,"*
May 15, 1985

"Plains Day" Proclaimed

CITY OF PLAINS DAY PROCLAMATION BY THE HONORABLE JOE FRANK HARRIS, GOVERNOR OF GEORGIA

WHEREAS: The City of Plains, Georgia, established in 1885, is celebrating its 100th anniversary this year; and

WHEREAS: In 1827, Plains of Dura was settled one mile North of its present location in southwest Georgia, and with the arrival of the railroad in 1885, the town relocatd to its present site and dropped the "of Dura" from its name; and

WHEREAS: Plains was a boomtown in the 1920's with a nationally known hospital and school, but with the coming of the Great Depression, it returned to a quiet, small town; and

WHEREAS: During the 1970s, however, Plains was awakened again when one of its citizens, Jimmy Carter, was first elected Governor of the State of Georgia and was then elected the 39th President of the United States; and

WHEREAS: Today, Plains is located in one of our state's most productive farming regions, and with a proud and friendly population of 693, it maintains the charm of a small Southern town, even admidst national attention and;

WHEREAS: To celebrate their rich heritage and achievements, the citizens of Plains will participate in festivities surrounding their Centennial on May 17-19, 1985; now

THEREFORE: I, Joe Frank Harris, Governor of the State of Georgia, do hereby proclaim the day of May 17, 1985, as "CITY OF PLAINS DAY" in Georgia, in honor of this historic occasion, and do further extend heartiest greetings and congratulations to all the good citizens of Plains on the celebration of their Centennial.

IN WITNESS WHEREOF, I have hereunto set my hand and affixed the Seal of the Executive Department to be affixed. This 29th day of April, 1985.

JOE FRANK HARRIS

Governor

TOM PERDUE

Chief Administrative Officer

—*Reprint from "Americus Times-Recorder,"*
May 15, 1985

Time Capsule

Will Be Buried This Weekend

One of the highlights of the Plains Centennial, and one which is attracting a lot of interest from the local townspeople, is the planned burial of an historic time capsule.

"Just think," one Plainsite recently remarked, "My grandchildren and great-grandchildren will be around when they dig this thing up."

And that certainly is the case, for in 2085, one hundred years from now, the capsule will be opened.

Dr. Jimmy Bagwell, Plains native and City Council member who teachs history at Georgia Southwestern College, is in charge of the event. According to Bagwell, the community is excited about this "little piece of history" and is actively contributing suggestions as to what should be contained in the capsule when it is buried.

Included in the capsule will be many issues of the Americus Times-Recorder, books written by President and Mrs. Jimmy Carter, pieces of clothing, letters, Coca-Cola bottles and numerous other articles.

Kyle Tindol of Reese Park Chapel, an Americus funeral home, graciously has agreed to donate the city of Plains a suitable vault to be used as a time capsule and also provide the necessary manpower and equipment for proper burial. The capsule will measure 25 inches long, 16 inches wide and 15 inches deep.

Jimmy Bagwell, city councilman, and Jimmy Carter with time capsule. Photo credit: Annette Wise

In addition, the city of Plains is also indebted to Roy Tallent of Tallent Monuments, Inc. for generously agreeing to donate a suitable stone marker to designate the site for future generations.

The burial of the time capsule is scheduled to take place on Sunday, May 18 at 1:45 P.M. in Logan Park under the watchful eye of the stone eagle that stands there. The Fort Benning infantry band from Columbus will present a concert in honor of the event and lend dignity to the occasion.

—*Reprint from "Americus Times-Recorder," May 15, 1985*

CSX Donates Historic Depot

in Plains, Georgia

The century old railroad depot where Jimmy Carter kicked off his presidential campaign in 1976 has been donated to the Plains, Georgia Historic Preservation Trust by CSX Transportation.

John W. Snow at podium; seated are Jimmy and Rosalynn Carter and P.J. Wise. Photo credit: CXS News

John W. Snow, president and CEO of CSX Rail Transport, presented a bill of sale for the depot to Rosalynn Carter as the former president looked on.

"Even though this station was closed after 88 years of service, its place in history was assured when it was leased by President Carter for his campaign headquarters," Snow said at the ceremony. "Our donation of this historic station building gives us a chance, in a small way, to say thank you to the people of Georgia for making the railroad an essential part of your lives for the past 150 years."

Snow pointed out that Carter was instrumental in passage of the Staggers Rail Act in 1980. "Thank you, Mr. President, for being a good friend of the railroads and the pubic that we serve."

The route through Plains that is now part of CSX Transportation was built by the Americus, Preston, and Lumpkin Railroad 100 years ago. Through a series of consolidations and acquisitions, the AP&L eventually became part of CSX.

—*Reprint from CXS NEWS, a publication of CSX Corporation, August 1986, page 12, Jacksonville, Floridia*

Over Years Four Banks Have Operated in City

The first of Plains' four banks was located in the brick building on the east side of South Bond Street, with Clint Timmerman the manager of the bank that was built by his father, Jesse Timmerman and an uncle, Edwin Timmerman, according to history compiled by Beth Walters.

Plains Bank was organized in 1901 in a one-story brick building located on Main Street, with R.S. Oliver as president, W.L. Thomas, vice president; and C.C. Lunsford, cashier. Frank Greer succeeded Lunsford as cashier.

After the failure of the Plains Bank, W. Alton Carter began offering facilities to his business, Plains Mercantile Co., adding a convenience to citizens of the area.

On December 16, 1974, the Plains Branch office of Citizens Bank of Americus was opened for business. The grand opening ceremonies were held January 4, 1975. Located in a new brick building on Main Street, and constructed on land which had been the site of Plains' first wooden stores. A large parking area is on the east side of the building.

James Harvey, vice president of the main branch, was named manager, and served until his death on March 4, 1975. The two tellers working with him were Eunice Griggs and Peggy Smith. J. Marvin Nation was named to the position of manager of the bank, and Beverly Johnson replaced Mrs. Smith. Beth Becton is presently branch manager and present teller is Ellen Harris.

Others serving as branch managers include Mrs. Marvin Griggs, Sr., Mrs. Al Williams, Eddie Howard, and Scott Ivey. Other tellers have been Mrs. Jack Everett, Amy Wise, Mrs. Raymond Lamb, Mrs. Mike Rushin, and Mrs. Harold Chavers.

—*Reprint from "Americus Times-Recorder," May 15, 1985*

Boyhood Chums

Like former President Jimmy Carter, Adrian Sidney Bacon grew up in Plains, Georgia. In Plains, the two boys debated and played basketball together and graduated from Plains High School. The two stayed in touch through the years.

Jimmy Carter's inaugural address had special meaning to the prominent St. Petersburg lawyer, Adrian Bacon. When the president quoted his favorite high school teacher, Julia Coleman, the words were taken from a Christmas letter that Miss Coleman wrote to Mr. Bacon in 1966.

"We must adjust to changing times and still hold to unchanging principles," Julia Coleman wrote to Mr. Bacon.

Impressed by the letter, Mr. Bacon saved it and sent a copy to Carter during the 1976 campaign. A month later, Carter sent Mr. Bacon a letter of thanks and told him that he used the quote in a speech to the American Bar Association.

—*Written by Craig Basse, St. Petersburg, (Florida), Times newspaper, June 4, 2001.*

Hudson Descendants Enjoy Plains Ceremony

This is to express our family's deepest appreciation for the most generous welcome and refreshing springs of hospitality offered by the people of Plains, Americus, and Sumter County. Your most famous citizens and America's most globally respected statespersons, President and Mrs. Jimmy Carter, provided us, the extended family of the late Milton Leander Hudson, an experience to be remembered for many generations.

Mary Jo C. Stout, great-granddaughter of M.L. Hudson, watches as Jimmy Carter unveils M.L. Hudson Street sign. Photo credit: Lawrence Smith

A small ceremony had been planned for Friday, October 11, 2002, to recognize the transfer of the Plains train depot site from M.L. Hudson's descendants to the National Park Service. We were delighted with the prospect of meeting the Carters, who we have always considered to be among the finest examples of faith, integrity, and courage to emerge from the South. Nevertheless, awaking on Friday morning, we had no idea what a fantastic day awaited us.

Zipping through Atlanta, our part of the family got the news that President Carter had just been awarded the Nobel Peace Prize. When we arrived in Plains, we found Main Street packed full of satellite TV trucks and the Carters surrounded by a swarm of international media representatives at the Historic Inn. Within minutes, the Carters ducked out of the global spotlight, into Mom's Kitchen for a quick lunch, and on to the Plains Train Depot. There, as the Times-Recorder reported, President Carter and the assembled National Park Service and Plains dignitaries contributed most generously to a thoughtful ceremony recognizing M.L. Hudson's many roles in the early life of the town.

President and Mrs. Carter and the other speakers took us into the station and unveiled a plaque honoring Mr. Hudson. They all greeted us as beloved community members coming home after an extended absence from our family circle. Many memories of decades long past were recalled, renewed, and passed forward to the next generation.

For our family, the simple acts of Jimmy and Rosalynn Carter on October 11 will forever powerfully illustrate their grace and profound generosity. They could have chosen to be anywhere in the world at that moment, enjoying the greetings and basking in the accolades of the world's most powerful and famous. Instead, they chose to hold to their plans for the day.

On the very day that the world was giving the Carters its greatest honor, the Carters chose to greet and honor the Hudsons, Campbells, Stouts, Stembridges, Polks and other practically unknown members of a small southern family. What a privilege it is for us to be able to renew M.L. Hudson's commitment to the life of this community, in honor of President Jimmy Carter! May this place forever be a fountain of renewal, hope and most of all, peace on earth.

—Reprint from "Americus Times-Recorder," Letter to the Editor October, 2002

Chapter 23: Reflections

Special Memories of Plains

In 1918, I was born on the second floor of the hospital located in downtown Plains. At that time, the hospital was on Main Street at the east end of the street. Patients would enter the hospital using the staircase located on Main Street.

The drugstore was located on the corner of Main Street and Hudson Street, and at one time it had a second story. The hospital moved from the east side of the downtown area, to the upstairs floor above the drugstore. There were three doctors' offices and four or five rooms upstairs for patients. Mrs. Mary Campbell ran the lab and Camilla Wise cooked for the three doctors, Dr. Sam Wise, Dr. Bowman Wise, and Dr. Thad Wise, at the hospital. Gas, tires, batteries, and paint were sold on the west side of the drugstore. Before my time there was a gas tank out front. On the west side of the drugstore, there was a wooden building.

Many of the stores in Plains were open Monday through Saturday. On Saturday, stores would stay open at night until midnight. Many farm hands would come into town to buy goods on Saturday. The sidewalks would be so crowded you could not even walk down the street! On Sunday the drugstore would open for a couple of hours in the morning, it would close for church, and then reopen from 3:00 to 6:00 in the afternoon.

Mill Jennings had a service station on the corner and across the street from the drugstore. This was before the Plains Branch of Citizens Bank was opened. Once Citizens Bank decided to build, they tore down the old wooden buildings for a new building and parking lot. Through the years many businesses have been located in this area of Plains:

the post office, café, a restaurant owned by Charlie Smith, a barbershop owned by William Spires (it had previously been owned by the Wellons family), and a pressing club (dry cleaners). The clothes were cleaned using gasoline, and they had a huge charcoal pot used for heating the pressing irons.

Murray Smith holding Boze Godwin beside Julian Booker on west side of Mill Jennings' filling station, 1944. Second picture: Boze Godwin on Main Street. Photo Credit: Pete Godwin

For many years the drugstore had a soda fountain. There were three large tables and one small table complimenting the soda fountain. When I was a young kid, they had a Victrola in the soda fountain area and I can remember the nurses in training coming down from the doctors' office and dancing in the afternoons. It was an afternoon affair!

The nurses in training boarded in the two-story house across the street at the first entrance to Plains High School. Plains was known for its outstanding doctors and the Wise Sanitarium. There was a wooden building located next to the clinic that served as a doctor's office for blacks. If an operation was needed, the patient would be transferred to the Wise Sanitarium operating room. After the Wise Sanitarium burned, Dr. Thad and Dr. Sam moved their office to Americus, and Dr. Bowman kept his office in Plains over the drugstore.

Another interesting place in the early 1920s in town was the gristmill, located near the railroad tracks and behind what is now known as Golden Peanut Co. (previously Carters Warehouse). There was a livery stable run by Pop M. Stevens that faced Bond Street. Edgar Smith later used that building for a garage. At one time this property was the site of a large livestock business. Livestock pens were located near the railroad tracks and cattle were shipped from this yard. Another business located in this area was a log company. Huge logs were brought in and stored near the tracks, and then the logs would be rolled onto train cars.

Cotton was grown in many of the fields around Plains. A cotton gin was located within a short drive of these fields. In the early 1930s it was not uncommon to see several two-horse drawn wagons lined up the street waiting their turn to unload the newly picked cotton at one of the gins. I can remember wagons lined up on the street in front of homes on South Bond Street waiting to be unloaded at Cranford's Gin. After the cotton was ginned and baled, it was a common sight to see kids playing on the large cotton bales, which would be stored along the sidewalk waiting to be railed from the platform behind the depot.

When I was young, Edgar Smith and George Smith operated two buses that picked up kids for Plains High School. The local school board controlled the operation of the school. They bought another bus around 1935, which was used to pick up students attending Plains High School. After those students were dropped off, it would take a load of students going to Georgia Southwestern College in Americus. This bus had to be back in Plains in the afternoon to take students back home.

As a teenager, I had a job making $10 a month driving the old school bus called the "cracker box" picking up children living on Old Plains Road. I picked up the Bacon, Carter and Watson children in the morning and carried them to school and then back home at the end of the school day. The ride could be quite exciting at times due to lack of adequate brakes on the bus. In order to stop the bus, you had to throw it into a different gear. Driving the bus was a good opportunity for me to make some money. The first person to run this route was James Cranford, and then I drove the route from 1936-1937. After graduating from Plains High School, I attended Georgia Southwestern College and was able to drive the bus to college.

In 1943, Dot and I moved back to Plains after I completed my degree in pharmacy. We looked for a place to live and rented a section of a house on Hospital Street. The house is located next to the Lutheran parish. We rented four rooms from Addie McGarrah for $8 per month. Three rooms that we rented were in a row on one side of the house and the fourth room was across the hall. We shared the kitchen and the bathroom with Mrs. McGarrah.

In the 1950s we bought the old hospital building and converted it into a nursing home. When we first opened it, patients paid $65 per month, and we had 75 beds. There were only five nursing homes in the state that were members of the Georgia Nursing Home Association when we first opened.

—*Submitted by Pete and Dot Godwin (2002) and a taped conversation with Ruth Godwin (1970s)*

Memories of Wise Sanitarium

I remember being a nurse in training at Wise Sanitarium. The hospital was divided into different wards. There was one area that had four beds in it and a patient paid $2 per day. The semi-private rooms cost $3 per day and the private rooms were the most expensive costing $5 per day.

Some of the people I remember working at the hospital include Miss Annie Mae Brannen and Miss Gussie Abrams. In 1929, when I was a nurse in training, Grace McCall was the director of nurses and then later, Miss Abrams. Mary Campbell was the lab technician. Ruth Harrison also worked at the clinic when I did.

The nurses' station was where we kept the charts for each patient and prepared the shots. We did not have disposable things, we had to boil things and reuse them. I remember the supply room had bolts of gauze. We would cut the gauze to make the size we needed. There was not a call button for nurses; if a nurse was needed, a small hand bell was rung. There were no numbers on the rooms and nurses were expected to know the patients' names. Nurses in training wore blue outfits with a white apron and the registered nurses wore white uniforms. Nurses got a good training at Wise Clinic.

The operating room had one big light for the doctors to do the surgery. You stayed in the hospital after an operation much longer back then. Someone having hernia surgery would stay for about 3 weeks. The patients did not turn over by themselves; a nurse had to turn them. Patients did not come to the hospital to have babies unless they were very rich or ill. Nurses were assigned weeks to go with Dr. Bowman to the homes.

When we had a black patient who needed surgery, the patient would be brought in the back door on a stretcher. There was a wooden building behind the clinic which was the hospital for the blacks. I remember the doctors' offices were in Americus before the clinic burned. Before then, the doctors' offices were located over the drugstore in Plains.

The clinic trained nurses and also had intern doctors. There was a doctor's room and the interns would sometimes spend the night in the hospital. I remember a Jack Cane, Dr. J.D. Martin and Dr.

Pendergrass. Patients needing an X-ray were sent to Dr. Pendergrass, who later had an office in Americus on the corner of Jackson and Church Street.

In addition to the main floor of Wise Sanitarium, there was a basement. The boilers were located there, which supplied heat to radiators located in each room and heat to the kitchen for cooking. We had a laundry chute on the main floor to drop the soiled linens in. A laundry service from Americus would pick up the soiled linens from the basement and deliver fresh linens. After surgery, the specimens were kept in jars in the basement. We had to keep them and there were a lot of them stored down there.

The day before the fire at the hospital, Carl Glover had a hernia operation and there was an old lady from Newnan who had an appendectomy. I also remember a man from Bronwood who had surgery the day of the fire for a ruptured ulcer. He was put to sleep in Plains at the clinic for surgery and he woke up in Americus!

It was such a cold day when the sanitarium burned. The fire started in the basement under the kitchen. The boiler exploded and the fire spread quickly. There were 13 patients in the hospital. Patients were scared when the fire broke out. I can remember Mr. Glover yelling for someone to come help him. We were able to get everyone safely out of the hospital.

Mr. Ross Dean was called and he brought his hearse from the funeral home to pick up patients and transport them to the hospital in Americus. One of the nurses, Ethel "Droopy" Jennings, lived across the street and she let us carry patients to her house while they waited to be transferred to Americus. It was scary seeing the hospital burning! It was a wonder that it did not burn down. Even some of the beams in the attic were charred from the fire. One thing I remember, the nurses at the Wise Clinic had just received a payraise. We were making $50 per month. After the fire, we transferred to Americus and only made $40 per month.

—*Taped conversation of Annie King Colbert on October 11, 1991, with Pete Godwin.*

The Mercantile

The Mercantile, a magical building in the midst of Main Street –
An enchanted land for the summer's child in bare feet.
It opened each day except Sunday and Wednesday afternoon.
Pale blue evening light glowed from arched windows on Saturday night.
As the people from Plains gathered and shopped.
There were dresses made of solids and splashy pastel prints-
"Miss Marilu" with her sweet southern ways-
complimented every choice and selection made.
Tan dungarees and blue overalls would soon turn red from clay.
The shoe area, midway the store, displayed six styles at the most.
The shoehorn, like a slide, shined from the heels that slid down.
A child saved their coins for a year to buy a gift-
Barely able to see over the glass counter top-
The barefoot child on tiptoes watched with delight
as their precious gift was wrapped!
Paper with designs and shiny ribbons were pulled off of large spools-
"Miss Betty" measured and cut each piece to a tee-
Then, with ribbon pressed between thumb and scissors-
She pulled and let go-curly ribbons springing and toppling.
"There you go, " she said with a wink and a smile
as she handed the beautiful box over the counter top.
A gift costing only a few dollars, now worth more than gold!
In the back of the store, at the end of a splintery aisle, was the town's bank.
There was a big black safe with a wheel on its door.
Mr. Alton was the town banker and picture-perfect he was.
He wore a green brim visor to cut the light bulb's glare-
and a black arm band to keep his sleeve out of ink.
Round spectacles sat on the very tip of his shiny nose.
He'd show one how to roll coins in a paper wrapper-
Under his scrutinizing eye, they had to be just right.
"Now, that's the way rolled coins should look."
His praise in the end made the effort worthwhile.
Children clamored in through the side door
finding a treasure of candy galore.
Bubble gum and fireballs costing a penny a piece-
While sodas in green bottles cost a nickel each.
Time goes by with its ups and downs, but
memories never lost can always be found!
—*Submitted by Amy Wise in memory of Beth Walters, Hugh Carter and Lon Wise*

Remembering Plains

I was born in Plains. My birth certificate only denotes Plains so I assume it was in the hospital. It was not uncommon to birth at home. My early childhood years were spent at my home about two miles outside of town on the road to Smithville. My grandfather's house was still standing on my last visit to the area. His name was J.L. Forrest. The house that I grew up in was across the road from his and was no longer standing on my last visit to Plains. I began school at Plains High School. I remember as only yesterday we would use our recess time in running to the Plains Mercantile operated by Alton Carter to spend our pennies. Good old days!

Somewhere about the time I was in the fifth or sixth grade, my parents moved about 7 miles farther south of town and that placed me in a district to attend school at Thompson School located at what was then known as "Croxton's Crossroads" across the road from Hebron Baptist Church. I attended there about two years, and as Thompson had no high school was bused to Plains.

At the age of 16, I drove the school bus. I well remember parking the bus on the corner of the church across the street from the school. When the last school bell rang I would drive the bus over to the school and the kids would scramble to get their favorite seat, almost to the point of danger! The bus had the usual window seats on each side and a long single row seat in the middle. My participation in school activities was greatly limited to my inability to practice after school. The years that I did not drive the bus, I would have to walk the 7 miles home. I did this many times – dirt road and no cars to catch a ride.

I have good memories of the agriculture workshop or Future Farmers of America, which was located in the rear of the gym. The instructor was Mr. Harvey Simpson. One project was to take a fresh cowhide and process it into leather. I think we first put it in a solution of lime to remove the hair and other material. Following this lengthy process and the skin was dry and ready for tanning, we would use chips from a red oak tree. Only red oak would give it the proper stain. As a participating member of the F.F.A., I remember attending a convention in Macon. That was quite an experience for a country boy as I had never been that far from home.

I graduated in the class of 1937 and for our graduation celebration we were given a trip to Warm Springs, Georgia. Another out-of-town journey was to Cuthbert for a visit to the college. I still have fond memories of Miss Julia Coleman and Mr. Sheffield. One in particular of Mr. Sheffield was when the hospital burned. Several of us could not resist the temptation of going across the street for a closer view. For this violation, we were called into the auditorium and after a stern lecture were given a choice of two punishments. One was to write several hundred words and definitions from the dictionary. The other choice was one of Mr. Sheffield's paddlings. Several of us boys, probably including Ernest Turner and George Harper, agreed among ourselves that the paddling was the boy's way to take our medicine. If memory serves me correct, I was the first one called upon for a choice of punishment. I promptly arose and made the paddling known as my choice. I hope I am correct in my memory, but no other boy made that stupid choice!

As a young boy, I can remember we had no electricity or plumbing. My father had a hole dug in the ground floor of a building about 2 feet by 2 feet and about 2 feet deep. On Saturday we would go to Americus and purchase a 50-pound block of ice and pack it well with cottonseed in the hole. This would probably last two or three days. That is about as country living as one can get!

Plowing fields was usually a 5½ day workweek. Usually on Saturday afternoon the sharecroppers would hitch the poor tired mules to a

Alton Carter at Plains Mercantile. Photo credit: Jimmy Carter National Historic Site

Mr. and Mrs. L.W. Wishard, 1928. Photo credit: James Forrest

wagon and go into town for their supplies. Much of the Saturday afternoon activities centered around Plains Mercantile operated by Alton Carter. I would like to take a moment to try to express the way Mr. Alton assisted my widowed mother during the Depression. Money was almost nonexistent in those days. My mother would give one of the sharecroppers a brief note to give to Mr. Carter asking that he allow the person to charge a certain amount (usually $10-$15) until harvest time. There was no alternative.

Farm produce prices in the 1930s were extremely low. I can vividly recall cotton prices at 5 cents per pound. It was a common sight to see the farm yards at home stacked with bales of cotton, in hopes of prices rising. I am not sure that this practice was successful. Day labor on the farm reached 50 cents a day; a loaf of bread, which we seldom had, was about 5 cents.

I recall Dr. Logan and his rural visitations. He made many visits to my grandfather Wishard's home some seven miles south of Plains. He was a familiar figure with his black medical bag. I knew nothing of the amount of charges but I do recall carrying a load of wood cut for use in his kitchen stove. I think a load delivered brought three dollars back then.

Many times I have gotten away from the history of Plains but there is a greater part of my life away from Plains. I want to give credit to one person for any accomplishments I might have made. That person is my wife, Augusta Powell Forrest. She served seven years as a Navy nurse prior to our marriage in 1948. Her Navy duty included one year in England near the Normandy invasion treating the wounded. She has held the family together during my many temporary assignments to include my tour flying over Korea and later a year in Vietnam. She has passed the test!

—*Submitted James E. Forrest*

Memories of Archery and Plains

When I was young, I would walk to Bishop Johnson's school. I was about 11 years old before my mama thought I was old enough to go to school. All of us kids would meet up on the dirt road and walk two miles to school. I remember going to that school with Ruby and Laura Lassiter and Ossie Bell Mays. There were a lot of students that went to that school. It was a big old building and it only had two teachers when I was going there. Some of the teachers were Mr. and Mrs. Hill, Ida Lowry, Mrs.

Johnson, Willie Johnson, Ollie Reddy, and Rosa Mae Williams. They ended up with a lot of teachers at that school.

Sometimes we would ride the train from Archery to Americus. If we wanted to catch a ride on the train, we would walk up to the church (St. Mark), stand out by the tracks and wave a white handkerchief. We'd flag down the train and ride to Plains and to Americus. We did not ride the train too often. My dad, Joe Kitchens, would drive a wagon to Plains to get groceries. One of the stores in Plains was Johnny Graham's store. He sold groceries, all kinds of dry goods, clothes, pretty cloth and notions. Our clothes were mostly made.

I remember working on the farm many a days with Miss Rachel Clark. We worked the fields in

Rachel Clark. Photo credit: Lillian Pickett

the Archery area hoeing, shaking peanuts and picking cotton. I was living in Webster County then on a farm. I think Mr. Earl Carter would come down to our house and pick us up on a pickup truck and we would ride to the fields on it. I used to love to shake peanuts. Picking cotton was the worst thing; it would hurt your back leaning over all day! When you would get started picking cotton, your fingers would get so sore trying to reach down and pull out the cotton, you'd hit those stickers! Later, they would get tough and not bother you so bad.

The Clarks lived in several places, off the Dawson Highway near the Sullivans, on the Carters' farm, the Burnette Place and then they moved to the housing project in town. I was living on the Downer farm about the 1960s. Earl Carter had sold it to the Downers. After the Clarks moved out, the

Home of Jack and Rachel Clark now part of the Jimmy Carter Boyhood Home Historic Site. Photo Credit: Annette Wise

Gardners lived there and Mr. Downer added an extra room for them. That's when we lived in that house for a while, after the Gardners. Years later, after we moved from the Downer farm, Miss Rachel came to live with Aunt Burt. She took care of Miss Rachel until she passed.

Inez worked at the old Stewart House, the one called the haunted house. I remember Leslie Schley working there for Dr. Wise. I don't know about that house being haunted. I never heard tales about it, but I can tell you about a *real* haunted house. Nobody stayed long in it and that is that old big Cox House down the road in Webster County. My mother told me somebody had to move out of that house 'cause they were scared. Back then, they'd bury people out in the back yard. There's a grave out there at the Kitchen House by the smokehouse; there are some big rocks out there around it. When people passed back then, the body would be brought back to the house and somebody would sit up all night by the casket.

—*Submitted by Annette Wise as told by Addie Josie Wright*

Joe Bacon's Store

circa 1938-1981

No one in the Bacon family can say for sure when the store that became my Granddaddy Joe Bacon's Store was first built. We think that my great-granddaddy may have built it in the early 1900s for a tobacco barn. My granddaddy decided to open a store around 1938 to provide extra income for his growing family. His sister in-law, Celestia Brown, served as store operator for a short time while my granddaddy continued to farm.

The old store, which sits on Highway 280 West, approximately 1.5 miles from the city of Plains, has always been referred to as "Joe Bacon's Store." Over the years a small motor court of four cabins and an office was added along with a barbeque shed. All that now remains is the old store building and a faded metal sign which reads "Bacon Motel."

Bacon's Motel in the 1950s
Photo credit: Dewey Paradise

The store had a long front counter with a "National" brand cash register sitting on top. There you would find my granddaddy talking with customers or getting them a homemade barbeque sandwich and a cold beer. Politics and crops were always the topic of conversations. In addition to the homemade barbeque which he cooked on his own

pit, he also sold beer, soft drinks, big sugar cookies, pickled pigs feet, pickled eggs, pickled sausage, potato chips and baked pork skins. And there was always his homemade barbeque sauce to pour over the baked skins.

The store was the gathering place of many and was occasionally the scene of a country social event called a "hat burning." This was a type of farming celebration that signified the end of the harvest season. Local farmers would gather, cook out and burn their old hats in a big bonfire. During Jimmy Carter's campaign days, several celebrities made occasional appearances at the store, including the Atlanta Braves.

My granddaddy ran the store until about the late 1960s or early 1970s. During Jimmy Carter's presidency, Joe Bacon's daughter, Nelle Mallard and her husband Norman, ran the store along with Nelle's brother, Gene Bacon. The store was named the Plains Country Club but will always be remembered as Joe Bacon's Store. Aunt Nelle attended to the store business and Uncle Gene did all of the barbequing. The store operated until the late 1970s or early 1980s when the doors closed for the last time.

—*Submitted by Dewey M. Paradise August 16, 2002*

A Special Marriage

In the early 1900s Young Thompson Sheffield came to Plains, Georgia. Miss Julia Coleman hired him to teach and coach at Plains High School. He was a young teacher and a recent graduate from Carson-Newman College in Jefferson City, Tennessee. Growing up in the small town of Pinehurst, Georgia, Plains must have seemed quaint and a reasonable place to begin his career. At that time, small town schools' athletic programs were not competitively organized. Y.T. took this opportunity to begin regional high school sports. He coached many youth as they attended Plains High, including

Y.T. Sheffield standing on basketball court at Plains High School. Photo credit: Michael Mallard

Lilloise Lunsford on outside basketball court at Plains High School. Photo credit: Michael Mallard

a young player, Lilloise Lunsford, who would later become his bride. The two also became my grandparents.

Young, single and motherless, Miss Julia greatly influenced Granddaddy's life. He spent many evenings and weekends with Miss Julia and her aunt, "Miss" Jesse McGee. Miss Julia hired him, advised him and she and "Miss" Jesse must have provided the mother-like guidance he missed growing up. Once, Miss Julia observed him as he walked by some young ladies and commented, "I'll need to polish him. Round off those rough edges." And she did her best.

My grandmother, Lilloise, graduated from Plains High in 1930 and attended the University of Georgia in Athens as a physical education major. A year later she returned home to complete her studies at Georgia Southwestern Teachers College in Americus. Even though her parents wanted her to continue at the university, Grandmamma thought she could get a good education and save the family money by living at home. On her return to Plains, Y.T. took new notice. They began group dates with friends. The friends would spend afternoons dancing at Magnolia Springs pavilion or at each other's homes listening to music and playing games. Eventually, Granddaddy proposed. According to Grandmamma the uneventful proposal went something like, "...so, do you want to give it a try?"

The 1930s were hard and Miss Julia confided to my grandmother that Y.T. would never make much money as teacher. Undaunted and without an engagement ring, the couple set out to elope. Miss Julia couldn't stand the thought of eloping, so Granddaddy agreed to marry in Plains if the wedding was kept secret. Granddaddy enjoyed playing practical jokes and he feared retribution if news of his wedding got out. My great grandmother (known to most as Nama), was sick and Miss Julia took the task of planning the wedding. Grandmamma wore a navy blue dress and the house was decorated with pink zinnias and pink crape myrtle from Nama's garden – Miss Julia called it the "wedding of the myrtles". Knowing Granddaddy's financial state, Miss Julia also bought the wedding rings. They were married June 29, 1932, at "Miss" Jesse and Miss Julia's home with only the preacher, Miss Julia and the McGees attending.

Grandmamma recalled, "... afterwards we stayed and had a cold drink – lemonade. We talked a few minutes. It was nice but not fancy at all." Still afraid of honeymoon pranks, Granddaddy instructed Miss Julia not to tell a soul until they had 30 minutes lead out of town. Grandmamma added, "Then she called her neighbors, Dot and Marjorie Andrews and told them." In a short time the news was all over town!

The newlyweds took off in Granddaddy's yellow Buick convertible and spent their honeymoon in Florida at his Aunt Lucy's house. Aunt Lucy owned a boarding house and rental cottages. The couple arrived unannounced at midnight. Aunt Lucy put them up in a room reserved by another couple who were supposed to arrive the next day. Of course, the guests arrived in the middle of the night. My grandparents had to relinquish their room to the early bird arrivals.

Y.T. and Lilloise Sheffield with children Tommy and Charlene. Photo credit: Michael Mallard

Soon they made it back to Plains, settling into the house they would live for the rest of their lives together. The home on Bond Street belonged to Grandmamma's aunt, Fannie Hiller. As a girl, Grandmamma took lunch to her two widowed aunts daily. Aunt Fannie willed the house to Grandmamma. My great-grandfather, Charles Lunsford, helped the new couple remodel the home. Y.T. planted the pecan trees in the triangle plot behind the house. The money the pecans generated later helped to make ends meet. In addition to teaching, coaching and farming, they took in boarders. Preparing meals and taking care of their new family kept my grandmother very busy.

—*Submitted by Michael Mallard*

Magnolia Springs

"One thing I remember – we were together in a group and we had been to Magnolia Springs pavilion, or at least to Magnolia Springs. I don't know if we were swimming or at a dance. I had a portable victrola (another boy had given me). We used my victrola to dance to. It started pouring rain and the roads were slick. The lights were out on the car so we had to follow behind another car to use their lights. We went up a hill and slid into the ditch. I was picked up and I said to Y.T. be sure and get the victrola! We then went on home. It wasn't far out from Plains."

—*Submitted by Michael Mallard as told by Lilloise Sheffield*

Miss Julia Goes to Washington D. C.

"Miss Julia had been invited to Washington to a committee meeting. She wanted to go. She told Mr. Sheffield – that's what she called him. She told him about it. He could pick up on the hint and he said, 'Well, Miss Julia, we'll take you.' So we went and Miss Julia attended the meetings. I remember the weather in Washington wasn't the best in the world – it was in June. She went to the White House. Y.T. carried her to the gate – he walked her to the gate and the White House staff escorted her in. We went back and picked her up."

—*As told by Lilloise Sheffield to Michael Mallard*

Miss Julia Coleman and Y.T. Sheffield worked together as a team for many years. I describe them as "an unbeatable team." They just seemed to compliment each other with both having special talents and ways to work with children. I remember when Miss Julia received an invitation to the White House. Everyone in town was so excited!

Y.T. and I decided that we would take Miss Julia to Washington, D.C. We drove right up in front of the White House and dropped Miss Julia off. Y.T. and I did some sightseeing and later we returned to pick up Miss Julia.

—*As told by Lilloise Sheffield to Annette Wise*

Summers in Plains

As a child I never lived in Plains except in the summers. During the 1960s my family lived in Louisiana where my parents were in college. Daddy would come home to Plains to work to make extra college money. I thought Plains was heaven. Both sets of grandparents lived there – the Sheffields and the Mallards.

Granddaddy Sheffield was a very "hands-on" grandfather. He usually had my sister, Marcia, and me with him everywhere he went. Errands with Granddaddy Sheffield were always a highlight. Seems like daily we were off to the bank, post office, schoolhouse, farm, or traveling to Preston, Leslie, or Americus to his favorite fishing hole.

The farm was a special place. The first thing we wanted to do was see Clarence and Alberta, the tenants on the farm. They took care of the pigs, chickens, etc. After we said our hellos, we went straight to the spring that originates on the property. This was the only source of water for Clarence and Alberta, and while I'm sure it was a chore to draw water daily, Marcia and I thought it was magic and we couldn't wait to get a drink from the spring. The ladle was kept in a small reservoir under a huge mulberry tree. The tree was almost as fascinating as the spring.

In the hot summer afternoons, Granddaddy took us to the pool to swim. He would give us swimming lessons and then we played. He entertained us by diving off the diving board – doing flips right along with all of the teenagers. Frozen candy bars, ice cream and bottled cokes were the pool treat that cooled us down at snack time. Granddaddy always had a deep tan.

Later in the afternoon, we would come home to 10 or 12 (seemed like a hundred) watermelons resting around the base of a huge pecan tree. Before we got out of our swimsuits, we often cut a watermelon. The sticky juice coated us just so we could get a scoot from the hose before drying and changing.

Returning to Louisiana was traumatic. Marcia and I dreaded leaving Plains every summer. We would say our goodbyes to our grandparents and make one last stop on the way out of town – at Mr. C. L.'s store. It was a ritual. Mr. C. L. always had two small brown paper sacks filled with candy waiting for us. We always looked forward to the candy but ate it sobbing.

—Submitted by Michael Mallard

Some "Twice Told Tales"

There are some stories concerning the early years of the Campbell boys in Plains that have been repeated many times. In those days they had a windmill and well in the back yard that supplied several families with water. Anytime the windmill squeaked, Mr. McDonald, their neighbor to the west, would phone: "Mary, send the boys up to oil that confounded thing!"

The Logans were their neighbors across Walters Street. This family consisted of four daughters: Ernestine, Geraldine, Gladys and Catherine, and two sons: Mitchell and John, Jr. When we were living in Panama City in 1964, Geraldine Logan Pope came to visit our church one Sunday, and recalled the following incident. It seems that there was a high wooden fence surrounding the Campbells' back yard. One Sunday afternoon Karl was riding his bicycle up and down the streets. His mother called to him, "Karl come in off the street and ride in the backyard!" To which he replied, "Mother, isn't it Sunday in the back yard, too?"

A few years later Karl often courted Catherine Logan in the swing on the Logans' porch. Mr. Logan would come to the front door and call "Catherine, tell that boy to go hone." Once in his haste, Karl remembers he jumped over the porch railing and landed in the rose bushes.

At one point Karl and Stewart had a beautiful white collie dog. Their mother was a firm believer in fresh air, so she put a bed on the sleeping porch upstairs for them to sleep in. This made it easy for them to slip "Lassie" in to sleep with them, much to their mother's chagrin.

The older brother, Milton, was desperately afraid of the dark. It has been said that he was even scared of his own shadow. It must have been a great joy to him when electricity came to Plains. He learned to help the crewmen and in fact, wired the home place. These lights consisted of a drop cord from the ceiling of each room, with one bulb which was turned on by the pull on a hanging cord – that is, if you could feel it in the dark.

When the Armistice finally came after World War I, the Campbell boys were in bed with flu, in the front bedroom across the hall from the parlor. Not wanting to be left out of the celebration, they persuaded their mother to get out their double-barreled shotgun, which she did. She succeeded in shooting several rounds from the front porch to add to the noise of the other residents of the community.

It seems that for some years cottages were maintained at Magnolia Springs for families who might want to spend a week or two out there during the summer. In remembering those days, Stewart recalls that they always looked forward to Uncle Ross coming in the late afternoons. He would drive out in his Cadillac, blowing the horn long before he reached the Springs and the boys rushed out to see what he had brought.

It was the custom for "Tot" and Frances Oliver to share a room. One night Stewart tells that he, Milton and Dolph Oliver slipped out and secured a billy goat from a farm nearby. They returned and put the goat in the room with "Tot" and Frances, causing quite a commotion.

Another story that Karl recalls bears a word or two. One rainy afternoon, his mother was driving their Cadillac back to Plains, when the car slid off into the ditch on the "famous" steep hill. After that experience, she rarely drove again and soon afterwards sold the car.

In later years a swimming pool and dance pavilion were added at the "Springs." This was always for many years a favorite picnic spot.

They all recalled many pleasant times at the Mill Pond, now owned by Leroy and Grace Young. Milton, on his visits to Plains in later years, wanted to go for a dip in the Mill Pond – even in dead of winter.

Finally this could not be ended without a word about "The Grove," the plot of ground that has been turned into a beautiful park. This piece of ground was about the size of a city block, bounded on the north by the main highway, on the west by Aunt Carrie's home, on the south by the S.A.L. Railway and on the east by Hudson Street. Mother Campbell received this property from the Hudson Estate, later selling it to Uncle Ross Dean, and he in turn selling it to the town of Plains. At some point a tennis court was added on the west side, but mainly it was crossed by a path, leading to the depot. This path was used by all as a shortcut to town. The Grove, as its name implies, contained many large, beautiful shade trees.

During the days of Gypsies, this was a favorite camping spot. At these times, the local people went the long way around, as there were always wild tales told about the Gypsy "goings on." Mary Marguerite recalls that she was terrified of the Gypsies, and would hardly go out of the house when they were camped in the Grove.

In the early days of the 1900s, the Chautauqua made an annual visit to Plains, and the Grove was just the right spot for their big tent. Karl remembers that they went when they were young boys.

—Submitted by Allene T. Haugabook, excerpts from the Campbell history book compiled by Rachel Winn Campbell, 1981.

Alton Carter's
Taped Comments About Plains
June 1976

Before our family moved to Plains in 1904, my father had about 10 acres of Concord Delaware grapes at Rowena, and made from 2,500 to 3,500 gallons of wine annually. It was sold quickly at 30 cents a quart. This was completely legal, before a 200-gallon, no sale law was passed.

After my daddy was killed in a gunfight, my mama Nina and the children moved from Cuthbert to the house behind the Methodist Church in Plains. Ethel was born in 1886, I came in '88, Lula in '91, Earl in '94, and Jeannette in '04, after Daddy was gone. They all came to Americus by train, then buggy to Plains, but I rode ahead of them on a horse.

Back in March '97, Ethel and I went from Rowena to Arlington school on a lumber wagon, because our new buggy had been damaged the day before by a blind mule that ran away. It started raining, and I and two boys went out to get the seats out of the buggy to keep them dry. They were gone, and we went back to the school. A tornado hit, blowing one boy 50 feet through the window, another had a nail driven into his back, and I was pinned under some beams, with a leg and arm broken and a 2X4 bradded across my face, mashing my nose. I was rescued, and put on a wagon with 3 dead and 2 other live children, and taken to a nearby home. Eventually, about 25 doctors came from Albany, Blakely, Cuthbert, Dothan, and other towns to treat all the hurt people. They set my leg, but forgot to put padding inside the plaster of paris. This soon began to squeeze my swelling leg, and it was cut off and replaced with wood splints. Of 35 students, 9 died, 19 were injured, and 7 were unhurt. I had two textbooks, one of which was found 24 miles away and returned to me.

The Bowman Wise House on the corner of Church and Bond was already here when the railroad was built. It was the main farmhouse, belonging to M. L. Hudson. I've got an old 1830 map that shows that Plains of Dura was about one-half mile north of Plains, at "Devil's Half Acre" where the Drue Murray place is (that Jack Slappey's family later owned.) There were three stores and a post office there, and those people and the ones at Magnolia Springs fought like the dickens to get the railroad to come by their places. The railroad folks, though, wanted to come the way it did – that was in 1890. In 1896, Mr. Hall began putting a building on what came to be Main Street and South Hudson, where the drugstore is now, and also began the brick building where we are now (Plains Mercantile building). Then everything moved from Plains of Dura, so there is now just a cemetery out there.

The town of Plains was incorporated in 1896. Mr. Hudson subdivided all this land. I bought my home lot from Mr. Hudson and Reese Andrews bought the one next door. I came here in 1904 and there is just one person who lived in Plains then who is still here – Annie Mae Brannen. She moved here in 1900 from down south of Plains where R.M. Story lives now. Oscar Williams and his family lived down on their farm near Choctahatchee Creek. Oscar was down in Florida, selling sewing machines. He had a buggy with two horses hitched to it, and carried two sewing machines at a time. He sold them for $65 each, on credit, and would go back and collect by the week. Ms. Lora Logan married when she was only about 15 – she was a Wilson. Her father was overseeing the Dodson place.

Plains had about 350 people in 1904. There were three passenger trains each way, at noon, 5 p.m., and 1 a.m. eastward, 9 a.m., 3 p.m., and midnight westward. A buggy trip to Americus was two hours each way, with a horse and buggy for the round trip costing $2. Regular live shows, music, drama, comedy were held at the opera house in Americus, also usually costing $2.

The depot has been remodeled several times — at first it had a high front porch. They had two waiting rooms, one for white and one for colored, and later tore them off. [We discussed Bishop William Johnson's family: sons Willy, Alvan, and Simeon (?), and his daughter Fannie Hill, whose husband was the first black legislator in Oklahoma.] I remember all the Packards, Cadillacs, and other big cars at Bishop Johnson's funeral. They even gave out programs for the funeral, which I had never known of before.

I knew Edgar Smith well [Rosalynn's father]. He was a good mechanic, and ran the garage down on South Bond Street for several years – Sonny Faircloth worked for him a long time. Bud Walters had a cobbler shop just west of the drugstore, and a Negro, Putt Tondee, also had one down by Johnny Graham's store [on South Hudson].

Edgar Smith. Photo credit: Rosalynn Carter

The first peanuts grown as a crop around Plains was 1920, by Wright Mims, down in the 17th District, on the Rufus Chappell place. The whole place was in peanuts. In those days, a ton to three acres was doing well. Right lately they've learned how to work them – or not to work them. They use that old medicine now to kill the weeds, and now they make a ton and a half or two per acre.

In 1918, Plains installed a 25-horsepower electric power plant; later it was increased to 37 and then 80 H.P. In the 1940s it was sold to Georgia Power Company.

After returning to Plains, I worked one season in Griffin, on a peach and grape farm owned by my Uncle Dave, and then four years for Oliver-McDonald Co. In 1907 I went into a kind of partnership with Mr. Oliver and Ross Dean to form Plains Mercantile Co. Mr. Dean and I would go to New York twice a year to buy dry goods and furniture. On one occasion, we joined in with four other southwest Georgia merchants and bought 15 carloads of furniture from High Point, N.C. In 1934, Oliver-McDonald Co. seemed to have faded, and Plains Mercantile moved down to occupy their building, where the present antique store is located. My store was open from daylight until dark on weekdays, and stayed open until 10 p.m. or midnight on Saturday. I sold the first gasoline from a 60-gallon tank for 15 cents/gallon. Bread was 5 cents, and 24 pounds of flour 65 cents.

I operated a banking operation from 1928, soon after the Plains Bank went broke, until 1965, when private banks were prohibited by the Legislature. I didn't lend money, but just ran a deposit and checking business for the town, often handling $40,000-$50,000 per day during the harvest season.

In 1938, I went in the mule business on halves with John Woodruff. I furnished the money, and John did the buying. I accompanied him and learned the business. We would buy mules in Atlanta, Montgomery, & Troy, Alabama, and "sell them like hot cakes." However, in 1939, I went to Athens to visit my son Don, and John went to Atlanta with the truck. When I arrived, I learned that John had been around to the mule merchants and asked for a $5 kickback on each mule. I didn't say anything until we returned to Plains, when I went around to the stable and we divided the five mules still in stock. At Woodruff's choice, I took my choice of two mules, and Woodruff kept the other three. From then on, until 1960, I was heavily in the mule business, usually selling from 500-800 each season (November to April). Until the last three or four years, mules sold 10:1 compared to horses. With everyone, even very small farmers, shifting to tractors, mules were being sold by them, not bought. Almost all went for dog food.

In 1918 I was elected to the town council, and from 1920 until 1954 served as mayor, with six years out of office. Twice, I was defeated. My annual salary rose from $20 to $25. I was a county commissioner from 1927-34, and also served on the hospital authority. I was a director of the Americus team and the Georgia-Florida baseball league for five years. Some seasons, I never missed any of the 80 or so games.

—*Submitted by Jimmy Carter*

Reflections of the Past

Among my many memories of my father, Joseph A. Bacon, Sr., better known as Joe Bacon or Mr. Joe, are these selections of conversations with daddy, remembering things of long ago relating to ways of life and how things were in the beginning settlements that later evolved into the little town of Plains, Georgia.

"Old Dr. Harper who lived west of Magnolia Springs, known as Brookside on Rabbit Creek, came back from the Civil War with just his horse, nothing more, living off peas and meat from the swamp. He kept corn for his horse. Times were very hard."

"The Cebe Walters family also lived here, early 1900s.

"Magnolia Springs was settled prior to the coming of the railroad to Plains, Georgia. There was a plentiful supply of water, which was a necessity; a cemetery south of Magnolia Springs northeast of O.A. Williams' farm; homes before you got to the springs; and homes beyond the springs.

"A Dr. Wise lived there, Magnolia tree in the front yard. School also there, but settlement moved in 1885 because of railroad coming through."

The Williams home built about 1877 near Magnolia Springs where Oscar Williams, Sr. was born. In this picture are Oscar Williams, Virginia Wellons, and Dorris Wise next to the Williams home in 1935. Photo credit: Frank Williams

"Black Home-Tanyard Hill"

(now George Whitten vicinity)

A tannery was there, boots and shoes were made. Kidds Mill known originally as Blacks Mill (now Youngs Mill).

Mr. Black was a remarkable man – his home and barns put together with wooden pegs."

Moving to Plains

"Papa had bought some land in Sumter County, Georgia, from a Mr. Rylander. Mama had got us up early. We were moving from Marion County, Georgia. Roads were bad, muddy, winding and many holes.

Boss Josey and Elbert French drove the animals. Household goods in wagon. Chickens in coops. Mama and the children rode in the buggy."

"The house – A Mr. Shinholser built the house about 1840. The Shinholser Cut on top of the hill and moved to its present location when the railroad came through Plains in 1884-1885. This home in its original location before it was moved to its present site was on the Stagecoach Road.

Signs of the Stagecoach Road are (were) still there (now destroyed) and on Downers' property in Webster County. Also two cemeteries.

The old Oliver Gristmill was where the old Stagecoach Road crossed Choctahatchee Creek and littered (light wood - fat pine) post still in the creek where the Stagecoach Road crossed, or was the last time I was there.

The mill race, over a mile long and dug before the Civil War, ran from the dam on Rabbit Branch which carried the water to the mill wheel which furnished power to grind corn.

"Stagecoach Road route – Americus and Preston – went by where Pink Jowers lived (grind corn on Sunday), came out by house in Preston, Georgia, where date is on house 1840." (now destroyed)

NOTE: Daddy and I along with my children walked part of this Stagecoach Road route. You could still see signs of it in some places, but is now destroyed.

"Plains Baptist Church (originally Lebanon) in what is now Lebanon Cemetery and a baptismal pool or pond, was what is now Bacon's Pond (original old pond). The church was later moved to Plains."

"Mr. Ed Stewart lived in the old Rylander Home (known as the haunted house) on the hill east of the cemetery. This home dates back before the Civil War, being built around 1858. At one time an old log crib was built by hand, the logs being hewn or hewed out by hand. An old blacksmith shop was there, a ram pump, an old syrup kettle and cane mill and three or four barns, and on the west of the cemetery Miss Anna Markette lived in the old Shinholser home (Bacon Homeplace) which was built on top of the hill and later moved to its present location when the railroad came through."

—*Sara B. Paradise, 2002*

Fun and Games of Earlier Days

Pop Guns

We made popguns using elderberry stems, chinaberries and sticks. There was soft material on the inside of the elderberry stem – this was pushed out with a hard stick such as oak or cherry. Then, we'd drop a chinaberry down into the stem and push it out quickly so that it would make a popping sound.

Rattles

After sopping up the syrup on biscuits, we'd take that empty can and fill it with small rocks, push the lid back on and punch a hole in each end. Then, a wire was run though it and it was pulled up and down the road making a loud rattling sound – small children loved these gizmos.

Tops

We'd make tops from empty thread spools. Spools used to be made of wood and we'd sharpen one end into a point. Then, we'd push a stick through the middle. The last thing to do was to wrap a string around it and pull – it would spin away.

Marbles

We'd spend hours playing with marbles – first of all, a circle was scratched into the dirt. The players dropped their marbles in the middle. A large marble, called the shooter marble, was used to knock marbles out of the circle. When you tucked your thumb into your fist, the marble would hold so that your thumb would flip it and knock other peoples' marbles out of the circle. You kept what you knocked out and the person with the most was the winner. Of course, out of courtesy, all the marbles were returned to the rightful owners.

Gangs

The boys from each side of town formed gangs and had their own gang name. Our gang was called the Night Hawks. We made clay balls and let them dry and whenever a member of another gang rambled into our part of town, we'd throw the clay balls at them.

We were really good friends the whole time and grew up to be even closer friends.

Bullhorns

We'd make what we called bullhorns out of syrup cans. We'd punch a hole through each end. Then we'd take a string of twine, coat it with pine rosin and string it through the can. When the string was pulled through the can, it made a loud, spooky sort of sound. We had fun scaring people with bullhorns.

—*Submitted by L.A. "Morgan" Wise*

Bicycling Around Town

Bicycles were not only a means of a fun time. They were also a means of getting to places one needed to go. Christmas was the time that most children received their bicycle. What fun, on Christmas morning, to go about the neighborhood and see who got a new bicycle for Christmas. Girls' bicycles usually had string guards on the rear wheel to keep the girls' dresses from being caught in the spokes as they didn't wear pants in those days. On the rear fender there was usually a seat for carrying a friend for a ride. On the handlebars a basket was attached for carrying mail or other goods picked up in town. If there was no basket, this was a place for a friend to ride. Helmets were unheard of and danger was never considered.

—*Submitted by Allene T. Haugabook*

Below: Mark Chambliss, on right side, and a friend (cir. 1900)

Above: Margaret, Gene, Betty and Burr Wise Jennings

Fun with bicycles. Photo credits: Wynelle Chambliss and Audra Jennnings

Roller Skating in the Park

Many people recall the days of roller skating in the park which is now the Maxine Newberry Reese Park. A large concrete square in the park was perfect for skating. Also remembered are the roller skates used back then which were made of metal. The skates were attached to the shoe by a leather strap across the ankle. Metal clamps on each side of the shoe held the front end of the skate in place. The clamps were loosened and tightened with a key.

After skating for a long time the clamps would sometimes become loose, so children usually kept the key handy. They'd string it on an old shoelace and wear it around their necks.

—*Submitted by Lonnie Wise*

Corncob Dolls

We'd make "corncob dolls" each summer. Since the silks on the ears of corn were different colors, we had a choice of blonde, brunette, or redheaded dolls. We'd braid the silks so that the doll would have a pretty long braid. Sometimes, there was a colored piece of string or ribbon around to tie on the end of the braid.

—*Submitted by Amy Wise*

Santa Claus

"Miss Allie" Smith told how when she was a little girl she was so excited because she saw Santa's boot prints in the back of the fireplace. When she grew older, she learned that someone had taken their shoes and pressed them against the back of the fireplace, leaving prints in the soot.

—Submitted by Amy Wise, as told to her by Mrs. Allie Smith

Legends and Stories Told Around Plains

Throughout history people have shared their memories with one another and the people from Plains are certainly no exception. They love to recall special times in their lives and to share them with others. Their stories vary in nature – some are funny, some are mysterious and some are even sad. These stories and legends are all very well deserving since they play a special part in the history of our beloved little town of Plains, Georgia.

—Submitted by Amy Wise

Garland, Elliott and Allie Anderson, 1922. Photo credit: Eunice Griggs

A Special Delivery

We received our mail on RFD Plains, Ga. My aunt lived on the same route about three miles before the postman got to our house. If she wanted to send us a message, she would put a card in the box with a 1¢ stamp. The postman would draw black lines over the stamp and leave it in our box that day. My Grandmother lived on our school bus route. If Mama wanted to send her anything, like a pound of butter, she would wrap it in a newspaper and tie a string around it and as the bus passed her house we would let a window down and throw it out. She was on her porch waiting. This is what we called "Special Delivery."

—Submitted by Eunice Griggs

He Tore the Door Off of the Hinges

One of the funniest events was when J.C. Webb and James Kennedy worked for Mr. Ross Dean's funeral home in Plains. One day they talked Bud Walters into helping them move a casket with a body inside from one room to another. Well, J.C. Webb got in the casket before it was moved and raised the lid. Bud turned around to look at the casket and when he did, he knocked the screen door off its hinges, ran out into the street and did some bad cursing.

—Submitted by L.A. "Morgan" Wise

Below: J.A. McDonald Home

Above: R.S. Oliver Home

Photo credits: Frank Williams and C.G. Haugabook, Jr.

The Legend of the Knot

In the early 20th century there arose a dispute as to which was the finest house in Plains. By common acclaim, it was either the house of J.A.

McDonald or R.S. Oliver, the two wealthiest men in Plains, both of whom are mentioned in the volume, Men of Mark in Georgia. To settle the issue, a committee of architectural experts was formed to inspect the two houses and render a decision. At length, they made their decision: the McDonald House was superior because it had no knots in the woodwork, the Oliver House had one knot. In every other way, the houses were of equal value. At present, Steve and Lisa Smith own the McDonald house and Mr. Frank and "Miss Virginia" Williams own the Oliver House.

—Submitted by Jimmy Bagwell

Jumping the Broom in the 1800s

Marriage between black slaves was not legally recognized, but it was encouraged by slaveholders who wanted to discourage runaways. Couples were usually married during Christmas week. The wedding couple jumped backwards over the broomstick. The one who landed on both feet without falling would always have "say-so" over the other.

—Told by my Great-Grandmother(Mamie Clark) to Liz Angry

Stuck in the Mud

Back in 1968, I rode with Mama and Maxine Reese over to Webster County to pick muscadines. We picked muscadines all right, but when we got ready to leave, the car got stuck in the mud. We gathered every stick we could find and stuck them under the tires.

"Miss" Maxine said, "Amy, let's you and me get behind the car and push." Well, we did and Mama hit the gas pedal. "Miss" Maxine and I were coated with mud – the only clean spots were around Maxine's eyes when she took off her glasses. We laughed all the way back to Plains. Maxine said the next pair of glasses that she got would have wipers on them.

—Submitted by Amy Wise

"J Who" The Depot Dog

Back in 1976, a young German shepherd showed up at the depot. She was named J Who since the phrase "Jimmy Who" was notorious at that time. J Who made the depot her home and what a life! She greeted visitors daily and enjoyed the many morsels of food she received. She even accompanied the police at night while making their rounds and they made sure she had extra food. J Who continued to live at the depot even after the election. She lived a long and happy life and became known as the Depot Dog. J Who is buried at the corner of Logan Park opposite the depot and historical marker.

—Submitted by Amy Wise

The Gypsies

Gypsies used to camp out around Plains. One of the places they camped was the field across from Jimmy Bagwell's house. They traveled in wagons and traded mules or painted houses for money. They'd camp out for about two weeks before moving on. It was funny how they would ask to borrow a stick of wood and end up getting a whole cord. Their outdoor cooking sure did smell good!

—Submitted by Millard Simmons, Bob Moss, Frank Williams

The Flimflammers

It was around 1957 when a couple of men told Miss Annie Mae Brannen they'd do repair work on her house. They pulled a board loose on her house and claimed that they saw a whole bunch of snakes. They scared Miss Annie Mae and pretty much forced her to pay them $800. She told me and I called Citizens Bank and stopped the check. The Americus police caught them and they ended up in jail.

—Submitted by Millard Simmons

Trains in Plains

The President of the S.A.M. Railroad, Samuel Hugh Hawkins, moved with his family from Jones County to the Plains area when he was 12 years old. He attended school near Magnolia Springs. His parents, Ezekiel Hawkins (1790-1868) and Nancy McKay Hawkins (1796-1861), are buried at Providence Cemetery near Plains.
—*Submitted by Ann Singer Lumpkin, Georgia*

A train ride from Archery to Plains cost 10¢ and a ride from Plains to Americus cost 20¢.
—*Submitted by Annie Mae Vaughn*

The train would stop in Plains to load and unload freight. Mail was delivered on the 3:00 stop. A two-wheel cart was rolled across the street to the Post Office loaded with mail. The drugstore also had a two-wheel cart to pick up the deliveries from the train. A lot of the medicine came in on the train; we got sulfur and Epson salt in 100 pound containers. Coke syrup came in 50-gallon containers and castor oil in 5-gallon containers. Cotton, peaches and watermelons were some of the crops shipped out of Plains. Later when the depot was not in such a demand and few trains came through, the two waiting rooms on the east side were removed as well as part of the office and platforms.

My grandfather was an engineer and sometimes I would ride in the engine with him. That was a real treat!
—*Submitted by Pete Godwin*

I rode the train to Americus on Saturday to take piano lessons. It left at 12:00 and came back to Plains at 3:00. If I couldn't catch the train back, I would go to the pharmacy where my uncle Brownie was a pharmacist and wait in his car and he'd bring me back home. I remember that there was a lot of soot in the train since it was fueled by coal and it was hot.
—*Submitted by Allene T. Haugabook*

One of the trains that came through Plains was called the Butt Head. And it ran west at 12:00. The other was called the Drummer and it ran east at 3:00.
—*Submitted by L.A. "Morgan" Wise*

I remember being in church and hearing the train whistle blowing. Everyone would look around indicating to the pastor that it was time for church to let out. If you were downtown and the train stopped, everyone looked to see who was getting off the train. This was an exciting time!
—*Submitted by Ruby Watson and Annie Mae Vaughn*

I can remember if you needed to catch a ride on the train, all you had to do was stand near the track waving a white handkerchief. The train would stop and you would pay your fare. There was not a ticket office at Archery.

Another fond memory was of a conductor who traveled from Americus to Montgomery on regular runs. As the train would near Archery, he would throw out a block of ice, it was a hundred-pound block. This was quite a treat for us! We had an icebox and with this drop-off of

E.H. Watson at Archery. Photo credit: Ruby Watson

ice three or four times a week, it kept us supplied. But my favorite thing was the candy bar he would toss me! As a young child, it was quite a treat to receive a Baby Ruth or piece of candy from him. Years later, I asked around and found that the conductor was Julian Suggs from Americus. This was not an arrangement where my dad asked for the ice to be delivered, Mr. Suggs just did it out of the goodness of his heart!

One year, Daddy decided he would go into farming on the side and planted watermelons. After

the watermelons were harvested, the watermelons were loaded on the boxcar and Daddy decided to put a note on one of the watermelons. The note said, "If you get this watermelon and note let me know." To Daddy's surprise a letter arrived one day from a man in New York stating he had received the watermelon and the note! That man and my dad corresponded for a number of years.
—*Submitted by Ruby Watson*

Sad Memories

A sad memory was when Lonnie Taylor, his wife, Teeny, their two children, Teeny's brother Bobby Ratliff and her sister, Lorraine, were all killed in an airplane crash at Junction City in 1948.
—*Submitted by Allene T Haugabook and Virginia Williams*

A sad event for everyone at Plains High School was when the Sheffield Stadium burned in 1940.
—*Submitted by Eunice Griggs*

The Tragic Death of Two Pilots

There used to be a landing field just below Plains on Highway 45, between the Colstons' house and town. The top of the barn was painted in a yellow checkerboard pattern so that pilots could see it and know to land there. One day there was this British pilot flying out there when his plane flipped and landed upside down. Joel Turner and I saw him and ran over to check on him. He was hanging upside down and had blood running out of his nose. Joel Turner opened the cockpit and unhooked his safety belts. We pulled him out and he was O.K. Later that year, this same pilot was training over at Southerfield. A fellow by the name of Holloway was the instructor. He said he would help this pilot get straightened out with his flying problems. Both of them went up and the plane fell back down, killing both of them.
—*Submitted by L.A. "Morgan" Wise*

A Telephone Tale

Buck Murchison ran the first telephone exchange in Plains. Ralph and Nina Wise were a couple who lived out at Magnolia Springs and owned one of the first phones in the area. Nina was afraid of a telephone and didn't particularly like talking on it. Well, her husband and Mr. Buck decided to have fun with this. Mr. Buck was to call their house that night after they had gone to bed. Ralph would pretend to be sick so that Nina would have to answer the telephone. The phone rang and she hesitantly said "Hello" and Mr. Buck asked her how she was doing and she said "Fine" and then he said, "You're looking fine, too." Well, she threw down the phone, ran through the house and yelled "Why didn't you tell me you could see over the blame thing?"
—*Submitted by Charles Medlock, as told to him by his grandfather*

School Days

"School days, school days
Dear old golden rule days
Reading and writing and 'rithmetic
All to the tune of a hickory stick"

The person from Plains who influenced me the most was Miss Julia Coleman. She tried to help poor children and other ones having problems. Earl Smith, Halley Smith and I worked in the schoolyard in the evening for 10¢ an hour. We worked around the shrubbery and planted trees. Miss Julia paid us out of her pocket.
—*Submitted by L.A. "Morgan" Wise*

Y.T. Sheffield arrived in Plains driving a four door yellow Buick. I remember the top would let down on his car. He coached the girls and boys basketball teams and baseball. We had some good teams back then! Basketball was a big sport for Plains. At that time Plains would play Preston and we were enemies on the court.

Mr. Sheffield engineered the building of the wooden floor for the basketball court. He got local people to put the floor down and then the money ran out so the teams played on that open court. It wasn't long until the W.P.A. came along and enclosed the gym. After that, we even had the Boston Celtics down here! During the winter, the gym was heated by coal burning stoves. In the back of the gym was a shop for the Future Farmers of America boys and that's where the fire started that destroyed the gym. That was a sad day in Plains.

Mr. Sheffield taught math, was the principal and the coach of Plains High School for many years.

—*Submitted by Pete Godwin*

Lavon Turner was a very popular senior at Plains High School. He was a lot of fun and had a wonderful personality. Lavon came down with typhus fever and therefore had to catch up with his schoolwork in order to graduate with the class. He later had a nervous breakdown and had to go away to Milledgeville for treatment. This was a sad situation for everyone. Mr. Sheffield was telling the school about Lavon's situation and became so upset that Miss Julia had to finish the announcement.

—*Submitted by Eunice Griggs*

One aspect of Miss Julia's versatility was her artistic drawings. When studying a piece of literature like Shakespeare's Macbeth or Blackmore's Lorna Doone, Miss Julia, using colored chalk and the entire blackboard, would recreate a scene or scenes to illustrate the novel or play under study. In addition, as we read and discussed passages from the works, Miss Julia would change her demeanor and voice to correspond with that of a particular character, such as Duncan, the king, Lady Macbeth, or John Ridd. Thus, Miss Julia's acting ability coupled with her art thrilled her students as literature came alive in the classroom.

—*Submitted by Jimmy Bagwell*

One April Fools Day, all of the high school students decided to skip school and go to Rabbit Branch. Well, we did and Miss Julia called in the school buses to take the elementary school students home. As for the high school students, we had to walk home.

—*Submitted by Charles Medlock*

The first school bus I remember in Plains was a Model T with seats running lengthwise. There were no windows, just a hard top with curtains attached. If it was raining you let the curtain down to try and keep the rain out. The children who lived in town did not ride the bus. We had to walk to school in the mornings, walk home for lunch, back to school for the afternoon classes and then when school was over walk back home. Sometimes I was jealous and wished I could bring my lunch to school instead of walking home for lunch.

—*Submitted by Pete Godwin*

The Williams boys and the Watson boys were always fussing with one another and nobody really knew why. They fussed from the 8th grade to the 11th grade.

—*Submitted by Ruby Watson*

"We fussed because somebody had a Ford and somebody had a Chevrolet."

—*Submitted by Frank Williams*

Albert Williams slid down the banister at school and broke the clock on the wall. His mother made him save up the money to buy a new clock.

—*Submitted by Allene T. Haugabook*

A plane flew over the schoolyard and dropped a parachute with a message attached to it. The boys ran out to get it and it was a note for Frances Conyers.

Another time a plane landed in the schoolyard and it was a fellow who knew Ebbie Nichols. She later married him.

—*Submitted by Eunice Griggs*

On cold nights when the temperature would drop really low, Y.T. would spend the night at

Plains High School. He would get up one or two times at night and add more coal to the furnace. On those really cold nights, it would be hard to keep the school warm and he knew students could not concentrate and learn if they were cold. Early in the morning, he would come back home, eat breakfast and then head back to school to start a new day.

—As told by Lilloise Sheffield to Annette Wise

The storm blew the Johnson School down and they had to have school in the church. I started school about 1949 and everybody was still having school in the church (St. Mark). I attended school there until about the 5th grade and then another storm came through and blew the church down. Then, we started having school down past the railroad in the old Johnson home. The house was empty then, so we had school there. I don't remember a name for that school; we just called it Webster County School. I went there about two years and then went to school in Plains until the 8th grade. After that I went to Staley to school. I rode a bus to Americus to go to Staley.

—Submitted by Pauline Kitchens

Depression Days

Everybody was in the same boat – nobody had any money.

—Submitted by Charles Medlock

Everybody had chickens and they'd buy feed in sacks. We'd pick out the feed sack that we liked and later on it was made into a dress. I went to Georgia Southwestern College in feed sack dresses.

—Submitted by Annie Mae Vaughn

Most people had cars when I was growing up, but during the Depression money was short. I heard of people filling the tires on their car with sawdust and strapping rawhide on the tires to keep them on the rim.

The stores in Plains as I remember didn't close during the Depression, people just didn't sell much. I remember my father saying he worked from 7

A.M. to midnight on Saturday and had as little as $14 in the cash register at the end of the day. People just didn't have money during the Depression. They paid bills with meat, meal or wood. Some people who had moved away from Plains moved back home because times were so bad.

—Submitted by Pete Godwin

During the Depression people raised nearly everything but sugar and salt. Everybody had a milk cow. Eggs were sold to the store. The sharecroppers would get stuff from the store and their boss would stand for the bill.

—Submitted by L.A. "Morgan" Wise

Old Matthew E. Rylander Home built circa 1850. Photo credit: Annette Wise

The Haunted House

Everyone in Plains gets a gleam in their eyes at the mention of the haunted house. It was built around 1849 by Mathew Edward Rylander and is located just west of Plains on the Old Plains Highway. People living in the house claimed to have seen ghosts, heard unwound clocks striking and had bed clothes snatched off their beds.

The known families who have lived in the antebellum house are the Ed Stewart family (grandson of Mathew Edward Rylander), Dr. Thad Wise, Jimmy Carter family, Howard Pantall family, Richard Hewitt family and Tommy Moncus family.

"I don't know when I first heard it was haunted. I just always knew it," explained Rosalynn Carter. "Over the years, there were many bizarre occurrences, but one story I remember was that a light in the attic window was a candle kept burning by a lady so soldiers would know where to hide during the Civil War.

"When I was a little girl, my best friend was Jimmy's sister, Ruth. We had to walk by here to visit each other because I lived in Plains and the Carters lived in the country. We were about 11 and we were so afraid of the house that we walked down in the woods. I'm sure the ghostly manifestations persisted, but I tended to forget them when Jimmy returned from the Naval Academy and we began to date. When we married, I moved about with him. Following the naval duty, we returned to Plains in 1953. It was during this time that we began to visit Dr. Thad Wise who was then living in the haunted house. Dr. Wise thoroughly enjoyed the psychic phenomena which continued to surround this house. When we visited him, he kept us amused with ghost stories. One was about the little white dog which would come up on the porch when you were sitting there. If anyone reached down to pat the dog, it would disappear."

"It was a real spook house," said Inez Laster. She cooked for Dr. Wise during the 1950s. "Things started happening when Dr. Thad was sick. I heard someone knocking on the door of that room. The door slammed open and then shut back. Then I heard walking. Later I saw a woman with a long white dress coming from towards the cemetery. I saw her for 12 whole months. Dr. Thad could see her, too. He would say it was our imagination and when we would speak to her, she would vanish. She would come in the daytime and when she came at night she carried a light as big as the moon. You would always see her coming but never see her leave because when she turned, she disappeared."

—Jacqueline Cook - Haunted House in Plains, "The Atlanta Journal and Constitution" Magazine, *Oct. 7, 1973*

Marriage Ceremony

The following notice was in the Americus Times-Recorder, January 8, 1990.

One Hundred Years Ago in 1890:

"Mr. Joe Buchanan and Miss Mattie Powell, were married yesterday afternoon at the residence of Mrs. E. R. Stewart of Plains of Dura. Rev. A. F. Stubbs presided."

—Submitted by Jack Cox

Legend of Annie Stewart

There is a legend that the old Ed Stewart home, on the left side of Lebanon Cemetery Road, where Jimmy and Rosalynn Carter lived briefly, is haunted. Several years ago at Sumter County Comprehensive High School, a young black female student told this story. She said her grandmother, when a young girl, was a maid to the Stewart family. Ed Stewart was Sunday school superintendent at Plains Methodist Church for 50 years and, it was said, never missed a Sunday during this time. The Stewarts had a daughter, their only child, who died at age 17. According to the young lady telling the story, her grandmother said the spirit of the Stewart girl would appear from time to time and she, the grandmother, had seen it once on the edge of the yard. The young Stewart girl, Annie, is buried in the Magnolia Springs cemetery. The house is now deserted so if Annie's restless spirit still wanders around the premises, only the wild creatures will know.

—Submitted by Jack F. Cox

Childhood Memories

When I was a little girl my Grand-Dad, Ernest Wright, made us roller skates. He would take 3 cans and cut the top and bottom out. Then, he would run wire through each can and tie them on a wood plank. We had a lot of fun sliding around on that hard red clay!

—*Submitted by Liz Angry*

A favorite childhood memory was swimming at the Shirley Place where we lived. The blacks built the pool to baptize in, so we also had a cold spring to swim in. I would swim with the sharecroppers' sons and we'd go swimming four or five times a day.

—*Submitted by L.A. "Morgan" Wise*

My wife Ann remembers when there was a ball diamond across the road from their house. One day the batter knocked a ball near their house. The outfielder ran and caught it, but when he turned around, he ran smack dab into a great big cactus. He sure was stuck up!

—*Submitted by Millard Simmons*

Growing up, we'd take syrup cans with a long wire tied to it and run around the yard pulling it behind us. To make a lot of noise, we would put rocks in the can. We would dig for doodlebugs singing, "Back, back dooblebug your house is on fire, back, back dooblebug your house is on fire." We would stir the hole with a stick and the bug would come up. Another thing, we would catch butterflies and tie a string on them and let them fly. We had fun going to each other's house playing. Mama would get out there on the road and she would call us. We'd hear her way down the road past the branch and when we heard her, we would come out running to the house!

—*Submitted by Addie Josie Wright*

A scary event for me was Richard Johnson and I crawled through the sewerage pipe by the highway. As we got nearly through, George Dodson went to throwing sand over the pipe opening. The dust was so bad, we couldn't breathe. I tried to back up, but Richard would not move back. George

finally opened the sewer and we got out. We all learned a lesson that day.

—*Submitted by L.A. "Morgan" Wise*

_____ ran a Model T into the Oliver-McDonald Store and hollered "Whoa, Whoa, Whoa!"

—*Submitted by Charles Medlock*

The circus would come to town every year. Once there was this wrestling bear at the circus. This bear didn't have claws or teeth and was really strong. One time the bear slung a man around so hard that he rolled out the door, knocking over the ticket booth.

—*Submitted by L.A. "Morgan" Wise*

As a young boy I can remember when Highway 280 was paved. The highway was cleaned out with dirt pans pulled by mules. After it was smooth, regular field rocks were put down on the road and then a layer of asphalt and gravel.

—*Submitted by Pete Godwin*

War Time Memories

Some of the women from Plains worked or went to school in Americus and since there wasn't much gas during the war, Margaret Harris bought a Blue Bird school bus to transport us back and forth and charged 15¢ one way. The bus caught on fire and burned one day on her way home.

—*Submitted by Virginia Williams*

I remember during World War II that German P.O.W. soldiers were brought over from Americus to work in the fields around Plains. There were a lot of men and young boys who were away fighting in the war and the fields had to be worked. I couldn't understand the Germans, but they were friendly. I still have a bucket that was used in our well to draw drinking water. The soldiers would take turns drawing a bucket of water. They were amazed at how the bucket opened at the bottom and would let the water out.

—*Submitted by Ernest Turner*

The Cannery

There used to be a canning plant in Plains. It was located west of the old gym by the road. It had a steam boiler. Each one brought wood for the boiler whenever they came to can food. They sold you the cans in pint, quart or gallon size. They had steam cookers. Someone would check on the boiler to see if it was working O.K. They had can sealers that you cranked by hand. My mother sent me 2 quarts of fried chicken to England in WWII. I took my knife and opened a can to see if it was O.K. We put it on a potbelly stove in the barracks and got it good and hot. "Them Yankees" went crazy over the fried chicken, so we opened the other can."

—*Submitted by L.A. "Morgan" Wise*

There was an old boiler that came from a sawmill and it was used in the canning plant to can vegetables. The agriculture teacher ran the canning plant. A lot of people in Plains used this plant to can their summer vegetables.

—*Submitted by Pete Godwin*

Stores in Plains

The stores would stay open on Saturday night until about 12:00. Some people would start buying their groceries around 11:00. The stores and street would be full of people. We liked to sometimes just sit in the car and watch everybody.

—*Submitted by Annie Mae Vaughn*

A fond memory that I have took place at the Mercantile where Wilburn Smith and I would put toys together for them every Christmas.

—*Submitted by L.A. "Morgan" Wise*

When I was a child, my grandmother sent me to Walters store to buy a few items. One of the items was oleo. Well, I didn't know what oleo was, so I came home with Oreos! Needless to say, I had to take them back to the store.

—*Submitted by Mary Evelyn Moncus*

President Jimmy Carter stops by to talk with Ernest Turner during visit home from the White House. Photo credit: Jimmy Carter Presidential Library

Johnny Graham's store was in a brick building behind the pharmacy. A lot of white people in town traded with him. He had cloth, shoes and dry goods. I remember he would drive to town and park his car next to his store. He was well respected in the community.

Other stores that I remember being located behind the pharmacy were a meat market run by Roy Brannen, Clark Wise and Oliver Spann had a grocery store located in the same building as the pharmacy, and Sis Tondee ran a hotel taking in boarders. The biggest business was the Cranford Gin.

—*Submitted by Pete Godwin*

Many stores have come and gone through the years, but one special to me was Turner Hardware and Used Furniture. Ernest and June Turner were owners and operators of this store for many years. During the Carter years, Mr. Ernest proudly displayed a sign that said, "The store that did not change." His sign was right, it did not change! The store catered to the community and in the last few years of operation carried only used furniture. One of my favorite memories is how Mr. Ernest always made any visitor to the town feel welcome. He always had time to talk and answer their questions.

He was asked time and time again the same questions, but he always smiled and gladly answered the endless questions with much delight. Through his kindness and generosity many lives have been touched.

—*Submitted by Annette Wise*

Stables

In the 1910s and 1920s, there were four stables in Plains at different times. Mr. Rolin Chambliss operated one on the west side of South Bond Street, from which a horse and buggy could be rented for a one day trip to Americus for twenty-five cents. Mr. Chambliss was an uncle of Mrs. Estes (Eleanor Chambliss) Forrest. Retiring from this stable work, he farmed for a few years on this farm about two miles south of Plains before moving to Homestead, Florida. He was married to Henrietta Davidson and their four children are: Florrie, Lois, Rolin, Jr. and Nadine.

John B. Clark, Sr. operated a stable in the same locale. The family lived at the corner of Church and Thomas street. The children are: John Bartow Clark, Jr., Miss Berta Will Clark, Lucy Kate C. Butterworth, Mrs. William Ed (Amise Clark) Carter, Mrs. Judson B. (Mary Clark) West, and Carol Clark Crook.

Louis Cato and a Mr. Croxton had a stable at one time and raised Texan ponies. No date available, remembered by Mrs. Morgan (Ann Slocumb) Wise as told to her when a child.

Emory Augustus Stephens ran a stable in the 1910s at same locale. The office area was on the south side of building and was a gathering place for the men to meet and enjoy conversation. He was the grandfather of Beth Walters, was married to Elizabeth Cheek and had two daughters: Florrie Estelle Stephens Murray and Eva Stephens Markette. He died at the home of his daughter, Mrs. Murray, in 1932.

John Woodruff also ran a stable on South Bond Street during the 1920s, in the same building. The children enjoyed climbing the ladder up to the hayloft to play. Mr. Woodruff was always happy to lend his pocketknife to the children with which to play mumblety-peg. He had one son named Jesse.

—*Excerpt from "History of Plains" by Beth Walters*

Tan Yard

Tan Yard was owned and operated by a Mr. Black (as remembered by Mozella Hicks) who presumably is the Major Black who owned nearby Black's Mill in the mid 1880s (Young's Mill). Knowledge of the Tan Yard was told to Mrs. George (Louise Price) Whitten by Hattie, the housemaid of Louise's mother, Mrs. Jim (Winnie Kidd) Price. The Yard was located in the area between Mrs. Whitten's and Mr. Young's farms. It was run by Turner Hicks, a first cousin to Abe Hicks, the husband of Mozella and a cousin of Juanita Hicks. At the Yard, hides were tanned for use as chair seats and other house purposes.

—*Excerpt from "History of Plains" by Beth Walters*

No Place Like Home – Memories of Plains

I was born in 1924. My parents were Anthony and Mattie Mitchner Ross. We lived on Dick Stewart's place out on Highway 30. We moved to Detroit in 1929 hoping that things would be better there. This was a mistake and my mother didn't like the snow. We moved back to Macon in 1930 and finally made our way back home to Plains.

My father Anthony Ross, or "Son" as everyone knew him, was a brick mason and made all sorts of things, even sundials. My mother, Mattie Mae Mitchner Ross, taught school in Archery and was the principal at Rosenwald School at one time.

A fond childhood memory of mine was chasing guineas. My sister, Toni, and I each had a doll. She named hers after Nancy Jones and I named mine after Della Franklin, who still lives here in Plains. During the Depression days, my sister Toni found a dime. We were so excited and ran back home to show it to our mother who was just as excited as we were.

Mama died when we were young and my grandmother helped raise us. She was "Aunt Laura" to everybody, both black and white. She helped look after sick folks and was the midwife in Plains.

I married Lonnie Cleveland and we had six children. Two of my children are no longer living. When Lonnie passed away, his dog would jump up to the window and look up toward the sky like he was thinking "I know my daddy's up there somewhere."

A dog showed up after the flood in 1994 and we named him Flood. He sure was an ugly dog, but we did't say that in front of him – we spelled it out U-G-L-Y. We knew he couldn't spell, but no one had ever told him he wasn't human.

—*Submitted by Mrs. Clydie Ross Cleveland*

Ebony Monts Story

Susie Barner tells the story of her little grandson, Ebony Monts, choking on a balloon. It seems that on October 10, 1999 the little boy was playing with a balloon when a piece of it got lodged in his throat. He was quickly taken to the Plains police chief, Benjie Conger, who breathed the breath of life in little Ebony. The child was without air for eight minutes but fortunately there was no brain damage. Mrs. Barner says the entire family is so grateful for the quick work done by Benjie to save Ebony's life.

—*Submitted by Susie Barner*

A Wednesday Wedding

On July 20, 1955, C.G. Haugabook, Jr. and Allene Timmerman were married at Plains Baptist Church. This does not seem newsworthy. However, in these times of having all weddings, it seems, on Saturday, ours is a bit different. We chose to marry at 3:00 on a Wednesday afternoon. Why Wednesday, you might ask. This was our choice because we wanted all the citizens of Plains and our friends in Americus and the New Era area as well as Ceegie's friends and family from Montezuma to attend. They could best attend on a Wednesday afternoon because this was when all the stores closed at noon, enabling all those who would like to, to be in attendance. Friends and family seemed glad we chose a Wednesday as the church was filled to capacity, even though we didn't send out invitations. The church was decorated, free of charge, by Ann Dodson and "Miss" Addie McGarrah. The reception was held at our house. Here, "Miss" Ruth Godwin decorated the table, which held the cake. Again, this was free of charge. This is just an example of how we all loved and supported each other in not only large events such as a wedding, but in smaller events, too.

—*Submitted by Allene T. Haugabook*

Getting Rid of Warts the Easy Way

When I was a child of about 9 or 10 I had several warts on my right hand. These were a bit worrisome and unattractive so I wanted them off. A good friend and neighbor, Mrs. Hewitt, said she knew how to talk them off. I took her at her word and we gave it a try. I went to her house, which at that time was located where the Citizens Telephone building is now. It was the Murray home, which has now been moved to Hospital Street across from the Lillian G. Carter Nursing Center. Mrs. Hewitt, whom I called just "Hewitt," took enough broom straws from her broom to touch each of my warts with a separate straw. She said a few words of magic, which I didn't understand. Then, she wrapped the straws in a piece of brown wrapping paper, tied them with a red string and handed them to me. My job was to walk down the street in front of her house, throw the package over my left shoulder and not look back. This I did with great care. I never knew who got my warts, but the "operation" got rid of mine.

—*Submitted by Allene T. Haugabook*

Alive, Not Dead

In 1977 Maranatha Baptist Church was formed and met down in St. Mark's Lutheran Church in the area known as Bottsford between Plains and Parrott. One night at a meeting of the Maranatha members, Mr. Alton Carter told the story of what he remembered of the Bottsford community. Mr. Alton came to Plains in 1904 and is telling the story in 1977. One funny story he tells on the tape is the story of Roscoe Lassiter. This took place perhaps around 1916 or 1917. It seems the Lassiter family lived in the Bottsford area as did the McTyier family. Roscoe Lassiter, who worked in Florida, called the McTyier family because they were the ones who had a telephone. His message was that he was coming home on the train next day. There were three passenger trains going east and three going west. He would be in on the 3:30 train. Somehow Mrs. McTyier got the message mixed up and reported to the Lassiter family that Roscoe had died and his body would be in on the 3:30 train. Mr. Ross Dean, the undertaker, was there to meet the train with his hearse drawn by a pair of beautiful gray horses. A crowd of about 150 people had gathered to see Roscoe's body taken from the train. As they waited the train pulled in and out walked Roscoe, suitcase in hand. He was only coming home for a visit.

Mr. Alton tells that every time the train came in many, many people gathered to see it.

—*Submitted by Allene T. Haugabook, as told by Alton Carter*

The Sin of Dancing

It seems that in the early days of the 1900s dancing was looked upon by many as a sin. Mr. Oscar Williams tells the story of some young people getting together at the home of my grandparents, Edwin and Alice Timmerman. There were five boys in the Timmerman family along with several Timmerman boys, sons of Jesse and Emma Timmerman. These young men, along with Mr. Oscar and others, were having an enjoyable time in the upstairs rooms of the Timmerman home, the two-story house on Walters Street. Mr. Oscar went downstairs for some reason. My grandfather asked in a concerned manner, "Oscar, the young people are not up there dancing, are they?" Mr. Oscar replied, "Oh no, Mr. Timmerman. They are only doing the two step." This seemed to satisfy Father Timmerman, as he said to Mr. Oscar, "Well, all right. Just so long as they are not dancing."

Seems Mr. Oscar and some other boys in town did some more dancing. The membership roll of Plains United Methodist Church shows that in 1910 three young men were dismissed from membership in the church by act of Quarterly Conference. These men were Oscar Williams, Jack Slappey, and Bob Andrews. Their offence? Dancing! Nobody seems to know what girls they were dancing with. Perhaps they were Baptist young ladies. My, how the times have changed in regard to what people feel is right and wrong.

—*Submitted by Allene T. Haugabook*

Community Tragedies

In the summer of 1948 a tragedy of gigantic proportions struck a family in Plains. The Robert Ratliff family had three daughters and one son. The third daughter, Eloise, nicknamed "Teeny," had married Lonnie Taylor, a young man in her high school graduating class. The Taylors had two little children born just a year apart. Lonnie was an airplane pilot and owned his own plane. He took his family of four,

Mrs. Johnson, mother of Mrs. Robert Ratliff, in her petunia garden to left of the Robert Ratliff home located on Main Street. Photo credit: Annette Howard

along with "Teeny's" sister, Lorraine, nicknamed "Doodle," and their young brother, Bobby, on a plane trip to Tennessee. On the way back the plane crashed killing all six on board. The funeral was held at Plains Baptist Church, where four caskets held the bodies. A heartrending sight, indeed, to see the four caskets at the front of the church holding the six family members.

Plains has experienced other tragedies that touched the lives of all. In 1935, Walter Jones was struck by lightning and died at the age of 10. In 1951, Walter's brother, Jack, was killed in an airplane crash in Alabama as he served in the United States Air Force. At the writing of this history, the third brother in that family, Howard, has just been killed in a car crash on November 3, 2001, along with his wife, Dollie. These brothers were all sons of W.L. and Zera Jones.

Another family struck by tragedy more than once was the J.W. Sewell family. In 1951 a group of young boys were fishing in a pond across the road from what we all refer to as "The Haunted House." The boat capsized and one of the young boys, John Sewell, drowned. It seems the entire town gathered on the bank of the pond, hoping it wasn't true, grieving with the family and each other. Then in April 1975 this same family was again struck by tragedy. This time Ross Sewell, son of J.W. and Martha Sewell, and brother of John, was struck as he rode his motorcycle in front of their house on Highway 280, just west of town and was killed. After J.W.'s death, Martha married again, and her husband was killed in a fiery car crash in Florida. Friends, neighbors and family have always pulled together to be a tower of strength in helping the grieving families through these difficult times.

—*Submitted by Allene T. Haugabook*

The Bank of Plains

Recently, the old Plains Bank Building, built in 1901, has been opened as "The Old Bank Café." This building has served the town in several ways. After being a bank and closing in 1926, it remained empty for some years. President Jimmy Carter tells us that he and his cousin, Hugh Carter, as young boys, sold hot dogs, hamburgers, and ice cream there on Saturdays. Later, in the 1930s, the post office was moved to this location from one of the small wooden buildings to the west of the row of brick stores. The building served as a post office until the present one was built in 1963. About this time, Hugh Carter began to use the building as the office for his worm farm. The farm was located in the rear of his house on the outskirts of Plains, but this building was used as the office. After Hugh's death in 1999 it closed and remained unused until 2002. The Better Hometown Program of Plains acquired the building and renovated it, first naming it "The Plains Coffee Shop," but deciding just before the grand opening that a better name would be "The Old Bank Café."

Good history is hard to come by, and the bank closing has been one of the things fitting this category. One source says that it closed in 1919, another in 1920. Word of mouth has the closing in 1925 and 1926. Knowing that the library in

Americus has copies of the *"Americus Times-Recorder"* on microfilm, the definite date of closing could possibly be found here. After scanning the 1919s and 1920s and not finding any mention of the closing of the bank, it seemed necessary to scan the issues for 1924, '25 and '26.

Being about ready to give up the search, the November 24, 1926 issue of the paper gave encouragement. In an article the first line says, "A grand jury, charged to specially investigate the failure this past summer of the Plains Bank, was convened at 2 o'clock this afternoon following a call by Judge Zera A. Littlejohn of the Sumter Superior Court." The possible reason for being unable to find the exact date of closing, was missing issues from July 9, 1926 through August 6, 1926. Since the article referred to the past summer, it was assumed the bank closed during the time of the missing issues of the paper.

The article goes on to say "The Plains Bank was one of the 83 in the chain in Georgia and Florida operated by the Banker's Trust Company of Atlanta, of which W.L. Manley was president. Manley was recently convicted in the Fulton Superior Court on one of the numerous indictments returned there in connection with the failure of the numerous institutions.

"The bank is operated by many of the prominent citizens of the county. R.S. Oliver, the president, is a former member of the county commissioners, and is well known through this section. Mr. Oliver has extensive business and farming interests throughout this section. W.L. Thomas, the vice president, is a prominent citizen of Plains. Frank H. Greer was the cashier."

The directors and officers of the bank were R.S. Oliver, president; W.L. Thomas, vice dresident, who with the following are directors: Dr. T.M. Merritt, of Americus; J.A. McDonald, Dr. B.T. Wise, Dr. S.P. Wise, Dr. B.J. Wise all of Plains. F.H. Greer was cashier of the bank which had a capital stock of $50,000 and at the time of its failure a surplus of $12,000.

The bank was considered one of the strongest institutions in this country and its failure was blamed by the local officers to the break of the parent institution in Atlanta.[1]

Headlines in the November 27 issue of the paper have big, bold letters stating "Sheriff Seeks Plains Banker." Within two days time, the closing of the bank was being blamed on Mr. F.H. Greer, the cashier. The Greers were close friends of my parents and according to stories told me by my mother, Mr. Greer was not a person who would be guilty of this behavior. I can remember Mother telling me that after the article came out in the paper stating Mr. Greer was missing and could not be found, my father, Frank, said, "I know exactly where he is." He immediately made a telephone call finding Mr. Greer at his boyhood home in Mansfield, knowing nothing of the charges brought against him.

In the November 30 issue of the *"Times-Recorder"* it seems the sheriff of Newton County had located Greer, and Greer would be in court to answer the indictment on Thursday.

The December 2, 1926 issue of the *"Times-Recorder"* had headlines stating "Greer Voluntarily Surrenders." In this article the paper says "True to his word, Frank Greer, former cashier of the defunct Plains bank, now under indictment here, charged with embezzling over $12,000 appeared in Americus today at noon and voluntarily surrendered to Sheriff W.P. McArthur."

He was immediately released on a bond of $2,500, fixed by Solicitor General Jule Felton. F.F. Timmerman (my father) and O.V. Hogsed, both of Plains, signed as securities.

Greer was accompanied here by his lawyer, Col. A.S. Thurman, of Monticello, Georgia, and several men from Plains.

"The first I knew of my indictment was when I read it in big letters in *The Atlanta Journal*," said Greer to a reporter. "Of course it was the surprise of my life."

He appeared to be in excellent spirits, laughing and talking with his companions and friends here.

"There are many things that will be straightened out," he said. "I will make a longer statement later on."

The entire party from Plains, after getting the bond completed, remained in Americus for lunch.[2]

Continuing the search on microfilm of the 1927 issues of the paper it was found in the June 4, 1927 issue headlines reading "JURY CLEARS PLAINS BANK CASHER HERE." The article reads "Frank H. Greer, formerly cashier of the Bank of Plains, was quickly cleared of a charge of embezzlement by a jury in the Sumter Superior Court late Friday afternoon, the jury being out only about thirty minutes."[3]

Mr. Greer went on to serve in many important positions, not the least of which was manager of the Atlanta agency of the Federal National Mortgage Association, having offices on two floors of the Georgia Power Building in Atlanta. The Greers remained friends of our family until their deaths.

—*Submitted by Allene T. Haugabook*

Endnote

[1] *Americus Times-Recorder*, Nov. 24, 1926, p. 1.
[2] Ibid, Dec. 2, 1926. p.1
[3] Ibid, June 4, 1927. p.1

⌘

Twins in Plains

For a town as small as Plains, we have had our share of twins. There were the Oliver twins, Catherine and Carrie, born in the 1800s to Aughtry and R.S. Oliver. Other twins have been Albert and Alice Ratliff, children of the Bernard Ratliffs, Billy and Betty Wise, son and daughter of Lon and Mae Wise; Faye and Kaye Harper, daughters of George and Georgia Harper; Dale and Gail McDonald, son and daughter of Ralph and Evelyn McDonald; Steve and Jeff Smith, sons of Phillip and Jessie Smith; Laura and Lynn Holloway, daughters of Marianna and Clinton Holloway; Brandon and Justin Smith, sons of Penny and Charles Smith, Jr. The Medlock family has two sets of twins. Polly and Molly Medlock are twin daughters of Pat and Patsy Medlock. Parks Medlock, son of Wade and Kathryn Medlock, has twin girls, Emma and Elise. Out from Plains were the Holston twins, Mae and Rae, who lived here while going to school in Plains in the 1940s. In more recent days, Cassie and Casey Lowell, a daughter and son, were born to Barbara and Stan Lowell. Twin daughters, Jesse and Jillian, were born to Joni and Tim Westberry. Beverly and Bruce Johnson have twins, Alan Ryan and Allison Ruth. However, the twins who brought notoriety to our town were another set of Smith twins born to Sue and Oliver Smith. They were named Will Rogers Smith and Wiley Post Smith, born August 14, 1935. The original plan was that they were to bear the names Oscar, for a grandfather, and Oliver, for the father. However, a tragedy that captured the attention of the world was the air crash in Alaska of humorist and philosopher Will Rogers, and record shattering, round-the-world aviator, Wiley Post. These two famous men were killed instantly as the engine on their plane failed. Since this happened about the time of the twins' birth in Plains, they were given the names Will Rogers Smith and Wiley Post Smith. These men

Twins Will Rogers Smith and Wiley Post Smith. Photo credit: Will Rogers Smith

are first cousins of Rosalynn Smith Carter. President Jimmy Carter remarked to Will recently that he and Wiley were the first people to make Plains famous.

—*Submitted by Allene T. Haugabook*

A Letter to Granddaddy

Happy Belated Birthday

Dear Granddaddy:

Amid all the hustle and bustle of another busy summer in the South, I looked across my calendar the other day, knowing there was some special reason for remembering this time of year. July in Georgia. July in Plains. Birthdays. Peaches. Peanuts. Gnats. So many memories. So many good times.

Walter Franklin Spann and Ada Brooks Spann, 1950s. Photo credit: Steve Short

Today is the first anniversary of your burial under that white marble gravestone in your hometown. I couldn't help but make a note of it, because I care too much to forget. The food. The flowers. The calls. The cards. All the relatives and friends, including the former president and first lady, who thought enough of you to come. Even Mr. (Larry) Hancock remarked as the funeral procession pulled into Lebanon Cemetery that, for an elderly person, you must have had lots of friends. I think he was enamored by the crowd.

The day after your funeral, Mama took two basketfuls of the flowers to place in your church and in our church that Sunday morning. It was reminiscent of your gift of sharing.

Granddaddy, you always were my hero. I was so happy last year when you turned 90. My prayers were answered. We didn't get to celebrate like I had planned because you were ill, but I still have the 3-foot-tall birthday card that we all signed. I'll always say with pride that "I had a grandfather who lived to be 90 years old." Just knowing you were always there, even after you and Grandma had "to give up housekeeping," meant a lot to all our family. You knew you had a place in our homes.

I thought of you last week on July 15. I thought about there wouldn't be a birthday card this year from Nena. It's sad to think you weren't here to get it, and she wasn't here to send it. So much has changed in one year, but so much more also has stayed the same.

I'm waiting for the orders of peaches to come in. You know, I've always claimed the Plains peaches are the best anywhere. I enjoyed going to the experiment station with you and helping pick.

And what about the pears on that tree in your back yard? Pharis has invited me to come and fill up when they ripen. I remember when your sister and Uncle Kinsey used to come from Columbus every August for pears. We loved for them to come and they always enjoyed the visits.

The crops – I know how you loved the land – are doing their best to survive the dry, dusty days of summer. The wheat has been harvested and a new crop planted in its place.

There's a new sign leading up to your house this year, Granddaddy, and it's called Spann Drive. I am glad to see it officially recognized. Two signs – one at each of the road – went up in March. I'm so proud. I took pictures.

Also, I have a new picture of the house hanging on my den wall. It's a 16-by-20 aerial view, taken by a man from Evansville, Ind. I think it's an incredible shot, the house embedded in fields of lush, green winter wheat. I couldn't pass on the opportunity to purchase it, though it was expensive. But if there is a prettier white-columned house in

Plains, I haven't seen it. You know how much I always loved your house and yard.

Cutting grass. Trimming hedges. Washing the car.

Granddaddy, we used to have such good times together. You used to buy us candy at Hugh Carter's store. We'd go fishing at the Revells' pond and picnicking at Miss Lillian's Pond House. You'd take us to the pool to swim. You did a lot for all of us. Who can forget you in your black tuxedo, walking Lisa down the aisle at her wedding in 1980? You were 78 at the time.

I think we all enjoyed spending time at your house. The Green Room. The Blue Room. All the rooms. Eating ice cream on Sunday afternoons. Listening to the whistle of a passing Seaboard train at night. The tales about Mr. Lowery.

I'll never forget how willing you and Grandma were to help me get started tracing the family tree back in the late '70s. Grandma was grand. We took trips to Lumpkin, Richland, Weston and Preston, among many others. What about all the trips to Parrott to see your cousin Bill Cole? He was a wealth of information.

And what about the time in 1987, not long after Grandma's death, that I got you to stand by the historical marker that bears your ancestors' names, on the courthouse square in Preston? Those pictures mean more to me every day. It's fun to recall the rich history of the family. So many people today don't seem to have the time, but I have never lost interest. In the Clarks. Montgomerys. Balls. Sapps.

Today's a new day, Granddaddy, and we are all keeping busy. It's still hot in Plains, but the crape myrtles are in bloom again. Walter keeps cool by riding his Harley. Yes, he's still going strong, despite a slip-up back in January. Melba and Anita and Mama keep working at their always-hectic paces.

We grandkids are fine. Anne, bless her heart, makes sure there are flowers kept on yours and Grandma's graves. All the great-grandchildren are following their non-stop schedules. Even Austin, the great-great grandchild, is growing like a weed.

Some things are changing, but others, like our regard for you, stay the same.

July in Georgia. July in Plains. Tourists. Family. Farms. Memories. Happy Belated Birthday, Granddaddy. I think you know we still care.
—*Written by Steve Short in memory of longtime Plains resident Walter Franklin Spann, who died July 23, 1992*

The Plexico House

In 1985 when I compiled the book on Plains for the Centennial, I was in contact with two of Bishop Johnson's relatives: Mrs. W.D. (Beatrice) Johnson of Atlanta and Della Franklin of Plains. They said the Archery settlement was first called Blind Barnabas. The Plains school two story frame building was bought in 1921 for $500 and moved to the Archery settlement.

About 1920 John Franklin Sr. and Minnie Plexico came from York, South Carolina to Plains and lived in a house at the northwest corner of Church and Thomas streets. He was in the sawmill work. They sold the house to Earl and Lillian Carter (located on Old Plains Road). The Plexicos moved back into Plains to live out their remaining life. The Plexicos had two sons and one daughter. This was told to me in 1988 by one of the Plexico sons, who I dated as a teenager. In 1989, Mr. Plexico died of a heart attack at his home in Edison, Georgia. Both sons are deceased and I do not know about the daughter, Francis Plexico Stewart.
—*A note from Beth Walters, February 2000*

The Story of Robert McGarrah

On June 21, 1908, Plains was blessed by the birth of James Robert McGarrah, son of James Samuel and Adella Wells McGarrah. Robert lived all his life in the little village of Plains. He died January 21, 1993. During those 84 years that he lived in Plains he blessed many lives of the citizens in many different ways.

Robert was a graduate of Stuby Pharmacy in Macon and during his younger years was affiliated with Plains Pharmacy. Later he began work at the

J. Robert McGarrah. Photo credit: Plains United Methodist Church Directory

Plains Post Office becoming the postmaster, where he retired after 20 years service there. As some of the citizens of Plains who worked in Americus gathered downtown in the cold early mornings to wait for Margaret Harris' shirt factory bus, he would allow those waiting to come in by the fire in the postoffice to keep warm as they waited. As people came into the postoffice during the day he would often greet them with "Well, what's the good word for today?" or maybe it would be "What do you know for sure?" Robert didn't seem to keep regular working hours at the post office. You could find him there early mornings, late afternoons, Saturdays after closing hours and even sometimes on Sunday afternoons. Never on Sunday mornings, as he was *always* at his church at that time.

C.L. Walters III tells that Robert always tried to learn one new word a week. One morning C.L. went into the post office and Robert greeted him with "Good morning, C.L. Is everything copacetic with you today?" C.L. said Robert let him chew on that a few days before telling him that it means "Is everything all right with you?"

It was a special treat for the children to come to the post office, always knowing Mr. Robert would treat them with a stick of Juicy Fruit chewing gum. After he retired from the post office, he carried this tradition over to his church, Plains United Methodist, where he was always a very active and faithful member. On Sunday mornings after Sunday school was dismissed, you could be sure to see Robert at the bottom of the stairs waiting to give each child a piece of Juicy Fruit gum. Another faithful member of the church, Beth Murray Walters, wrote to The Wrigley Gum Co. telling them of Robert's tradition of giving gum to the children of Plains. The Wrigley Co. responded with a nice letter along with several boxes of Juicy Fruit Gum. You can be sure this gum went to treat the children.

Robert never married but lived with and cared for his mother very faithfully all of her life. His house has now been torn down but was located on Bond's Trail just north of the house where Rosalynn Smith Carter grew up.

—*Submitted by Allene T. Haugabook*

Fond Memories of Plains

Rachel Williams was born in 1917 and raised in Plains, Georgia. Her father, Joseph Henry Williams, was owner and operator of a store in Plains. She lived next door to her grandmother and grandfather Dodson. Rachel attended school in Plains and was very active in basketball and one act play. Her last year in school she was in the play and won a medal for Best Actress.

Later, Rachel married Billy Ferguson and moved to DeSoto. In January 1977, Rachel and Billy flew to Washington, D.C. for the inauguration of Jimmy Carter. Rachel's younger sister, Rebecca, and her husband Irvin Karr from New Jersey met them in Washington. Rebecca and Jimmy Carter were classmates during their school days at Plains High School.

Beth Ferguson, daughter of Rachel and Billy Ferguson, also went to Washington for the inauguration of Jimmy Carter. She rode the "Peanut Special." Upon arriving in Washington they found out the hotel that had been reserved for all that made the trip on the train had many problems. There was panic with some people and they made reservations in other places.

—*Submitted by Beth F. Usry*

Longtime Citizen of Plains, Linton Slappey

The history of Plains would not be complete without some mention of one of the special citizens of the town, Linton Slappey. Slappey, as he was called by many people, was the son of Jack and Ethel Carter Slappey. Many people also called him Leonard, though his given name was really Linton and he appreciated those people who really knew and used his name. He was born August 4, 1912 and died August 2, 1982

Linton had a brilliant mind but was handicapped because of a nervous condition. Today there are many kinds of medications with which he could be helped, enabling him to attend school. This was not the case in the days he was growing up in Plains. One of his special hobbies that necessitated a keen mind was that of ham radio operator. He spent many hours communicating with friends he made in this manner.

Being unable to drive a car, he hitch-hiked from place to place. Often he could be seen at the intersection of Highways 280 and 19. Local citizens were always glad to give him a lift. The story is told that at one time a man going to Albany stopped and asked Linton directions. Linton replied, "If you will give me a lift, I will show you the way." Getting in the car, he directed the man to Plains. At this point, Linton got out, turned to the man and said, "If you will go back to the place you picked me up and keep going straight in the direction you were heading, you will come to Albany." Is that not smart? He was always quick with an answer or response to anyone who made a derogatory remark about him. In the drugstore one day he complimented a young girl on how pretty she was. The girl replied, "I'm sorry I can't say the same about you." His quick reply, "You could if you would lie like I did." One day he was seen rolling a wheelbarrow upside down. When questioned about the reason for this he replied, "If I turned it upright somebody would put something in it."

Unfortunately, there being no facilities for caring for his type problem, he often had to be admitted to the mental institution of Central State Hospital in Milledgeville, Ga. After being treated there for a period of time, he would be able to return to Plains. Upon his return home, he sold packages of needles as a means of income, often giving away more packages than he sold.

Some people were afraid of Linton. That was to their detriment. He meant no harm and if he thought people were afraid of him, he would make up songs about them, singing the song as he walked up and down the streets of Plains wringing his hands and rubbing his head.

Linton Slappey was a very important part of the lives of people of Plains and surrounding areas. He endeared himself to many citizens and it was with a degree of sadness when he was no longer a part of the lives of the people here. He is buried in the Slappey family plot at Lebanon Cemetery west of Plains.

—*Submitted by Allene T. Haugabook*

A Teacher Remembered

Nancy Daniell Sheppard

The school year 1937-38 began at Plains High School with a new teacher for third-grade pupils. Her name was Nancy Daniell. She taught in Plains for many years and was loved and appreciated by those who sat in her class.

Nancy Daniell Sheppard's third-grade class, 1937-38. Front: Harold Wise, George Mims, Jerry Smith, Jimmy Whaley, Allman Hogsed, Betty Wise, Allene Timmerman and Ruth Carter. Back: Joe Bacon, Jack Jones, Freddie Chavers, Billy Wise, Hazel Hobgood, Polly Smith and Helen Coleman. Photo credit: Allene T. Haugabook

Since it was my privilege to be one of her first pupils that year of '37-'38, I have reflected on some of the things she did for and with our class. Going on a field trip to Americus on the train were the 15 boys and girls in third grade. They were: Joe Bacon, Jr., Ruth Carter, Freddie Chavers, Helen Coleman, Hazel Hobgood, Allman Hogsed, Jack Jones, George Mims, Jerry Smith, Polly Smith, Allene Timmerman, Jimmy Whaley, Betty and Billy Wise, who were twins, and Harold Wise. We all boarded the train, which was called " The Butthead," at noon, rode to Americus where we visited the fire department and the post office. We then boarded the afternoon train for our return trip. What a wonderful experience for children of "The Depression" who seldom had a trip out of Plains.

At the beginning of our school year she made a promise to her pupils. This promise was that any pupil who was not absent or tardy the entire year would earn a trip to her home in Leary for several days the next summer. The three earning that privilege were Harold Wise, George Mims and Allene Timmerman. Since I was the only girl earning this trip, she let me invite my friend and classmate, Ruth Carter, sister of President Carter. As we traveled to Leary she took us by Albany to visit the airport and on by Radium Springs. Then it was on to Leary. Her family home in the country impressed us by the fact it straddled the county line. We slept in Baker County and ate in Calhoun County. Also, the water was sulphur water, so she took us to a nearby neighbor to draw water that was more suited to our taste.

She taught in Plains for many years, but the second year she was here she married C.C. Sheppard. She taught my brother, Edwin, in four different grades – third, fourth, fifth, and seventh. She also served as librarian some of the years she taught, keeping the door of her classroom open between it and the library. What a pity if she had been a poor teacher, but this was certainly not the case. She had the love and respect of her pupils.

My mother thought Nancy could do almost anything. An example is something that happened during World War II when many commodities were in short supply. Mother worked in the lunchroom in the upstairs part of the school building. Being the accommodating person that she was, Mrs. Sheppard came and asked if she could get anything for the ladies as she went to Americus that afternoon. Mother, in a joking way said, "Yes, bring me back three yards of cloth, blue with a white dot," feeling sure this would be impossible. Not so, as here came Mrs. Sheppard back with the material from which Mother made a dress, wearing it for many years.

After I married and was living out from Americus, Mrs. Sheppard called one day to tell me that she and her daughter, Jeanette, had come by to pay Mother for Jeanette's piano lessons, finding her very sick from a number of bee stings. Mrs. Sheppard and Jeanette stayed there with Mother until I could come over to see about her and Dr. Smith could come to the rescue from Americus.

It was with a degree of sadness that many of us attended her funeral on September 4, 2002. Many good memories flooded the minds of those who knew her and had learned many lessons under her direction.

—*Submitted by Allene T. Haugabook*

My Hometown

Many people in Plains worked very hard, long hours traveling to some of the coldest states campaigning for Jimmy Carter. Others devoted hundreds of hours volunteering at the old train depot in Plains which was the Presidential Campaign Headquarters. In 1976, Jimmy Carter was elected president of the United States, and the community rejoiced in the victory! We had seen many changes in our community through the years, but Jimmy Carter's bid for president, by far, was the biggest changing factor in the history of our town. No longer was it a sleepy, little town; now the entire world looked over our shoulder. As the Carters prepared to leave Plains for Washington, several from our community – Phil Wise, Bernstine Hollis, Sonny Carter, and Mary Prince – would also make the move. In addition, Jody Powell from Vienna, Georgia, and Hamilton Jordan from Albany, Georgia, moved to be part of the Carter Administration. To say it was an adjustment would be an understatement to the changes which would occur in our lives over the course of the next four years. In 1981, many of us would return to Georgia when President Carter was defeated by Ronald Reagan.

This is a time of reflecting Jimmy and Rosalynn Carter's return home, as Plains welcomed them back from serving as the CEO of our nation. Returning home was a much simpler style of living. A warm reception was planned for the Carters' return home. We had a lot to celebrate and celebrate we did! Our reasons for celebrating were varied: 1) Our hometown had made history – Plains, Georgia is now on printed maps of the United States. We can now look for Plains and not Americus or Columbus as a major site to visit. 2) Plains became a tourist attraction. Many people had never heard of Plains, but after *"Jimmy Who?"* became known as President Jimmy Carter, the world began traveling Interstate 75 South following the signs to Plains, Georgia – home of Jimmy Carter.

The citizens of Plains are just regular folks – they live a simple life. With a population of less than 1,000, it is pretty simple living! There is only one street, Main Street, where you can locate the Post Office, pharmacy, several businesses and then the farm center which caters to the needs of our local farmers. The streets are not fancy. There is only one light and it blinks all the time – a caution light.

Since the Carters' return home they have remained active in the development of their hometown. The majority of the residents have gained even a deeper respect for them after observing their involvement in numerous community projects as well as world wide projects. The Carters have devoted many hours of community service to Plains. In addition to their commitment to their hometown, they also looked at a broader project which would enable them to continue their work on human rights issues, health, and world peace. Thus, the idea for The Carter Center was developed and Atlanta was selected as the site for this center. Often times, we do not realize what talents and gifts we have in the midst of us!

The Carter Center was established in the early 1980s and demonstrates a love for people, the less fortunate, people of color and their love for Jesus Christ. Even in the midst of assisting Third World countries they continue to do mission work here in the state and at home, teaching others to become self-sufficient and to be able to have a better quality of life.

Through the years, we have seen many projects around Plains, including the restoration of Plains High School, the revitalization of the downtown area, and the establishment of a Boys and Girls Club which is used by all of the citizens of Plains. The Plains Boys and Girls Club is a facility assisting with the needs of our local youth, providing a place for them to go after school and in the summer. Numerous programs are offered for youth as well as continuing education programs for adults. This facility is a center for the entire community – black, white, and hispanic working together as a *team* disbanding segregation.

There have been many people who have played key roles in Plains. One who was instrumental as the town was thrown into the public light was Maxine Reese. She was instrumental in getting people to work together and pulling events together to benefit the needs of the community and the presidential campaign. She worked tirelessly in campaigning for the Carters and then making arrangements to get residents of Plains to Washington to witness the inauguration ceremony. A train was hired to carry people from Plains to Washington, D.C. for the event. The day for departure finally arrived with a trainload of excited friends and supporters. The train was affectionately named "The Peanut Special."

The residents of Plains have seen many changes through the years with businesses coming and going as the town has changed to meet the needs of the community as well as the thousands of tourists who visit the hometown of the 39th president of the United States of America. There is now soul food for the soul found right in the heart of downtown Plains with Maggie Crimes running "Mom's Kitchen" and located right on the edge of town is Henry Tatum's meat market.

Many churches have revivals, singings, vacation bible schools, and homecomings inviting those in the community to rejoice with one another. Through the support of our churches working together, special assistance programs, the forming of sister churches and missions have occurred. One special relation exists between Maranatha Baptist Church and Lebanon Baptist Church with these churches gathering to fellowship from time to time through revivals and Sunday school lessons. Maranatha reaches into the black community to assist the less fortunate.

Each September the citizens come together to host the "Plains Peanut Festival." The activities pull the community together outside of work and church. This is a time all can be free and meet new friends. The event is advertised statewide and many visitors are in our midst. The Carters attend one night of a three-night event as stories are retold of our past with a folk play that is performed by the residents of Plains. This is a special treat for the community as we celebrate our past, laughing about some of the funny things that have occurred and even shedding tears as we recall some of the tragedies that have touched our lives. On the Saturday of the festival, everyone enjoys the parade, road races, arts and crafts booths and visiting with friends. Kids especially enjoy hayrides, participating in the parade, and the special activities which have been planned for them.

The Plains Historical Preservation Trust was established in 1977 and actively works with the city and Park Service to ensure that the town of Plains is preserved the way the citizens want it. Trust members have actively lobbied for the establishment of the Jimmy Carter National Historic Site, raised several million dollars for the restoration of Plains High School, which serves as the main visitors center for the National Park Service, and have placed historical markers around Plains just to name a few projects. Residents of Plains take much pride in their hometown and the preservation of its unique history. Trust board members meet monthly and hold four general meetings each year. One of the Trust's charter board members, P.J. Wise, has been instrumental in many developments around town. Since the presidential years, P.J. as well as many others, dreamed of having a tourist train running from Plains to Archery connecting these two historical sites. Due to his commitment to the train idea and the fact that the Boyhood Farm of President Carter had recently opened for visitation, the Trust approached the railroad company in 1999 asking if it would be possible to operate a tourist train on the existing tracks running through Plains. Surprisingly, the local train company was interested and began to research the idea. In July 1999, the Trust invited representatives from the National Park Service and local city government to meet at a Trust board meeting and discuss this possibility. Thus the idea grew and in 2002 an excursion train began operating as a tourist train running through our hometown connecting our historical sites. In addition, visitors can visit Americus and Cordele on the train ride. This will be beneficial to the economy of Plains.

The Boyhood Home is very educational and a great site to visit, giving the visitor an opportunity to look back to the 1930s to see how Jimmy Carter once lived. Through this story, one can see how families were bonded together as one unit. With the many opportunities becoming available in Plains this gives the local residents the chance to work closer to their home, have an impact on how the town is operated and get more involved taking active roles in the political arena.

May 11, 2002, will be marked as an important part of our history as the Main Street of downtown Plains had a grand opening for a restored Plains Inn and Antiques Mall, café, and Community Center. The Plains Better Hometown Program purchased several building from Hugh Carter's family for this project. In the efforts that have gone into the restoration of Plains, the Carters have been very involved having many hands-on experiences. Jimmy and Rosalynn Carter worked tirelessly juggling meetings and trips in order to spend as much time as possible in Plains working on the downtown project. Visitors were surprised and delighted to see them darting from one work site to another – planning, selecting and working on the restoration of the

buildings. During those long months, it was not unusual to see one or both of them right in the middle of the operation, not as bystanders, but actively participating and working. Decisions had to be made and a quality operation was desired. The Troyer brothers, Leroy and Lloyd, were just the persons to see that this was the case. Leroy designed the plans and Lloyd was the overseer. These two men donated their time and talents. Prison labor was used throughout the project.

We are appreciative of the hard work that has gone into the development and restoration of the town of Plains through the years. We have been blessed to have citizens who are dedicated and hard working and willing to share their hometown with the world. No job can ever be completed without the cooperation of the *team* players. Surely, we may face obstacles and challenges that are set before us but relying on the help of our Lord and Savior Jesus Christ "all things are possible" only if you believe. We must believe in ourselves and in the people of our community.

—*Submitted by Bernstine Hollis*

Houses of Plains

There are many beautiful and historic homes in Plains. The following are the ones that were submitted.

Hudson House

The first settler of Plains was Milton Leander Hudson who built on the northeast corner of Bond's Trail and Church Street around 1883. Mr. Hudson gave land for the store area, the depot, schoolhouse, and the Plains Methodist Church. He was the first postmaster, first railroad agent and a member of the first Mercantile Company. His daughter, Mary Hudson Campbell, was the first white baby born in Plains on February 9, 1884.

In the early 1900s the house was sold to Dr. Bowman J. Wise. Bowman was one of the three

Wise brothers who were doctors in Plains. He married Mozelle Baldwin and had one daughter, Marguerite.

The house is presently owned by Mr. and Mrs. Frank Williams.

See Chapter 2 for picture of the Hudson House.

—Submitted by Virginia Williams

Edwin Timmerman House on Walters Street, built circa 1893. Photo credit: Allene T. Haugabook

Timmerman House

This house was built about 1890 by Edwin and Alice Forth Timmerman. Here they reared their family. After the death of Edwin, Alice continued to live there with her son, Brownie, and his wife, Lillian, until her death in 1937. Brownie and Lillian lived there until 1946 at which time they moved to Americus and sold the house to Frank and Virginia Williams. The Williams family lived there with their family until 1977 at which time they moved to the home of Frank's parents on Church Street. The house was rented for several years. In 1981 Rev. Dan Ariail, pastor of Maranatha Baptist Church, and his wife, Nelle, bought the house and are living there at the time of this writing in 2003.

—Submitted by Allene T. Haugabook

The Hudson-Campbell House located on northeast corner of Church and Walters streets. Photo credit: Frank Williams

Hudson-Campbell House

This house was built by Milton Leander Hudson. After his death his two daughters, Mary Hudson Campbell and Marguerite "Tot" Hudson, lived here. Mrs. Campbell's sons were Milton, Karl, and Stewart. After the boys were grown "Miss" Mary rented part of the house out as apartments. Some who had apartments here were C.L. and Beth Walters, L.L. and Valrie Spence, and Fred and Lula Peacock.

It was later bought by Mrs. Gordon Mills who lived there for several years in the 1950s. Her nephew, Billy Melvin, continued living there after her death. It was sold to the Plains Historical Preservation Trust which used it as a meeting place until the Plains High School was restored. It was bought from the Trust by Sherrie Stokes.

—Picture submitted by Frank Williams, description by Allene T. Haugabook

C.L. Walters House

This home was built by George Jennings in the 1890s. From that point, several families claimed this house as home, including the Rees Mahone

Andrews, Sr. family. In the mid-1930s, the house was purchased by Claude Leonard Walters, Sr. and Bernice Harper Walters. The house was then sold to Claude Leonard Walters, Jr. and Beth Murray Walters. They, in turn, sold the house to the current owners, Claude Leonard Walters III and Sandra Harrell Walters. This home is located at 308 Church Street.

—*Submitted by Craig Walters*

The C.L. Walters House, 308 Church Street
Photo credit: Lawrence Smith

Mrs. William Edgar (Allie Murray) Smith House

Built by W.H. Crawford in 1900s, who with children, returned to Plains when his wife, Ida Hiller, died. Children: Blanche C. Watkins, Myrtle C. Wise, Charlie Crawford, Lucile C. Morris, Dixie C. Stallings, Sarah C. McGrit. Mr Crawford later married Fannie Wise. Later residents, Walter Kennedy family, Drue and Maude Jennings Murray, Robert and Bernard Ratliff and families. In late 1920s J.W. Murray bought and spent last years there with his daughter, Allie and Edgar Smith, whose children are Rosalynn S. Carter, Jerry and Aino Smith, Murray and Helen Smith and Allethea S. Wall.

—*Copied from Beth Walters' "History of Plains Georgia 1885-1985" pp. 106-107*

Allie Smith House located on east side of South Bond Street, home in which Rosalynn Smith Carter grew up. Photo credit: Annette Wise

Marvin Griggs House

Marvin Griggs House

210 S. Bond Street

John and Ella Jennings bought land in 1900 to build their house. Over the years owners have included: Jessie McGarrah, Annie G. Jones, A.B. Moore and Corrie Moore, Luma L. Smith and Mary D. Smith, James K. Sproull and Doris E. Sproull,

Jack Pugh, Jr., and Jean S. Pugh. In 1963 James Marvin Griggs,Sr. and Eunice Anderson Griggs bought it. Their children are Maxine, Marvin, Jr. and Gail.

—*Submitted by Eunice Griggs*

Home of Frank and Virginia Williams, northwest corner of Church and Thomas streets. Photo credit: Frank Williams

Frank Williams House

The home of Mr. and Mrs. G. Frank Williams on Church Street in Plains is one of the town's older homes. It was built by Rodolph Oliver about 1905. In 1939, the home was purchased by Oscar A. and Leila Earle Williams and later sold to George Frank and Virginia Harris Williams in 1976. The home is still the residence of Frank and Virginia Williams.

—*Submitted by Virginia Williams*

Howell-Bagwell House

This Georgian cottage on the corner of Thomas and Paschall streets is owned by Jimmy and Cindy Bagwell. The house was built by Jimmy's grand-parents, Mr. and Mrs. James Ira Howell, in 1908. Floy Howell Bagwell inherited the house and left it to her son, Jimmy, and his wife, Cindy. The timber was cut from the Howell farm in Sasser and brought to Plains by mule-drawn wagons. The architect who built the house was Rev. Augustus Wellons.

—*Submitted by Jimmy Bagwell*

The Howell House, on the corner of Thomas and Paschall streets. Photo credit: Jimmy Bagwell

The Alford House, 213 N. Bond St. Photo credit: Annette Wise

Alford House

This house was built built by Jesse Timmerman 1910. Mrs. Lou Wise ran a boarding house. The house was used as a home for nurses who trained at Wise Sanitarium with Mrs. Lillie Jennings as house mother. Other occupants have included Mr. & Mrs. Jesse Woodruff, Virgil and Sara Shierling

Chambliss, school principal Tubbs, Ronald and Marilyn Gray and Thomas Spring. The property was purchased by Elizabeth Corine "Rena" and Greg Alford from Mary Jo Sanborn Blackwood on October 29, 1993. The present owners are Rena and Greg Alford and their children Courtney, Jeremy and Bryan.

—*Submitted by Josephine Medlock*

Martha Tidd Harris House, 213 W. Church Street.
Photo credit: Martha T. Harris

Martha Tidd Harris House

This house was built by George Washington Montgomery in the 1910s, burned later and rebuilt by Mr. Montgomery. After Mrs. Montgomery (Irene Alston) died, the daughter, Grace Young, and family lived there with her father. Mr. and Mrs. Walter Leroy Young have three children, Roy II, Bill and Jane. Wade and Kathryn Cape Medlock lived there at one time, then Bill and Betty Raybon Medlock. Mrs. Young sold to John and Jerri Bailey, son Bill, in the 1940s, they in turn sold later to the Tidds. Their children are 1. James H. Rushin Tidd m. Mary O'Reiley; 2. Edgar Lee Tidd m. Ernestine Bailey; 3. William Earl Tidd m. Nancy Cleverdon; 4. Mrs. Tom (Myrtice Ann Tidd) Allgood.

—*Copied from Beth Walters' "History of Plains, Georgia 1885-1985" p. 125*

The Moncus House, 212 S. Bond Street
Photo credit: Annette Wise

Moncus House

This house, 212 S. Bond St., was built in 1910 by Mrs. Mattie Caughman. Laura and Hewlitt Carlton and children Jacob and Jency lived here after the death of Mrs. Caughman, the mother of Mrs. Carlton. William "Billy" Wise bought the property from the heirs of Mrs. Laura Carlton on February 1, 1963. The property was inherited by Keith Moncus on July 20, 1992. The present owners are Mary Evelyn and Keith Moncus and their children Michael, Lindsay and Will.

—*Submitted by Josephine Medlock*

Wellons House

Built in 1910 by Rev. A.C. Wellons on the northwest corner of Church and Hudson streets. Due to the fact that Rev. Wellons was the architect for many homes in Plains, and the fact that he has no living descendants here, his home has been included in this history. After his death, the daughter, Bessie Wellons Crozier, husband Arthur Hood Crozier and son Arthur Hood Crozier, Jr. lived here with Mrs. Wellons. It was here that Jimmy Carter's parents, Earl and Lillian, lived until just before the birth of their son, Jimmy. People who had apartments here were Mettauer and Ruby Timmerman Davidson, the W.L. Jones family, Gladys Murray and Ann Phagan Gay, before her marriage to Clarence Dodson. Mrs. Agnes Webb Dennard ran an antique house here for a short period of time. The Maggios lived here and later sold the house to Buck and Grace Jackson, who converted it into the Plains Bed and Breakfast. At the time of this writing in 2003, it is owned by Janet Nixon and is still a bed and breakfast.

—*Submitted by Allene T. Haugabook*

Joe Wise and daughters, Florence and Minnie, in front of home which he built, presently owned by Morgan Wise. Photo credit: Morgan Wise

Spann-Lowery House

154 Spann Drive
"Plains' Olympic Home"

The Spann-Lowery House, built in 1912, has long been considered one of the Plains community's most beautiful houses. During the past 90-plus years, several families have called it home. Its place in local lore was accentuated when it was seen worldwide on NBC on August 3, 1996, during the Summer Olympic Games in Atlanta, thus earning the distinct label as "Plains' Olympic Home."

Land on which the house was built was sold by R.S. Oliver, a prominent Plains businessman and a former councilman and mayor, to Thomas H. Lowery on Janurary 19, 1912. Lowery purchased 667½ acres of land in the 6th District of Sumter County, just outside the Plains city limits, from Oliver for $25,365. Oliver was the first president of Plains Bank.

The very late Victorian-style farmhouse includes neoclassical features that include a one-story porch with eight Tuscan columns. The porch originally wrapped around the house, but was divided into three separate porches in the early 1950s.

The A.C. Wellons House.
Photo credit: Lawrence Smith

Morgan Wise House

This home was built by Joseph Patrick Wise in 1911. His wife was Anna Josephine Derrick. The lumber for the house came from woods south of Plains and was milled by Will Everett. Two of Joe and Anna's daughters, Minnie and Florence, continued to live in the house until 1956. Morgan and Ann Wise purchased the house in 1957 and continue to live there.

—*Submitted by Lonnie Wise*

The house's cedar shake hipped roof has three connecting gables.

Spann-Lowery House, 154 Spann Drive
Photo credit: Steve Short

The attic, though never furnished or used as a room, features a high ceiling, striking shingles underneath and an impressive view overlooking the yard, which for many years included a picket fence. Fireplaces originally were built to provide heat for seven rooms, including the three bedrooms that were known as the Yellow Room, Green Room and Blue Room. A 440-square-foot parlor, now referred to as the living room, is the focus of the front-porch entry. Ceilings throughout the house are 12½ feet tall. Transoms for cross-ventilation purposes complement the wide doors throughout.

According to Dr. John Huff, an associate professor of art at the University of Georgia, the house "was very elegant for its day." It was built with enduring products and was typical of a "prosperous Georgia family," according to Huff. The house sits on brick piers, typical of its period. The underpinning added in the 1950s consists of rocks that most likely came off the farmland, Huff said.

A two-story barn, a commissary and at least four tenant houses were also part of the original farm. The initials of Lowery's son, Wade Hampton Lowery – WHL – and the date 1912 were engraved in concrete near the barn's foundation from that time until the early 1990s, when the grounds were cleared.

Wade Lowery, who was 10 at the time, later was married to Jeanette Carter, the aunt of former President Carter. She died in 1984 at age 80. Wade Lowery died in 1967.

Families other than the Thomas Lowerys who have lived in the house over the years include the Shorts, Chaverses, Davises, Fosters, and Hogseds.

In 1951, Frank Spann purchased the home and 200 acres of farmland from E.P. Jacobs of Floral City, Florida, the owner at the time. The deed states the land was "bounded on the South by public road and property of Mrs. Rosa Fussell and on the West by lands of Alton Carter; on the North by right-of-way of the Seaboard Air Line Railroad; and on the East by land sold to Charles C. Wise."

Frank and Ada Spann moved into the house on December 19, 1952, and occupied the house for nearly 40 years, longer than any other residents. Improvements were made, and meticulous care was taken to the yard, including the planting of hedges. Cedar, holly and china berry trees, crape myrtles, nandinas, petunias, water lilies, roses, azaleas, marigolds and ivy were staples over the years.

The Spanns celebrated their 50th, 55th and 60th wedding anniversaries at parties in the home. Birthdays, Christmases and Thanksgivings were notable family gatherings during their lifetimes. For several years in the 1970s and through 1980, "Miss" Lillian Carter observed Thanksgiving dinner there with her daughter and son-in-law, Gloria and Walter Spann.

Today, the Spanns' grandson and granddaughter-in-law, Jackie and Pharis Short, reside in the house. In recent years, the Shorts have repainted ans re-roofed the house, in addition to adding banisters to the porch. Renovations also have been made on the inside.

Extensive landscaping has enhanced the grounds, all adding to its unique country charm.

—*Submitted by Steve Short*

The Chapman House, on northeast corner of Paschall and Walters streets. Photo credit: Evelyn McDonald

Chapman House

First remembered to live here was Mrs. Fannie Jennings, an aunt of Mrs. Betty Jennings Carter. When she died, her niece, who had lived with her, retained the home. Mr. and Mrs. Carlton (Pharis) Walton and children, Renee, Michele and Tara, lived there in the 1970s, then selling to the Chapmans, who have a young son, Ronny.

—*Copied from Beth Walters' "History of Plains, Georgia 1885-1985" p. 132*

Ralph McDonald House

This house is just off South Bond Street. First known to live in it was Mrs. Sam (Lillie) Jennings. Mr. Toms lived in it. J.W. Sewell owned it and sold to McDonald in 1959. He had come from Florida to teach school. McDonald had moved to Plains with his family. He has a been councilman for several years, is present mayor. He married Evelyn Jacobs, and thier children are Angela Althea, Gail Evelyn and Dale Ralph, who are twins.

—*Copied from Beth Walters' "History of Plains, Georgia 1885-1985", p. 106*

Ralph McDonald House. Photo credit: Lawrence Smith. Picture submitted by Evelyn McDonald

Mrs. Ralph McDonald submitted the following write-up on the Bloxham Kearse House at 308 S. Bond St. The house was built in 1960s by Kearse, who lived there many years. Now owned by Mrs. Ralph McDonald. *No picture summitted.*

*Y.T. Sheffield House
Photo credit: Charlene Sheffield Mallard*

Y.T. Sheffield House

Built by Philip Johnson Wise (grandfather of P.J. Wise); sold to Mrs. Fannie Susanne Wise Hiller, who moved from the May Shirley Wise House. Y.T. bought the house from wife's aunt, Fannie. The Sheffield children are Charlene, wife of a Baptist minister, Rev. James Mallard, and Tommy Sheffield, Jr.

—*Copied from Beth Walters' "History of Plains Georgia 1885-1985" p. 110*

Annie Mae Watson Vaughn and Clayton "Kit" Watson. Section foreman house at Archery where the Watson family lived. Photo credit: Ruby Watson and Annie Mae Vaughn

Watson House

About five miles east of Plains, along the railroad track, at what was known as New Point, was a group of houses provided for families of section foremen who worked for the Seaboard Airline Railroad. To the west of Plains in the community of Archery was another group of houses for the same purpose. Mr. Watson was the head foreman. The Watson family was one of the few white families living as neighbors of the Carter family at Archery. Members of the Watson family were: Mr. and Mrs. Watson and their two daughters, Annie Mae and Ruby, and their sons, Clayton,

called "Kit," and Bernice, called "Wat." The Watson boys were two of the best basketball players to ever attend Plains High School.

—*Submitted by Allene T. Haugabook with approval of Ruby Watson and Annie Mae Vaughn*

The Timmerman-Haugabook House, 215 Walters St. Photo credit: Lawrence Smith

Timmerman-Haugabook House

Frank and Ida Lee Timmerman had this house built in 1923 by Mr. Leonard Jennings. The architect was Dennis and Dennis of Macon, Georgia. It was the first brick house in Plains. After Frank's death in 1939, Ida Lee continued to live here until her death in 1986. The following year their daughter, Allene and husband, C.G Haugabook, Jr., restored the house and retired to Plains.

—*Submitted by Allene T. Haugabook*

Carter House

Built in 1961, this has been the home of Jimmy and Rosalynn Carter. Designed by Albany architect, Hugh Gaston, the house was altered several times. The modest 4 bedroom, 2 ½ bath house has hosted some of the most famous political figures in the world. A complete wood working shop and tennis court reflects the Carter's leisure interests. The wooded landscape that surrounds the home gives the home a cool feel in an otherwise hot environment. Across Woodland Drive is the Pond Lot. Its primary feature is a small pond. In 1994 the Carter's donated the home and associated lands to the National Park Service. The Carter's retain a life estate agreement on the property. This was done in much the same fashion as was done with the Truman, Eisenhower and Johnson families.

—Submitted by Fred Boyles

Home of Jimmy and Rosalynn Carter on Woodland Dr. Photo credit: Fred Sanchez

Chapter 24: Cemeteries

Sites Where our Loved Ones Rest

From North or from South, from East or from West,
We know not from where he shall come,
The Old Grim Reaper, better known as death,
Eventually shall call on everyone.

It may be a babe in swaddling clothes
or a girl in the prime of her life.
It may be a man who has never known fear
It could be a soldier's wife.

He has visited this area we hold so dear,
The town of Plains is the center of it all,
So we honor these heroes who paved our way,
With kind words and their names to recall.

Take a look back at things in the past,
There was nothing a neighbor wouldn't do,
They took food to the family, with tears in their eyes,
The deceased would be missed they all knew.

When church services were over, the procession began
With headlights glaring in the sun,
Other cars would pull over, and their drivers salute
They knew a family had lost a loved one.

The Cemeteries get bigger as time moves on,
Where we honor these loved ones so dear,
Several places are reserved for their resting place,
So there is nothing for a person to fear.

The first one we recall is named the Devils Half Acre,
Located one mile north of our town
It was established in the early eighteen hundreds,
Not many records of these souls are around.

St. Mark's was founded beside a Lutheran Church
Four miles as the crow flies southwest,
About one mile North of Kincheefoonee Creek,
Where many a good soul's laid to rest.

Another St. Mark is located out at Archery,
Where a train whistle blows every day.
These souls lying here are still held very dear
For they worked hard to help pave our way.

Last but not least where all face the east,
Is two Lebanons sitting side by side,
One for the colored and one for the white,
Where all now take there last ride.

There is one thing we know for those interred below,
All the true things our dear Lord has said,
Christ died for our sins, so there is never an end,
That's why he so willingly bled.

Some of the founders of our Plains of Dura,
As our small town was really once named,
Are resting in peace, North of Magnolia Springs
Some of our residents are kin to these same.

There is just one more, we dare not look over,
Bottsford is four miles Southwest of our town
Their names I'll not mention, but bring to your attention
They were present, when our streets were laid down.
—By Millard Simmons

Devil's Half Acre

Surveyed by Jack F. Cox March 1, 2001

Devil's Half Acre is located on Jack Slappey Road near intersection of Highway 45 about one half mile from Plains, Ga. Mazie Harvey refers to this as Cook's Half Acre and Jimmy Bagwell of Plains states that this was the Universalist Cemetery and called "Devil's Half Acre" by town people who were opposed to the Universalists. This cemetery is much overgrown with ivy and covered with fallen trees and briars. I went into this cemetary on March 1, 2001 and found parts of marble copings of the type that surrounded cemetery plots but could find no graves even though many years ago I did see several slabs with names engraved. Mrs. Larry Hancock told me that Hancock Funeral Home had moved two graves from this cemetery about 18 or 20 years ago.

The information below is from Mazie Harvey's "Sumter County, Georgia Cemetery Records."

KING, A. R.
(Not successful in getting to grave.)
PICKETT, Emma H. 05/13/1852   08/15/1923
(Wife of A. R. King)
COOK, Emmett
(Impossible to get to grave.)
STEWART, Rev. Tom.

Mrs. Larry Hancock found a video tape on March 15, 2002 that was made when the graves were moved. The video, narrated at the time of the removal, was by Larry Hancock as the graves were being disinterred and later being re-interred in Preston, Ga. City Cemetery stated that the two graves being moved were John Rufus King and Emma Pickett King and that Frank King, whose father, John Amos King, Sr., was having this done. Larry stated in the narration that a Louise Harvey, who died in 1903, was also buried in Devil's Half Acre.

On March 17, 2002, I went to Preston City Cemetery and found the following: A large marble marker, the original, by the looks of it. On one side was John Rufus King February 6, 1834 - May 3, 1905. On the other side was Emma H. Pickett Wife of J. R. King May 13, 1852 - August 15, 1923. Covering each of the graves was a marble slab, original by the looks, and on one was: JRK and on the other: EHK.

Lebanon Cemetery (Section One)

Surveyed by Jack F. Cox October 31, 2001

Section One is located on the right side of the road going to the Carter Boyhood Home.

NAME	BIRTH	DEATH
(???? = Could not read tombstone)		
ADAMS, William (Age 85)	????	08/08/1920
ADDY, Mrs. Mary	00/00/1874	00/00/1963
ANGRY, Cleveland	09/??/1889	12/12/1963
ANGRY, Eliza M.0	02/3/1893	01/02/1983
ANSLEY, Louise J.	01/01/1929	10/28/1992
BAKER, Lynn	10/24/1924	08/13/2000
BANKS, Della Glass	????	02/14/1962
BATTLE, Annie Lou	07/27/1878	01/08/1975
BATTLE, James	05/23/1938	03/04/1969
BATTLE, Noon	12/25/1900	12/07/1975
BELL, Alan	????	09/25/1961
BELL, Anna	????	12/31/1946
BELL, Mr. Odie B.	10/11/1911	11/15/1979
BERRY, Amanda	????	05/19/1961
BERRY, Annie Laura	00/00/1908	00/00/1954
BERRY, Bertha	????	02/09/1951
BERRY, Cooper	10/12/1910	05/27/1981
BERRY, Cooper	10/12/1910	05/27/1981
BERRY, Ed	04/15/1892	04/22/1976
BERRY, Emory	04/15/1887	04/14/1974

BERRY, John Ed	????	03/11/1957
BERRY, Laura	07/15/1915	05/17/1988
BERRY, Mary Alice	????	06/29/1965
BERRY, Olie	00/00/1865	00/00/1945
BERRY, Preston	00/00/1856	00/00/1944
BIGGINS, Angeline	00/00/1852	00/00/1942
BIGGINS, Clark	05/15/1890	06/5/1973
BIGGINS, Mary Lizzie	03/31/1894	04/11/1985
BIGGINS, Sr., Clark	01/15/1852	04/09/1894
BILLUPS, Eliza	????	05/27/1962
BISHOP, David	00/00/1888	00/00/1954
BISHOP, Mamie L.	????	05/13/1965
BISHOP, Melvin	05/31/1903	03/30/1969
BRIDGES, Charlie	????	05/10/1954
BRIDGES, Ealie	????	02/21/1958
BRIDGES, Emmett	????	01/27/1953
BRIDGES, JR., Emmett	10/12/1927	02/11/1981
BRIDGES, SR., Willie A.	04/06/1914	10/16/1993
BRIDGES, Tommy Lee	01/22/1955	12/11/1996
BRONER, March	03/15/1902	11/02/1985
BRONER, Will	00/00/1900	10/22/1975
BROWN, Amos	????	04/13/1954
BROWN, Eddie D.	04/02/1908	07/12/1990
BROWN, Lewis	05/04/1903	02/11/1995
BROWN, Magnolia Givins	????	02/28/1982
BROWN, Marguerite	09/19/1911	06/05/1993
BROWN, Mis Onnie	05/12/1908	02/08/1974
BROWN, Mollie	????	04/20/1964
BROWN, Will	????	02/04/1959
BRYANT, Bessie L.	05/11/1896	06/02/1998
BRYANT, Jessie B.	02/12/1934	10/15/1999
BRYANT, Johnnie	09/15/1928	11/01/1995
BRYANT, JR., Burland	03/30/1920	09/17/2001
BRYANT, Otis	????	09/19/1950
BRYANT, SR., Burlond	11/7/1895	11/02/1968
BURKE, Polly	????	06/15/1905
BURKS, Riley	10/10/1915	10/11/1998
BURTON, Rosa Mae	07/29/1944	08/26/1985
BUSH, Charlotte	????	01/16/1921
BUSH, Ira Mae	No date	No date
BUSH, Leila	00/00/1889	00/00/1945
BYRD, Willie Curts	05/22/1939	04/24/1974
CALLAHON, Mary	05/20/1909	11/11/1963
CARTER, Harper	????	????
CARTER, Mamie	00/00/1893	00/00/1952
CARTER, Sally M.	02/04/1917	08/30/1989
CHAMBLISS, Brenda J.	10/22/1955	04/04/1992
CHAMPION, Sarah Ann	01/03/1846	09/15/1988
CHEATHAM, Minnie B.	08/10/1894	02/25/1981
COLWELL, Alfred (Age 15 mos.)	????	12/20/1950
COLWELL, Alphonzo	01/14/1972	03/11/1990
COLWELL, Alphonzo	03/28/1956	01/24/1981
COLWELL, Annie	????	10/17/1968
COLWELL, Bowman	01/28/1948	08/4/1959
COLWELL, Michael K.	05/30/1965	02/05/1967
CORLEY, B. H.	????	09/26/1947
CORLEY, Drucilla	????	11/25/1969
COTTLE, Willie M.	????	08/17/1957
COWELL, Avis Shantiell	10/25/1975	12/13/1975
CRITTINDEN, Mary	????	12/03/1961
CUTTS, Daniel	07/21/1885	12/31/1887
CUTTS, Mary	10/26/1878	11/15/1883
DANIEL, ????	????	05/29/1924
DANIEL, Bessie M.	06/23/1942	06/25/1998
DANIEL, Betsy	No date	Nodate
DANIEL, Ida Smith	06/01/1870	07/09/1884
DANIEL, Levi (Age 64)	????	12/29/1911
DANIEL, Mary Lee	????	05/29/1930
DANIEL, Sam	12/01/1843	05/30/1901
DAVIES, Benjamin Carl	12/30/1941	06/17/1994
DAVIS, Alvin	09/23/1926	01/08/1985
DAVIS, SR., James A.	04/29/1954	03/05/1985
DIXON, Mary L. Mike	????	03/09/1954
DYOUS, Jim	09/01/1887	12/17/1967
EDGE, Charlie	00/00/1921	00/00/1943
EDGE, Lawsie	01/14/1930	11/14/1995
EDGE, Maggie R.	07/09/1909	11/10/1986
EDGE, Rose Lee	????	10/23/1969
EDGE, SR., Dea. Judson	02/16/1932	01/07/1998
EDGE, SR., John C.	08/20/1909	05/27/1984
EDMONDS, Sallie B.	10/15/1911	01/06/1997
EDMONDS, SR., William	12/24/1908	03/15/1990
EDWARDS, Eddie J.	07/19/1959	11/04/1973
EDWARDS, Eddie L.	10/02/1921	02/17/1980
ENGLISH, Bessie Mae	01/04/1927	01/11/1988
EVANS, Angie S.	08/26/1910	06/13/1993
FLOYD, Annie B.	????	04/01/1971
FLOYD, Clayton	00/00/1912	00/00/1985

FLOYD, Essie	00/00/1881	00/00/1949
FLOYD, Eugene	????	10/06/1952
FLOYD, James H.	00/00/1921	00/00/1943
FLOYD, M. J.	00/00/1850	00/00/1922
FLOYD, Peter	????	12/06/1958
FLOYD, Will	????	10/08/1955
FLOYD, William	????	10/27/1946
FLOYD, Virginia	????	01/01/1922
FRANKLIN, S. D.	01/21/1924	08/26/1969
FRANKLIN, SR., Floyd	10/15/1906	12/06/1971
FUDGE, Floyd	????	06/14/1977
GALLOWAY, Willie Belle	03/13/1936	05/19/2001
GARDNER, James	04/01/1919	01/13/2000
GARDNER, Vera Mae	04/17/1923	05/25/1997
GIBSON, Annie Lucy	08/02/1906	04/18/1983
GIBSON, Donald T.	09/08/1976	08/08/1992
GIBSON, Frank	03/12/1946	08/09/1985
GIBSON, O'Neal	02/16/1945	07/18/1980
GIBSON, Walter	05/30/1910	06/05/1990
GILFORD, Autry	06/15/1925	08/13/1981
GILFORD, Henry	02/04/1924	02/17/1991
GIVINS, Berther L.	12/25/1919	07/30/1970
GLOVER, Aaron	08/30/1919	09/18/1981
GLOVER, Herbert	01/18/1946	11/10/1978
GLOVER, Viola W.	07/03/1918	08/27/1986
GORDON, Roy Lee	06/10/1945	02/14/1964
GRAHAM, James L.	00/00/1918	00/00/1935
GRAHAM, John B.	08/31/1872	07/2/1950
GRAHAM, Lottie B.	10/15/1881	01/10/1959
GREEN, Catherine Ross	09/23/1908	11/03/1960
GREEN, Eliza	????	07/13/1957
GREEN, Henry	11/12/1900	12/25/1960
GREEN, Wesley	00/00/1858	04/31/1904
GREENE, Emmet	00/00/1877	00/00/1946
GRIFFIN, Ed	02/22/1894	03/22/1968
HALL, Ethel	00/00/1906	00/00/1961
HALL, L. C.	????	06/31/1968
HALL, Mackie D.	????	10/31/1972
HALL, Mary	????	06/12/1953
HARRIS, Drucilla	00/00/1848	00/00/1935
HART, Anita N.	09/22/1983	09/28/1994
HARVER, Rev. W. H.	????	00/00/1940
HARVEY, Agnes	02/13/1930	02/22/1996
HARVEY, Alex	05/05/1843	12/04/1911
HARVEY, Alice R.	10/02/1906	06/04/1967
HARVEY, Christine	????	12/08/1958
HARVEY, Ed	04/01/1929	04/12/1991
HARVEY, Emma L.	10/12/1912	05/23/1993
HARVEY, Joseph D.	10/11/1925	01/25/1979
HARVEY, Lonnie	07/04/1916	02/16/1976
HARVEY, Mary R.	05/20/1892	06/27/1979
HARVEY, Otic C.	02/02/1925	04/07/1997
HARVEY, William	08/26/1939	02/02/2000
HAWK, Mannie B.	03/01/1920	03/27/1978
HAWK, Vet. Luther A.	04/15/1920	03/21/1991
HENDERSON, Curry	10/05/1898	12/16/1983
HENDERSON, Jesse	00/00/1923	00/00/1988
HENDERSON, Laura	????	11/12/1947
HENDERSON, Roberta	09/01/1898	06/12/1973
HICKS, Beverly	09/26/1961	09/01/1964
HICKS, Emma L.	12/07/1902	05/23/1964
HICKS, Majorie	03/02/1929	02/21/1996
HICKS, Mrs. Mozelia	12/24/1900	04/14/1952
HIGHTOWER, George W.	00/00/1873	00/00/1951
HIGHTOWER, Martha	00/00/1877	00/00/1950
HIGHTOWER, Mimmie	00/00/1850	00/00/1928
HIGHTOWER, Remus	00/00/1898	08/09/1941
HILL, Arthur	????	11/11/1950
HILL, Roy	????	02/13/1956
HILL, Victoria	????	06/09/1955
HOLLIS, Benjamin	01/06/1926	01/01/1982
HOLLIS, George E.	12/16/1926	10/06/1981
HOLLIS, Hannah	????	06/08/1953
HOLLIS, Lillie	????	07/13/1955
HOLLIS, Lois D.	02/14/1956	05/13/2000
HOLLIS, Reatha M.	03/21/1935	02/12/1993
HOLLIS, Willie James	07/06/1922	11/15/1991
HOLSEY, Beatrice	????	04/26/1956
HOOKS, Annie	????	10/20/1955
HUBBARD, Silas	11/25/1915	09/08/1985
HUDSON, Eli (Age 70)	????	12/16/????
JACKSON, Alberta	????	12/30/1976
JACKSON, Clarence	08/28/1802	03/15/1878
JACKSON, Dea. Arzell	11/25/1920	06/22/1993
JACKSON, Este	10/29/1939	10/30/1997
JACKSON, Estella	????	08/07/1956
JACKSON, Irma S.	10/14/1951	08/05/1992
JACKSON, Lenward	04/19/1914	02/05/1986

JACKSON, Marzell	05/07/1951	02/15/1987
JACKSON, Rosa Lee	08/02/1928	03/22/1991
JACKSON, Sis. Annie R.	01/28/1922	06/08/1997
JACKSON, Sr., Joe	04/14/1925	12/01/2000
JACKSON, Willie Frank "Bud"	07/27/1946	05/01/1993
JAMES, Thelma M.	05/21/1955	11/04/1993
JENKINS, Alferd	07/09/1887	12/18/1958
JENKINS, Angeline	00/00/1870	00/00/1952
JENKINS, Isaac	05/06/1851	05/10/1916
JENKINS, Jessie	????	12/04/1967
JENKINS, Lucy	????	04/25/1964
JOHNSON, C. J.	00/00/1851	12/22/1906
JOHNSON, Cleaveland	????	10/30/1957
JOHNSON, Daisy	01/01/1899	08/09/1974
JOHNSON, Don	03/25/1889	06/26/1964
JOHNSON, Jay	01/??/1896	02/06/1986
JOHNSON, Mammie	????	01/09/1946
JOHNSON, Mrs. Lillie B.	????	10/3/1966
JOHNSON, Peter	00/00/1852	02/06/1890
JOHNSON, Rachel M.	12/13/1930	01/30/1980
JOHNSON, Robert	04/15/1918	04/25/1950
JOHNSON, Sampson	????	00/00/1889
JOHNSON, Samuel H.	00/00/1922	00/00/1922
JOHNSON, Stella Hollis	No dates	No dates
JONES, Cee Bell	02/16/1916	10/09/1985
JONES, Charlie	09/27/1910	04/02/1973
JONES, E. K.	????	06/06/1957
JONES, Merica	????	03/28/1907
JONES, Sarah	????	10/11/1967
JONES, Tom	????	05/23/1957
JORDAN, Dea. Joe	05/20/1917	06/02/1999
JORDAN, Rosa L.	07/16/1914	02/23/1995
JORDAN, Willie Frank	????	01/08/1961
JOWERS, Lillian	????	08/10/1960
KING, (Stillborn baby)	????	04/15/1965
KING, Betty J.	01/05/1950	11/09/1990
KING, David Lee	????	08/28/1967
KING, Richard Morgan	08/10/1922	05/24/1987
KING, Ruby	????	06/29/1957
KING, SR., James	02/02/1943	01/02/1998
KITCHEN, Emma	No date	No date
KITCHEN, George	No date	No date
KITCHEN, JR., George	02/17/1936	12/10/1976
KITCHEN, Thaid	01/06/1936	03/16/1980
KITCHEN, Willie Clyde	12/26/1937	09/21/1989
KITCHEN, Willie Pearl	01/20/1914	07/10/1977
KITCHENS, George	00/00/1875	00/00/1948
KITCHENS, George	03/25/1946	03/26/1997
KITCHENS, Mamie	10/08/1882	02/21/1964
LAMPKIN, JR., Ben	12/15/1925	04/11/1982
LASTER, Alzora	12/10/1871	12/27/1974
LASTER, Emmit	????	12/18/1858
LASTER, Joe	00/00/1883	00/00/1945
LASTER, John M.	09/26/1917	07/25/1989
LASTER, Robert	03/04/1918	06/18/1960
LAUSON, Mrs. Lula	????	08/11/1968
LAWSON, Eddie	06/02/1906	12/01/1977
LESTER, Flora	????	03/26/1970
LEWIS, Annie B.	05/04/1930	12/10/1992
LEWIS, Birda Lee	????	01/30/1962
LEWIS, Darryl	04/14/1962	12/27/1999
LEWIS, Hessie B.	08/18/1916	11/19/1985
LEWIS, SR., James	08/15/1918	11/19/1970
LITTLE, Annie Bell	????	03/26/1960
LUNDY, Frank	03/28/1930	09/24/1944
LUNDY, Ida	????	06/06/1955
MACKEY, Alfred	07/09/1894	02/25/1935
MAHONE, Della Edmond	01/12/1903	11/15/1985
MAHONE, Fletcher	????	10/01/1962
MAHONE, Janie	????	02/11/1937
MAHONE, Jimmie Lee	09/30/1933	07/10/1975
MAHONE, Luellen	12/12/1900	02/20/1988
MAHONE, Sidney	????	05/15/1951
MANSFIELD, Ethel	04/22/1898	05/01/1996
MANSFIELD, Henry	07/28/1922	06/25/1997
MANSFIELD, Mattie	02/14/1885	12/29/1905
MATHIS, Eddie	06/15/1893	04/21/1966
MATHIS, Eddie Clint	????	09/01/1955
MATHIS, Ruby Lee	????	04/26/1926
MATHIS, Tillie Floyd	05/22/1908	09/08/1988
MAY, Gearfield	????	09/30/1967
MAY, (Infant)	????	10/23/1953
MAY, John Jacob	????	06/03/1953
MAY, Johnny M.	11/26/1962	09/11/1995
MAY, Lucile	????	11/20/1971
MAY, Moses	00/00/1901	06/06/1948
MAY, Mrs. Alice M.	10/03/1873	01/30/1968
MAY, Vet. Charlie Moses	05/05/1913	08/05/1987

MAY, W. D.	00/00/1884	00/00/1940
McCOY, A. J.	11/09/1994	11/09/1994
McCOY, Lee	????	11/18/1949
McGARRAH, Eva Mae	04/30/1914	06/16/1982
McGARRAH, Reliford	????	12/17/1959
McGRADY, Dea. Leo	12/15/1890	03/26/1988
McGRADY, Joe	00/00/1927	00/00/1943
McGRADY, Onie	????	01/22/1961
McGRADY, Rachel	????	06/05/1955
McGRADY, Wesley	????	06/11/1896
McMURRAIN, Lonnie M.	07/07/1918	04/12/1991
MERRITT, Bobby	08/06/1938	12/02/1971
MILLER, Annie	????	09/30/1947
MILLER, Blance Angry	08/24/1920	01/15/1983
MILLER, Rufus	No date	No date
MINION, Mary W. Wright	????	11/01/??62
MINTER, Beatrice K.	05/29/1906	09/07/1997
MINTER, Carbin	00/00/1893	00/00/1980
MINYARD, Bettie	????	05/26/1947
MOCK, George	????	00/00/1936
MOGAN, Walter	12/18/1945	02/15/1964
MOORE, Alfred	04/30/1953	01/07/1979
MOORE, Rachel B.	04/08/1888	08/18/1988
MOORE, Rev. E. J.	00/00/1884	07/28/1953
MOORE, SR., James	05/11/1921	04/03/1980
MORGAN, Ella (Age 44)	????	04/20/1907
MORGAN, Fleeola	03/18/1933	08/09/1999
MORGAN, Ruth F.	04/15/1901	03/07/1980
MURPHY, Christeen	01/30/1966	09/01/1989
MURPHY, Shawnda	12/23/1984	09/01/1889
MURRAY, Carie	????	11/19/1960
NAPIER, Joseph	????	06/11/1950
NEWSOME, Jennye H.	03/04/1925	01/08/1991
NORWOOD, Ruby H.	03/28/1929	03/26/1990
OATES, Andre Carlus	02/09/1969	06/16/1981
OATES, Ann Hicks	12/03/1927	05/11/1981
PERRY, Ruthie D.	02/13/1919	03/19/1993
PERRY, Walter J.	08/31/1964	05/20/1989
PHILLIPS, Willie B.	03/15/1914	12/26/1983
PICKETT, Buster	07/23/1954	06/04/1979
POLK, Annie L.	12/05/1899	11/22/1936
POLK, Willie Lee	11/10/1935	04/29/1978
PORTER, Archie B.	07/15/1924	12/16/1978
PORTER, Mattie M.	05/12/1912	03/24/2001
PORTER, Susie	05/??/1888	08/23/1984
PRINCE, (Baby)	No date	Nodate
PRINCE, Mattie	05/08/1877	07/01/1960
PRINCE, Stokes H.	04/04/1874	02/20/1961
PRYOR, Eddie	03/05/1902	02/26/1981
RAVEN, Eddie Lee	????	07/04/1952
REID, Denia	12/14/1890	10/28/1891
RIGGINS, Carrie	05/03/1908	10/23/1972
RIGGINS, Sim	06/10/1899	08/12/1961
ROBERTS, Hatte L.	????	06/13/1966
ROBERTS, Joe B.	01/27/1936	08/13/1990
ROBERTS, SR., Ernest	11/04/1940	06/27/1980
ROGERS, Este	10/15/1945	01/04/1995
ROGERS, Lula Mae	12/25/1919	11/25/1982
ROGERS, Reather	03/07/1907	04/05/1975
ROGERS, Willie Lee	08/23/1938	02/10/1985
ROSS, Anthony	????	07/24/1966
ROSS, Essie Mae	06/13/1913	03/31/1989
ROSS, John	06/17/1883	01/13/1976
ROSS, John W.	01/14/1884	03/15/1931
ROSS, Laura Berry	????	05/24/1949
ROSS, Silvia	????	07/08/1900
RUTHERFORD, Josie	????	09/03/1940
RUTHERFORD, Willis	????	09/15/1954
SALES, Madeline S.	03/05/1910	12/28/1996
SCHLEY, Betty	No date	No date
SCHLEY, Booker Biggins	07/15/1908	01/22/1984
SCHLEY, Chester	02/03/1948	01/28/1978
SCHLEY, Clifford	05/13/1896	05/07/1966
SCHLEY, Dora	No Date	Nodate
SCHLEY, Emma	????	09/1933
SCHLEY, Frances L.	12/18/1942	12/24/1962
SCHLEY, Francis Leanor	????	12/24/1962
SCHLEY, James W.	05/13/1904	01/07/1971
SCHLEY, Lessie W.	02/25/1906	12/12/1998
SCHLEY, Levonia	00/00/1875	00/00/1944
SCHLEY, Minnie M.	07/30/1910	03/08/1987
SCHLEY, Mrs. Lucy	10/??/1894	05/16/1926
SCHLEY, Paul	????	12/28/1945
SCHLEY, Rev. B. D.	00/00/1874	00/00/1946
SCHLEY, Saul	????	12/28/1945
SCHLEY, Seaborn	00/00/1874	00/00/1946
SCHLEY, Wiley	00/00/1874	00/00/1946
SHANNON, Myrtice	02/1801907	06/15/1969

SHEPPARD, Georgia Lee	12/01/1918	11/01/1974
SIMMONS, Azzie Lee	01/01/1921	11/06/1975
SIMS, Ethel Lee	05/25/1913	07/24/1985
SIMS, George L.	03/01/1928	09/29/1974
SIMS, Geraldine T.	03/24/1949	05/28/1998
SIMS, Robert L.	04/05/1935	09/02/1974
SIMS, Willie L.	03/03/1900	02/21/1974
SLAPPY, Florie Lee	????	06/13/1960
SNIPES, Lucy	????03/	09/1956
STATEM, Johnnie	09/02/1918	08/24/1970
STATHAM, Florence	No date	No date
STATHAM, Henry	????	05/21/1951
STATHAM, Lonnie B.	????	04/13/1957
STATHAM, Mumford	No date	No date
STATHAM, Rosie	06/??/1900	03/??/1901
STATHAM, Sallie	????	04/02/1900
STATHAM, Tellis	00/00/1898	00/00/1958
STREETER, Antoinette	08/06/1975	03/08/1976
STREETER, Johnnie M.	12/10/1928	04/12/2001
STREETER, Zachary T.	03/06/1979	07/31/1998
STYLES, Arthur J.	10/05/1961	06/28/1976
SWINNEY, Leroy	09/09/1909	05/26/1985
SWINNEY, Willie	00/00/1880	00/00/1943
TATUM, Alex	????	08/09/1958
TATUM, Alveta	????	08/07/1957
TATUM, Dan (Age 60)	????	05/20/1902
TATUM, James	05/17/1925	02/22/1991
TATUM, Jennie	00/00/1880	00/00/1947
TATUM, Mary	04/10/1858	11/28/1906
TATUM, Verlie Ann	12/12/1891	03/15/1985
TAYLOR, Eula	06/01/1921	10/22/1984
TAYLOR, JR., Olay	07/27/1940	07/28/1988
TENNIE, Verlie	07/10/1914	07/26/1985
THOMAS, Eddress	09/01/1904	11/14/1993
THOMAS, Matie	????	02/25/1951
THOMIE, Lillie B.	02/19/1886	03/17/1987
THOMIE, O. C.	00/00/1886	00/00/1937
TONDEE, C. H.	04/??/1894	????
TONDEE, Laster	03/13/1873	01/04/1905
TONDEE, Odies	09/12/1867	09/30/1894
TONDEE, P. B.	08/17/1898	01/05/1899
TYSON, Bernice C.	11/10/1950	10/06/1998
TYSON, Larry Dean	08/13/1959	08/16/1978
TYSON, Rosa M.	02/13/1938	03/07/1998
TYSON, Sr. Robert L.	11/08/1914	07/06/1988
WAKEFIELD, Alphonso	10/18/1903	11/19/1987
WAKEFIELD, Mary P.	05/28/1934	03/29/1993
WARREN, Daisy	10/06/1890	01/11/1971
WARREN, Louise	10/26/1895	10/03/1984
WARREN, Sidney M.	????	08/26/1963
WATSON, Gladys Bryant	????	06/02/1960
WHITE, Clifford	10/30/1899	07/01/1948
WHITE, Katie	00/00/1886	00/00/1937
WILLIAMS, Sammie T.	10/11/1927	04/25/1991
WILLIAMS, Susie Wright	06/19/1900	05/27/1987
WILSON, Governor	09/09/1909	11/06/1999
WILSON, Hattie S.	01/18/1912	03/15/1997
WILSON, James	05/06/1930	05/07/1930
WILSON, Lawrence	12/07/1908	06/29/1976
WILSON, Lillie M.	02/19/1930	07/15/1997
WILSON, Ola B.	10/16/1920	08/14/1986
WILSON, Sr., Bobby L.	02/12/1965	07/29/1992
WILSON, Willie	12/03/1907	09/10/1985
WILSON, JR., Governor	07/09/1948	08/18/1989
WOODS, James H.	????	05/07/1943
WOODS, Bettie	03/08/1863	06/22/1901
WOODS, Dennis	10/08/1892	08/25/1944
WOODS, Dock	????	11/17/1962
WOODS, Mamie Louise	????	04/29/1966
WOODS, Ramson	????	12/03/1918
WRIGHT, Amos	05/20/1930	09/07/1954
WRIGHT, Charlie	????	04/01/1954
WRIGHT, James B.	06/18/1931	12/29/1997
WRIGHT, Katie C.	????	06/27/1962
WRIGHT, Mahala Addie	06/13/1886	06/06/1964
WRIGHT, Mrs. Safronia	????	06/20/1969
WRIGHT, Olivia	????	00/00/1942
WRIGHT, Oscar	08/??/1923	02/23/1973
WRIGHT, Rosa Lee	03/11/1901	04/23/1972
WRIGHT, SR., Leonard	12/06/1926	04/18/1983
WRIGHT, Wesley	11/04/1898	05/21/1979
WRIGHT, Willis	03/26/1902	03/27/1980

Lebanon Cemetery (Section Two)

Surveyed by Jack F. Cox October 29, 2001

Section Two is located on both sides of the road going to the Carter Boyhood Home.

NAME	BIRTH	DEATH
(???? = Could not read tombstone)		
ADDY, Joey	11/12/1862	03/16/1893
ALLEN, Freeman Walker	01/18/1808	01/19/1879
ANDERSON, Allie A.	01/11/1891	02/10/1977
ANDERSON, Dorothy Whiteley	08/29/1926	No date
ANDERSON, Elizabeth	02/10/1866	11/13/1949
ANDERSON, Elliott F.	11/14/1921	02/12/1972
ANDERSON, Garland D.	09/12/1886	06/02/1968
ANDERSON, T. G.	06/18/1855	12/19/1898
ANDERSON, Thomas Durell	01/08/1924	01/16/2000
ANDREWS, Maybelle Timmerman	11/08/1887	11/14/1980
ANDREWS, Rees Mahone	10/11/1879	08/25/1958
BACON, Edmund David	09/15/1882	02/28/1915
BACON, Eugene F.	04/01/1934	10/16/1992
BACON, Jennie Lind	04/22/1890	01/08/1941
BACON, Joseph Abner	01/9/1899	02/02/1983
BACON, Joseph Edmund	10/29/1856	10/29/1939
BACON, Leila K. Wells	05/01/1861	02/08/1940
BACON, Martha Elizabeth Pennington	05/03/1899	09/09/1977
BAGWELL, Floy Howell	12/18/1901	02/7/1986
BAGWELL, Henry Taylor	07/??/1943	
BALDWIN, Claude S.	02/05/1912	11/28/1970
BALDWIN, JR., Claude S.	02/11/1938	04/7/1970
BARKER, ?		
BARKER, ?		
BARKER, Mary		
BARTLEY, Henry T.	09/30/1861	12/10/1937
BARTLEY, John P.	12/14/1905	10/17/1925
BARTLEY, Myra M.	07/30/1851	07/22/1931
BARTLEY, Sallie M.	01/28/1870	03/31/1957
BARTLEY, Susan	12/20/1829	12/28/1903
BARTLEY, Thomas	02/16/1829	11/25/1903
BARTLEY, Thomas	01/05/1895	01/25/1966
BEAMON, Gerome T.	03/19/1868	02/25/1952
BEAMON, Lavina	00/00/1850	00/00/1922
BEAMON, Virginia V.	01/11/1875	12/12/1935
BLAND, J. T.	00/00/1879	00/00/1972
BLAND, Ruby	00/00/1898	00/00/1968
BLANTON, Aaron Loren	09/24/1927	04/14/1989
BLANTON, James Ellis III	07/03/1970	10/28/1983
BRADLEY, Horry T.	00/00/1870	00/00/1918
BRADLEY, Mamie McDonald	00/00/1876	00/00/1967
BRANNEN, Annie Mae	00/00/1893	00/00/1977
BRANNEN, Bertha H.	02/01/1896	01/23/1987
BRANNEN, David C.	00/00/1858	00/00/1940
BRANNEN, Roy D.	00/00/1894	00/00/1955
BRANNEN, Victoria L.	00/00/1862	00/00/1940
BROWN, Mary Paul	09/14/1904	04/14/1977
BROWN, R. A.	12/22/1894	11/05/1974
BROWN, Russell C.	10/22/1925	09/19/1998
BRUCE, Betty	05/23/1933	11/01/1999
BRYANT, Arthur C.	09/14/1912	06/12/1963
BRYANT, Bayard B.	01/02/1887	12/07/1955
BRYANT, Lula R.	01/18/1887	03/31/1957
BRYSON, Christine S.	00/00/1898	00/00/1987
BRYSON, Clifton E.	00/00/1894	00/00/1951
BRYSON, John F.	01/09/1932	07/30/1932
BUEHLER, Dorothy W.	09/02/1916	Living
BURNETT, Marilu McTyier	08/16/1889	07/16/1982
BURNETT, Sanford Frank	05/28/1877	05/30/1961
CADY, Francis W.	05/26/1914	01/09/1990
CAMPBELL, Mary Hudson	02/09/1884	07/28/1965
CAMPBELL, SR., Karl C.	02/17/1880	04/09/1916
CAPPS, Edna Frances	03/14/1916	01/02/1984
CAPPS, George A.	04/14/1909	12/14/1995
CARLTON, Hewlette B.	05/27/1897	05/11/1967
CARLTON, Laura C.	10/22/1904	02/02/1959
CARTER, Annie Laurie Gay	00/00/1895	00/00/1940
CARTER, Billy	03/29/1937	09/25/1988
CARTER, Elizabeth Jennings	00/00/1909	00/00/1993
CARTER, Emma M. Wife of Joel H.	11/16/1858	05/??/1890
CARTER, James Earl	09/12/1894	07/22/1953
CARTER, Lillian Gordy	08/15/1898	10/30/1988
CARTER, Nina Pratt	00/00/1863	00/00/1939

CARTER, SR., Hugh Alton	00/00/1920	00/00/1999
CARTER, William Alton	00/00/1888	00/00/1978
CATO, Dr. James F.	11/04/1883	08/28/1910
CATO, Florence	07/22/1878	03/02/1882
CATO, George E.	04/02/1871	02/21/1898
CATO, Mary E.	12/08/1836	12/14/1881
CAUGHMAN, Mattie H.	00/00/1873	00/00/1953
CHAMBLISS, Florrie Bell	00/00/1898	00/00/1911
CHAMBLISS, Henrietta	00/00/1869	00/00/1949
CHAMBLISS, J. R.	00/00/1863	00/00/1937
CHAMBLISS, Leila Arrington	07/09/1874	03/18/1950
CHAMBLISS, Mark A.	01/07/1896	02/05/1965
CHAMBLISS, Melba Valrie Lunsford	09/09/1898	06/01/1979
CHAMBLISS, Sara S.	02/13/1912	01/29/1983
CHAMBLISS, Virgil H.	07/08/1904	04/18/1981
CHAPMAN, Michael Todd	00/00/1961	No date
CHAPPEL, Ammie	12/15/1882	08/31/1976
CHAPPEL, Armstid William	11/08/1919	09/16/1998
CHAPPEL, Armstid William	09/17/1891	04/10/1932
CHAPPEL, Homer	07/13/1887	04/27/1969
CHAPPEL, Mrs. Emma E.	12/25/1825	09/17/1904
CHAPPEL, Neva Holley	04/10/1891	04/01/1973
CHAPPEL, Rhodabel Gay	04/22/1918	06/11/1999
CHAPPEL, Rubye M.	08/28/1885	02/04/1972
CHAPPEL, Ruth	01/28/1894	02/23/1994
CHAPPELL, Alexander Aged 81	????	02/28/1905
CHAPPELL, Edwin Lewis	08/14/1861	06/29/1862
CHAPPELL, Eliza D.	02/29/1856	05/31/1942
CHAPPELL, Florence	10/26/1891	12/10/1893
CHAPPELL, Georgia A.	09/22/1829	05/12/1891
CHAPPELL, Homer Alonzo	10/16/1867	06/09/1887
CHAPPELL, Ida Adelia	05/31/1863	09/12/1887
CHAPPELL, John A.	04/04/1852	07/13/1913
CHAPPELL, Rufus	02/26/1846	01/01/1874
CHAVERS, Annie Belle	10/09/1890	01/22/1956
CHAVERS, Arthur Clyde	03/20/1920	Living
CHAVERS, Fred M.	09/22/1926	10/25/1989
CHAVERS, James Oscar	05/18/1915	02/14/1994
CHAVERS, Jeanette P.	08/01/1928	10/09/1994
CHAVERS, Martha Louise Toms	11/21/1923	01/25/1987
CHAVERS, W. H.	04/20/1883	03/06/1947
CHILDERS, William Robert	00/00/1892	00/00/1938
CHRISTIE, Clara W.	00/00/1858	00/00/1921
CLARK, Berta Will	08/27/1890	07/07/1963
CLARK, Elizabeth S.	00/00/1855	00/00/1924
CLARK, John Bartow	10/11/1861	09/13/1930
CLARK, Maggie A	03/09/1857	11/25/1907
CLARK, Mary Spann	09/01/1864	11/13/1920
CLARK, Wm. Lawson	00/00/1851	00/00/1878
CLEMENTS, John David Jr.	02/13/1928	02/25/1984
CLEMENTS, Melba Spann	10/14/1933	Living
CLINGENPEEL, Marvelyn Murray	10/08/1951	12/18/1998
COKER, Epsey	07/06/1831	01/30/1903
COLEMAN, Julia L.	00/00/1889	00/00/1973
COLEMAN, Julia Lewis	00/00/1850	00/00/1905
COLEMAN, Rev. T. N.	00/00/1843	00/00/1914
COLSTON, Howard	08/10/1917	01/10/1995
COLSTON, Stella	09/18/1917	07/7/1971
COOGLE, Leon James	11/17/1890	01/10/1919
COOGLE, Lucy Chambliss	06/13/1898	12/05/1962
CORNWELL, Dollie Hough	11/16/1917	01/22/1992
CORNWELL, Joel Hardy	08/12/1915	08/16/1964
CORNWELL, Sr., Ralph Lee	08/10/1911	05/26/1990
COX, Annie Hale (wife of John Morgan)	08/14/1894	05/21/1977
COX, Carey Thomas (son of Chappell)	00/00/1821	00/00/1856
COX, Chappell	12/20/1799	00/00/1863
COX, Charlie Crisp (son of John Augustus)	05/03/1890	08/14/1957
COX, Hettie Fulbright (wife of Charles C.)	09/13/1903	03/18/1962
COX, John Augustus (husband of S. M.)	06/25/1845	12/31/1918
COX, John Morgan (son of John Augustus)	05/23/1876	06/19/1943
COX, Mrs. S. M. (Sarah Missouri)	03/10/1850	09/01/1908
COX, Thomas Matthew	08/14/1882	02/5/1940
COX, Willie Daniel (son of John & Sarah)	11/11/1880	11/28/1897
CRANFORD, James w.	10/15/1915	09/08/1944
CRANFORD, Joseph M.	00/00/1908	00/00/1939
CRANFORD, Luther J.	00/00/1872	00/00/1957
CRANFORD, Mary W.	00/00/1887	00/00/1968
CRANFORD, William H.	00/00/1860	00/00/1953

CRAWFORD, Fannie W.	00/00/1871	00/00/1954
CRAWFORD, Joseph W.	03/05/1900	11/09/1984
CROXTON, George Lewis	06/10/1862	06/26/1914
CROZIER, Bessie Wellons	00/00/1900	00/00/1961
CROZIER, JR., Arthur Hood	10/19/1925	07/28/1976
CROZIER, SR., Arthur Hood	00/00/1898	00/00/1965
DANIEL, Clarence D.	no data	04/06/1930
DAVENPORT, Henry	11/05/1809	04/04/1874
DAVENPORT, Julia Caroline	01/11/1810	03/07/1899
DAVENPORT, Lavonia Geraldine	04/30/1845	07/29/1862
DAVIDSON, Mettauer Edward	05/23/1891	05/11/1956
DAVIDSON, Ruby Timmerman	10/08/1892	01/04/1992
DAVIS, John Walter	09/29/1942	08/07/1988
DAVIS, Joseph T.	09/13/1904	09/08/1974
DAVIS, JR., Perry	00/00/1960	00/00/1981
DAVIS, Lillian K.	10/15/1908	02/20/1998
DAVIS, Perry C.	00/00/1912	00/00/1982
DAVIS, Ruby T.	02/19/1913	03/27/1999
DAVIS, Rufus H.	07/02/1897	09/04/1970
DEAN, Carrie Turner	00/00/1869	00/00/1939
DEAN, Ernest M.	11/22/1875	08/29/1944
DEAN, Georgia A.	06/16/1852	02/03/1917
DEAN, Henry Rufus	07/26/1870	05/05/1885
DEAN, Henry Rufus	11/13/1828	12/25/1900
DEAN, James Crawford	10/22/1885	08/22/1903
DEAN, Lillie Ruth	03/11/1906	06/04/1907
DEAN, Rose M.	11/17/1880	03/23/1956
DEAN, Ross	00/00/1876	00/00/1941
DODSON, A. Cecil	????	04/13/1905
DODSON, A. Chappell	04/11/1879	11/22/1923
DODSON, Ann Gay	04/22/1912	09/23/1999
DODSON, Armstid	09/18/1849	09/30/1942
DODSON, Bob W.	08/02/1909	10/23/1988
DODSON, Clarence	01/17/1915	10/12/2000
DODSON, James H.	03/28/1877	10/21/1956
DODSON, Jessie Parham	12/08/1897	07/23/1982
DODSON, Jr., James Henderson	08/05/1907	01/09/2000
DODSON, Mary Cordelia Valentine	01/30/1915	03/24/1995
DODSON, Mary Ella	12/15/1912	08/22/1914
DODSON, Mary Sue	05/07/1931	09/17/1931
DODSON, Maude Wells	02/09/1884	07/27/1986
DODSON, Minnie H.	03/30/1886	02/01/1931
DODSON, Sara Elizabeth	07/18/1850	11/20/1922
DODSON, Susie L.	09/30/1910	11/23/1998
DOMINICK, Helen Walters	03/14/1914	02/06/1969
DOMINICK, Henry C.	11/05/1879	01/15/1958
DOMINICK, James Guy	10/01/1909	03/27/1986
DOMINICK, Lovie Jewel	07/14/1910	06/28/2001
DOMINICK, Minnie N.	07/09/1882	09/10/1961
DOMINICK, SR., George T.	11/01/1905	11/06/1999
DORN, Mrs. Emil	11/24/1817	06/07/1885
DOWNER, Ella Parker	00/00/1927	Living
DOWNER, J. T.	00/00/1921	Living
DOWNER, John A.	09/05/1912	09/08/1957
DOWNER, John A.	08/13,1875	07/03,1955
DOWNER, John Mack	01/05/1949	01/05/1949
DOWNER, Lena G.	04/18/1878	02/09/1961
DOWNER, Roy O.	01/31/1919	02/27/1947
DOWNER, S. Colley	10/6/1914	01/27/1959
DOYAL, Anne W.	08/30/1904	01/30/1981
DOZIER, John Clide	10/04/1875	08/29,1896
DOZIER, Mary D.	03/23/1921	07/30/1985
DOZIER, W. Clyde	10/08/1921	06/13/1970
DUKE, James Errold	11/20/1875	11/11/1905
DUPREE, J. Mallie	07/20/1879	03/22/1967
DUPREE, Jennie	08/02/1880	11/24/1939
DUVALL, Lucia H.	08/15/1894	11/14/1973
DUVALL, William W.	10/08/1890	04/06/1964
ELLIS, ??	07/10/1892	08/07/1892
ELLIS, Lula G.	05/15/1867	07/16/1892
ENGLISH, Ida B.	10/19/1921	09/29/1992
EUBANKS, W. E.	02/08/1884	09/14/1908
EVANS, Martha Cody	07/08/1909	05/15/1994
EVANS, Ola Munro	03/23/1859	06/16/1928
EVANS, Oliver Wing	03/24/1896	09/06/1897
EVANS, Ora C.	00/00/1876	00/00/1953
EVANS, R. B.	07/03/1855	03/31/1902
EVANS, Raymond A.	08/16/1892	02/28/1894
EVANS, Robert P.	00/00/1867	00/00/1952
EVERETT, Mary Helen Paul	05/29/1930	Living
EVERETT, Bertha Witt	07/09/1893	11/30/1943
EVERETT, Clarence Coleman	09/10/1928	02/13/1989
EVERETT, Edward C.	09/25/1924	05/19/1992
EVERETT, James W.	07/11/1893	04/25/1982
EVERETT, Oliver Clyde	04/27/1926	07/18/1985
EVERETT, William L.	05/02/1919	04/22/1973
FAIRCLOTH, G.T. Jr.	No date	00/00/1937

FAIRCLOTH, Geo. Thomas	07/26/1868	03/19/1928
FAIRCLOTH, Leila Mae	07/12/1913	06/30/1972
FAIRCLOTH, Mattie Wallis	11/05/1874	05/30/1950
FAIRCLOTH, Rudolph "Sonny"	02/02/1901	03/25/1969
FAUST, Daniel Floyd	10/20/1837	08/11/1911
FINLEY, James G.	07/12/1921	12/05/1972
FISHER, Mary Louise	00/00/1943	00/00/1987
FITE, Charle H.	11/12/1914	04/14/1978
FITE, Estelle Sellers	07/07/1886	08/25/1941
FITE, James B. Jr.	11/07/1909	11/12/1986
FITE, James B. Sr.	00/00/1884	10/11/1933
FITE, John Daniel	11/29/1925	07/25/2000
FLANAGAN, Lois	09/28/1900	11/15/1982
FOREST, A. L.	10/16/1891	10/01/1916
FOREST, Fannie Jennings	08/20/1874	03/26/1913
FOREST, Mrs. Claud	00/00/1882	00/00/1899
FORREST, Clara H.	00/00/1896	00/00/1931
FORREST, Eleanor Chambliss	11/05/1901	11/08/1988
FORREST, Estese D.	07/26/1894	07/26/1946
FORREST, James E.	04/20/1893	08/15/1931
FORREST, Ruby Ratliff	09/05/1881	04/04/1976
FORREST, William G.	00/00/1858	00/00/1912
FORREST, Leila Mae	03/13/1895	10/11/1966
FORTH, F. W.	08/15/1860	06/01/1909
FORTH, Henry B.	11/15/1850	08/17/1872
FRENCH, George Age 1 yr. 6 mos.	No date	No date
FRENCH, Marion King Age 4 yrs. 11 mo	No date	No date
GERALD, PERRY C.	No date	No date
GODWIN, Lynton E.	09/08/1892	10/13/1954
GODWIN, Ruth S.	06/26/1897	12/2/1995
GREEN, Alice Nix	01/31/1897	12/03/1992
GREEN, Ethel	12/29/1893	11/28/1992
GREEN, Walton	07/10/1891	06/29/1983
GREENE, Julia Ann	03/12/1868	02/16/1916
GREENE, Thomas J.	01/10/1865	05/22/1954
GRIFFIN, Lyman Son of F. W. & C. R.	06/10/1890	10/03/1890
GRIFFIN, Willie T.	01/27/1888	03/10/1888
Son of F. W. & C. R		
GRIGGS, James Marvin Sr.	11/07/1921	08/26/1985
GURR, Hattie C.	00/00/1874	00/00/1964
GURR, Thomas J.	00/00/1872	00/00/1924
HALE, Annie Cox	06/25/1894	12/02/1973
HALE, Fletcher Frank	11/11/1934	06/19/1971
HALE, Frank	01/09/1891	05/24/1948
HALE, Robert	03/14/1889	08/17/1981
HAMLIN, Guy Rucia	00/00/1892	00/00/1938
HAMLIN, Kattie Dean	00/00/1855	00/00/1930
HAMLIN, SR., J. W.	00/00/1858	00/00/1896
HAMLIN, Thomas Washington	01/06/1886	03/16/1960
HAMLIN, Thomas Wesley	02/14/1918	08/10/1989
HANCOCK, Mary Lavera	03/11/1891	10/21/1933
HAND, Alfred B.	00/00/1926	00/00/1977
HAND, Janie H.	06/12/1889	06/14/1956
HANNER, Eliza H.	00/00/1855	00/00/1943
HARPER, George Amos	08/21/1920	03/04/2001
HARPER, Georgia Brightwell	08/06/1923	Living
HARPER, James Emmett	00/00/1872	00/00/1954
HARPER, Jewell Kidd	00/00/1889	00/00/1980
HARRELL, L. W.	10/23/1849	06/23/1921
HARRELL, Mrs. L. W.	04/08/1856	02/24/1938
HARRIS, Alice M.	05/18/1926	05/02/1995
HARRIS, Homer McCook	02/10/1888	10/07/1975
HARRIS, Mattie Johnston	01/29/1895	06/04/1964
HARRISON, Louis Patrick	09/01/1928	12/03/1977
HARROD, Mary Hale	11/21/1915	04/23/1980
HAUTMAN, Majorie Mays Jennings	12/01/1911	11/24/1941
HEWITT, Bertha M.	09/25/1911	09/09/1990
HEWITT, Fleta	00/00/1895	00/00/1985
HEWITT, James Henry	00/00/1893	00/00/1960
HEWITT, John T.	00/00/1867	00/00/1930
HEWITT, Luther C.	00/00/1888	00/00/1977
HEWITT, Richard J.	09/10/1897	06/29/1973
HEWITT, Sheryl Lynn	00/00/1963	00/00/1964
HEWITT, Wealthy J.	00/00/1863	00/00/1949
HEWITT, Winnie F.	00/00/1904	00/00/1964
HILLER, Fannie W.	00/00/1852	00/00/1934
HINSON, George Wendell	00/00/1902	00/00/1987
HINSON, Jessie Commander	00/00/1908	00/00/1991
HOBGOOD, Infant son of Lark & Laura	00/00/1915	No date
HOBGOOD, Lark C.	04/26/1884	01/24/1950
HOBGOOD, Laura G.	00/00/1890	06/16/1916
HOBGOOD, Marjorie Slocumb	11/07/1930	Living
HOBGOOD, Rosa G.	10/24/1902	12/13/1992

HOBGOOD, Theron	05/20/1921	05/30/1986
HOBGOOD, Thomas L.	08/21/1914	08/21/1987
HOGSED, Brenda Emma Bunton	06/02/1959	Living
HOGSED, Francis W.	00/00/1860	00/00/1933
HOGSED, JR., Carman Francis	12/30/1927	02/20/1998
HOGSED, Lula L.	00/00/1889	00/00/1973
HOGSED, Martha L.	00/00/1860	00/00/1950
HOGSED, Olgia V.	00/00/1885	00/00/1971
HOGSED, SR., Carman Francis	03/16/1887	03/15/1968
HORN, John M.	10/26/1943	10/07/1996
HOWARD, Adam Patrick	No date	12/17/1995
HOWARD, Oscar Edward	02/13/1913	03/29/1961
HOWARD, Robert I	07/26/1943	03/04/1997
HOWARD, Sara H. Leuty	02/07/1921	01/08/1983
HOWELL, Annie Harper	02/25/1866	04/17/1924
HOWELL, John Emmett	09/03/1907	04/05/1966
HOWELL, L.P.	12/06/1835	09/12/1890
HUDSON, Cassie Clark	12/11/1857	12/29/1896
HUDSON, Douglas C.	02/04/1886	03/21/1956
HUDSON, Edward T.	12/18/1896	05/18/1897
HUDSON, Florence Lucile	03/06/1881	08/07/1884
HUDSON, Lewis N.	10/26/1890	02/28/1898
HUDSON, Marguerite	00/00/1894	00/00/1969
HUDSON, Milton L.	10/06/1953	06/30/1912
HUDSON, Stewart C.	07/24/1879	01/11/1900
HUDSON, Thomas G.	09/12/1825	04/30/1856
HUDSON, Willie Cato	Nodate	No date
HULSE, Elizabeth M.	10/22/1932	05/15/1990
HULSE, John E.	12/31/1932	Living
JACKSON, Edward	10/08/1875	01/02/1963
JACKSON, Victoria Mims	08/03/1878	03/10/1949
JAMES, Willie B.	09/26/1896	04/25/1957
JENNINGS, B.T.	08/27/1830	08/01/1900
JENNINGS, Barbary	01/30/1803	12/11/1881
JENNINGS, Ethel. L.	12/13/1907	02/14/1966
JENNINGS, Geo. W.	12/28/1842	01/13/1913
JENNINGS, George S.	00/00/1872	00/00/1919
JENNINGS, J. W.	11/10/1866	11/21/1931
JENNINGS, John (B.)	02/04/1797	09/15/1878
JENNINGS, John A.	07/18/1860	11/22/1890
JENNINGS, Lillie M.	00/00/1876	00/00/1960
JENNINGS, Mrs. Ella Dorn	06/24/1850	09/15/1890
JENNINGS, Mrs. Fannie C.	11/21/1858	07/19/1944
JENNINGS, Mrs. J. W.	05/15/1858	08/13/1936
JENNINGS, Susan	04/09/1838	07/14/1905
JENNINGS, Sybil Kendrick	00/00/1882	00/00/1964
JENNINGS, William L.	07/03/1904	08/13/1927
JENNINGS, William Leonard	00/00/1877	00/00/1947
JOHNSON, A. M.	06/12/1857	11/14/1916
JOHNSON, David E.	05/22/1876	0712/1951
JOHNSON, Ella R.	09/05/1874	08/16/1960
JOHNSON, George W.	05/09/1869	03/23/1929
JOHNSON, Homer	07/13/1889	08/19/1890
JOHNSON, Kyle	08/08/1901	06/17/1958
JOHNSON, Mamie	05/15/1860	No date
JOHNSON, Mollie K.	05/14/1878	08/14/1964
JONES, Arthur G.	01/10/1894	12/13/1975
JONES, Irene Murray	06/05/1904	07/03/1979
JONES, Jack Burton	03/20/1929	11/20/1951
JONES, Maggie Coker	05/04/1876	04/08/1956
JONES, Thaddeus Marion	11/17/1901	01/24/1972
JONES, Thomas Marion	02/22/1858	08/09/1934
JONES, Walter Linwood	08/21/1895	11/30/1975
JONES, Walter Linwood Jr.	03/13/1925	07/17/1935
JONES, Zera Smith	04/08/1896	03/11/1980
KEARSE, Infant son of M/M G. C.	02/02/1927	02/04/1927
KEARSE, Rosa Thornton	10/11/1886	05/27/1928
KENDRICK, Almon Gage	03/12/1853	08/30/1931
KENDRICK, Amanda E.	03/25/1870	01/01/1906
KENDRICK, Callie Cason	10/14/1881	12/12/1960
KENDRICK, Cecil Virginia	11/19/1878	12/03/1953
KENDRICK, Douglas B.	02/03/1877	08/18/1939
KENDRICK, Edgar M.	11/08/1862	08/14/1908
KENDRICK, Embry Mayes	11/28/1902	05/26/1959
KENDRICK, Flora Markette	12/11/1873	11/30/1950
KENDRICK, Florence Huntington Beall	04/05/1906	05/07/1984
KENDRICK, Mabel B.	10/01/1880	11/30/1929
KENDRICK, Martha Anne	No date	05/29/1976
KENNEDY, J.W.	09/18/1867	05/11/1925
KENNEDY, James Walter Jr.	09/04/1903	07/25/1942
KENNEDY, Jolly H.	10/04/1894	04/22/1967
KENNEDY, Mary Lou Harling	03/14/1870	04/23/1944
KENNEDY, Willie Kate	01/23/1906	04/26/1923
KINARD, John T.	07/03/1848	08/11/1892
KINARD, Oral Osmond	06/03/1905	07/09/1905
KINARD, Susan Rebecca	08/28/1901	12/30/1901

KIRKLAND, D. L.	00/00/1876	00/00/1928
KIRKLAND, Della Smith	00/00/1889	00/00/1940
KIRKLAND, L. W.	12/02/1901	04/24/1966
KIRKLAND, Olar	09/30/1903	08/13/1961
KNOWLTON, H. Walter	11/13/1919	10/02/1988
KNOWLTON, Hiram W.	05/16/1875	03/13/1930
KNOWLTON, Lillie C.	12/18/1878	08/03/1971
KNOWLTON, Margie	01/26/1914	08/30/1989
LAMB, Joyce Hawkins	08/15/1943	Living
LAMB, JR., William Coney	11/26/1940	12/01/1994
LANE, Polly A. Smith	07/20/1929	06/17/1996
LANSFORD, Gladys	12/23/1918	01/01/1919
LARGE, Evelyn F.	08/08/1912	Living
LARGE, J. G. (Jerry)	09/27/1939	11/30/1981
LARGE, James T.	00/00/1870	00/00/1964
LARGE, Levie T.	00/00/1878	00/00/1950
LARGE, Paul M.	01/14/1909	03/14/1957
LEROY, Henry Howard	00/00/1927	00/00/2001
LESSLEY, Martha E.	00/00/1860	00/00/1942
LESSLEY, Robrt I.	00/00/1847	00/00/1928
LEUTY, Reggie Neal	11/05/1926	02/11/1986
LEWIS, Ida C.	00/00/1869	00/00/1965
LORENTZSON, Bettie T.	07/02/1926	Living
LORENTZSON, Thomas R.	05/30/1926	07/02/1972
LOWERY, Jeanette C.	00/00/1904	00/00/1984
LOWERY, Wade H.	00/00/1902	00/00/1967
LUNSFORD, Bertha G.	10/26/1890	12/13/1908
LUNSFORD, Charles C.	05/06/1886	03/31/1947
LUNSFORD, Cora Dean Spann	12/06/1868	03/31/1942
LUNSFORD, Ethel W.	06/01/1890	07/12/1964
LUNSFORD, Everett	01/20/1862	05/25/1916
MALLARD, George Dewey	09/03/1945	06/21/1969
MALLARD, James W.	00/00/1935	00/00/2001
MALLARD, Linda Henderson	04/25/1945	06/20/1969
MALLARD, Mamie Hodge	01/18/1904	01/18/2001
MALLARD, William Fletcher	07/20/1903	01/28/1970
MANGHAM, Charles B.	12/23/1859	09/09/1930
MANGHAM, J. Willis	12/22/1882	08/09/1970
MANGHAM, John Scott	????	08/23/1952
MANGHAM, JR., James W. (Pete)	12/20/1918	03/16/1987
MANGHAM, Laura May	05/26/1923	01/26/1924
MANGHAM, Maria Emma	05/09/1859	02/05/1924
MANGHAM, Mary Mogridge	10/20/1920	No date
MANGHAM, Milford S.	02/24/1886	06/25/1977
MARCHANT, Katherine Hale	04/13/1918	07/26/1947
MARKETT, Eva S.	00/00/1883	00/00/1928
MARKETT, Z. F.	06/23/1845	12/06/1906
MARKETTE, John Wise	07/25/1876	10/30/1919
MASK, John F.	11/20/1906	05/17/1985
MASK, Lora Forrest	12/04/1878	01/25/1958
MASK, Margaret Edwards	05/31/1916	07/25/1942
MASK, Sarah J.	09/29/1910	02/26/1999
MASK, William B.	09/05/1863	08/20/1931
MATHEWS, Elizabeth Dodson	09/27/1907	04/24/1991
MAYES, B. B.	02/17/1816	06/26/1889
MAYES, Georgia V.	04/14/1848	03/29/1925
MAYES, Infant dau. of B. B. Mayes	????	00/00/1884
MAYES, Nora Benning	00/00/1879	06/19/1883
MAYES, Stephen Douglas	09/27/1852	11/08/1885
MAYS, Mary A.	11/29/1818	10/30/1865
McBRYDE, Floy	00/00/1891	00/00/1968
McCOLLUM, G. W.	00/00/1915	00/00/1995
McCOLLUM, Grace H.	00/00/1925	Living
McDONALD, Cornelia	00/00/1851	00/00/1923
McDONALD, Evelyn J.	12/11/1928	Living
McDONALD, John A.	00/00/1848	00/00/1930
McDONALD, Ralphard Willis	10/05/1924	03/23/1988
McGARRAH, Addie L. Wise	06/10/1879	08/16/1966
McGARRAH, James Albert	00/00/1883	00/00/1917
McGEE, Henry P.	00/00/1876	00/00/1952
McGEE, Infant dau of H. H. & T.	03/01/1898	09/12/1899
McGEE, Jessie Coleman	01/09/1881	12/30/1953
McGILL, Dr. John	00/00/1884	00/00/1915
McTYEIR, Infant dau. of M/M Uriah	No date	No date
McTYIER, Susie Clay	01/11/1861	01/26/1946
McTYIER, Uriah Kendrel	02/05/1847	06/03/1929
McTYLER, Clarence	06/13/1871	08/30/1891
MEDLOCK, Betty R.	01/18/1929	04/15/1985
MENSHON, Elsie K.	10/26/1917	04/30/1982
MIDDLETON, Mary Isabel	00/00/1870	00/00/1956
MIDDLETON, Mary Katherine	00/00/1947	No date
MILLER, Emily	04/28/1994	No date
MIMS, George T.	08/21/1886	02/09/1955
MIMS, Minnie Carroll	05/18/1899	01/14/1989
MINICK, Cora Lee	00/00/1880	00/00/1921

MINICK, Francis Hair	11/27/1848	05/31/1940
MINICK, J. B.	09/15/1912	03/21/1975
MINICK, Marshal	10/23/1877	01/10/1929
MINICK, Marshall	01/25/1904	No date
MINICK, Sybyl Hale	06/14/1913	03/10/1989
MINICK, Tearcey B.	00/00/1888	00/00/1982
MINNICK, Ellieree	00/00/1889	00/00/1897
MINNICK, Fannie	00/00/1869	00/00/1917
MINNICK, James Ross	00/00/1866	00/00/1957
MOMAN, Harvwell B.	12/29/1892	02/16/1977
MOMAN, Lavert Minnick Smith	01/20/1896	03/14/1984
MONTGOMERY, Eudora C. Lester	12/01/1899	03/08/1945
MONTGOMERY, Geo. W.	00/00/1864	00/00/1949
MONTGOMERY, George A.	06/08/1921	10/08/1994
MONTGOMERY, George A.	09/07/1896	02/07/1961
MONTGOMERY, Irene A.	00/00/1871	00/00/1939
MONTGOMERY, James Douglas	00/00/1935	00/00/1944
MOORE, Andrew B.	00/00/1892	00/00/1950
MOORE, Annie Wise	00/00/1882	00/00/1948
MOORE, Clarence Williams	05/26/1921	05/27/1921
MOORE, Dennis Markette	08/28/1888	04/12/1928
MOORE, Geo. G.	01/21/1854	10/15/1887
MOORE, Luther	00/00/1876	00/00/1958
MOORE, Mary Louisa Markette	08/28/1851	11/08/1936
MOORE, William Sampson	03/20/1842	10/21/1927
MORRELL, Allis	03/15/1887	01/12/1890
MORRELL, Jennie T.	02/15/1870	04/19/1952
MORRELL, Joseph C.	06/23/1907	12/31/1962
MORRELL, Rufus V.	11/09/1853	11/08/1916
MORRIS, C. B.	00/00/1879	00/00/1910
MORRIS, Callie	00/00/1885	00/00/1907
MORRIS, John Ed	09/22/1889	04/22/1900
MORRIS, Mariah Clark	06/13/1851	09/25/1926
MORRIS, W. R.	07/14/1853	03/12/1907
MORRIS, W. W.	00/00/1876	00/00/1910
MURRAH, Rosa Kathryn Wise	03/19/1918	07/02/1990
MURRAY, Almer C.	00/00/1879	00/00/1937
MURRAY, Annie Marguerite	07/23/1900	09/03/1901
MURRAY, Drue Parker	09/09/1868	10/10/1944
MURRAY, Edythe Harris	04/25/1912	01/24/1971
MURRAY, Florrie S.	00/00/1885	00/00/1935
MURRAY, Gladys E.	09/25/1908	02/13/1991
MURRAY, Grace McConnell	03/08/1904	10/22/1981
MURRAY, Griffin Almer	02/18/1944	11/21/1999
MURRAY, Infant of Mr. & Mrs. D.P.Murray	No date	No date
MURRAY, Infant son of Norman & Edyth	No date	03/17/1939
MURRAY, J.W. (Captain)	06/12/1871	07/15/1966
MURRAY, John Cato	09/15/1902	12/18/1971
MURRAY, JR., Drue Parker	08/27/1908	11/03/1956
MURRAY, Maude Erin Jennings	10/29/1871	12/25/1958
MURRAY, Rosa Wise	10/12/1880	09/30/1941
MURRAY, SR., Norman Clyde	09/23/1904	04/30/1983
NATION, Ruth Lane	12/13/1943	06/25/1985
NELMS, Minerva Hillsman	11/23/1832	02/23/1886
NICHOLSON, Lizzie	00/00/1856	00/00/1949
NIGHT, Joseph Alton	01/04/1901	01/04/1901
NIX, Ray W.	00/00/1900	00/00/1966
OLIVER, Annie Laurie	10/08/1898	02/02/1899
OLIVER, Aughtry Rylander	03/27/1864	11/16/1898
OLIVER, Edmund M.	09/16/1888	11/29/1930
OLIVER, Effie Turner	04/01/1868	10/28/1958
OLIVER, Jessie	08/19/1884	08/20/1884
OLIVER, Jno. W.	06/22/1857	10/19/1893
OLIVER, John Wesley	00/00/1893	00/00/1957
OLIVER, Katherine Schallwig	05/05/1898	06/12/1981
OLIVER, R. S.	12/02/1859	05/30/1928
OLIVER, Walter Harvey	07/15/1883	10/21/1883
PANTALL, Elsie Jane	09/04/1863	09/11/1912
PANTALL, Gene T.	02/12/1896	08/22/1982
PANTALL, Howard	04/29/1889	08/04/1953
PANTALL, Howard Jr.	01/16/1921	10/13/1926
PANTALL, Roy W.	02/09/1925	09/06/1983
PARADISE, Dewey Wright	01/28/1922	03/25/2000
PARADISE, Fannie Belle D.	09/13/1901	10/08/1998
PARADISE, Lorraine Ratliff	11/26/1922	07/16/1948
PARKER, Clarence Edwards	04/04/1871	01/21/1924
PARKER, Infant son of W.R. & Leola	No date	No date
PARKER, Irene Jennings	04/19/1878	07/16/1915
PARKER, Kittie Wise	01/06/1899	12/16/1982
PARKER, Leola Chappell	03/04/1871	01/27/1946
PARKER, Miriam	10/24/1891	09/20/1893
PARKER, Walter Raleigh	03/11/1866	03/1/1926
PASCHAL, Infant dau of Dr. & Mrs W. C	No date	No date

PASSMORE, Allie Mae	00/00/1926	00/00/1932
PASSMORE, Ammis L.	04/23/1922	07/12/2001
PASSMORE, Arliffa L.	00/00/1892	00/00/1932
PASSMORE, Cordelia	No date	No date
PASSMORE, John F.	00/00/1920	00/00/1921
PASSMORE, JR., John	00/00/1882	00/00/1936
PASSMORE, Robert	00/00/1928	00/00/1932
PASSMORE, SR., John	No date	No date
PASSMORE, Walkr J.	????	02/02/1918
PATE, Lillie G.	00/00/1881	00/00/1979
PAUL, Ernest E.	08/03/1912	08/28/1982
PAUL, Joseph Robert	10/14/1906	09/24/1990
PAUL, Mary Lena T.	12/02/1881	12/30/1964
PAUL, Teavy	06/23/1912	05/25/1986
PAUL, Virgie Coggins	09/18/1911	01/29 1994
PAUL, William H.	10/09/1878	07/16/1952
PEEL, Katherine	No date	00/00/1912
PERRY, Annola Murray	00/00/1906	00/00/1988
PERRY, Henry Camp	00/00/1894	00/00/1965
PERRY, Norma Ann	00/00/1930	No date
PHILLIPS, Charles	06/08/1910	07/03/1912
PITTMAN, Thelma T.	11/10/1912	11/29/1979
POWELL, Louise McL.	06/21/1902	03/03/1996
POWELL, W. J.	07/01/1902	10/19/1966
PRATT, Cowan	00/00/1858	00/00/1918
PRESKITT, Nellie M.	10/20/1900	07/19/1974
PRICE, James H.	10/02/1881	12/01/1956
PRICE, Laverne	00/00/1920	00/00/1937
PRICE, Winnie Kidd	00/00/1887	00/00/1939
PRITCHARD, Eva May	00/00/1891	04/14/1913
PUGH, Esther K.	05/10/1904	04/10/1989
PUGH, SR., Jack S.	05/09/1900	12/18/1981
PYLE, Gordon C.	12/02/1917	07/09/2000
RATLIFF, Cathryn D.	01/21/1916	05/05/1993
RATLIFF, Edgar Lee	12/19/1883	01/27/1973
RATLIFF, Herman J. "Mother"	08/08/1896	11/09/1961
RATLIFF, J. Bernard	08/21/1890	07/27/1970
RATLIFF, Jessie Albert	02/13/1916	03/24/1997
RATLIFF, Nona Deriso	12/19/1891	07/07/1955
RATLIFF, Robert S.	05/05/1893	05/21/1978
RATLIFF, Robert S. Jr.	06/22/1936	07/16/1948
RATLIFF, Rosa Mae A.	11/16/1887	03/03/1972
RAWSON, Edmond P.	No date	No date
RAWSON, Joseph G.	No date	No date
RAWSON, Miss Mary A.	No date	No date
RAWSON, Mrs. Mary	No date	No date
REESE, Buford H.	12/27/1930	08/26/1986
REESE, Maxine N.	06/10/1931	05/25/2000
REESE, Sallie, Dau. of H.P. & Becky	04/23/1908	08/23/1916
REEVES, Charlie G.	07/24/1905	08/20/1954
REEVES, Luna Mae	02/24/1899	07/02/1955
REVELL, Margaret W.	09/8/1924	Living
REVELL, William W.	01/25/1918	05/24/1995
ROGERS, Margaret Bath	03/24/1917	10/31/2000
ROGERS, Everett Lloyd	10/27/1912	10/29/1994
RYAN, Clarence B.	07/06/1906	04/11/1972
RYAN, Jewel Agnes	09/04/1921	12/17/1984
RYAN, Joseph Michael	11/13/1961	
SALTER, Jesse	03/26/1824	12/21/1900
SALTER, Lillie Leola	05/27/1878	09/21/1891
SALTER, Mrs. Victoria	03/13/1842	09/08/1917
SANDOCK, Beth Tyler	07/31/1954	09/24/1994
SAXON, Lois Wellons	05/09/1926	06/3/1946
SCOGGINS, Robert Charles	07/14/1917	05/11/1982
SEWELL, Anella C.	08/23/1913	10/08/1998
SEWELL, Charles Ross	08/11/1961	04/17/1975
SEWELL, John W.	07/17/1914	03/04/1975
SEWELL, JR., John W.	04/10/1940	05/19/1951
SEWELL, M. H.	07/31/1910	11/17/1979
SHEALY, Guy C.	00/00/1900	00/00/1942
SHEFFIELD, Lilloise L.	12/13/1912	Living
SHEFFIELD, Young T.	06/24/1904	09/21/1967
SHROPSHIRE Olivia Rymes	10/27/1860	12/23/1869
SHROPSHIRE, Dr. J.W.	01/16/1835	10/20/1871
SHROPSHIRE, James Clay	08/13/1863	12/07/1887
SHROPSHIRE, James H.	04/15/1867	07/20/1867
SHROPSHIRE, Josephine Cassandra	01/23/1838	01/05/1893
SHROPSHIRE, Julia Caroline	10/07/1869	01/26/1949
SIMPSON, Charles	11/01/1856	09/02/1868
SIMPSON, Lydia	03/11/1822	01/11/1888
SIMPSON, Saluda J.	10/03/1847	07/14/1864
SIMPSON, Thomas	12/16/1816	12/24/1886
SLAPPEY, Ethel Carter	02/05/1887	01/09/1972
SLAPPEY, Jack Linton	03/13/1883	09/25/1947
SLAPPEY, Linton Alton	08/04/1912	08/02/1982
SLOAN, David U.	04/07/1862	07/03/1909

SLOAN, Mrs. Julia A.	02/08/1842	03/27/1909
SMITH, Eddie A.	10/13/1941	03/09/1969
SMITH, Virgil	00/00/1923	00/00/2000
SMITH, Ambrose Jackson	08/04/1919	03/18/1994
SMITH, Charles Wilburn	03/25/1916	07/17/1978
SMITH, Evan Thomas	09/23/1883	05/08/1928
SMITH, Frances Allethea Murray	12/24/1905	04/01/2000
SMITH, Hazel Hobgood	05/17/1929	Living
SMITH, Henry Grady	12/23/1892	05/06/1921
SMITH, Henry Wilburn	00/00/1924	Living
SMITH, James Henry	11/08/1921	06/23/1923
SMITH, James Newton	05/07/1920	01/28/1921
SMITH, John Oliver	11/08/1918	01/03/1919
SMITH, Jr., J. Harrison	04/26/1929	09/16/1996
SMITH, Leila Teressa	08/20/1894	12/05/1994
SMITH, Louise Everett	08/09/1920	Living
SMITH, Lumus Leonidas	07/13/1903	11/22/1969
SMITH, Mary Dominick	04/07/1907	03/12/1952
SMITH, Mrs. Grace	10/08/1903	08/15/1939
SMITH, Oliver C.	02/26/1906	03/14/1979
SMITH, Patsy Miller	10/25/1926	No date
SMITH, Ruby Parker	00/00/1923	Living
SMITH, Sarah Bell	07/27/1875	03/16/1951
SMITH, Sarah Ellen	01/07/1905	11/10/1918
SMITH, Sarah Louisa	08/01/1877	11/12/1918
SMITH, Sue Senn	12/02/1908	Living
SMITH, W. Edgar	11/20/1896	10/22/1940
SMITH, W. Tennyson	04/25/1901	06/07/1923
SMITH, Wilburn J.	11/27/1853	11/25/1918
SMITH, William C.	00/00/1930	00/00/1934
SMITH, William Ronald	05/30/1934	12/14/1975
SPANN, Gloria Carter	10/22/1926	03/05/1990
SPANN, Ada Brooks	07/07/1904	06/05/1987
SPANN, Ernest Linwood	09/17/1892	07/24/1984
SPANN, Jerry Ernest	10/03/1941	10/13/1943
SPANN, JR., Oliver Williama	04/16/1953	04/20/1953
SPANN, Lizzie May	00/00/1888	00/00/1906
SPANN, Nannie E. Fletcher	11/23/1847	06/05/1936
SPANN, P. H.	12/25/1814	03/20/1908
SPANN, Theodosia N.	00/00/1858	00/00/1948
SPANN, Walter Franklin	07/15/1902	07/23/1992
SPANN, William H.	00/00/1858	00/00/1933
SPEEGLE, Loease R.	01/15/1928	Living
SPEEGLE, Ralph G.	07/16/1927	11/09/1986
SPIRES, Lucile Sewell Harrison	10/04/1910	11/24/1971
SPIRES, Mattie Beth Anderson	08/25/1928	04/21/1988
SPIRES, William Arthur	05/11/1909	07/16/1982
SPROULL, Jessie Kennedy	03/24/1893	02/14/1973
SPROULL, William Jeff	08/31/1890	05/12/1968
STEPHENS, Emory A.	00/00/1861	00/00/1932
STEPHENS, Lizzie C.	00/00/1864	00/00/1947
STEPHENSON, Claud	02/07/1911	01/08/1939
STEPHENSON, Etta Belle Carter	02/23/1873	09/12/1935
STEPHENSON, Hugh Pittman	09/13/1907	02/28/1959
STEPHENSON, I. Johnson	12/16/1877	11/26/1944
STEPHENSON, Roberta Bryant	04/20/1908	10/23/1972
STEVENS, Alma C. H.	11/22/1895	11/10/1955
STEVENS, Betty Eloise	02/10/1926	07/30/1981
STEVENS, Evelyn Minnick	12/22/1900	07/01/1990
STEWART, Ed. R.	02/02/1863	08/25/1939
STORY, Augusta R.	11/16/1857	09/03/1885
STORY, Rufus M.	08/16/1904	12/05/1995
STORY, Vida S.	09/27/1908	01/19/1991
STUBBS, Sallie Cox Dau. of John Augustus	03/11/1887	00/00/1913
SUTHERLIN, Mary Lewis	00/00/1853	00/00/1934
TAYLOR, Eloise	00/00/1924	00/00/1948
TAYLOR, Harold Wayne	10/29/1924	10/18/1945
TAYLOR, Irene H.	06/15/1902	06/19/1978
TAYLOR, Lonnie	00/00/1922	00/00/1948
TAYLOR, Lonnie F.	12/06/1893	05/14/1973
TAYLOR, Patrick	00/00/1947	00/00/1948
TAYLOR, Tommy	00/00/1946	00/00/1948
THARP, Benjamin	09/05/1818	07/15/1883
THOMAS Theodore C.	09/18/1883	02/22/1957
THOMAS, Allie Maude Murray	07/25/1901	09/16/1994
THOMAS, Lavonia Shrophire	09/27,1867	02/03/1953
THOMAS, Lucy Stokes	No date	12/09/1923
THOMAS, Lula Toms	04/22/1902	10/14/1975
THOMAS, Robert E.	12/23/1888	10/13/1969
THOMAS, Ruth	03/09/1892	05/08/1893
THOMAS, William H.	08/11/1874	12/25/1951
THOMAS, William Lang	07/23/1859	0708/1943
THOMPSON, Allie Inez	03/15/1906	04/29/1991
THOMPSON, SR., Robert F.	04/18/1903	11/03/1973
TIETJEN, Annie Carol H.	08/03/1944	Living
TIETJEN, David W.	08/03/1941	11/22/1988
TIMMERMAN, Ida Lee Pritchard	04/27/1890	05/24/1986

TIMMERMAN, James E. 09/27/1913 01/03/1964
TIMMERMAN, Joyce Fuller .... 05/01/1933　　Living
TIMMERMAN, Alice Cody 03/03/1894 11/06/1980
TIMMERMAN, Alice Forth.......... 01/19/1856 01/03/1937
TIMMERMAN, Alice Ruth.......... 07/03/1895 04/03/1926
TIMMERMAN, Alton Wells .... 06/05/1881　　No date
TIMMERMAN, Alvin J. 04/03/1890 08/02/1927
TIMMERMAN, Edgar 08/14/1882 12/19/1941
TIMMERMAN, Edwin................. 10/14/1854 06/11/1922
TIMMERMAN, Edwin Cody 09/24/1920 10/08/1988
TIMMERMAN, Effie M. 07/2/1887 02/20/1967
TIMMERMAN, Emily Lucille 12/14/1893 05/14/1897
TIMMERMAN, Emma Woodham . 02/25/1862 02/14/1936
TIMMERMAN, Ernest William 01/25/1895 01/15/1942
TIMMERMAN, Frank F. 08/09/1885 06/04/1939
TIMMERMAN, Jessie W. 10/9/1859 01/18/1934
TIMMERMAN, John Clinton 03/11/1883 09/25/1943
TIMMERMAN, Lillian Templeton 10/03/1907 08/05/1995
TIMMERMAN, Louie B. 02/07/1892 04/15/1961
TIMMERMAN, Lyman Crisp .... 07/18/1888　　No date
TIMMERMAN, Martha Fish 08/11/1919 12/12/1995
TIMMERMAN, Rosa May............ 04/06/1884 01/23/1910
　Phillips
TIMMERMAN, S. H. 12/04/1886 11/03/1951
TIMMERMAN, Virginia 07/31/1888 08/24/1973
　Randolph
TMMERMAN, Lily French 03/26/1886 11/01/1957
TORBET, D. M. 04/29/1861 01/04/1894
TURNER, Arthur V. 04/21/1881 01/19/1938
TURNER, Augustus L. 01/02/1899 03/13/1944
TURNER, Bennie F. 10/17/1907 09/18/1994
TURNER, Carlton Leroy 01/24/1885 01/08/1923
TURNER, David M. 00/00/1859 00/00/1934
TURNER, Dennis 10/09/1904 09/16/1972
TURNER, Jas. H. 09/10/1874 12/31/1919
TURNER, Jewel Sears 07/11/1907 07/27/1999
TURNER, Lavon 06/07/1927 04/13/1995
TURNER, Leila M. 07/07/1875 04/20/1963
TURNER, Mamie P. 09/07/1887 01/14/1973
TURNER, Melanie 09/18/1941 01/02/1967
TURNER, Nancy M. 00/00/1872 00/00/1946
TYLER, Ralph D. 03/14/1918 02/05/1999
UNGER, Emily Rachel 01/06/1985 03/21/1985
VAUGHN, Charles J. 12/11/1906 08/09/1983

VAUGHN, John P. 07/10/1911 07/12/1983
WALL, Eva Johnson 08/15/1904 06/30/1955
WALTERS, Bernice Harper.......... 01/29/1881 09/1/1968
WALTERS, Caroline Rhymes 08/04/1886 12/25/1923
WALTERS, Claude L. 01/31/1878 02/04/1955
WALTERS, Florrie Elizabeth 05/07/1913 06/11/2001
　Murray
WALTERS, Homer T. 04/06/1900 09/20/1915
WALTERS, How...................... 02/12/1876 11/21/1877
WALTERS, JR., Claude Leonard .. 10/06/1904 11/25/1980
WALTERS, Mary Alice 00/00/1879 00/00/1920
WALTERS, Mary Emily Forth 11/09/1847 05/15/1887
WALTERS, Milbry J. 03/15/1874 11/10/1953
WALTERS, Mildred.................. 01/25/1917 05/09/1917
WALTERS, Mrs. Maria D. 03/06/1847 01/12/1940
WALTERS, Nellie Maude............ 00/00/1883 00/00/1980
WALTERS, Pearl 00/00/1870 00/00/1952
WALTERS, Seaborn J. 03/23/1843 05/16/1894
WALTERS, Thomas C. 09/20/1841 05/20/1914
WALTERS, Thomas W. 10/13/1874 03/12/1937
WALTERS, Wiley Ross 09/25/1843 10/13/1901
WATSON, Bernice L. 00/00/1917 00/00/1940
WATSON, Carrie M. 07/30/1893 08/14/1970
WATSON, Clayton (Kit)............ 12/19/1919 10/12/1975
WATSON, Edward H. 05/08/1891 02/02/1949
WEBB, Marcella W. ....???? 11/07/1968
WEBB, Susan Clements 10/29/1953 01/12/2000
WELLONS, Anna B. 09/22/1855 01/03/1942
WELLONS, Barbara Murray 00/00/1947 00/00/2000
WELLONS, Blannie 00/00/1881 00/00/1907
WELLONS, Broadus A. 00/00/1889 00/00/1952
WELLONS, Ethel McGarrah 01/22/1899 11/07/1971
WELLONS, Grady Mills 10/06/1919 09/05/1988
WELLONS, Mary Ella M. 00/00/1897 00/00/1991
WELLONS, Otis O. 07/01/1893 12/23/1930
WELLONS, Rev. A. C. 06/16/1854 03/20/1932
WELLS, J.W. .... 00/00/1829 09/??/1904
WELLS, Mrs. M.E. Timmerman 01/25/1834 09/15/1908
WHALEY, Willie E. 00/00/1901 00/00/1970
WHALEY, Eugene W. 00/00/1874 00/00/1938
WHALEY, Everdine.................. 00/00/1908 00/00/1989
WHALEY, Jewell Doris 00/00/1904 00/00/1983
WHALEY, Johnny Gus .... 00/00/1910　　Living
WHALEY, Mary Cox................. 00/00/1873 00/00/1959

WHALEY, Robert E.	00/00/1898	00/00/1906
WHALEY, Rose Bud	00/00/1902	00/00/1982
WHALEY, Sarah M.	00/00/1912	00/00/1990
WHEELER, Walter P.	12/20/1918	12/23/1971
WHITTEN, George L.	03/28/1914	12/28/1980
WHITTEN, Infant of Louise & George	No date	11/20/1944
WIGGINS, Ralph C.	06/03/1917	04/09/1993
WILLCOX, Mary E.	09/11/1924	02/20/1989
WILLIAMS, Bertha Dodson	10/27/1884	04/02/1958
WILLIAMS, Betty Dodson	03/26/1934	10/20/1996
WILLIAMS, James B.	09/09/1932	Living
WILLIAMS, Jeremiah Gabe	10/01/1999	10/01/1999
WILLIAMS, Joseph Henry	07/21/1880	02/24/1936
WILLIAMS, Leila Earl	04/28/1892	03/8/1975
WILLIAMS, Mary Susie	07/20/1962	07/20/1962
WILLIAMS, Oscar Albert	12/19/1884	03/29/1975
WILLIAMS, Pamela Gayle	11/11/1981	08/05/1998
WILLIAMSON, Mable Claire	04/12/1893	09/20/1979
WILLIAMSON, Orion M.	08/14/1900	01/28/1976
WILLIAMSON, Tululah	00/00/1857	00/00/1931
WILLIAMSON, W. J.	00/00/1855	00/00/1927
WILLIAMSON, William Overton	12/27/1888	04/03/1978
WISE, Minnie Clara	10/17/1884	10/17/1956
WISE, Walter James	11/25/1890	03/09/1964
WISE, Alma C.	00/00/1883	00/00/1942
WISE, Ann E. Slocumb	04/14/1927	Living
WISE, Anna Josephine	03/02/1852	11/07/1918
WISE, Armenia Eloise	04/28/1925	02/26/1926
WISE, Burr Thaddeus	07/19/1882	04/06/1956
WISE, Burr Thomas	08/27/1858	02/12/1910
WISE, Calvin	00/00/1906	00/00/1941
WISE, Carrie Bowers	03/30/1886	09/21/1970
WISE, Charles Crawford	05/14/1922	12/07/1996
WISE, David	04/30/1809	06/08/1882
WISE, Elizabeth F.	09/25/1907	02/07/1964
WISE, Eola Anderson	08/28/1888	08/13/1972
WISE, Florence Dallas	01/11/1880	11/05/1956
WISE, James H.	06/20/1913	01/29/1983
WISE, John Calhoun	08/07/1885	07/31/1977
WISE, Joseph P.	12/26/1847	01/04/1926
WISE, JR., Burr Thaddeus	10/31/1917	06/20/1920
WISE, JR., Luther A. "Morgan"	06/09/1922	Living
WISE, Laura Rachel Addy	04/06/1864	03/15/1943

WISE, Lilla	07/09/1869	09/12/1899
WISE, Lottie Meadows	09/17/1901	12/15/1981
WISE, Lou Chappell	01/11/1866	12/20/1953
WISE, Louise Lamar	02/01/1886	03/29/1931
WISE, Luther Alonzo	08/02/1888	04/12/1940
WISE, Luther D.	03/21/1863	02/14/1926
WISE, Luther E.	09/08/1888	10/21/1922
WISE, Luther Elmore	04/19/1930	05/09/1997
WISE, Martha Holcombe	12/09/1936	Living
WISE, Mary Irene	10/10/1876	06/21/1887
WISE, Mary Wynn	12/01/1920	Living
WISE, May Shirley	06/25/1896	02/19/1991
WISE, Mildred Lucille	01/14/1920	Living
WISE, Myrtle C.	08/01/1893	12/30/1978
WISE, Philip Johnson	01/11/1861	12/18/1907
WISE, Ray H.	00/00/1908	00/00/1937
WISE, Rosa	02/01/1821	01/15/1900
WISE, Samuel D.	10/23/1869	06/30/1891
WISE, Samuel Paul	06/21/1884	11/03/1943
WISE, SR., David Thomas	03/12/1915	11/01/1986
WISE, SR., Phillip Joseph	04/10/1917	Living
WISE, T. Phillip	10/24/1901	09/17/1969
WISE, Tyre Patrick	01/05/1874	12/08/1960
WISE, W. T.	00/00/1878	00/00/1941
WISE, Warren Wallace	08/26/1918	09/10/1977
WISE, William E.	06/05/1924	04/13/1992
WOODHAM, Mrs. N. C.	03/26/1837	12/25/1915
WOODS, JR., James Buck	03/03/1952	06/09/1999
WOTEN, Mary	03/13/1869	01/12/1919
YOUNG, Grace Montgomery	08/15/1905	06/05/1990
YOUNG, Walter Leroy	08/09/1990	04/26/2001
YOUNG, Walter Leroy	10/07/1904	09/23/2000
ZORN, Irene "Rene" Jones Smith	08/11/1937	04/04/1996

Magnolia Springs

Surveyed by Jack F. Cox November 10, 2001

NAME	BIRTH	DEATH
ANDREWS, Alice Williams	10/08/1891	11/01/1912
ARGO, Effie	05/03/1878	08/29/1905
COKER, James P.	03/12/1836	06/15/1899
COKER, Mary Ida	09/23/1897	02/17/1898
COKER, Sarah J.	01/24/1836	11/09/1883

COKER, William B.	01/10/1888	06/06/1889
GLASS, Elizabeth	12/05/1829	09/19/1889
GLASS, S. B.	11/18/1821	09/08/1894
HARPER, C. A. (MD)	09/31/1837	06/12/1917
HARPER, J. L.	11/18/1861	06/23/1906
HARPER, M. E.	10/25/1841	04/29/1899
JOHNSON, R. E.	05/03/1830	04/11/1910
JOHNSON, Rosa Lee	11/10/1823	08/13/1876
JOHNSON, Willie E.	04/13/1869	01/15/1896
KIDD, Georgia	01/09/1859	11/11/1907
KIDD, W. M.	03/09/1861	11/06/1926
MOORE, Sarah A.	04/19/1820	03/15/1891
POWELL, Mr. Clestia	10/06/1854	06/27/1905
POWELL, Richard E.	05/31/1894	01/15/1913
STEWART, Sallie E.	03/15/1866	03/29/1897
Wife of E.R. Stewart		
STEWART, Annie Lou	05/04/1889	10/28/1906
STUBBS, U. M.	01/09/1855	04/10/1926
WALLACE, Jim Newt	11/03/1883	10/14/1912
WILLIAMS, Charlotte Bryson	11/02/1823	10/15/1899
WILLIAMS, Fannie Moore	09/21/1858	02/01/1908
WILLIAMS, George H.	10/27/1853	01/05/1900
WILLIAMS, Robert	02/27/189?	12/16/1892

Providence Cemetery

Surveyed by Jack F. and Earlene Cox
November 20, 2001

Located 4.3 miles from Plains, Ga. On Hwy 45 S.
(corner of Bottsford Rd. & Hwy. 45 S.)

NAME	BIRTH	DEATH
(???? = Could not read tombstone)		
BIRD, J.C.	06/19/1875	05/29/1905
BIRD, J.M.	No date	05/13/1897
Died May 13, 1897 age 70		
BIRD, Mary E.	No date	No date
BYRD, Elizabeth Worsham	09/20/1880	07/23/1943
Wife		
BYRD, George H.	03/13/1907	04/20/1993
BYRD, Henry M.	01/06/1865	11/07/1922
BYRD, Lee C.	05/12/1905	06/02/1987
CALDWELL (4 graves)	No date	No date
N.A.C. - W.T.C. - R.H.C. - T.C.		

CALDWELL, J.W.	No date	No date
Age 50 years		
CALDWELL, Nancy (Mitchell)	No date	No date
Age 41 years		
COLLUM, James R.	00/00/1843	00/00/1916
Co. H.59 Regt. Ga. Inf. C.S.A.		
COLLUM, Pvt. Uriah	00/00/1824	00/00/1868
Co. G. 1 Regt. Ga. Inf.		
Mexican War		
DAVISON, Ann B.	00/00/1812	08/29/1862
Wife of W.H. Davison		
DAVISON, Eugenie	01/08/1866	10/00/1866
Daughter of W.H. & L.C.		
DAVISON, Henry	03/07/1875	04/00/1876
Son of W.H. & L.C. Davison		
DAVISON, John Ira	Age 9 mos.	00/00/1855
Son of W.H. & A.R. Davison		
DAVISON, Lucretia	11/04/1844	11/03/1911
Wife of W.H. Davison		
DAVISON, Mamie Griffin	12/17/1852	05/12/1890
Wife of T.A. Davison		
DAVISON, Samuel E.	00/00/1850	12/08/1866
Son of W.H. & A.R. Davison		
DAVISON, T.A. Sr.	08/09/1842	08/07/1922
DAVISON, Talbot B.	03/16/1842	11/11/1870
Son of W.H. & A.R. Davison		
Co. A 11 Bn. Ga. Arty. C.S.A.		
DAVISON, Pvt. Thomas A.	08/09/1842	08/07/1922
Co.A 11Bn. Ga. Arty. C.S.A.		
DAVISON, William H.	04/02/1820	01/19/1889
DAVISON, William H.J.	00/00/1859	02/28/1863
Son of W.H. & A.R. Davison		
DUCKWORTH, Francis M.	No date	No date
Co. E 25 Ga. Inf. C.S.A.		
FAUST, James Madison	02/00/1849	08/00/1912
FAUST, Martha Ann Ratliff	12/??/1848	08/??/1912
FINCH, Pvt. John W.	03/21/1841	02/25/1903
Co. C 10 Batt. Ga. Inf. C.S.A.		
FINCH, Maggie Walters	09/00/1838	08/00/1917
FINCH, W.P.	08/18/1816	12/15/1911
HARGROVE, J.T.	06/09/1852	04/02/1917
HATFIELD, Martha Jane	04/28/1837	09/08/1891
Wife of E.B. Cheek		
HAWKINS, Ezekiel	12/25/1790	08/31/1868
HAWKINS, Isabella	01/22/1852	07/17/1869
HAWKINS, J.H.	04/03/1876	01/17/1903

HAWKINS, Nancy 12/25/1796 09/15/1861
    Consort of E. Hawkins

HAWKINS, Neill 11/11/1840 10/04/1843

HAWKINS, R.W. 09/27/1820 12/31/1864

HAWKINS, Robt. E. 02/13/1848 07/07/1851

HAWKINS, Pvt. W.J. 04/03/1846 01/17/1903
    Co. G 2 Ga. Inf. Regt. C.S.A.

HILL, Lula Davison 09/14/1888 07/21/1917
    Dau. of T.A. & Mamie Davison

HILSMAN, Herman 04/15/1907 03/17/1909
    Son of E.C. & W.C. Hilsman

HOWELL, C.L. 09/04/1850 11/09/1917

HOWELL, Henrietta 03/03/1853 01/11/1929

HOWELL 08/15/1911 08/15/1911
    Infant son of Mr. & Mrs. G.B.

HUCKABAY, Lizzie M. 08/07/1861 08/17/1920

JENNINGS, T.P. 01/12/1884 08/27/1912

JENNINGS, Tilman .... No date   No date
    Son of T.P. & Virginia

JENNINGS, Virginia 08/02/1852 04/03/1892
    Wife of T.P. Jennings

JENNINGS, Virginia .... No date   No date
    Dau. T.P. & Virginia Jennings

JOHNSON, Chas. M. 05/26/1909 01/17/1910
    Son of C.F. & L.V. Johnson

MARKETT, Pvt. Benjamin F. 05/17/1838 12/20/1915
    Co. A 12 Ga. Vol. C.S.A.

MARKETT, Jannie K. 04/26/1866 10/09/1881

MARKETT, John F. 02/04/1804 09/02/1882

MARKETT, John Ira 02/11/1853 09/03/1853
    Age 6 mos. and 22 days

MARKETT, Wealthy Ann .... ??/??/???? 01/06/1854
    Age 17 yrs. 2 mos. & 26 days

MARKETTE, Capt. Joseph 12/24/1834 02/18/1898
    Co. A 12 Ga. Vol. Inf. C.S.A.

MARKETTE, Mary 11/05/1842 11/24/1926

MARKETTE, Sarah H. 11/10/1810 11/18/1890

MARSHALL, Eliza. 05/06/1847 01/00/1870
    Daughter of W.H. & A.R

MARSHALL, M.T. 03/23/1800 08/26/1873

McCAY, Daniel .... No date 08/31/1874
    Age about 70 years

McCAY, Neill 08/15/1801 11/28/1873

MORTON, Mary Annis 12/14/1867 09/30/1898
    Dau. of B.F. & Mary Markette

MULHOLLAND, Pvt. Joseph 00/00/1822 00/00/1898
    Webster Co. Militia C.S.A.

MULHOLLAND, Mrs. Annie 00/00/1824 08/09/1884
    Age 60 years

NOBLES, Annie L. 07/09/1903 10/09/1904
    Daughter of W.R. & N.C.

PATTON, James J. 08/26/1845 01/19/1892

PRICE, Jane 07/14/1823 08/03/1904

PURVIS, Lucy L. 02/20/1894 12/31/1897
    Daughter of J.M. & S.U. Purvis

PURVIS, Mary .... No date   No date
    In memory of my aunt by Cecil Purvis

RATLIFF, Freddie 10/21/1886 10/03/1887
    Son of J.T. & E.A. Ratliff

RATLIFF, Jesse T. 09/13/1854 09/05/1926

RATLIFF, Mary Ann 06/14/1828 11/13/1908

RATLIFF, S.B. 12/29/1851 04/29/1911

RATLIFF, Thomas 02/13/1814 05/07/1886

RATLIFF, W.S. 01/12/1847 05/01/1907

RATLIFF, Eugenia 04/06/1856 06/30/1941

RATLLIFF W.H. 09/07/1888 11/30/1916
    Son of J.T. & E.A. Ratliff

SMALLPIECE, J.M. 06/28/1848 02/16/1907

SMALLPIECE, James W. 12/21/1877 12/13/1880

SMALLPIECE, Jimmie 06/11/1881 04/30/1903

SMALLPIECE, Laura T. 12/09/1879 08/13/1900

SMALLPIECE, Lavinia 12/25/1840 09/13/1906
    Dau. of Thos & Elizabeth

SMALLPIECE, Leila 03/27/1879 11/08/1949

SMALLPIECE, Thomas 11/03/1812 08/20/1882

SMALLPIECE, Elizabeth 12/25/1812 07/07/1878
    Wife of Thomas

SMALLPIECE, Laura Lugenia 05/19/1850 01/12/1918
    Wife of J.M. Smallpiece

SMITH, Mrs. Georgia Ann 10/24/1829 05/03/1887

SMITH, Roan 03/11/1826 08/28/1910

SNELLGROVE, Lottie E. .... No date   No date
    Age 70 years

SNELLGROVE, W.H. 07/19/1862 12/12/1888

SPENCER, William M. 07/23/1826 08/13/1895

STEPHENS, Jacob S. 12/18/1832 04/04/1911
    Co. B 11 Bn. Ga. Arty.

STEPHENS, Stafford 12/18/1832 04/04/1911

WESSON, Elenora E. 11/24/1880 09/02/1888
    Daughter of P.V & A.M.

NAME	BIRTH	DEATH
WESSON, Lucy A.C.	11/13/1861	10/02/1866
Daughter of P.V.& A.M.		
WISHARD, Elizabeth	11/25/1834	12/19/1912
Wife of Thos. G. Wishard		
WISHARD, Mary Elizabeth	05/14/1846	01/22/1920
Wife of J.M. Wishard		
WISHARD	10/10/1882	10/10/1882
Infant son of Mr.&Mrs.J.M. Wishard, Jr.		

Rural Hill Methodist Cemetery

Survey December 28, 2001 by Jack F. Cox

This cemetery is located 4.3 miles from Plains, Ga. on Highway 45 S. Rural Hill Methodist Church was originally located next to this cemetery. The church was moved to a new location on a road now named Rural Hill Road. The cemetery is sometimes referred to as Bottsford.

NAME	BIRTH	DEATH
(???? = Could not read tombstone)		
BRANNEN, infant son of D.C. & Victoria	No date	No date
BRASWELL, Robert H.	06/??/1901	07/??/1931
BROXTON, J.W.	03/18/1862	05/08/1892
BROXTON, Mattie	10/08/1862	11/08/1911
CALLAWAY, R.S.	10/13/1836	12/05/1913
CRAPP, Mrs. Ellen	11/10/1832	06/01/1869
DILLARD, Alice Irene	10/25/1864	11/15/1898
DILLARD, Ina Bell	03/16/1895	06/03/1895
DILLARD, Sallie	02/14/1875	04/08/1875
DILLARD, Susan Harriett	02/09/1866	08/15/1889
EVERETT, James J.	11/03/1853	04/19/1923
EVERETT, Mattie Randall	09/11/1858	04/29/1950
EVERETT, Mrs. Will (age 50)	No date	11/29/1943
FLETCHER, Mark H.	09/12/1818	08/30/1883
FLETCHER, Martha	04/24/1823	06/15/1870
FOUST, Peter (age 85)	No date	06/07/1854
FRAZIER, Martha M.	11/23/1832	12/10/1897
GREEN, David H.	12/23/1862	08/13/1890
HALE, Hungter H.	??/??/1859	10/25/1929
HALE, Mrs. Dolly Callaway (aged 80)	No date	07/29/1935
JACKSON, Sallie	01/30/1853	04/15/1887
JENNINGS, George P.	06/13/????	12/25/1869
LASSITER, Amos	11/04/1824	10/28/1897

NAME	BIRTH	DEATH
LASSITER, Anna McLain (age 75)	No date	02/07/1936
LASSITER, Annette	10/30/1860	09/30/1903
LASSITER, Annie	09/30/1903	01/15/1904
LASSITER, Charlie	No date	??/??/1933
LASSITER, Elizabeth J.	12/09/1829	12/15/1902
LASSITER, Henry	10/06/1852	05/23/1925
LASSITER, James	07/12/1857	01/25/1928
LASSITER, Joseph E.	04/15/1885	11/17/1885
LASSITER, Marguret	12/05/1854	01/29/1934
LASSITER, Mary	04/23/1850	10/23/1927
LASSITER, Victoria	02/20/1863	08/22/1894
McLAIN, Mrs. Maria	06/25/1835	01/29/1885
McLAIN, P.W.	05/19/1819	06/03/1868
MILLER Jr., J.A.	06/11/1852	06/02/1885
MILLER, Mrs. Peggy	No date	02/08/1895
MILLER, William	07/22/1811	10/30/1859
MIMS, Martin H.	01/27/1842	12/17/1908
MIMS, Mrs. Sallie	??/??/1808	03/15/1893
MIMS, Sarah Amanda	03/28/1846	05/07/1908
MOORE, J.M.	10/25/1846	08/12/1878
SIEG, Carl	09/19/1892	06/04/1893
SKELTON, Ella Mims	08/16/1878	04/21/1901
WITT, Earl W.	02/17/1892	11/23/1917
WITT, Lawrence R. (age 62)	No date	12/30/1936
WITT, Lucy Hale (age 60)	No date	11/28/1946
YOUNGBLOOD, Thomas V.	1810	03/23/18??

St. Mark Archery

Surveyed by Jack F. Cox October 31, 2001

St. Mark is located at Archery, Georgia just past the Carter Boyhood Home.

NAME	BIRTH	DEATH
(???? = Could not read tombstone)		
ADDY, George E.	09/16/1906	03/15/1972
BARNES, Rev. G. W.	10/20/1881	01/11/1973
BATY, Margaret	00/00/1865	00/00/1950
BERRY, Fred D.	No date	08/07/1970
BERRY, Lucy Mae	01/09/1919	11/02/1988
BERRY, Rosie Lee	02/08/1917	12/27/1991
BROWN, James	No date	03/10/1960

BROWN, Mrs. Mollie	10/28/1868	03/01/1949
CLARK, Alice D.	12/03/1904	12/09/1977
CLARK, Earnest	06/30/1941	05/08/1974
DEW, John	00/00/1888	00/00/1946
DODSON, Mamie	04/03/1911	07/18/1974
DOTSON, ??	No date	00/00/1932
DOTSON, Hershel	11/29/1902	11/25/1987
DOTSON, Linda	No date	00/00/1911
DOTSON, Lizzie	No date	09/29/1913
DOTSON, Mattie	02/09/1909	04/04/1944
DUNNING, James C.	06/28/1921	06/13/1994
DUNNING, Rev. J. C.	00/00/1888	00/00/1925
DUNNING, Rosa	No date	06/30/1959
FRENCH, Rosa	12/25/1890	07/05/1974
GRAHAM, George	00/00/1877	00/00/1944
HARRELL, Rev. C.	08/25/1912	12/12/1982
HARRIS, Alice Ruth Smith	00/00/1915	00/00/1932
HARROLD, David	08/24/1910	03/15/1974
HARROLD, Lillie	08/28/1885	05/14/1945
HARVEY, Alice	No date	10/19/1969
HARVEY, Daisy	12/15/1887	04/18/1978
HARVEY, Henry Lee	04/14/1917	03/17/1975
HARVEY, John	04/20/1908	09/17/1968
HARVEY, Toy	No date	02/25/1976
HARVEY, Toy	No date	10/18/1959
HAWKINS, George	05/19/1892	02/25/1963
HAWKINS, Mrs. Josephine	04/23/1902	03/30/1976
HILL, Joseph	No date	01/14/1955
HINTON, Essie	04/20/1882	05/??/1888
HOLLEY, Dock	09/30/1918	12/28/1999
HOLLEY, Fannie	No date	05/15/1941
HOLLEY, John Henry	12/02/1927	09/10/1996
HOLLEY, Larry	No date	06/30/1941
HOLLEY, Mary Lee	10/??/1906	10/28/1964
HOLLEY, Michael A.	09/13/1964	00/00/1993
HOLLEY, Teresa	01/11/1975	12/16/1998
JAMES, Felton	08/28/1919	03/01/1998
JAMES, Frank	04/04/1895	08/22/1992
JAMES, Joseph	04/05/1925	11/15/1982
JAMES, Mary Eliza	00/00/1886	00/00/1948
JAMES, Rufus	No date	12/15/1954
JAMES, Willie	03/15/1906	07/30/1971
JAMES, Willie Mae	No date	09/18/1963
JOHNSON, Corene	No date	03/23/1947

JOHNSON, D. C.	No date	02/15/1954
JOHNSON, William Decker II	11/15/1869	06/16/1936
JOHNSON, Willie	No date	09/30/1949
JOHNSON, Winnifred E.	12/25/1879	09/23/1950
KITCHEN, Joe	05/27/1893	07/03/1964
KITCHEN, Lora Bell	No date	02/12/1956
KITCHEN, Willie	11/24/1916	07/30/1955
KITCHENS, Rosa Lee	07/14/1890	01/29/1886
KLECKLEY, Anna	No date	08/04/1959
KLECKLEY, Rev. A. C.	04/01/1913	12/04/1989
LASTER, Bud	05/02/1909	08/23/1970
LASTER, Charlie	00/00/1906	00/00/1952
LASTER, Georgia	04/06/1891	11/05/1974
LASTER, John E.	05/29/1912	03/22/1982
LASTER, Ruby	12/02/1916	06/02/1935
LASTER, Will	No date	05/06/1967
LESTER, Sally	No date	12/08/1956
MARSHALL, Mamie Ruth	No date	07/29/1942
MARSHALL, Pauline	No date	00/00/1916
MARTIN, James	No date	03/15/1957
McNEAL, Minnie	No date	07/16/1946
MILES, Mary Lee	05/03/1908	10/28/1972
MILLER, Lucy M.	5/22/1936	08/06/1999
MONTS, Annie Lou	No date	11/23/1962
MONTS, Edward	08/12/1920	09/11/1975
MONTS, George H.	No date	06/23/1962
MONTS, Horace C.	07/12/1919	07/23/1966
MONTS, Ida Bell	No date	11/25/1956
MONTS, Johnie	03/02/1896	04/22/1958
MONTS, Rebecca	No date	01/18/1966
MONTS, Sammie T.	10/26/1907	10/17/1964
MOORE, Mary G.	00/00/1883	00/00/1942
MORGAN, Anthony	07/01/1888	09/04/1951
ODUM, Tobe	10/22/1931	No date
PERRY, Ida Maude	09/22/1904	06/21/1983
RAVAN, Cliffart	12/14/1906	03/??/1936
RAVAN, Clinton T.	11/27/1912	03/02/1987
RAVAN, Floyd Clyde Jr.	05/30/1929	04/07/1998
RAVAN, Lavonia Edge	09/11/1934	11/10/1996
RAVEN, Johnnie Sr.	10/06/1891	12/16/1968
RAVEN, Lillie A.	12/25/1888	05/01/1966
REDDICK, Letha Barnes	No date	09/??/1916
REID, Anna	04/06/1893	04/01/1938
REID, Clevon	00/00/1861	00/00/1926

REID, Silver Sr.	No date	12/07/1956
REID, Willie	02/14/1891	11/22/1972
RICHARDSON, Wiley Jr.	06/24/1948	10/19/2001
RIGGIN, Edward	07/10/1889	12/10/1959
RIGGINS, Carrie B. Ford	12/17/1899	02/14/1986
ROBERTS, Tom	07/20/1895	02/06/1950
ROBINSON, Mrs. Rose Lee	No date	07/22/1973
SHEPARD, Johnnie	00/00/1910	05/13/1951
SIMPSON, Charle G.	06/1/1880	04/30/1971
SIMPSON, George Sr.	No date	07/11/1957
SMITH, Edith	00/00/1877	00/00/1953
SMITH, Frank E.	02/04/1917	08/30/1998
SMITH, Frank E. Jr.	08/12/1946	03/31/1985
SMITH, George	No date	08/17/1968
SMITH, Lue	No date	08/07/1959
SMITH, Shade J.	00/00/1910	00/00/1946
TAYLOR, Eliza	No date	00/00/1932
TOMMIE, Blummie	No date	05/19/1998
TOMMIE, Blummie	04/20/1915	07/27/1966
TOMMIE, Joe T.	06/10/1911	09/09/1965
TOOMER, May Agnes	No date	11/08/1965
TRAMELL, Reanor	06/30/1936	04/20/1968
WAKEFIELD, Arrena	12/21/1901	04/18/1936
WAKEFIELD, Berthal	01/26/1907	02/01/1972
WAKEFIELD, Eula Mae	00/00/1910	00/00/1922
WAKEFIELD, Levi W.	02/02/1874	12/01/1956
WAKEFIELD, Paul R.	09/18/1927	06/16/1957
WAKEFIELD, Rena	11/08/1947	01/20/2001
WAKEFIELD, Rev. Sid	00/00/1862	00/00/1946
WAKEFIELD, Rev. T. R. Sr,	04/23/1901	08/20/1977
WAKEFIELD, Zenobia	01/15/1867	10/21/1962
WALTON, Earnestine	No date	08/26/1966
WALTON, Emma L.	No date	09/21/1966
WHITE, Calvin Jr.	08/27/1948	09/11/1994
WHITE, Clifford	05/20/1947	04/20/1999
WHITE, Mary A.	No date	09/13/1956
WHITFIELD, Alice	00/00/1868	00/00/1923
WHITFIELD, Charlie	06/06/1900	04/19/1970
WHITFIELD, J. M.	00/00/1850	00/00/1922
WHITFIELD, Julia	00/00/1886	00/00/1949
WHITFIELD, Ollie Simpson	08/15/1896	06/13/1994
WILLIAMS, Ophelie	00/00/1900	00/00/1940
WILLIS, Mrs. Carrie A.	06/23/1900	03/22/1982
WRIGHT, Ernest	03/31/1922	03/23/1969

St. Mark's Luthern Church

Surveyed by Jack F. Cox November 1, 2001

The St. Mark's Luthern Church at Bottsford, Georgia was established in 1870. Travel south on Highway 45 from Plains, Georgia and go to Thomas Mill Road, turn left and you will find the church and cemetery on the left.

Name / Note	Born	Died
???? = Could not read tombstone)		
ADDY,	No date	No date
ADDY, Fanny	11/16/1834	05/18/1916
ADDY, George	02/25/1814	08/09/1877
ADDY, Herman T.	07/25/1906	05/10/1937
ADDY, Rosa Lula	11/24/1866	07/25/1949
ADDY, W. P.	08/25/1861	10/24/1936
Infant child of Levi W. & Elizabeth		
CLINKSCALES, Lucius Oscar	07/01/1874	02/07/1968
CRAWFORD, Ida Hiller	00/00/1873	00/00/1906
CULPEPPER, Miline	07/28/1892	05/18/1893
Daughter of W. & M. Z.		
DERRICK, Annie Laura	05/26/1883	08/06/1894
DERRICK, David S.	08/27/1841	08/04/1926
(Co. C 15 S. C. Reg. Jackson Core)		
DERRICK, Hattie Eugenia	02/07/1863	04/07/1887
Wife of H. D.		
DERRICK, Martha A.	05/29/1846	11/04/1925
DERRICK, Pauline Melissa	12/10/1886	10/??/1887
DERRICK, Willie May	01/24/1887	12/19/1887
Daughter of H. D. & H. E.		
ELMORE, G. Ernestine	03/25/1871	07/17/1890
Daughter of J. S. & M.		
HILLER, Charlie A.	07/04/1886	07/29/1902
HILLER, G. E.	11/24/1839	10/21/1924
HILLER, G. E.	10/17/1887	05/06/1889
HILLER, Hattie A.	09/06/1846	06/12/1901
Wife of Geo. E.		
HILLER, Hattie E.	03/10/1890	05/20/1890
HILLER, Jacob P.	02/17/1876	03/06/1876
Son of W. W. & A.		
HILLER, Joseph E.	09/13/1877	11/05/1878
Son of Joseph & Callie		

HILLER, Mary A. 09/30/1871 11/10/1871

HILLER, Rena Mae 08/20/1886 05/20/1896

HITE, Martha Pauline 10/07/1906 11/29/1906
    Daughter of D. I. & Camilla

JENNINGS, ... No date   No date
    Infant son of B. T. & M. M.

JENNINGS, ... 12/21/1896 01/02/1897
    Infant son of J. L. & M. M

JENNINGS, Charlie Caughman 04/01/1891 09/23/1891
    Son of L. J. & M. M

JENNINGS, Lott 08/31/1828 05/26/1899
    Husband of Mary

JENNINGS, Lott S. 07/21/1878 06/18/1879
    Son of W. & M.

JENNINGS, Mark S. .... 05/31 & Died 08/10/1876
    Son of W. S. & M

JENNINGS, Mary 08/02/1829 10/09/1910
    Wife of Lott

JENNINGS, Mary E. 02/02/1842 05/28/1898
    Wife of Wm

JENNINGS, Mary Melissa 02/25/1843 06/14/1917
    Wife of Philp

JENNINGS, Joseph E. 10/09/1870 11/24/1871

JENNINGS, Philip 02/19/1846 05/14/1894

JENNINGS, William 11/20/1836 12/30/1905

JOHNSON, Sarah Ellen 01/16/1927 03/10/1927

KENNEDY, ... 06/23/1888 11/18/1888
    Baby of J. J. & Carrie

KENNEDY, Hattie 09/20/1875 07/12/1879
    Daughter of H. C. & ??

KENNEDY, Jesse Joseph 00/00/1852 00/00/1921

KENNEDY, Little Pete 09/18/1886 04/20/1890
    Son of J.J Carrie

KENNEDY, M. M. Caroline 08/15/1858 08/15/1896

MARKETT, ...No date 01/06/1884
    Infant son of S. A. & L. J.

MARTIN, Mamie Lorena 01/09/1870 02/12/1907
    Wife of W. R. Martin

McGILL, Laura J. 08/17/1854 09/07/1911

MURRAY, ... 12/26/1907 01/08/1908
    Infant son of J. W. & R. N.

RAUCH, Mary 07/12/1886 05/18/1887

RAUCH, Mattie M. ....No date 09/24/1884

RAVAN, Emma Hill ....No date   1918

RAVAN, Francis

RAVAN, Levi Simeon 1865   1925

WISE, ... Age 1 day 09/??/1874
    Infant daughter of G. C. & R. A.

WISE, Camilla Addy 01/11/1857 02/15/1947
    Wife of Samuel P.

WISE, Frances Coogle 03/09/1857 11/24/1942

WISE, George Calhoun 04/17/1844 05/25/1898

WISE, Jency 08/17/1821 07/17/1886

WISE, Joel 06/28/1820 05/26/1895

WISE, R. A. 03/27/1853 05/22/1875
    Wife of G. C.

WISE, Samuel P. 04/10/1851 09/11/1887
    Born Newberry Co., S. C.

Section V: Bibliography and Index

Bibliography

Act of Incorporation and Ordinances of the Town of Plains, Georgia. (Americus, Georgia: Herald Job Department. Americus, Georgia. March 1, 1897).

Americus Times Recorder. October 31, 1952.

Bagwell, Dr. James E., Professor of History. Georgia Southwestern State University. Mayor of Plains 1984-1985. City Council of Plains 1978 to present. *Of Time and Mayors: A Sketched History of Plains' Mayors and the World Beyond.*

Carter, Jimmy. *An Hour Before Daylight.* (New York, NY: Simon & Schuster. Rockefeller Center, 1230 Avenue of the Americas, New York, NY 10020. copyright 2001).

_____, *Why Not the Best?* Nashville: Broadman Press, 1973.

Carter, Mrs. Hugh A. Sr. *A History of the Railroad in Plains, Georgia*: As Told by Mrs. Hugh A. Carter, Sr. Copyright by Mrs. Hugh A. Carter, Sr. July 26, 1986

Coulter, E. Merton. *A Short History of Georgia.* Univeristy of North Carloina Press-1933.

Cox, Jack F. *History of Sumter County, Georgia.* (Roswell, Georgia: Wolfe Publishing, In association with the Sumter Historic Preservation Society. 1983).

Gibson, Dot Rees. *Plains, Georgia – Carter Country, U.S.A.* (Waycross, Georgia: Dot Gibson Publications,PO Box 935 Waycross, Ga. 31502, 1977).

Haugabook, Allene T. *Remembering Plains in the 1930's, 1940's, 1950's and a Little Beyond.* (Americus, Georgia: Copyright by Allene T.

_____,*History of Plains.* (Americus, Georgia: Gammage Print Shop, Published under auspices of Lebanon Baptist Church, Plains Baptist Church, Plains United Methodist Church, St. Andrews Evangelical Lutheran Church, St. John A.M.E. Church, The House of God. 1st ed. , October

Hoffmeyer Ralph *A. History of St. Marks.* Unpublished manuscript. 1985.

Klenbort, Marcia and Daniel Klenbort. Text. Smith, Jack. Drawings and Map of Plains. Klenbort, Photos.*The Road to Plains : A Guide to Plains and Nearby Places of Interest in Southwest Georgia.* (Atlanta, Georgia: Avery Press, P.O. Box 7396. 1977).

Masonic Records of the Grand Lodge of Georgia. Macon

McCullar. This Is Your Georgia. Viewpoint Publications, Inc. 1971.

Morris, Kenneth E. *Jimmy Carter, American Moralist.*(Athens and London: The University of Georgia Press. Athens, Georgia 30602. 1996).

National Park Service. *General Management Plan/Development Concept Plan*, National Park Service, 1993.

O'Brien, William Patrick. *Special History Study.* (Jimmy Carter National Historic Site and Preservation District. National Park Service. November 1991).

Plains Historical Preservations Trust, Inc. *A Self-Guided Tour of Plains, Georgia.*(Atlanta, Georgia: Darby Printing Company).

Short, Steve. Interview with Alan Anderson, June 6, 2002

Short, Steve. Interview with Mary Carol Bagwell. June 2002

Short, Steve. Interview with Oliver W. Spann. March 2002.

United States Census. Sumter County, Georgia. 1850 and 1860.United States Department of the Interior/ National Park Service. National Register of Historic Places.Inventory - Nomination Form. Form prepared by Andrea Niles, Survey and Research Specialist. Historic Preservation Section. Georgia department of Natural Resources. 270 Washington St.,S.W Atlanta, Georgia 30334. April 23, 1984.

United States Department of the Interior/National Park Service. National Historic Site and Preservation District. Special History Study - Jimmy Carter. 1991.

United States Department of the Interior / National Park Service. National Register of Historic Places.Registration Form. Form prepared by Jill K. Hanson,(Atlanta, Georgia: National Park Service, Southeast Support Office. Atlanta Federal Center. 1924 Building , 100 Alabama St. S.W., Atlanta, Ga. 30303. May 1998).

Walters, Mrs. C.L., Jr. (Beth M.) *History of Plains, Georgia 1885-1985*, (Americus, Georgia: Gammage Print Shop, 1985).

Wise, Amy. *Colored Schools of Plains, Georgia*, (Unpublished paper, July 2002).

Wishum, Keith. "Plains High Reopens to Students", *SCS School Notes* (Oct., 1996; 1-2.

Index

The index does not include detailed listings of school rosters, cemeteries, and club members. Please refer to table of contents for these listings.